AI for Sustainable Business

This essential guide empowers readers to leverage artificial intelligence (AI) as a tool for efficiency, financial viability, growth, and innovation and as a force for positive social and environmental impact, creating sustainable shared value for all stakeholders. It explores the transformative role of AI in advancing business sustainability and explains how technology and the use of AI, including generative AI (GenAI) and large language models (LLMs), can foster and promote sustainability initiatives as well as measure, report, and analyze key performance indicators in sustainability.

AI for Sustainable Business offers a strategic roadmap for integrating AI to foster responsible, long-term sustainable business practices. Using straightforward language, the book helps unpack the sometimes complex theoretical and practical concepts and procedures. As businesses increasingly recognize the importance of sustainability, the challenge lies in effectively integrating sustainable practices with advanced technologies. The book addresses this challenge by offering practical insights, frameworks, and case studies that illustrate the successful implementation of AI in various business contexts. It highlights the potential of AI to optimize resource use, reduce environmental impact, and improve corporate governance while maintaining a competitive advantage. This book enables businesses to make more informed decisions, optimize their operations, and promote sustainable practices, ultimately contributing to a more sustainable future by providing practical insights for leaders, managers, and policymakers.

This book should be a mandatory desktop reference for corporate directors, officers, advisors, legal counsel, accountants, and auditors who are engaged in sustainability factors of planning, performance, risk, reporting, and assurance. It also provides business leaders, academics, and students with a comprehensive understanding of how AI can be strategically integrated into business operations to enhance sustainability, drive innovation, and create long-term value.

Zabihollah Rezaee is the Thompson-Hill Chair of Excellence and a professor of accountancy at the University of Memphis and served on the Standing Advisory Group of the Public Company Accounting Oversight Board. Dr. Rezaee holds ten certifications, including Certified Public Accountant, and has served as the editor of the *Journal of Forensic Accounting Research* and is currently serving on the Hong Kong Accounting and Financial Reporting Council Panel. Professor Rezaee has published over 280 articles and written 18 books. He is currently in the top 2% of the Stanford-Elsevier Ranking and received certifications of "Highly Ranked Scholar in Sustainability" from Scholar GPD and "High Impact Scholar" from the University of Memphis.

Salem L Boumediene is an associate professor of accounting and the accounting department chair at the University of Illinois Springfield (UIS). Professor Boumediene is the guest editor for Forensic Accounting and Artificial Intelligence.

Saeid Homayoun is a senior lecturer in accounting with a focus on sustainability at the University of Gävle in Sweden. He has over 20 years of academic teaching and research experience.

Salma Boumediene is an adjunct professor at the UIS. Previously, she served as a faculty research associate in the Department of Defense Management at the Naval Postgraduate School in Monterey, California. She specializes in AI and delivering software and hardware solutions.

AI for Sustainable Business

Leveraging Technology for a Better Future

Zabihollah Rezaee, Salem L Boumediene, Saeid Homayoun, and Salma Boumediene

Routledge
Taylor & Francis Group
LONDON AND NEW YORK

First published 2026
by Routledge
4 Park Square, Milton Park, Abingdon, Oxon OX14 4RN

and by Routledge
605 Third Avenue, New York, NY 10158

Routledge is an imprint of the Taylor & Francis Group, an informa business

British Library Cataloguing-in-Publication Data
A catalogue record for this book is available from the British Library

ISBN: 978-1-041-00858-3 (hbk)
ISBN: 978-1-032-98730-9 (pbk)
ISBN: 978-1-003-61198-1 (ebk)

DOI: 10.4324/9781003611981

Typeset in Times New Roman
by Apex CoVantage, LLC

Access the Support Material: www.routledge.com/9781032987309

This book is dedicated to the authors' family.

Dr. Rezaee wishes to honor the memory of his late parents Fazlollah and Fatemeh, sister Monireh, brother Heshmat, and cousin, Mohamad Reza Rezaee, and dedicates this book to his wife Soheila and children Nick and Rose.

Dr. Salma and Salem L Boumediene dedicate this book to their parents. Thank you for grounding us in love and reminding us of what truly matters. To their daughters, Synda and Cyrine, you are our brightest source of hope for the future.

Dr. Homayoun dedicates this book to his family, with heartfelt wishes to honor his parents, Toran and Hemmat, wife Elham, and siblings, for their love, support, and inspiration.

And to our readers, thank you for opening your minds and hearts. May this book inspire you to care more deeply for the planet we share and to guide technology with wisdom, purpose, and compassion.

Contents

About the authors

Zabihollah Rezaee is Thompson-Hill Chair of Excellence and a tenured Professor of Accounting at the Crews School of Accountancy, University of Memphis. He served on the Standing Advisory Group (SAG) of the Public Company Accounting Oversight Board (PCAOB) from 2004 to 2006 and has been the editor of the *Journal of Forensic Accounting Research* from 2019 to 2025. Additionally, he serves as the Honorary Advisor to the Financial Reporting Council in Hong Kong, a position he has held since December 2019 and will continue through September 2026. Dr. Rezaee earned his B.S. from the Iranian Institute of Advanced Accounting, an M.B.A. from Tarleton State University in Texas, and a Ph.D. from the University of Mississippi. His teaching expertise spans a wide range of topics, including Business Sustainability, Corporate Governance, Financial Accounting, Financial Reporting, Financial Statement Analysis, Forensic Accounting, Internal and External Auditing, International and Managerial Accounting, Organizational Ethics, and Accounting Systems Applications including artificial intelligence (AI), across undergraduate, graduate, Executive M.B.A., International M.B.A., and Ph.D. programs.

Dr. Rezaee has published over 285 articles in prestigious academic and practitioner journals, including recent papers in the Accounting Review (September 2023) and the British Accounting Review (January 2025). He has delivered more than 305 research presentations at universities and regional, national, and international conferences, frequently as a keynote speaker. Dr. Rezaee is highly ranked among leading scientists in business and management, holding positions #510 in the United States and #1095 worldwide according to the 2023 Research.com Ranking of Best Scientists. His work is also recognized in the Stanford-Elsevier 2023 Top 2% Most-Cited Researchers (https://www.memphis.edu/mediaroom/releases/2023/december/uofm-research-top-2-percent-stanford-elsevier.php), and as of May 2024, he is ranked in the top 0.05% of scholars worldwide by ScholarGPS, *View your scholar profile and rankings*. Dr. Rezaee's research has real-world impact, extending beyond citation counts to drive positive change in the accounting profession and society. He holds numerous certifications, including CPA, CMA, CIA, CFE, CGFM, CSOXP, CGOVP, CGRCP, CGMA, and CRMA. He is the author of 17 books on topics such as Financial Statement Fraud, Mergers and Acquisitions, Corporate Governance, Internal Auditing, Business Sustainability, Organizational Ethics, Audit Committees, Forensic Accounting, Business Analytics, and Artificial Intelligence. Many of these books have been translated into Spanish, Chinese, Persian, and Korean, broadening their global reach. Dr. Rezaee has also contributed to numerous international and national professional organizations and served on various university, college, and departmental committees including chaired the Budget and Finance Committee of the Faculty Senate at the University of Memphis from 2020 to 2024. Recipient of the 2025 High Impact Scholar Award at the University of Memphis.

Salem L Boumediene is an associate professor of accounting and the department chair at the University of Illinois Springfield (UIS), College of Business and Management. He previously served as the president of the Western Decision Sciences Institute. He has participated in various committees for the American Accounting Association and the Decision Sciences Institute. Professor Boumediene is the guest editor for the Forensic Accounting and Artificial Intelligence Special Topic of the *Journal of Forensic Accounting Research* and has organized several academic conferences.

Saeid Homayoun is a senior lecturer in accounting with a focus on sustainability at the University of Gävle in Sweden. He has over 20 years of academic teaching and research experience, with an h-index of 18, alongside practical experience as a finance manager.

Salma Boumediene is an adjunct professor at the UIS. Previously, she served as a faculty research associate in the Department of Defense Management at the Naval Postgraduate School in Monterey, California. Salma has over 15 years of experience as a solutions architect, project manager, systems auditor, and international consultant, specializing in AI and delivering software and hardware solutions.

Preface

The convergence of artificial intelligence (AI) and sustainability represents one of the most transformative frontiers of our time. As the global community grapples with mounting environmental, social, governance, and economic challenges, the role of intelligent technologies in shaping a more sustainable future has never been more critical. This book *AI for Sustainable Business: Leveraging Technology for a Better Future* is born from the urgent need to explore how AI can serve as a catalyst for positive, sustainable, and systemic change. As companies navigate an era of AI technologies, the need for adaptive AI-related sustainability strategies has never been greater. This groundbreaking book offers an in-depth exploration of how AI revolutionizes financial economic sustainability and nonfinancial environmental, social, and governance (ESG) sustainability practices, driving innovation, efficiency, and impactful change. This book explores the transformative role of AI in advancing business sustainability and explains how machine learning (ML) tools and the use of AI can foster and promote sustainability initiatives. Our aim is to provide a comprehensive and multidisciplinary examination of the intersection between AI technologies and sustainability factors of strategic planning, performance, risk, reporting, and assurance, including sustainable development goals (SDGs). We delve into how ML, natural language processing (NLP), computer vision, and business analytics are being harnessed to address complex global issues ranging from climate change and energy efficiency to ethical governance, circular economy, biodiversity conservation, and sustainable urban development.

In a world increasingly shaped by data, algorithms, and sustainability efforts, business leaders and professionals face both extraordinary opportunities and unprecedented challenges. The convergence of AI and business sustainability and ethical imperatives is reshaping how decisions are made, products are built, and organizations compete. This book brings together contributions from leading scholars, industry practitioners, policy experts, and technologists who share a commitment to responsible innovation and sustainable performance. We emphasize the importance of transparency, fairness, and accountability in AI systems to ensure they align with the values of sustainability and ethics. This book offers a comprehensive guide to understanding, implementing, and leveraging AI and business sustainability. It bridges foundational theories, concepts, and real-world applications, equipping students, professionals, and decision-makers with the knowledge and tools necessary to lead in a data-driven, sustainability-centric, and ethically responsible future. Covering core technologies, strategic implementation, and emerging trends, the book also includes timely chapters on responsible AI, ESG performance, and sustainability. Each chapter not only highlights groundbreaking applications and case studies but also addresses critical ethical, social, and environmental implications of AI adoption.

Our approach balances technical insight with business practicality. Each chapter builds progressively from basic concepts to real-world applications, with an emphasis on strategy, ethics, and sustainability. We not only explain how AI and business analytics work but also explore why they matter and how they can be deployed responsibly and effectively to ensure sustainable financial and nonfinancial performance. Organizations of all types, sizes, and complexities can benefit from comprehensive AI and business sustainability. Whether you are a student, researcher, policymaker, entrepreneur, sustainability advocate, data scientist, business analyst, or corporate decision-maker, this book will equip you with the foundational knowledge, applied tools, and critical thinking required to thrive in a data-driven and sustainability-focused economy. This book offers valuable insights into how AI can be purposefully directed to build a resilient, inclusive, and thriving world. It challenges readers to think beyond technological advancement alone and to consider the deeper question: how can we ensure that AI works for the planet and with humanity?

This book offers a strategic roadmap for integrating AI to foster responsible, long-term, sustainable business practices. Using straightforward language, the book helps unpack the sometimes complex theoretical and practical concepts and procedures. As businesses increasingly recognize the importance of sustainability, the challenge lies in effectively integrating sustainable practices with advanced technologies. The book addresses this challenge by offering practical insights, frameworks, and case studies that illustrate the successful implementation of AI in various business contexts. It highlights the potential of AI to optimize resource use, reduce environmental impact, and improve corporate governance while maintaining a competitive advantage. This book enables businesses to make more informed decisions, optimize their operations, and promote sustainable practices, ultimately contributing to a more sustainable future by providing practical insights for leaders, managers, and policymakers.

This book should be a mandatory desktop reference for corporate directors, officers, advisors, legal counsel, accountants, and auditors who are engaged in sustainability factors of strategic planning, performance, risk, reporting, and assurance. It also provides business leaders, academics, and students with a comprehensive understanding of how AI can be strategically integrated into business operations to enhance sustainability, drive innovation, and create long-term value. This essential guide empowers readers to leverage AI as a tool for efficiency, financial viability, growth, and innovation and as a force for positive social and environmental impact, creating sustainable shared value for all stakeholders. We hope you find this book relevant in inspiring action, fostering collaboration across disciplines, and contributing meaningfully to the global dialogue on building a sustainable future through the power of AI.

Acknowledgments

This book has also benefited, inter alia, from permission to quote from several references and publications of a variety of professional organizations and standard-setting bodies, including the Securities and Exchange Commission, the Public Company Accounting Oversight Board, the Financial Accounting Standards Board, the International Accounting Standards Board, the American Institute of Certified Public Accountants, the International Sustainability Standards Board, the Sustainability Accounting Standards Board, the Global Reporting Initiative, the Big-Four public accounting firms (Deloitte & Touche, Ernst & Young, KPMG, and PricewaterhouseCoopers), national stock exchanges (NYSE, Nasdaq, and AMEX), Google, the Organization for Economic Co-operation and Development, the United Nations Educational, Scientific and Cultural Organization, the European Union, the Global Partnership on Artificial Intelligence, the US National Institute of Standards and Technology, the UK Office for Artificial Intelligence, White House Office of Science and Technology Policy, OpenAI, explainable AI, Alphabet/Google, Meta, Microsoft, Hugging Face, Nvidia, Anthropic, Mistral AI, DeepSeek AI, JGraph and draw.io, Napkin, GitHub, Responsible AI Institute, and IEEE Global Initiative on Ethics of Autonomous and Intelligent System.

Many of the materials used in this book come from *The Sustainable Business Blueprint: Planning, Performance, Risk, Reporting, and Assurance*, a book authored by Zabihollah Rezaee and published by Routledge, Taylor & Francis Group, summer 2024. Many people have generously contributed their time, knowledge, and talents during the development, writing, revisions, and production stages of this book. We are most grateful to all of them, and without their valuable assistance and contributions, this book would not have come to fruition. We would also like to thank the members of the editorial staff of Routledge, including the editorial guidance of Rebecca Marsh, Grace Collier, and the graduate assistant, Joshua Bittner, for their hard work and invaluable assistance. We thank Nick J. Rezaee and Majid Behravan, and Seyed Mahmoud Hosseinniakani for reviewing all 11 chapters and providing constructive comments in refining the chapters. Sincere thanks are due to Rezaee's family: wife Soheila, son Nick, and daughter Rose; Boumediene's family: daughters, Synda and Cyrine; and Homayoun's family: father Hemmat, mother Toran, and wife Elham.

1 Introduction to business sustainability and artificial intelligence

1.1 Introduction

Businesses have traditionally operated under a shareholder primacy model, where maximizing shareholder wealth by achieving financial returns was the primary objective. However, recent shifts toward a stakeholder primacy model have expanded the scope of corporate responsibility in creating shared value for all stakeholders. Business sustainability focuses on creating wealth for shareholders by achieving financial economic sustainability performance (ESP) and protecting the interests of other stakeholders by obtaining environmental, social, and governance (ESG) sustainability performance. In this regard, the primary purpose of business sustainability is to create shared value for all stakeholders, including shareholders, creditors, customers, suppliers, society, regulators, communities, and the environment. This chapter examines the transition from shareholder to stakeholder capitalism, highlighting how contemporary businesses are redefining success by embracing a broader set of goals that promote long-term resilience and sustainable growth in creating shared value. In exploring the multifaceted nature of business sustainability initiatives and performance, this chapter provides insights into the strategies and practices that organizations can adopt to build sustainable business models (SBMs) with technology integration. It covers essential sustainability issues such as sustainability performance, corporate culture, sustainability reporting, and sustainability governance. Furthermore, the chapter addresses the role of technological advancements, including the integration of artificial intelligence (AI) in enhancing sustainability initiatives and driving positive economic, social, and environmental outcomes. It presents a comprehensive understanding of how business sustainability is reshaping the corporate landscape, the fundamental principles that underpin it, the use of AI in business sustainability, and the ways in which organizations can effectively embed technology and sustainability into their strategic and operational frameworks. This chapter presents an overview of business sustainability and AI's role in promoting sustainable development within organizations.

DOI: 10.4324/9781003611981-1

1.2 Business sustainability definition and factors

1.2.1 Definition

Organizations of all types and sizes focus on a strategic approach to business sustainability planning, performance, risk, reporting, and assurance. Business sustainability has become a strategic imperative as investors demand, regulators require, and companies report their sustainability information in areas of financial ESP and nonfinancial ESG sustainability performance, with ethics integrated into both ESP and ESG dimensions of business sustainability. The persisting challenges for business organizations are the identification and measurement of key performance indicators (KPIs) of economic, ESG dimensions of business sustainability. Business sustainability is defined in many ways, with the common theme of a process and practice of managing an organization's operations, resources, and strategies to achieve long-term financial success while considering the social, environmental, and governance impacts. A sustainable business typically focuses on the triple bottom line of economic (profit), social (people), and environmental (planet) factors and integrates them into its core strategies, making decisions that balance financial profitability with prosperity, social, ethical, and ecological responsibility. Business sustainability is defined "as a process of generating financial ESP to create shareholder value while achieving nonfinancial ESG sustainability performance in protecting the interests of other stakeholders, including creditors, customers, employees, suppliers, government, society, communities, and the environment."[1]

This definition is adopted in this book with keen focus on: (1) financial ESP to ensure economic viability consistent financial performance and profitability in the long term; (2) environmental sustainability performance in minimizing environmental impact through resource efficiency, reducing waste, and protecting ecosystems and leaving a better environment for the next generations; (3) social sustainability performance of meeting the needs and well-being of employees, customers, communities, and other stakeholders; (4) corporate governance sustainability performance of achieving the effectiveness of governance measures in creating shared governance and value for all stakeholders; and (5) ethical sustainability performance of adherence to the utmost ethical principles and values in conducting business affairs. This definition of business sustainability aligns with the goals of creating shared value for all stakeholders, including shareholders, corporate governance effectiveness, and ethical behavior, to ensure that businesses achieve sustainable growth while contributing positively to society and the environment.

AI should be integrated into the aforementioned definition of business sustainability and its components by leveraging AI technologies to enhance decision-making, optimize operations and utilization of resources, achieve sustainability strategic plans, and improve sustainability performance across the economic, social, and governance, ethical, and environmental dimensions. AI should be incorporated into all five components of business sustainability performance dimensions as described in the following:

- **ESP Sustainability and Economic Viability:** AI enables businesses to achieve long-term financial success by improving efficiency, reducing costs, ensuring long-term business viability and driving innovation by: (1) promoting AI-driven automation that can streamline manufacturing, logistics, and service processes, reducing resource consumption and labor costs; (2) forecasting market trends, demand patterns, and consumer behavior enabling companies to make informed decisions and reduce financial risk; (3) analyzing vast amounts of data (big data) to optimize supply chains, minimizing operational disruptions, reducing waste, and improving inventory management; (4) automating repetitive tasks, increasing efficiency, and allowing human workers to focus on value-adding activities; (5) forecasting equipment failures, reducing downtime and extending asset lifecycles; and (6) supporting research and development (R&D) by simulating product performance and identifying sustainable materials or designs.
- **Environmental Sustainability Performance and Stewardship:** AI can improve environmental sustainability performance and support environmental sustainability by (1) enhancing resource efficiency, reducing waste, and improving environmental monitoring; (2) reducing resource consumption, energy use, and waste generation; (3) optimizing energy usage in buildings, factories, offices, and data centers by monitoring and controlling energy consumption in real time; (4) monitoring air quality, carbon emissions, and resource use, enabling proactive measures to reduce carbon footprints; (5) optimizing recycling, reuse, and waste management systems, helping businesses transition from linear to circular production models; (6) facilitating real-time data processing in smart grids to balance energy loads and integrate renewables; and (7) tracking deforestation, water pollution, and emissions.
- **Social Sustainability Performance and Responsibility:** AI tools enable businesses in meeting the needs of employees, customers, and communities by promoting fairness, equity, transparency, and inclusivity by: (1) analyzing employee performance data, hiring patterns, employee engagement to promote diversity, equity, and inclusion within the organization; (2) addressing customer needs and preferences, enabling them to offer personalized, ethical products and services that meet societal expectations and have positive impacts and are not detrimental customers and society; (3) reducing bias in recruitment and identifying gaps in diversity and inclusion; and (4) identifying and verifying labor conditions and human rights practices through data analysis and third-party verifications.
- **Ethical Sustainability Performance:** AI can foster ethical considerations by: (1) improving data transparency, compliance monitoring, and decision-making integrity; (2) implementing AI systems with fairness and transparency can help address biases, ensuring that social benefits extend to all stakeholders; (3) analyzing stakeholder feedback, social media data, and public sentiment, helping businesses maintain open and transparent communication with stakeholders;

and (4) integrating ethical AI principles ensures decisions made by AI systems align with societal values and corporate responsibility.

- **Governance Sustainability Performance and Compliance:** AI can improve the effectiveness of corporate governance measures to create shared governance and value for all stakeholders by: (1) assisting all corporate governance participants from the board of directors to managers, accountants, and auditors with reliable data to fulfill their responsibility; (2) assessing and detecting unethical behavior, compliance risks, and fraud early, enabling businesses to uphold high standards of corporate governance; (3) simulating and optimizing product designs for sustainability, reducing materials usage and ensuring products are eco-friendly to improve operations and decision-making processes; (4) optimizing renewable energy use, and support carbon-neutral strategies, contributing to broader environmental sustainability efforts; and (5) identifying ESP and ESG-related risks in real time, aiding compliance with applicable regulatory frameworks.

Overall, integrating AI into the definition of business sustainability and its components enhances an organization's ability to balance economic success with governance and ethical, social, and environmental responsibilities. AI's data-driven insights, platforms, and automation capabilities make it a key tool for achieving sustainable economic growth and maintaining long-term business resilience while addressing the multiple bottom lines (MBL) of profit, planet, people, and prosperity of sustainability.

1.2.2 Sustainability factors

The four essential sustainability factors of sustainability planning, performance, risk, and disclosure are collectively enabling business organizations to create shared value for all stakeholders, including shareholders, creditors, employees, customers, suppliers, communities, society, and the environment.[2] These four sustainability factors are the drivers of sustainability trends, including sustainability disclosure standards, litigation risk, energy and affordability, net-zero carbon emissions commitments, circular economies, and social sustainability trends in sustainability that are influencing corporate decision-making.[3] These trends highlight the complex and evolving landscape of sustainability, requiring companies to be proactive and adaptive in their approaches. By addressing these key trends, businesses can enhance their sustainability performance, build trust with stakeholders, and contribute to a more sustainable future. The other ten prevailing sustainability trends that are expected to shape the business landscape in 2024 and beyond include decarbonization efforts, valuing human capital, integrating ESG factors, safeguarding natural systems, streamlining sustainability disclosures, building sustainable supply chains, enabling sustainable consumption and production, applying technology to sustainability, respecting fundamental rights, and navigating the evolving political landscape.[4] The integration of AI into the four sustainability factors can significantly enhance various aspects such as corporate strategic planning, performance, risk, and disclosure. The use of AI in sustainability factors of planning, performance, risk management, and disclosure offers businesses a powerful tool to improve their financial viability, environmental, and social outcomes. AI enables business organizations to analyze complex datasets, automate processes, and provide real-time insights to achieve their sustainability goals more efficiently and transparently, as well as facilitating the alignment of corporate practices with global sustainability standards, enhancing long-term resilience and shared value creation for all stakeholders.

Sustainability planning refers to the process of developing goals, strategies, and practices to achieve both ESP and ESG sustainability performance by focusing on activities and processes that are sustainable in the long term while maintaining mid-term and short-term outcomes for economic resources, society, and the environment. Sustainability planning consists of (1) assessment of existing business activities and setting priorities for future activities; (2) establishment of goals and objectives based on the concept of profit-with-purpose; (3) engagement of stakeholders in the sustainability planning and implementation processes engagement; (4) communication with stakeholders; (5) implementation and monitoring; and (6) reevaluation, reassessment, adaptation, and refinement of sustainability strategic plans. AI can help business organizations to: (1) analyze vast amounts of data from economic, ESG sources to aid in better planning of sustainability initiatives, identifying patterns, risks, and opportunities not possible by manual human process, allowing businesses to develop more efficient sustainability strategies; (2) utilize predictive models to forecast the future impact of current business operations on financial ESP and nonfinancial ESG sustainability KPIs and related metrics, allowing them plan for long-term sustainability goals by simulating various scenarios and outcomes; and (3) plan and optimize scarce resources, reduce waste, and improve energy efficiency by using smart grids or supply chain logistics to ensure sustainable resource utilization.

The second factor is sustainability performance, consisting of financial ESP and nonfinancial ESG sustainability performance, with the ethics component integrated into both ESP and ESG dimensions of sustainability performance. The primary objective of any business organization is to create wealth for shareholders by maximizing the achievement of financial ESP sustainability performance. However, business organizations should establish the right balance between the ESP achievement and the ESG attainment because achieving nonfinancial ESG sustainability performance, including social and environmental, and governance performance, managing their activities more effectively with effective corporate governance, and conducting activities ethically can significantly contribute to financial viability in the long term and add to the bottom-line earnings. AI platforms, algorithms, and data-driven automation enable business organizations to effectively and efficiently improve their financial ESP and nonfinancial ESG sustainability performance by (1) monitoring sustainability performance in real-time, using sensors and Internet-of-things (IoT) devices to oversee financial performance, track energy usage, water consumption, waste production, and carbon emissions to ensure more accurate and timely ESP and ESG performance data compared to traditional methods; (2) improving operational efficiency by reducing human error and energy usage and optimizing production processes to reduce emissions and resource consumption; and (3) measuring and comparing their sustainability performance against industry benchmarks to ensure continuous improvement (CI).

The third factor is sustainability risk, which represents the likelihood that an organization is not achieving its financial ESP and nonfinancial ESG sustainability performance targets. Sustainability risks include: (1) strategic risk, which reflects the failure of strategic plans to achieve sustainability goals of creating shared value for all stakeholders; (2) operation risk of disruptions in the sustainability supply chain are also relevant to financial ESP and nonfinancial ESG dimensions of sustainability performance; (3) financial risk of issuing materially misstated financial reports that is detrimental to the sustainability of corporations; (4) compliance risk of not adhering to applicable laws, rules, regulations and regulations; and (5) reputational risk of losing public trust, stakeholder confidence and customer satisfaction. AI-driven tools can: (1) predict and identify sustainability risks including supply chain disruptions, environmental damage, or regulatory noncompliance by assessing and managing these risks to avoid financial losses and reputational damage; (2) model climate change risks and assist in develop adaptation strategies to prevent the effects of climate change that can pose significant risks to long-term sustainability; and (3) evaluate different risk mitigation strategies and scenario analyses allowing organizations to make informed decisions about investment in sustainable initiatives and related resource allocation.

The last factor is sustainability disclosure, which reflects sustainability reporting, assurance, ranking, rating, and indexing. Sustainability reporting and assurance (SRA) processes refer to the continuous process of promoting, measuring, recognizing, enforcing, reporting, and auditing sustainability performance in both financial ESP and nonfinancial ESG dimensions of sustainability. AI can improve the reliability, relevance, and transparency of sustainability reports and objectivity and credibility of sustainability assurance by: (1) automating the collection, recognition, and reporting of sustainability data, making the process more efficient, accurate, and transparent in disclosing both ESP and ESG information; (2) tracking the entire supply chain and making it easier to verify and disclose environmental impacts, labor practices, and reputation and social impacts; (3) generating tailored sustainability reports for different stakeholders, including shareholders, creditors, regulators, and consumers, offering insights that are specific to their concerns and interests; and (4) promoting the use of electronic and continuous auditing and assurance processes.

1.3 Sustainability models and AI integration

In today's global business landscape and technological advances, regulatory and technology challenges have become increasingly complex and demanding to ensure compliance with regulations and technological advances. Business organizations have adopted a proactive approach to compliance with regulations and the integration of technology into their corporate culture to streamline compliance processes. The purpose of business organizations has also transformed from profit maximization and shareholder wealth creation to the generation of shared value for all stakeholders, with the mission of profit-with-purpose. Two distinct models of shareholder primacy and stakeholder primacy are suggested to achieve corporate mission and purpose effectively.[5]

1.3.1 Shareholder primacy model and governance

The shareholder primacy model of business sustainability advocates shareholder wealth maximization and value creation, with the main mission of creating value primarily for shareholders. Under this model, the board of directors, as representatives of shareholders, is responsible for protecting shareholders' interests with less focus on addressing social and environmental impacts. This model has been criticized for focusing on generating short-term profits for shareholders while compromising long-term sustainability performance that creates shared value for all stakeholders and promotes innovation, growth, and social and environmental impacts. The shareholder primacy model focuses on maximizing shareholders' interest rather than considering the interests of other stakeholders, such as creditors, employees, customers, society, community, consumers, and the environment. The agency theory defines the relationship between corporate owners (shareholders) and the agent management, whereas shareholders elect the board of directors, and the board appoints managers to manage the organization for the benefit of its owners. Under the agency theory of the relationship between owners and management, it is possible that directors and executives use their discretion to advance their interests at the expense of shareholders, thus creating a potential conflict of interest between shareholders and management. Sufficient corporate governance measures should be designed to minimize this potential conflict of interest. Therefore, the shareholder primacy model suggests that the primary responsibility of a corporation is to maximize shareholder value with minimal efforts to protect the interests of other stakeholders, including employees, customers, suppliers, and the broader community.

Some of the features of the shareholder primacy model are as follows: (1) the business of business is to make profit, and thus, business organizations should focus on strategies, actions, and decisions and maximize shareholder wealth; (2) the primary fiduciary duties of the board of directors and executives are to shareholders to protect their interests; and (3) the focus on maximizing shareholder wealth can indirectly contribute to overall economic growth and societal well-being that benefit other stakeholders and generate positive social and environmental outcomes. Thus, shareholders (principals) provide financial capital to the company, which is run by management (agents) to achieve the desired rate of returns for them. The principal–agent problem exists because agents (management) need physical capital (investment funds), and investors need skilled human capital (management) to manage the company. Shareholder governance consists of the principles, mechanisms, measures, functions, and processes that should be developed and implemented through which shareholders can exercise their voting rights to elect the board of directors to represent them, participate in decision-making, make investment decisions, and hold corporate directors and management accountable for protecting their interests.

Shareholders, as owners of public companies, should be attentive and protect their investments by attending shareholders' annual meetings (in person and virtually) to vote on corporate governance issues as reflected in management and shareholders' resolutions. Shareholders play a crucial role in corporate governance through their voting rights and engagement in meetings and discussions with the board of directors and management. Effective shareholder governance measures are essential for maintaining a balance of power between shareholders, directors, and management within corporations, ensuring that the interests of shareholders are aligned with the long-term sustainability of the company, and promoting overall corporate responsibility and accountability. Some of the measures of effective shareholder governance are as follows: (1) shareholders possess certain rights, including voting on electing directors and key issues and receiving information about the company's financial performance that enable them to participate in corporate governance; (2) shareholders discuss important matters, voice concerns, and express their views on corporate decisions, vote on resolutions, and receive updates from the management regarding the strategic plans; (3) shareholders have the right to propose resolutions that are put to the vote during annual meeting that can influence corporate policies and practices; (4) directors represent shareholders and have fiduciary duties of care and loyalty to protect the interests of shareholders which require the directors to use informed, deliberate decision-making, and use good faith and independent judgment to act in the best interest of the company and its shareholders; and (5) directors and executives compensation should be linked to their performance. The conventional governance models can be adapted to integrate sustainability at their core, promoting long-term value creation and ethical business practices.

AI can promote the shareholder primacy model by enhancing the efficiency and profitability of firms to achieve their goals of maximizing shareholder value. In the shareholder primacy model, the primary objective of corporate governance is to increase shareholder wealth, and an AI-centric approach supports the classic goals of shareholder primacy, which prioritizes maximizing the financial returns of equity holders above other considerations. AI can advance the shareholder primacy model by: (1) enabling operational efficiency and cost reduction through AI-driven automation and process optimization that automates repetitive tasks, streamlines supply chains, and improves productivity, leading to higher profit margins and, consequently, greater shareholder returns; (2) analyzing large datasets quickly and accurately, identifying trends, risks, and opportunities in real-time that enables management to make more informed decisions relevant to investment strategies, resource allocation, or risk management that align with shareholders' interests; (3) improving the accuracy of financial forecasting models by considering vast amounts of data and uncovering complex patterns that enables firms optimize their capital structure and avoid financial pitfalls in pursuing strategies that maximize shareholder wealth; (4) analyzing consumer behavior and preferences using AI tools and machine learning (ML) algorithms, enabling firms to better target their products and services to increase sales, customer satisfaction, and revenue growth that generate shareholder returns; (5) improving communication with shareholders, ensuring transparency and faster responses to shareholder concerns that promote investor confidence in the management team and financial reports, which may positively impact stock prices and investor sentiment; and (6) optimizing investment strategies of predicting market trends and optimizing asset allocation to maximize investment returns for shareholders.

1.3.2 Stakeholder primacy model and governance

Business organizations are encouraged by investors, social activists, and stakeholders to pay attention to the interests of customers, suppliers, employees, society, and the environment, among others, to create shared value for all stakeholders, including shareholders. Corporations should focus on creating the right balance between wealth maximization for shareholders under the shareholder primacy model, while achieving welfare maximization for all stakeholders under the stakeholder primacy model. The mission of profit-with-purpose should be pursued by corporations under the stakeholder primacy model, and the board of directors should assume fiduciary duties to all stakeholders. Thus, stakeholder governance measures are intended to protect the interests of all stakeholders who have a stake (interest) in the company and assume some risks. The World Economic Forum highly recommends that companies move from the traditional model of "shareholder capitalism" to the model of "stakeholder capitalism" and supports the stakeholder governance concept in the context of the stakeholder primacy model.[6] The stakeholder primacy model focuses on the broader view of the company as the nexus of contracts among all stakeholders with the common goal of creating shared value and pursuing the mission of profit-with-purpose. Under the stakeholder primacy model, public companies must be financially viable, socially responsible, environmentally conscious, and good citizens. Thus, the performance of public companies is measured in terms of financial and nonfinancial key financial indicators (e.g., earnings, market share, stock price, employment, customer satisfaction, fair trading with suppliers, proper business culture, corporate governance measures, executive compensation, director independence, business code of conduct, antipollution, and preservation of natural resources).

The stakeholder primacy model promotes the impact investing concept of generating desired financial returns on shareholders' investments while protecting the interests of other stakeholders and achieving social and environmental impacts. The corporate purpose is transformed from shareholder wealth creation to stakeholder welfare creation under the stakeholder primacy model. Shareholders are considered the primary recipients of the company's reports on economic performance. However, stakeholders are now becoming more engaged and interested in the company's MBL performance on various economic, governance, ethical, social, and environmental issues. Shareholders' initiatives, proposals, and resolutions on environmental and social issues are being considered by the board of directors and incorporated into the corporate governance structure. Important features of the stakeholder primacy model are as follows: (1) protecting interests of all stakeholders by recognizing that business organizations create shared value for all stakeholders including shareholders; (2) communication with stakeholders in decision-making processes to ensure that decisions involve all concerned stakeholders; (3) focus on the mission of profit-with-purpose; (4) compliance with the principles of corporate social responsibility (CSR) by taking take actions on a voluntary basis beyond what is required by law to benefit society; and (5) adherence to stakeholder governance measures and recognition of the importance of considering societal and environmental concerns and impacts by adopting adopt sustainable and environmentally friendly and socially responsible practices.

The stakeholder primacy model requires the development and implementation of stakeholder governance, which consists of governance measures, mechanisms, practices, and processes to protect the interests of all stakeholders. Stakeholder governance is a process of managing an organization for the benefit of all its stakeholders by considering the interests and perspectives of various stakeholders. Stakeholders consist of individuals, groups, or entities such as shareholders, creditors, employees, customers, suppliers, communities, and governmental bodies, among others, that have an interest or stake in the organization, and they assume risks as they are affected by its decisions and actions. Unlike the shareholder governance model, which focuses primarily on shareholders, stakeholder governance considers the interests of a broader range of stakeholders when making decisions, rather than primarily focusing on maximizing shareholder value under the traditional approach in corporate governance. Stakeholder governance is a holistic approach to corporate governance that recognizes that a company's success is linked to the well-being of various stakeholders.

Some of the essential features of stakeholder governance are: (1) identification of all stakeholders that have stake in the company and take risk including shareholders, creditors, employees, customers, suppliers, society, and the environment; (2) effective involvement and engagement of all concerned stakeholders by seeking input, feedback, and collaboration from them to understand their interests and concerns and ensure a more comprehensive and diverse perspectives of decision-makings and actions; (3) creation of corporate governance measure that protect interests of all stakeholders; (4) improving transparent and open communication with stakeholders by providing clear and accessible information about the company's strategic planning, activities, and impacts; (5) implementation of governance mechanisms for ongoing engagement with all stakeholders through regular meetings, surveys, feedback channels, and other means to ensure proper communication and responsiveness to stakeholder concerns; and (6) ensure compliance with all financial and nonfinancial law, rules, regulations, standards, and best practices including financial guidelines and principles as well as social, governance, and environmental guidelines. Corporate governance has transformed from the governance of sustainability, which often entails isolated efforts, to sustainable corporate governance, where sustainability principles are embedded in every aspect of corporate strategy and operations.[7] This transition is crucial for businesses aiming to meet the growing expectations of stakeholders and regulatory requirements, as well as encompassing transparent reporting, stakeholder engagement, and strategic alignment with sustainability goals. Under the emerging sustainable corporate governance practices, boards of directors can take two distinct functional and foundational approaches to integrate sustainability into corporate governance.[8] The functional approach involves incorporating sustainability into existing corporate governance structures. Boards create specific committees or roles dedicated to sustainability, set sustainability targets, and report on sustainability performance. While this approach can drive incremental improvements, it may not fundamentally change the governance framework. The focus is on integrating sustainability as a function within the existing governance model rather than rethinking the model itself. The foundational approach goes beyond integrating sustainability into existing structures and aims to embed sustainability into the core principles of corporate governance. It involves rethinking governance practices to prioritize long-term sustainability over short-term financial gains. This approach can lead to more profound and systemic changes in how companies operate and make decisions. By embedding sustainability into the foundation of corporate governance, companies can ensure that sustainability considerations are at the heart of all decision-making processes. Thus, there is a need for a transition from the functional approach to the foundational approach, emphasizing the need for boards to adopt sustainable corporate governance practices to address the pressing challenges of sustainability and the integration of technology such as AI into sustainable stakeholder governance, as explained in the next paragraph.

AI can promote the stakeholder primacy model and governance by enabling organizations to balance the interests of a broader set of stakeholders, including shareholders, creditors, employees, customers, communities, suppliers, and the environment. AI can advance the stakeholder primacy model and governance by enabling firms to operate more ethically and sustainably, considering the diverse needs of shareholders, creditors, employees, customers, communities, suppliers, and the environment by tracking, stakeholder engagement, and risk management, supporting a governance structure that values long-term, sustainable value creation for all stakeholders. AI can play an important role in supporting the stakeholder primacy model and governance in many ways including: (1) enabling business organizations to analyze vast amounts of data from various sources, enabling more holistic decision-making that considers the interests of all stakeholders by integrating nonfinancial ESG data with financial data to align business strategies with both profitability and stakeholder well-being and issues; (2) tracking of ESG performance, assessing supply chains to ensure compliance with environmental standards, fair labor practices, and human rights, and addressing stakeholder concerns related to sustainability and corporate responsibility; (3) optimizing business processes to reduce environmental impacts while maintaining or enhancing profitability which aligns with the goals of stakeholder governance, where long-term sustainability is prioritized over short-term shareholder returns; (4) facilitating better communication and engagement with a wide range of stakeholders, identifying their concerns, and ensuring that their voices are heard and integrated into governance processes; (5) assessing the long-term impacts of business decisions on environmental sustainability, community welfare, and employee well-being and helping companies build strategies that align with the mission of profit-with-purpose, stakeholder interests, and long-term sustainability goals in creating long-term shared value for all stakeholders; (6) identifying and mitigating various sustainability risks that affect all stakeholders, including financial risks, reputational risks, compliance risks, and strategic risks, supply chain risks, and operational risks; (7) supporting the development of innovative products and services that address social and environmental challenges, improving worker safety by detecting potential hazards before they occur, thus prioritizing employee well-being, reducing environmental impact, and benefiting both customers and society; and (8) ensuring that the use of AI itself adheres to ethical standards and corporate governance measures by implementing AI governance frameworks that emphasize fairness, transparency, and accountability to protect interests of all stakeholders. Thus, business organizations should integrate AI into their core business sustainability strategies and operations by creating cross-functional governance, fostering a culture of sustainability, and ensuring that governance functions and measures support sustainability goals to achieve financial performance, create shared value for all stakeholders, enhance stakeholder trust, and effectively manage risks.

1.4 Global drivers and initiatives of sustainability

Several mandatory and voluntary global initiatives are aimed at guiding business organizations in their sustainability efforts, performance, and reporting. There is a move toward the establishment of a globally accepted reporting and assurance framework for sustainability information that creates uniformity in objectively reporting both financial ESP and nonfinancial ESG sustainability performance.[9] Mandatory business sustainability initiatives are those requirements and regulations imposed by governments or regulatory bodies that compel businesses to integrate sustainability factors of planning, performance, risk, and disclosure into their corporate culture, business environment, managerial decisions, and operations. These initiatives are intended to address both financial ESP and nonfinancial ESG issues and concerns and ensure the creation of shared value for all stakeholders.

Regulators worldwide have issued mandatory sustainability rules and guidelines addressing social, environmental, and governance issues. For example, in the United States, the SEC on March 21, 2022, released its proposed rule changes requiring registrants to disclose certain climate-related information in their registration statements and periodic reports.[10] Subsequently, on March 6, 2024, the SEC released its Final Rules Regarding Mandatory Climate Risk Disclosures that require: (1) climate risk disclosures be included in a company's SEC filings, such as annual reports and registration statements by making the filings more reliable; (2) disclosure of material climate-related risks faced by a company as well as any governance and processes used by the company to manage climate-related risks by updating Regulation S-K to require; (3) larger registrants, specifically large accelerated filers and accelerated filers, to disclose direct greenhouse gas (GHG) emissions (Scope 1) and emissions associated with energy purchases (Scope 2) when those emissions are material; (4) important financial statement footnote disclosures on expenditures resulting from severe weather events and disclosure of disclose capitalized costs, expenses, charges, and losses as a result of such events; (5) a disclosure of material impacts on financial estimates and assumptions; and (6) a level of third-party review subject to attestation standards of those emissions data to increase their veracity and reliability to disclose a quantitative dataset of GHG emissions subject to a gatekeepers' review.[11] In 2025, the SEC signaled a shift away from federal ESG mandates by halting the proposed climate disclosure rule.[12]

On September 29, 2014, the European Commission (EC) endorsed the adoption of the Council Directive on disclosure of nonfinancial sustainability information for more than 6,000 large public companies for their financial year 2017.[13] The primary objectives of the Directive are to (1) increase transparency in sustainability reporting, (2) increase sustainability performance on social and environmental matters, and (3) contribute effectively to long-term economic growth and employment. In addition to reporting on their operations, covered organizations will need to include information about their supply chain. Affected companies should report their environmental performance, social and employee-related information, human rights policies, anticorruption and bribery issues, and diversity on the Board of directors. In January 2023, the EU Corporate Sustainability Reporting Directive (CSRD) was released, which would require mandatory sustainability reporting for European companies and their counterparts and trading partners worldwide.[14] The CSRD requires covered companies to disclose historical and forward-looking information relevant to sustainability matters, including ESG issues and information about sustainability risk management, metrics, and value chain due diligence for EU companies starting July 2023 and onward. The first sustainability reports in compliance with CSRD requirements covering non-EU companies are not due until 2029, and early compliance is encouraged. The CSRD also defines the concept of double materiality to include both the financial implications of sustainability issues and the environmental and social impacts of their operations. The adoption of the double materiality concept can provide a more comprehensive view of a company's sustainability performance by focusing on the importance of transparent reporting and stakeholder engagement in implementing double materiality to ensure that companies address both financial and nonfinancial aspects of their business activities.[15] There is a need for robust data collection, stakeholder engagement, and transparent disclosure practices to implement double materiality successfully to enhance a company's ability to manage risks and seize opportunities associated with ESG sustainability.[16] Double materiality assessment can be achieved by using AI-driven tools and digital technologies.

The European Financial Reporting Advisory Group (EFRAG) adopted the European Sustainability Reporting Standards (ESRS) in July 2023 under the CSRD of the European Union (EU).[17] These standards are intended to enhance and harmonize the reporting of ESG factors of performance and risk by companies within the EU, ensuring greater transparency and consistency in sustainability reporting and assurance. The objectives of ESRS are to (1) improve the transparency of companies' ESP and ESG sustainability performance; (2) ensure consistency and comparability of sustainability information across different companies and sectors; and (3) provide stakeholders, including shareholders, creditors, customers, suppliers, employees, regulators, and policymakers, with relevant and reliable sustainability information. These standards focus on providing guidelines for (1) environmental reporting relevant to environmental matters and areas such as climate change mitigation and adaptation, biodiversity, pollution, water and marine resources, and circular economy; (2) social reporting of issues and matters like customer reputation and satisfaction, employee well-being, diversity and inclusion, human rights, and community impacts; and (3) governance reporting of corporate governance matters relevant to corporate governance structures, measures, functions, business ethics, anti-corruption measures, and risk management. The core guiding principles of these standards are: (1) double materiality of considering both financial materiality relevant to sustainability issues affect the company's financial performance and environmental/social materiality reflecting how the company impacts the environment and society; (2) sector-specific standards of customized requirements for different sectors to address industry-specific sustainability challenges and impacts; and (3) forward-looking information of focusing on reporting future-oriented data, such as sustainability targets, strategic planning, and trajectories. Overall, the ESRS aims to provide comprehensive and standardized sustainability reporting and assurance in Europe, reflecting the EU's commitment to sustainable development and responsible business practices.

Voluntary business sustainability initiatives are guidelines provided by individuals, professional organizations, and companies that go beyond regulatory requirements to address financial ESP and nonfinancial ESG sustainability performance. These initiatives reflect a company's commitment to both ESP and ESG sustainability and involve activities such as promoting financial viability, reducing GHG emissions, minimizing waste generation, supporting community development, and promoting ethical labor practices. Voluntary sustainability initiatives refer to business organizations' programs, strategic plans, actions, or projects to address their ESP and ESG sustainability performance. Several organizations worldwide, including the Global Reporting Initiative (GRI), International Integrated Reporting Council (IIRC), Sustainability Accounting Standards Board (SASB), the United Nations (UN) Global Compact, and the International Sustainability Standards Board (ISSB), have issued guiding principles and standards regarding voluntary disclosure of sustainability performance information. The effective implementation of these voluntary initiatives can demonstrate corporations' commitments to promoting business sustainability, enhance financial viability, improve corporate credibility and reputation, ensure social and environmental impacts, and prevent excessive mandatory government sustainability initiatives.

In September 2015, the UN proposed a holistic framework of the Sustainable Development Goals (SDGs) to design indicators and an integrated monitoring framework to address all three dimensions of economic development, social inclusion, and environmental sustainability.[18] The 17 SDGs build on the UN Millennium Development Goals of 2000–2015 and involve new areas such as climate change, economic inequality, innovation, sustainable production and consumption, and peace and justice.[19] These SDGs are relevant to three dimensions of sustainability development: economic, social, and environmental development, and thus can be linked to all economic, governance, social, ethical, and environmental (EGSEE) dimensions of sustainability performance. A total of 169 targets and 232 indicators support the SDGs and are aligned with GRI G4 performance indicators.[20] Some of the SDGs (e.g., SDGs 5, 10, and 16) are applicable to the nature of life below the water and life on land, and others (e.g., SDGs 14 and 15) are relevant to human rights and equality. Corporations frequently use these goals and link them to sustainability performance from the sourcing of raw materials and inputs for production to product innovations that lead to positive impacts on the environment, health, or society; employee safety, training, and diversity; compliance with ethical principles and human rights standards; and community initiatives in the areas of health and well-being, education, employment, and economic empowerment. The 17 UNSDGs are related to sustainability reporting and assurance as they address economic, social, ethical, governance, and ecological sustainability performance.

In April 2021, the International Financial Reporting Standards (IFRS) released its exposure draft proposing targeted amendments to the Foundation's Constitution to create IFRS sustainability standards. In this exposure draft, the suggested proposals include expanding the Foundation's efforts to create a new board to set sustainability standards, creating the ISSB under IFRS governance, and amending the Foundation's governance structure. The exposure draft also included several pieces about the IFRS Foundation, including its objectives, governance, trustees, and further information about the International Accounting Standards Board (IASB), the Monitoring Board, and the Interpretations Committee. The ISSB's mission is to establish sustainability-related financial reporting standards to satisfy investors' information demands and needs for sustainability reporting and operate on four key principles: comprehensive global baseline, consolidation, and building on existing initiatives (e.g., GRI, SASB), informed by the ISSB reporting expert advice and global footprint. In March 2022, the ISSB issued two exposure drafts of proposed general sustainability-related disclosure requirements (IFRS S1) and climate-related disclosure requirements (IFRS S2). IFRS S1 establishes overall standards for disclosing sustainability-related financial information to provide stakeholders, including investors, with a complete set of sustainability-related financial disclosures. IFRS S2 establishes the requirements for identifying, measuring, and disclosing climate-related risks and opportunities. These two proposals are driven by the recommendations of the Task Force on Climate-Related Financial Disclosures (TCFD) and industry-based disclosure requirements of the SASB Standards. In June 2023, the ISSB issued its inaugural global sustainability disclosure standards of IFRS S1 and IFRS S2 to establish a common language for disclosing the effect of climate-related risks and opportunities on a company's prospects. IFRS S1 provides a set of disclosure requirements intended to assist companies in communicating with their investors about sustainability-related risks and opportunities. IFRS S2 establishes specific climate-related disclosures and is intended to be used with IFRS S1.

Overall, business sustainability initiatives, both mandatory and voluntary, are intended to address many sustainability factors of: (1) long-term financial viability; (2) CSR programs; (3) environmental issues including energy efficiency and renewable energy adoption to reduce their carbon footprint and dependence on fossil fuels including implementing smart building technologies, installing solar panels, and upgrading to energy-efficient lighting and appliances; (4) corporate governance measures to ensure effective management of the company in creating shared value for all its stakeholders; (5) sustainable product design and development by focusing on material selection, product lifespan, and end-of-life disposal, using recycled or biodegradable materials, designing products for easy disassembly and recycling, and offering take-back programs for used products; (6) green supply chain management (GSCM) of adopting sustainable practices throughout their supply chain to reduce environmental impacts by sourcing materials and components from environmentally responsible suppliers, optimizing transportation routes to minimize emissions, and reducing packaging waste; and (7) transparency and reporting to enhance transparency and reliability of both financial ESP and nonfinancial ESG sustainability performance information to build trust with stakeholders and empower accountability in achieving sustainability goals.

It is expected that more sustainability-related rules and regulations will be established to standardize the four sustainability factors of strategic planning, performance, risk, and disclosure. Business organizations worldwide should address the relevance and importance of regulatory compliance in ensuring business sustainability by: (1) understanding the significance of regulatory compliance because companies that fail to comply with regulations face severe consequences, including financial penalties, reputational damage, and legal actions; (2) implementing proactive compliance strategies in all business areas including data protection, environmental regulations, labor laws, financial reporting, and consumer protection; (3) establishing a culture of compliance within the organization for core business processes, conducting regular risk assessments, and implementing internal controls to prevent and detect noncompliance risks; and (4) leveraging technology such as AI, big data, and IoT, presented in the next section, to enhance sustainability efforts by providing innovative solutions for energy management, resource optimization, and environmental monitoring that meet their legal obligations and gain a competitive advantage.[21]

The role of AI in promoting both voluntary and mandatory sustainability initiatives is essential by enhancing data processing, predictive capabilities, and decision-making and enabling organizations to meet sustainability goals effectively. AI can play an important role in voluntary sustainability initiatives where organizations go beyond compliance to showcase their commitment to economic, social, environmental, and governance responsibilities by: (1) tracking analyzing, and reporting ESG performance through automating data collection from various sources (such as sensors, IoT devices, and corporate data), and ensuring more accurate and timely ESG reports; (2) enabling organizations to optimize the use of resources such as energy, water, and raw materials to reduce waste and improve efficiency, aligning with voluntary sustainability goals; (3) tracking carbon emissions, helping organizations reduce their carbon footprint voluntarily, identifying energy inefficiencies and suggesting measures to decrease emissions, and making it easier for companies to adopt green practices; (4) promoting innovative eco-friendly products and processes and aligning with voluntary sustainability goals by reducing waste and using recyclable materials; and (5) assessing and monitoring complex global supply chains to ensure that companies voluntarily meet their sustainability commitments by identifying and eliminating unethical or unsustainable suppliers, thus promoting transparency and ethical practices.

AI can also play an essential role in the design and implementation of mandatory sustainability initiatives intended by regulators by: (1) automating compliance with sustainability laws such as emissions caps, water use, and waste management to ensure accurate and continuous monitoring and helping firms stay compliant with environmental regulations; (2) analyzing large datasets to predict environmental, social, or governance-related risks and to proactive assess and manage risks of noncompliance with mandatory sustainability regulations, such as environmental impact assessments or waste disposal standards; (3) automating audits related to sustainability practices, providing real-time data, and ensuring that companies meet mandatory disclosure requirements to improve compliance and accountability in reporting practices mandated by laws such as the EU's CSRD; and (4) monitoring compliance with regulations by minimizes the risk of violations, which can lead to penalties or fines.

Digital technologies, including AI, business analytics, blockchain, and the IoT, are influencing the way businesses approach sustainability to improve resource management, enhance efficiency, reduce waste, and promote sustainable practices across various industries. AI can assist organizations in managing both voluntary initiatives, such as self-directed ESG goals, and mandatory sustainability requirements by offering tools that automate processes, improve data accuracy, and support decision-making. As AI technology advances, it will continue to drive sustainability practices, helping businesses adapt to evolving regulations while exceeding voluntary targets, to foster collaboration between companies and governments to achieve global sustainability goals by harmonizing data collection, tracking global supply chains, and enhancing transparency, and to optimize the reuse, recycling, and remanufacturing of materials, contributing to both voluntary and mandatory circular economy initiatives by tracking the lifecycle of products and helping firms meet recycling standards set by regulations while exceeding voluntary commitments to waste reduction. The integration of technology (AI) into sustainability initiatives and efforts can lead to transformative outcomes by leveraging technological innovations and AI-driven tools to reduce environmental footprint, improve resource efficiency, optimize resource utilization, and enhance competitive advantage.

1.5 Evolution of AI in corporate and sustainability reporting

Corporate reporting in general and sustainability reporting in particular have undergone significant changes and transformation in the past decades, evolving from traditional financial statements and related audit reports to reports on financial information and internal control over financial reporting and now encompassing integration of financial and nonfinancial ESG disclosures. In this context, AI has enabled business organizations to enhance the quality, efficiency, and transparency of their corporate reporting and auditing processes. This section traces the evolution of AI in corporate and sustainability reporting, highlighting its applications, benefits, and challenges over time, as well as the future use of AI in corporate and sustainability reporting. In the early 2000s and 2010s, AI was employed to automate repetitive and data-heavy reporting tasks with the use of early-stage ML and robotic process automation. AI-powered tools have been developed to automate the collection and aggregation of data from disparate financial systems, identifying inconsistencies in large datasets to ensure compliance with accounting standards, to increase efficiency in producing financial reports, but have limited ability to collect and analyze nonfinancial information.

During the late 2010s and early 2020s, AI enables the expansion to advanced analytics by leveraging predictive analytics for deeper insights. AI technologies, including advanced ML models, NLP, and data visualization tools, enable organizations to assess and predict risks related to financial health and stability, regulatory compliance, and ESG issues. AI-powered tools such as automated narrative generation software were used to prepare financial and sustainability reports or sections of annual reports. Companies began reporting on UNSDGs, supported by AI, to align sustainability data with global sustainability frameworks to enhance stakeholder confidence and improve decision-making through predictive insights.

In recent years, AI-powered real-time data reporting and monitoring technologies such as NLP, computer vision, IoT, and deep learning (DL) enable the use of databases such as Refinitiv ESG or Asset4, which is currently changed to LSEG ESG, Morgan Stanley Capital International (MSCI), and Bloomberg to generate financial and ESG reports. These databases contain comprehensive global repository of environmental, social, and governance data designed for investment, regulatory compliance, and corporate reporting. NLP tools can be used to analyze stakeholder sentiments from news, investor communications, and social media to improve corporate disclosures. Integration of AI and IoT devices enables real-time tracking of emissions, energy use, and waste management, identifies anomalies in ESG disclosures to detect potential greenwashing practices and misstatements, and prepares assurance services for sustainability reports to improve timeliness, accuracy, and reliability of integrated sustainability ESP and ESG information.

Soon, GenAI will play an important role in transforming how companies communicate their sustainability initiatives and narratives to all stakeholders. AI-powered tools, including GenAI (e.g., ChatGPT), advanced neural networks, and autonomous AI systems, are now capable of tailoring sustainability reports for different stakeholders, such as shareholders, creditors, regulators, employees, suppliers, and consumers. There are several applications of AI-assisted tools for business organizations that can be employed to: (1) enhance measurement and reporting on governance factors of board diversity, compensation, ethics, and anti-corruption; (2) monitor biodiversity loss and other emerging metrics to align with global standards such as Taskforce on Nature-related Financial Disclosures; (3) customize communication and interactive reporting with all stakeholders; and (4) prepare sustainability reports and assurance statements of both financial ESP and nonfinancial ESG disclosures.

Overall, there are several benefits of using AI-assisted techniques and tools in corporate sustainability reporting and assurance, including: (1) minimizing human errors in processing large datasets; (2) automating to reduce reporting costs, improve efficiency and accelerate timelines; (3) employing predictive analytics to provide actionable insights for strategic planning; (4) creating real-time monitoring to foster trust among stakeholders; and (5) ensuring alignment with global sustainability frameworks (e.g., GRI, SASB, ISSB, TCED, and CSRD). However, there are some challenges in using AI-powered tools, including ethical concerns over data privacy and transparency in AI algorithms, a lack of standardization in ESG metrics globally, and potential over-reliance on AI, undermining human judgment that needs to be considered. Some of specific challenges are: (1) data quality, reliability, and availability, as sustainability data often lacks standardization, completeness, and consistency across organizations and industries; (2) AI models often require large, high-quality datasets to function effectively, and unreliable inputs can lead to inaccurate or biased reporting; (3) there is a risk of algorithmic bias, where AI tools may unintentionally favor certain outcomes or overlook context-specific sustainability concerns; (4) the complexity and opacity of some AI systems such as deep learning systems, pose difficulties in ensuring transparency and explainability; (5) integrating AI into existing sustainability frameworks requires significant investment in technology, skills, and governance structures, which can be challenging for smaller organizations; and (6) ethical considerations around data privacy, accountability, and the potential misuse of AI-generated insights further complicate its deployment in sustainability reporting. Lack of proper responses to these challenges can have detrimental impacts on stakeholder trust and regulatory compliance. The evolution of AI in corporate and sustainability reporting has significantly transformed how companies collect, analyze, and present sustainability information. The emerging AI-powered platforms, tools, and algorithms enable real-time monitoring, predictive insights, and enhanced transparency to meet the growing demands of stakeholders for reliable and meaningful financial ESP and nonfinancial ESG disclosures in chapters throughout this book. As AI technologies continue to advance, they will play an essential role in driving reliable corporate reporting, accountability, stakeholder trust, and long-term sustainability.

1.6 Transforming sustainability reporting and assurance with AI tools

Sustainability reporting is an integral component of corporate reporting and is a process of providing information about the organization's financial ESP (ESP disclosing profit) and nonfinancial ESG (ESG disclosing impact on the planet, people, and governance practices and prosperities).[22] Corporate reporting, either mandatory on financial ESP and/or voluntary on nonfinancial ESG, is intended to provide investors and other stakeholders with reliable, useful, transparent, and relevant financial and nonfinancial information in evaluating risks and opportunities of their investment and making sound investment decisions. Public companies in the United States have traditionally reported a set of financial statements to their shareholders under the corporate mandatory disclosure regime and have recently provided voluntary corporate disclosures on ESG information to enable their shareholders to make sound investment and voting decisions. Investors typically value meaningful and reliable mandatory and voluntary disclosures and use them to make investment decisions. Mandatory ESP financial statements have traditionally been audited by independent auditors, lending more credibility to financial reports presented by management. Independent auditors are expected to express their opinion on the fair presentation of financial statements in conformity with a set of globally accepted accounting principles and standards.

SRA on nonfinancial ESG sustainability performance information require effective assessment of sustainability risks and accurate measurement, as well as reliable disclosure of sustainability performance. AI tools can help in effective risk assessment and accurate measurements of ESG sustainability performance. Several standard-setters and organizations worldwide, including the GRI, IIRC, SASB, and ISSB, have issued guidelines regarding voluntary/mandatory disclosure of sustainability information. There are two ESG sustainability reporting regimes: mandatory (European, some Asian, and South African countries) and voluntary/semi-mandatory (United States and some other countries). Disclosure of ESG sustainability performance information is expected to affect the firm's financial performance and corporate governance. European companies are required to disclose their nonfinancial ESG sustainability performance and diversity information for their financial year 2017 and onward.[23] In the United States, the Securities and Exchange Commission (SEC) released its final related rules in March 2024 that require public companies to disclose certain climate-related risks that are considered to have material impacts on their business, results of operations, or financial condition, and other climate-related financial statement metrics such as GHG emissions.[24]

In January 2023, the EU CSRD was issued, requiring mandatory sustainability reporting for European companies, and could apply to their counterparts and trading partners worldwide.[25] The CSRD is intended to complement existing sustainability reporting standards and voluntary frameworks of the GRI, the SASB, and the ISSB and will have a global implication. The CSRD requires covered companies to disclose historical and forward-looking information relevant to sustainability matters, including ESG issues and information about sustainability risk management, metrics, and value chain due diligence for EU companies. The ESRS were adopted by the EFRAG in July 2023, under the CSRD of the EU.[26] These standards are intended to enhance, standardize, and harmonize the reporting of ESG sustainability performance information by companies within the EU, ensuring greater transparency and consistency in sustainability reporting. These mandatory sustainability reporting standards are intended to promote environmentally friendly practices, social justice, reduce carbon emissions, conserve resources, mitigate the impacts of climate change and global warming, and consistently report to inform stakeholders about social and environmental impacts. These mandatory sustainability reports enable stakeholders, including shareholders, creditors, consumers, employees, and communities, to make informed decisions.

AI can play an important role in promoting *mandatory sustainability reports* on financial ESP and nonfinancial ESG sustainability performance information by enhancing the efficiency, accuracy, reliability, and scope of data collection, analysis, and reporting processes. AI can promote mandatory ESP and ESG sustainability reports by making them more efficient, reliable, transparent, and aligned with globally accepted and regulatory frameworks (GRI, SASB) to ensure accountability and stakeholder trust. AI can contribute to mandatory sustainability reporting by: (1) automatically collecting sustainability ESP and ESG data from a variety of sources, including financial reports, corporate governance, supply chain management systems, environmental monitoring sensors, and social media platforms that effectively reduces human error and accelerates the process of gathering reliable data to prepare mandatory sustainability reports; (2) analyzing large volumes of financial ESP and nonfinancial ESG sustainability data, identifying patterns and trends that might be missed through manual analysis, and enabling ML algorithms to provide predictive insights into future sustainability outcomes and tackling potential compliance issues and improve ESG reporting quality; (3) improving the transparency of ESP and ESG sustainability reporting by tracking the provenance of ESP and ESG data and ensuring that the reported information is accurate, consistent, and reliable auditable; (4) analyzing stakeholder feedback and align corporate sustainability reporting with stakeholder expectations and priorities that can result in more effective communication of sustainability efforts and fosters better relationships with investors, suppliers customers, and regulators; (5) enabling real-time monitoring of sustainability metrics of carbon emissions, energy consumption, and waste management to comply with applicable laws, rules, regulations and standards and preparing sustainability reports that reflect real-time performance; (6) standardizing and harmonizing a sustainability reporting frameworks by analyzing different sustainability standards and guidelines (e.g., ISSB, GRI, SASB, and TCFD) to ensure compliance with various mandatory reporting requirements; and (7) reducing sustainability reporting costs by streamlining data collection, processing, and reporting activities needed for mandatory sustainability reports.

Voluntary ESG sustainability reporting is the practice of disclosing ESG information to all stakeholders. These voluntary sustainability reports are often published alongside financial reports with the purpose of providing stakeholders with comprehensive information about the company's sustainability, ESG activities, and impacts. Voluntary sustainability reporting provides a platform and mechanism for business organizations to communicate with stakeholders on a broad range of economic, social, ethical, environmental, and governance matters and share their sustainability efforts, initiatives, and outcomes. Voluntary ESG sustainability reporting demonstrates an organization's commitment to ethical and sustainable business practices by contributing positively to society, minimizing environmental impact, and building trust and reputation with stakeholders, including investors, customers, employees, communities, and suppliers. Currently, there are several voluntary sustainability reporting initiatives and standards to guide business organizations worldwide in disclosing their ESG performance information. These initiatives provide frameworks, standards, and structured processes for companies to communicate their ESG sustainability efforts, activities, and achievements to their stakeholders. Several global organizations, including GRI, the IIRC, the SASB, ISSB, the UN Global Compact (UNGC), and the International Organizations for Standardization (ISO, 26,000), have issued guidelines and frameworks for voluntary reporting of ESG sustainability information. Business organizations worldwide can apply these frameworks in producing stand-alone integrated sustainability ESG reports. These guidelines can align business practices with stakeholder expectations, business models, and industry specifications. These voluntary sustainability initiatives are essential for fostering transparency and accountability and contributing to the shared value creation for all stakeholders. Table 1.1 presents a comprehensive list of the leading sustainability frameworks that can guide business organizations in the preparation of sustainability reports, and AI can enable compliance with these frameworks.[27] By understanding and leveraging AI in these top sustainability frameworks, organizations can enhance their sustainability reporting, improve transparency and accountability, and contribute to a more sustainable future.

AI can play an important role in promoting and enhancing voluntary ESG sustainability reporting by improving data collection, analysis, and communication. AI tools and platforms enable business organizations to access and manage large datasets, predict trends, and communicate insights for the preparation of voluntary ESG sustainability reports. Furthermore, AI can help organizations assess and manage their sustainability efforts, ultimately fostering greater stakeholder trust and long-term business success by improving the efficiency, accuracy, and transparency of ESG data. AI-powered systems and ML algorithms can contribute to the preparation of voluntary ESG reporting by: (1) automatically collecting ESG data from various sources including financial reporting processes, supply chain records, internal reports, and social media to reduce the manual effort required for gathering sustainability data in areas such as carbon emissions, waste management, and water usage; (2) tracking and monitoring ESG KPIs in real-time in areas of energy consumption, GHG emissions, and social impact metrics without manual intervention; (3) standardizing ESG data from different sources, departments, and formats to ensure consistency across reports and compliance with applicable rules and standards (e.g., ISSB, GRI, and SASB); (4) identifying anomalies, irregularities or errors in ESG data, improving data accuracy, and reducing the risk of misrepresentation or greenwashing; (5) analyzing historical ESG data to predict future performance trends in the areas of carbon footprint over many years to predict and set more accurate sustainability targets and goals;(6) benchmarking and automatically comparing a company's ESG performance against industry benchmarks or peer companies to identify areas for ESG sustainability improvement; (7) assisting in writing ESG sustainability reports through converting data into coherent narratives and generate sections of reports to ensure that complex ESG data is

Table 1.1 Prevailing sustainability frameworks

Framework/Guideline	*Description*	*Implications for Sustainability*
EU CSRD (ESRS)	The European Sustainability Reporting Directive and its standards provide a comprehensive framework for sustainability reporting in the EU, requiring companies to disclose detailed information on their ESG practices.	Enhances transparency and accountability, ensuring companies provide thorough and standardized sustainability disclosures. Compliance may be complex, but it drives consistent reporting.
ISSB (IFRS)	The ISSB offers a global framework based on the IFRS for sustainability reporting.	Facilitates global consistency in sustainability reporting, integrating ESG factors into financial reporting, and helping companies align with international standards.
CDP	The Carbon Disclosure Project (CDP) focuses on environmental impact, particularly climate-related disclosures, helping companies measure and manage their carbon footprints.	Drives transparency in corporate climate actions, encourages companies to address climate-related risks and opportunities, and fosters improved environmental management.
GRI	The GRI provides comprehensive guidelines for reporting economic, environmental, and social impacts, widely adopted for sustainability reporting.	Enhances transparency and accountability, helping organizations report on a broad range of sustainability issues and improve overall sustainability performance.
SASB	The SASB offers industry-specific standards focused on material sustainability issues relevant to financial performance.	Enhances the relevance of sustainability information for investors and stakeholders by highlighting key ESG factors specific to each industry.
TCFD	The TCFD provides recommendations for disclosing climate-related financial risks and opportunities.	Emphasizes the financial impact of climate change on companies, promoting structured and comprehensive climate-related disclosures that inform better risk management.
IRIS	Impact Reporting and Investment Standards offer a catalog of standardized metrics for measuring and reporting on social, environmental, and financial performance.	Ensures consistency and comparability in impact measurement, facilitating transparent and reliable sustainability reporting across organizations.

(*Continued*)

Table 1.1 (Continued)

Framework/Guideline	*Description*	*Implications for Sustainability*
ISO 14001	An international standard for environmental management systems (EMS), ISO 14001 provides a framework for companies to manage their environmental responsibilities systematically.	Demonstrates a company's commitment to CI in environmental performance, enhancing resource efficiency and reducing environmental impact.
UNSDGs	The UNSDGs provide a global framework addressing social, economic, and environmental challenges, comprising 17 interconnected goals.	Guides organizations in aligning their sustainability efforts with global development goals, promoting comprehensive and multi-faceted sustainability initiatives.
B Corp Certification	B Corp certification is awarded to companies that meet high standards of social and environmental performance, accountability, and transparency.	Signifies a strong commitment to sustainability and ethical business practices, enhancing corporate reputation and stakeholder trust through rigorous assessment.

communicated clearly and in a way that is understandable to stakeholders; (8) helping in modeling different climate scenarios and their outcomes and impacts to support more effective decision-making regarding climate-related risks and to analyze ESG risks across supply chains; (9) analyzing ESG data to identify areas for efficiency and improvements where a company can improve its ESG sustainability performance; (10) optimizing sustainability processes in areas of waste management, energy use, and water conservation to contribute to better environmental performance and enhanced sustainability reporting; (11) tailoring sustainability reports to corporate culture and strategic plans to meet the requirements of different ESG reporting frameworks and comply with regulations; and (12) adapting sustainability reporting processes to incorporate new initiatives, metrics or changes in regulatory guidelines to ensure that ESG sustainability reports are complete, accurate, and up-to-date.

Audit of financial statements disclosing financial ESP sustainability information and assurance statements on nonfinancial ESG sustainability performance information can play an important role in lending credibility to ESP and ESG sustainability reports. Objectivity, reliability, transparency, credibility, and usefulness of sustainability reports are important to all stakeholders, including shareholders, creditors, employees, customers, suppliers, and communities. Audit services and reports are typically provided by independent auditors. Sustainability assurance on ESG performance information can be provided internally by internal auditors or external assurance providers, including public accountants. Current auditing standards provide guidelines for auditors to present reasonable assurance on financial and internal control reports prepared by management. Assurance standards on different dimensions of sustainability performance reports vary in terms of rigorousness and general acceptability, and these assurance standards on ESG dimensions of sustainability have yet to be fully developed and globally accepted.

The current sustainability assurance statement consists of: (1) an introductory paragraph of presenting the purpose and scope of the assurance engagement, explaining the responsibilities of both the organization and the assurance provider; (2) a scope paragraph of outlining the criteria and standards used by organizations and assurance providers (e.g., GRI, SASB, and ISSB) in providing assurance statements and aspects of the sustainability report that were subject to assurance procedures; (3) assurance procedures, describing the methodology used by the assurance provider to assess the organization's sustainability performance including details of sampling techniques, data verification procedures, interviews conducted, and any other relevant assurance procedures; (4) assurance findings and conclusion paragraph of presenting findings based on the assurance procedures performed, any material discrepancies or areas of concern identified during the assurance engagement, and the conclusion reached regarding an overall assessment of the reliability and accuracy of the organization's sustainability report; (5) an assurance limitations paragraph of outlining any limitations or constraints encountered during the assurance engagement to assist stakeholders understand the scope and boundaries of the assurance provided; and (6) an assurance opinion paragraph of expressing a reasonable or limited assurance on the organization's sustainability report that could range from unqualified (meaning that the report is reliable and transparent) to qualified or adverse (suggesting significant issues, deficiencies, noncompliance, or limitations). Sustainability assurance statements can play an important role in lending more credibility to sustainability reports to build trust and confidence among stakeholders and demonstrate a commitment to transparency, reliability, objectivity, and accountability in addressing ESG sustainability factors of planning, performance, and risk.

The role of AI in auditing financial ESP sustainability reports and assuring nonfinancial ESG sustainability reports is increasingly essential as both sustainability and assurance gain prominence in corporate reporting. AI tools and ML algorithms can be integrated into auditing and assuring sustainability reports to transform the way companies report and assure their ESG sustainability performance. AI can strengthen the overall credibility of sustainability reports by enhancing data accuracy, efficiency, and real-time monitoring. Furthermore, AI can provide auditors and assurance providers with more sophisticated tools for audit planning, risk assessment, anomaly detection, and continuous auditing to improve audit and assurance quality of sustainability reporting. Specifically, AI-driven NLP tools and ML algorithms can contribute to the improved audit and assurance quality by: (1) automating the collection, sorting, and analysis of large volumes of unstructured ESG sustainability data to enable auditors and assurance providers to focus on interpreting results rather than gathering and processing the information; (2) improving the accuracy of audit and assurance processes by identifying discrepancies or inconsistencies more effectively than traditional manual audit processes; (3) enabling the use of continuous auditing and assurance of investigating sustainability data in real time rather than periodically to monitor ESG sustainability performance more closely and to provide ongoing assurance rather than waiting for annual reviews; (4) standardizing the ESG performance metrics to compare companies across industries and regions and benchmark a company's sustainability performance against peers or industry standards that assist auditors assess a company's assertions the existence, completeness, valuation, and disclosure of ESG sustainability performance; (5) identifying potential misrepresentation, fraud, or greenwashing in sustainability reporting by analyzing historical data and applying predictive models to ensure that ESG sustainability information is presented accurately and not misleadingly; (6) analyzing the narrative portions of sustainability reports, such as management discussions or qualitative ESG disclosures to identify red flag inconsistencies between narrative disclosures and quantitative data; (7) fostering the effectiveness of assurance services by automating components of the assurance process including validating data against third-party sources, tracking compliance with sustainability standards (e.g., ISSB, GRI, and SASB), and verifying the alignment of a company's sustainability efforts with its intended goals; and (8) ensuring that business organizations are complying with an increasingly complex set of sustainability regulations and reporting standards by automatically tracking changes in ESG regulations and assessing whether sustainability practices align with current legal requirements.

The accounting profession should improve the effectiveness of governance and control activities to enhance the quality and quantity of sustainability disclosures. The International Federation of Accountants (IFAC) and We Mean Business Coalition, in partnership with the Global Accounting Alliance on December 19, 2024, published "*Building Trust in Sustainability Reporting and Preparing for Assurance: Governance and Controls for Sustainability Information* guide" that highlights how to establish effective governance and control measures to build confidence in sustainability information.[28] This guide is intended to: (1) provide a roadmap for improve the effectiveness of governance and control systems of corporate reporting; (2) enable business organizations to issue sustainability disclosures simultaneously with financial statements; (3) reduce the likelihood of modified assurance statements or audit opinions; (4) ensure that sustainability reporting is prepared with the same rigor, robustness, and ethical approach as financial statements; (5) align sustainability and financial reporting in terms of quality, timing, transparency, reliability, and connectivity; (6) support the adoption of the IFRS Sustainability Disclosure Standards issued by the ISSB and the ESRS; and (7) address the urgent need for actionable sustainability strategies by business organizations, regulators, the accounting profession, and stakeholders including investors. Many companies are now leveraging AI in financial statement preparation and ESG reporting to improve accuracy, efficiency, and compliance with regulatory standards. Table 1.2 presents several examples of companies that use AI in the preparation of their financial statements and ESG reporting. These companies demonstrate how AI-driven automation, predictive analytics, and data processing tools

Table 1.2 Organizations that use AI-powered tools in sustainability reports

Organizations	*Financial Statements (Economic Sustainability Performance)*	*Sustainability Reports (Environmental, Social, Governance, ESG Performance*
IBM	AI-based Watson platform to automate financial statement analysis and preparation. Watson assists IBM's finance team by analyzing vast datasets, identifying trends, and flagging anomalies, which helps streamline financial reporting and ensure accuracy.	Integrates AI into its ESG reporting, using advanced data analytics to track and measure its sustainability initiatives. AI helps IBM automate data collection across its global operations, which is essential for meeting compliance and transparency standards in ESG reporting.
	IBM Envizi ESG Suite, a cloud-based AI platform for automated ESG data capture, Scope 1–3 GHG accounting, and compliance reporting.	Envizi supports frameworks like ESRS, GRI, SASB, and TCFD, providing AI-driven GHG emissions accounting, customizable dashboards, and audit-ready ESG disclosures.
Microsoft	Applies AI and power platform with Copilot for various aspects of financial reporting, including forecasting and scenario analysis. Its Azure AI platform supports financial modeling by automating data analysis and providing predictive insights, which helps Microsoft's finance team make informed decisions and prepare more accurate financial statements.	Leverages AI tools to monitor and analyze data on its environmental impact, such as carbon emissions, energy usage, and waste reduction. This AI-driven approach enables Microsoft to generate detailed ESG reports that align with global standards like the GRI. Application of Azure AI and Power Platform with Copilot for financial forecasting.
Google	Uses ML in its finance functions, particularly for financial statement preparation. The company uses AI algorithms to streamline the consolidation of financial data from different regions, automate routine processes, and detect discrepancies in real-time, which helps in maintaining accuracy and consistency.	Utilizes AI to track its environmental impact, monitor renewable energy usage, and quantify emissions reductions. AI tools enable the company to gather and analyze this data automatically, providing transparency for stakeholders and aligning with Google's commitment to carbon neutrality.
Unilever	Employs AI in financial reporting to automate data processing and reduce manual work and to assist in analyzing large volumes of transaction data and highlighting errors or unusual patterns, leading to faster and more accurate financial reporting.	Uses AI to collect and analyze sustainability data across its supply chain to monitor key sustainability metrics like water usage, waste, and GHG emissions, to meet reporting standards, and to provide insights for making sustainability improvements.
Deloitte	Uses AI tools to support clients in the preparation of financial statements. Deloitte's AI-based solutions can automate tasks like data extraction, classification, and analysis, which are time-consuming in traditional accounting.	Deloitte's AI-powered platforms assist clients in gathering and analyzing sustainability data, ensuring consistency and compliance with ESG frameworks like the TCFD and SASB to automate these processes in reducing reporting errors and enhancing data accuracy.

(*Continued*)

Table 1.2 (Continued)

Organizations	*Financial Statements (Economic Sustainability Performance)*	*Sustainability Reports (Environmental, Social, Governance, ESG Performance*
PwC	Uses AI-powered tools, like the "GL.ai" solution, to leverage ML in detecting anomalies in financial statements and to process and review vast amounts of financial data quickly, improving the accuracy of audits and financial reporting for clients.	Uses AI to help clients track and report their sustainability performance and to measure metrics like carbon emissions, water use, and waste management, facilitating accurate and transparent ESG disclosures.
SAP	Integrates AI into its financial software, SAP S/4HANA, to assist companies with financial close processes, reconciliations, and regulatory compliance and to automate data processing and reduce manual errors, improving the speed and reliability of financial statement preparation.	Offers AI-driven sustainability solutions, enabling companies to collect, analyze, and report ESG data seamlessly. For example, SAP's AI-based tools help organizations track CO_2 emissions and measure their environmental impact, allowing for accurate and timely ESG reporting aligned with global standards.
Salesforce	Uses AI within its own financial operations and provides AI-based tools for clients' financial and ESG reporting. Salesforce's AI platform, Einstein, automates various aspects of data analysis, helping organizations prepare financial reports more accurately and identify potential risks.	Leverages AI for ESG reporting, particularly in tracking carbon emissions and monitoring energy consumption across its data centers. Salesforce's Sustainability Cloud, powered by AI, helps organizations gather and analyze ESG metrics, supporting compliance with sustainability reporting standards.
HSBC	Uses AI in financial reporting and auditing processes to enhance efficiency and compliance. By applying ML models, HSBC can streamline financial statement preparation, improve the accuracy of reconciliations, and detect anomalies across complex financial datasets.	Uses AI to monitor and report on its carbon footprint and other sustainability metrics. AI-driven data processing enables HSBC to capture ESG data across its global operations and provide transparent reporting for investors and regulators.
PepsiCo	Leverages AI to optimize its financial reporting by automating the consolidation of data and identifying trends across financial statements. This approach helps the company reduce manual errors and improve the speed of reporting.	Uses AI to track its environmental and social impact, particularly in areas such as water conservation, GHG emissions, and waste management. AI tools help PepsiCo gather data and automate reporting, allowing for greater transparency and alignment with sustainability goals.

are transforming both financial and ESG reporting, making them more efficient, accurate, and aligned with regulatory standards.

1.7 Sustainability development goals and AI applications

The UN, in September 2015, released a comprehensive framework of the SDGs (UNSDGs) in addressing the three dimensions of economic development, social inclusion, and environmental sustainability.[29] The 17 SDGs build on the UN Millennium Development Goals of 2000–2015 and involve areas such as climate change, economic inequality, innovation, sustainable production and consumption, and peace and justice.[30] UNSDGs are a collection of 17 global goals established by the UN as part of the 2030 Agenda for Sustainable Development. The purpose of the UNSDGs is to address global challenges and promote sustainable development in social, economic, and environmental dimensions. The UNSDGs are intended to guide governments, organizations, businesses, and individuals in contributing to a more sustainable, equitable, and peaceful world by 2030 by serving as a blueprint for integrating sustainability into policies and practices at all levels. These goals are interconnected and aim to end poverty, protect the planet, and ensure prosperity and peace for all. A total of 169 targets and 232 indicators support the SDGs, and they are aligned with GRI G4 performance indicators.[31] Some of the SDGs (e.g., SDGs 5, 10, and 16) are applicable to the nature of life below the water and life on land, and others (e.g., SDGs 14 and 15) are relevant to human rights, education, equality, and environmental issues. Corporations frequently use these goals and link them to sustainability performance from the sourcing of raw materials and inputs for production to product innovations that lead to positive impacts on the environment, health, or society; employee safety, training, and diversity; compliance with ethical principles and human rights standards; and community initiatives in the areas of health and well-being, education, employment, and economic empowerment.

The 17 UNSDGs address no poverty, zero hunger, good health and well-being, quality education, gender equality, clean water and sanitation, affordable and clean energy, decent work and economic growth, industry, innovation, and infrastructure, reduced inequality, sustainable cities and communities, responsible consumption and production, climate action, life below water, life on land, peace, justice, and strong institutions, and partnerships for the goals. These 17 SDGs are related to sustainability reporting and assurance as they address economic, social, ethical, governance, and ecological sustainability performance. In November 2016, the IFAC published a policy document that considers many of the 17 SDGs relevant to the accounting profession, including those that address quality education, gender equality, economic growth, innovation, production, climate action, and societal issues.[32] Unfortunately, the United States has formally rejected the UNSDGs, which is a set of 17 global objectives to address economic, social, and environmental challenges, in March 2025, whereas other countries are aiming to meet these SDGs by 2030.[33] The US withdrawal of support for the SDGs reflects a broader shift toward ESG sustainability efforts, as many US companies align with the SDGs. However, the US withdrawal from the SDGs may accelerate the fragmentation and politicization of the global sustainability landscape.

AI can play a transformative role in advancing the achievement of the 17 UNSDGs by providing innovative solutions, improving efficiencies, and enabling data-driven decision-making across various sectors. AI-driven NLP tools and ML algorithms have immense potential to accelerate progress on the UNSDGs by making processes more efficient, enabling better decision-making, and providing innovative solutions to complex global challenges. Table 1.3 lists all 17 UNSDGs, their descriptions, and AI roles in achieving these goals.

1.8 Ethical considerations of business sustainability and AI

Integration of AI into business sustainability offers opportunities to enhance efficiency and decision-making, but comes with ethical responsibilities and raises several ethical considerations of transparency, accountability, equity, and environmental impact. Business organizations should consider these ethical aspects to ensure that AI tools are used responsibly and effectively to reinforce rather than undermine business sustainability missions and goals. Addressing these considerations enables companies to balance technological advancements with their commitment to sustainable and ethical practices to ensure that AI serves as a tool for positive, inclusive, and enduring impact on business, the environment, and society. Some of these important ethical considerations are as follows:[34]

1.8.1 Digital amplification and accountability

AI technologies can amplify the outcomes of business operations, making them more efficient and scalable. However, this amplification can also magnify negative effects, such as spreading misinformation or perpetuating errors. For instance, if an AI model used for customer service is not properly trained, it could misinterpret user queries on a large scale, leading to widespread dissatisfaction. Responsible AI usage involves continuous monitoring, testing, and updating of AI systems to ensure that they produce desired outcomes without unintended consequences. Assigning responsibility for AI-generated outcomes is vital, as AI systems that make or recommend decisions affecting sustainability should have clear accountability frameworks. There should be mechanisms to correct or refine those recommendations when an AI model suggests actions or recommendations that could be harmful to society, the environment, or contradict sustainability goals.

1.8.2 Algorithmic bias and transparency

Algorithmic bias occurs when AI systems reflect the biases present in the data they are trained on. These biases can lead to discriminatory practices in areas such as hiring, lending, and law enforcement. For example, if an AI system is trained on historical hiring data that contains gender bias, it may continue to favor male candidates over female ones. Addressing algorithmic bias requires diverse and

Table 1.3 UNSDGs, their description, and AI integration

Goals	*Title*	*Description*	*AI-Powered Platforms*
SDG 1	**No Poverty**	End poverty in all its forms worldwide	• Identify poverty patterns through satellite imagery and other data sources. • Enhance access to credit and banking services for underbanked populations, reducing economic inequality.
SDG 2	**Zero Hunger**	End hunger, achieve food security, improve nutrition, and promote sustainable agriculture.	• Optimize planting, watering, and harvesting by analyzing soil, weather, and crop data, leading to increased agricultural productivity and reduced food waste. • Improve supply chain management to reduce food loss during transportation and ensure equitable distribution of food.
SDG 3	**Good Health and Well-being**	Ensure healthy lives and promote well-being for all at all ages.	• Increase access to healthcare services in remote areas and detect diseases and pandemics. • Accelerate drug R&D, reducing costs and time for bringing new treatments to market.
SDG 4	**QUALITY EDUCATION**	Ensure inclusive and equitable quality education and promote lifelong learning opportunities for all determined based on literacy rate, primary school enrolment rate, and population with tertiary education among others.	• Adapt learning materials to individual student needs, enhancing the learning experience and making education more accessible. • Create educational content in local languages, bringing quality education to underserved communities.
SDG 5	**GENDER EQUALITY**	Achieve gender equality and empower all women and girls. Based on the proportion of seats held by women in national parliaments, female labor force participation rate, gender wage gap, and female years of education among others.	• Analyze large datasets to monitor gender disparities by providing data for informed policymaking. • Assist in identifying and reducing gender bias in hiring, financial services, and public policies.

(*Continued*)

Table 1.3 (Continued)

Goals	*Title*	*Description*	*AI-Powered Platforms*
SDG 6	**Clean Water and Sanitation**	Ensure the availability and sustainable management of water and sanitation for all.	• Optimize water distribution systems, reduce waste, and forecast water needs based on environmental data to ensure more efficient use of water resources. • Monitor water quality and predict pollution incidents, enabling quicker responses to contamination.
SDG 7	**Affordable and Clean Energy**	Ensure access to affordable, reliable, sustainable, clean, and modern energy for all.	• Manage energy grids more efficiently, predicting demand, and integrating renewable energy sources into the grid. • Optimize energy usage in industries, homes, and cities, reducing waste and carbon emissions.
SDG 8	**Decent Work and Economic Growth**	Promote sustainable economic growth, full and productive employment, and decent work for all.	• Boost economic growth by creating new markets and industries for all sectors, including technology, energy, and healthcare. • Improve productivity and safety in all industrial sectors.
SDG 9	**Industry, Innovation, and Infrastructure**	Build resilient infrastructure and sustainable industrialization, and foster innovation.	• Revolutionize manufacturing by optimizing production processes, reducing waste, and increasing product quality. • Predict the failure of infrastructure systems and recommend timely maintenance, saving costs and improving safety.
SDG 10	**Reduced Inequality**	Reduce inequality within and among countries.	• Create fairer systems by enabling access to financial services, healthcare, and education for disadvantaged communities. • Identifying and mitigating discriminatory practices in hiring, lending, and other systems.

(Continued)

Table 1.3 (Continued)

Goals	*Title*	*Description*	*AI-Powered Platforms*
SDG 11	**Sustainable Cities and Communities:**	Make cities and human settlements inclusive, safe, resilient, and sustainable.	• Optimize urban planning, transportation, waste management, and energy use in cities, making them more sustainable and resilient. • Enhance disaster response by predicting natural disasters, managing emergency resources, and coordinating relief efforts.
SDG 12	**RESPONSIBLE CONSUMPTION AND PRODUCTION**	Ensure sustainable consumption and production patterns determined based on the percentage of anthropogenic wastewater, municipal solid waste, and non-recycled municipal solid waste among others.	• Optimize supply chains for sustainability, promote recycling, and track resource use. • Identify inefficiencies and opportunities for reducing waste in industries and consumer practices.
SDG 13	**CLIMATE CHANGE**	Take urgent action to combat climate change and its impacts determined based on energy-related CO2 emissions per capita and climate change vulnerability monitor among others.	• Enhance climate modeling and forecasting by providing better insights into the effects of climate change and helping to develop effective mitigation strategies. • Optimize energy usage in sectors such as transportation and manufacturing, reducing carbon footprints.
SDG 14	**Life Below Water:**	Conserve and sustainably use the oceans, seas, and marine resources for sustainable development.	• Monitor ocean health by tracking marine species populations, pollution levels, and illegal fishing activities, helping to protect marine ecosystems. • Predict changes in marine ecosystems due to climate change, enabling proactive conservation efforts.

(*Continued*)

Table 1.3 (Continued)

Goals	*Title*	*Description*	*AI-Powered Platforms*
SDG 15	**LIFE ON LAND**	Protect, restore, and promote sustainable use of terrestrial ecosystems, combat desertification, halt and reverse land degradation, and halt biodiversity loss manage forests sustainably, determined based on red list index of species survival, annual change in forest area, terrestrial sites of biodiversity importance, and bird life international among others.	• Track wildlife populations, monitor deforestation, and predict the impact of human activities on ecosystems, supporting conservation efforts. • Optimize land use in agriculture and forestry to balance economic activities with environmental preservation.
SDG 16	**PEACE AND JUSTICE**	Promote peaceful and inclusive societies for sustainable development, provide access to justice for all, and build effective, inclusive and accountable institutions at all levels determined based on Homicides, prison population (per 100,000 people), proportion of the population who feel safe walking alone, corruption perception Index, transparency international, government efficiency, and property rights among others.	• Improve public services, detect fraud, and enhance transparency in government operations, contributing to stronger institutions. • Analyze conflict indicators to predict potential unrest and help guide peace-building efforts.
SDG 17	**PARTNERSHIPS FOR THE GOALS**	Strengthen the means of implementation and revitalize the global partnership for sustainable development determined based on high-income and all OECD DAC countries, which are countries with low or moderate incomes that are entitled to public development aid, international concessional public finance and health, education, and R&D spending among others.	• Facilitate collaboration between governments, businesses, and non-profits by analyzing global datasets and identifying areas where joint efforts can have the greatest impact. • Enable better tracking of SDG progress by analyzing global data and reporting on goal achievements, helping partners coordinate more effectively.

representative training data, regular audits, and adjustments to the algorithms to ensure fairness and equity. Techniques like fairness-aware ML can help mitigate these biases. AI algorithms, especially those used for sustainability performance optimization, reporting, emissions tracking, or predicting environmental impact, must be transparent to build trust with stakeholders and improve accountability. AI systems can perpetuate biases in the data they use, which can lead to unfair or unsustainable decisions. Thus, businesses should be clear about how AI systems operate, the data they use, and the criteria they employ to make decisions.

1.8.3 Data privacy and security

AI systems often rely on vast amounts of data, raising concerns about user privacy and data protection. Compliance with data protection regulations such as the General Data Protection Regulation (GDPR) is essential to ensure that personal data is collected, processed, and stored responsibly. Transparent data handling practices involve informing users about how their data will be used, obtaining their consent, and allowing them to control their data. Techniques such as differential privacy and federated learning can help protect user privacy while enabling data-driven insights. Sustainability-related AI often uses data about company operations, consumer behavior, and environmental conditions. Protecting this data is vital, particularly when it includes sensitive information about individuals or communities. Ethical AI implementation should include robust privacy policies and data protection measures to prevent misuse or unauthorized access.

AI systems can be vulnerable to a range of cyber threats such as data breaches, model inversion attacks, and adversarial attacks because, they rely heavily on data, complex algorithms, and interconnected infrastructures. Data breaches can expose sensitive information, while adversarial attacks involve manipulating AI inputs to produce incorrect outputs. For example, subtle modifications to an image can fool an AI-based image recognition system. Ensuring robust cybersecurity involves implementing measures like encryption, access controls, regular security audits, and incident response plans. It also includes training employees to recognize and respond to potential threats. AI-specific cyber risks also exist. Examples include: (1) data breaches of unauthorized access to training data or model outputs can expose sensitive business, environmental, or user-specific data used in AI-driven sustainability analytics; (2) model inversion attacks where an attacker can infer sensitive information from the AI model's outputs, compromising privacy in sustainability reporting systems; (3) adversarial attacks of slightly altering AI input data such as modifying satellite imagery or sensor readings that can mislead environmental AI models used for carbon monitoring or deforestation detection; (4) data poisoning attacks where attackers inject manipulated or mislabeled data into AI training sets; (5) model extraction attacks where a competitor or attacker might repeatedly query a company's ESG reporting AI system to reverse-engineer the underlying proprietary model used for emissions prediction or risk assessment; and (6) backdoor attacks that can occur during AI model training, hidden triggers may be inserted that, when activated cause the AI system to output false sustainability metrics or ignore violations. These threats highlight the need for robust cybersecurity strategies tailored to AI, including data validation pipelines, secure training environments, model auditing, access controls, encryption, and employee training to recognize manipulation attempts. In sustainability-focused contexts, these safeguards ensure the reliability and trustworthiness of AI-generated insights.

1.8.4 Inclusiveness

Inclusiveness in AI development ensures that AI systems benefit a diverse range of users and do not exclude or disadvantage any groups. This involves considering the needs and perspectives of various demographic groups, including those based on gender, race, socioeconomic status, and physical abilities. Inclusive AI design requires diverse teams and inclusive datasets, as well as accessibility features to ensure that AI technologies are usable by people with disabilities. For example, incorporating voice recognition that works well across different accents and languages can make AI tools more inclusive. AI should be applied in ways that are inclusive and equitable. Marginalized groups may face disproportionate impacts from environmental challenges, and AI solutions should be developed to consider these groups' needs. Ensuring equitable access to AI-driven sustainability benefits, like improved resource management or disaster response, is an ethical imperative.

1.8.5 Environmental impact

AI-powered tools and systems may require large-scale data processing and ML, consume significant energy, which may conflict with sustainability goals. Environmental impacts of AI should be considered in developing energy-efficient models, optimizing computing power, and using renewable energy sources.

1.8.6 Human labor and skill development

Using advanced AI tools in sustainability-focused businesses may displace certain jobs or change the nature of work. Human resource department and its leaders can adopt AI-powered tools to improve and customize employee experience by addressing employees' individual needs and preferences, attract talented employees, support the retention and engagement of employees, and suggest rewards and compensation packages based on peer firms. Indeed, AI platforms can provide applications for several HR functions of talent acquisition, hiring, onboarding, rewards and compensation, mentoring and coaching, promoting diversity, equity, and inclusion, and career management and retention.[35] GenAI can significantly reshape the way HR functions and the way work is carried out. HR professionals should assist their organizations in addressing AI applications with employees in communicating the introduction of AI and its effects on workplace, the need for training for new AI-supported roles, addressing bias in AI, automation where AI can potentially replace employees' jobs, augmentation where there is the opportunity for an effective collaboration between employees and AI tools to increase efficiency and improve employees' lives, the impact of AI on mental health and autonomy of employees, and the tasks that are best to offload to AI, the retainment of potentially displaced workers. Ethical AI integration involves considering the impact on employees, retraining them, and promoting skill development so they can work alongside AI rather than being replaced by it to ensure the broader social sustainability goal of supporting human capital.

These ethical considerations are vital for businesses to navigate the complexities of AI and ensure that their use of AI technologies is responsible, fair, and beneficial to society. In addition, AI can drive efficiencies that may seem beneficial in the short term but might have adverse long-term business, environmental, or social effects. Implementing a clear ethical framework and governance structure for AI within sustainability programs ensures that businesses ensure AI capabilities are aligned with commitments to responsible innovation and sustainability principles. For example, IBM's focus on AI Ethics in Sustainability determines how it is balancing the advancements in AI with ethical considerations, particularly in the realm of sustainability by; (1) leveraging AI to significantly reduce environmental footprints for various organizations including optimizing energy consumption to ensure that systems run efficiently without unnecessary waste, reducing overall waste by improving supply chain logistics, and enhancing resource management to make better use of available resources; (2) emphasizing the development of AI that is transparent, fair, and accountable including includes rigorous testing to ensure that AI algorithms do not perpetuate bias, maintaining clarity on how AI decisions are made, and establishing mechanisms for accountability in case of AI-induced errors or failures; (3) analyzing vast datasets to provide actionable insights for conserving water in drought-prone areas to aid nonprofit and government organizations in tackling sustainability challenges and to devise innovative solutions for issues such as water conservation, energy efficiency, and agricultural sustainability; (4) involving experts from various fields such as law, sociology, and environmental science to ensure that AI developments are not only technically sound but also socially responsible and legally compliant and to foresee and mitigate potential ethical dilemmas that could arise from AI deployment; and (5) advancing responsible AI through its foundation model ethics framework and developing AI models that adhere to ethical standards and are designed for positive societal impact.[36] The IBM foundation models are built with ethical considerations from the ground up, ensuring that they are used responsibly and ethically in real-world applications. For instance, AI used in healthcare should be ensured to respect patient privacy and deliver unbiased outcomes. IBM's comprehensive focus on AI ethics in sustainability is a testament to its commitment to harnessing technology for the betterment of both the planet and society. By integrating ethical principles into AI development and deployment, IBM aims to lead by example in creating a sustainable and ethically responsible future.

Properly balancing the sustainable advantages and ethical considerations of AI-powered tools enables businesses to benefit from using AI and address the ethical challenges of integrating AI into sustainability efforts in the following context:[37]

- **AI for Sustainability:** AI technologies can significantly enhance sustainability by optimizing resource use, reducing waste, and improving energy efficiency. For example, AI can analyze large datasets to identify patterns and suggest ways to reduce energy consumption in manufacturing processes.
- **Ethical Considerations:** While AI offers many benefits, it also raises ethical concerns. These include issues related to data privacy, algorithmic bias, and the potential for job displacement. Ensuring that AI systems are transparent, fair, and accountable is crucial to addressing these concerns.
- **Interdisciplinary Collaboration:** Collaboration between technology experts, sustainability professionals, and ethicists is essential in integrating AI in sustainability. This multidisciplinary approach helps ensure that AI systems are developed and deployed responsibly, with a focus on transparency, accountability, and fairness.
- **Balancing Benefits and Risks:** Organizations must carefully balance the advantages of AI with its ethical implications. This involves implementing robust data protection measures, conducting regular audits to detect and mitigate biases, and ensuring that AI systems are used in ways that benefit society.
- **Promoting Ethical AI Use:** By fostering partnerships and prioritizing ethical considerations, organizations can maximize AI's potential to drive sustainable outcomes while minimizing its negative impacts. This approach promotes the responsible use of AI and helps build trust with stakeholders.

1.9 The growing importance of AI in sustainable business practices

By the integration of AI-driven platforms into their business culture, corporate environment, and operations, businesses can not only enhance their sustainability efforts but also improve their bottom line in the long term. The important, unique, and compelling aspects of the use of AI in sustainability are efficiency and risk, among others, discussed in this section.

- **Efficiency:** Digital transformation (especially through AI) typically aims to improve operational efficiency. While initial costs of AI implementation might raise concerns among investors and other stakeholders, the long-term gains, such as reduced marginal costs and improved performance, should generate a positive response from these groups. AI algorithms can enable business organizations to achieve efficiency optimization by analyzing operations and identifying inefficiencies, reducing waste and energy consumption, and optimizing supply chain logistics, leading to lower emissions and resource use.
- **Risk Assessment:** It is critical for companies to understand how AI can help them better assess the risks associated with sustainability and how these digital tools can assist in more effective risk management. AI can enhance operational efficiency across different business functions.

- **Predictive Analytics:** AI tools can forecast demand more accurately and manage resources more sustainably by minimizing overproduction, excess inventory, and reducing waste.
- **Resource Optimization and Management:** AI platforms can constantly monitor and manage resources in real time by identifying and managing energy and water usage and adjusting consumption patterns based on usage data, ensuring more efficient resource use. AI platforms can analyze data to optimize resource usage and reduce waste in materials, energy, and water, predicting energy needs for manufacturing processes.
- **Robust Product Design:** AI can assist in creating more sustainable products by analyzing materials, lifecycle impacts, and end-of-life options and simulating the environmental impact of different materials and design choices.
- **Supply Chain Process Efficiency:** AI tools can enhance supply chain management and improve supply chain processes and their transparency by predicting demand, optimizing logistics, and identifying sustainable suppliers and tracking materials from their initial sources to the production processes and final products to ensure production efficiency and ethical sourcing and reduce environmental impact.
- **Predictive Maintenance:** AI systems can be used for predictive maintenance, enabling companies to monitor equipment health and predict failures before they occur to extend the lifespan of machinery and minimize downtime and waste.
- **Consumer Behavior and Sentiments:** AI systems can collect and analyze consumer patterns, preferences, and trends to suggest for products and services that align with the company's sustainable mission, products, and services.
- **Environmental Issues:** AI tools can help businesses collect, track, and analyze their carbon emissions, providing insights on where to make reductions and improve sustainability efforts, and enhance recycling and waste management processes by improving sorting technologies and identifying recyclable materials more effectively. AI technologies can analyze waste streams and identify patterns by enabling businesses to implement recycling and recovery processes more effectively, and track and analyze their carbon emissions across operations.
- **Stakeholder Engagement:** AI-driven systems and platforms can help companies engage their stakeholders from shareholders to employees, customers, suppliers, and communities in their sustainability initiatives, efforts, and performance to achieve financial ESP and nonfinancial ESG sustainability performance.

Several studies have addressed the role of AI in business sustainability and the power of integration. One study explores how AI technologies can address sustainability challenges while also driving business growth and value creation in the following ways:[38]

- **AI for sustainability:** AI technologies are being harnessed to tackle critical sustainability challenges. For instance, AI can optimize energy usage in manufacturing by analyzing data to predict and reduce energy consumption peaks, thus lowering overall energy costs and environmental impact. AI algorithms can also help in managing waste more efficiently by predicting waste generation patterns and optimizing waste collection routes. AI technologies can provide businesses with valuable insights and real-time visibility as they work toward achieving net-zero emissions. By analyzing large datasets, AI helps identify patterns and suggests ways to optimize energy use, reduce waste, and improve resource management. This leads to more efficient and sustainable business operations.

- **Integration with business operations:** Companies are embedding AI into their core business operations to achieve sustainability and economic goals simultaneously. This integration involves using AI to streamline operations, reduce costs, and improve efficiency. For example, AI can be used to monitor supply chain emissions in real time, helping companies to identify areas where they can reduce their carbon footprint.
- **Collaboration between CSOs and CTOs:** Effective implementation of AI-driven sustainability solutions requires close collaboration between chief sustainability officers (CSOs) and chief technology officers (CTOs). This partnership ensures that sustainability goals are supported by the latest technological advancements. For example, CTOs can provide the technical expertise needed to develop AI tools, while CSOs ensure that these tools align with the company's sustainability objectives.
- **Supporting suppliers:** AI can assist companies in supporting their suppliers to adopt more sustainable practices. By providing suppliers with AI-driven tools and insights, companies can help them improve their environmental performance. This collaborative approach fosters a more sustainable supply chain. For instance, AI can help suppliers optimize their production processes to minimize waste and energy consumption.
- **Upskilling staff:** To successfully integrate AI into sustainability initiatives, companies need to invest in upskilling their staff. This involves training employees in how to use AI tools and understand the data they generate. By building AI competencies within the workforce, companies can drive more effective and innovative sustainability solutions.
- **Winning the race for future supply:** With constraints on green energy supplies becoming more pronounced, companies must act quickly to secure their future energy needs. AI can help by forecasting energy demand, optimizing energy use, and identifying alternative renewable energy sources. This proactive approach ensures a stable and sustainable energy supply for the future.
- **Delivery value to customers:** AI can enhance customer value by enabling companies to offer more sustainable products and services. For example, AI can help develop eco-friendly products by analyzing consumer preferences and market trends. This not only benefits the environment but also strengthens customer loyalty and trust in the brand.

Another study addresses the role of AI in business sustainability and sustainable business practices in the following context:[39]

- **AI for Sustainability:** AI technologies can provide businesses with valuable insights and real-time visibility as they work toward achieving net-zero emissions. By analyzing large datasets, AI helps identify patterns and suggests ways to optimize energy use, reduce waste, and improve resource management. This leads to more efficient and sustainable business operations.

- **AI in Various Sectors:** AI is applicable across various economic sectors to address environmental challenges. In agriculture, AI aids precision farming techniques that optimize the use of water and fertilizers, reducing environmental impact. In the energy sector, AI enhances the management of renewable energy sources and improves the efficiency of energy grids.
- **AI and Climate Change:** AI plays a significant role in mitigating climate change. AI reduces GHG emissions by optimizing energy use and improving resource management. Additionally, AI is used for environmental monitoring and enforcement, ensuring adherence to environmental regulations.
- **Economic Impact of AI:** The economic impact of AI is broad, multifaceted, and rapidly evolving into all sustainability performance dimensions from productivity and efficiency to labor market transformation, macroeconomic considerations, innovation, government, and environmental impacts. The integration of AI in environmental applications has a substantial economic impact. A PwC UK study found that applying AI to manage the environment in sectors such as water, agriculture, transport, and energy could increase global GDP by $5.2 trillion by 2030.[40] This represents a 4.4% increase relative to business as usual and helps limit global GHG emissions.
- **Challenges and Opportunities:** While AI offers numerous benefits for sustainability, it also presents challenges. These include the energy consumption required to train and operate AI models, potential biases in AI algorithms, and the need for robust cybersecurity measures. Addressing these challenges is crucial for maximizing the positive impact of AI on sustainability.

By integrating AI into sustainability efforts, companies can achieve significant environmental benefits while also driving business growth and innovation. The collaborative approach between various stakeholders within the organization ensures that AI technologies are effectively utilized to meet sustainability targets.

1.10 A case study of using AI-powered tools and techniques throughout the book

In this section, we provide an example of using AI-powered techniques and tools by companies in the oil and gas (O&G) industry for sustainability factors of planning, performance, risk, and disclosure. We select the XYZ company in the O&G industry, specifically for adopting AI-powered techniques and tools to address sustainability factors of planning, performance, risk management, and disclosure. The unique characteristics of the industry shape the sustainability efforts of O&G companies as they face distinct challenges and opportunities due to the nature of their operations, the resources they utilize, and their position in the global economy. However, the presented case examples of using AI-assisted tools and techniques are relevant and applicable to any company in any industry, and these specific case studies can be tailored to all companies in all industries worldwide.

1.10.1 Introduction of the case study

The case study is introduced to illustrate the application of AI-powered tools and techniques for sustainability factors of strategic planning, performance, risk, and disclosure presented throughout the book. XYZ company in the O&G industry is selected because: (1) its sustainability efforts are unique in its scale, complexity, and potential impact as it must balance its traditional operations with sustainability goals as key players in the global transition to a low-carbon economy; (2) it can contribute meaningfully to sustainable development while addressing its distinct challenges by leveraging innovation, embracing renewable energy, and enhancing transparency; and (3) the preparation of its sustainability reporting and assurance is complex that can be fundamentally shaped by the use of AI-powered tools and techniques. The financial and sustainability attributes of XYZ company are presented earlier. We examine the particularity, sustainability efforts, and factors, as well as the use of AI-assisted techniques and tools to address and improve ESP and ESG sustainability performance in the following subsection in general and throughout the chapters in particular.

- **High environmental impact:** The O&G industry is inherently resource-intensive and environmentally impactful, contributing significantly to GHG emissions, water use, and land degradation. Companies in the O&G industry have (1) adopted carbon capture and storage (CCS) technologies to reduce emissions; (2) transitioned to renewable energy sources, such as wind, solar, and hydrogen production; and (3) reduced methane leaks through real-time monitoring with AI-powered sensors.
- **Long supply chain and complexity:** XYZ company in the O&G industry operates complex supply chains involving exploration, extraction, refining, transportation, and distribution. Thus, it can employ AI and ML to reduce energy consumption and waste, optimize supply chain logistics, and use blockchain platforms for transparency and traceability of sustainably sourced resources.
- **High capital intensity and long-term investments:** Sustainability efforts and projects of XYZ in the O&G industry require significant financial investment that makes it challenging to pivot quickly to sustainable practices, adopt strategic integration of sustainability goals into long-term investment decisions, and develop hybrid business models, balancing fossil fuel revenues with renewable energy projects.
- **Resource dependency and geopolitical risks:** XYZ company relies heavily on finite resources, and operations in geopolitically sensitive regions expose companies to risks. Thus, its sustainability efforts are well-diversified in energy portfolios to include renewable energy projects and integrate sustainable risk management systems into its business environment and corporate culture to address geopolitical, operational, and climate-related risks.

- **Public perception and brand image:** XYZ company faces reputational challenges due to public perception as major polluters, prompting greater emphasis on sustainability efforts with the increased investment in CSR initiatives focused on local communities and branding itself as a leader in the energy transition through visible sustainability projects.
- **Technological innovation:** XYZ company is highly reliant on technological advancements for efficiency and exploration. Its sustainability efforts consist of integrating AI, IoT, and big data to optimize operations, address climate change, reduce environmental footprints, and develop smart grids and low-carbon technologies to enhance energy efficiency.
- **Workforce and community impact:** XYZ company employs a large, diverse workforce and operates in areas often economically dependent on O&G activities. Thus, its sustainability efforts are centered around investment in reskilling programs to prepare workers for the renewable energy sector and supporting local economies through community development programs and infrastructure investments.
- **Regulatory and stakeholder pressures:** XYZ company operates under intense scrutiny from governments, non-governmental organizations (NGOs), and the public, with increasing regulatory requirements for environmental and social compliance. Its sustainability initiatives and efforts are influenced by regulatory reforms and stakeholder expectations, including Comprehensive ESG disclosures using AI to ensure transparency and alignment with global standards and collaboration with regulators to align operations with climate goals, such as the Paris Agreement.

1.10.2 AI applications for sustainability in O&G

The following are synopses of examples of using AI to examine four planning, performance, risk, and disclosure factors of sustainability. The complete application of AI to these factors is presented in the next several chapters of the book.

1.10.2.1 Sustainability planning: AI-driven resource optimization

Companies in the O&G industry (e.g., BP, ExxonMobil, and Shell) use AI to optimize resource allocation and project planning for sustainability initiatives, which is thoroughly addressed in Chapter 8. AI-assisted tools and techniques can be employed to analyze large datasets from geological surveys, operational data, and environmental conditions to:

- Predict optimal drilling sites with minimal environmental impact.
- Reduce water usage and energy consumption by suggesting more sustainable production processes.
- Incorporate CCS planning into operational workflows.

1.10.2.2 Sustainability performance: monitoring and efficiency

AI-powered algorithms (e.g., IoT-enabled AI platforms) enable O&G companies to monitor their financial ESP performance and nonfinancial ESG performance, particularly environmental performance, in real time. The complete application of AI in examining ESP and ESG sustainability performance is presented in Chapter 9. For example,

- Companies in the O&G industry can utilize AI-driven predictive maintenance to enhance equipment efficiency, reducing energy waste and CO_2 emissions.
- ML models analyze sensor data from equipment and pipelines to detect inefficiencies, enabling immediate adjustments to improve operational sustainability.

1.10.2.3 Risk assessment and management: Predicting environmental hazards

AI-powered predictive analytics enable O&G companies to assess and mitigate environmental risks as thoroughly examined in Chapter 6. For example,

- Companies in the O&G industry can apply ML models to analyze historical data and satellite imagery, predicting the likelihood of oil spills or methane leaks.
- AI-integrated early-warning systems alert operators to potential hazards, enabling proactive mitigation and minimizing environmental harm.

1.10.2.4 Sustainability disclosures: AI for the integrated sustainability reporting of ESP and ESG information

Companies in the O&G industry can use NLP tools to improve the quality and quantity of both ESP and ESG sustainability disclosures, as presented in Chapter 9, to ensure completeness, accuracy, transparency, and compliance with financial and nonfinancial sustainability disclosure. For example:

- O&G companies can leverage AI-powered platforms to analyze internal sustainability reports, extract relevant data, and automate the generation of comprehensive integrated ESP and ESG disclosures.
- AI tools can benchmark company performance against global financial accounting standards and ESG standards, helping identify areas for improvement and ensuring accurate reporting.

1.10.2.5 Sustainability assurance: AI for sustainability assurance statements

Accounting firms use AI-powered organisms to assist their clients in preparing financial and nonfinancial sustainability reports, audit reports, and assurance statements, as presented in Chapter 9.

Overall, by integrating AI-powered techniques into their sustainability efforts of planning, performance, risk, and disclosure, O&G companies can achieve the following:

- Establish robust sustainability strategic plans.
- Improve the quality and quantity of both ESP and ESG sustainability information.
- Effectively assess and manage sustainability risk.
- Improve audit and assurance quality of sustainability information.
- Reduced carbon footprints.
- Enhanced operational efficiency.
- Improved stakeholder trust through transparent ESG disclosures.
- Proactive risk management, reducing the likelihood of catastrophic environmental events.

These examples throughout the next several chapters showcase how AI can transform sustainability in traditionally high-impact industries like O&G, aligning their operations and sustainability information with global sustainability goals.

1.11 Summary

Business sustainability focuses on the creation of wealth for shareholders by achieving financial ESP while protecting the interests of other stakeholders by obtaining ESG sustainability performance. Thus, the primary purpose of business sustainability is to create share value for all stakeholders, including shareholders, creditors, employees, customers, suppliers, society, regulators, communities, and the environment. AI technologies have transformed many industries. This chapter explores the evolving intersection between business sustainability and AI, highlighting how AI-powered tools and techniques are reshaping sustainable business practices. It begins by defining business sustainability as the pursuit of long-term value creation through the integration of EGSEE considerations into core business operations and strategy. The chapter then examines the transformative role of AI in enabling organizations to meet sustainability goals more effectively and efficiently. The role of AI tools and techniques in promoting business sustainability is increasingly significant, offering transformative capabilities across ESP and ESG sustainability performance dimensions.

The chapter outlines key applications of AI in sustainability, including environmental monitoring, predictive analytics for resource optimization, intelligent supply chain management, sustainable product design, ESG risk assessment, and automated sustainability reporting. By leveraging ML, NLP, and advanced data analytics, businesses can identify patterns, predict risks, reduce emissions, and enhance transparency in ESG performance. In addition, the chapter discusses ethical considerations surrounding the use of AI in sustainability efforts, such as algorithmic bias, data privacy, and responsible AI governance. It emphasizes the importance of aligning AI initiatives with sustainability values and corporate responsibility principles. Through real-world examples and case studies, the chapter illustrates how leading companies are integrating AI into their sustainability strategies, achieving both competitive advantage and positive societal impact. It concludes by proposing a framework for integrating AI into sustainability strategy, encouraging business leaders to adopt AI not only as a technological tool but as a strategic enabler for sustainable transformation.

1.12 Takeaways

- Business sustainability focuses on achieving financial ESP and nonfinancial ESG sustainability performance.
- The primary purpose of business sustainability is to create shared value for all stakeholders, including shareholders, employees, creditors, customers, suppliers, communities, and the environment.
- AI is a powerful enabler of business sustainability, offering tools to analyze, predict, and optimize ESP and ESG sustainability performance.
- ML and data analytics enhance decision-making, allowing businesses to identify sustainability risks, forecast environmental impacts, and optimize resource use.
- AI improves transparency and accountability through automated sustainability reporting, real-time monitoring, and enhanced ESG data analysis.
- Intelligent supply chains and smart manufacturing, powered by AI, reduce waste, improve efficiency, and lower carbon footprints.
- NLP supports stakeholder engagement, enabling companies to analyze public sentiment and improve communication around sustainability efforts.
- AI helps companies design more sustainable products and services, driven by consumer data, lifecycle analysis, and demand forecasting.
- Ethical AI use is critical, requiring governance structures to manage bias, ensure data privacy, and align AI applications with sustainability principles.
- Integration of AI into sustainability strategy creates competitive advantages, such as cost savings, enhanced brand reputation, regulatory compliance, and investor appeal.
- Case studies show leading companies are already applying AI successfully in areas like emissions tracking, energy efficiency, and CSR impact analysis.
- A strategic framework is needed to guide AI-sustainability integration, ensuring alignment with corporate values, stakeholder expectations, and long-term sustainability goals.

Notes

1 Rezaee, Z. 2024. The Sustainable Business Blueprint: Planning, Performance, Risk, Reporting, and Assurance, g Routledge, Taylor & Francis Group, summer 2024. Available at https://www.routledge.com/The-Sustainable-Business-Blueprint-Planning-Performance-Risk-Reporting-and-Assurance/Rezaee/p/book/9781032571270.

2 Rezaee. *The Sustainable Business Blueprint*

3 Ly, L., Hall, L., Bastit, B., Ellis, T., Munday, P., Thomson, B., Sugrue, D., Whieldon, E., & Laidlaw, J. 2023. Key sustainability trends that will drive decision-making in 2023. *S&P Global*. https://www.spglobal.com/esg/insights/featured/special-editorial/key-sustainability-trends-that-will-drive-decision-making-in-2023
4 ERM. 2024. 10 sustainability trends impacting business in 2024 and beyond. *ERM*. https://www.erm.com/insights/10-sustainability-trends-likely-to-shape-the-business-landscape-in-2024-and-beyond/
5 Rezaee, Z. 2025, February. *Business Sustainability Framework: Theory and Practice*. Routledge, Taylor & Francis Group
6 *Davos Manifesto 2020: The Universal Purpose of a Company in the Fourth Industrial Revolution*. 2019, 2 December. https://www.weforum.org/agenda/2019/12/davos-manifesto-2020-the-universal-purpose-of-a-company-in-the-fourth-industrial-revolution/
7 Board Foundation. 2021. *From Corporate Governance of Sustainability to Sustainable Corporate Governance*. https://boardfoundation.org/en/insight/from-corporate-governance-of-sustainability-to-sustainable-corporate-governance/
8 Board Foundation, *From Corporate Governance of Sustainability to Sustainable Corporate Governance*
9 Rezaee, *Business Sustainability Framework*
10 Securities and Exchange Commission (SEC). 2022, 21 March. *SEC Proposes Rules to Enhance and Standardize Climate-Related Disclosures for Investors*. https://www.sec.gov/news/press-release/2022-46
11 Securities and Exchange Commission (SEC). 2024, 6 March. *The Enhancement and Standardization of Climate-Related Disclosures for Investors*. 17 CFR 210, 229, 230, 232, 239, and 249, [Release Nos. 33-11275; 34-99678; File No. S7-10-22]. Final Rules. https://www.sec.gov/files/rules/final/2024/33-11275.pdf
12 US Securities and Exchange Commission (SEC), 2025, February 11. *Statement: Acting Chairman Statement on Climate-Related Disclosure Rules, Commissioner Mark T. Uyeda*. https://www.sec.gov/newsroom/speeches-statements/uyeda-statement-climate-change-021025
13 European Commission. 2014. *Disclosure of Non-financial Information: Europe Information: Europe Council, the European Economic and Social, Environmental Issues*. http://ec.europa.eu/internal_market/accounting/non-financial_reporting/index_en.htm
14 European Commission (EC). 2023, 5 January. *The Corporate Sustainability Reporting Directive (CSRD)*. https://finance.ec.europa.eu/capital-markets-union-and-financial-markets/company-reporting-and-auditing/company-reporting/corporate-sustainability-reporting_en
15 PwC. 2024. *What Is Double Materiality under CSRD?* https://www.pwc.com/us/en/services/esg/library/csrd-double-materiality.html
16 Deloitte. 2024. *Applying the Double Materiality Principle*. https://www2.deloitte.com/us/en/blog/accounting-finance-blog/2024/double-materiality.html
17 European Commission (EC). 2023, 31 July. *The Commission Adopts the European Sustainability Reporting Standards*. https://finance.ec.europa.eu/news/commission-adopts-european-sustainability-reporting-standards-2023-07-31_en
18 UN Sustainable Development Goals Report (UNSDGs). 2015. *Indicators and a Monitoring Framework for the Sustainable Development Goals Launching a Data Revolution for the SDGs*. http://unsdsn.org/wp-content/uploads/2015/03/150320-SDSN-Indicator-Report.pdf
19 UN Sustainable Development Goals Report (UNSDGs). *Indicators and a Monitoring Framework for the Sustainable Development Goals Launching a Data Revolution for the SDGs*

20 Global Reporting Initiative (GRI). 2017. *Linking the GRI Standards and the European Directive on Non-financial and Diversity Disclosure*. https://www.globalreporting.org/standards/resource-download-center/linking-gri-standards-and-european-directive-on-non-financial-and-diversity-disclosure/
21 Binsaeed, R. 2023. Navigating regulatory challenges: Compliance and business sustainability. *Entrepreneurship & Organization Management*, 12(3), 1–10. https://www.hilarispublisher.com/open-access/navigating-regulatory-challenges-compliance-and-business-sustainability−100507.html
22 Rezaee, *Business Sustainability Framework*
23 European Commission, *Disclosure of Non-financial Information*
24 Securities and Exchange Commission (SEC), *SEC Proposes Rules to Enhance and Standardize Climate-Related Disclosures for Investors* and SEC Final Rules, *The Enhancement and Standardization of Climate-Related Disclosures for Investors*
25 European Commission (EC), *The Corporate Sustainability Reporting Directive (CSRD)*
26 European Commission (EC), *The Commission Adopts the European Sustainability Reporting Standards*
27 ESG The Report. 2024. *Top Sustainability Frameworks for Organizations*. https://esgthereport.com/the-top-sustainability-frameworks-for-organizations/
28 International Federation of Accountants (IFAC). 2024, 19 December. *Building Trust in Sustainability Reporting and Preparing for Assurance: Governance and Controls for Sustainability Information*. https://www.ifac.org/publications/building-trust-sustainability-reporting-and-preparing-assurance-governance-and-controls?utm_source=Main+List+New&utm_campaign=e81b800203-EMAIL_CAMPAIGN_2024_12_18_06_41&utm_medium=email&utm_term=0_-e81b800203–80664632
29 UN Sustainable Development Goals Report (UNSDGs), *Indicators and a Monitoring Framework for the Sustainable Development Goals Launching a Data Revolution for the SDGs*
30 UN Sustainable Development Goals Report (UNSDGs). *Indicators and a Monitoring Framework for the Sustainable Development Goals Launching a Data Revolution for the SDGs*
31 Global Reporting Initiative (GRI), *Linking the GRI Standards and the European Directive on Non-financial and Diversity Disclosure*
32 International Federation of Accountants. 2016. *The 2030 Agenda for Sustainable Development: A Snapshot of the Accountancy Profession's Contribution*. International Federation of Accountants, New York. https://www.ifac.org/publications-resources/2030-agenda-sustainable-development
33 United States Mission to the United Nations. 2025, 4 March. *Remarks at the UN meeting entitled 58th Plenary Meeting of the General Assembly, Consideration of Draft Resolution (A/79/L.57/Rev.1)*. https://usun.usmission.gov/remarks-at-the-un-meeting-entitled-58th-plenary-meeting-of-the-general-assembly-consideration-of-draft-resolution-a-79-l-57-rev-1/
34 Harvard Business School Online. 2024. *5 Ethical Considerations of AI in Business*. https://online.hbs.edu/blog/post/ethical-considerations-of-ai
35 The Conference Board. 2024. *AI for HR*. https://www.conference-board.org/topics/AI-HR
36 IBM. 2024. *For the Planet and People: IBM's Focus on AI Ethics in Sustainability*. https://www.ibm.com/blog/for-the-planet-and-people-ibms-focus-on-ai-ethics-in-sustainability/
37 The Sustainable Times. 2024. *Balancing the Sustainable Advantages and Ethical Considerations of AI Technology*. https://thesustainabletimes.com/transparency-and-reporting/data-and-reporting/balancing-the-sustainable-advantages-and-ethical-considerations-of-ai-technology/

38 Bain & Company. 2024. *AI and Sustainability: The Power of Integration*. https://www.bain.com/insights/ai-and-sustainability-power-of-integration-ceo-sustainability-guide-2024/
39 Institute of Sustainability Studies. 2023. *The Role of AI in Business Sustainability*. https://instituteofsustainabilitystudies.com/insights/guides/the-role-of-ai-in-business-sustainability/
40 PwC. 2019. *Using AI to Better Manage the Environment Could Reduce Greenhouse Gas Emissions, Boost Global GDP by Up to US $5 Trillion and Create Up to 38m Jobs by 2030*. https://www.pwc.com/gx/en/news-room/press-releases/2019/ai-realise-gains-environment.html

2 Theoretical foundations of business sustainability and AI ethics considerations

2.1 Introduction

The integration of AI into business sustainability is underpinned by several theoretical foundations and frameworks that explain how organizations can leverage technological advancements to achieve SDGs and performance. Sustainability theories, principles, and concepts present foundations for the achievement of SGDs, which emphasize meeting the needs of the present without compromising future generations' ability to meet their own needs. When sustainability theories are combined with AI, they enable organizations to include the development of intelligent systems that optimize resource use, minimize environmental impact, and reduce waste while supporting social equity and governance goals. Key theories that inform the use of AI for business sustainability include systems theory, stakeholder theory, and the triple bottom line framework as described in this chapter. These sustainability theories provide a comprehensive overview of how AI can be harnessed to drive sustainable business practices by examining the strategic implications of AI adoption, the role of data and analytics in sustainability reporting, and the potential of AI to foster innovation in areas such as supply chain management, energy efficiency, and CSR. Understanding the theoretical underpinnings of AI and business sustainability enables business organizations to gain insights into how technology can be leveraged to create sustainable value in a rapidly changing world. This chapter also examines the ethical considerations of the use of AI in sustainable business practices, as while AI offers powerful tools for promoting sustainability, it also poses risks related to privacy, bias, accountability, and the potential for unintended consequences. Understanding AI ethical considerations and developing frameworks for ethical AI governance is crucial for ensuring that AI applications align with broader sustainability goals.

2.2 Sustainability theories and AI

Several sustainability theories are presented in the literature that provide guiding principles and foundations for understanding and implementing sustainable initiatives and practices. The six commonly dominant sustainability theories are

DOI: 10.4324/9781003611981-2

shareholder/agency, stakeholder, signaling/disclosure, legitimacy, institutional, and stewardship, which are relevant to sustainability factors of planning, performance, risk, and disclosure.[1] Shareholder theory postulates that corporations exist primarily to maximize shareholder value and thus managers (agents) are expected to act in the best interests of owners (principals). Under this theory, sustainability activities relevant to ESG are supported only if they contribute to long-term shareholder wealth in reducing risk, enhancing reputation, or improving financial performance. Stakeholder theory posits that business organizations have a responsibility to multiple stakeholders including shareholders, employees, customers, communities, and the environment and they must balance the interests of diverse stakeholders to ensure long-term success and social legitimacy. Signaling/disclosure theory suggests that sustainable organizations voluntary disclosure their sustainability performance to signal their quality, values, or prospects to external stakeholders. Legitimacy theory indicates that organizations seek to align their operations and disclosures with societal norms and values to gain or maintain legitimacy. Institutional theory suggests that organizational behavior is shaped by external institutional pressures such as regulatory, normative, and cultural expectations and thus organizations adopt sustainability efforts due to coercive (laws), normative (industry standards), or mimetic (peer imitation) pressures. Stewardship theory explains that managers are stewards of all sustainability capitals including financial, environmental, social, operational and the organization, motivated by a desire to do what is best for the firm and its stakeholders. While these sustainability theories are relevant to AI integration, the rest of this section focuses on stakeholder theory.

Shareholder/agency theory focuses on the relationship between shareholders (principals) and management (agent) and the potential conflicts of interest between management and shareholders when agents are charged with the responsibility of managing the business affairs in the best interest of owners. Shareholder/agency theory aims at creating shareholder value by maximizing positive externalities and minimizing negative externalities of sustainability activities. The implications of shareholder/agency theory for sustainability performance are that management incentives and activities may be focused on meeting short-term financial performance at the expense of achieving sustainable and long-term performance for all stakeholders. Thus, nonfinancial ESG sustainability performance is viewed as the allocation of firm resources in pursuit of activities that are not in the best financial interests of shareholders, even though they may create value for other stakeholders. Agency theory posits that ESG activities can create shareholder value when they increase future cash flows by increasing revenue (better customer satisfaction), reducing costs (reducing waste, better quality and cost-effective products and services, maintaining talented and loyal employees), and reducing risks (complying with regulations, avoiding taxes and fines).

AI can play a transformative role in integrating agency theory into sustainability activities and performance by addressing several key challenges associated with the principal–agent relationship, where agents may not always act in the best interest of the principals. Thus, implementation of AI in sustainability process mitigate and resolve agency problems. Specifically, AI-driven tools and technologies (e.g., NLP and ML) can: (1) provide real-time monitoring and analytics to minimize information asymmetry between shareholders and executives by analyzing vast amounts of data (e.g., financial statements, management reports, or social media trends) enabling shareholders to detect potential mismanagement or misalignment with their interests more quickly and accurately; (2) optimize decision-making processes by both shareholders and management by analyzing large datasets relevant to internal performance metrics, market conditions, competitors, and recommending strategies that maximize shareholder value; (3) assist in designing executive compensation schemes that are more aligned with performance metrics that truly reflect shareholder value by automating performance tracking and providing dynamic adjustments to incentives; (4) predict and manage risks on on-going bases and more effectively than traditional methods by tracking excessive risks and providing risk assessments that better align with long-term shareholder value creation; (5) provide timely information by continuously analyzing transactions and financial data for anomalies to reduce the chances of executives engaging in unethical behavior such as financial fraud; and (6) enable management to focus on more strategic initiatives that align with long-term shareholder value by allowing shareholders to engage more proactively with management. Thus, AI-driven tools and platforms have the potential to promote agency theory by strengthening the alignment between shareholders and managers and improving transparency, decision-making, risk management, and executive compensation. Furthermore, AI can reduce agency costs and assist in creating governance structures that favor long-term shareholder value creation while minimizing conflicts of interest inherent in the principal–agent relationship.

The stakeholder theory promotes the corporate mission of profit-with-purpose that creates shared value for all stakeholders, including shareholders, creditors, employees, customers, suppliers, communities, government agencies, and the environment. Under the stakeholder theory, all stakeholders have a reciprocal relationship with a company in providing financial, human, social, and environmental capital. The application of the stakeholder theory to business sustainability suggests that a company should be viewed as a nexus of all constituencies in creating shared values for them by integrating all business activities from the supply chain, inbound and outbound logistics, processes and operations, finished products and customer interface, distribution channels services, and financial reporting processes to achieve both financial economic sustainability performance (ESP) and nonfinancial environmental, social, and governance (ESG) sustainability performance. In the context of business sustainability, stakeholders are those who have a direct interest (stake) and bear risks associated with business activities through their investments in the form of financial capital (shareholders), human capital (employees), physical capital (customers and suppliers), social capital (the society), environmental capital (environment), and regulatory capital (government). By addressing the needs and concerns of diverse stakeholders, businesses can create shared value for all stakeholders while enhancing long-term financial performance and generating positive social and environmental outcomes. The legitimacy and institutional theories are closely related to the stakeholder theory in the sense that only those with legitimate claims and institutional identification can be considered stakeholders. Stakeholders are those who have property/legal claims (shareholders), contractual agreements (creditors, employees, management, suppliers), moral responsibilities (society, customers), and presumed/legal claims (the environment, government, competitors) as promoted by other sustainability theories of signaling/disclosure, legitimacy, institutional, and stewardship.

AI-driven algorithms and tools can play an important role in helping business organizations manage and integrate the diverse needs of all stakeholders by focusing on maximizing shareholder value and creating long-term shared value for all stakeholders. Specifically, AI systems can assist business organization in: (1) better understanding and engagement with all stakeholders by analyzing vast amounts of data from different sources (e.g., financial, social media, surveys, and public sentiment) and stakeholder opinions; (2) tracking and improving their ESG sustainability performance to optimize resource usage (e.g., energy and water), reduce waste, and track carbon emissions and achieve social and environmental sustainability goals more effectively; (3) ensuring the alignment of strategic decisions with ethical standards and stakeholder interests by identifying potential ethical issues in supply chains (e.g., labor violations and environmental harm) and fulfilling CSR; (4) improving risk management by identifying risks that may affect different stakeholder groups and forecasting financial, environmental, or reputational risks and their potential impact on employees, customers, suppliers, and communities; (5) improving employees workplace by enhancing training, optimizing workforce management, and promoting work–life balance, personalizing learning experiences, recommending career paths, predicting employee burnout that enable management to take actions that improve employee satisfaction and productivity; (6) driving innovation that enhances the customer experience, a core stakeholder group in any business and customizing products and services to individual customer preferences, improving satisfaction and loyalty; (7) improving efficiency, reducing waste, and ensuring ethical sourcing that generate positive environmental impacts; and (8) managing and optimizing CSR initiatives, assessing the effectiveness of their CSR programs, monitoring the real-world impact of these initiatives on communities, and ensuring that resources are being allocated in ways that maximize benefits for stakeholders. Overall, AI offers powerful tools to enhance stakeholder theory by improving engagement, decision-making, ethical standards, and transparency across various stakeholder groups, enabling organizations to create long-term shared value for all stakeholders and better balance the needs of shareholders, creditors, employees, customers, suppliers, communities, and the environment with stakeholder-driven governance models. AI can assist companies in addressing stakeholder-related issues in their sustainability activities.

Other AI sustainability-related theories are systems, Green AI, and the lifecycle assessment (LCA) theories. Systems theory highlights the interconnectedness of business activities with the broader environmental and social systems, emphasizing the importance of holistic approaches that account for complex interactions between various elements. Stakeholder theory expands the concept of value creation beyond shareholders to include all parties affected by a company's operations, advocating for AI solutions that enhance stakeholder engagement, transparency, and trust. The triple bottom line framework underscores the need for organizations to balance economic growth with social responsibility and environmental stewardship, suggesting that AI technologies can help optimize decision-making processes to achieve this balance.

The Green AI theory[2] emphasizes the importance of prioritizing computational efficiency in AI research alongside accuracy. Driven by the rapid and massive increase in the computational cost of DL, growing by 300,000 times in just six years, and the resulting serious environmental and financial impacts, Green AI promotes the adoption of more sustainable and inclusive approaches to AI research. Unlike Red AI, which seeks state-of-the-art accuracy through massive computation ("buying" performance), Green AI aims to achieve comparable results with less computation or reduce costs without sacrificing effectiveness. This theory underscores the importance and relevance of efficiency metrics, such as floating-point operations that should be standard in reporting AI research, enabling transparency and encouraging energy- and cost-saving innovations. This shift would help democratize AI research, allowing broader participation, including those with limited resources, moving the field toward environmentally friendly and cognitively plausible directions inspired by the brain's efficiency.

The LCA theory[3] is a systematic method to evaluate the environmental impacts of products or processes throughout their entire lifecycle, from resource extraction, production, and use to disposal. LCA aims to identify environmental hotspots across global value chains to inform better decision-making in policy, product development, and consumption, avoiding burden shifting between impact categories or phases. The process consists of four main phases: goal and scope definition, inventory analysis (compiling inputs and outputs), life-cycle impact assessment (grouping and quantifying impacts like climate change and toxicity), and interpretation. LCA integrates complex cause–effect environmental relationships and utilizes international consensus on data and modeling standards. Despite its strengths as a screening tool, LCA faces challenges such as data gaps, uncertainties, and simplifications inherent in broad system boundaries. Future improvements include enhancing regional accuracy and incorporating economic and social dimensions, making LCA increasingly relevant to producers, consumers, and policymakers.

These AI-sustainability-related theories can establish a foundation for Doughnut Economics, a model that presents a compass for the 21st-century economy to show how organizations can utilize sufficient resources to provide essential needs for everyone while safeguarding nature and our planet.[4] The concept of the "donut economy" is linked to understanding what our planetary body can handle. Economic growth might be at the core of the problem because it has reached planetary limits as society is currently consuming more than both humans and the planet can sustain. This continued push for growth occurs even in mature economies, seeking more expansion even if it leads to disasters. Within the structure of the donut model, there appears to be an "inside." This is described as human rights not always being protected, such as in the fashion industry, where people live and work "on the inside of the donut model." Moving into the doughnut requires greater equity in resource distribution, especially reducing consumption by the richest, and improved resource efficiency. Well-designed policies can eradicate poverty without stressing planetary boundaries. This suggests that the inner boundary of the donut represents a social foundation that everyone must meet.[5] This model suggests that AI should operate within a "safe and just space for humanity," balancing social foundations and ecological ceilings.

2.3 Emerging sustainability initiatives

The global ESG regulatory landscape is evolving as both the United States and the EU are moving toward more robust and structured sustainability initiatives. However, their approaches differ as the EU tends to adopt more comprehensive, mandatory frameworks at the supranational level, whereas the United States currently leans toward a mix of debatable federal mandates, state leadership, and voluntary corporate action. These emerging initiatives signal a major global shift toward integrating sustainability into the business environment, corporate culture, core business, investment, and supply chain practices. In recent years, both the United States and the EU have significantly accelerated their efforts to promote business sustainability through new initiatives, regulatory frameworks, and strategic policy reforms. These sustainability initiatives reflect growing recognition of the urgent need to support long-term economic resilience and global prosperity, address climate change, protect ecosystems, and promote social responsibility. This section presents emerging sustainability initiatives in the United States and the EU.

2.3.1 United States

In the United States, sustainability initiatives and regulations are advancing and driven by federal rules, state-level initiatives, and market forces as follows:

- **SEC Climate Disclosure Rules:** The US SEC has introduced new rules requiring publicly listed companies to disclose material climate-related risks, GHG emissions, and governance practices related to sustainability. On March 6, 2024, the SEC released its Proposed Final Rules Regarding Mandatory Climate Risk Disclosures that require: (1) climate risk disclosures be included in a company's SEC filings; (2) disclosure of material climate-related risks faced by a company and its efforts in managing climate-related risks; (3) larger registrants to disclose direct Greenhouse Gas (GHG) emissions (Scope 1) and material emissions associated with energy purchases (Scope 2); (4) important financial statement footnote disclosures on expenditures resulting from severe weather events and disclosure of disclose capitalized costs, expenses, charges, and losses as a result of such events; and (5) a level of third-party review subject to attestation standards of those emissions data to increase their veracity and reliability to disclose a quantitative dataset of GHG emissions subject to a gatekeepers' review (Scope 3).[6] These rules are intended to enhance the disclosures needed by investors to make their investment decisions as they benefit from the consistency, comparability, and reliability of these disclosures. This move aims to enhance transparency and allow investors to better assess companies' environmental risks and strategies. Federal initiatives in the United States are increasingly becoming fragmented, with federal climate disclosure rules stalled in the United States, while European mandates gain momentum. In 2025, the US SEC signaled a shift away from federal ESG mandates by halting the proposed climate disclosure rule.[7] The United States has formally rejected the UNSDGs, which are a set of 17 global objectives to address economic, social, and environmental challenges, in March 2025, whereas other countries are aiming to meet these SDGs by 2030.[8] The US withdrawal of support for the SDGs reflects a broader shift toward ESG sustainability efforts, as many US companies align with the SDGs. However, the US withdrawal from the SDGs may accelerate the fragmentation and politicization of the global sustainability landscape.

- **State-Level Regulations:** States such as California are leading independently with laws like the California Climate Disclosure Act (SB 253 and SB 261), mandating detailed emissions reporting and climate risk disclosures for large companies operating in the state. California's emerging climate-related disclosure laws (SB-253 and SB-261)continue to promote far-reaching effects by being applied to large public and private companies with operations in the state and effectively becoming the standard for climate disclosure in the United States.[9] Given California's economic influence, these climate change regulations are becoming de facto standards for corporate climate disclosure in the United States, as about 10,000 companies will be subject to SB 261, of which 5,000 are also subject to SB 253. Specifically, SB 253 requires annual public disclosure of scope 1, 2, and 3 GHG emissions by US-organized entities doing business in California with total annual revenues exceeding $1 billion. Under that Act, the first disclosures are required in 2026 for fiscal 2025. For public companies in the United States, this means increased compliance obligations, particularly around scope 3 emissions tracking for the wider value chain, which equates to about 75% of Fortune 1,000 companies being covered by SB 253, while 73% are covered by both SB-253 and SB-261 acts. The new Senate Bill (SB) 285 was introduced in March 2025 in California, requiring that offsets counted for purposes of GHG emissions reporting under the Climate Corporate Data Accountability Act meet specified requirements. This Bill is intended to help California achieve its 2045 carbon reduction goals by enabling it to better measure progress against its targets.[10] The carbon dioxide removal (CDR) process under SB 285 requires minimizing: (1) copollutant emissions from facilities where carbon capture, use, and storage or CDR technology is deployed; and (2) local water pollution or air pollution from construction- and transportation-related impacts from the projects in communities adjacent to the projects.

Other states in the United States that are implementing or considering implementing pro-ESG measures are Colorado, Florida, Illinois, Maine, Maryland, New Hampshire, New York, Oregon, and Utah. However, there are more than 40 anti-ESG bills that have been enacted in 21 states that are aimed at Prohibit public pension funds, state and local government authorities, and their investment managers from considering nonfinancial ESG factors when investing state assets.[11] Thus, moving forward, public companies in the United States should closely monitor legislative developments in the jurisdictions in which they operate and engage with state policymakers to stay informed on potential impacts. Businesses must also navigate conflicting state-level ESG policies by balancing compliance in states with pro-ESG regulations against restrictions in states with anti-ESG regulations, creating operational and strategic complexities.

- **Corporate Sustainability Reporting:** The United States yet to established a unified national sustainability reporting standard equivalent to the EU's CSRD. However, there is increasing adoption of voluntary frameworks like the Task Force on Climate-related Financial Disclosures (TCFD), Sustainability Accounting Standards Board (SASB) standards, and Global Reporting Initiative (GRI) frameworks among American companies. The International Sustainability Standards Board (ISSB) standards, S1 and S2, are adopted by many public companies in the United States. Several major U.S. companies voluntarily adopt sustainability frameworks including Apple Inc that discloses climate-related risks and opportunities following TCFD recommendations, aligns its sustainability disclosures with SASB standards for the Hardware industry, and provides select disclosures aligned with GRI, particularly for labor practices and energy usage. Another example is Microsoft Corporation that Fully aligns with TCFD in its annual sustainability reports, discloses material metrics according to the Software and IT Services SASB standards, and uses GRI indicators for broader stakeholder reporting. Walmart Inc. uses TCFD to disclose climate risks and opportunities, follows SASB for consumer goods/retail sector metrics, and uses of GRI standards to report on human rights, community engagement, and supply chain issues. These companies are also transitioning toward ISSB compliance, particularly for climate-related disclosures (S2). It is expected that ESG disclosure regulations in the EU will impact not only EU-based companies but also large US multinationals and their subsidiaries. Thus, the emerging ESG regulations will continue to impose compliance burdens and costs, and companies should prepare by integrating regulatory requirements into broader sustainability strategies and strengthen governance and data management for effective compliance.

2.3.2 European Union

The EU has positioned itself as a global leader in sustainability regulation, developing comprehensive and binding frameworks that are reshaping corporate behavior across industries and worldwide. Major emerging initiatives in the EU include the following:

2.3.2.1 EU Disclosure of nonfinancial information

In 2014, the EC adopted the Council Directive on disclosure of nonfinancial sustainability information for more than 6,000 large public companies for their financial year 2017.[12] This Directive requires large EU companies to (1) increase transparency in sustainability reporting, (2) increase sustainability performance on social and environmental matters, and (3) contribute effectively to long-term economic growth and employment. Additionally, these companies should report on their operations, and covered organizations will need to include information about their supply chain.

2.3.2.2 Corporate Sustainability Reporting Directive

In January 2023, the EU CSRD was released, which would require mandatory sustainability reporting for European companies and their counterparts and trading partners worldwide.[13] Effective from 2024, the CSRD expands on previous requirements by mandating large companies, and eventually many small- and medium-sized enterprises (SMEs), to disclose detailed information on their ESG impacts using standardized formats aligned with the ESRS. In recent years, the EU has enacted comprehensive sustainability reporting regulations that are expected to affect thousands of companies, including multinationals headquartered in the United States that operate in or do business with the EU. For example, the CSRD was adopted in 2022, which mandates comprehensive ESG disclosures for in-scope companies, requiring reporting on sustainability performance risks and governance using standardized ESRS. The Corporate Sustainability Due Diligence Directive (CSDDD) was adopted in 2024, which requires in-scope companies to identify, prevent, mitigate, and account for human rights and environmental risks across their operations and value chains.

- **EU Taxonomy for Sustainable Activities:** This classification system establishes clear criteria to determine whether an economic activity is environmentally sustainable, helping investors, companies, and policymakers channel capital toward green activities and avoid "greenwashing." These EU sustainability regulations require all in-scope companies to: (1) disclose their governance, strategy, impact, risk, and opportunity management and (2) conduct a double materiality assessment to determine additional disclosures, assessing both financial materiality of impact of ESG factors on company's financial performance and impact materiality of impact on environmental and social factors. This double materiality assessment determines reporting on climate, pollution, water and marine resources, biodiversity and ecosystems, consumers, end-users, business conduct, workforce, workers in the value chain, affected communities, and resource use and circular economy. These companies should also obtain "limited assurance" to verify that ESG disclosures are free from material misstatements.[14]

2.3.3 Asia

Standards and regulations on sustainability and climate change in Asia are diverse and evolving and vary significantly by country, which reflects differing levels of economic development, environmental challenges, and political commitment. Examples of these climate change regulations in Asia: (1) China Dual Carbon Goals of Carbon peaking by 2030 and carbon neutrality by 2060; (2) Japan's Climate Act:

Japan aims for carbon neutrality by 2050; (3) South Korea Net-Zero 2050 Goal; and (4) India Energy Conservation Act Amendments (2022).[15]

2.4.4 International Sustainability Standards Board

The ISSB is a sustainability standard-setting body created by the IFRS Foundation in November 2021.[16] The ISSB's mission is to establish sustainability-related financial reporting standards to satisfy investors' sustainability information demands. The primary mission of the ISSB is to establish global sustainability-related disclosure standards that provide investors and other capital market participants with material and relevant sustainability information about companies' sustainability information. The ISSB has issued two standards of proposed general sustainability-related disclosure requirements (IFRS S1) and climate-related disclosure requirements (IFRS S2). IFRS S1 establishes overall standards for disclosing sustainability-related financial information to provide stakeholders, including investors, with a complete set of sustainability-related financial disclosures. IFRS S2 establishes the requirements for identifying, measuring, and disclosing climate-related risks and opportunities. IFRS S1 provides a set of disclosure requirements intended to assist companies in communicating with their investors about sustainability-related risks and opportunities, whereas IFRS S2 establishes specific climate-related disclosures and is intended to be used with IFRS S1.

It is expected that as climate risks intensify, more companies worldwide are embedding emissions reduction and climate governance into their core business strategies, corporate culture, business environment, and supply chains. Both the United States and the EU are moving toward more robust and structured sustainability initiatives as climate disclosures across all industries continue to improve, highlighting trends in GHG reporting, target setting, regulatory preparedness, and board oversight. However, their approaches differ as the EU tends to adopt more comprehensive, mandatory frameworks at the supranational level, whereas the United States currently leans toward a mix of debatable federal mandates, state leadership, and voluntary corporate action. Together, these emerging initiatives signal a major global shift toward integrating sustainability into the business environment, corporate culture, core business, investment, and supply chain practices. In recent years, both the United States and the EU have significantly accelerated their efforts to promote business sustainability through new initiatives, regulatory frameworks, and strategic policy reforms. These sustainability initiatives reflect growing recognition of the urgent need to support long-term economic resilience and global prosperity, address climate change, protect ecosystems, and promote social responsibility. It is expected that: (1) most global public companies continue to disclose their exposure to climate risk, particularly in high-exposure sectors; (2) US companies are likely reinforce climate risk and reporting as a board-level issue despite a US federal shift away from climate regulation; (3) US companies continue to comply with emerging state disclosure laws like California's SB 261 and international mandates such as in the EU; (4) US companies continue to increase their carbon disclosures and attempt to reduce scope 1 (direct) and scope

2 (indirect) GHG emissions, due largely to renewable energy purchases, operational efficiency improvements, and grid decarbonization; (5) continue to disclose their scope 3 (value chain) emission by engaging their key suppliers, enhancing data quality, and using external assurance to ensure integrity; and (6) global public companies to set public climate targets of becoming carbon neutral by 2030.

2.4 Global perspectives on AI and sustainability

Global perspectives on AI and sustainability highlight the role of AI in addressing sustainability challenges while fostering economic growth across different countries. Nations have integrated AI into sustainability, demonstrating improved resource efficiency and reduced environmental impact. For example, the United Kingdom's "Green AI" initiative has improved energy management efficiency by over 20%, significantly reducing carbon emissions and operational costs. Germany's Industrie 4.0 framework has achieved a 30% reduction in resource consumption and a 50% decrease in waste during the production cycle. Japan has reduced water waste by as much as 40% in urban areas, resulting in billions saved in treatment costs. At the same time, global collaborations between developed and developing countries are crucial for knowledge exchange and resource sharing, enabling tailored solutions to specific sustainability issues. However, developing nations often face challenges such as inadequate infrastructure and limited access to advanced technologies, which necessitate focused capacity-building initiatives.[17]

Effective policy and regulatory frameworks are essential to ensuring the safe development and deployment of AI while promoting innovation. An interdisciplinary approach that encompasses various perspectives is vital for creating resilient solutions to complex global challenges like climate change. Looking ahead, the integration of AI into sustainable practices has the potential to transform multiple sectors, emphasizing the need for inclusivity and equity in technology deployment to benefit all communities. However, the synergy between AI and sustainability presents transformative opportunities for advancing global sustainability goals.

2.5 Ethical considerations of using AI in sustainability

Using AI-driven tools in sustainability initiatives not only presents significant possibilities and opportunities but also requires careful ethical consideration. Addressing ethical considerations is vital to ensuring that AI is leveraged responsibly in sustainability. Ethical guidelines should be established to ensure transparency, data privacy and security, and a transformative role in advancing sustainability initiatives while respecting societal values and responsibilities. Some of the AI ethical considerations that should be addressed are: (1) personal data sensitivity as AI for sustainability often involves data collection from various sources, such as IoT devices in smart cities or energy usage in homes and industries; (2) security vulnerabilities as AI systems are often vulnerable to hacking and data breaches, which can undermine sustainability efforts and harm individuals or communities if data is misused; (3) algorithmic opacity as many AI models are not fully transparent and often are "black boxes" where decision-making processes are not easily understood creating lack of transparency that may result in distrust among stakeholders and raise questions about accountability; (4) environmental impact of AI development and usage as large AI models can consume vast amounts of energy, sometimes contradicting sustainability goals; (5) accountability and liability that can arise when AI systems make errors, it can be difficult to assign responsibility and lack of AI accountability can lead to ambiguity in legal and moral obligations; (6) AI-driven automation in sustainable industries can displace jobs that should be considered by supporting affected workers through retraining or job transition programs; (7) over-reliance on AI automated systems could undermine human judgment, leading to ethical challenges if the AI's goals do not fully align with human values; (8) AI-driven greenwashing can happen when AI enables companies to appear more sustainable than they are; and (9) lack of trust by stakeholders regarding AI outputs, these insights may have limited influence, especially if there's a lack of clarity in how AI arrived at its conclusions.

Several studies address the underlying ethical concerns and dilemmas that arise from the increasing reliance on AI to help businesses achieve sustainability goals. There are several high profile incidents that highlight the ethical concerns of AI being used in business including Amazon's AI-driven recruitment tool demonstrated bias against women, Microsoft's chatbot, Tay, had to be discontinued due to racist and misogynistic remarks, and Tesla's autonomous systems have been involved in fatal accidents, leading to calls for greater public scrutiny.[18] These AI-related incidents highlight the need for integrating ethical considerations into the design of AI systems to prevent harm and promote equitable outcomes. Thus, the development of guidelines and frameworks for ethical AI that not only mitigate risks but also enhance the sustainability of AI applications across various industries, ensuring that technological advancements align with societal values. A survey uses business journal articles published between 2000 and mid-2021 to help identify some of the main ethical dilemmas dealing with AI in business and finds that foundational issues regarding AI seem to be one of the most dominant topics in the literature that can inform discussions on the ethical implications of AI technologies, particularly regarding their impact on employment and foundational societal issues.[19] A survey of 3,000 Americans aged 18 years and older conducted by the Markkula Center for Applied Ethics reveals that: (1) more than 80% of respondents indicated that they do care whether AI is ethical or not; (2) about 86% of these respondents believe that there needs to be government regulation on AI companies; (3) over half of the survey participants believe that these Ai companies are not even considering ethics when they are developing this technology; and (4) public trust in these AI companies is murky at best as 41% answered that they only somewhat trust these companies and 38% said they do not really rust them with only 8% said they have complete trust in this companies.[20] Overall, these studies suggest a more macro look at AI rather than just focusing on the impact it can have on business.

2.5.1 Ethical AI and potential biases in AI systems

Ethical AI and potential biases in AI systems are one important area, particularly as AI becomes increasingly integrated into decision-making processes across various domains, which have an impact on societal sectors such as bank loan management, stock analyses, healthcare, personnel hiring, and so on. AI tools include ML algorithms, robotics, autonomy, and other related AI platforms. Since the advent of AI, scholars have debated its potential risks, limitations, and negative and ethical effects. Ethical frameworks must be established to guide the development and deployment of AI, ensuring that these systems operate within acceptable moral boundaries and contribute positively to society.

The ethical implications of AI systems are deeply related to CSR. Ethical AI also extends to the broader societal impacts of these technologies. Organizations are expected to fulfill both economic and ethical responsibilities, which include the ethical deployment of AI technologies. Research indicates that robust corporate governance and efficient CSR strategies significantly contribute to translating the advantages of emissions reduction initiatives into enhanced financial performance. Essentially, companies that effectively manage their governance and implement strong CSR initiatives are more likely to achieve financial gains from decreasing their carbon emissions.[21] Regulatory frameworks and international policies can enhance corporate incentives to engage in sustainability practices, thereby leading to more substantial financial benefits. AI can improve corporate governance by integrating with existing frameworks such as data governance and risk management. This involves using AI to monitor compliance and ethical standards, thereby enhancing transparency and accountability within organizations.[22] Ethical AI can significantly improve a company's reputation, long-term value, and sustainability, fostering responsible AI practices that help minimize adverse effects that could lead to reputational damage, such as biased decision-making or compliance failures.[23]

Ethical AI is tied to responsible AI, which reflects a broader commitment to good governance and societal well-being. This approach often attracts stakeholders who prioritize CSR, potentially leading to increased loyalty and higher sales, positively impacting profitability. The ethical considerations should be embedded into AI development and deployment for building and maintaining a positive company reputation through increased public and stakeholder trust and for mitigating potential risks and liabilities, which can contribute to long-term success and sustainability. CSR initiatives should be designed with a focus on achieving greater social impact, which can be relevant when considering the deployment of AI systems in organizational contexts. The ethical deployment of AI should align with CSR principles, ensuring that technological advancements contribute positively to society rather than exacerbate existing inequalities.

ESG and CSR are related and often overlap. ESG focuses on measurable metrics and criteria used for investment and evaluation, while CSR encompasses the overall philosophy and ethical practices of a business regarding its stakeholders. In literature and practice, firms may use either term depending on the context of their discussions about social and environmental responsibilities.[24] They refer to a company's efforts and commitments to operate in a socially responsible manner. Superior ESG performance can enhance valuation in the eyes of investors and stakeholders and contribute to increasing firm value by improving the firm's reputation, building stakeholder trust, and potentially leading to better financial performance. In today's marketplace, there is a growing expectation for companies to operate ethically and sustainably; this expectation shapes investment decisions and consumer preferences alike. To further boost sustainability efforts, organizations increasingly integrate AI into their ESG strategies. The synergy between ESG and AI technologies is significant, offering organizations innovative ways to improve sustainability, social responsibility, and governance practices.[25] However, the ethical use of AI is crucial for fostering trust and maximizing the positive impacts of AI technology on society. This includes principles such as transparency, accountability, fairness, data privacy, and safety. AI systems should allow users to understand decision-making processes, and organizations must take responsibility for AI outcomes. Ensuring fairness involves avoiding biases through diverse datasets and regular audits. Protecting individual privacy is crucial, requiring informed consent and strong data protection. Additionally, AI should prioritize beneficial outcomes for society, addressing challenges in healthcare, education, and the environment. By adhering to these principles, AI can be developed and used responsibly, minimizing risks while maximizing societal benefits.[26]

2.5.2 Responsible AI and ethical AI

2.5.2.1 Responsible AI

Responsible AI contributes to minimizing harm, maximizing benefits, and building trust. It means the development of AI in an ethical, fair, and safe way for humans and society. The development includes transparent and accountable AI systems that respect human rights. It is basically about ensuring the safe use of AI technology in a manner that is good for and does not harm individuals or society. Although AI comes with risks, it may also have tremendous benefits to society. It assists developers and organizations in developing AI systems that are creative, functional, and compliant with the norms of ethics and societal values. Responsible AI is concerned with ethical considerations that rest on three pillars: accountability, responsibility, and transparency (ART).[27] Accountability refers to the need to explain and justify decisions. Responsibility refers to the role of people and the capability of AI systems to answer their decisions and identify errors. Transparency refers to the need to describe, inspect, and reproduce the mechanisms through which AI systems make decisions and learn. These principles are sensitive to human values, highlighting the ethical dimension of responsible AI.

Responsible AI refers to a paradigm that emphasizes the inclusion of ethical values in the design, development, and deployment of AI systems. It involves the responsibility to consider the risks and consequences that AI technologies may impose on individuals and societies. The goal is to create AI systems that prioritize the needs and requirements of people while mitigating potential harm through a human-centered approach to making trustworthy decisions.[28], [29], [30] This includes several key commitments of responsible AI:

1. Prioritization of stakeholder needs involves addressing the needs of all stakeholders, particularly those who are marginalized or disadvantaged, to ensure that the interests, rights, and well-being of all individuals affected by AI systems are considered during the design, development, and deployment of these technologies.
2. Trustworthy decision-making refers to the expectation that AI algorithms will make decisions that are reliable, fair, and aligned with ethical standards, thereby earning the trust of users and society at large. This implies that the algorithms are expected to make decisions that can be trusted by users and society.
3. Information and protection include obligations to protect users and adequately inform them about the AI systems they interact with. This means that AI systems have two obligations: they must safeguard users from harm and give them information about the technology they use.
4. Mitigating negative impacts refers to the expectation that AI will prevent and mitigate any negative consequences that may arise from using AI technologies. The goal is to ensure that AI systems positively contribute to society while minimizing potential harm.
5. Maximizing the long-term advantages focuses on designing and implementing AI systems to produce positive, sustainable societal impacts over time. The goal is to enhance the long-term beneficial impact of AI systems on society.
6. Continuous feedback means that responsible AI algorithms are designed to receive continuing feedback from users to ensure they align with expected social values while improving accuracy and relevance.

Responsible AI practices are informed by ethical concepts, and moral judgments about what is good or bad, right or wrong, should govern AI technology development and use.

2.5.2.2 Ethical AI

Ethical AI is defined through the values of responsible AI. AI ethics guidelines typically highlight five key values: transparency, fairness, safety, accountability, and privacy.[31] While there is a convergence on these core values, different guidelines and frameworks may interpret these values and concepts in various ways, addressing similar ethical areas; they might define or emphasize these areas differently, potentially leading to a lack of standardization. Even when various groups utilize the same terminology, their comprehension of the implications of that term in practical application may differ.[32] Additionally, other frameworks, such as the EC's ethical guidelines for Trustworthy AI, include a broader set of principles such as human agency and oversight, technical robustness and safety, privacy and data governance, transparency, diversity, non-discrimination and fairness, societal and environmental well-being, and accountability.[33] The OECD AI Principles also set out five complementary principles for responsible stewardship of trustworthy AI: inclusive growth, sustainable development, and well-being; respect for the rule of law, human rights, and democratic values, including fairness and privacy; transparency and explainability; robustness, security, and safety; and accountability.[34]

However, these values may not reflect the priorities of a wider and more diverse population that engages with AI technologies. Studies show that people's value preferences are influenced by their experiences and backgrounds; nevertheless, as uniform groups commonly create AI systems, this can result in biases in the definition and application of responsible AI.[35] The absence of reliable data regarding the priorities of various demographic groups suggests that practitioners may unintentionally embed their own biases into the development of responsible AI.

We can define ethical AI as a framework that emphasizes the inclusion of ethical values in the design, development, and deployment of AI systems. The focus should be on ensuring that AI technologies are developed and used in ways aligned with moral principles and societal values, considering the potential impacts on individuals and communities. This includes the importance of privacy, ensuring that personal data is protected and that individuals have control over how their information is used. Ethical AI focuses on the moral aspects integrated into AI development and application. It is guided by moral guidelines and practices that ensure the responsible use of AI technologies. Data bias, lack of transparency, and potential unintended consequences make developing and applying ethical AI quite challenging. Organizations can achieve this by establishing moral guidelines, conducting bias audits, prioritizing explainability, ensuring human oversight, and, finally, promoting AI literacy. For example, regarding fair hiring, an HR ethical AI application should be developed. In summary, ethical AI is the process of creating and applying AI systems in accordance with morality and ethics, designed to maximize the benefits society can achieve while reducing harm and protecting individual rights. The terms "ethical AI" and "responsible AI" are often viewed as interchangeable, but some nuances in their focus and scope are presented in Table 2.1.

Ethical AI is a subset of responsible AI, as illustrated in Figure 2.1. While ethical AI focuses on moral principles, responsible AI ensures that AI is developed and used in a way that benefits society. Responsible AI is important because it ensures that AI technologies are consistent with social values and ethical standards. As AI becomes a part of everyday life, these systems must follow the ethics of fairness, openness, and responsibility. Incorporating these principles into AI development helps build trust with users and stakeholders, which is essential for AI technology adoption and success. Overall, integrating AI ethics with sustainability initiatives and reporting is pivotal for ensuring responsible and transparent use of emerging technologies in advancing ESG initiatives. Ethical AI frameworks promote fairness, accountability, transparency, and inclusiveness, which align closely with the principles of sustainable development. Ethical and responsible AI can enhance the credibility of ESG reporting by ensuring that data collection, analysis, and decision-making processes are free from bias and respect stakeholder rights. Furthermore, AI systems guided by ethical principles can help organizations identify

Table 2.1 Responsible AI versus ethical AI

	Ethical AI	*Responsible AI*
Core Focus	Mainly focuses on the moral implications of AI. Primarily concerned with the moral principles and values that should guide the development and application of AI. Focuses on ensuring that AI behaves ethically.	Includes many more considerations than just ethics. Encompasses a broader perspective, including the ethical principles but also extending to the processes, governance, and accountability mechanisms needed for ethical development and deployment. Focuses on prioritizing stakeholder needs and mitigating negative impacts.
Scope	It mainly aims to ensure that AI maintains social values, avoids causing damage, and encourages fairness. Might be seen as more focused on the inherent ethical qualities of the AI system itself, such as fairness, privacy, transparency, and respect for human rights.	In addition to ethical dimensions, it includes privacy, reliability, safety, transparency, as well as accountability. Addresses the entire lifecycle of AI, from design and development to deployment and use, emphasizing the responsibilities of various stakeholders involved. Considers the broader societal impact and the need for continuous feedback and improvement.
Relationship	Can be considered a component of responsible AI. Achieving responsible AI often requires building ethical AI systems that adhere to moral norms. Some refer to responsible AI as ethical AI.	Sometimes used interchangeably with ethical AI and trustworthy AI. It builds upon the foundation of ethical principles by adding layers of ART in practice.
Example	Developing AI algorithms that do not convey any form of bias.	Implementing/enacting stringent data procedures for the protection of user privacy.

risks, optimize resource use, and monitor sustainability performance in real time. This integration fosters stakeholder trust, strengthens regulatory compliance, and supports long-term value creation through responsible innovation.

2.5.3 *Managing bias, fairness, and transparency*

Bias, fairness, and transparency have become important areas since the increase in public scrutiny and standards. These factors significantly influence the efficiency and equity of various systems, from human resource management and public policy to corporate strategy and social resource allocation. Managing bias, fairness, and transparency in AI systems has gained increasing attention across various industry

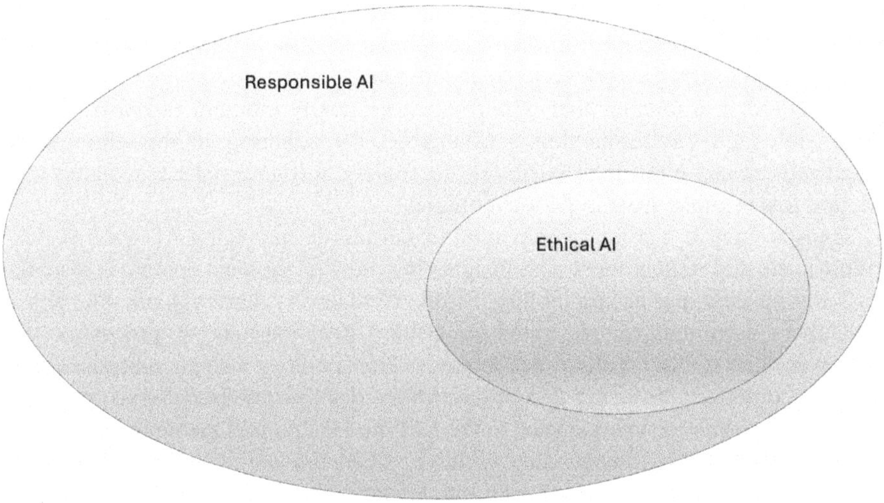

Figure 2.1 Graphic depicting responsible AI versus ethical AI

sectors, including healthcare, finance, and human resources. The integration of AI into decision-making processes has the potential to enhance efficiency and accuracy; however, it also raises significant ethical issues, particularly regarding bias and fairness.

Bias in AI systems often stems from the data used to train these models. For instance, many studies have shown that AI-based decision-making systems can exhibit gender bias, adversely affecting individuals and societal structures. This bias is not merely a technical flaw; it reflects deeper societal inequalities perpetuated through algorithmic processes.[36] Bias in AI can lead to unfair treatment based on race, gender, or socioeconomic status, as algorithms may mirror existing societal biases in the training data. Implicit biases against AI can shape user perceptions and interactions with these systems, suggesting that biases may stem not only from the data but also from user attitudes toward AI and their perception of bias, which can vary depending on cultural contexts, social settings, and use cases. This interaction between human biases and algorithmic outputs raises significant ethical questions about the fairness and equity of AI applications, which can pose risks of discrimination.[37]

Fairness in AI requires a nuanced understanding of how it is defined in different contexts. As various stakeholders may have differing perspectives on fairness, inclusive stakeholder engagement throughout the development process is essential. This engagement ensures that diverse voices contribute to defining fairness, which can inform how AI systems are designed and deployed.[38] Moreover, adopting fairness metrics and frameworks can guide practitioners in assessing and improving the equitable performance of AI systems.[39] The AI ethics and sustainability framework refers to a structured approach that combines ethical considerations and sustainability principles in the development, deployment, and governance of AI systems. This framework seeks to ensure that AI technologies are designed and implemented in a manner that is not only technically efficient but also socially responsible and environmentally sustainable. By adhering to this framework, organizations can contribute positively to society, mitigate risks associated with AI, and foster public trust in AI technologies.

Transparency is a crucial companion to fairness in managing AI systems. Providing users and stakeholders with insights into how AI systems operate is essential for building trust and accountability. Efforts to make AI more explainable, where developers communicate the rationale behind decision-making processes, can empower users to hold systems accountable. Transparency also encompasses clear reporting practices, ensuring that organizations disclose methodologies, potential biases, and evaluation criteria used in their AI models. AI transparency is generally related to algorithmic transparency, which involves the visibility of the algorithms themselves, allowing users to see and understand the decision-making processes within the AI. However, understanding the learning processes of AI systems, particularly those using DL models, poses significant challenges. These systems often function as "black boxes," making it difficult for users to translate their operations into understandable terms. The opaque nature of these models can hinder comprehensive understanding and effective governance of AI.[40]

To effectively manage these dimensions, bias, fairness, and transparency, organizations must embed ethical considerations into every stage of the AI lifecycle. This includes ongoing evaluations of AI systems post-deployment, enabling continuous monitoring and adjustment for biases that may arise over time. Additionally, fostering a culture of ethical consciousness within organizations through training and interdisciplinary collaboration can enhance the ethical management of AI. Managing bias, fairness, and transparency in AI systems is a multifaceted challenge that requires continuous effort from researchers, practitioners, and policymakers, and adopting a systematic approach that combines proactive data collection, stakeholder engagement, fairness frameworks, and transparent practices can significantly mitigate bias and enhance fairness and transparency in AI systems. The integration of ethical frameworks, transparency measures, and human oversight is essential to mitigate the risks associated with AI bias. As organizations continue to adopt AI technologies, it is imperative to prioritize fairness and transparency to build trust and ensure that AI serves as a tool for positive societal impact.

2.6 Legal and societal implications of AI deployment

The implementation of AI technologies brings numerous legal and societal implications that require careful consideration by entities engaged in AI development and application. As AI becomes more entrenched in various sectors, critical issues surrounding regulatory compliance, accountability, and societal impact have emerged as fundamental concerns. The rapid progress of AI technologies has outpaced current legal frameworks, raising significant concerns about the security of personal data and potential privacy violations.[41] A key legal implication of AI is compliance with regulations. Companies that implement AI systems must contend with a complex array of regulations, which encompass data protection laws, intellectual property rights, and safety standards. For instance, the GDPR in Europe enforces strict guidelines on data collection, processing, and user consent. Failure to adhere to these regulations may result in substantial legal penalties and harm to a business's reputation, highlighting the necessity of following these legal requirements.

Accountability and liability represent another key challenge in the deployment of AI technologies. As AI systems become more autonomous, determining who is responsible when an AI system causes harm or makes mistakes becomes increasingly complex. Questions arise regarding whether liability lies with developers, users, or the AI itself, leaving many jurisdictions grappling with the need for legal frameworks that effectively allocate responsibility. Additionally, intellectual property issues must be considered, as the generation of creative content by AI raises questions about ownership and rights. Legal systems must adapt to clarify whether AI can be credited with copyrights or patents, complicating existing intellectual property laws. Privacy and data protection concerns further emphasize the legal landscape surrounding AI. The reliance of AI on data raises significant issues about user privacy, as organizations are required to adhere to laws establishing clear guidelines for data usage, user rights, and informed consent. This is particularly important as AI applications often require large datasets that may contain sensitive information. Moreover, anti-discrimination laws become pertinent in the context of AI, given that biased datasets can lead to discriminatory outcomes in areas such as employment and lending. Therefore, legal frameworks need to address these implications to ensure that AI systems promote fairness and do not perpetuate societal inequities.

The societal implications of AI deployment are equally significant. For instance, the introduction of AI into various industries can exacerbate existing inequalities if marginalized communities are disproportionately impacted. Ensuring that AI systems promote fairness and do not widen the gap between different societal segments is vital. Furthermore, the impact of AI on employment raises concerns, particularly as automation is set to displace jobs in repetitive task roles. While new job opportunities may emerge, there is growing apprehension regarding the necessity for reskilling workers affected by these shifts. Societies must proactively invest in education and workforce development to address the challenges posed by automation. Another pressing concern surrounding AI is its potential to disseminate misinformation, which can erode public trust. Particularly, with the emergence of GenAI technologies, the proliferation of deepfakes and the spread of misinformation have emerged as significant threats to the integrity of information ecosystems worldwide.[42] It is crucial to promote transparency in AI applications to ensure that users can rely on the accuracy and integrity of information generated by these systems. In addition to misinformation, the ethical considerations surrounding AI technologies raise numerous dilemmas regarding privacy, autonomy, and the use of AI in sensitive areas such as law enforcement. Thus, it is essential for society to establish ethical standards that protect human rights while embracing technological advancements.

The European regulation on AI suggests a comprehensive, horizontal approach that aims to regulate AI technologies by balancing legal, ethical, and socio-economic considerations while pursuing geopolitical objectives. Despite the intention to safeguard rights and values, the regulations' applicability could impose challenges, especially on smaller firms within the sector.[43] To effectively build trust in AI, nuanced and context-sensitive regulatory approaches are essential. Policymakers need to understand the multifaceted nature of trust and how different regulatory strategies can positively or negatively impact the human–automation relationship. This awareness can guide the development of regulations that not only govern AI technology but also foster trust in its use. Regulating for trust is not straightforward; it requires deliberate design that recognizes trust's dynamic and context-dependent character, enabling more effective regulatory strategies that can adapt to changing societal perceptions and technological developments.[44]

2.7 Strategies for building fair and transparent AI systems

Building fair and transparent AI systems requires a multi-faceted approach that integrates ethical considerations into every stage of the development and deployment process, integrating principles of algorithmic fairness, transparency, and user engagement. The strategies employed to achieve these objectives should be grounded in empirical research and best practices from various fields, including information systems, human resources, and ethical governance.

One of the foundational strategies for ensuring fairness in AI systems is implementing robust algorithmic fairness frameworks. Algorithmic fairness has been framed as a technology that can mitigate systemic discrimination in automated decision-making processes. This involves not only the technical design of algorithms but also the social context in which these technologies operate. For instance, integrating fairness measures into the design and evaluation of AI systems can help identify and mitigate biases that may arise from historical data or flawed assumptions embedded in the algorithms. In the context of ML-based AI systems, fairness is often conceptualized in terms of groups rather than individuals. This distinction arises from the nature of algorithms and their reliance on statistical patterns derived from data. However, the limitations of current fairness frameworks in AI often fail to address individual circumstances effectively, raising important questions about the definition and implementation of fairness in algorithmic systems. Organizations should adopt a sociotechnical perspective, recognizing that fairness is not merely a technical issue but also a social construct that requires stakeholder engagement and accountability.[45]

As discussed earlier, transparency is a very important component to develop fairness in AI systems. Transparency in AI systems includes the clarity of the algorithms themselves and the processes by which decisions are made and communicated to users. For example, providing clear explanations of how algorithms function and the criteria they use for decision-making can help users understand and trust the outcomes generated by these systems. This implies that developing AI systems with transparency in mind includes documenting the decision-making processes and providing clear explanations of how decisions are made. Making the underlying models accessible for scrutiny can enhance trust, with techniques like explainable AI (XAI) helping users understand the rationale behind AI decisions.[46] Transparency can also be implemented through the user interface, which is designed to facilitate effective management of the level of automation employed in these systems. This means that AI systems should not operate in a vacuum without human involvement, but as tools that enhance and serve human needs while upholding principles of human dignity and personal autonomy.[47]

Another strategy is to actively involve diverse stakeholders in the design and implementation of AI systems. Engaging diverse perspectives, especially from underrepresented groups, helps identify potential biases and ensures that AI systems are fair and inclusive.[48] Involving community representatives, ethicists, and policymakers can offer valuable insights into the ethical implications of the technology and help shape a more equitable system. This approach can be facilitated through workshops, focus groups, and collaborative design sessions, allowing stakeholders to voice their concerns and contribute to developing fair AI practices. Additionally, organizations should consider implementing diversity and inclusion training for employees involved in AI development to raise awareness of ethical implications and foster a culture of fairness.

Furthermore, establishing governance frameworks prioritizing ethical considerations in AI development and deployment is another strategy to implement fair and transparent AI systems. This includes creating policies and guidelines that outline the ethical use of AI technologies, as well as mechanisms for accountability and oversight. Frameworks for ongoing monitoring and evaluation of AI systems enable organizations to track their performance, fairness, and societal impact over time, allowing for adjustments to models and processes as new issues arise. Furthermore, establishing clear accountability structures for AI systems ensures that individuals or teams responsible for ethical deployment are held accountable for outcomes. The goal is to foster accountability, enhance public trust in AI technologies, and ensure that individuals have recourse should they feel impacted by the automated systems. Human oversight plays a critical role in the deployment and operation of AI systems, ensuring that there are mechanisms in place for accountability, transparency, and user engagement. For example, mechanisms for feedback and appeals should be implemented to address injustices when they occur: if a person believes they have been unfairly treated or affected by an algorithmic decision, they should have the option to challenge that decision through a formal procedure.[49]

Organizations can greatly benefit from developing and adhering to ethical frameworks and guidelines for AI development. This can include creating an internal code of conduct that defines principles of fairness, accountability, and transparency. Prioritizing user-centric design principles ensures that AI systems are built with the end user in mind, considering user needs, values, and context throughout the design process. Establishing a robust ethical code guides AI practices in a manner that considers societal impacts and moral responsibility.[50] Governance frameworks should also address issues related to data privacy, security, and the potential for misuse of AI technologies, ensuring that organizations comply with legal and ethical standards. By integrating ethical considerations into the governance of AI systems, organizations can better navigate the complexities of algorithmic decision-making and promote fairness and transparency.

Additionally, ongoing monitoring and evaluation of AI systems are necessary to maintain fairness over time. As AI systems are used in the real and complex world, it becomes vital to evaluate their effectiveness and efficiency frequently. This enables businesses to gather prompt feedback from users, assess results for bias, and implement necessary changes to algorithms and procedures. Organizations should develop the necessary resources and metrics to evaluate fairness and transparency, empowering stakeholders to track progress and identify areas for improvement. As smart cities and societies emerge, AI-driven systems must follow ethical principles prioritizing human dignity, autonomy, and fairness.[51] Adhering to pertinent regulations and standards concerning AI usage is essential, which includes complying with data protection legislation, guidelines on fairness and transparency, and collaborating with regulatory bodies to ensure conformity with legal requirements.

In addition to these strategies, fostering a culture of ethical AI within organizations and forming partnerships with academic institutions and industry leaders focused on ethical AI research can facilitate the sharing of best practices, contributing to the creation of robust frameworks for fair AI development. This involves promoting awareness and understanding of the ethical implications of AI technologies among all stakeholders, from developers to decision-makers. Understanding AI capabilities and limitations empowers users to make informed decisions and hold organizations accountable for their systems. These strategies underscore the importance of developing AI systems that allow users to maintain agency over their interactions with technology, ensuring that humans can oversee operations, make informed decisions, and intervene when necessary.

2.8 Building ethical AI frameworks for responsible business sustainability practices

Building ethical AI frameworks for responsible business sustainability practices involves a comprehensive understanding of the principles underpinning AI ethics and sustainability. As organizations increasingly rely on AI technologies to drive efficiency and innovation, they must ensure that these technologies are implemented in ways that are ethical and aligned with sustainable practices. This requires a deliberate focus on the integration of ethical principles such as accountability, transparency, fairness, and respect for human rights. Ethical AI principles are critical guidelines that govern the development, deployment, and use of AI systems to ensure that they operate in a manner that is fair, transparent, accountable, and respects user rights. These principles are increasingly recognized as essential for fostering trust and mitigating the risks associated with AI technologies. Building ethical AI frameworks in business sustainability practices requires integrating responsible AI principles with sustainability goals.

Aligning AI with sustainability goals requires a comprehensive understanding of how AI technologies can contribute to sustainable development while addressing environmental, social, and economic challenges, thereby supporting the UNSDGs. This alignment is crucial as organizations increasingly recognize the need to adopt sustainable practices in response to global environmental challenges. One of the primary ways AI can contribute to sustainability is through the optimization of resource management. For instance, AI technologies can analyze vast amounts of data to improve decision-making processes in sectors such as agriculture, energy, and waste management. By using big data analytics, organizations can enhance their operational efficiency, reduce resource consumption, and minimize environmental impacts. In the agricultural sector, AI can facilitate precision farming, which optimizes water usage and reduces chemical inputs, thus promoting sustainable agricultural practices. Similarly, in energy management, AI can optimize energy consumption patterns, leading to reduced GHG emissions and enhanced energy efficiency.[52]

As organizations increasingly rely on AI technologies, it is essential to ensure that these systems are designed and implemented responsibly. Ethical AI principles, such as fairness, accountability, and transparency, must be integrated into AI systems to prevent biases and ensure equitable outcomes. Organizations should emphasize sustainability within their AI practices and are encouraged to develop AI solutions that reinforce sustainable business practices by improving resource efficiency and reducing environmental impact. Such an alignment supports broader sustainability objectives while complying with ethical guidelines and providing guidance on AI design and outcomes systems.[53] Moreover, companies need to create mechanisms for monitoring AI systems and establishing who is responsible for decisions made by these technologies. This involves developing clear guidelines that clarify accountability in the decision-making processes and align organizational policies with ethical commitments. For instance, when AI is used in decision-making processes related to resource allocation or environmental assessments, it is crucial to ensure that these systems do not generate existing inequalities or harm marginalized communities. By adhering to ethical AI principles, organizations can enhance public trust and foster a collaborative approach to sustainability.

Ethical AI frameworks should require businesses to provide accessible and understandable documentation regarding the functionality of their algorithms. This documentation should detail data usage, from collection to application in decision-making processes. Ensuring that stakeholders can review and comprehend this information promotes ethical engagement and cultivates an accountable culture within organizations. In addition, organizations must implement strategies to identify and mitigate biases in their AI applications to prevent existing inequalities from being perpetuated or new forms of discrimination from arising. They should inform their target audience about their data privacy policies.[54] The use of fairness metrics and continuous assessment of AI systems can help businesses ensure adherence to ethical standards and foster equitable outcomes.

The role of governance in aligning AI with sustainability goals is vital. Effective governance frameworks can facilitate the responsible deployment of

AI technologies while ensuring that they contribute positively to sustainability outcomes. Policymakers and organizations should collaborate to establish regulations and guidelines that promote the responsible use of AI in sustainability initiatives. By integrating insights from various sectors and considering both environmental and societal factors, the collaboration aims to develop comprehensive strategies that facilitate a balanced transition toward sustainability and responsible AI implementation.[55] This collaborative approach is essential for addressing the complexities of ESG challenges associated with AI technologies. This includes fostering partnerships between the public and private sectors to leverage AI for addressing complex sustainability challenges, such as climate change and resource depletion. By creating a conducive environment for innovation and collaboration, stakeholders can harness the full potential of AI in driving sustainable development.

Finally, fostering human oversight in AI decision-making processes is vital. AI should be viewed as a supportive tool that enhances human judgment rather than completely replacing it. By ensuring that there are mechanisms for human intervention in automated decision-making, businesses can maintain ethical considerations at the forefront. This reinforces the notion that responsibility for ethical decisions ultimately rests with humans rather than algorithms.

The impact of AI on sustainability extends beyond organizational boundaries. The increase of AI technologies can influence societal behaviors and attitudes toward sustainability. For instance, AI-driven platforms can raise awareness about environmental issues and encourage pro-environmental behaviors among consumers. By utilizing AI for educational purposes, organizations can engage communities and promote sustainable practices at the first level, thereby fostering a culture of sustainability. This societal engagement is crucial for achieving long-term sustainability goals, as it empowers individuals to make informed choices that align with environmental stewardship. Overall, when the use of AI technologies is more responsible, organizations can better enhance their sustainability performance, drive innovation, and contribute to the achievement of the SDGs. As the global community faces environmental challenges, integrating AI into sustainability initiatives offers a promising pathway toward a more sustainable and equitable future. Initiatives have been taken to address ethical AI. One example is Ethical AI Integration in Google's Gemini and Gemma Models.[56] Google's development of the Gemini and Gemma models demonstrates a robust application of ethical AI principles such as fairness, accountability, transparency, and safety. These models were designed with responsibility embedded throughout the entire lifecycle, from training data preparation to post-deployment evaluation.

2.9 Summary

This chapter explores the intersection of business sustainability and AI through two primary lenses of theoretical underpinnings and ethical considerations. The first part establishes the theoretical foundations linking AI and sustainability, drawing on key sustainability theories such as stakeholder theory, institutional theory, legitimacy theory, and resource-based theory. These frameworks are adapted to understand how AI technologies can enhance both financial ESP and nonfinancial ESG sustainability performance, drive innovation, and enable data-driven sustainability strategies. The second part of the chapter addresses AI considerations in the context of sustainable business. It discusses the challenges and opportunities of embedding ethical and responsible AI practices.

This chapter establishes a robust theoretical framework for business sustainability that integrates the principles of business sustainability with the ethical dimensions of AI. It begins by exploring foundational theories underpinning sustainable business practices, including stakeholder theory, institutional theory, and legitimacy theory, as these theories collectively emphasize the need for organizations to align economic performance with social responsibility and environmental stewardship. The second part of the chapter then transitions to the ethical challenges posed by the rapid adoption of AI technologies in corporate environments. Ethical considerations address issues of algorithmic bias, transparency, accountability, data privacy, and fairness. It highlights the growing necessity for ethical governance and oversight mechanisms to ensure responsible AI and innovation. By synthesizing sustainability theories with AI ethics, the chapter proposes a conceptual foundation for ethical AI integration into sustainable business strategies and sustainability factors of planning, performance, risk, and disclosure. It emphasizes the role of corporate culture, leadership, and regulatory frameworks in fostering ethical AI applications that support long-term stakeholder value and achieve shared value for all stakeholders. The chapter concludes with the need for interdisciplinary collaboration and continuous ethical evaluation as AI becomes an integral driver of sustainable transformation in business.

2.10 Takeaways

- AI can be a powerful enabler of business sustainability by improving both ESP and ESG sustainability performance through data-driven insights, risk prediction, and operational efficiency.
- Theoretical frameworks such as shareholder theory, stakeholder theory, legitimacy theory, and resource-based theory provide a foundation for understanding how AI supports sustainable business objectives.
- Stakeholder theory highlights the importance of aligning AI development with the interests of diverse stakeholders, including shareholders, customers, employees, regulators, suppliers, communities, and the environment.
- Institutional and legitimacy theories explain how companies adopt sustainable AI practices to gain legitimacy, meet societal expectations, and comply with evolving norms.
- Resource-based theory suggests that AI can be a strategic asset for sustainability, offering firms a competitive advantage through superior data capabilities and innovation.
- Governance of AI is critical for ensuring ethical, fair, and transparent use of AI in business sustainability initiatives and practices.

- Responsible AI requires oversight mechanisms that address data privacy, algorithmic bias, accountability, and transparency.
- Effective AI frameworks must integrate ethical principles, corporate governance structures and functions, and sustainability goals to ensure long-term value creation.
- Regulatory compliance and stakeholder trust are central to governing AI systems in ways that support sustainable development and performance.
- Case studies demonstrate that businesses integrating AI within robust sustainability and ethics frameworks are better positioned to achieve both ethical and performance-driven outcomes.

Notes

1 Rezaee, Z. 2025, Spring. *Business Sustainability: Theory and Practice*. Routledge, Taylor & Francis Group

2 Schwartz, R., Dodge, J., Smith, N.A., & Etzioni, O. 2020. Green AI. *Communications of the ACM*, 63(12), 54–63

3 Hellweg, S., & Milà i Canals, L. 2014. Emerging approaches, challenges and opportunities in life cycle assessment. *Science*, 344(6188), 1109–1113

4 VPRO Documentary. 2017. *Doughnut Economics by Kate Raworth—VPRO documentary—2017*. https://www.youtube.com/watch?v=qYpkRkPjZnM

5 Raworth, K. 2012. *A Safe and Just Space for Humanity. Can We Live Within The Doughnut?* Oxfam Discussion Papers. www.oxfam.org/grow

6 Securities and Exchange Commission (SEC). 2024, 6 March. *The Enhancement and Standardization of Climate-Related Disclosures for Investors*. 17 CFR 210, 229, 230, 232, 239, and 249, [Release Nos. 33-11275; 34-99678; File No. S7-10-22]. Final Rules. https://www.sec.gov/files/rules/final/2024/33-11275.pdf

7 US Securities and Exchange Commission (SEC). 2025, 11 February. *Statement: Acting Chairman Statement on Climate-Related Disclosure Rules, Commissioner Mark T. Uyeda*. https://www.sec.gov/newsroom/speeches-statements/uyeda-statement-climate-change-021025

8 United States Mission to the United Nations. 2025, 4 March. *Remarks at the UN Meeting Entitled 58th Plenary Meeting of the General Assembly, Consideration of Draft Resolution (A/79/L.57/Rev.1)*. https://usun.usmission.gov/remarks-at-the-un-meeting-entitled-58th-plenary-meeting-of-the-general-assembly-consideration-of-draft-resolution-a-79-l-57-rev-1/

9 California, Legislative Information. 2023. *SB-253 Climate Corporate Data Accountability Act and SB-261 Greenhouse Gases: Climate-related Financial Risk*. https://leginfo.legislature.ca.gov/faces/billNavClient.xhtml?bill_id=202320240SB253 and https://leginfo.legislature.ca.gov/faces/billNavClient.xhtml?bill_id=202320240SB261

10 California Air Resource Board. 2025. *California Releases Final Proposal for World-leading Climate Action Plan that Drastically Reduces Fossil Fuel Dependence, Slashes Pollution*. https://ww2.arb.ca.gov/news/california-releases-final-2022-climate-scoping-plan-proposal

11 Ropes & Gray. 2024, 5 November. *The New Battleground in the Fight over ESG's Role in Public Pension Investments: The Courtroom*. https://www.ropesgray.com/en/insights/viewpoints/102jniy/the-new-battleground-in-the-fight-over-esgs-role-in-public-pension-investments

12 European Commission. 2014, 29 September. *Disclosure of Nonfinancial Information: Europe Information: Europe's Largest Companies to be More Transparent on Social and Environmental Issues*. ec.europa.eu/commission/presscorner/detail/en/STATEMENT_14_291

13 European Commission (EC). 2023, 5 January. *The Corporate Sustainability Reporting Directive (CSRD)*. https://finance.ec.europa.eu/capital-markets-union-and-financial-markets/company-reporting-and-auditing/company-reporting/corporate-sustainability-reporting_en

14 The Conference Board. 2025. *The Most Comprehensive Library of Disclosure Data Extracted from US Companies' SEC Filings, CSR Reports, and Organizational Documents*. https://conferenceboard.esgauge.org/login

15 Ullah, S., Arif, M., Hussain, S., & Al-Faryan, M.A.S. 2024. Climate change, governance, and economic growth in Asia: A panel cointegration analysis. *Cogent Economics & Finance*, 12(1). https://doi.org/10.1080/23322039.2023.2299125

16 International Sustainability Standards Board (ISSB). 2021, November. *The IFRS*. IFRS - International Sustainability Standards Board

17 World of Conferences (WOC). 2024. The modern vector of the development of science. In *XVI International Scientific Conference, Philadelphia, PA, USA*. WOC. ISBN 978-92-44514-22-1. https://doi.org/10.5281/zenodo.13919106

18 Sison, A., Ferrero, I., García Ruiz, P., & Kim, T.W. 2023, 12 September. Editorial: Artificial Intelligence (AI) ethics in business. *Front Psychology*, 14, 1258721. https://doi.org/10.3389/fpsyg.2023.1258721. PMID: 37771802; PMCID: PMC10523296.

19 Daza, M.T., & Ilozumba, U.J. 2022, 19 December. A survey of AI ethics in business literature: Maps and trends between 2000 and 2021. *Front Psychology*, 13, 1042661. https://doi.org/10.3389/fpsyg.2022.1042661. PMID: 36600712; PMCID: PMC9806431.

20 University, Santa Clara. 2023. *Ethics in the Age of AI Survey Results*. Markkula Center for Applied Ethics. www.scu.edu/institute-for-technology-ethics-and-culture/ethics-in-the-age-of-ai/

21 Issa, A. 2024. Do emissions reduction initiatives improve financial performance? Empirical analysis of moderating factors. *International Journal of Accounting & Information Management*, 32(2), 228–257.

22 Stahl, B.C., Antoniou, J., Ryan, M., Macnish, K., & Jiya, T. 2022. Organisational responses to the ethical issues of artificial intelligence. *Ai & Society*, 37(1), 23–37.

23 Eitel-Porter, R. 2021. Beyond the promise: Implementing ethical AI. *AI and Ethics*, 1(1), 73–80.

24 Fatemi, A., Glaum, M., & Kaiser, S. 2018. ESG performance and firm value: The moderating role of disclosure. *Global Finance Journal*, 38, 45–64.

25 EY. 2023. *Artificial Intelligence ESG Stakes*. Discussion Paper. https://www.ey.com/en_us

26 EY. *Artificial Intelligence ESG Stakes*.

27 Dignum, V. 2020. Responsibility and artificial intelligence. *The Oxford Handbook of Ethics of AI*, 4698, 215.

28 Barletta, V.S., Caivano, D., Gigante, D., & Ragone, A. 2023, June. A rapid review of responsible AI frameworks: How to guide the development of ethical AI. In *Proceedings of the 27th International Conference on Evaluation and Assessment in Software Engineering* (pp. 358–367). Association for Computing Machnary (ACM). https://doi.org/10.1145/3593434.3593478

29 European Commission. 2019. *High-level Expert Group on Artificial Intelligence. Ethics Guidelines for Trustworthy AI.* European Union

30 Jakesch, M., Buçinca, Z., Amershi, S., & Olteanu, A. 2022, June. How different groups prioritize ethical values for responsible AI. In *Proceedings of the 2022 ACM Conference on Fairness, Accountability, and Transparency* (pp. 310–323)

31 Jakesch et al. How different groups prioritize ethical values for responsible AI

32 Jakesch et al. How different groups prioritize ethical values for responsible AI (p. 15)

33 Jakesch et al. How different groups prioritize ethical values for responsible AI (p. 16)

34 OECD. 2024. *Recommendation of the Council on Artificial Intelligence*, OECD/LEGAL/0449.

35 OECD. *Recommendation of the Council on Artificial Intelligence*; Jakesch et al. How different groups prioritize ethical values for responsible AI

36 OECD. *Recommendation of the Council on Artificial Intelligence*; Jakesch et al. How different groups prioritize ethical values for responsible AI
37 AI Action Summit. 2025. *Rapport international sur la sûreté de l'IA Rapport scientifique international sur la sûreté de l'IA avancée*. https://assets.publishing.service.gov.uk/media/67af5a7363d7f4cceef9e236/International_AI_Safety_Report_2025_executive_summary_french.pdf
38 AI Action Summit. *Rapport international sur la sûreté de l'IA Rapport scientifique international sur la sûreté de l'IA avancée*, 16
39 Cumming, D., Saurabh, K., Rani, N., & Upadhyay, P. 2024. Towards AI ethics-led sustainability frameworks and toolkits: Review and research agenda. *Journal of Sustainable Finance and Accounting*, 1, 100003.
40 Camilleri, M.A. 2024. Artificial intelligence governance: Ethical considerations and implications for social responsibility. *Expert Systems*, 41(7), e13406.
41 Chesterman, S. 2024. From ethics to law: Why, when, and how to regulate AI. In *Handbook on the Ethics of Artificial Intelligence* (pp. 113–127). Edward Elgar Publishing
42 Shoaib, M.R., Wang, Z., Ahvanooey, M.T., & Zhao, J. 2023, November. Deepfakes, misinformation, and disinformation in the era of frontier AI, generative AI, and large AI models. In *2023 International Conference on Computer and Applications (ICCA)* (pp. 1–7). IEEE.
43 Finocchiaro, G. 2024. The regulation of artificial intelligence. *AI & Society*, 39(4), 1961–1968.
44 Tamò-Larrieux, A., Guitton, C., Mayer, S., & Lutz, C. 2024. Regulating for trust: Can law establish trust in artificial intelligence? *Regulation & Governance*, 18(3), 780–801
45 Pfeiffer, J., Gutschow, J., Haas, C., Möslein, F., Maspfuhl, O., Borgers, F., & Alpsancar, S. 2023. Algorithmic fairness in AI: An interdisciplinary view. *Business & Information Systems Engineering*, 65(2), 209–222
46 Pfeiffer et al. Algorithmic fairness in AI, 16
47 Pfeiffer et al. Algorithmic fairness in AI, 37
48 Pfeiffer et al. Algorithmic fairness in AI, 33
49 Pfeiffer et al. Algorithmic fairness in AI, 34
50 Boddington, P. 2017. *Towards a Code of Ethics for Artificial Intelligence Research*. Berlin: Springer.
51 Zwitter, A., & Helbing, D. 2024. Ethics of smart cities and smart societies. *Ethics and Information Technology*, 26(4), 1–5.
52 Javed, A.R., Shahzad, F., ur Rehman, S., Zikria, Y.B., Razzak, I., Jalil, Z., & Xu, G. 2022. Future smart cities: Requirements, emerging technologies, applications, challenges, and future aspects. *Cities*, 129, 103794
53 Javed et al. Future smart cities, 27
54 Javed et al. Future smart cities, 33
55 Javed et al. Future smart cities, 27
56 Pichal, S., & Hassabis, D. 2024. Our next-generation model: Gemini 1.5. February 15. https://blog.google/technology/ai/google-gemini-next-generation-model-february-2024/

3 Corporate governance in AI sustainability integration

3.1 Introduction

Governance of AI integration into business sustainability encompasses a range of issues, from AI-value-adding activities, the responsible use of data, and the prevention of algorithmic bias to the protection of privacy, the impact on employment, and compliance with applicable laws, rules, regulations, and standards. While AI's transformative potential offers substantial opportunities, including benefits of new business opportunities, enhanced efficiency, and improved decision-making, it also presents challenges and complexities that necessitate effective and robust governance measures and ethical oversight. As AI systems often operate as "black boxes," where decision-making processes are opaque and difficult to interpret, organizations worldwide face heightened risks related to bias, discrimination, and accountability. Ensuring that AI applications are reliable, fair, equitable, and transparent is crucial for maintaining stakeholder trust and complying with evolving applicable laws, rules, regulations, and standards. Corporate governance structures, including principles, mechanisms, and functions, play an essential role in overseeing AI integration, providing the necessary checks and balances to mitigate potential risks. Effective governance requires the establishment of robust measures and effective policies, procedures, and accountability mechanisms that address the specific challenges posed by AI technologies. This includes the oversight function of directors and executives in setting up cross-functional teams to oversee AI initiatives and goals, defining roles and responsibilities to achieve the intended goals, and implementing regular audits and assessments of AI systems to ensure that they operate within ethical and legal boundaries.

Organizations must consider the fairness of AI decisions, the potential for reinforcing existing inequalities, possible challenges, and the need for transparency in how AI models are trained and deployed. Developing and adhering to governance and ethical guidelines and standards is crucial for fostering responsible AI practices and ensuring that AI technologies contribute positively to sustainable financial performance and societal outcomes. Furthermore, the integration of AI in business operations presents regulatory and legal challenges. Organizations must navigate a complex landscape of data protection laws, intellectual property rights,

DOI: 10.4324/9781003611981-3

and emerging AI regulations. Compliance with AI-applicable laws, rules, and regulations is essential to ensure a firm commitment to ethical practices and stakeholder interests and avoid unethical practices and potential legal penalties. This chapter addresses the critical aspects of corporate governance in the context of AI integration by examining the principles, measures, and functions of effective AI governance, the development of effective governance frameworks, and the challenges associated with regulatory compliance.

3.2 Evolution of corporate governance and AI integration

The evolution of corporate governance in the context of recent AI advancements reflects a shift from the shareholder primacy model and governance toward more dynamic, data-driven, and transparent practices of the stakeholder primacy model and governance.[1] Corporate governance has traditionally centered on balancing the power sharing between shareholders, the board of directors, and management in protecting the interests of stakeholders under the shareholder primacy model. Over the years, this model evolved to include more stakeholder-centric views, focusing on creating shared value for all stakeholders. The evolution of corporate governance from the shareholder to the stakeholder model with AI integration reflects a convergence of governance with technology and ethical and responsible business practices that are reshaping how businesses operate, manage, report, and engage with stakeholders. This shift is expected to continue directing corporate governance into a more stakeholder-centric, transparent, efficient, and sustainable future.

3.2.1 Shareholder governance

Traditionary, corporate governance models prioritized shareholder primacy, focusing on maximizing profits, creating shareholder value, and ensuring compliance. However, with growing interest in sustainability and societal and environmental impact, stakeholder governance has gained momentum, encouraging companies to balance interests across all stakeholders, including shareholders, creditors, employees, customers, suppliers, and the broader community. This shift has influenced governance frameworks to incorporate ESG criteria.

The shareholder governance model is driven by the agency theory that corporate directors and executives' fiduciary duties are to shareholders who provide financial capital and have a residual claim on the company's assets and cash flows.[2] The principal–agent problem exists because corporations are separate entities from their owners, where management needs physical capital (investment funds), and investors need skilled human capital (management) to run the company, and corporate governance measures should be implemented to ensure management works in the best interest of shareholders. Under the shareholder primacy model, the primary objective of the company is to maximize shareholder wealth, and thus, the role of corporate governance is to ensure the enhancement of shareholder wealth. The shareholder corporate governance structure consists of internal and external mechanisms aimed at effectively aligning the interests of management (agents) with the desires of the principals (shareholders). The shareholder governance measures are intended to reduce the agency costs and align the interests of management with those of investors through: (1) empowering shareholder to monitor, control, and discipline management through incentive compensation plans, enforceable contracts, or legal protection; (2) holding the board of directors fiduciary responsible to shareholders in protecting their interests; and (3) improving the board oversight function to effectively overseeing corporate strategic plans, operations and performance, and reliability of financial and auditing processes. Shareholders play an important role in corporate governance by electing directors who appoint management to manage the company for the best benefits of shareholders. Thus, effective shareholder governance is essential for maintaining a balance of power between shareholders, directors, and management within corporations to ensure that the interests of shareholders are aligned with the long-term sustainability of the company and promote overall corporate responsibility and accountability.

Several research studies have criticized the relevance of traditional shareholder governance to the emerging AI technologies. A paper published in the Harvard Business Review presents five important challenges of AI integration into the traditional corporate governance including: (1) companies cannot rely on traditional corporate governance to protect the social good; (2) even creative governance structures will struggle to tame the profit motive; (3) independence and social responsibility do not necessarily converge; (4) corporate governance should try to solve for the alignment of profit and safety; and (5) AI companies' boards must maintain a delicate balance in cognitive distance.[3]

3.2.2 Stakeholder governance

The stakeholder primacy model considers the interests of all stakeholders, including shareholders, creditors, customers, employees, suppliers, and communities with the primary mission of creating shared value for all stakeholders.[4] The stakeholder primacy model is driven by the concept of impact investing of generating desired financial rates of returns for shareholders while protecting other stakeholders' interests and achieving social and environmental impacts. Stakeholder governance is a process of managing an organization for the benefit of all its stakeholders by considering the interests and concerns of various stakeholders, including shareholders, creditors, employees, customers, suppliers, communities, and governmental bodies, among others, that have an interest or stake in the organization. They assume risks as they are affected by their decisions and actions. Stakeholder governance is a holistic approach to corporate governance that recognizes that a company's success is linked to the well-being of various stakeholders. Stakeholder governance represents a broader trend in corporate governance practices by emphasizing a more inclusive, holistic, and sustainable approach to corporate governance. Some of the important aspects and attributes of stakeholder governance are: (1) identification of all stakeholders that have stake in the company and take risk including shareholders, creditors, employees, customers, suppliers, society, and the environment; (2) active involvement and engagement of all stakeholders; (3) focus on the social and environmental responsibilities and impacts of the company by maximizing its positive outcomes for society and the environment and minimizing its negative impact of society and the environment; (4) meeting expectations of all stakeholders by gaining their trust; and (5) holding corporate decision-makers including directors and executive fiduciary responsible and accountable to all stakeholders including shareholders.

The primary oversight function of the board of directors under stakeholder governance is to protect the interests of all stakeholders by appointing competent, accountable, ethical, and responsible executives to manage the business for the benefit of all stakeholders. Internal and external governance mechanisms, including rules, regulations, policies, and procedures, should be established to achieve the organization's purposes, mission, vision, values, and goals. Internal mechanisms consist of a vigilant and independent board of directors overseeing the organization's purpose, mission, objectives, strategies, and performance and executives' commitments to implement proper strategies to minimize the negative impacts and maximize positive impacts of the organization's activities, operations, and performance. External mechanisms of rules and regulations established by policymakers, regulators, and standard setters can play an important role in stakeholder governance, such as establishing applicable laws, regulations, rules, and standards intended to benefit all stakeholders and protect their interests.

3.3 Business sustainability governance

Business sustainability has advanced from the focus on ESG sustainability performance to governance of business sustainability in creating shared value for all stakeholders. Governance of business sustainability refers to creating frameworks, policies, and practices that ensure a company's long-term success by balancing financial, social, and environmental responsibilities. It extends beyond traditional governance, which focuses on power-sharing among shareholders, the board of directors, and management to protect investors' interests, to include a broader set of stakeholders (e.g., employees, customers, suppliers, communities, and the environment) and protecting their interests. Effective governance of business sustainability integrates all five dimensions of sustainability performance of EGSEE into decision-making processes to ensure that business organizations operate responsibly and sustainably.

Some of the important aspects and attributes of governance for business sustainability are intended to:[5]

1. Develop long-term sustainability investment strategies focusing on long-term and sustainable investments rather than short-term market movements. Business organizations should promote the concept of impact investing and socially responsible investing to generate desired rates of return for shareholders while ensuring social and environmental outcomes. To accomplish impact investing and socially responsible investment strategies, corporations should modify their traditional corporate governance principles and functions by trying to maximize

financial performance as well as to have positive and measurable effects on the environment and society (positive screening, investing in employees, communities, and environment) and minimize the possible negative impacts of business operations on communities, society, and the environment. Sustainability governance requires companies to integrate ESG initiatives into their core business strategies to align sustainability goals with overall corporate strategic plans and corporate objectives. Business organizations that focus on the governance of sustainability and integrate sustainability into their business strategies often gain a competitive global advantage by responding to global market demands for socially responsible and environmentally friendly products and services. A corporate culture that values sustainability is vital to embedding sustainable strategies and practices throughout the organization.

2. Set tone at top by promoting sustainability by the board of directors (sustainability board committee, a director with sustainability focuses and experience) to improve board-level leadership and oversight. The board of directors plays an important role in overseeing a company's sustainability initiatives, strategies, and efforts by setting the tone at the top, integrating sustainability into the company's overall strategy, business environment, and corporate culture to ensure that the company's ESG performance is aligned with its business objectives. Investors are interested in risks and opportunities associated with ESG activities, and boards as their representative should ensure that sustainability risks and opportunities are properly assessed and managed, and that long-term shared value creation for all stakeholders is achieved. The board of directors can effectively fulfill its sustainability responsibilities by promoting impact investing and socially responsible investing by electing at least one director with sustainability interests and skills, creating a board sustainability committee consisting of directors with adequate sustainability expertise, and engaging the entire board of directors in sustainability issues and initiatives, being held accountable for achieving sustainability performance and to provide the needed sustainability leadership. The board of directors plays a key role in fostering the sustainability culture by promoting ethical behavior, encouraging innovation in sustainable practices, and setting clear sustainability targets that align with the company's long-term goals. Corporate directors and executives who prioritize sustainability and set the right tone at the top can inspire employees to adopt sustainable practices and align their actions with the company's sustainability vision.
3. Ensure commitments by executives in promoting financial ESP and nonfinancial ESG sustainability performance. Executive commitments to sustainability can be achieved through the active oversight function of the board of directors, demanding sustainability performance from executives, including a sustainability performance target clause in the executive compensation contract to ensure generation of both ESP and ESG sustainability performance, and rewarding sustainability executive leadership and punishing managerial short-termism. Effective governance of business sustainability emphasizes commitment by management to transparency in ESG sustainability reporting and accountability to stakeholders. Management should comply with global frameworks such as

the ISSB, the GRI, SASB, TCFD, and Integrated Reporting (IR) to ensure providing credible, comparable, and comprehensive sustainability reports. These sustainability reports should be accompanied by assurance statements obtained from independent assurance providers to lend more credibility to these reports, to ensure their accuracy, completeness, and reliability, providing stakeholders with confidence in the company's sustainability reports.

4. Promote stakeholder engagement in sustainability factors of planning, performance, risk management, and disclosure. Governance principles and practices for business sustainability emphasize the importance of engaging with a wide range of stakeholders from shareholders to employees, customers, local communities, regulators, and the environment. Effective stakeholder engagement enables businesses to identify and prioritize the ESG initiatives most relevant to their business model, strategic plans, and stakeholders to ensure that sustainability initiatives are aligned with stakeholder expectations and concerns. Sustainability governance includes identifying, assessing, managing, and mitigating risks associated with ESG sustainability initiatives, including climate change, resource depletion, and labor rights violations. Governance of business sustainability focuses on climate-related risks, including physical risks (global warming, extreme weather) and transition risks (regulatory changes, compliance). The governance of business sustainability emphasizes creating long-term shared value for all stakeholders by balancing financial ESP with nonfinancial ESG sustainability performance, which is a shift from the traditional governance of focus on short-term profits to ensuring that the governance of business operates in a way that is sustainable over the long run. In this regard, companies are moving away from the shareholder primacy model and toward the stakeholder primacy model of adopting a stakeholder-centric model of focus on creating value for all stakeholders rather than prioritizing shareholder returns alone.
5. Initiate and design sustainable innovation and technology by emphasizing the important role that innovation and technology play in promoting business sustainability. Governance frameworks should encourage investment in sustainable innovations and technologies of AI, blockchain, circular economy practices, and renewable energy to improve the sustainability of products, services, and processes. AI can help companies monitor and manage their ESG performance by analyzing large datasets and providing insights into areas such as resource efficiency, carbon emissions, and supply chain transparency.
6. Comply with regulatory and voluntary sustainability initiatives and global sustainability governance frameworks to ensure compliance with local, national, and international regulations related to corporate governance, environmental protection, and human rights. Business organizations should also voluntarily adhere to sustainability standards and initiatives such as the UNSDGs and UNGC to their commitment to responsible business practices as part of corporate governance.

Overall, the governance of business sustainability is an integrated and holistic approach that integrates financial, social, ethical, and environmental considerations into the core operations and strategy of a business. It requires setting the right tone at the top, strong executive leadership and commitments, active stakeholder engagement and impact, transparency, and innovation to ensure long-term shared value creation for all stakeholders, aligning business practices with sustainability goals, and building resilient and sustainable organizations.

The 2024 Blue Ribbon Commission (BRC) report provides the guidance and tools needed to strengthen technology oversight in the boardroom.[6] The 2024 BRC report makes several recommendations for establishing technology governance capabilities and leadership across three key areas of oversight, insight, and foresight of the board of directors to fulfill their fiduciary duty of protecting the interests of shareholders and creating sustainable value for shareholders. The report recommends boards of directors strengthen their oversight of the organization's use of technology and data by: (1) ensuring trustworthy technology use by aligning it with the organization's purpose and values and consider stakeholder trust as part of technology decision-making; (2) upgrading board structures for technology governance by establishing an effective technology committee with outlined clear scope, roles, responsibilities, and authority; (3) clearly defining the board's role in data oversight to ensure that the data is protected and its risks and opportunities are assessed and managed; (4) defining decision-making authorities for technology at board and management levels to ensure that technologies are used to create value; (5) establishing and maintaining necessary technology proficiency among the board through hiring either external technology advisors or recruiting directors with technology and innovation expertise to the board to help maintain proficiency; (6) evaluating director and board technology proficiency to ensure that the board recruitment process considers the necessary level of technology proficiency of new director candidates and proper technology trainings for existing directors; (7) ensuring appropriate and clear metrics for technology oversight including progress metrics tied to time-bound goals and related financial metrics; (8) recognizing technology as a core element of long-term strategy through continuously monitoring emerging technologies and their implications, regularly reviewing emerging competitors, including if and how they change the nature of the firm's business, frequently reviewing management's technology-and data-driven assumptions underlying strategy, and determining new ways to win through technology and data; (9) enabling exploratory board and management technology discussions by hosting a guest speaker about a relevant technology and then have a facilitated set of questions to guide the board and managers through "what-if" questions; and (10) designing board calendars and agendas to ensure appropriate focus on forward-looking discussions by establishing a new agenda approach for the annual board calendar and refining individual meeting agendas.[7]

3.4 Sustainability governance and internal controls

On December 19, 2024, the IFAC issued its guidance and support tools for governance and controls for sustainability information.[8] This guidance is intended to: (1) enable ESG sustainability reports to be issued at the same time as financial statements; (2) reduce the likelihood of modified assurance statements or audit opinions; and (3) ensure that sustainability reporting is prepared with the same rigor, robustness, and ethical approach as financial statements. Effective governance and internal control processes of sustainability reports are vital to improving the quality of sustainability information and achieving the integration of sustainability and financial information. This is aimed at meeting investors' expectations and understanding the financial effects of ESG sustainability risks and opportunities, and aligning sustainability reporting with the requirements of ISSB and CSRD. This guidance is structured based on the Institute of Internal Auditors' Three Lines Model of "clarifying and strengthening the underpinning principles, broadening the scope, and explaining how key organizational roles work together to facilitate strong governance and risk management."[9] The IIA model helps ensure the effectiveness of governance and internal control processes for sustainability, clear allocation, segregation of internal control roles and responsibilities, and the prevention of inefficiency and inconsistent and unreliable sustainability reporting.

The guidance uses an annual cycle of governance and control activities to ensure an effective governance and internal control system for sustainability information. This suggested annual cycle consists of: (1) materiality assessment of determining important sustainability factors, and issues that should be included in sustainability reports, which is a key requirement of most sustainability reporting standards and regulations; (2) risk assessment and material misstatement of determining the sustainability porting process and the scope of the control environment and underlying data, technology, and the internal control process; (3) control objectives that are determined based on risk assessment and materiality of answering questions of "what can go wrong or has gone wrong"? and directing the control design, and employees understand the purpose of the controls; (4) control catalogues consisting of nature and types of control activities, performance, and effectiveness that should be established based on control objectives; (5) standard operating procedures (SOPs) are more detailed versions of control catalogues, which describe each control in detail to improve the maturity of sustainability reporting processes; (6) monitoring plan is designed to ensure the effective implementation of control activities that are typically overseen by the audit committee; and (7) external assurance by independent assurance providers to ensure the confidence in the effective, reliable, and objective sustainability reports.

The aforementioned suggested annual cycle model is intended to ensure the effectiveness of corporate governance and internal controls for maintaining a balance of power between stakeholders, directors, and management to protect the interests of shareholders and align them with the long-term sustainability of the company and promoting overall corporate responsibility and accountability for all stakeholders. The governance and control structure consists of governance measures, control activities, and processes used to protect the interests of all stakeholders by managing the company's relationships and interactions with various stakeholders through robust sustainability reports. In the context of business sustainability, the governance and control structure focuses on the maximization of wealth and creation of shared value for all stakeholders, including shareholders, creditors, suppliers, customers, and employees, the local community, society and global partners, local, state, and federal governments, and the environment. The annual cycle of governance and control guides corporate gatekeepers and participants, from the board of directors to executives, investors, legal counsel, financial advisors, and auditors, to discharge their responsibility effectively and fulfill their accountability, ensure the preparation of both financial statements and ESG reports with applicable laws, rules, regulations and standards, and the integration of audit opinion on financial statements and assurance statement on ESG sustainability reports.

The use of AI platforms in governance and control structures significantly improves the quality of business sustainability performance, reporting, and assurance by streamlining processes, fostering decision-making, and ensuring compliance with sustainability goals and standards. AI-powered tools and techniques can: (1) enhance the governance and control structure through data-driven insights by analyzing historical and real-time data to predict risks and opportunities related to governance practices, supporting boards by providing dashboards with real-time metrics on sustainability performance, ESG compliance, and risk management, and monitoring and ensuring adherence to governance frameworks by flagging deviations in corporate policies, particularly in areas like ethical practices and regulatory compliance; (2) strengthen internal controls by continuously monitor transactions and operations to detect anomalies, such as fraud, data breaches, or policy violations, enhancing the accuracy of internal and external audits by quickly processing large volumes of financial and operational data, identifying discrepancies, and ensuring compliance with sustainability reporting standards, and predicting and mitigate risks related to financial instability, environmental hazards, or governance challenges; (3) promote business sustainability by automating ESG data collection, integration, and analysis, making sustainability reporting more accurate and less labor-intensive, enhancing engagement with stakeholders, such as investors, employees, and communities, by providing tailored, data-driven insights on sustainability efforts and governance practices, and simulating the outcomes of different governance and sustainability strategies, enabling companies to select approaches that align with long-term sustainability goals; and (4) ensure compliance with all applicable sustainability laws, rule, regulations, and standards by assisting businesses in staying compliant with complex and dynamic regulatory ESG sustainability frameworks, and benchmarking corporate governance practices against global standards and recommend adjustments to improve compliance. Overall, AI platforms can transform governance and control structures by offering robust, rigorous, data-driven, and adaptive tools that enhance business sustainability to enable companies to meet their ESG goals, mitigate risks, and build a resilient governance framework for long-term sustainable success.

3.5 Impact of technology on corporate governance

The digital transformation era introduced more transparency and accountability. Data analytics, for instance, enabled real-time monitoring of business practices, helping executives make evidence-based and data-driven decisions while complying with regulatory standards. Particularly, AI integration in corporate governance brings significant improvements and advancements including: (1) enhanced decision-making by the board of directors and executives as AI algorithms can analyze vast amounts of data, trends, identifying patterns and assessing risks that enable directors and executives to make more informed, robust, and proactive decisions; (2) stakeholder engagement as AI tools can analyze stakeholder sentiment and feedback across platforms enabling companies to obtain a clearer understanding of public perception and areas for improvement; (3) improved corporate reporting as AI technologies can generate accurate, transparent, and easy-to-understand reports for stakeholders by using NLP and data visualization; (4) automated compliance as AI can ensure regulatory compliance by automating processes, monitoring regulatory changes, and identifying potential noncompliance in real time to reduce the risk of fines or reputational damage; and (5) robust risk assessment and management and fraud detection as AI-powered tools can identify errors, irregularities, and potential fraud by analyzing transaction patterns and predicting risk factors that make governance more robust.

Several studies attempt to determine the use of AI-driven platforms in business. A research survey was conducted in 2024 to determine the adoption of AI in business and how value creation can be obtained from the use of this technology. The results of this online survey reveal that: (1) 981 of the respondents indicated that their company was utilizing AI in at least one business function, with 878 saying they were regularly using gen AI in at least on business area; (2) organizations are equally as likely to invest more than 5% of their digital budgets in GenAI and analytical AI; and (3) despite vast challenges with AI, those who are able to utilize it are excelling in their respective fields.[10] The results of this survey add to the knowledge about AI use and adoption in business and how companies are utilizing AI-driven tools to create value for the business. Another study presents an update on the current state of AI in business and the initiatives these companies are taking to advance their business utilizing GenAI. Another study provides an update on the current state of AI in business and the initiatives these companies are taking to advance their business utilizing GenAI by conducting a survey of 2,770 senior leaders in businesses, which includes members of boards, C-suites, presidents, and VPs, among others, in 14 countries. Some key points among the results of this survey are that businesses are building on the initial success and potential of AI, businesses are looking for ways to scale AI into more of their operations, and a majority of the respondents believe that there needs to be more regulation in the AI space.[11] Specifically, more than 65% of organizations surveyed indicated that they are increasing their investments in GenAI as they have seen a strong return thus far. The survey respondents also indicate that the main risk with AI that they are concerned with is regulatory compliance, followed by difficulty managing risks and lack of a governance model.[12]

AI can play a transformative role in shareholder governance by improving transparency, enabling data-driven decision-making, and enhancing corporate accountability. There are several ways that AI-driven technologies and tools can influence shareholder governance measures including: (1) analyzing vast datasets to offer insights into market trends, business operations, and financial risks to enable shareholders make informed decisions regarding potential risks and opportunities associated with their investments; (2) enabling more effective and tailored communication with shareholders by providing shareholders with personalized information on company's governance practices, performance, and financial viability; (3) supporting the effectiveness of corporate governance by optimizing board composition and enhancing diversity in terms gender, ethnicity, skills and backgrounds; (4) supporting AI-driven shareholder election systems by streamlining proxy voting, making it easier for shareholders to participate in governance processes; and (5) aligning corporate affairs, actions, and performance with shareholder expectations by enabling robust and transparent governance structure that can adapt to a rapidly technological advances and evolving business environment. A study addresses how AI can enable a sustainable future by using bottom-up and top-down analysis and finds that: (1) using AI for environmental applications has the potential to boost global GDP by 3.1–4.4% while also reducing global GHG emissions by around 1.5–4.0% by 2030; and (2) AI applications in energy (up to −2.2%) and transport (up to −1.7%) have the largest impact on GHG emissions reduction of our sectors covered, but water and agriculture still have an important role to play for the environment more broadly.[13]

AI-powered platforms can play an important role in stakeholder governance by aligning corporate governance practices with the interests of all stakeholders, including shareholders, creditors, employees, customers, suppliers, communities, and the environment. There are several ways that AI serves as a powerful tool in improving the effectiveness of stakeholder governance including: (1) helping companies to engage and communicate with diverse stakeholder groups by analyzing feedback from shareholders, employees, customers, and the public, providing insights into stakeholder, expectations, satisfaction, and concerns; (2) tracking and analyzing financial ESP and nonfinancial ESG metrics from multiple sources in real time, identifying trends and sustainability issues to align corporate actions with sustainable and ethical goals that matter to stakeholders; (3) improving supply chain processes by tracking the origins and sustainability of materials, ensuring ethical labor practices, and assessing supplier risks to ensure commitments to social and environmental standards that resonate with stakeholder values; (4) enabling the use of predictive analytics for economic, social, and environmental impacts by analyzing employee satisfaction, workload, and productivity to improve workplace conditions and forecasting the environmental effect of production methods or the societal impact of layoffs or factory relocations; (5) helping companies gauge public sentiment on environmental and social issues such as climate change or diversity, equity, and inclusion to adjust their strategies to align with stakeholder priorities; and (6) helping to take ethical, social, and environmental considerations into corporate governance processes to make companies more responsive to a broad range of stakeholder needs and expectations that foster trust and accountability and create long-term shared value creation for all stakeholders.

3.6 AI governance

AI technologies have been extensively used across various corporate functions, including recruitment, profitability assessment, information management, investment strategy development, budgeting and pricing in accounting and auditing, product quality monitoring, labor productivity evaluation, and so on. Corporate governance is the structure that is intended to make sure that the right questions get asked and that checks and balances are in place to make sure that the answers reflect what is best for the creation of long-term, sustainable, renewable value. When that structure gets subverted, it becomes too easy to succumb to the temptation to engage in self-dealing.[14] AI has a positive impact on enhancing corporate governance. For example, the impact of AI on the economy and industry has gradually expanded from the macroeconomic level to the microeconomic level. AI technology has introduced significant innovations in corporate operations and management, playing a crucial role in enhancing corporate governance. The application of AI can substantially improve governance standards, with higher levels of AI adoption correlating to more effective corporate governance. The application of AI in corporate governance has many different effects in different areas. From an impact perspective, AI technology could potentially reduce information asymmetry,[15] which is a key factor in corporate governance. Asymmetric information refers to a situation in which one party involved in a transaction or decision-making process possesses more or better information than the other party, leading to an imbalance that can distort outcomes. This phenomenon often results in issues such as adverse selection and moral hazards, affecting market efficiency and decision-making quality.[16] An AI-driven approach can help mitigate asymmetric information by leveraging data analysis and insights to reduce reliance on subjective opinions and ensure decisions are informed by objective data. By utilizing advanced data analysis and ML techniques, AI facilitates better signaling and screening processes, leading to more informed decisions. This helps reduce information gaps and improve data accessibility for both external and internal users of financial and nonfinancial information; AI provides favorable technical conditions and decision-making support that strengthen governance structures. Through its ability to enhance information symmetry, AI has a positive and transformative impact on corporate governance.

Second, AI has a positive effect in terms of data-driven decision-making. The impact of AI on corporate governance involves a lot more than simply facilitating data analysis. AI increases the precision and efficiency of decision-making processes.[17] The adoption of AI models enables organizations to effectively analyze vast amounts of structured and unstructured data, enhancing decision-making and addressing sustainability challenges in areas like climate. For environmental management,

AI aids climate change modeling, monitors deforestation through satellite imagery, and optimizes energy management. Using advanced AI algorithms, AI allows companies to predict future values of their shares in markets and reduce potential business. AI can quickly process massive amounts of data with the help of ML algorithms, extract valuable information from it, and provide accurate data support for corporate decision-making. For example, by analyzing historical sales data, market trends, and customer feedback, AI can predict sales trends of different products in different regions and time periods, helping companies in recommendations or decisions, such as planning production and inventory, and avoid wasting resources rationally.

AI can be employed to monitor compliance with regulations and ethical standards. For example, AI systems can analyze transactions in real-time to detect anomalies that may indicate potential fraud or unethical practices. This capability not only enhances accountability but also supports organizations in adhering to legal and regulatory requirements.[18] By predicting compliance issues, businesses can proactively address them, thus avoiding fines and enhancing their public image. In the energy sector, AI plays a crucial role in managing renewable energy sources, optimizing the operations of wind and solar power installations, and allowing for a higher percentage of renewable energy to be integrated into the grid. This capability is vital for reducing the carbon footprint of energy production.

Finally, risk management is also one of the important applications of AI in corporate governance. By collecting and analyzing internal and external multi-source data, including market fluctuations, industry dynamics, and competitor information, AI can build accurate risk assessment models. These models can assess the various risks faced by enterprises in real time, such as market risk, credit risk, and operational risk, and issue early warning signals based on the severity of the risk. Enterprises can formulate response strategies in advance based on early warning information to reduce the possibility and impact of risks. Risk management should also include strategies that mitigate potential harms, such as AI biases, data privacy, intellectual property, and cyber vulnerabilities. While this encourages flexibility and innovation, it relies on companies and governments to adopt and enforce these principles of sustainability. Risk management, governance, workforce transformation, trust, and data management are critical within AI-powered sustainability. Past methods may not work with new AI technologies, especially GenAI. There will be a transitional phase that transforms potential benefits into value while also exposing challenges as barriers.[19]

Several academic research studies provide evidence of AI governance measures pertaining to the design, control, and oversight of AI systems to ensure that they achieve their intended use and purpose, and they are safe, fair, and beneficial for society. Various aspects of AI governance, providing insights into frameworks, ethical considerations, and implementation challenges, are studied at the team, organization, industry, national, and international levels, highlighting gaps in stakeholder involvement and ethical considerations.[20] Corporate governance measures should provide a comprehensive understanding of AI governance from various perspectives, including ethical, legal, organizational, compliance with applicable laws, rules, regulations, standards, and global viewpoints. The multifaceted nature of

AI governance in identifying key themes, knowledge gaps, the integration of AI into various sectors, and the corresponding governance challenges should be considered when advocating for a comprehensive approach that aligns AI governance and deployment with organizational strategies, legal requirements, and ethical principles.[21] Public companies may consider establishing an AI board committee or assigning the responsibility for AI integration and its opportunities and risks to either audit or risk committees. Effective board oversight is essential for companies to realize the potential opportunities of AI for business efficiency, profitability, and shareholder value creation, as well as assessing and managing potential risks and disruptions to their business, including human rights and privacy, or to avoid costly financial losses. Ever-growing AI applications in businesses demand proactive and responsible oversight of the board of directors to realize AI advantages, avoid risk, manage investor expectations, and remain resilient and competitive. There is a need for holistic governance frameworks in providing comprehensive coverage of all aspects of AI in addressing questions of accountability, governance elements, timing within the AI lifecycle, and implementation mechanisms.[22]

AI governance has received considerable attention from regulators, investors, and businesses in recent years. For example, in 2024, the percentage of companies providing some disclosure of board oversight of AI systems increased by more than 84% year over year and more than 150% since 2022. Shareholder proposals related to AI and its impacts on businesses more than quadrupled compared with 2023 and are expected to intensify further in 2025.[23] AI governance attributes, regulations, and aspects are categorized and summarized as follows:

- **Regulations, policies, and compliance:** Regulators worldwide have established regulations and rules (e.g., the EU AI Act and US AI regulations) that set standards and requirements for the development and use of AI systems, including safety testing, data protection, and accountability. As more business organizations are leveraging complex AI technologies of GenAI and AI agents, there is an urgent need for regulations and standards to ensure transparency and fairness of AI applications. There are currently several AI standards, such as the EU's AI Act, the Open Web Application Security Project GenAI, LLM Security Guidance and Initiatives, and the National Institute of Standards and Technology (NIST) AI Risk Management Framework. Compliance with these and other forthcoming AI rules and regulations ensures responsible AI governance through structural, relational, procedural, and effective governance measures.
- **Ethical principles:** Organizations often adopt ethical guidelines for AI, including fairness, transparency, privacy, human oversight, and sustainability, to guide how AI should be built and deployed. However, there is an urgent need to establish international AI governance frameworks and regulatory structures that support the development of responsible AI by addressing ethical considerations and challenges.
- **Accountability and liability:** AI governance should foster a framework for focusing on extending current regulatory and liability approaches to ensure that if an AI system causes harm (e.g., a self-driving car crash), there are

effective mechanisms and clear processes for investigating these incidents, preventing their further occurrences, assigning responsibility, and compensating victims.

- **Transparency and explainability:** AI governance should provide transparency and explainability in addressing AI challenges and problems, offering options, and making recommendations to ensure ethical and responsible AI systems, and require AI systems to be understandable to users and regulators in assisting in decision-making.
- **Risk assessment, management, and monitoring:** AI governance should require the establishment of adequate and effective AI internal control systems to assess, manage, and continuously monitor AI risks and behavior, implement internal audit models for preventing and detecting bias or errors, and correct them when needed.
- **International coordination:** The International theoretical and practical frameworks should be for AI governance and address the challenges in developing and enforcing such frameworks for countries to work together to handle global AI issues, such as AI arms races, cyberattacks, or unfair global advantages.
- **Stakeholder engagement:** An effective and robust AI governance demands the involvement and engagement of all stakeholders, from AI system developers to technology companies, businesses, governments, civil society groups, academics, researchers, and the public, in determining and influencing how AI is governed.

3.7 Challenges and opportunities of AI in governance

In today's complex and ever-changing business environment, corporate governance and ethical business practices have become the cornerstone of sustainable development for enterprises. As global economic integration deepens, businesses now face increasingly fierce market competition and stringent regulatory requirements. Ensuring compliance, transparency, and fairness in corporate operations while pursuing economic benefits has become an urgent challenge for corporate managers. Meanwhile, AI technology is advancing at an astonishing pace and is being widely applied across industries, profoundly transforming business operations and management practices. From intelligent decision support systems to automated compliance management, AI holds immense potential in corporate governance. AI has been increasingly used for managerial decision-making across various business sectors, particularly in financial services. Additionally, AI plays a crucial role in ethical business practices. As many stakeholders, such as investors, consumers, and suppliers, place greater emphasis on CSR and ESG, companies must maintain ethical standards in areas such as data privacy protection, supply chain transparency, and fair competition, fostering a more responsible and sustainable business ecosystem. For example, AI-powered algorithms can monitor transactions and behaviors to detect unethical activities such as financial fraud, insider trading, and bribery.

The use of AI-delivered technologies can improve the effectiveness of corporate governance and bring new challenges. For example, the board of directors should consider ethical aspects of AI governance in maintaining a balance between automated and human oversight, address potential biases in AI algorithms, and protect data privacy. The board of directors should evaluate accountability in AI-driven decisions to ensure AI's outputs align with corporate culture, ethical standards, and organizational missions and goals. Management should ensure the proper use of AI technologies in measuring and reporting on their environmental and social impact, employee well-being, customer satisfaction, and other nonfinancial metrics. Regulators should also establish rules and standards for ethical AI use, emphasizing transparency, accountability, and fair practices. Despite these challenges, studies suggest that: (1) 65 of chief executives globally see AI as a force for good, but they also believe that there is more work the be done to prevent adverse outcome; (2) the majority of CSOs view data and technology as an accelerator to their organization's sustainability initiatives; (3) integrating AI into sustainability initiatives could enhance organizational effectiveness and societal impact; and (4) there is a need for a balanced approach, emphasizing not only the benefits of AI but also the importance of addressing potential negative consequences.[24]

AI technologies have been extensively used across various corporate functions, including recruitment, profitability assessment, information management, investment strategy development, budgeting and pricing in accounting and auditing, product quality monitoring, labor productivity evaluation, and so on. Corporate governance is the structure that is intended to make sure that the right questions get asked and that checks and balances are in place to make sure that the answers reflect what is best for the creation of long-term, sustainable, renewable value. When that structure gets subverted, it becomes too easy to succumb to the temptation to engage in self-dealing.[25] AI has a positive impact on enhancing corporate governance. For example, the impact of AI on the economy and industry has gradually expanded from the macroeconomic level to the microeconomic level. AI technology has introduced significant innovations in corporate operations and management, playing a crucial role in enhancing corporate governance. The application of AI can substantially improve governance standards, with higher levels of AI adoption correlating to more effective corporate governance. The application of AI in corporate governance has many different effects in different areas. First, from an impact perspective, AI technology could potentially reduce information asymmetry,[26] which is a key factor in corporate governance. Asymmetric information refers to a situation in which one party involved in a transaction or decision-making process possesses more or better information than the other party, leading to an imbalance that can distort outcomes. This phenomenon often results in issues such as adverse selection and moral hazards, affecting market efficiency and decision-making quality.[27] An AI-driven approach can help mitigate asymmetric information by leveraging data analysis and insights to reduce reliance on subjective opinions and ensure decisions are informed by objective data. By utilizing advanced data analysis and ML techniques, AI facilitates better signaling and screening processes, leading to more informed decisions. This helps reduce information gaps and improve data accessibility for both external and internal users of financial and nonfinancial information; AI provides favorable technical conditions and decision-making support that strengthen governance structures. Through its ability to enhance information symmetry, AI has a positive and transformative impact on corporate governance.

Second, AI has a positive effect on data-driven decision-making. The impact of AI on corporate governance involves a lot more than simply facilitating data analysis. AI increases the precision and efficiency of decision-making processes.[28] The adoption of AI models enables organizations to effectively analyze vast amounts of structured and unstructured data, enhancing decision-making and addressing sustainability challenges in areas like climate. For environmental management, AI aids in climate change modeling, monitoring deforestation through satellite imagery, and optimizing energy management. Using advanced AI algorithms, AI allows companies to predict future values of their shares in markets and reduce potential business. AI can quickly process massive amounts of data with the help of ML algorithms, extract valuable information from it, and provide accurate data support for corporate decision-making. For example, by analyzing historical sales data, market trends, and customer feedback, AI can predict sales trends of different products in different regions and time periods, helping companies in recommendations or decisions, such as planning production and inventory, and avoid wasting resources rationally.

AI can be employed to monitor compliance with regulations and ethical standards. For example, AI systems can analyze transactions in real time to detect anomalies that may indicate potential fraud or unethical practices. This capability not only enhances accountability but also supports organizations in adhering to legal and regulatory requirements.[29] By predicting compliance issues, businesses can proactively address them, thus avoiding fines and enhancing their public image. In the energy sector, AI plays a crucial role in managing renewable energy sources, optimizing the operations of wind and solar power installations, and allowing for a higher percentage of renewable energy to be integrated into the grid. This capability is vital for reducing the carbon footprint of energy production.

Finally, risk management is also one of the important applications of AI in corporate governance. By collecting and analyzing internal and external multi-source data, including market fluctuations, industry dynamics, and competitor information, AI can build accurate risk assessment models. These models can assess the various risks faced by enterprises in real time, such as market risk, credit risk, and operational risk, and issue early warning signals based on the severity of the risk. Enterprises can formulate response strategies in advance based on early warning information to reduce the possibility and impact of risks. Risk management should also include strategies that mitigate potential harm, such as AI biases, data privacy, intellectual property, and cyber vulnerabilities. While this encourages flexibility and innovation, it relies on companies and governments to adopt and enforce these principles of sustainability. Risk management, governance, workforce transformation, trust, and data management are critical within AI-powered sustainability. Past methods may not work with new AI technologies, especially GenAI. There will be a transitional phase that transforms potential benefits into value while also exposing challenges as barriers.[30]

3.8 How AI improves sustainability performance

Several studies have examined the use of AI in improving ESG sustainability performance. For example, a paper reviewed various AI techniques used in the context of sustainability and the SDGs and concludes that: (1) artificial neural networks (ANNs) are the most frequently applied AI techniques inspired by the biological neural networks of animal brains that can be used in various sustainability-related tasks, such as predicting renewable energy production, optimizing resource allocation, and modeling environmental phenomena; (2) key areas where AI can contribute include climate action, clean energy, sustainable cities, and responsible consumption and production and AI has been successfully applied to address specific sustainability challenges to optimize energy consumption in smart grids, predict deforestation patterns, and improve waste management systems; (3) there are many several challenges associated with integrating AI into sustainability efforts including data availability and quality, the need for interdisciplinary collaboration, and the potential for unintended consequences; and (4) there are numerous opportunities for advancing the use of AI in sustainability to harness the full potential of AI in achieving the SDGs including the development of more accurate and efficient models, the integration of AI with other emerging technologies (such as the IoT and blockchain), and the establishment of frameworks for ethical AI deployment.[31] Another study examines the Current Landscape of AI and Sustainability Literature by identifying key trends and addressing gaps and challenges and concludes that: (1) several key trends in AI and sustainability research are the importance of collaborative and inclusive research that bridges regional differences, the interconnection of AI, technology, and sustainability topics, and the major research themes related to sustainability; (2) hybrid approaches that combine AI, data-driven techniques, and expert knowledge for multi-level, multi-dimensional decision-making are crucial for addressing complex, interconnected sustainability challenges; and (3) the necessity of addressing ethical concerns and ensuring the sustainable use of AI and big data in sustainability research including preventing monopolization of AI resources and technology and ensuring environmentally friendly AI development.[32] Another paper highlights that AI and DL have the potential to contribute to 134 out of the 169 targets across all SDGs and concludes that: (1) AI-driven technologies can play a significant role in achieving goals related to climate action, clean energy, sustainable cities, and responsible consumption and production; (2) in the renewable energy sector, AI and DL have been effectively utilized to optimize energy management, fault detection, and power grid stability, waste management, and predictive analysis in photovoltaic power plants; and (3) the integration of AI and DL has facilitated the analysis of complex spatial data, improving exposure modeling and disease prediction. This can help better understand and mitigate environmental health risks.[33]

3.9 Engagement of Leadership in AI and sustainability

Recent progress and advances of business sustainability and integration of AI into business sustainability require “tone at the top” commitments to business sustainability strategies and actions, and AI-driven tools and platforms. The leadership of the board of directors and executives plays a vital role in promoting business sustainability and AI integration. Businesses are more likely to achieve their financial ESP and nonfinancial ESG performance when they use AI-delivered technologies and directly report their sustainability performance to a CEO who is committed to sustainability initiatives. A CSO is a top-level executive responsible for leading, overseeing, and managing sustainability strategic plans, initiatives, efforts, risk assessment, performance, and reporting. The role of a CSO has become increasingly important as businesses integrate sustainability into their overall business strategy, corporate culture, business environment, and operations. To effectively achieve financial ESP performance to create value for shareholders and obtain nonfinancial ESG to ensure some positive social and environmental impacts, business organizations have established a new executive position of "Chief Sustainability Officer" to be responsible for (1) participating with the board of directors and other executives in developing and implementing the organization's sustainability strategy plans; (2) promoting achievement of both ESP and ESG sustainability performance to ensure a desired rate of return for shareholders and have social and environmental impacts; (3) assessing and managing the sustainability-related risks including strategic, financial, reputation, compliance, social, and environmental; (4) ensuring compliance with all applicable laws, rules, regulations, and standards to achieve financial viability and protect safety and well-being of all stakeholders, particularly customers, suppliers, and employees; (5) managing business continuity of establishing and implementing sustainability policies and procedures to achieve economic viability and prosperity, environmental impact, social responsibility, governance effectiveness, and ethical business conduct; (6) preventing possible disruption in supply chain by leveraging company strengths, such as technology, manpower, expertise, resources, and market positions, evaluating the effectiveness of existing sustainability initiatives, identifying areas for improvement, and staying informed about emerging sustainability initiatives, trends, and best practices; (7) effectively communicate sustainability information to all stakeholders by engaging with various stakeholders, including shareholders, employees, customers, suppliers, and communities, by building relationships, understanding stakeholder expectations, and finding ways to reach out to new stakeholders or increase participation and communication with existing stakeholders; (8) complying with all the growing government guidelines and regulations by communicating effectively to other officers and employees about best practices in sustainability and enforce compliance with them; (9) engaging in long-term strategy and sustainability performance by discussing and shaping long-term business strategies within corporations and having an open, transparent dialogue with investors regarding sustainability strategies; and (10) collaborating with other executives (CEOs and CFOs) in the preparations of sustainability reports and obtaining assurance statements on these reports in compliance with applicable and globally accepted accounting, auditing and financial standards.[34]

An ever-increasing and growing use of AI in business organizations, from strategic planning to designing policies and procedures, assessing their risks, and implementing operations, necessitates the establishment of a position of chief AI officer (CAIO). The CAIO is a senior executive position responsible for leading an organization's AI strategy, development, innovation, and implementation. The evolving responsibilities of the CAIO are to: (1) design and implement a comprehensive AI strategy that aligns with the organization's overall missions, goals, and integration of AI-tools into business sustainability initiatives; (2) develop and lead AI efforts across the organization, including establishing AI sustainability and governance frameworks, policies, and ethical guidelines to ensure responsible AI applications; (3) manage the deployment and implementation of AI technologies and solutions including staying up-to-date with the latest AI trends, tools, and best practices; (4) collaborate with other executives particularly with the CSO, Chief Data Officer (CDO), the CTO, and other executives (CEOs, CFOs) to ensure data quality, availability, and governance to support AI initiatives; (5) ensure that AI solutions are in compliance with legal and regulatory requirements; and (6) identify, assess, and manage risks associated with AI, including cybersecurity threats, data privacy issues, and operational risks by developing risk management frameworks and contingency plans for AI-related challenges.[35]

Integrating the roles of the CSO and the CAIO enables business organizations to create synergies that align sustainability initiatives and goals with cutting-edge AI technology. This integration could lead to a strategic partnership where AI becomes a vital tool in advancing sustainability initiatives by fostering collaboration between these two positions to achieve more innovative solutions, improved efficiencies, and stronger alignment between technology and sustainability goals. The role of the CSO and the CAIO should be harmonized to: (1) create a shared vision for sustainability by leveraging AI technologies to enhance sustainability initiatives, optimizing energy usage, reducing waste, predicting environmental impacts, and ensuring sustainability goals; (2) streamline ESG data collection, analysis, reporting, and assurance in ensuring more accurate and timely sustainability disclosures; (3) establish data-driven sustainability solutions by integrating AI into sustainability strategies using predictive analytics to anticipate environmental risks, supply chain vulnerabilities, and resource consumption, enabling proactive decision-making; (4) measure, assess, and manage carbon footprints, support the transition to net-zero emissions, and monitor compliance with environmental regulations; (5) monitor and optimize supply chains for sustainability, reducing waste, inefficiencies, and emissions; (6) develop circular economy models by identifying opportunities for recycling, tracking the lifecycle of products, and reducing resource consumption; (7) ensure that AI implementations align with business sustainability principles and practices in promoting social and environmental ethics within the organization; (8) improve the efficiency of renewable energy systems by predicting supply and demand, optimizing grid distribution, and improving storage by prioritizing the use of these AI-driven solutions to meet sustainability target; (9) enable stakeholder engagement by providing real-time data and insights on sustainability performance and ensuring that the AI tools are used to prepare sustainability reports in communicating sustainability efforts transparently and effectively to stakeholders and in complying with sustainability reporting and assurance frameworks; and (10) develop real-time dashboards for tracking ESP and ESG sustainability KPIs and metrics across the organization by allowing both internal and external stakeholders to monitor progress.

Business organizations need to hear from an AI leader to define and implement their AI strategy. Although many businesses are considering hiring a CAIO to define and implement an AI strategy for their organization, it may not be right for every business. Organizations may hire a Chief Information Officer or CDO to implement their AI strategy. The organization's focus should determine the type of AI leader, as many organizations have advanced from technology to business transformation and radical product innovation opportunity. Thus, the selection of an AI leader depends on the organization type, size, and focus on strategic goals, product innovation, or business innovation. However, an AI leader is a strategic systems thinker within an organization.

The active involvement of C-suite executives, including the CEO, CFO, and CSO, is essential for achieving AI-related sustainability goals. The C-suite's active engagement in AI and sustainability initiatives is vital for driving innovation, improving operational efficiency, managing risks, ensuring alignment with global sustainability goals, transforming challenges into opportunities, and positioning organizations for success in a rapidly evolving world. These leaders should establish a comprehensive approach, ensuring that they can effectively address challenges while fostering innovation and sustainability by prioritizing the following actions:

1. **Driving Growth:** Invest in innovation, launch new products and services, and leverage technology (including AI) as core strategies to overcome recent material challenges and future risks while driving profitability.
2. **Aligning AI and Sustainability Goals:** Setting a clear vision that integrates AI technologies with sustainability objectives by identifying areas where AI can drive efficiencies, reduce carbon footprints, and enhance sustainability performance.
3. **Navigating AI Advancements:** Address the rapid evolution of AI technology, which may exacerbate geopolitical tensions (e.g., among the United States, EU, and China), slow global economic growth, create regulatory challenges, and heighten sustainability demands.
4. **Promoting Organizational Commitment:** Foster a culture that prioritizes sustainability and innovation, ensuring that these values permeate all levels of the organization.
5. **Funding AI Initiatives:** Allocating resources to AI projects that support sustainability, such as predictive analytics for resource management or AI-powered tools for monitoring environmental impacts.
6. **Encouraging Sustainable Innovation:** Investing in R&D by creating AI-enabled products and services that contribute to sustainability goals.
7. **Managing Geopolitical and Regulatory Risks:** Navigate complex geopolitical environments and emerging regulations related to AI and sustainability by balancing innovation with risk mitigation, and consider intensified trade wars, foreign cyberattacks, and the increased risk of global conflict as leading geopolitical business threats.
8. **Addressing Ethical AI Use:** Oversee the ethical deployment of AI, ensuring **Greening the Supply Chain:** Executives guide efforts to use AI in optimizing supply chains, reducing emissions, improving efficiency, and promoting

circular economy principles, transparency, fairness, and compliance with global regulations.

9. **Optimizing Supply Chains:** Alter supply chains to reduce risks and costs, improve proximity to customers, and promote environmentally sustainable practices.
10. **Assessing and Managing Risk:** AI-driven analytics help executives proactively identify and address risks within the supply chain, such as disruptions due to climate change or geopolitical tensions.
11. **Preparing for Economic Uncertainty:** Evaluate the potential for a global economic downturn or recession while anticipating slower economic growth in both emerging and mature markets.
12. **Addressing Labor Challenges:** Respond to labor shortages, rising labor costs, and demographic shifts by attracting and retaining top talent by developing strategies to attract, train, and retain talent with expertise in AI and sustainability to ensure productivity and alignment with sustainability goals.
13. **Accelerating Digital Transformation:** Advance digital transformation, including the adoption of AI, to enhance sustainability performance, workforce productivity, customer satisfaction, and innovation.
14. **Focusing on Sustainability:** Prioritize climate risk management, compliance with AI-related regulations, and adherence to sustainability disclosure requirements.
15. **Leveraging AI for Sustainability:** The adoption of AI-powered tools and technologies, such as ML and IoT, enables organizations to monitor and reduce their environmental impact, improve energy efficiency, and enhance sustainability reporting.
16. **Driving Customer-Centric Innovation:** AI-powered insights enable executives to develop sustainable products and services that meet emerging consumer demands for environmentally friendly solutions.
17. **Transparency in Reporting:** Ensure the organization adheres to sustainability reporting standards (GRI, SASB, ISSB, and CSRD) by leveraging AI to enhance the accuracy and timeliness of ESG disclosures.
18. **Building Trust:** Demonstrate the organization's commitment to sustainability and responsible AI usage by engaging with stakeholders, including investors, regulators, customers, and employees.
19. **Promoting Long-Term Resilience and Adaptation:** Integrate AI and sustainability into business strategies by adapting to challenges such as climate change, economic shifts, and anticipating and responding to disruptions, ensuring long-term sustainability and stability, and meeting consumer expectations, investor needs, and stakeholder expectations.

3.10 AI and multiple risk assessment and management

Multiple risks refer to the assessment and management of financial risk as well as strategic, reputational, compliance, ethical, technical, operational risk among others. AI-powered systems play a transformative role in multiple risk assessment and management by enabling organizations to detect, evaluate, and respond to a broad spectrum of risks with greater accuracy and efficiency. AI can analyze vast and diverse datasets in real time to identify emerging threats across financial, operational, cybersecurity, environmental, and compliance domains by leveraging machine learning algorithms, natural language processing, and predictive analytics. AI capabilities can detect patterns and anomalies that might be missed by traditional methods, enabling proactive risk mitigation and faster decision-making. Furthermore, AI-driven tools support continuous monitoring and adaptive learning, allowing risk management strategies to evolve dynamically in response to new data and changing conditions. Ultimately, AI enhances both the strategic and operational aspects of risk management, promoting resilience, agility, and informed governance. This section examines multiple risks in the context of business sustainability using ML and AI platforms and their implications in financial reporting and auditing processes. Multiple risk assessment and management in the context of AI generally involves evaluating the following risks:

1. **Financial Risks:** Financial risks are risks relevant to financial and economic factors such as market volatility, inflation, currency fluctuations, economic downturns, and financial instability. These risks encompass various types of uncertainties or potential losses that companies, investors, or individuals may encounter and can arise from various internal and external factors, including economic downturns, market volatility, material financial misstatements, financial mismanagement, and structural weaknesses. For example, market risk can arise from fluctuations in market prices, including stock prices, interest rates, exchange rates, and commodity prices. Effectively managing economic and financial sustainability risks is essential for businesses to ensure financial viability, resilience, profitability, and shared value creation over time for all stakeholders.
2. **Nonfinancial Risks:** Nonfinancial risks are risks relevant to ESG factors. Nonfinancial risks encompass a range of risks that are not directly tied to financial performance but can significantly impact an organization's strategic planning, operations, reputation, and long-term sustainability. Emerging nonfinancial risks relevant to ESG sustainability can include climate risks affecting asset values, reputational risks from social issues, and governance risks from regulatory noncompliance. With increasing ESG-focused policies and AI in sustainability, there is a push to integrate these nonfinancial factors into risk assessment. Corporate practice of risk management could be extended to cover sustainability (environmental risk) risks using AI technologies. AI could be used as a tool for predictive analytics, helping businesses anticipate environmental risks, thus enabling better decision-making.
3. **Technical Risks**: These risks relate to robustness, reliability, safety, and performance of the AI systems, consisting of issues such as algorithmic bias, model accuracy, robustness against adversarial attacks, cybersecurity attacks, and

compliance with regulations. These risks arise from rapid technological change, reliance on specific technology, or the failure of IT systems, which can disrupt operations and data integrity.

4. **Ethical and Societal Risks**: These risks focus on the broader implications of utilizing AI systems, such as privacy concerns, job displacement, societal impact, and adherence to ethical standards.

3.10.1 Steps for multiple risk assessment and management

Business organizations with sustainability-focused can employ AI-powered tools to monitor and manage these risks in real time using the following steps:

1. **Identify Risks**:
   - **Technical:** Analyze potential failures, biases, and data security issues.
   - **Financial:** Assess the risk of materially misstated financial information generated by using AI applications.
   - **Nonfinancial:** Analyze the risk of material ESG information.
   - **Ethical:** Evaluate impacts on privacy, fairness, and societal well-being.
2. **Assess Risks**:
   - Use quantitative and qualitative methods to assess the likelihood and impact of each identified risk.
   - Assess the negative outcomes for financial, nonfinancial, technical, and ethical risks.
   - Engage stakeholders to understand different perspectives and concerns.
3. **Manage Risks**:
   - Implement technical safeguards such as rigorous testing, validation, and continuous monitoring.
   - Design accounting processes to mitigate financial and nonfinancial risks.
   - Establish ethical guidelines and frameworks for responsible AI use, including transparency and accountability measures.
4. **Monitor and Review**:
   - Regularly revisit the risk assessment to adapt to new challenges and advancements in AI technology.
   - Continuous monitoring of all types of risks.
   - Solicit feedback from users and affected communities to ensure ongoing alignment with ethical standards.
5. **Documentation and Reporting**:
   - Maintain clear records of risk assessments and management strategies.
   - Update risk documentation.
   - Communicate findings transparently to stakeholders to foster trust and collaboration.

Effectively assessing and managing these multiple risks is essential for ensuring that AI technologies enable businesses to achieve financial viability and have social and environmental impacts. Integrating and balancing innovation with responsibility enables businesses to build public trust and encourages the responsible adoption of AI.

3.11 AI and double fraud prevention, detection, and reporting

Fraud is commonly defined as an intentional, wrongful act to deceive, harm, or injure others.[36] Fraud can be classified into: (1) occupational/employee fraud, which is fraud against the company, usually involving misappropriation of assets, theft, and embezzlements; (2) financial statement and management fraud, which is intentional misstatements or omissions of amounts or disclosures in financial statements to deceive investors; and (3) nonfinancial ESG fraud, which is intentional misstatements or omissions of amounts or disclosures in reporting ESG performance. Greenwashing is the most important challenge preventing progress toward reducing carbon footprint, an important problem that also damages the trust in the sustainability environment of claiming "net zero" emissions. Carbon offset schemes could be considered an intentional accounting fraud (net-zero emissions) or unintentional greenwashing accusations (reducing carbon footprint).

Common forms of fraud in carbon offset schemes are: (1) false claims of reducing emissions without actual, verifiable reductions; (2) false claims of offsetting for actions that would have occurred anyway without the carbon offset funding; (3) double counting of the same emission reduction by multiple parties; (4) exaggeration of the amount of reduced CO_2; and (5) not provide clear, transparent reporting and verification can hide fraudulent activities.

Double fraud in ESP and ESG sustainability performance refers to the simultaneous occurrence of deceptive practices in both financial and nonfinancial reporting by a company. This means the company is misleading stakeholders about both its financial health and its commitment to sustainable and ethical practices, including social and environmental impacts. Double fraud can severely undermine investor confidence, damage the company's reputation, and lead to legal and regulatory consequences. Examples of double fraud in sustainability reporting include: (1) overstating financial performance, where a company might inflate its financial results to appear more profitable while simultaneously exaggerating its ESG achievements to attract socially conscious investors; and (2) greenwashing and financial misreporting, where a company could engage in greenwashing by falsely claiming environmental initiatives while manipulating its financial statements to hide losses or inflate profits.

Financial ESP reflects how a company reports its economic and financial activities, focusing on long-term sustainability and economic viability to create wealth for shareholders. Financial reporting fraud may involve manipulating financial statements to present a misleading picture of the company's economic health and sustainability. This could include overstating revenues, understating expenses, or engaging in practices like big bath accounting to distort financial results.

Nonfinancial ESG performance measures a company's commitment to environmental protection, social responsibility, and governance practices, which generate environmental and social impacts. Fraud in this area may involve providing false or exaggerated information about a company's environmental impact, social initiatives, or governance practices. For example, a company might falsely claim to have reduced carbon emissions or misrepresent its labor practices and corporate governance standards.

Double fraud refers to situations when a company engages in fraud in both ESP and ESG reporting. This means that the company is misleading stakeholders about both its financial health and its commitment to sustainable and ethical practices, including social and environmental impacts. Double fraud can severely undermine investor confidence, damage the company's reputation, and lead to legal and regulatory consequences. It can mislead stakeholders into believing the company is more sustainable and financially healthy than it is, potentially leading to poor investment decisions and misallocation of resources. Examples of double fraud are as follows: (1) a company might inflate its financial results to appear more profitable while simultaneously exaggerating its ESG achievements to attract socially conscious investors; and (2) a company could engage in greenwashing by falsely claiming environmental initiatives and at the same time manipulate its financial statements to hide losses or inflate profits, inflating the value of carbon credits, using modern slavery for production, making illegal political donations. Companies must ensure that their sustainability reports are accurate and free from misleading information, which requires robust internal controls, regular audits, and adherence to reporting standards to prevent fraudulent practices. Noncompliance with legal and regulatory requirements related to sustainability reporting can result in both financial and nonfinancial fraudulent practices. Companies need to communicate transparently with stakeholders, address their concerns, and incorporate their feedback into their sustainability initiatives. These foster trust and collaboration, leading to more sustainable business practices.

The identification and prevention of double fraud is important for: (1) protecting investors from receiving misstated financial and nonfinancial information and ensuring that they have accurate information for decision-making; (2) ensuring companies adhere to financial and ESG reporting standards and comply with all applicable laws, rules, regulations, and standards that help maintain market integrity and trust; (3) producing accurate reporting on both financial and ESG metrics is essential for promoting genuine sustainable development and corporate responsibility; and (4) enabling stakeholders, including investors, regulators, and policymakers, to better evaluate the true performance and sustainability of a company, thereby fostering a more transparent and accountable business environment.

Examples of double fraud cases are as follows:

- **Volkswagen Emissions Scandal:** In 2015, Volkswagen was found to have installed software in diesel engines to cheat emissions tests. The software allowed the vehicles to emit lower levels of pollutants during testing than they did in real-world driving conditions. This deceit affected around 11 million cars worldwide. The scandal led to significant legal penalties, a massive recall of vehicles, and severe reputational damage. It highlighted the need for stricter oversight in environmental claims by corporations. AI technologies are playing an increasingly critical role in monitoring real-time vehicle emissions, leveraging advancements in AI, the IoT, and ML models, for example, the On-Board Diagnostics (OBD-II) system, which allows for the continuous monitoring of various parameters directly from vehicles. Like TinyML soft-sensor technique that retrieves data from vehicles through OBD-II, enabling real-time detection and monitoring of emissions in urban settings. This methodology can be integrated with edge processing hardware, facilitating immediate data analysis and emissions assessment, thereby improving air quality monitoring.[37]

Moreover, advances in ML have enabled more sophisticated approaches to emissions prediction. For example, by employing DL models, frameworks have been built to develop driving cycle-based emission models for diesel vehicles, addressing the challenges posed by differing driving styles and engine performance.[38] These models use vast datasets to create accurate emission inventories, further supporting real-time analysis.[39]

Combined with sensor networks, AI makes the ability to monitor things much better. There is a particular system that brings together different data sources along with AI technologies. This system does not just keep track of emissions; it can also monitor noise pollution. This shows how flexible these solutions can be in smart transportation systems.[40] The cooperation among different AI algorithms makes it possible to conduct spatial-temporal analysis. Thanks to this, it is feasible to make accurate and up-to-date predictions about the emissions from vehicles in urban areas.

- **BP Deepwater Horizon Oil Spill:** In 2010, BP's Deepwater Horizon oil rig exploded, causing one of the worst environmental disasters in history. The company was found to have ignored safety protocols and environmental concerns, which are key components of environmental and governance practices. BP faced substantial fines, cleanup costs, and long-term reputational damage. The disaster highlighted the importance of environmental responsibility and robust safety governance. AI technologies, particularly DL and LLMs, could have played a crucial role in preventing or mitigating the BP Deepwater Horizon oil spill by enhancing real-time monitoring, predictive analysis, and automated decision-making.[41]

AI has the potential to significantly boost real-time monitoring during oil extraction and transportation. Sophisticated ML models can analyze vast amounts of data obtained from drilling operations. They can spot patterns and abnormalities that might signal equipment breakdowns or unsafe situations. AI plays a crucial role in predicting failures within engineering systems. Predictive maintenance, as suggested, can avert disasters such as oil spills by identifying problems proactively before they turn into major catastrophes.[42] For instance, AI systems can examine sensor data from drilling rigs to keep track of well pressure and temperature. This allows for earlier action in case of any irregularities.

In addition, when remote sensing technologies, especially Synthetic Aperture Radar (SAR), are integrated, it becomes easier to detect oil spills over large regions. SAR imagery works by analyzing the surface features of water bodies. This allows it to accurately identify oil spills, making it an extremely useful tool for spotting spills early and taking quick action.[43] And geographic information systems combined with AI models can analyze regions susceptible to spills, visually mapping key risk factors and vulnerabilities.[44]

3.12 AI and double materiality assessment and consideration

Materiality in sustainability refers to what is important and meaningful to all stakeholders, including sustainability issues and factors that could influence investors' assessment of sustainability information. Double materiality considers both financial materiality—how sustainability issues affect the company's financial performance—and environmental/social materiality—how the company impacts the environment and society. The concept of double materiality, as introduced by the EU's CSRD, encompasses both financial and nonfinancial materiality.[45] Double materiality requires companies to assess both the financial impact of sustainability issues on the company (financial materiality) and the company's impact on the environment and society (impact materiality). This dual approach ensures a comprehensive understanding of sustainability, addressing both external and internal factors that influence the business. This means that companies need to assess both how sustainability matters affect their financial performance (financial materiality) and how their operations impact the environment and society (impact materiality).

Financial materiality focuses on how sustainability matters, such as climate change, resource scarcity, and social responsibility, may pose either a prospective material risk or opportunity that could affect a company's financial performance and position over the short, medium, and long term. Sustainability matters are considered material for primary users of a company's financial reports if omitting or misstating the information could influence their decisions. For instance, regulatory changes, market demands, and environmental risks can pose financial threats or opportunities. Companies need to disclose these potential impacts to provide a complete picture of their financial health and sustainability initiatives.

Impact materiality focuses on the actual or potential short-, medium-, and long-term impacts on people or the environment that are directly linked to a company's operations and its value chain. These impacts can be both positive and negative. Impact materiality examines how a company's operations affect the environment and society. This includes evaluating the direct and indirect effects of activities such as emissions, waste management, labor practices, and community engagement. Companies must disclose these impacts to demonstrate their commitment to sustainability and accountability, fostering trust among stakeholders.

To comply with the CSRD, companies need to conduct a double materiality assessment. To apply the double materiality principle effectively, companies must conduct a thorough assessment that incorporates both financial and impact perspectives. This involves identifying material sustainability impacts, risks, and opportunities from both financial and impact perspectives. The ESRS detail the reporting requirements and mandate that companies independently assess if a sustainability matter is material from one or both perspectives. Conducting a double materiality assessment adds complexity to materiality assessments. Implementing the double materiality principle presents challenges, such as the complexity of assessing diverse sustainability issues and ensuring accurate reporting. Companies need to understand sustainability matters in their value chain to measure and assess financial and impact materiality. However, this process also provides valuable insights for shaping company strategy and ensuring compliance with sustainability reporting standards. By understanding and applying the double materiality concept, companies can enhance their sustainability reporting and contribute to a more transparent and accountable business environment. Companies that successfully apply double materiality can enhance their sustainability reporting, improve stakeholder trust, and drive long-term value creation. This comprehensive approach allows businesses to anticipate and manage risks more effectively, aligning their strategies with both regulatory requirements and stakeholders' expectations. By adopting the double materiality principle, companies can provide a more holistic and transparent view of their sustainability efforts, aligning with the requirements of the CSRD and enhancing their overall sustainability performance. By understanding and applying the double materiality principle, companies can enhance their sustainability reporting, manage fraud risks, and contribute to a more transparent and accountable business environment.

3.13 AI applications in fraud detection and risk analysis

The rapid evolution of technology has introduced significant challenges in fraud detection and risk analysis. With increasingly sophisticated fraud tactics and a growing volume of digital transactions, organizations are compelled to adopt advanced solutions. AI and its subsets act as game-changing tools in this context.

As global economies become more interconnected, the dynamics of fraud are growing increasingly complex. The increasing use of AI and GenAI has significantly empowered cybercriminals by providing them with advanced tools and techniques that enhance their fraudulent activities. Financial institutions, e-commerce platforms, and various organizations are facing serious threats from different fraud schemes, including identity theft, transaction fraud, and data breaches. At the same time, stakeholders demand rigorous ESG risk management to align with sustainability objectives. AI has surfaced as a groundbreaking solution, facilitating proactive fraud detection, real-time risk analysis, and compliance with regulatory and sustainability frameworks.

Traditional fraud detection methods, often marked by static rules and historical data analysis, are no longer effective against these evolving threats. In this context, AI technologies provide a strong framework for improving detection mechanisms and conducting real-time risk assessments through advanced analytics to enhance organizational resilience. AI's transformative potential offers innovative solutions for fraud detection and risk analysis in diverse fields. We will explore AI techniques, applications, and benefits while addressing challenges, ethical considerations, and best practices for CEOs, managers, and sustainability specialists across various industries. The integration of AI technologies allows organizations to enhance their capabilities in identifying fraudulent activities, managing risks, and safeguarding consumer trust. AI encompasses a range of technologies, including ML, NLP, and anomaly detection techniques, enabling systems to learn from data, identify patterns, and make decisions with minimal human intervention.[46, 47] The commonly employed AI algorithms and techniques are detailed in the following. Table 3.1 summarizes the AI algorithms for fraud detection and financial risk assessment.

Table 3.1 AI algorithms used for fraud detection and financial risk assessment

Algorithm/Technique	*Description*	*Application*
Decision trees	Splits data into branches to make decisions based on features	Identifying patterns that may indicate fraud
Random forests	Ensemble method using multiple decision trees for improved accuracy	Aggregating outputs to detect fraudulent transactions
SVMs	Classifies data points by finding the optimal hyperplane that separates classes	Distinguishing between legitimate and fraudulent behavior
Neural networks	Analyzes complex data patterns; excels at unstructured data recognition	Detecting fraud through analysis of transaction data
KNN	Identifies anomalies by comparing transactions to similar data points	Detecting outlier behavior indicative of fraud
Isolation forest	Anomaly detection algorithm that isolates anomalies instead of profiling normal data	Identifying fraudulent transactions in datasets
Autoencoders	Neural networks that compress and reconstruct data; used to spot deviations from normal behavior	Detecting potential fraud by analyzing reconstruction errors
Logistic regression	Regression analysis for binary classification (e.g., fraudulent vs. non-fraudulent)	Credit scoring and risk assessment.
Bayesian networks	Uses probabilities to assess relationships among variables; predicts the likelihood of fraud	Predicting risk based on prior data
NLP	Analyzes textual data to identify risks or fraudulent claims based on semantic content	Analyzing transaction descriptions or communications for fraud
RL	Develops systems that adapt and improve over time based on feedback from predictions	Proactive fraud detection improving strategies over time
Clustering algorithms (e.g., K-means)	Group transactions based on similarity to identify clusters with fraudulent characteristics	Detecting clusters that exhibit fraudulent behavior
Behavioral biometrics	Analyzes unique patterns in human behavior for authentication.	Detecting fraudulent activities and enabling proactive measures

3.13.1 Various ML algorithms used for fraud detection

- **Decision Trees:** These algorithms split data into branches to make informed decisions based on specific features, helping to identify patterns that may indicate fraud. The data is divided into subsets based on feature values, creating a tree structure that is easy to interpret but can be prone to overfitting.
- **Random Forests:** An ensemble method that uses multiple decision trees to improve prediction accuracy and reduce the likelihood of overfitting. It is effective in identifying fraudulent transactions by aggregating outputs from various decision trees.
- **Support Vector Machines (SVMs):** This algorithm classifies data points by finding the optimal hyperplane that separates classes, making it useful for distinguishing between legitimate and fraudulent behavior.
- **Neural Networks:** Particularly DL models can analyze complex and high-dimensional data. They excel at recognizing patterns in unstructured data (like text or images) and have been successful in detecting fraud from transaction data. While capable of capturing intricate patterns, they tend to be less interpretable than simpler models.
- **K-Nearest Neighbors (KNN):** This algorithm identifies anomalies by comparing a given transaction to the most similar transactions in the dataset, helping detect outlier behavior indicative of fraud.

3.13.2 Anomaly detection techniques

- **Isolation Forest:** This algorithm is specifically designed for anomaly detection and isolates anomalies instead of profiling normal data points. It focuses on isolating observations to identify outliers and works particularly well with high-dimensional datasets.
- **Autoencoders:** A type of neural network that learns to compress and reconstruct data. It can be trained on normal transaction patterns; deviations from the reconstructed data can signal potential fraud. They are used for unsupervised anomaly detection by learning efficient representations of input data. They are particularly useful for detecting rare events, but require a deeper understanding of the model for explainability.

3.13.3 Statistical techniques

- **Logistic Regression:** This is a regression analysis used for binary classification (fraudulent vs. legitimate). A classical statistical method that serves as a baseline due to its interpretability and wide acceptance in regulatory environments. It provides coefficients that can be easily understood, allowing for clear feature importance assessments. It is often used in credit scoring and risk assessment.
- **Bayesian Networks:** Using probabilities to represent relationships among variables, these networks can assess risk by predicting the likelihood of fraudulent activities based on prior data. These probabilistic models are based on applying

Bayes' theorem with the assumption of independence among predictors. Naive Bayes is commonly used for classification tasks and helps in understanding the underlying probabilities of classes.

3.13.4 Natural Language Processing

NLP encompasses various algorithms to analyze and interpret human language, enhancing the accuracy of AI systems in financial fraud detection. By leveraging traditional ML techniques, NLP analyzes textual data, such as transaction descriptions and user communications, to identify potential risks and fraudulent claims through semantic analysis. It identifies keywords indicative of fraud and flags suspicious activities, significantly reducing false positives and negatives. NLP analyzes data from various sources, including social media and customer interactions, to uncover fraud indicators based on language patterns. Additionally, NLP supports sentiment analysis, language translation, and chatbots through advanced models like transformers. By recognizing linguistic nuances, NLP can detect phishing attempts and social engineering tactics, facilitating proactive fraud mitigation. Ultimately, NLP enhances organizations' capabilities in detecting fraudulent activities, enabling them to safeguard financial systems and maintain security in customer interactions. Modern NLP systems increasingly leverage advanced models such as BERT, RoBERTa, and other large language models (LLMs) for deep contextual understanding of text data. These models excel at capturing subtle meanings, variations in syntax, and context-dependent semantics, which significantly improves fraud detection performance in complex language scenarios. Additionally, techniques like Named Entity Recognition (NER) are employed to extract and classify critical information such as names, locations, account numbers, or organizations from unstructured data. This helps in identifying fraudulent actors, fake identities, and suspicious claims more efficiently. By integrating these state-of-the-art models, NLP systems can detect more sophisticated forms of fraud, including fabricated transaction narratives or impersonation schemes, with greater accuracy.

3.13.5 Reinforcement learning

Reinforcement learning (RL) is utilized to create proactive fraud detection systems that adapt and improve based on feedback from their predictions. Within this framework, an agent learns to make decisions by receiving rewards or penalties related to its actions, allowing it to refine strategies over time. In fraud detection, RL models enhance their effectiveness by learning from past experiences and outcomes, continuously optimizing their strategies as new fraud patterns emerge. These models evaluate prior actions, determining the accuracy of identifying fraudulent versus legitimate transactions. Positive outcomes lead to reinforcement, while incorrect flags result in penalties. This dynamic learning process enables the system to improve its detection methods, operating in real time to quickly address emerging fraud threats. By leveraging RL, organizations can develop resilient fraud detection systems that evolve to meet the challenges posed by new fraudulent tactics. Common RL techniques applied in fraud detection include Q-Learning and Deep Q-Networks (DQN). Q-Learning is a value-based method that helps an agent learn optimal actions by estimating the expected rewards for each state-action pair. DQN extends this approach by using deep neural networks to approximate these values, enabling effective decision-making in high-dimensional environments like real-time transaction monitoring. These methods allow systems to adaptively learn detection strategies without requiring labeled data for every possible fraud scenario.

3.13.6 Clustering algorithms

Clustering algorithms are unsupervised learning techniques that identify patterns and anomalies in large datasets, making them effective for detecting new fraud schemes. They group transactions based on similarity to highlight clusters with potentially fraudulent characteristics. Common algorithms include K-means, which partitions data into K clusters by minimizing variance, and DBSCAN, which identifies clusters of varying shapes and densities while handling noise and outliers effectively. Hierarchical clustering also aids in fraud detection by building a hierarchy of clusters to uncover hidden relationships. In risk analysis, clustering helps identify high-risk profiles by grouping similar customer behaviors, enabling organizations to develop targeted risk management strategies. The flexibility and adaptability of AI clustering algorithms make them essential tools in the ongoing fight against fraud and in enhancing risk analysis processes. They enable organizations to continuously adapt their detection systems to new threats, improving their overall fraud prevention strategies.

3.13.7 Gradient boosting algorithms

Gradient boosting algorithm, like XGBoost, is an ensemble learning technique that builds models incrementally by combining weak learners (typically decision trees) through optimization. Gradient boosting algorithms are highly effective for complex predictive tasks like fraud detection due to their incremental learning approach, ability to compose weak learners, and capability to uncover intricate feature relationships. Gradient boosting techniques are known for their ability to capture complex patterns within data, resulting in high levels of predictive accuracy. This is particularly important in fraud detection, where the identification of fraudulent transactions often relies on subtle and intricate patterns among various features. Fraud detection requires understanding interactions among multiple variables (e.g., transaction amounts, locations, and user behavior). Gradient boosting can effectively model these nuanced interactions, improving the detection of fraudulent activities that may not be obvious when analyzing individual features in isolation. Common implementations of gradient boosting include LightGBM and CatBoost, which are optimized for performance and can handle large-scale data efficiently. LightGBM is known for its speed and ability to manage categorical features with minimal preprocessing. CatBoost is especially effective at handling categorical data natively, without requiring manual encoding. These models are widely used in production-level fraud detection systems and in data science competitions due to their high accuracy and scalability. In addition, feature engineering is critical for maximizing the effectiveness of gradient boosting algorithms. Creating meaningful features such as transaction frequency, customer spending patterns, or location-based metrics can significantly improve the model's ability to detect fraudulent behavior.

3.13.8 Behavioral biometrics

Behavioral biometrics refers to technology that analyzes unique patterns in human behavior to create a digital profile for authentication. Unlike traditional biometrics, such as fingerprints or retinal scans, behavioral biometrics focuses on dynamic actions such as typing patterns, mouse movements, and touchscreen interactions. This technology provides an additional layer of security that is difficult to replicate. Unlike passwords or PINs, behavioral patterns are unique to each individual and are not easily mimicked by fraudsters. This makes behavioral biometrics a robust tool for securing digital transactions and protecting sensitive information. By continuously monitoring these behaviors, the system can authenticate users in real time and identify any suspicious activities. This technology enhances security by observing user behavior throughout a session, which helps prevent account takeovers and dynamically detect unauthorized activities. By establishing a baseline of normal behavior, the system can identify significant deviations that may signal potential fraudulent actions, triggering alerts as necessary. Additionally, it reduces false positives by recognizing subtle behavioral cues, ensuring that legitimate users are not inconvenient. Behavioral biometrics improves security while enhancing user experience and supports increased loss mitigation by enabling proactive measures, such as blocking suspicious transactions or freezing accounts based on unusual behavior. Unlike static authentication methods such as passwords or one-time codes, behavioral biometrics enables continuous authentication by monitoring user behavior throughout an entire session. This approach helps detect fraud in real time, such as account takeovers or unauthorized access after login. Tools like BioCatch have successfully implemented behavioral biometrics in production environments to enhance fraud detection capabilities across banking and financial platforms. However, since behavioral data includes highly personal interaction patterns, it raises important concerns around data privacy and user consent. Organizations must ensure compliance with privacy regulations and transparently communicate how such data is collected and used to maintain user trust while enhancing security.

The combination of these algorithms allows companies to analyze large datasets, detect anomalies, and create robust systems for both fraud detection and risk assessment. The adaptability and real-time processing capabilities of these

AI methods enhance the effectiveness of fraud prevention and financial risk management strategies. Table 3.1 shows AI algorithms used for fraud detection, their description, application, and risk assessment and management.

3.14 GenAI for fraud detection and risk analysis

GenAI is rapidly evolving and showing great promise in various fields, particularly in fraud detection and prevention. Its impressive capabilities suggest limitless future applications that can sometimes seem overwhelming. However, while anti-fraud professionals use GenAI to identify and combat fraudulent activities, criminals are also quick to leverage this technology for their own deceptive purposes. This creates an ongoing conflict between those fighting fraud and those exploiting it, highlighting the dual-edged nature of GenAI. Fraudsters exploit GenAI to create realistic fake documents and misleading data, complicating audits.

GenAI plays a transformative role in fraud detection and prevention, particularly in the context of the growing reliance on digital platforms. It employs various algorithms, such as variational autoencoders (VAEs) and generative adversarial networks (GANs), which enable the creation of synthetic data, allowing for rigorous testing of detection algorithms while protecting real data privacy.[48] The combination of both models addresses the limitations of traditional supervised techniques that typically struggle with class imbalance and the dynamic nature of fraudulent patterns. This integration allows for the capabilities of GANs to complement the anomaly detection and feature extraction strengths of autoencoders and VAEs, leading to improved performance metrics such as accuracy, recall, and area under the curve.[49]

3.14.1 VAEs in enhancing fraud detection

VAEs are valuable for their probabilistic interpretation and their ability to generate synthetic data that reflects real transactions, assisting in anomaly detection. When new transactions are evaluated, those with low reconstruction probabilities (i.e., those that do not fit well into the learned distribution) can be flagged as potential fraud. VAEs have the ability to capture complex data patterns and help to model both normal and fraudulent transactions by providing a latent space representation, which can identify anomalies based on reconstruction error. They are particularly effective in situations where labeled data is scarce, as they allow the system to learn from the inherent structure of the data without requiring vast amounts of labeled examples. By analyzing the reconstruction loss during the test phase, the VAE can assign anomaly scores to transactions. During the training phase, a VAE learns to reconstruct input data by compressing it into a latent space and then reconstructing it back to the original space. The reconstruction error, which is the difference between the actual input and the reconstructed output, serves as an anomaly score. Transactions with high reconstruction errors are flagged as potential fraud, as they deviate significantly from learned normal patterns.

3.14.2 GANs in enhancing fraud detection

GANs enhance fraud detection through several key mechanisms that improve model performance and address common challenges in the field of anomaly detection. GANs excel in producing realistic data and adapting to new fraud schemes, making them particularly useful for real-time fraud detection and minimizing false alarms. They are used to generate realistic synthetic fraudulent transactions that are then mixed with original datasets to create a more balanced training set. This alleviates issues related to imbalanced class labels, which are a common problem in fraud detection. The synthetic data produced by GAN models allows for training VAEs and other models on a larger, more representative dataset, hence improving the accuracy and effectiveness of the detection models. By mixing the synthetic data generated by GANs with real transaction data, the learning process of models such as VAEs and autoencoders is enhanced. The GAN-generated data provides additional examples for the model to learn from, which can improve the overall detection performance and reduce the false positive rate. By training on a mix of normal and generated fraudulent data, GANs can improve detection accuracy and reduce the number of legitimate transactions incorrectly flagged as fraudulent (false positives). The main advantage of these models is their capacity to produce highly realistic synthetic data, which is beneficial when real fraudulent transaction samples are scarce or imbalanced. They are particularly effective in detecting subtle and emerging fraud patterns due to their adaptive nature.

3.15 Agentic AI and AI agents for fraud detection

Agentic AI refers to autonomous AI systems designed to pursue complex goals with minimal human intervention. These systems differ from traditional AI, which typically relies on structured instructions and close oversight. Agentic AI demonstrates adaptability, advanced decision-making capabilities, and self-sufficiency, allowing it to operate dynamically in changing or uncontrolled environments.[50] Unlike conventional AI systems, which are task-specific and operate within defined parameters, agentic AI can independently manage resources and make judgments to achieve long-term objectives over extended periods without pre-specified behavior or human supervision. Agents are specialized and purpose-driven modules trained for specific tasks.[51] They are autonomous software programs that observe their environment, make decisions, and act to achieve specific goals, having the ability to interface with other agents. In their environment, they take sensory information and generate actions that affect it. This interaction is typically continuous and non-terminating.[52] AI agents represent a significant advancement in AI, blending the power of AI with human-like interaction and decision-making capabilities. They can range from simple rule-based systems to complex ML models and are designed to operate independently, without constant human control or supervision.[53] AI agents reshape how businesses interact with their digital and real-world environments,[54] with key functions including the following:

1. **Perception:** detecting changes or anomalies in their environment.
2. **Responsive actions:** taking actions to influence their environment, adjusting strategies as needed.
3. **Reasoning and interpretation:** interpreting complex datasets to support decision-making.
4. **Problem-solving:** offering solutions and strategies to address challenges.
5. **Inference and learning:** analyzing past and present data to predict future outcomes and enhance performance.
6. **Action and outcome analysis:** planning actions considering various scenarios and their impacts.

AI agents can be powerful fraud detection and prevention tools by providing sophisticated, real-time solutions that can adapt to evolving threats. They can mimic human self-reflection and evaluation. They offer significant advantages over traditional methods by leveraging advanced analytics, ML algorithms, and real-time monitoring capabilities. They can detect fraud by scrutinizing vast amounts of data, identifying complex and subtle patterns, including those not easily recognizable by humans. They can pinpoint unusual behaviors and discrepancies that may indicate fraud. By analyzing transactional data, user behavior, and other relevant metrics in real time, they can detect and flag suspicious activities much faster and more accurately than traditional methods. By integrating GenAI, AI agents continuously refine fraud detection algorithms, combine with an organization's proprietary data to provide context-aware insights, and create a tailored approach to fraud prevention. For example, they can be used in card fraud, where AI agents analyze transaction patterns and identify anomalies such as unusual spending habits or geographic locations. Another significant application is malware detection, where AI agents monitor files and network activities to spot signs of malware, analyze file behaviors, and track network traffic to detect patterns indicative of malware spread. AI agents can detect document forgery by employing sophisticated image analysis and pattern recognition techniques. AI agents can also continuously learn and adapt to new fraud techniques to autonomously handle fraud detection processes.[55] This includes identifying anomalies and suggesting mitigation actions, allowing teams to focus on high-value activities. This enables organizations to take immediate action to prevent potential financial losses and mitigate damage.

3.16 Summary

This chapter explores the critical role of corporate governance in effectively integrating AI into sustainability strategies and practices. As organizations increasingly adopt AI technologies to address ESG challenges, robust governance frameworks are essential to ensure ethical, transparent, and responsible implementation. The chapter begins by defining the intersection of AI and sustainability, highlighting the potential of AI to enhance sustainability performance through predictive analytics, real-time monitoring, and optimized resource management. The discussion then shifts to corporate governance structures, emphasizing the importance of board oversight, audit committees, risk management systems, and ethical codes in guiding AI deployment. Special attention is given to the responsibilities of the board of directors in aligning AI initiatives with long-term ESG goals and stakeholder interests. The chapter also reviews best practices for data governance, algorithmic accountability, and compliance with emerging AI regulations, as well as risk assessment and fraud detection.

Key governance issues include algorithmic transparency, data privacy, bias mitigation, accountability, and stakeholder engagement. The chapter outlines emerging frameworks for AI governance that align with sustainability goals, emphasizing the importance of aligning AI oversight with principles of ethical leadership, regulatory compliance, and long-term value creation. It illustrates how businesses can implement governance mechanisms that ensure AI technologies support, not undermine, sustainable development and the achievement of sustainability goals. Together, various sections of this chapter provide a comprehensive understanding of how theoretical insights and robust governance systems can guide the ethical integration of AI in advancing sustainable business practices. Main key challenges, such as bias in AI systems, lack of transparency, and potential misuse of AI, are addressed, along with governance mechanisms designed to mitigate these risks. Real-world case studies illustrate how companies are integrating AI into their sustainability agendas under strong governance models. The chapter concludes with a forward-looking framework for AI-sustainability governance, advocating for a multi-stakeholder approach that includes ethical AI committees, independent audits, CSO, CAIO, and ESG-aligned KPIs. By embedding AI within a robust governance system, businesses can drive innovation while ensuring responsible, sustainable growth.

3.17 Takeaways

- AI can significantly enhance sustainability efforts by enabling data-driven decision-making, predictive modeling, and real-time environmental and social monitoring.
- Strong corporate governance is essential to ensure that AI applications align with ethical standards, stakeholder interests, and long-term ESG goals.
- Boards of directors play a critical role in overseeing AI strategy, risk management, and the integration of sustainability priorities into technological innovation.
- Transparent and accountable data governance frameworks help mitigate risks such as algorithmic bias, privacy breaches, and regulatory noncompliance.

- Ethical oversight mechanisms, including AI ethics committees and independent audits, are vital to ensure the responsible deployment of AI in sustainability contexts.
- Governance structures must adapt to the complexity and rapid evolution of AI technologies while maintaining a focus on corporate accountability and public trust.
- Multi-stakeholder engagement, including input from regulators, communities, and civil society, strengthens AI governance and supports inclusive sustainability outcomes.
- KPIs aligned with ESG objectives should be used to measure the effectiveness of AI initiatives and ensure CI.
- Case studies demonstrate the value of proactive governance, showing how leading organizations use governance to balance innovation with responsibility in AI adoption.
- Future governance frameworks should be dynamic and forward-looking, fostering agility, resilience, and ethical stewardship in the integration of AI and sustainability.

Notes

1 Rezaee, Z. 2025, Spring. *Business Sustainability: Theory and Practice*. Routledge, Taylor & Francis Group

2 Rezaee, *Business Sustainability*

3 Tallarita, R. 2024, 18 April. Ai is testing the limits of corporate governance. *Harvard Business Review*. hbr.org/2023/12/ai-is-testing-the-limits-of-corporate-governance.

4 Rezaee, *Business Sustainability*

5 The Conference Board. 2025. *The Most Comprehensive Library of Disclosure Data Extracted from US Companies' SEC Filings, CSR Reports, and Organizational Documents*. https://conferenceboard.esgauge.org/login

6 National Association of Corporate Directors (NACD). 2024. *2024 Blue Ribbon Commission Report. Technology Leadership in the Boardroom: Driving Trust and Value*. https://www.nacdonline.org/all-governance/governance-resources/governance-research/blue-ribbon-commission-reports/BRC/2024/tech-leadership-in-the-boardroom/

7 National Association of Corporate Directors (NACD). 2024. *Blue Ribbon Commission Report*

8 International Federation of Accountants (IFAC). 2024, 19 December. *Building Trust in Sustainability Reporting and Preparing for Assurance: Governance and Controls for Sustainability Information*. https://www.ifac.org/publications/building-trust-sustainability-reporting-and-preparing-assurance-governance-and-controls

9 Institute of Internal Auditors (IIA). 2024, September. *The IIA's Three Lines Model: An Update of the Three Lines of Defense*. https://www.theiia.org/en/content/position-papers/2020/the-iias-three-lines-model-an-update-of-the-three-lines-of-defense/

10 Chui, M., Hall, B., Singla, A., Sukharevsky, A., & Yee, L. *The State of AI in Early 2024: Gen AI Adoption Spikes and Starts to Generate Value*. McKinsey and Co. https://www.mckinsey.com/capabilities/quantumblack/our-insights/the-state-of-ai

11 Deloitte. 2024, August. *Now Decides Next: Moving from Potential to Performance*. www2.deloitte.com/content/dam/Deloitte/us/Documents/consulting/us-state-of-gen-ai-q3.pdf

12 Deloitte. *Now Decides Next.*
13 Herweijer, C., Combes, B., & Gillham, J. 2024. *How AI Can Enable a Sustainable Future*. Retrieved October 1, 2024, from www.pwc.co.uk/sustainability-climate-change/assets/pdf/how-ai-can-enable-a-sustainable-future.pdf
14 Monks, R.A., & Minow, N. 2011. *Corporate Governance*. John Wiley & Sons.
15 De la Peña, N., & Granados, O.M. 2024. Artificial intelligence solutions to reduce information asymmetry for Colombian cocoa small-scale farmers. *Information Processing in Agriculture*, 11(3), 310–324.
16 Marwala, T. & Hurwitz., E. "Artificial Intelligence and Asymmetric Information Theory." ArXiv abs/1510.02867 (2015): n. pag
17 Marwala & Hurwitz. Artificial Intelligence and Asymmetric Information Theory, 27.
18 Balcıoğlu, Y.S., Çelik, A.A., & Altındağ, E. 2024. Artificial intelligence integration in sustainable business practices: A text mining analysis of USA firms. *Sustainability*, 16(15), 6334.
19 EY. 2024. *AI for Good Impact Report. International Telecommunication Union.* https://s41721.pcdn.co/wp-content/uploads/2024/10/AI-for-Good-Impact-Report.pdf
20 Batool, A., Zowghi, D., & Bano, M. 2025, January. AI governance: A systematic literature review. *Journal: AI and Ethics.* https://doi.org/10.1007/s43681-024-00653-w
21 Birkstedt, T., Minkkinen, M., Tandon, A., & Mäntymäki, M. 2023. AI governance: Themes, knowledge gaps, and future agendas. *Internet Research*, 33(7), 133–167. https://doi.org/10.1108/INTR-01-2022-0042.
22 Batool, A., Zowghi, D., & Bano, M. 2023, December. Responsible AI governance: A systematic literature review. *arXiv*. https://arxiv.org/abs/2401.10896
23 ISS-Corporate. 2024, 21 March. *AI and Board of Directors Oversight: AI Governance Appears on Corporate Radar*. https://www.iss-corporate.com/library/ai-and-board-of-directors-oversight-ai-governance-appears-on-corporate-radar/
24 Brachio, A., & Hinish, S. 2023, 5 December. How AI can help accelerate the pace of change. *EY*, MIT OpenCourseWare. www.ey.com/en_gl/insights/sustainability/how-can-ai-help-us-accelerate-the-pace-of-change-the-world-needs
25 Monks, & Minow, *Corporate Governance*
26 De la Peña, N., & Granados, O.M. 2024. Artificial intelligence solutions to reduce information asymmetry for Colombian cocoa small-scale farmers. *Information Processing in Agriculture*, 11(3), 310–324.
27 Marwala & Hurwitz, Artificial intelligence and asymmetric information theory
28 Marwala & Hurwitz. Artificial intelligence and asymmetric information theory, 27
29 Balcıoğlu, Çelik, & Altındağ, Artificial intelligence integration in sustainable business practices, 6334.
30 EY. 2024. *AI for Good Impact Report*. International Telecommunication Union. https://s41721.pcdn.co/wp-content/uploads/2024/10/AI-for-Good-Impact-Report.pdf
31 Greif, L., Röckel, F., Kimmig, A., & Ovtcharova, J. 2024. A systematic review of current AI techniques used in the context of the SDGs. *International Journal of Environmental Research*, 19(1), 2025
32 Tripathi, S., Bachmann, N., Brunner, M., Rizk, Z., & Jodlbauer, H. 2024. Assessing the current landscape of AI and sustainability literature: identifying key trends, addressing gaps and challenges. *Journal of Big Data*, 11, 65
33 Fan, Z., Yan, Z., & Wen, S. 2023. Deep learning and artificial intelligence in sustainability: A review of SDGs, renewable energy, and environmental health. *Sustainability*, 15(18), 13493
34 Rezaee, Z. 2025. *Corporate Governance: A Guide for Students*. Routledge, Taylor & Francis Group, Chapter 8
35 Rezaee. *Corporate Governance*

36 Rezaee, Z., & Riley, R. 2019, Summer. *Financial Statement Fraud: Prevention and Detection* (2nd ed.). John Wiley & Sons, Inc.
37 Andrade, P., Silva, I., Silva, M., Flores, T., Cassiano, J., & Costa, D.G. 2022. A tinyml soft-sensor approach for low-cost detection and monitoring of vehicular emissions. *Sensors*, 22(10), 3838
38 Xu, Z., Wang, R., Kang, Y., Zhang, Y., Xia, X., & Wang, R. 2021. A deep transfer NOx emission inversion model of diesel vehicles with multisource external influence. *Journal of Advanced Transportation*, 2021(1), 4892855
39 Le Cornec, C.M., Molden, N., van Reeuwijk, M., & Stettler, M.E. 2020. Modelling of instantaneous emissions from diesel vehicles with a special focus on NOx: Insights from machine learning techniques. *Science of the Total Environment*, 737, 139625
40 Rauniyar, A., Berge, T., Kuijpers, A., Litzinger, P., Peeters, B., Van Gils, E., . . . Håkegård, J.E. 2023. NEMO: Real-time noise and exhaust emissions monitoring for sustainable and intelligent transportation systems. *IEEE Sensors Journal*, 23(20), 25497–25517
41 Tharayil, S.M., Qarni, S.A., Thubaiti, L.A., Dossary, B.A., & Shahada, M. 2024, November. Oil spill detection and understanding using deep learning and large language models. In *Abu Dhabi International Petroleum Exhibition and Conference* (p. D021S048R002). SPE
42 Ochella, S., Shafiee, M., & Dinmohammadi, F. 2022. Artificial intelligence in prognostics and health management of engineering systems. *Engineering Applications of Artificial Intelligence*, 108, 104552
43 Taravat, A., & Oppelt, N. 2014. Adaptive Weibull multiplicative model and multilayer perceptron neural networks for dark-spot detection from SAR imagery. *Sensors*, 14(12), 22798–22810
44 Abid, S.K., Sulaiman, N., Chan, S.W., Nazir, U., Abid, M., Han, H., . . . Vega-Muñoz, A. 2021. Toward an integrated disaster management approach: How artificial intelligence can boost disaster management. *Sustainability*, 13(22), 12560
45 PwC. 2024. *What Is Double Materiality under CSRD?* https://www.pwc.com/us/en/services/esg/library/csrd-double-materiality.html
46 Craja, P., Kim, A., & Lessmann, S. 2020. Deep learning for detecting financial statement fraud. *Decision Support Systems*, 139, 113421
47 Ghosal, A., Nandy, A., Das, A.K., Goswami, S., & Panday, M. 2020. A short review on different clustering techniques and their applications. *Emerging Technology in Modelling and Graphics: Proceedings of IEM Graph 2018*, 69–83
48 Joseph, S. 2024. Generative AI in financial fraud detection. Financial fraud detection. *International Journal on Recent and Innovation Trends in Computing and Communication*, 12(2), 351–359
49 Chen, Z., Soliman, W.M., Nazir, A., & Shorfuzzaman, M. 2021. Variational autoencoders and wasserstein generative adversarial networks for improving the anti-money laundering process. *IEEE Access*, 9, 83762–83785
50 Shavit, Y., Agarwal, S., Brundage, M., Adler, S., O'Keefe, C., Campbell, R., Lee, T., Mishkin, P., Eloundou, T., Hickey, A., & Slama, K. 2023. *Practices for Governing Agentic AI Systems*. Research Paper, OpenAI
51 Shah, C., & White, R.W. 2024. Agents are not enough. *arXiv preprint* arXiv:2412.16241.
52 Wooldridge, M. 1999. Intelligent agents. *Multiagent Systems: A Modern Approach to Distributed Artificial Intelligence*, 1, 27–73
53 AI Action Summit. 2025. *Rapport international sur la sûreté de l'IA Rapport scientifique international sur la sûreté de l'IA avancée*. https://assets.publishing.service.gov.uk/media/67af5a7363d7f4cceef9e236/International_AI_Safety_Report_2025_executive_summary_french.pdf

54 Acharya, D.B., Kuppan, K., & Divya, B. 2025. Agentic AI: Autonomous intelligence for complex goals–a comprehensive survey. *IEEE Access*, 13, 18912–18936. https://doi.org/10.1109/ACCESS.2025.3532853

55 LeewayHertz. *AI Agents for Fraud Detection: Key Components, Use Cases and Applications, Benefits, Implementation and Future Trends*. https://www.leewayhertz.com/ai-agents-for-fraud-detection/

4 AI tools and techniques and their application for sustainability

4.1 Introduction

In an era defined by global need for economic growth, resource scarcity, accelerating climate change, and social inequality, sustainability has emerged as a central priority for governments, businesses, and civil society. Addressing complex sustainability opportunities and challenges requires not only a commitment to responsible practices but also the adoption of innovative technologies that can drive systemic and CI. Among these technologies, AI stands out as a transformative force with the potential to reshape many industries in understanding, managing, and responding to economic challenges and environmental and social issues. AI encompasses a broad set of tools and techniques, including ML, DL, NLP, computer vision, and optimization algorithms, that enable machines to learn from data, identify patterns, and make informed decisions. These capabilities are being increasingly harnessed to support sustainability efforts across various sectors. From predicting climate-related risks and optimizing energy usage to monitoring deforestation and enhancing the transparency of corporate sustainability reports (CSRs), AI offers powerful solutions that enhance both the efficiency and effectiveness of sustainability strategies.

This chapter provides a comprehensive examination of the intersection between AI and sustainability by outlining the core AI techniques most relevant to sustainability applications and proceeds to explore their use in key domains such as environmental monitoring, sustainable agriculture, smart cities, green supply chains, and ESG reporting. Furthermore, the chapter addresses critical challenges, including data governance, algorithmic bias, and ethical concerns that must be considered when deploying AI for sustainable outcomes. By presenting both theoretical insights and practical examples, this chapter aims to present an understanding of how AI can contribute to achieving global sustainability goals. It also emphasizes the importance of responsible AI implementation, where transparency, inclusivity, and accountability guide the integration of technology into sustainable development efforts.

DOI: 10.4324/9781003611981-4

4.2 Artificial Intelligence

AI, coined by John McCarthy in 1955, is defined as the "science and engineering of making intelligent machines, especially intelligent computer programs."[1] It can be described as a field of research and study aimed at creating machines that can perform tasks that require human intelligence (HI). AI includes computer science, mathematics, cognitive science, linguistics, and neuroscience, emphasizing systems that can mimic HI. AI aims to develop algorithms, models, and technologies that enable machines to learn, understand, reason, make decisions, and solve complex problems in the same way as human beings.[2]

AI is categorized into three main types: narrow AI, artificial general intelligence (AGI), and artificial superintelligence (ASI). ASI represents a perspective on the future development of AI that could lead to the creation of systems possessing general reasoning abilities without cognitive limitations, surpassing human cognition. These systems would not be constrained by human-like cognitive limits, allowing them to process information and solve problems in ways that humans cannot.[3] AGI refers to an advanced form of AI that can perform any given task, similar to HI. It is expected to have the ability to comprehend, learn, reason, solve problems, make decisions, and execute tasks using cognitive abilities like those of humans and leveraging prior knowledge. This suggests that AGI could potentially undertake a variety of tasks rather than focusing on a single narrow objective. Once AGI is achieved, where machines exhibit human-like intelligence, ASI will quickly follow. This implies that AGI could evolve or develop into a form of intelligence that vastly exceeds human capabilities in all areas, including creativity, problem-solving, and emotional intelligence. Currently, AGI is more of a theoretical concept and a subject of ongoing research for future advancements. However, narrow AI is specifically designed to complete a defined task or a set of tasks as determined by the programmer. Within the scope of narrow AI, various disciplines and components contribute to its functionality, with ML being the most prominent among them.[4]

4.2.1 Machine learning

ML is a subset of AI that focuses on developing algorithms and models that learn from experience and improve machines' performance.[5] ML employs algorithms to learn from data continually, make predictions and informed decisions, and adapt its behavior based on new information to improve accuracy without requiring specific instructions. These algorithms include support vector machines, decision trees, and neural networks. They are sets of rules or instructions that determine how an AI system learns, analyzes data, and makes decisions. ML is the basis for many useful applications, such as web search, NLP, computer vision, speech recognition, and product recommendations. Four learning techniques are utilized in ML: supervised learning, unsupervised learning, semi-supervised learning (SSL), and RL. AI is a broad field that employs various techniques to create intelligent systems capable of mimicking human-like capabilities. To understand AI's potential, it is beneficial to break it down into its key subfields, as depicted in Figure 4.1.

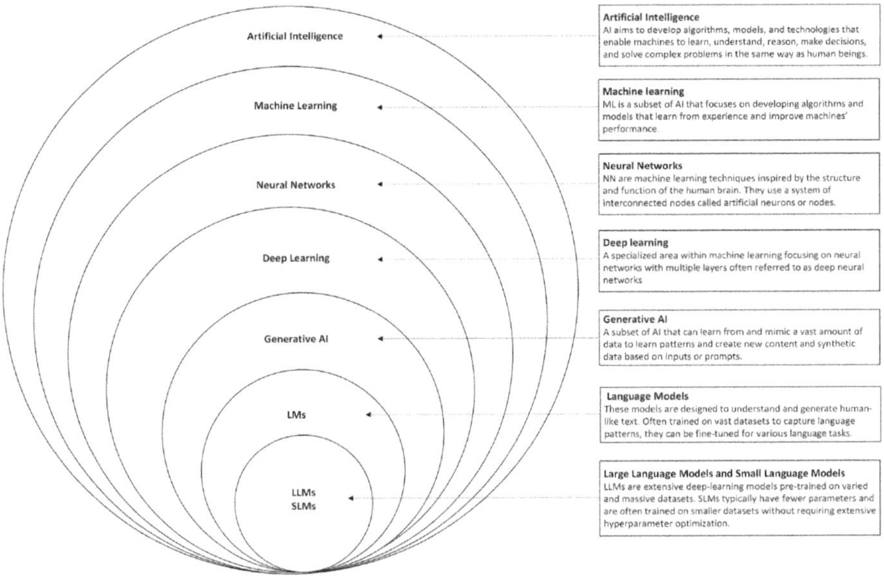

Figure 4.1 AI and key subfields

4.2.1.1 Supervised learning

In supervised learning, a model is trained on a labeled dataset, where the labels reflect the expected output based on the input data.[6] Each training example is paired with an output label. The model aims to learn the mapping from inputs to outputs to predict the output for new, unseen data. For instance, if we want our ML model to classify images of animals as cats or dogs, we provide pictures labeled as such. This method relies heavily on expert knowledge to define the state labels and requires significant human effort in the labeling process. The algorithm learns from the training data by adjusting its parameters to minimize the difference between its predictions and the actual labels. Supervised learning can be used for classification, such as identifying which category an input belongs to (e.g., spam detection in emails), and for regression, like predicting a continuous value (e.g., forecasting house prices based on features such as size and location). While it offers better computational efficiency and often converges more quickly than unsupervised methods, the effectiveness of the model is heavily dependent on the quality of the labeling; subjective judgment can introduce biases and inaccuracies, particularly in contexts where the underlying cognitive states of operators are not directly observable.

4.2.1.2 Unsupervised learning

Unsupervised learning involves training models without labeled data, allowing the algorithm to identify patterns and structures within the data autonomously.[7]

In unsupervised learning, the model is trained on data that lacks labeled outputs, where the goal is to identify patterns or structures within the data without any prior knowledge of what those patterns might be. This approach does not require predefined labels, which mitigates the biases and inaccuracies often associated with human labeling. The algorithm first performs model selection to determine the optimal number of hidden states, after which it uses techniques such as the Baum-Welch algorithm for training. The algorithm analyzes the input data to uncover hidden structures or groupings, as it does not have a specific target to predict. Unsupervised learning could play a role in inferring the model during training by allowing it to explore data and identify underlying structures, relationships, or conjectures without being explicitly trained on labeled examples, like in a mathematical context. Unsupervised learning is used for clustering, such as grouping similar data points together (e.g., customer segmentation in marketing), and for dimensionality reduction, which involves decreasing the number of features in a dataset while preserving important information.[8]

4.2.1.3 Semi-Supervised Learning

SSL combines elements of both supervised and unsupervised learning. It enables models to learn from labeled and unlabeled data, enhancing performance in scenarios where labeled data is scarce. SSL offers a robust framework for improving classification tasks by effectively leveraging both labeled and unlabeled data, resulting in better performance across various applications such as image classification and NLP. The model is trained on a dataset that includes labeled examples (where the output is known) and unlabeled examples (where the output is unknown). SSL methods can be categorized into two primary paradigms: transductive learning and inductive learning.[9] Transductive learning focuses on applying the trained classifier to unlabeled instances present during training, without generalizing to new, unseen instances. This approach is often utilized in specific contexts, such as graph-based methods. Inductive learning aims to create a model that generalizes effectively to unseen instances in testing. It trains both labeled and unlabeled data to predict new data points. Inductive learning is more commonly applied in practical settings, as it allows effective deployment in real-world scenarios where future data may differ from the training set. In SSL, the training dataset comprises a small amount of labeled data with known outputs, alongside a larger amount of unlabeled data lacking known outputs. This dual data composition enables the model to learn from both types of data. SSL is employed in various applications where acquiring labeled data is costly or time-consuming while unlabeled data is abundant, including image classification, NLP, speech recognition and understanding, medical diagnosis, and fraud detection.

4.2.1.4 Reinforcement Learning

RL involves training an agent to make decisions by performing actions in an environment to achieve a goal. The agent learns to map situations to actions on its own through trial and error, receiving feedback in the form of rewards or penalties based on its actions, which guides its learning process. The agent explores the environment, acts, and receives feedback. It uses this feedback to learn which actions lead to better outcomes over time. The agent learns from the rewards and penalties it receives, adjusting its behavior to maximize those rewards. It uses policies to decide actions and value functions to evaluate the long-term rewards of actions. This process is characterized by two main features: the need for exploration via trial-and-error search and the concept of delayed rewards, where actions influence not just immediate responses but future situations and rewards as well. RL has a variety of applications across different domains, including game playing, like training an AI to play games like chess, where it learns strategies to win, and robotics, where RL is used to teach robots to perform tasks by rewarding them for successful actions (e.g., maze navigation tasks).[10]

4.2.2 Neural networks

Neural networks are ML techniques inspired by the structure and function of the human brain.[11] They use a system of interconnected nodes called artificial neurons (or nodes). They consist of interconnected layers of neurons, including an input layer, one or more hidden layers, and an output layer, as depicted in Figure 4.2. Each neuron receives input, processes it, and produces an output. The processing typically involves applying a weighted sum of the inputs, followed by a nonlinear activation function. They are designed to recognize patterns and make decisions based on input data. Neural networks are powerful tools for modeling complex relationships in data and are particularly effective for tasks such as image recognition, NLP, and speech recognition. Their ability to learn from large datasets, model complex relationships, and generalize to new data makes them a cornerstone of advanced ML and AI models, particularly DL applications.

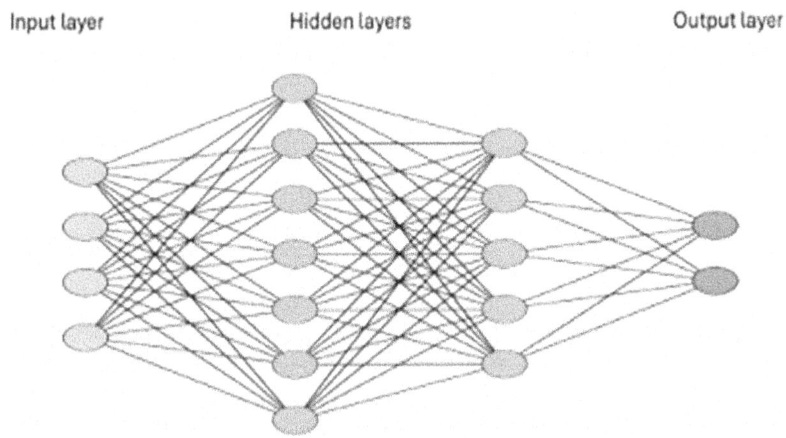

Figure 4.2 An example of a neural network with two hidden layers

4.2.3 Deep learning

DL is a specialized area within ML focusing on neural networks with multiple layers, often referred to as deep neural networks. This multi-layered architecture allows DL models to automatically learn and extract high-level features from raw data and representation learning, which is crucial for effectively solving complex tasks. In DL, multi-layer networks are employed to identify complex patterns and improve performance in tasks such as speech and visual recognition. These architectures change the input space to make classes more easily separable, which is crucial for handling the intricacies of real-world data variations, such as differences in image lighting or shapes, thus enabling better classification accuracy.[12] This capability has transformed how machines understand and interact with the world and has enabled significant progress in areas such as autonomous driving, medical diagnosis, and personalized recommendations.

4.3 Generative AI

GenAI is a subset of AI that can learn from and mimic a vast amount of data to learn patterns, create new content, including audio, video, images, text, code, simulations, and synthetic data, based on inputs or prompts. GenAI was first introduced in chatbots throughout the mid-1960s with the creation of ELIZA in 1966 by Joseph Weizenbaum.[13] ELIZA was designed to mimic a psychotherapist and engaged in text-based conversations. Early text-based chatbots like ELIZA (1966) mimicked conversation but did not generate novel content; true generative models emerged with GANs in 2014. However, it was not until 2014, with the advent of GANs,[14] a category of ML algorithms, that GenAI was able to produce realistic photos, videos, and sounds of real people. This technology utilizes algorithms and models designed to learn patterns and structures from training data, enabling them to produce novel outputs that maintain the characteristics of the original data.

The field encompasses various applications, such as image synthesis, text generation, and even music composition, and has significant implications across multiple industries, including entertainment, healthcare, finance, and sustainability.[15] The advancements in DL techniques and the availability of large-scale datasets have propelled the rapid development of GenAI, making it a prominent area of study and application in recent years. Many types of GenAI models exist and can be categorized based on their underlying architecture and the types of data they generate. Some common types include transformers, diffusion models, VAEs, and GANs.

4.4 Language Models

Language models (LMs) are systems designed to predict the next element in a sequence of text (tokens, which can be characters, words, or strings). They work by assessing the likelihood of a token appearing based on its context—using either preceding tokens (as in traditional models) or both preceding and following tokens (as in bidirectional and masked models). These models are typically unsupervised, meaning that they learn from unannotated data without explicit labels or feedback.

When these models are operational (deployed), they process input text and predict subsequent tokens or provide confidence scores for those predictions. The origins of language modeling can be traced back to Claude Shannon, who first proposed the concept in 1948 through a mathematical framework for understanding communication, with the goal of reproducing messages at different points, regardless of their meanings or context.[16] The early implementations of LMs occurred in the 1980s, where they found applications in various computational tasks, including automatic speech recognition and machine translation (MT), organizing and categorizing documents, information retrieval, spelling correction, optical character recognition, and handwriting recognition.[17]

LMs are designed to understand and generate human-like text. Often trained on vast datasets to capture language patterns, they can be fine-tuned for various language tasks. LMs are foundational to many NLP applications, enabling machines to interact with human language meaningfully. They can perform several tasks, such as generating new natural language, answering questions, summarizing text, translation, comparing semantic text similarity, and sentiment analysis.[18]

LMs differ primarily in size, architecture, performance capabilities, and computational requirements. LLMs are trained on large, varied datasets, while smaller language models (SLMs) use smaller, more focused datasets. While LLMs offer versatility, enhanced capabilities, and performance due to their scale and training, SLMs offer efficiency and accessibility, making them valuable in many contexts, especially for specific applications where resource constraints are a concern or where simpler models suffice.

4.4.1 Large Language Models

LLMs are extensive deep-learning models pre-trained on diverse and massive datasets.[19] LLMs, such as OpenAI's GPT series, utilize extensive training data and advanced techniques such as chain-of-thought (CoT) prompting hundreds of billions of parameters, enabling them to capture complex language patterns and perform well on a wide range of tasks, including reasoning. The underlying transformer architecture consists of a collection of neural networks capable of unsupervised training, including an encoder and a decoder with self-attention mechanisms. These encoders and decoders comprehend word and phrase relationships while extracting meanings. Transformers learn fundamental grammar, language, and general knowledge through self-learning. LLMs focus on language-based tasks such as text comprehension, summarization, and translation, and they can generate predictions from a limited set of prompts or inputs. Their large size allows them to capture complex patterns and nuances in language. Generally, LLMs exhibit superior performance on a wide range of tasks, including reasoning, understanding context, and generating coherent text. They harness their extensive training data to excel at complex queries, capture deeper patterns in data, and perform effectively on a broader spectrum of tasks. LLMs are also capable of producing content based on input prompts in human language, and they are commonly employed in applications requiring high accuracy and versatility, including advanced chatbots, content generation, and sophisticated language understanding tasks.

4.4.2 Small Language Models

SLMs typically have fewer parameters and are often trained on smaller datasets without requiring expensive hyperparameter optimization. SLMs require less computational power, and their memory can be fine-tuned for specific tasks with fewer labeled examples, making them more accessible for deployment in resource-constrained environments. SLMs are designed to be lightweight and efficient, which can lead to faster inference times and lower operational costs.[20] For example, models like DistilBERT are designed to be compact and efficient. While they can perform well on simpler tasks, they often struggle with more complex reasoning and understanding compared to LLMs. However, SLMs can benefit from techniques like knowledge distillation, which allows them to be fine-tuned on outputs from larger models to improve their performance without needing to be as large themselves. Recent research has shown that smaller models can also achieve competitive performance on NLP tasks, often using fewer resources and having a smaller carbon footprint. These models can be fine-tuned or adapted for specific applications while maintaining efficiency. SLMs are suitable for applications where speed and efficiency are critical, such as mobile applications, real-time systems, or environments with limited computational resources.

4.5 Multimodal GenAI

Multimodal GenAI (MGenAI) is a type of AI that combines GenAI with multimodal AI capabilities to enhance its understanding of real-world scenarios. A multimodal model is an ML model that processes various types of information, such as like text, images, video, audio, and sensory inputs, and creates any type of output.[21] Expanding on the capabilities of traditional GenAI, MGenAI can process and generate content from multiple modalities simultaneously, effectively mimicking how humans process information from different senses. Multimodality allows AI systems to interpret and understand diverse forms of sensory input, such as combining images, videos, and text in a single request, allowing the extraction of insights and patterns from diverse sources. This means that users are not confined to providing just one type of input or expecting one type of output; they can interact with these models in a more versatile and flexible manner. For example, a user might input a written description and receive an image or upload a video and receive a summary in text form. Multimodal LLMs can simultaneously process and generate diverse types of data, such as text, images, and audio, making resources more accessible to a wider audience. They can perform complex tasks, such as understanding the sentiment behind text, identifying objects in images, and interpreting audio signals, effectively integrating these diverse inputs to develop a comprehensive understanding of the context. These models can rapidly analyze and synthesize data from tables, charts, and graphs. This ability facilitates faster, more informed decision-making for businesses, allowing them to navigate complex information landscapes effectively.

MGenAI models broaden the potential applications of generative technologies, making them more useful and adaptable in various contexts, including enhancing creative possibilities across industries such as sustainability, education, and entertainment. They improve reasoning, problem-solving, and content generation capabilities, allowing developers and users to create innovative applications that can significantly transform sustainability practices and outcomes. These models can integrate diverse data sources, including satellite imagery, sensor readings, weather data, and textual reports. By combining these inputs, MGenAI provides a comprehensive view of environmental issues and potential solutions and actively contributes to environmental and social sustainability initiatives by analyzing complex datasets, identifying patterns, and proposing solutions across sectors such as energy efficiency, waste management, and sustainable agriculture, all while leveraging the strength of multiple data modalities.

4.6 The IoT and business sustainability

The IoT offers many potentials for transforming industries and daily life by connecting devices to collect, share, and act on data. There are several ways the IoT can be used across different sectors including: (1) the use of IoT sensors to monitor traffic flow and optimize signal timing, reducing congestion and emissions and rerouting traffic based on current road conditions, improving urban mobility; (2) the application of IoT-enabled smart grids to manage electricity distribution more efficiently, balancing demand and reducing outages; (3) the use of IoT sensors in waste bins to signal when they are full, allowing for optimized collection routes and reducing fuel use to improve sanitation services while lowering costs; (4) promoting patient monitoring through wearable devices to track vital signs such as heart rate, blood pressure, and oxygen levels, enabling healthcare providers to monitor patients remotely; (5) IoT tags can help track medical equipment, improving inventory management and ensuring critical tools are always available when needed; (6) the use of IoT sensors to measure soil moisture, temperature, and nutrient levels, allowing farmers to adjust irrigation and fertilization precisely; IoT-enabled wearables on livestock can track health, location, and breeding cycles, helping farmers manage herds more efficiently and reduce losses; (7) IoT weather stations on farms provide localized data that improves weather prediction, helping farmers plan planting and harvesting schedules more accurately; (8) IoT sensors on machinery detect potential issues before they cause breakdowns; by analyzing machine performance data, manufacturers can conduct maintenance only when necessary, reducing downtime and repair costs; (9) IoT devices can monitor product quality during production by tracking factors such as temperature, pressure, and vibration to ensure consistent quality, reduces waste, and boosts efficiency; (10) IoT can automate inventory tracking, reducing the risk of shortages or overstocking; real-time data allows manufacturers to adapt quickly to supply chain changes; (11) IoT-enabled grids can distribute energy more efficiently by monitoring usage patterns and predicting demand to reduce energy wastage and integrates renewable energy sources effectively; (12) IoT-based meters provide real-time data on energy or water usage, allowing consumers to monitor and manage their consumption; (13) IoT sensors monitor environmental factors for solar panels or wind turbines, maximizing energy generation based on weather conditions and system health; (14) IoT sensors provide real-time location and condition updates for goods in transit, reducing loss and improving supply chain transparency; (15) IoT sensors monitor engine health, tire pressure, and other critical metrics, preventing unexpected breakdowns and improving vehicle safety; (16) IoT sensors track stock levels and automate reordering, ensuring shelves are stocked and reducing excess inventory; (17) smart thermostats, lighting systems, and appliances can adjust based on occupancy and user preferences, reducing energy consumption and lowering utility bills; (18) IoT security cameras, smart locks, and alarm systems can be monitored remotely, enhancing home security and enabling real-time alerts; (19) IoT sensors can monitor pollution levels, air quality, and water quality in real-time, helping authorities respond to environmental threats; (20) IoT sensors detect early signs of natural disasters, such as earthquakes, floods, and wildfires. This allows for faster response and potentially saves lives; and (21) IoT devices can track wildlife movement and habitat changes, providing data to support conservation efforts. Overall, IoT presents potential for data-driven decision-making and process automation by enabling efficiency, safety, and convenience across numerous sectors, reshaping traditional practices for a connected future.

4.7 Overview of key algorithms

4.7.1 ML algorithms for ESG

ML offers a wide variety of algorithms that enable computers to learn from data and subsequently make informed predictions or decisions. These algorithms are classified by the type of learning, with each serving distinct purposes.[22] Each algorithm possesses unique strengths and is particularly suited for specific tasks. In the following, we categorize the algorithms based on their learning types and explain each one along with its applications in the ESG context. Figure 4.3 summarizes the common ML algorithms by learning type with an ESG focus. This classification provides a valuable framework for understanding their diverse capabilities and practical applications. Table 4.1 presents a structured comparison of ML models and their applications in ESG.

- **Supervised learning:** Supervised learning serves as the foundation for numerous predictive applications, particularly in classification and regression tasks.
- **Linear regression:** Linear regression is a statistical method that models the relationship between a dependent variable (what you want to predict) and one or more independent variables (your input). It operates by identifying the best-fitting straight line through your data points that minimizes overall prediction error. This algorithm captures the relationship between variables by fitting a linear equation to the observed data. Its goal is to find the best-fitting straight line (or hyperplane in higher dimensions) that reduces the difference between predicted and actual values. For example, linear regression can be

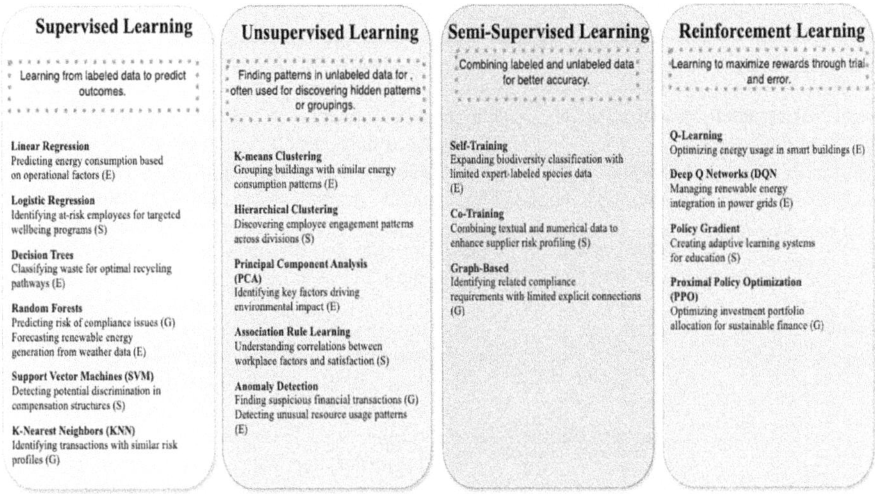

Figure 4.3 Common ML algorithms by learning type for ESG

Table 4.1 Common ML algorithms and their applications in ESG

Learning Type	*Algorithm*	*Recommended Use*	*ESG Example*
Supervised	Linear regression	Predicting numerical values	Forecasting carbon emissions
	Logistic regression	Binary classification	Waste classification
	Decision trees	Rule-based decision-making	Sustainability index inclusion
	Random forest	Complex classification and regression	Renewable energy generation prediction
	SVMs	High-dimensional classification	Governmental risk assessment
	KNN	Instance-based classification	Environmental monitoring and land use planning
Unsupervised	K-means clustering	Data clustering	Grouping companies based on sustainability performance
	Hierarchical clustering	Identifying nested clusters	Grouping industries based on carbon footprint
	PCA	Dimensionality reduction	ESG factor analysis
	Anomaly detection	Identifying unusual patterns	Detecting corporate greenwashing

(*Continued*)

Table 4.1 (Continued)

Learning Type	*Algorithm*	*Recommended Use*	*ESG Example*
Semi-Supervised	Self-training	Handling limited labeled data	Predicting missing ESG scores
	Co-training	Multi-modal learning	Improving ESG classification using multiple data sources
	Graph-based learning	Relationship modeling	Mapping corporate relationships in supply chain
Reinforcement	Q-learning	Optimizing sequential decisions	Smart grid energy optimization
	DQN	Handling complex decision spaces	Sustainable supply chain management
	Policy gradient	Continuous decision-making	Implementing dynamic carbon pricing
	PPO	Real-time optimization	Adapting corporate ESG policies dynamically

used in environmental contexts to predict energy consumption based on operational factors such as building occupancy, weather conditions, or production levels. This can help optimize energy efficiency and reduce the carbon footprint.

- **Logistic regression:** Despite its name, logistic regression is primarily used for classification problems rather than regression. It predicts the probability that an observation belongs to a particular category (e.g., "yes" or "no," "high risk" or "low risk"). The algorithm transforms a linear equation using the logistic function (also known as the sigmoid function), predicting the likelihood of an instance belonging to a specific class, which maps any real-valued number to a value between 0 and 1. Logistic regression can be used to identify employees at risk of burnout or attrition based on factors such as workload, work–life balance, and survey responses. This allows for proactive interventions to enhance employee well-being and reduce turnover.
- **Decision trees:** Decision trees are hierarchical models that make decisions by following a tree-like structure of conditions, resembling a flowchart. Starting from a root node, they split the data based on feature values, creating branches until they reach leaf nodes that provide predictions. These algorithms construct a tree-like model of decisions, where the leaf nodes represent the final classification for the problem statement. Each internal node represents a test on an attribute, each branch reflects the test's outcome, and each leaf node indicates a class label or predicted value. Decision trees are interpretable and can handle both categorical and numerical data. Decision trees can be used to classify waste streams for optimal recycling pathways based on material composition, contamination levels, and the availability of recycling infrastructure.

- **Random forests:** Random forests are ensemble learning methods that construct multiple decision trees during training and output the mode of classes (for classification) or the mean prediction (for regression) from the individual trees. This method leverages the power of multiple decision trees (weak classifiers) to create a strong classifier, improving accuracy and generalization by combining their predictions. This ensemble learning method builds on decision trees by creating various trees, each trained on a random subset of the data and features.[23] The final prediction is made by aggregating the predictions of all individual trees, often through majority voting for classification or averaging for regression. Random forests are robust, reduce overfitting, and typically offer high accuracy. Random forests can be used to predict renewable energy generation (solar, wind) based on weather data, time of day, and seasonal variations, thereby improving grid management and energy planning.
- **Support Vector Machines:** SVMs are powerful algorithms for both linear and nonlinear classification and regression. They aim to find an optimal hyperplane that separates different classes, maximizing the margin (distance) between the boundary and the closest points from each class, known as support vectors. For nonlinear problems, SVMs can utilize kernel functions to map data into higher-dimensional spaces where linear separation becomes feasible. SVMs can be used to classify corporate disclosures (e.g., sustainability reports) to detect instances of greenwashing or misleading ESG claims by examining textual content and numerical data.
- **K-Nearest Neighbors:** KNN is a non-parametric, instance-based learning algorithm used for classification and regression. Given N training vectors, the KNN algorithm identifies the KNN. It classifies a new data point by considering the classes of its "k" nearest neighbors in the training dataset. The class that appears most frequently among the "k" neighbors is assigned to the new data point. KNN is simple to implement and effective for datasets with complex decision boundaries. For example, KNN can be used to identify financial transactions that share similar risk profiles with past fraudulent activities by comparing features such as amount, location, and time against historical data on fraudulent transactions. KNN could classify land cover types from satellite imagery by assessing spectral similarity to known land cover samples, thus aiding in environmental monitoring and land use planning.

4.7.1.2 Unsupervised learning

These algorithms are essential for exploratory data analysis, dimensionality reduction, and discovering hidden relationships without explicit guidance.

- **K-means clustering:** This algorithm divides data points into "k" distinct clusters. It iteratively assigns each data point to the nearest cluster centroid and updates the centroids based on the mean of the points assigned to each cluster. Points are assigned to the nearest centroid, indicating similarity, and the algorithm iteratively recalculates centroids by averaging the points assigned to each one. This process continues until data point assignments stabilize and no longer change. The goal is to minimize the within-cluster sum of squared distances. For example, K-means clustering can group buildings with similar energy consumption patterns based on energy usage data, building characteristics, and operational parameters. This enables targeted energy efficiency programs for specific building clusters. It can also assist in clustering companies based on sustainability performance to identify industry leaders and laggards.

- **Hierarchical clustering:** This method builds a hierarchy of clusters. It can be agglomerative (bottom-up), starting with each data point as a separate cluster and iteratively merging the closest clusters, or divisive (top-down), starting with a single cluster containing all data points and recursively splitting clusters.[24] Hierarchical clustering generates a tree-like structure (dendrogram) that represents the clustering process. For example, hierarchical clustering can identify employee engagement patterns across various departments or divisions using employee survey data and engagement metrics, revealing organizational units with particularly high or low levels of engagement. In governance, it can group industries based on their environmental impact and carbon footprint.
- **Principal Component Analysis:** Principal component analysis (PCA) is a dimensionality reduction technique that transforms high-dimensional data into a lower-dimensional space while preserving maximum variance. It identifies principal components, which are orthogonal linear combinations of the original features, ordered by the amount of variance they explain. PCA also serves as a unifying concept across various perspectives in representation learning, like a simple form of linear manifold learning, characterizing lower-dimensional regions in the input space where the density of the data is significant.[25] For example, PCA can identify the key factors driving environmental impact from a large set of environmental indicators (e.g., emissions, resource consumption, and waste generation). By reducing dimensionality, PCA simplifies analysis and highlights the most significant drivers of environmental performance. In governance, it can reveal the most important ESG factors that influence sustainability performance.
- **Anomaly detection:** These techniques aim to identify data points that deviate significantly from the normal or expected patterns in a dataset.[26] They help in detecting unusual patterns in data without relying on labeled examples. Anomalies can represent errors, outliers, or significant events that require attention. Various methods exist, including statistical methods, ML models, and proximity-based techniques. For example, isolation forests are specialized ensemble ML algorithms designed specifically for anomaly detection that work by explicitly isolating outliers in the data. For example, anomaly detection can flag suspicious financial transactions or unusual trading activities that might indicate fraud or insider trading or detect discrepancies in CSRs that could suggest greenwashing.

4.7.1.3 Semi-supervised Learning

SSL, a mix of supervised and unsupervised learning, is used to improve learning accuracy.

- **Self-training:** This is an iterative approach in which a supervised learning model is initially trained on a small set of labeled data. The trained model is then used to predict labels (pseudo-labels) for the unlabeled data. High-confidence pseudo-labeled instances are then added to the labeled dataset, and the model is retrained. This process is repeated iteratively, gradually expanding the labeled dataset.[27] For example, self-training can be applied to classify satellite imagery for deforestation detection. Initially, a small set of labeled images (deforested vs. non-deforested) is used to train a model. This model then predicts the likelihood of deforestation on a larger set of unlabeled images. High-confidence predictions are added to the training set, and the model is retrained, enhancing its ability to identify deforestation patterns over time with limited labeled data. In governance, self-training can be used to predict missing ESG scores for companies with incomplete sustainability data.
- **Co-training:** Co-training extends self-training by employing multiple supervised classifiers. In this approach, two or more classifiers are trained iteratively on labeled data, where each classifier adds its most confident predictions of unlabeled data to the other's labeled dataset during each iteration. A critical requirement for successful co-training is that the classifiers should not be highly correlated in their predictions; this condition is known as the diversity criterion. For example, for governance risk assessment, co-training could involve two classifiers: one trained on financial data and another on textual data from news articles and reports, to predict corporate ESG risk. Each classifier can leverage its strengths in its respective data domain and collaboratively enhance the overall risk prediction by utilizing high-confidence predictions from the other classifier on unlabeled data. This method can also combine financial reports and environmental impact assessments to improve ESG risk classification.
- **Graph-based learning:** Graph-based methods are techniques that utilize graph structures to model relationships between data points for the purpose of label propagation and classification. Consisting of three main steps: graph creation, graph weighting, and inference, they typically use a local similarity measure to create a graph of all data points. These methods represent data points as nodes in a graph, with edges connecting nodes that exhibit some level of similarity based on predefined measures. The overarching idea is to leverage the connections between labeled and unlabeled data points to propagate information and make predictions. For example, in social network analysis aimed at assessing ESG impact, graph-based SSL can predict the ESG stance or engagement level of individuals or organizations within a network. In governance, mapping corporate relationships is utilized to analyze the sustainability impacts of supply chains.

- **Reinforcement learning:** RL is particularly well-suited for problems involving sequential decision-making, where the optimal action relies on both the current state of the environment and previous actions.
- **Q-learning:** Q-learning is an RL algorithm that learns the value (quality) of taking specific actions in particular states, with the goal of maximizing cumulative rewards over time. Q-learning iteratively updates the Q-function based on observed rewards and transitions in the environment. This algorithm is ideal when an agent must learn optimal decision-making through trial and error, without requiring a model of the environment. Q-learning equips agents with the capability to learn optimal strategies over time by interacting with and adapting to their environment based on received rewards and penalties, making it applicable in various fields such as robotics, game playing, and resource management in smart grids.[28] For example, Q-learning can optimize energy usage in smart buildings by learning control policies for heating, ventilation, and air conditioning (HVAC) systems, lighting, and appliances based on real-time occupancy, weather conditions, and energy prices.
- **Deep Q Networks:** Deep Q network (DQN) extends Q-learning by employing deep neural networks to approximate the Q-value function, enabling the handling of large and high-dimensional state spaces. DQNs combine Q-learning with deep neural networks to approximate the Q-function, enabling RL to handle high-dimensional state spaces, such as images or complex sensor data. Deep neural networks provide the function approximation capability to generalize from limited experiences to unseen states. DQNs are suitable for complex decision-making problems where the state space is too large for traditional Q-learning.[29] For example, DQNs can manage dynamic supply chain logistics to minimize their carbon footprint.
- **Policy gradient methods:** Policy gradient methods aim to directly maximize the cumulative reward and can easily integrate with nonlinear function approximators like neural networks. These RL algorithms optimize the policy directly, which maps states to actions, without explicitly learning a value function like Q-learning. Instead of relying on a value function to derive the policy, these methods parameterize the policy (often using neural networks) and adjust its parameters by estimating the gradient of expected returns with respect to those parameters. Policy gradient methods adjust the policy parameters iteratively to increase the probability of actions that lead to higher rewards. They are effective in continuous or complex action spaces and are particularly useful when smooth policy updates are desired, especially in systems with many possible actions.[30] For example, in governance, they are useful for implementing dynamic carbon pricing models that adapt to market conditions.
- **Proximal Policy Optimization:** Proximal policy optimization (PPO) is a policy gradient method that enhances training stability and sample efficiency compared to basic policy gradient algorithms. PPO introduces constraints on the policy update process to ensure that policy changes are not overly drastic in each iteration, resulting in more robust and reliable learning. This method aims to improve the efficiency and simplicity of existing approaches in RL. It is

recommended for training RL agents in environments that require stable learning with continuous actions.[31] For example, PPO can optimize logistics routes for transportation companies to minimize emissions and fuel consumption. The state space may encompass traffic conditions, road networks, vehicle characteristics, and delivery schedules. The actions would involve route selections, and the reward function would seek to minimize fuel consumption and emissions while meeting delivery deadlines. In governance, they can dynamically optimize corporate sustainability policies in response to regulatory changes.

4.7.2 DL algorithms

DL utilizes various types of neural networks to perform specific tasks. Figure 4.4 depicts the DL algorithms for ESG applications. Many different types of DL models are available, each employing the types of learning. Some models are generative, meaning that they can create new data like their training data. In the following, we present some of the most common types of DL algorithms. Table 4.2 summarizes key DL algorithms.

4.7.2.1 Convolutional Neural Networks

Convolutional neural networks (CNNs) are neural networks specialized for processing grid-like data, such as images and spatial data, designed to detect important features without human intervention automatically. These algorithms primarily utilize supervised learning for tasks such as image classification and object recognition, where they learn features from data through filter optimization. They use convolutional layers to automatically learn hierarchical features within images, from basic edges to complex objects. CNNs maintain spatial relationships, making them highly effective for computer vision tasks.[32] For example, CNNs can monitor deforestation trends using satellite imagery. By analyzing these images over time,

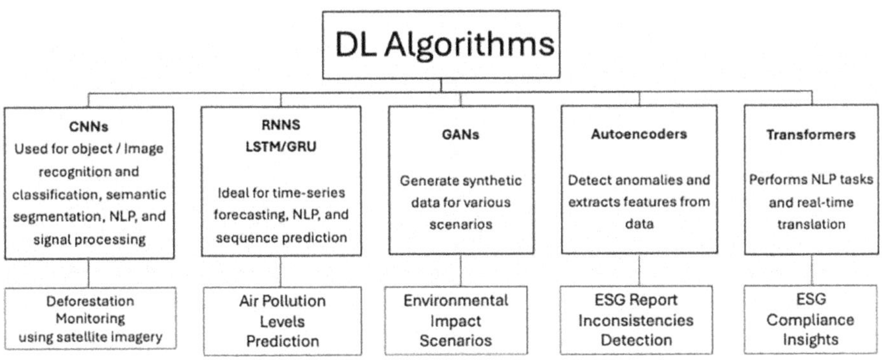

Figure 4.4 Common DL algorithms for ESG applications

Table 4.2 Key DL algorithms and their applications in ESG

Algorithm	*Recommended Use*	*ESG Example*
CNNs	Object detection, image recognition and classification, semantic segmentation, NLP, and signal processing	Monitoring deforestation trends using satellite imagery
RNNs/LSTM/GRU	Time-series forecasting, NLP, and sequence generation and prediction	Predicting air pollution levels
GANs	Synthetic data generation	Generating future environmental impact scenarios
Autoencoders	Anomaly detection and feature extraction	Detecting inconsistencies in corporate ESG reports
Transformers	NLP tasks, translating text and speech in near real-time	Extracting ESG compliance insights from reports

CNNs detect and quantify deforestation, providing crucial data for environmental conservation and policy enforcement.

4.7.2.2 Recurrent neural networks/long short-term memory/gated recurrent unit

Recurrent neural networks (RNNs) are neural networks designed to recognize patterns in data sequences by capturing temporal dependencies through their internal memory, making them suitable for time-series, text, and other sequential data. They are trained using supervised learning. While RNNs incorporate "memory," they can struggle with long-term dependencies. Long short-term memory (LSTM) and gated recurrent units (GRUs) are advanced RNN architectures that address this limitation with gating mechanisms. These architectures are designed to mitigate the vanishing gradient problem, which can hinder standard RNNs from learning long-term dependencies in sequential data.[33]

LSTMs are primarily used to learn and process sequential data, particularly those with long-term dependencies, making them suitable for NLP, time-series prediction, and speech recognition. They excel at identifying long-term dependencies in data, allowing them to retain information from earlier parts of a sequence when predicting later segments. LSTMs achieve this by utilizing "memory cells" and "gates" to control the flow of information, enabling them to retain or discard data as needed selectively. In NLP, LSTMs can be applied to text classification, text generation, MT, sentiment analysis, and language modeling, which involves predicting the next word in a sequence and facilitating tasks like auto-completion. For time-series analysis, LSTMs can predict future values based on past data, such as stock prices or weather patterns. They can also be used for anomaly detection, identifying unusual or unexpected patterns in time-series data. Additionally, LSTMs are employed for speech recognition, handwriting recognition, video analysis, robot control, analysis of sustainability data, and prediction of regulatory violations.

GRUs are a simplified version of LSTM networks, featuring fewer gates (reset and update gates) in their architecture. GRUs are designed to handle sequential data, which refers to data that has a specific order or time dependency, such as sentences, audio recordings, or stock prices. They are utilized to process and comprehend sequential data like text, speech, and time series by selectively remembering and forgetting information over time. Similar to LSTMs, GRUs are employed in NLP for tasks such as MT, text generation, and sentiment analysis. In speech recognition, GRUs assist in understanding and transcribing spoken language. They are applied in time-series forecasting to predict future values in datasets, including stock prices, weather patterns, and demand forecasts. Generally, GRUs are computationally more efficient than LSTMs, requiring fewer parameters and less processing time while still achieving high performance. For example, RNNs, particularly LSTMs and GRUs, can predict future air pollution levels based on historical environmental data trends. By analyzing time-series air pollutant data, these models can forecast pollution levels, aiding in proactive environmental management and public health planning.

4.7.2.3 Generative Adversarial Networks

GANs consist of two neural networks—a generative model (generator) and a discriminative model (discriminator) that compete to produce realistic synthetic data, resembling the training data. The two models are trained simultaneously: one to generate data and the other to discriminate between real and generated data. In this scenario, the generator creates data that looks realistic and is indistinguishable from real data. At the same time, the discriminator evaluates the authenticity of that data and attempts to identify any fakes. Its role is to classify data as real or fake accurately. Through this competition, they create increasingly realistic scenarios. GANs have been widely used in a variety of fields, including image generation, video generation, and even text generation. They are known for their ability to produce high-quality samples that closely resemble the input training data.[34] GANs excel at generating synthetic data for ESG scenario planning, thereby augmenting limited datasets.

4.7.2.4 Autoencoders

Autoencoders are a special type of unsupervised neural network designed to encode input data into compressed representations before decoding it back to approximate the original input.[35] They are trained to compress and reconstruct their input data, learning efficient representations in the process. Autoencoders reconstruct their input in an unsupervised manner, providing informative representations for applications such as clustering. They can be either linear or nonlinear, with nonlinear autoencoders serving as generalizations of PCA. Training methods can vary; some autoencoders are trained end-to-end, while others are built layer by layer to achieve greater depth. They consist of an encoder and a decoder that work together to transform input data into a useful representation and then revert it to a form that resembles the original data, enabling various applications such as dimensionality reduction, feature extraction, image denoising, image compression, image search, anomaly detection, and handling missing values.

Autoencoders function by encoding input data into a lower-dimensional representation through an encoder. It then decodes this representation back to its original form using a decoder, aiming to minimize reconstruction error. There are various types of autoencoders, including contractive, denoising, and sparse autoencoders. Generally, the previously mentioned autoencoders are not generative; they replicate the input rather than generate new data. However, VAEs are generative variant models that encode input data into a latent space and decode it back. [36] They are valuable for anomaly detection, generating synthetic data, and enhancing fraud detection systems. For example, autoencoders are used for anomaly detection in manufacturing and noise reduction in environmental sensor data.

4.7.1.5 Transformers

Transformers represent a modern architecture designed for processing sequential data. Unlike RNNs, they employ a self-attention mechanism to process entire sequences simultaneously to improve both performance and training efficiency. Transformers are particularly effective at capturing long-range dependencies without the constraints of RNNs and advanced NLP models. Transformers are typically first pretrained as LMs, using self-supervised learning on large amounts of raw text, followed by supervised fine-tuning on a small dataset for specific tasks.[37] Transformers are trained on sequenced data to generate extended sequences of content (such as words in sentences, shapes in an image, frames in a video, or commands in software code). They are considered the foundational architecture behind most modern GenAI tools, such as ChatGPT, Gemini, Copilot, and BERT, enabling them to effectively process and generate human-like text, images, and other forms of content by leveraging the attention mechanism to understand the context within data sequences. This key feature allows the model to focus on the most relevant parts of an input sequence when generating output. Notable examples include (1) BERT, which stands for Bidirectional Encoder Representations from Transformers (BERT), which focuses on Natural Language Understanding, which is understanding and representing text. BERT is versatile and improves the efficiency of NLP tasks. It is ideal for tasks such as text generation, translation, summarization, sentiment analysis, Q&A, and text classification; (2) GPT, a Generative Pre-trained Transformer that excels at handling sequential data like text; and (3) the Text-to-Text Transfer Transformer (T5), an encoder–decoder model pre-trained on a mixture of unsupervised and supervised tasks, where each task is formatted as text-to-text.[38] For example, transformers can analyze CSRs to extract key ESG compliance insights and detect potentially misleading claims within textual disclosures. By processing and understanding the nuances of textual data in ESG reports, transformers can enhance the accuracy and depth of ESG analysis.

4.8 Strategy for selecting the appropriate AI algorithm for ESG applications: the five-step decision framework

Selecting the right AI algorithm for your ESG initiatives requires a systematic approach that balances business objectives, data characteristics, and organizational capabilities. The appropriate algorithm choice depends on your specific objective (prediction, classification, detection, understanding, or optimization) and the nature of your available data (structured, text, image, or time series). For effective implementation, consider both the algorithmic fit for your problem and the explainability requirements for stakeholder communication. We developed a five-step conceptual framework that provides a structured methodology for managers to make informed decisions when implementing AI solutions for sustainability challenges. The structured approach to choosing the right AI algorithm for business problems, particularly with an ESG focus, is depicted in Figure 4.5.

4.8.1 The five-step decision framework for using AI in sustainability

4.8.1.1 Step 1: Clearly define your objective

Defining your objective establishes the fundamental purpose of your AI initiative and provides clear direction for all subsequent decisions. This critical first step prevents wasting resources on sophisticated algorithms that do not address your actual business needs. The objective you select directly determines the category of algorithms that will be most effective for your ESG challenge. Without a well-defined objective, even the most advanced AI implementation

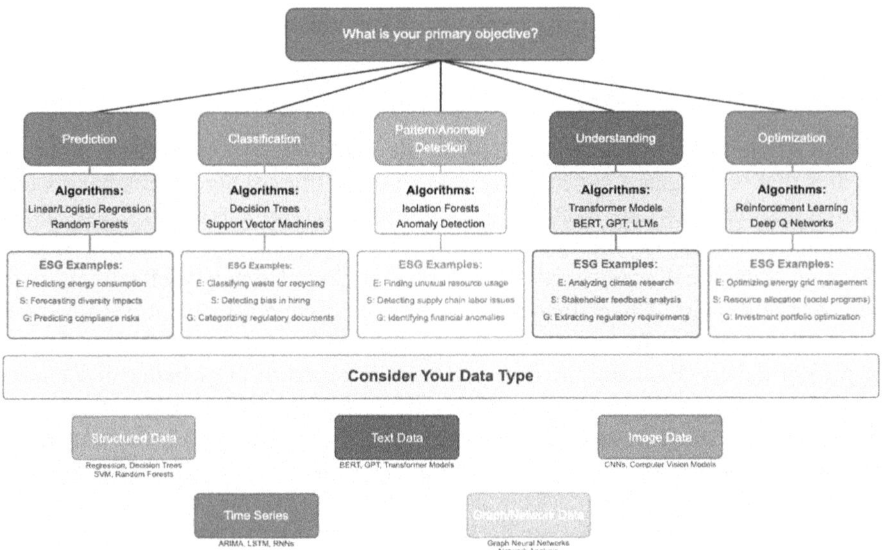

Figure 4.5 Structured approach to choosing the right AI algorithm for ESG

will fail to deliver meaningful business value. Begin by asking yourself what business question you are trying to answer. Is it about predicting future outcomes? Categorizing information? Discovering hidden patterns? Understanding complex documents? Or finding optimal solutions? Your answer determines your algorithm direction.

A well-defined objective narrows your algorithm options significantly. Start by categorizing your ESG challenge into one of these fundamental objectives and by clearly articulating the fundamental objective of your ESG initiative:

- **Prediction:** do you need to forecast a future value or outcome?
  For example, predicting energy consumption, estimating future carbon emissions, and forecasting diversity metrics
- **Classification:** do you need to categorize items into predefined groups?
  For example, identifying high-risk suppliers, classifying waste for recycling, and detecting policy violations
- **Pattern detection:** do you need to discover hidden patterns or anomalies?
  For example, finding unusual resource consumption, detecting financial irregularities, and identifying emerging risks
- **Understanding:** do you need to extract insights from unstructured information?
  For example, analyzing sustainability reports, processing stakeholder feedback, and interpreting regulatory documents
- **Optimization:** do you need to find the best solution among many possibilities?
  For example, optimizing energy usage, improving resource allocation, and enhancing portfolio sustainability

A well-defined objective narrows your algorithm options significantly.

4.8.1.2 Step 2: Assess your data situation

Assessing your data characteristics reveals the fundamental constraints and opportunities that will shape your algorithm selection. Different algorithms have varying requirements for data quantity, quality, and structure, making this assessment essential for identifying feasible options. This step prevents the common pitfall of selecting theoretically powerful algorithms that cannot function effectively with your available data. Understanding your data landscape also identifies potential preparation needs before implementation can begin, potentially saving months of project delays. Evaluate the data you have in terms of (1) whether it includes labeled examples with known outcomes, (2) its format (tables, text, images, and time sequences), (3) its quantity and quality, and (4) how well it represents the problem you are trying to solve. Your available data significantly narrows your algorithm options.

Evaluate the nature of your available data to further refine algorithm selection:

- **Labeled data availability:** do you have historical examples with known outcomes?

- **High availability:** choose supervised learning, for example, linear/logistic regression, decision trees, and random forests.
- **Limited availability:** consider semi-supervised approaches, for example, self-training and co-training.
- **No labels:** use unsupervised methods, for example, clustering and anomaly detection.

- **Data type and structure:**
  - **Structured tabular data:** traditional ML algorithms, for example, regression and decision trees
  - **Text documents:** NLP models, for example, transformers like BERT
  - **Images/visual data:** computer vision models, for example, CNNs
  - **Time series:** specialized models, for example, ARIMA and LSTM
  - **Network/relationship data:** graph-based methods

- **Data volume and quality**:
  - **Small, high-quality datasets:** simpler algorithms often perform well, for example, linear models and KNN.
  - **Large datasets with noise:** more complex models can extract signals, for example, random forests and DL.
  - **Imbalanced data:** require specialized approaches, for example, SMOTE and cost-sensitive learning.

4.8.1.3 Step 3: Consider explainability requirements

Evaluating explainability requirements addresses the critical balance between algorithm performance and transparency needed for your specific context. This step prevents implementing "black box" solutions in situations where stakeholders, regulators, or ethical considerations demand clear explanations of AI decision-making. Understanding explainability needs to be addressed early in the process, allowing for appropriate algorithm selection rather than retrofitting explanations to inherently opaque models. In the ESG context, particularly, explainability often affects stakeholder trust and the perceived legitimacy of your sustainability initiatives. Be open about the importance of understanding how your AI system makes decisions for you and your stakeholders. Regulatory contexts, public-facing applications, and high-stakes decisions typically require more explainable algorithms. Assess how crucial it is for stakeholders to comprehend how the model works.

Determine the level of transparency and interpretability needed for your application:

- **High explainability needed,** like regulatory compliance, public reporting, and stakeholder trust:
  - **Recommended:** linear/logistic regression, decision trees, and rule-based systems

  - **Avoid:** complex neural networks and ensemble methods without explainability tools

- **Moderate explainability needed,** like internal operations and non-critical decisions:

  - **Recommended:** random forests with feature importance and gradient boosting with SHapley Additive exPlanations (SHAP) values, which are a method used to explain the output of machine learning models
  - **Can use:** more complex models with post-hoc explanation methods

- **Low explainability needed,** like back-office optimization and minimal human intervention:

  - **Can use:** any algorithm, including complex "black box" models, if they deliver superior performance

4.8.1.4 Step 4: Evaluate implementation constraints

Assessing implementation capabilities ensures that your algorithm selection aligns with your organization's real-world constraints and abilities. This crucial step prevents selecting sophisticated algorithms that your team cannot effectively implement, maintain, or interpret. Understanding your technical limitations helps identify whether you need to build internal capacity, engage external partners, or select more accessible approaches. Realistic capability assessment also enables accurate project planning, resource allocation, and timeline development for your ESG initiative. Be realistic about your organization's technical capabilities and resources. Assess your organization's technical capabilities, computing resources, and time constraints honestly. Sometimes the "best" algorithm on paper is not the best for your specific situation. Choose approaches that your team can successfully implement and maintain.

Realistically evaluate your organization's technical capabilities and resources:

- **Technical expertise:**

  - **Limited AI expertise:** start with simpler, established algorithms, for example, regression and basic decision trees.
  - **Strong expertise:** can implement more advanced models, for example, DL and RL.

- **Computing resources:**

  - **Limited computing power:** choose computationally efficient algorithms, for example, linear models and KNN.
  - **Strong computing infrastructure:** can utilize resource-intensive methods, for example, DL and complex simulations.

- **Time constraints:**

  - **Quick implementation needed:** use pre-built solutions and simpler models.
  - **Longer timeline available:** can develop custom models and tune parameters extensively.

4.8.1.5 Step 5: Select, implement, and iterate

Developing an implementation strategy transforms your algorithm selection from theoretical to practical by establishing a structured pathway for deployment. This step ensures that your AI implementation includes appropriate testing, validation, and monitoring to confirm real-world effectiveness for your ESG objectives. A well-designed implementation strategy mitigates the risk of project failure by identifying potential issues early and establishing feedback mechanisms for CI. This approach recognizes that successful AI implementation is an iterative process rather than a one-time decision, particularly in the rapidly evolving ESG landscape.

Follow these practical steps when implementing your selected algorithm for ESG applications:

1. **Establish a Baseline—Start Simple:** Begin with the simplest algorithm that could solve your problem. Then, a performance baseline must be established before moving to more complex approaches.
2. **Comparative Evaluation—Test Multiple Approaches:** For critical ESG applications, compare two to three different algorithm types. Evaluate each model based on both performance metrics and practical usefulness.
3. **Validation Protocol—Validate Thoroughly:** Test against historical data where outcomes are known. You can perform scenario testing for extreme or edge cases. Then, conduct bias audits, especially for social applications.
4. **Implement with Monitoring:** Deploy with continuous monitoring for performance drift. Set up alerts for unexpected patterns or results and establish regular review cycles.
5. **CI—Iterate and Improve:** Enhance capabilities incrementally rather than making dramatic changes. Collect feedback from users and stakeholders and update models as new data becomes available.

4.9 GenAI for sustainable practices

4.9.1 X.1 The importance of prompts for GenAI systems

GenAI can generate new content in response to a user's request. The user communicates with the system using natural language prompts. A prompt is essentially the user's input into a GenAI system. It serves as the primary means by which users communicate their intentions to the AI. It serves as a conversation starter that guides the GenAI in generating specific responses. GenAI system responds to prompts by leveraging its core technologies, primarily NLP and ML. When given a prompt, the GenAI analyzes the text to grasp the user's request's context, intent, and specific details. This understanding is crucial for generating a relevant response.[39]

The GenAI interprets the words and phrases in the user's prompt, identifying key elements such as the subject matter, tone, and any specific instructions the user has provided. Many GenAI systems are also designed to remember previous interactions within a session, allowing them to maintain context from earlier prompts. This capability enables a more coherent and fluid dialogue; for instance, if the user asks a follow-up question, the GenAI system can reference its previous responses without needing the user to restate the context.

Once the GenAI system understands the prompt and context, it generates a response by predicting the most appropriate output based on patterns learned from vast amounts of data. Algorithms are employed to formulate coherent and relevant sentences to the user's request. Additionally, GenAI systems can learn from user interactions over time. As the user provides feedback or refines the prompts, the GenAI system can adapt and improve its responses, becoming more aligned with the user's preferences and needs.

4.9.2 How to prompt?

GenAI systems, like LM, apply text generation to engage in conversations with users, responding to queries in a natural, conversational manner. This interaction can enhance sustainability engagement, facilitate better communication between organizations and their stakeholders, and promote transparency and understanding of sustainability efforts. Writing effective prompts is often a trial-and-error process for users, as the effectiveness of prompts can vary significantly based on their structure and content.[40] Moreover, prompts optimized for one generative model, like ChatGPT, may not perform well with another (Gemini, Copilot, Mistral, etc.), leading to potential lock-in effects where users feel confined to a specific system. Different AI models are designed for various tasks and have unique areas of expertise. For instance, an LM like ChatGPT excels in generating text-based responses, while an image generation model like Dall-E or Midjourney is optimized for creating visual content. Using the same prompt across these different systems may not yield the best results because each model interprets and processes prompts according to its design and training.

A prompt can range from a simple phrase to complex sentences and paragraphs. Prompts are crucial because they determine how the LM system interprets the user's request and then determines its output quality. They can be thought of as instructions or questions we provide to the system to elicit a desired response. The effectiveness of the LM system's output largely depends on how well a prompt is crafted. For instance, a well-defined prompt with clear context and specificity can lead to more relevant and useful responses, while vague prompts may yield less satisfactory results. To achieve optimal results, a prompt should be tailored to align with the specific strengths of the AI system, which requires understanding the model's strengths and weaknesses to help tailor prompt crafting. Effective prompt engineering involves recognizing the unique characteristics of each AI system and adjusting the approach to maximize the quality and relevance of the responses received.

Example: Sam, the XYZ Ltd. O&G sustainability Director, is preparing the annual ESG report. Sam is working with an AI system to gather information about the company's sustainability metrics. Sam submits the following prompt to the LM.

4.9.2.1 What sustainability metrics do we report?

When requesting information about sustainability metrics and reporting frameworks, the clarity and structure of the prompt significantly impact the quality of the response. The prompt is too broad and unfocused and lacks crucial context, boundaries, and specific requirements that would guide a comprehensive response.

A well-crafted prompt, on the other hand, acts like a detailed project brief, guiding the AI through exactly what information you need, in what format, and for what purpose. A structured prompt helps both the user and the AI understand the scope, expectations, and desired outcomes. It enables the AI to provide organized, relevant information that aligns with reporting standards and stakeholder needs. A better prompt should be clear and direct and should include context, intent, and specific details while motivating the model to produce original and perceptive answers. Here is an example of an improved prompt to achieve better results:

As a senior sustainability analyst specializing in the O&G industry, your goal is to create a comprehensive overview of the company's current sustainability metrics. Follow these step-by-step instructions:

1. Map the current sustainability metrics to relevant frameworks, including GRI, SASB, TCFD, and SDGs. Identify which metrics align with each framework and highlight any discrepancies.
2. Indicate the data quality and verification status for each metric. Specify whether the data is internally verified, externally audited, or estimated.
3. Assess the alignment of the current metrics with the results of the materiality assessment. Identify any metrics that are not aligned with material issues and suggest adjustments.
4. Review the metric selection against stakeholder requirements. Ensure that the metrics address the information needs and expectations of key stakeholders, including investors, regulators, and community groups.
5. Compare the company's metric coverage against industry standards specific to the O&G sector. Identify any gaps or areas where the company's metrics fall short of industry benchmarks.
6. Identify gaps in the current measurement capabilities. Suggest improvements to enhance data collection, analysis, and reporting processes, particularly in areas such as GHG emissions, water management, and community engagement.
7. Provide clear and actionable recommendations for enhancing the sustainability metrics and measurement systems. Suggest strategies for improving data quality, alignment with frameworks, and stakeholder engagement.

4.9.2.2 The overview should be approximately 2,000 words long

Just as a clear project scope leads to better deliverables, a structured prompt results in more comprehensive, useful responses. The output quality significantly improves when the user provides context, specifies frameworks, requests data quality levels, and outlines how the information will be used. By incorporating specific elements such As timeframes, framework requirements, and data quality considerations, the prompt creates a clear pathway for generating actionable insights. This approach ensures that responses are not just informative but also practical and aligned with business objectives. Table 4.3 reports a comparative analysis between a poor-crafted and a better prompt.

This comparative analysis demonstrates the significant advantages of using well-structured prompts for sustainability reporting. Key observations include the following:

1. The well-crafted prompt improves information quality and provides more comprehensive and usable information.
2. Better prompts improve the system's efficiency and reduce the need for follow-up questions and clarifications.
3. Well-structured prompts have a greater business impact and align better with strategic objectives and compliance requirements.
4. Detailed prompts result in more actionable and practical recommendations.

The well-crafted prompt can significantly influence the response quality and relevance of a GenAI system by clearly defining the role and goal, which guides the AI in generating appropriate and insightful responses. Detailed step-by-step instructions ensure that all necessary aspects are covered, leading to a comprehensive and organized analysis. Specifying the report length helps balance detail and conciseness, ensuring that all relevant information is included without overwhelming the reader. By providing clear and specific guidelines, the prompt helps the AI understand the context and generate outputs that are accurate, contextually appropriate, and aligned with the user's needs, particularly in complex industries like O&G. This approach enhances the overall effectiveness and usefulness of the AI's responses, making them more targeted and valuable for the user. Table 4.4 explains how and why the improved prompt helps the AI system tailor its output to the user's intended audience.

4.9.2.3 Strategies for crafting effective prompts

Well-crafted prompts can help prevent hallucinations and inaccuracies and guide the model to provide more focused and relevant responses.[41] Well-structured prompts can minimize back-and-forth clarifications. They help maintain consistency in output format and style while ensuring resource efficiency: better prompts often mean fewer iterations to get desired results and can reduce token usage by being more specific. LM needs specific instructions because it cannot infer unstated requirements or preferences. In this example, the better prompt

Table 4.3 Comparative analysis between a poorly crafted prompt and a better prompt

Aspect	*Poor Prompt*	*Better Prompt*
User Impact		
Information quality	Receives generic, unfocused data	Gets comprehensive, framework-aligned information
Decision support	Limited context for decision-making	Clear basis for action and planning
Framework alignment	May miss critical reporting requirements	Ensures coverage of all relevant frameworks
Resource planning	Difficult to assess resource needs	Clear view of implementation requirements
Gap analysis	Gaps may not be identified	Systematic identification of reporting gaps
Stakeholder communication	Limited ability to explain approach	Clear communication of methodology
LLM Impact		
Context understanding	Minimal context for response generation	Clear understanding of purpose and scope
Framework reference	Uncertain which frameworks to include	Specific frameworks identified
Temporal scope	No clear reporting period	Defined temporal boundaries
Output structure	No guidance on response format	Clear structure for response
Detail level	Uncertain depth requirements	Specified level of detail needed
Verification requirements	No clarity on assurance needs	Clear verification requirements
Response Characteristics		
Comprehensiveness	Often incomplete or scattered	Systematic and thorough
Actionability	Generic recommendations	Specific, implementable suggestions
Organization	Potentially disorganized	Clearly structured information
Relevance	May include unnecessary information	Focused on specific needs
Practicality	May lack practical application	Implementation-focused
Repeatability	Difficult to replicate	Creates consistent approach
Business Value		
Strategic alignment	May miss strategic objectives	Aligned with business goals
Resource efficiency	Potential waste of resources	Efficient use of resources
Compliance	May miss compliance requirements	Ensures regulatory alignment
Benchmarking	Limited comparison capability	Clear peer comparison framework
Risk management	May overlook key risks	Systematic risk identification
CI	Limited basis for improvement	Clear pathway for enhancement

Table 4.4 Well-crafted prompts' influence on the output quality and relevance

Aspect	*Explanation*	
	Why	*How*
Role specification	Defining the role ensures that the LLM understands the context and the level of expertise required. This helps in generating responses that are appropriate for a senior sustainability analyst in the O&G industry.	The LLM will tailor the language, depth of analysis, and recommendations to match the expertise of a senior analyst, ensuring the output is relevant and insightful.
Clear goal	A clear goal provides direction and focus for the analysis. It ensures that the LLM understands the primary objective and can structure the response accordingly.	The LLM will prioritize the key aspects of the analysis, such as mapping metrics to frameworks, assessing data quality, and providing recommendations, making the output more targeted and useful.
Step-by-step instructions	Detailed instructions guide the LLM through the analysis process, ensuring that all necessary steps are covered. This helps in generating a comprehensive and structured response.	The LLM will follow the instructions to map metrics, assess data quality, align with materiality, review stakeholder requirements, compare with industry standards, identify gaps, and provide recommendations, resulting in a well-organized and thorough analysis.
Report analysis length	Specifying the length ensures that the LLM provides a detailed and comprehensive analysis without being too brief or overly lengthy.	The LLM will generate an overview that is approximately 2,000 words long, ensuring that all relevant information is included without overwhelming the reader.

helps generate responses that meet the user's specific interests and needs. Here are some strategies:

1. Be specific:
   - Clearly define the task and provide all necessary details.
   - Include specific data, goals, and requirements.
2. Provide context:
   - Include background information to help the LLM understand the task.
   - Specify the role, audience, and purpose of the analysis.
3. Use clear language:
   - Use simple and straightforward language to avoid ambiguity.
   - Ensure that the prompt is easy to understand.

4. Set constraints:
   - Specify any limitations or requirements, such as word count, format, or style, and explain how you want the AI to present the output.
   - Include guidelines or rules the AI should follow.
5. Consider Tone and Audience:
   - Provide the AI with specific information about your audience and the tone you would like to set. Adding more specificity and context will further improve the output.
   - Example: "You are a senior sustainability analyst presenting to a board of directors. The tone should be formal, professional, and authoritative. The analysis should highlight key metrics, trends, and actionable recommendations for improving sustainability performance."
6. Test and refine:
   - Test the prompt with the AI and review the output. If possible, provide examples and scenarios.
   - Adjust the prompt based on the results to improve relevance and accuracy.
7. Iterate and optimize:
   - Continuously refine the prompt based on feedback and the AI's performance.
   - Experiment with different phrasing, keywords, and structures to find the most effective prompt.

4.10 Boosting GenAI effectiveness

GenAI systems like LLMs may generate text to simulate human interaction and answer user questions in a natural, conversational way. This capability enables them to respond effectively to user queries, making interactions more fluid and user-friendly. However, the effectiveness of AI-generated text depends on several factors, including the model's complexity, the training data quality, adaptation and learning, the contextual understanding, the language and cultural nuances, the user engagement, and the nature of the prompts. LLM usefulness and alignment can be increased through prompting, fine-tuning, and RL.[42] While prompting refers to the process of providing specific inputs or instructions to a GenAI system to guide its output, fine-tuning involves taking a pre-trained model and further training it on a specific dataset to adapt it to a particular task or domain. This process allows the model to specialize in a specific area, improving its performance on certain tasks such as data analysis, text summarization, video analytics, audio analysis, data extraction, sentiment analysis, and code generation.

Providing new data and more focused feedback can help the model learn and adapt to the desired output, style, and content. Tailoring and refining prompts enhance the clarity and effectiveness of interactions with GenAI systems by encouraging users to articulate their intent and goals more clearly. This approach leads to responses that are better aligned with user expectations and specific needs. For example, prompts used for data analysis should focus on analytical tasks, whereas those for creative writing should encourage the development of narratives. By providing constructive feedback, users can identify weaknesses in the outputs, which can then be addressed through iterative prompt refinement. This is particularly relevant in specialized applications where the AI needs to understand niche topics or specific user preferences. For example, to create a model that summarizes sustainability reports, it is trained on a dataset of sustainability reports. We then provide the model with many examples of sustainability reports (input) and their desired output, guiding the model to become better at sustainability report summarization. LLMs can adapt and learn from their interactions, improving over time by recognizing patterns and adjusting their responses based on feedback and new information. This capability allows AI to develop a form of situational awareness (SA), enhancing its effectiveness in generating relevant and contextually appropriate text.

4.11 SA for LLMs

SA is the ability to perceive and interpret what is happening in the current scenario and appropriately respond to the context, nuances, and implications of a given situation or conversation.[43] For LLMs, SA involves context understanding, conversational memory and coherence, and appropriate response calibration. LLMs need to recognize the broader setting and circumstances and understand the social, cultural, and temporal context while focusing on subtle cues and implications to better respond to user expectations.[44]

Furthermore, an LLM should maintain consistency across a conversation and be able to track previous exchanges and references. In the meantime, an LLM must be able to understand how new information relates to what was discussed before. Adjusting tone and content based on context is an important feature that ensures that the information provided is relevant, appropriate, and effective. This feature involves tailoring the responses to fit the specific situation, audience, and purpose of the communication, for example, recognizing when to be formal versus informal and understanding when detailed versus brief responses are needed. The following example illustrates SA for LLM.

AI can significantly enhance cross-functional communication by synthesizing information, facilitating collaboration, and providing comprehensive solutions. By crafting effective prompts that bridge different functional areas, business users and leaders can leverage the LLM to address complex business challenges, make informed decisions, and drive innovation and efficiency across the organization. This holistic approach ensures that the organization can develop integrated solutions that consider the insights and expertise of multiple departments, leading to better outcomes and a more cohesive strategy. The art and science of crafting effective prompts for AI systems is called prompt engineering, which can play a crucial role in harnessing AI's potential for sustainability. Well-designed prompts can guide AI models to produce relevant, innovative, and impactful solutions that address specific environmental problems.

4.12 Case study

This case aims to demonstrate the difference between poor and well-crafted prompts through a sustainability reporting scenario.

- **The company:** Founded in 1963, XYZ Ltd. is one of the largest conventional O&G companies with a net worth of USD 75.61 billion. The enterprise value is approximately 87.68 billion. With an average production of approximately 573,000 barrels of oil equivalent per day, they are the largest producer in the region. Furthermore, XYZ is the fourth-largest natural gas producer and the largest producer of condensate.
- **The challenge:** In 2024, XYZ faced a critical challenge: they needed to reduce their environmental impact while maintaining profitability and supporting local communities. Like many companies in the industry, they had to navigate complex relationships with different groups—from environmental activists to Indigenous communities to longtime employees worried about their future.
- **The situation:** Sam, XYZ's sustainability Director, aims to understand the big picture, helping to create effective sustainability strategies. Sam quickly realized that successful sustainability initiatives required more than just technical solutions.

  Sam needs to analyze the company's GHG emissions and highlight key metrics, trends, and actionable recommendations for improving sustainability performance. Sam submitted the following prompts to ChatGPT, Gemini, Copilot, Mistral, and DeepSeek. The output is shown in Chapter 2, Appendix A.
- **Prompt 1:** Analyze our GHG emissions provided in the following:

Scope	*As of December 31, 2024 (tons CO2e)*	*As of December 31, 2023 (tons CO2e)*	*Changes from December 31, 2023 to December 31, 2024 (tons CO_2e)*
Total Scope 1	1,947,756	1,939,060	8,696 increase in Scope 1 GHG emissions
Total Scope 2	58, 419	50, 351	8,068 increase in Scope 2 GHG emissions

4.12.4 Outputs analysis

The outputs from ChatGPT, Gemini, Copilot, Mistral, and DeepSeek analyze GHG emissions data, focusing on Scope 1 and Scope 2 emissions. We analyzed the output focusing on four aspects: the structure and style, the depth of details analyzed, the recommendations provided by each LLM, and the focus area of each model.

1. **Structure and Style:**

- **ChatGPT:** Presents a detailed breakdown of emissions data with a clear interpretation of changes between 2023 and 2024. The analysis is thorough and multifaceted, concluding with actionable recommendations for further action based on the findings.
- **Gemini summarizes key findings more concisely**, highlighting the increases in both Scope 1 and 2 emissions and their implications. While it offers recommendations, it is less detailed than ChatGPT and maintains a straightforward narrative.
- **Copilot** provides a structured summary of data points, emphasizing the overall changes in emissions. The tone is direct and focused on clarity, and the presentation style efficiently communicates essential information without extensive elaboration.
- **Mistral:** Similar to ChatGPT, it breaks down emissions data and provides insights. It emphasizes the examination of changes and potential factors contributing to variations while offering suggestions for mitigation strategies, maintaining an analytical tone.
- **DeepSeek** offers a comprehensive analysis but with a more analytical and broader perspective. It combines specific data metrics with discussions on regulatory and market expectations. While it structures information well, it strives for a higher-level analysis of trends.

2. **Details Analyzed:**

- **ChatGPT:** Offers comprehensive interpretations of both scopes, delving into operational impacts and suggesting conducting energy audits to identify areas for improvement.
- **Gemini:** Focuses more on the implications of the emissions increase, including environmental and reputational risks. It provides actionable recommendations without going deeply into operational details.
- **Copilot:** Presents a concise and factual breakdown of emissions data, emphasizing overall increases. It highlights the urgency of addressing these increases, but does not provide extensive analysis.
- **Mistral:** Similar in depth to ChatGPT, it emphasizes the percentage increases and provides a general overview of potential factors influencing changes in emissions, aligning closely with operational dynamics.
- **DeepSeek:** Combines specific emissions metrics with broader context and implications. It analyzes potential causes for the increases and considers external factors such as regulatory pressures, offering a more nuanced understanding.

3. Recommendations:

- **ChatGPT:** Offers a wide range of recommendations, including ongoing monitoring, conducting energy audits, transitioning to renewable energy sources, and assessing operational efficiencies.
- **Gemini:** Highlights the need for thorough investigations into emissions sources and developing a reduction plan with SMART targets, though it is less detailed compared to ChatGPT's multifaceted approach.
- **Copilot:** Emphasizes the importance of addressing underlying causes behind emissions through specific focus areas such as energy consumption and operational efficiency, although it lacks depth in its recommendations.
- **Mistral:** Provides both mitigation strategies and suggestions for continued monitoring, stakeholder engagement, and prevention of future increases, echoing recommendations found in ChatGPT and Gemini.
- **DeepSeek:** Stresses the necessity of a detailed emissions audit, exploring innovative strategies for emissions reduction, and aligning with regulatory expectations, placing emphasis on optimized energy management.

4. Focus Area:

- **ChatGPT and Mistral:** Both focus on detailed analysis and operational recommendations. They aim to provide a comprehensive understanding of emissions trends and strategies for reduction, showing strong alignment in their approaches.
- **Gemini:** Prioritizes implications and overarching risks associated with increased emissions, providing a quicker overview that serves executive decision-making.
- **Copilot:** Focuses on straightforward data presentation and high-level insights, emphasizing clarity and simplicity in communications about emissions trends.
- **DeepSeek:** Aims to blend specific data analysis with broader discussions on implications, exploring risks and operational impacts more comprehensively than some of the other outputs.

ChatGPT and Mistral provide more detailed and comprehensive analyses, while Gemini presents a summary with implications, and Copilot offers clear, straightforward data. DeepSeek enhances the discussion by incorporating broader regulatory and market implications, highlighting the need for alignment with external expectations as well as internal operational efficiencies. All outputs recognize the importance of addressing the increase in GHG emissions and suggest pathways for mitigation. Table 4.5 presents a comparative summary of the outputs from ChatGPT, Gemini, Copilot, Mistral, and DeepSeek regarding the analysis of GHG emissions.

Table 4.5 provides a clear comparison of each analysis approach's strengths and focus areas, illustrating how they each contribute to understanding GHG emissions and strategies for mitigation.

Table 4.5 Prompt 1 output summary

Aspect	*ChatGPT*	*Gemini*	*Copilot*	*Mistral*	*DeepSeek*
Structure/style	Systematic breakdown, clear and coherent	Direct and terse, focuses on key findings	Straightforward summary format	Clear layout with detailed analysis	Comprehensive analysis, thorough and strategic
Details analyzed	Both Scope 1 and 2, context on operational implications	Focuses primarily on overall emissions increase	Basic numerical data	Percentage analysis, connects to operations	Specific sources and operational efficiency
Recommendations	Monitoring, investigating operational factors	Evaluate electricity procurement strategies	Suggests examining emission rise causes	Energy efficiency and stakeholder engagement	Detailed strategies (energy audits, renewables, etc.)
Focus area	Balanced focus on Scope 1 and 2	Overall GHG emissions increase	Equal focus on both scopes	Highlights operational changes	Investigates both scopes, implications emphasized
Emphasis on Scope 1 increase	Discussed within emissions trends narrative	Brief mention, less analytical depth	Reports increases without probing reasons	Specific percentage increase, connects to inefficiencies	Analyzes operational growth and seeks reductions
Emphasis on Scope 2 increase	Significant emphasis on potential causes	Highlights increase with less detail	Mentions increase without deeper exploration	Connects to energy consumption and changes	Examines reliance on carbon-intensive sources
Conclusion	Need for addressing emissions increase	Importance of sustainability awareness	Urgency in addressing emissions	Emphasis on reducing carbon footprint	Stresses the need for alignment with regulations and detailed auditing

Prompt 2: As a senior sustainability analyst specializing in GHG emissions for the O&G sector, provide a comprehensive analysis of the following emissions data for XYZ for presentation to the Board of Directors:

Scope	*As of December 31, 2024 (tons CO_2e)*	*As of December 31, 2023 (tons CO_2e)*	*Changes from December 31, 2023, to December 31, 2024 (tons CO_2e)*
Total scope 1	1,947,756	1,939,060	8,696 increase in Scope 1 GHG emissions
Total scope 2	58, 419	50, 351	8,068 increase in Scope 2 GHG emissions

Structure your response as follows:

1. Executive Summary (150 words)
    - Key findings
    - Material risks and opportunities
    - Critical trends
2. Emissions Performance Analysis (400 words)
    - Scope 1, 2, and 3 emissions breakdown
    - Year-over-year performance
    - Benchmark against industry peers
    - Progress against targets
    - Intensity metrics analysis
3. Framework Compliance Assessment (300 words)

    Evaluate our performance against:

    - ISSB S2 Climate-Related Disclosures
    - GRI 305: Emissions
    - SASB EM-EP-110a.1–3 (O&G)
    - TCFD Risk Management and Metrics

    Identify any gaps in reporting or compliance:
4. Risk Analysis (250 words)
    - Regulatory risks (carbon pricing, emissions trading)
    - Transition risks
    - Physical risks
    - Market risks
    - Reputational risks
5. Strategic Recommendations (300 words)

    Provide three to five actionable recommendations:

    - Short-term actions (0–2 years)
    - Medium-term strategy (2–5 years)

- Long-term positioning (5+ years)

Focus on:

- Emissions reduction opportunities
- Technology solutions
- Cost–benefit analysis
- Implementation timeline

6. Performance Metrics Dashboard

   Present key metrics, including:

   - Absolute emissions by scope
   - Emissions intensity per production unit
   - Year-over-year change
   - Industry benchmark comparison
   - Progress against targets
   - Carbon price exposure

Ensure:

- Professional, authoritative tone suitable for board presentation
- Data-driven insights
- Industry-specific context and benchmarks
- Clear linkage between metrics and business impact
- Actionable recommendations with implementation pathways
- Visual representations where appropriate
- Maximum length: 1,500 words

Specific requirements:

- Use standard industry terminology
- Include quantitative targets where applicable
- Highlight material financial implications
- Reference relevant industry standards and frameworks
- Incorporate peer comparison data
- Identify both risks and opportunities

4.12.5 Outputs analysis

The outputs from ChatGPT, Gemini, Copilot, Mistral, and DeepSeek present summarized insights regarding XYZ's GHG emissions performance, but with varying focuses and structures. In the following, we present the output analysis of each model.

1. ChatGPT Output

- **Structure**: Focused on a clear executive summary and structured analysis.
- **Key Highlights**: Emphasizes the slight increase in Scope 1 and significant increase in Scope 2 emissions. It discusses risks (regulatory and reputational) alongside opportunities (efficiency and renewable energy).

- **Compliance Assessment**: Mentions partial compliance with reporting frameworks and gaps needing attention.
- **Risk and Strategic Recommendations**: Discusses regulatory and transition risks but does not delve deeply into specific actions or timelines beyond general recommendations.

2. **Gemini Output**

- **Structure**: Divided into executive summary and emissions performance analysis.
- **Key Highlights**: Similar to ChatGPT with a recognition of the need for energy efficiency improvements and potential risks regarding regulatory scrutiny.
- **Risk Analysis**: More emphasis on risks associated with operational emissions and the need for immediate attention.
- **Recommendations**: Suggests leveraging emerging technologies and improved operational efficiencies, but lacks detailed strategic elements.

3. **Copilot Output**

- **Structure**: Includes an executive summary that outlines key findings and discusses material risks and opportunities.
- **Key Highlights**: Clearly states the increases in Scope 1 and Scope 2 emissions, reinforcing the need for strategic interventions due to the increase.
- **Performance Metrics**: Provides a concrete dashboard of metrics, addressing absolute emissions, intensity metrics, and progress against targets.
- **Compliance Alignment**: It offers a more detailed section on compliance with ISSB, GRI, SASB, and TCFD standards.

4. **Mistral Output**

- **Structure**: Presents findings in a structured executive summary with separate sections for risks and recommendations.
- **Key Highlights**: Similar to others, but goes into specific recommendations and timelines for actions more comprehensively.
- **Risk Analysis**: Includes depth in discussing reputational and transition risks along with compliance challenges.
- **Strategic Focus**: Offers a balanced view of short-, medium-, and long-term strategies with actionable recommendations.

5. **DeepSeek Output**

- **Structure**: Provides a clear and concise executive summary followed by a detailed emissions performance analysis and risk assessment.
- **Key Highlights**: Acknowledges the overall increase in emissions, stressing the importance of addressing both Scope 1 and Scope 2 increases in the context of global decarbonization trends.
- **Risk Analysis**: Focuses heavily on regulatory risks, market expectations, and the implications of failing to meet net-zero commitments.

- **Strategic Recommendations**: Emphasizes the need for innovative approaches such as adopting renewable energy solutions and carbon capture technologies, aiming for both short-term and long-term improvements.
- **Compliance Gaps**: Identifies specific areas where the reporting and compliance frameworks can be enhanced, notably in Scope 3 emissions and governance disclosures.

While all four models' outputs share common themes regarding the increase in emissions and the need for proactive strategies, they vary in their depth of analysis, focus areas, and specificity of recommendations. Table 4.6 presents a comparison summarizing the key aspects of the outputs from ChatGPT, Gemini, Copilot, Mistral, and DeepSeek regarding XYZ's GHG emissions performance.

6. Comparison summary

- **Depth and Detail**: Copilot and Mistral provide more structured dashboards and insights regarding compliance and performance metrics than ChatGPT and Gemini, which are more generalized. Mistral offers a comprehensive approach that includes actionable strategies and timelines, enhancing its depth of analysis.
- **Focus on Compliance**: All outputs recognize the importance of compliance, but ChatGPT and Mistral emphasize addressing gaps in reporting more explicitly. Copilot provides detailed alignment with various standards, while Gemini outlines partial compliance without firm recommendations for improvement.
- **Risk Assessment**: Mistral provides an extensive analysis of risks, including regulatory, transition, and reputational risks, while others touch upon risks without detailing them as extensively. ChatGPT and Gemini acknowledge risks but do not delve into the complexity of risk implications to the same depth.
- **Recommendations**: Mistral and Copilot focus on actionable recommendations with specific timelines, offering clear strategies for improvement. ChatGPT provides general recommendations for energy efficiency, while Gemini suggests leveraging technologies but lacks the detailed actions and timelines found in the other outputs.
- **Metrics and Performance Monitoring**: Copilot and DeepSeek emphasize the importance of performance metrics and provide concrete dashboards for tracking emission performance. In contrast, ChatGPT and Gemini summarize emissions performance qualitatively, lacking the granular detail that aids in monitoring and assessing progress effectively.

4.13 Summary

This chapter examines the dynamic intersection of AI tools and sustainability by highlighting how advanced AI techniques can be leveraged to promote economic viability, environmental protection, social responsibility, and effective governance. It began by introducing core AI technologies such as ML, DL, NLP, computer vision, and optimization algorithms, and describes their relevance in addressing sustainability challenges. The chapter then explored real-world applications of AI across several critical sectors. In environmental sustainability, AI is used for climate prediction, energy optimization,

Table 4.6. Prompt 2 outputs summary

Aspect	*ChatGPT*	*Gemini*	*Copilot*	*Mistral*	*DeepSeek*
Structure	Executive summary and structured analysis	Executive summary and emissions performance analysis	Executive summary with key findings	Executive summary with detailed sections	Executive summary with detailed emissions performance analysis
Key highlights	Scope 1 increase (0.45%), significant Scope 2 increase (16%). Discusses risks and opportunities.	Notes increase in both scopes, emphasize energy efficiency.	Highlights increases, stresses need for strategic interventions.	Similar findings, with a comprehensive approach to recommendations.	Acknowledges total emissions increase, focusing on compliance risks and market expectations.
Compliance assessment	Partial compliance mentioned, gaps identified.	Outlined partial compliance and gaps.	Detailed alignment with ISSB, GRI, SASB, and TCFD standards.	Comprehensive assessment of compliance with gaps highlighted.	Identifies significant gaps in Scope 3, governance disclosures, and metrics.
Risk analysis	Discusses regulatory and transition risks, but limited detail.	General recognition of risks associated with emissions.	Emphasizes regulatory risks and financial implications.	Extensive analysis of regulatory, transition, and reputational risks.	Focuses on regulatory risks and the financial impact of emissions compliance.
Strategic recommendations	General recommendations for energy efficiency.	Suggests leveraging technologies but lacks detailed actions.	Concrete dashboard with performance metrics, actionable recommendations.	Balanced view with short-, medium-, and long-term strategies.	Emphasizes innovative solutions like renewable energy and carbon capture technologies.
Depth and detail	Moderate depth, clear but general insights.	Moderate depth, focused on immediate attention.	High depth with a focus on metrics and compliance.	High depth with actionable strategies and timelines.	High depth with a strong emphasis on regulatory and compliance aspects.
Performance metrics	Summarizes emissions performance qualitatively.	Outlines increases but less focus on metrics.	Provides a concrete metrics dashboard.	Discusses metrics and performance improvement clearly.	Comprehensive analysis of emissions data and performance metrics.

biodiversity monitoring, and pollution control. In the social domain, AI supports sustainable agriculture, public health, education access, and ethical labor practices. On the governance front, AI enhances transparency in ESG reporting, supports risk management, and assists in regulatory compliance and stakeholder engagement.

This chapter also addresses key challenges in applying AI for sustainability, including data limitations, algorithmic bias, ethical concerns, and the need for transparent, explainable systems. It emphasized the importance of responsible AI development guided by principles such as fairness, accountability, inclusivity, and sustainability-by-design. In conclusion, the chapter considers AI as both a technological enabler and a strategic tool in the global pursuit of sustainability and suggests interdisciplinary collaboration among technologists, policymakers, industry leaders, and sustainability professionals to ensure that AI is harnessed ethically and effectively to support the UNSDGs and foster long-term societal well-being.

4.14 Takeaways

- AI is a catalyst for sustainability by offering powerful tools to support ESG objectives by enabling data-driven decision-making, predictive analytics, and process optimization.
- AI technologies should already be applied in diverse areas such as climate modeling, renewable energy management, smart agriculture, sustainable urban planning, and corporate ESG reporting.
- Core AI techniques such as ML, NLP, and computer vision play a central role in extracting insights from complex data and automating sustainability-related tasks.
- AI helps organizations reduce waste, improve resource allocation, detect risks early, and enhance transparency in sustainability reporting and stakeholder communication.
- Successful AI adoption for sustainability requires addressing concerns related to data privacy, algorithmic bias, explainability, and equitable access to AI solutions.
- Implementing responsible AI practices ensures that the deployment of technology aligns with sustainability values, promotes social inclusion, and avoids unintended negative consequences.
- Interdisciplinary collaborations among technologists, sustainability experts, businesses, and regulators are key to maximizing the positive impact of AI on sustainable development.
- AI can significantly contribute to achieving the UNSDGs by providing innovative solutions to complex global challenges when guided by ethical principles.

Notes

1 McCarthy, J. 2007. *What Is Artificial Intelligence?* Stanford University. http://www-formal.stanford.edu/jmc/whatisai.pdf. Accessed 05.11.2024

2 Bengio, Y., & Malkin, N. 2024. Machine learning and information theory concepts towards an AI Mathematician. *Bulletin of the American Mathematical Society*, 61(3), 457–469

3 Narain, K., Swami, A., Srivastava, A., & Swami, S. 2019. Evolution and control of artificial superintelligence (ASI): A management perspective. *Journal of Advances in Management Research*, 16(5), 698–714

4 Frerichs, J.T. 2019. *Empowering Our Recruiters: Leveraging Narrow Artificial Intelligence and Cloud-based Customer Relationship Management Tools to Enhance Systematic Recruiting*. USMC School of Advanced Warfighting. Marine Corps University. Quantico, Virginia, USA
5 Mitchell, T.M. 2006. *The Discipline of Machine Learning* (Vol. 9, p. 3). Pittsburgh: Carnegie Mellon University, School of Computer Science, Machine Learning Department
6 Boussemart, Y., Cummings, M.L., Fargeas, J.L., & Roy, N. 2011. Supervised vs. unsupervised learning for operator state modeling in unmanned vehicle settings. *Journal of Aerospace Computing, Information, and Communication*, 8(3), 71–85
7 Boussemart et al. Supervised vs. unsupervised learning for operator state modeling in unmanned vehicle settings
8 Ghahramani, Z. 2003. *Unsupervised Learning. In Summer School on Machine Learning* (pp. 72–112). Berlin, Heidelberg: Springer Berlin Heidelberg
9 Ouali, Y., Hudelot, C., & Tami, M. 2020. An overview of deep semi-supervised learning. *arXiv preprint* arXiv:2006.05278
10 Sutton, R.S., & Barto, A.G. 1998. *Reinforcement Learning: An Introduction* (Vol. 1, No. 1, pp. 9–11). Cambridge: MIT Press
11 O'shea, K., & Nash, R. 2015. An introduction to convolutional neural networks. *arXiv preprint* arXiv:1511.08458
12 LeCun, Y., Bengio, Y., & Hinton, G. 2015. Deep learning. *Nature*, 521(7553), 436–444
13 Weizenbaum, J. 1966, January. ELIZA—a computer program for the study of natural language communication between man and machine. Commun. *ACM*, 9(1), 36–45. https://doi.org/10.1145/365153.365168
14 Goodfellow, I.J., Pouget-Abadie, J., Mirza, M., Xu, B., Warde-Farley, D., Ozair, S., Courville, A., & Bengio, Y. 2014. Generative adversarial nets. *Advances in Neural Information Processing Systems*, 27
15 Ooi, K.B., Tan, G.W.H., Al-Emran, M., Al-Sharafi, M.A., Capatina, A., Chakraborty, A., Dwivedi, Y.K., Huang, T.L., Kar, A.K., Lee, V.H., & Loh, X.M. 2025. The potential of generative artificial intelligence across disciplines: Perspectives and future directions. *Journal of Computer Information Systems*, 65(1), 76–107
16 Shannon, C.E. 1948. A mathematical theory of communication. *The Bell System Technical Journal*, 27(3), 379–423
17 Rosenfeld, R. 2002. Two decades of statistical language modeling: Where do we go from here? *Proceedings of the Institute of Electrical and Electronics Engineers (IEEE)*, 88(8), 1270–1278. https://doi.org/10.1109/5.880083
18 Paaß, G., & Giesselbach, S. 2023. *Foundation Models for Natural Language Processing: Pre-trained Language Models Integrating Media* (p. 436). Springer Nature
19 Lehman, J., Gordon, J., Jain, S., Ndousse, K., Yeh, C., & Stanley, K.O. 2023. Evolution through large models. In *Handbook of Evolutionary Machine Learning* (pp. 331–366). Singapore: Springer Nature Singapore
20 Brown, T., Mann, B., Ryder, N., Subbiah, M., Kaplan, J.D., Dhariwal, P., Neelakantan, A., Shyam, P., Sastry, G., Askell, A., & Agarwal, S. 2020. Language models are few-shot learners. *Advances in Neural Information Processing Systems*, 33, 1877–1901
21 Baltrušaitis, T., Ahuja, C., & Morency, L.P. 2018. Multimodal machine learning: A survey and taxonomy. *IEEE Transactions on Pattern Analysis and Machine Intelligence*, 41(2), 423–443
22 Juyal, A., Bhushan, B., & Hameed, A.A. 2023. Towards applications of machine learning algorithms for sustainable systems and precision agriculture. *Data Analytics for Smart Grids Applications—A Key to Smart City Development*, 313–350
23 Reinders, C., Ackermann, H., Yang, M.Y., & Rosenhahn, B. 2019. Learning convolutional neural networks for object detection with very little training data. In *Multimodal Scene Understanding* (pp. 65–100). Academic Press
24 Ghosal, A., Nandy, A., Das, A.K., Goswami, S., & Panday, M. 2020. A short review on different clustering techniques and their applications. *Emerging Technology in Modelling and Graphics: Proceedings of IEM Graph 2018*, 69–83

25 Bengio, Y., Courville, A., & Vincent, P. 2013. Representation learning: A review and new perspectives. *IEEE Transactions on Pattern Analysis and Machine Intelligence*, 35(8), 1798–1828
26 Braei, M., & Wagner, S. 2020. Anomaly detection in univariate time-series: A survey on the state-of-the-art. *arXiv preprint* arXiv:2004.00433
27 Van Engelen, J.E., & Hoos, H.H. 2020. A survey on semi-supervised learning. *Machine Learning*, 109(2), 373–440
28 Yadav, K. 2023. Design, optimization and performance analysis of microgrids using multi-agent Q-learning. In *Data Analytics for Smart Grids Applications—A Key to Smart City Development* (pp. 15–24). Cham: Springer Nature Switzerland
29 Yadav. Design, optimization and performance analysis of microgrids using multi-agent Q-learning
30 Schulman, J., Moritz, P., Levine, S., Jordan, M., & Abbeel, P. 2015. High-dimensional continuous control using generalized advantage estimation. *arXiv preprint* arXiv:1506.02438
31 Schulman, J., Wolski, F., Dhariwal, P., Radford, A., & Klimov, O. 2017. Proximal policy optimization algorithms. *arXiv preprint* arXiv:1707.06347
32 Zhao, X., Wang, L., Zhang, Y., Han, X., Deveci, M., & Parmar, M. 2024. A review of convolutional neural networks in computer vision. *Artificial Intelligence Review*, 57(4), 99
33 Fu, R., Zhang, Z., & Li, L. 2016, November. Using LSTM and GRU neural network methods for traffic flow prediction. In *2016 31st Youth Academic Annual Conference of Chinese Association of Automation (YAC)* (pp. 324–328). IEEE
34 Fu, Zhang, & Li. 2016. Using LSTM and GRU neural network methods for traffic flow prediction, In *2016 31st Youth Academic Annual Conference of Chinese Association of Automation (YAC)* (pp. 324–328). IEEE
35 Bank, D., Koenigstein, N., & Giryes, R. 2021. *Autoencoders*. https://arxiv.org/abs/2003.05991
36 Kingma, D.P., & Welling, M. 2013. *Auto-encoding Variational Bayes*. https://doi.org/10.48550/arXiv.1312.6114
37 Vaswani, A., Shazeer, N., Parmar, N., Uszkoreit, J., Jones, L., Gomez, A.N., Kaiser, L., & Polosukhin, I. 2017. Attention is all you need. *Advances in Neural Information Processing Systems*, 30
38 Minaee, S., Mikolov, T., Nikzad, N., Chenaghlu, M., Socher, R., Amatriain, X., & Gao, J. 2024. Large language models: A survey. *arXiv*. https://arxiv.org/abs/2402.06196
39 Acar, O.A. 2023. AI prompt engineering isn't the future. *Harvard Business Review*. https://hbr.org/2023/06/ai-prompt-engineering-isnt-the-future
40 Zamfirescu-Pereira, J.D., Wong, R.Y., Hartmann, B., & Yang, Q. 2023. Why Johnny can't prompt: How non-AI experts try (and fail) to design LLM prompts. In *Proceedings of the 2023 CHI Conference on Human Factors in Computing Systems* (pp. 1–21). Association for Computing Machinery. https://doi.org/10.1145/3544548.3581388
41 OpenAI. 2023. *A Guide to Crafting Effective Prompts for Diverse Applications*. https://community.openai.com/t/a-guide-to-crafting-effective-prompts-for-diverse-applications/493914
42 Bill, D., & Eriksson, T. 2023. *Fine-tuning a LLM Using Reinforcement Learning from Human Feedback for a Therapy Chatbot Application*. KTH Royal Institute of Technology
43 Munir, A., Aved, A., & Blasch, E. 2022. Situational awareness: Techniques, challenges, and prospects. *AI*, 3(1), 55–77
44 Laine, R., Chughtai, B., Betley, J., Hariharan, K., Balesni, M., Scheurer, J., Hobbhahn, M., Meinke, A., & Evans, O. 2025. Me, myself, and AI: The situational awareness dataset (sad) for LLMs. *Advances in Neural Information Processing Systems*, 37, 64010–64118

5 AI technologies and sustainability factors

5.1 Introduction

The growing sustainability demand by investors, requirements by regulators, and disclosure by businesses have spurred a wave of technological advancements, including renewable energy solutions and smart infrastructure, digital platforms, and circular economy models that enable more transparent and accountable business sustainability practices. These innovations are reshaping business organizations and their industries and driving a shift toward more sustainable production and consumption patterns. For example, renewable energy technologies such as hydroelectric power, solar, wind, and are reducing reliance on fossil fuels and decreasing carbon footprints. Similarly, advances in energy storage and smart grid technologies are enhancing the efficiency and resilience of energy systems. Digital technologies, including the IoT, blockchain, AI, and big data analytics, are revolutionizing how organizations monitor, measure, and manage their sustainability performance. IoT devices enable real-time monitoring of environmental conditions and resource use, providing critical data that can be used to optimize operations and reduce waste. Blockchain technology offers new ways to ensure transparency and traceability in supply chains, thereby supporting ethical sourcing and responsible consumption. AI and ML algorithms are driving predictive analytics that help organizations anticipate and mitigate sustainability risks, such as supply chain disruptions or climate-related impacts. The technological innovations examined in this chapter present significant opportunities for advancing sustainability while posing new challenges. The development, deployment, and scaling of these technologies require careful consideration of their environmental and social impacts, from the carbon footprint of digital infrastructure to issues of data privacy, equity, and inclusivity.

This chapter also provides business organizations with a comprehensive understanding of how technology can drive sustainable transformation by exploring a range of technological innovations and their applications in sustainability and covering the potential of emerging technologies to enhance resource efficiency, reduce environmental impact, foster social inclusion, and create new business models that align with the principles of sustainable development. This chapter aims at inspiring organizations to leverage technology not just as a tool for compliance or cost

DOI: 10.4324/9781003611981-5

reduction but also as a catalyst for creating long-term value and positive impact in a rapidly changing world by examining opportunities and challenges of technological innovations and highlights the importance of adopting a holistic approach that integrates technological innovation with sustainable business strategies and ethical governance frameworks.

5.2 AI and sustainability strategic planning

Four sustainability factors, as mentioned in Chapter 1, are planning, performance, risks, and disclosures. These four sustainability factors enable business organizations to create shared value for all stakeholders.[1] Sustainability planning involves developing sustainability goals, strategies, and practices to balance "shareholder value maximization," of improving earnings for shareholders, and broader "stakeholder/ society welfare maximization" of creating shared value for all stakeholders. Sustainability planning focuses on sustainability initiatives, activities, and processes that are sustainable in the long term. Sustainability planning consists of (1) evaluation and assessment of business activities and priorities to determine economic, environmental, and social impacts; (2) establishment of goals and objectives of balancing profit, people, planet, and prosperity to achieve the corporate mission of profit-with-purpose; (3) stakeholder engagement and communication to understand and identify sustainability opportunities, preferences, concerns, and expectations; (4) implementation and monitoring to ensure the effective achievement of sustainability goals; and (5) reevaluation, reassessment, and adaptation to pursue the mission of profit-with-purpose for business organization which enables them to implement short-term and long-term plans for making a profit while pursuing long-term strategic plans with social and environmental impacts.

The use of AI platforms in developing sustainability strategic planning is essential in transforming how organizations approach sustainability goals and initiatives by empowering organizations to establish the five strategic planning processes mentioned in the previous paragraph and create, implement, and monitor sustainability strategies more effectively by leveraging data-driven insights and predictive analytics. AI-powered tools and techniques enable business organizations to establish their sustainability strategic plans by: (1) collecting, aggregating, and processing large volumes of data from various sources, including environmental monitoring systems, corporate ESG reports, supply chain data, and stakeholder feedback; (2) providing a comprehensive view of sustainability-related issues to identify gaps and opportunities; (3) predicting future trends in ESG performance to anticipate risks and opportunities; (4) forecasting carbon emissions, energy consumption, or water usage trends, allowing businesses to make proactive adjustments to their operations; (5) assessing various scenarios based on changes in regulatory policies, market conditions, or environmental risks to evaluate the potential impact of different sustainability strategies and choose the most resilient and effective approach; (5) optimizing resource allocation by analyzing operational data to reduce waste, improve energy efficiency, and minimize environmental impact and suggesting energy-saving measures or optimize supply chain logistics for reduced carbon footprints; (6) enabling real-time monitoring of sustainability performance metrics, such as GHG emissions, waste levels, or diversity and inclusion benchmarks and automating sustainability reporting, ensuring compliance with global standards and improving transparency with stakeholders; (7) analyzing stakeholder sentiments from social media, surveys, or public comments, providing valuable insights into societal expectations and concerns by using NLP tools to support interactive platforms for engaging with stakeholders and co-creating sustainability initiatives; (8) making informed decisions by presenting actionable insights and recommendations based on complex datasets to align sustainability initiatives with broader corporate objectives, ensuring both financial ESP and nonfinancial ESG goals are achieved; (9) identifying opportunities for product lifecycle extension, material recycling, and waste reduction to find innovative ways to repurpose waste materials or optimize product designs for sustainability; (10) assessing climate-related risks, such as flooding, heatwaves, or supply chain disruptions, and providing mitigation strategies to develop climate-resilient business strategies; and (11) ensuring that sustainability strategies align with global ESP and ESG frameworks such as Financial Accounting Standards Board, GRI, SASB, TCFD, CSRD, and ISSB by tracking and benchmarking performance against these standards to identify key areas for improvement to enhance ESG disclosures. Overall, AI-assisted algorithms and platforms can play a pivotal role in sustainability strategic planning by offering advanced tools for data-driven decision-making, risk assessment, and performance optimization to enhance ESP and ESG performance in building resilient and future-ready business models.

5.3 Dimensions of sustainability performance and AI

Sustainability performance is typically classified into financial and nonfinancial performance and grouped into five dimensions: Economic (E), Governance (G), Social (S), Ethical (E), and Environmental (E), abbreviated as EGSEE.[2] These five EGSEE dimensions of business sustainability performance can be classified into two general categories of financial ESP and nonfinancial ESG; sustainability performance with the ethics component is integrated into both ESP and ESG performance dimensions. Each industry has its own applicable set of sustainability, financial, and nonfinancial ESG sustainability performance. Each business organization must carefully identify its own social and environmental responsibilities, given the context of the industry and community in which it operates, in identifying, measuring, and reporting ESP and ESG key sustainability performance indicators (KSPIs). The list of financial and nonfinancial sustainability KSPIs depends on a variety of factors: industry, legal regimes, cultural background, corporate mission and strategy, corporate culture, political infrastructure, managerial philosophy, and sustainability reporting frameworks.

5.3.1 AI and financial economic sustainability projects, performance, and stability

AI-powered tools can play a vital role in promoting financial economic sustainability by improving both performance and stability across various aspects of financial markets, corporate finance, and economic management. Integrating AI-driven platforms into financial economic sustainability initiatives and efforts improves performance metrics and enhances the overall resilience and stability of financial systems, which may contribute to a more sustainable economy. There are several ways that AI can contribute to the achievement of financial sustainability projects, performance, and stability. First, AI-driven predictive models can identify investment opportunities aligned with ESG criteria by processing large datasets, including ESG reports, financial disclosures, and market data, to assess whether a company is likely to deliver long-term, sustainable returns. Second, AI algorithms, especially ML and anomaly detection, can assist in identifying irregular transactions and potential fraud more efficiently than traditional methods by assessing and managing financial risks and protecting investor confidence, which can contribute to the stability of financial systems. Third, AI-powered tools can track financial ESP metrics, market trends, and sector-specific risks in real time by anticipating market shifts and performance drops, and companies can proactively adjust strategies to maintain stability. Fourth, AI-powered algorithmic trading platforms now incorporate ESG factors of strategic plan, performance, risk, and disclosure into trading decisions that may contribute to market stability and promote socially responsible investing. Fifth, AI technologies can automate repetitive financial processes, reducing costs and minimizing human error by enabling companies to allocate resources to innovation and long-term growth rather than administrative tasks. Finally, AI-powered tools enable more advanced stress testing and scenario analysis by stimulating economic and environmental scenarios to predict the resilience of financial entities under different conditions and support a more robust and stable financial environment.

The use of AI platforms in identifying, measuring, and reporting financial ESP is essential in achieving sustainability goals to enhance financial and ESP. AI-assisted tools and techniques can be used to financial ESP by: (1) collecting, processing, and analyzing extensive financial, economic, and sustainability data to identify KSPI including profitability, environmental impacts, social contributions, and governance practices; (2) detecting financial risks tied to environmental and social factors, such as climate change, resource scarcity, or regulatory shifts; and (3) mapping and mining unstructured data (e.g., social media, news articles, and ESG reports) to identify stakeholder concerns and public perception regarding sustainability. AI can revolutionize the measurement of ESP by: (1) tracking real-time financial and sustainability metrics, such as carbon emissions, waste reduction, and energy consumption; (2) standardizing ESP to ensure that diverse data points from various sources are harmonized and aligned with global standards such as the GRI, the SASB, the CSRD, the ISSB, or the TCFD; and (3) predicting long-term financial and sustainability outcomes based on historical data and scenario analysis. AI can improve the ESP reporting process by: (1) creating customized, real-time sustainability reports tailored to stakeholders' needs, reducing the manual workload; (2) ensuring that reported data is accurate, traceable, and immutable, boosting stakeholder confidence; (3) generating interactive dashboards and visualizations that make financial and sustainability performance more comprehensible to non-experts; and (4) detecting discrepancies or potential issues in reporting to ensure compliance with sustainability disclosure regulations. Several benefits of using AI-powered algorithms in identifying, measuring, and reporting financial ESP are to: (1) improve efficiency and cost reduction by reducing the time and resources needed to collect, analyze, and report sustainability data; (2) enable organizations to align sustainability goals with financial performance in making a better financial decision; and (3) improve stakeholder trust by producing high-quality, transparent sustainability reporting fostering trust among investors, customers, and regulators. Some of the challenges in using AI for ESP are: (1) reliance on high-quality data, which may not always be available or standardized; (2) risk that AI systems may not integrate with existing platforms and processes; and (3) ethical concerns that AI tools themselves may not align with sustainability and ethical principles, avoiding biases and unintended negative impacts. Companies should leverage AI to provide real-time ESP sustainability dashboards for stakeholders, reflecting both economic and sustainability performance metrics, because AI platforms represent a transformative approach to achieving financial ESP by bridging the gap between financial performance and ESG imperatives. The integration of AI enhances ESP identification, measurement, and reporting, empowering business organizations to drive meaningful change and prepare robust sustainability reports while meeting regulatory and stakeholder demands.

One empirical study provides an in-depth analysis of how AI is driving economic development through various applications and research areas and finds that: (1) AI systems are increasingly being used to support and automate decision-making processes in various economic sectors to leverage data analytics and ML in providing accurate and timely insights, enhancing the efficiency and effectiveness of economic decisions; (2) AI technologies can be applied to improve social governance, helping governments and organizations manage social resources more effectively; (3) AI is transforming labor markets and capital allocation by optimizing workforce management and investment decisions, leading to increased productivity and economic growth; and (4) AI fosters innovation by providing new tools and methodologies for developing novel solutions and products, which can accelerate the pace of innovation and opens up new avenues for economic growth.[3]

Another paper examines how AI technologies are being integrated into various economic subfields and the factors influencing their adoption and finds that: (1) AI methods, such as ML, DL, and neural networks, are increasingly being incorporated into economic research and becoming a crucial tool for economic analysis, providing more sophisticated and accurate insights a wide range of economic issues, from forecasting and modeling to policy analysis and financial economics compared to traditional methods; (2) there is a positive association between the quality of an institution's affiliation and its engagement with AI in economics often with better access to resources and expertise, which underscores the importance of institutional support and investment in fostering AI research in economics; and (3) there is a negative correlation between a country's human development index (HDI) and the share of learning-based AI papers, which suggests that countries with lower HDI may face barriers in accessing or adopting advanced AI technologies for economic research.[4]

5.3.2 AI and nonfinancial ESG sustainability

AI-powered tools can play an important role in enhancing ESG performance and stability and could offer valuable insights, especially given their potential for predictive analytics, real-time monitoring, and automation. A comprehensive analysis of AI's transformative potential across multiple sectors should consider any challenges, like data quality or ethical concerns, that could affect AI's effectiveness in ESG applications. Focusing on AI-powered tools such as ML models for predictive insights, NLP, and AI-driven platforms for real-time environmental monitoring is increasingly vital for ESG data collection, analysis, and reporting. Integrating ML, NLP, and real-time monitoring should provide a powerful framework for understanding and improving ESG performance.

AI platforms play a transformative role in identifying, measuring, and reporting nonfinancial ESG sustainability performance. The integration of AI into ESG sustainability efforts is expected to grow significantly as organizations recognize the value of data-driven decision-making. AI platforms offer an unparalleled opportunity to enhance the credibility and efficiency of ESG reporting while supporting organizations in meeting their sustainability goals by effectively identifying, measuring, and reporting ESG sustainability performance.

AI-powered legalisms can be utilized to identify key ESG issues across industries and organizations through advanced data processing capabilities including: (1) NLP to analyze unstructured data such as sustainability reports, media articles, social media posts, and regulatory documents to detect ESG-related risks and opportunities and identify sentiment and public perception regarding ESG practices; (2) image recognition to assesses visual data (e.g., satellite images) to track ESG factors such as deforestation, carbon emissions, or water usage, social injustice, and workplace environment; (3) and predictive analytics to identify emerging ESG trends by analyzing large datasets, including historical data and real-time feeds.

AI platforms can be used to enhance the precision and scope of ESG performance measurement, enabling business organizations to capture complex, multi-dimensional metrics through: (1) data integration to aggregate data from diverse sources, such as IoT sensors, internal systems, and external datasets, for comprehensive ESG measurement, and facilitate data standardization and harmonization, addressing inconsistencies in ESG metrics; (2) AI-powered metrics to calculate nonfinancial ESG metrics, such as GHG emissions, diversity and inclusion indices, and social impact scores, and assist in benchmarking ESG performance against industry standards or peer organizations; and (3) real-time monitoring to track environmental data, such as air and water quality, in real time using IoT and AI-powered environmental monitoring tools, and detect anomalies or deviations in ESG performance metrics for early intervention.

AI-assisted tools and techniques can be employed to prepare and streamline ESG reporting to ensure, completeness, accuracy, transparency, compliance, and alignment with global frameworks through: (1) automation of reporting to automate the generation of ESG reports by pulling data from multiple systems, saving time and reducing manual errors and supports reporting in compliance with major ESG frameworks such as GRI, SASB, TCFD, CSRD, and ISSB; (2) AI for text generation (NLP) to draft ESG narratives and summaries for annual reports and sustainability disclosures and tailor ESG reports to specific audiences, such as investors, regulators, and other stakeholders; (3) data visualization to generate advanced visualizations, dashboards, and infographics to make ESG data accessible and actionable; and (4) audit and assurance to lend more credibility to ESG reports, enhance data accuracy by identifying inconsistencies and anomalies in reported metrics, and facilitate ESG data audits to verify compliance with reporting standards.

5.4 Prompt engineering and techniques for LM fine-tuning

Prompt engineering and techniques for LM fine-tuning are essential strategies for optimizing model performance and aligning outputs with specific tasks or domain requirements. Prompt engineering involves crafting input queries or templates that effectively guide the model's responses without altering its underlying parameters. This technique is particularly valuable in zero-shot learning (ZSL) or few-shot learning (FSL) scenarios, where minimal labeled data is available. In contrast, LM fine-tuning refers to retraining a pre-trained model on a domain-specific dataset to adapt its knowledge and behavior to a particular application, such as legal document analysis or medical diagnosis. Fine-tuning can be supervised or unsupervised and often requires careful data curation, learning rate selection, and evaluation metrics to avoid overfitting or bias amplification. Together, these approaches enhance the model's adaptability, accuracy, and usability across diverse real-world contexts.

5.4.1 Prompt engineering

Prompt engineering is the practice of crafting and refining inputs, queries, or prompts to guide AI models, especially LMs, in producing desired outputs.[5] This is achieved by providing clear instructions, context, and examples, thus optimizing the model's responses to specific tasks and questions. Prompt engineering is both an art and a science focused on effectively communicating with AI to obtain the most accurate and relevant results. It serves to optimize the model's responses to particular tasks and questions.[6] It involves understanding how different elements of a prompt, such as word order and context length, can influence the results. The model's output can be enhanced by providing the model with specific instructions, examples, role, context information, and teaching the model how to prioritize various types of inputs. Effective prompt engineering aims to optimize the interaction with generative models, ensuring that the prompts lead to more accurate and relevant outputs. This practice is essential for improving the performance of LLMs in various applications. Figure 5.1 depicts the prompt engineering process. The quality and relevancy of the AI's response can be significantly affected by the wording of queries or prompts since these models do not have a set of predetermined instructions. A well-crafted prompt can unlock the full potential of the model, guiding it toward generating outputs that are not only accurate but also relevant, insightful, and tailored to the specific needs of the user. Conversely, a poorly constructed prompt can lead to ambiguous, inaccurate, or irrelevant responses, hindering the model's ability to contribute meaningfully to the task at hand.

Prompts are text-based inputs that guide the output of your GenAI assistant (LLMs, like ChatGPT, Gemini, Copilot, or other assistants like Midjourney and DALL-E). Essentially, they are a set of instructions given to the model that can include input data, relevant context, and a specification for the desired output format to guide the model in achieving a desired task. A prompt can be audio, but it is transcribed into text before being fed into the model. A well-structured prompt typically comprises five key components (Figure 5.2):

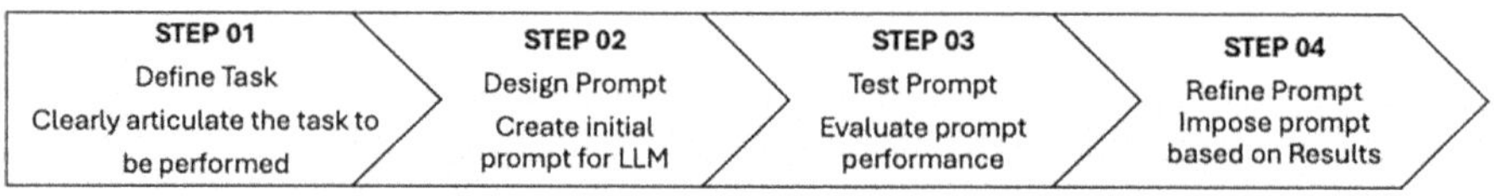

Figure 5.1 Prompt engineering process

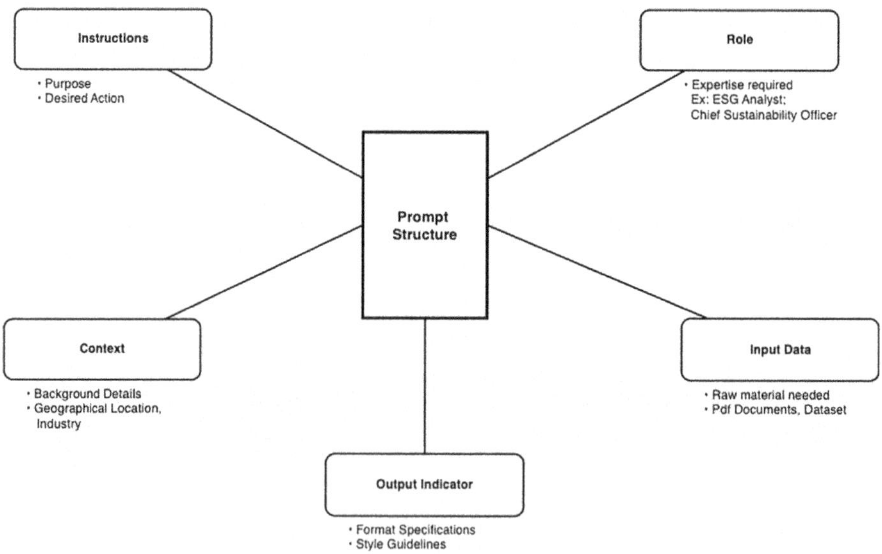

Figure 5.2 Anatomy of a prompt

1. **Instructions:** this element clearly articulates the task the GenAI assistant is expected to perform, establishing a clear path to follow. Specify the role that impacts how the model may interpret the input. This component sets the stage for interaction, defining the purpose, desired action, or outcome. Examples include "Summarize the following article," "Analyze the provided data," "Generate a list of recommendations," or "Translate this text into Spanish."
2. **Role:** specify the expertise required to ensure that the GenAI assistant generates content with suitable depth and authority. The role impacts how the GenAI assistant may interpret the input. Examples of roles include ESG Analyst, CSO, Director of Corporate Social Responsibility, ESG Director, Sustainable Finance Manager, Sustainable Finance Consultant, ESG and Climate Data Analyst, Sustainability Communication Manager, and ESG and Financial Reporting Officer.
3. **Input Data:** this component provides the GenAI assistant with the raw material it needs to work with. It could be a text document, a PDF file, a dataset, a code snippet, or any other information relevant to the task.
4. **Context:** this element offers background information that helps the GenAI assistant understand the broader context of the task. It provides relevant details, constraints, or assumptions that shape the model's understanding and guide its response. For instance, in a sustainability context, this could include information about the specific industry, geographical location, or period under consideration.
5. **Output Indicator:** this component specifies the desired format or type of output. You can provide sample outputs and specify your target audience. This component clarifies the user's expectations regarding the AI assistant's response structure, tone, style, or content. Examples include "a concise summary," "a detailed report," "professional tone," "technical one," "a bulleted list," "a table of data," or "a creative story."

5.4.1.1 Importance of prompt engineering for sustainability

Sustainability reporting and setting carbon targets have become standard practice, with a trend toward increased transparency and responsibility in sustainability reporting among large corporations, influenced by both market pressures and impending regulations. The introduction of mandatory sustainability reporting, particularly through the EU's CSRD, has significantly transformed companies' practices. Businesses are increasingly publishing ESG data and carbon reduction targets, with a proactive approach becoming the norm among major companies. Many companies have begun aligning their sustainability reporting with CSRD guidelines and the EU Taxonomy ahead of the regulatory deadline. This shift indicates that reporting on sustainability has become standard practice for major companies globally and within various jurisdictions.[7] The mandatory reporting landscape drives companies to enhance their sustainability practices, improve transparency, and engage more meaningfully with stakeholders regarding their ESG goals and performance. As sustainability becomes increasingly critical for corporate strategy, prompt engineering offers a powerful tool for transforming environmental initiatives while maintaining profitability. LLMs have immense potential as tools for

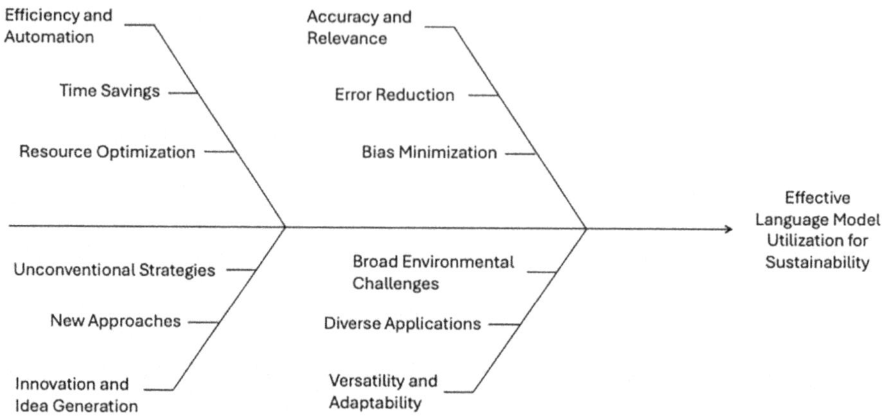

Figure 5.3 Harnessing LLMs for sustainability through prompt engineering

addressing sustainability challenges, but they need clear and precise guidance to be effective in this area. Prompt engineering allows companies to harness the power of these models by creating specific instructions that steer them toward performing sustainability-related tasks. It plays a vital role in harnessing AI effectively for sustainability reporting, ensuring that the outputs are reliable, transparent, and useful for various stakeholders.[8] Figure 5.3 shows an example of how we can harness LMs for sustainability through prompt engineering.

The strategic implementation of prompt engineering can drive both sustainability goals and business performance, with multifaceted advantages:

5.4.1.2 Efficiency and automation

Efficiency and automation revolve around using carefully crafted prompts to streamline environmental monitoring and resource management. Well-crafted prompts can automate the creation of sustainability-related materials, including sustainability reports, plans, and data analyses, saving time and resources. For example, LLMs can automate the process of creating sustainability reports. This allows companies to generate narrative content quickly and efficiently, helping to meet the increasing demands for transparency and detail in corporate sustainability disclosures. When analyzing environmental data, well-designed prompts can help AI systems quickly identify patterns in energy consumption, waste production, or carbon emissions. For example, an LLM can be prompted to analyze a company's energy consumption data and automatically generate an analysis report outlining areas for improvement and potential cost savings. A manufacturing facility can use prompt engineering to continuously monitor its production processes—the system could automatically flag energy inefficiencies or suggest optimal equipment operation times, leading to significant reductions in energy usage and operational costs. This automation frees up experts to focus on more strategic and complex tasks.

5.4.1.3 Innovation and idea generation

Smartly designed prompt engineering practices and tools can create an environment conducive to innovation and enhance the capability of users to generate and develop new ideas. Innovation and idea generation become particularly powerful when prompts are structured to explore novel sustainability solutions. By designing prompts that encourage divergent thinking, users can stimulate creative processes, leading to novel solutions. For example, crafting a prompt that encourages users to think broadly and creatively about various aspects of sustainability, such as energy sources, urban planning, transportation, and community engagement. By having to consider multiple dimensions, participants may generate unique ideas such as vertical gardens, smart waste management systems, eco-friendly public transport options, or community education initiatives to promote sustainable habits. Such prompts can lead to novel, interdisciplinary solutions for urban sustainability challenges. Furthermore, the iterative refinement of prompts allows for rapid prototyping and experimentation, encouraging exploration of different angles. Exploring different prompt variations and experimenting with diverse perspectives can uncover new ideas and innovative approaches to sustainability problems. LMs can be prompted to brainstorm solutions, generate alternative scenarios, and explore unconventional strategies that might not have been considered otherwise. This can lead to breakthroughs in areas such as waste reduction, renewable energy adoption, and sustainable resource management (SRM). For example, a prompt might explore how biomimicry principles could be applied to urban water management, leading to nature-inspired solutions for water conservation.[9] The key is to design prompts that encourage lateral thinking while maintaining focus on practical sustainability outcomes.

5.4.1.4 Accuracy, transparency, and relevance

Prompt engineering plays a crucial role in enhancing the effectiveness of interactions with LMs, ensuring that they produce high-quality outputs. It promotes accuracy, transparency, and relevance, keeping sustainability initiatives focused and effective. By carefully designing prompts, we guide LMs in generating quality outputs, minimizing ambiguity, and improving the precision of the model's responses while fostering transparency by clarifying the underlying logic of the model outputs. Techniques like "chain-of-thought" prompting can break down the reasoning process into understandable steps, allowing users to see how conclusions are drawn.[10] This clarity can build trust in the model's outputs. Prompt engineering involves crafting prompts that explicitly consider environmental impact metrics and sustainability goals. Clear and well-crafted prompts ensure that LMs provide more precise and relevant information, reducing the risk of errors, biases, or misinterpretations in sustainability-related outputs.[11] For instance, strategies such as using specific examples help models focus on relevant information, thereby enhancing accuracy. By clearly defining the task, providing relevant context, and specifying the desired output format, the prompt can guide the model toward generating outputs directly applicable to the sustainability challenge. For example, when analyzing a company's supply chain, well-engineered prompts can assist AI systems in accurately identifying areas of high environmental impact while filtering out less relevant factors. This precision helps organizations prioritize their sustainability efforts where they will have the greatest effect. To ensure that prompts yield relevant outputs, they can be tailored to include specific context or constraints relevant to the task at hand. For example, by optimizing prompts using templates, we can enhance the likelihood of generating relevant responses. Additionally, prompts can be iteratively refined based on performance metrics, further improving relevance over time.

5.4.1.5 Versatility and adaptability

Versatility and adaptability of prompt engineering are particularly valuable in sustainability applications because environmental challenges often require flexible, context-sensitive solutions. They can transform sustainability initiatives across any industry. A prompt framework designed for reducing energy consumption in office buildings might be adapted for industrial facilities or residential complexes. This adaptability extends to handling different types of environmental data and varying regulatory requirements across regions. For example, a prompt structure developed for tracking carbon emissions in North America could be modified to accommodate different reporting standards in Asia or Europe. Prompt engineering can be applied to various sustainability tasks, making it a versatile tool for addressing diverse environmental challenges. Some key applications include the following:

- ***Identifying Sustainable Solutions***: Prompt engineering systems to adapt to specific industry contexts while identifying sustainable solutions. LMs can be prompted to research and identify best practices, innovative technologies, and effective strategies for addressing specific sustainability issues, such as reducing plastic waste, promoting sustainable transportation, or conserving water resources. Let us consider a practical example:

  A retailer implemented an adaptive prompt system to identify sustainability opportunities across their operations. The system automatically adjusted its focus between:

  - Store locations (urban vs. rural energy needs)
  - Supply chain (transportation optimization)
  - Packaging (material reduction strategies)
  - Waste management (recycling opportunities)

  The same system, when deployed in a healthcare setting, seamlessly shifted its priorities to:

  - Medical waste reduction
  - Energy-efficient medical equipment

  - Water conservation in sterilization processes
  - Sustainable procurement of medical supplies

  This versatility enables organizations across different sectors to improve their ability to identify industry-specific sustainable solutions while maintaining operational efficiency.

- ***Analyzing Sustainability Data***: Modern organizations generate massive amounts of sustainability-related and other data, including emails, stakeholders' feedback, and social media data, making them especially valuable for sustainability initiatives. AI systems can analyze various data types and process vast amounts of information, enabling smarter decisions that drive data-driven sustainability initiatives. Prompt engineering's adaptability is demonstrated in making sense of this data across different contexts and industries. For example, LLMs can analyze complex datasets related to energy consumption, waste generation, carbon emissions, and other environmental indicators. They can identify trends, patterns, and anomalies, providing valuable insights for informed decision-making.
- ***Developing and Evaluating Sustainability Plans***: The adaptability of prompt engineering enables sophisticated plan development and evaluation. Moreover, AI systems, especially LM, can adapt to different planning contexts, making them invaluable for strategic sustainability initiatives. They can act as experts who instantly understand the industry's unique challenges and opportunities. LMs can assist in developing comprehensive sustainability plans by generating outlines, drafting content, and evaluating the feasibility and potential impact of different strategies. For example, a company's AI system can adapt to create sustainability plans for different operational scales (individual facility optimization or global corporate strategy), various timeframes, and multiple stakeholder requirements while maintaining operational efficiency.
- ***Generating Educational Materials***: The versatility extends to creating targeted educational content for different audiences. Prompt engineering can help create customized sustainability education materials to ensure that everyone understands their role in achieving sustainability goals. LMs can be used to create engaging and informative educational materials, such as articles, reports, presentations, and social media content, to raise awareness about sustainability issues and promote environmentally responsible behaviors. For example,

  - For the executive level, LMs can create:

    - Strategic briefings on sustainability trends
    - Region-of-interest (ROI) analysis of green initiatives
    - Competitive advantage assessments
    - Risk management strategies

- For the operational teams, prompt engineering can help generate:
  - Technical training materials
  - Best practice guides
  - SOPs
  - Emergency response protocols
- For community stakeholders, well-crafted prompts will help create:
  - Environmental impact reports
  - Community engagement materials
  - Progress updates and achievements
  - Future initiative explanations

5.5 Techniques for LM fine-tuning

Instruction tuning enhances model performance by fine-tuning a pretrained LM on a diverse set of tasks that are expressed in the form of natural language instructions. These techniques are essential for leveraging LLMs in flexible and dynamic interactions. They allow users to guide outputs effectively without needing to retrain or fine-tune the model extensively for every specific task and to improve the output results. During instruction tuning, the model learns to associate specific instructions with the appropriate outputs across various tasks. This training utilizes a mixture of instruction-based data, ensuring that the model develops a broad understanding of how to respond to different prompts. By training on a wide range of instructions, the model can better generalize its capabilities to handle tasks it has not explicitly seen during training. The intuition is that once the model learns how to follow instructions, it can apply this learning to new, unseen instructions.

Research has shown that LLMs can operate effectively without fine-tuning for specific tasks.[12] Users can simply provide a short prompt to instruct the system on what to generate. ZSL, one-shot learning (OSL), and FSL are approaches used in ML, particularly in the context of NLP and generative models, to enhance the model's ability to perform tasks without extensive retraining.[13]

5.5.1 Zero-shot learning

In ZSL, a model is required to perform a task without having seen any specific examples for that task during training. Instead, it relies on its understanding of language and the context provided in the prompt. The ZSL allows models to recognize or classify instances of classes that were not present in the training data. In this approach, the system uses pre-defined semantics or attributes of unseen classes to make predictions, enabling classifiers to identify unseen classes without specific training. The ZSL heavily relies on the model's pre-existing knowledge.

Prompt Example:

Classify the following material as biodegradable or non-biodegradable: "graphene-infused bioplastic."

OSL and FSL are extensions of the zero-shot paradigm, where models are provided with one or a few examples of a new class or task, respectively. These approaches aim to improve model performance with minimal additional training data. The characteristics of OSL and FSL include:

- Leveraging the model's ability to generalize from limited examples to new tasks or classes
- Utilizing techniques like in-context learning, where models are given a few examples within the input prompt to guide their responses
- Improving performance as more examples are provided, particularly in few-shot scenarios

5.5.2 One-shot learning

OSL refers to scenarios where the model is given a single example of a task to learn from. This means that the model can adjust its outputs based on one specific instance. For example, if a user provides one sentence as a key example and then requests similar sentences, the model learns to generalize from that one instance to produce similar outputs. With this approach, we leverage the model's ability to generalize from a single example, balancing between zero-shot capabilities and traditional supervised learning. OSL improves the model's performance compared to ZSL, but with minimal additional data.

Prompt Example:

Here is an example of a renewable energy source: "Solar panels convert sunlight into electricity."

Now, classify the following as renewable or non-renewable: "Tidal turbines harness ocean currents to generate power."

5.5.3 Few-Shot Learning

FSL involves providing the model with a small number of examples, usually between two to a handful. This additional context helps the model better understand the task and improves the quality and relevance of the generated output. For example, a user might supply two or three examples before asking the model to generate new content based on those examples. In this scenario, the model is fine-tuned or adapted based on limited examples, providing a balance between zero-shot capabilities and traditional supervised learning. In FSL, the performance of generative models improves as more examples are provided. However, FSL depends on the model's enhanced capacity to learn from a limited dataset, leading to more accurate and contextually appropriate outputs.

Prompt Example:

Classify the following actions as eco-friendly or not:

1. Using a reusable water bottle—eco-friendly.
2. Taking short showers—eco-friendly.
3. Leaving lights on when not in use—not eco-friendly.

Now classify: "Composting food scraps."

These learning techniques are essential for leveraging LLMs in flexible and dynamic interactions. They allow users to guide outputs effectively without needing to retrain or fine-tune the model extensively for every specific task. Table 5.1 highlights the main differences between ZSL, OSL, and FSL approaches, emphasizing the trade-offs and considerations for each approach.

We will use the same example in a mini-case study to illustrate how the different prompting techniques influence the model's output. We tested the different prompts on ChatGPT. All outputs are provided in **Appendix B, Output 1**.

Table 5.1 Main differences between ZSL, OSL, and FSL

Aspect	*ZSL*	*OSL*	*FSL*
Training data	No labeled examples of target class/task	One labeled example of target class/task	2–10 labeled examples of target class/task
Prior knowledge	Heavily relies on pre-existing semantic information	Uses both prior knowledge and a single example	Leverages prior knowledge and multiple examples
Adaptability	Least adaptable to new tasks	Limited adaptability based on a single example	More flexible in adapting to new tasks
Generalization	Requires the strongest generalization ability	Moderate generalization from a single example	Better generalization from multiple examples
Performance	Generally lowest performance	Improved performance over zero-shot	Best performance among the three
Auxiliary information	Often requires extensive attribute descriptions	Less reliant on auxiliary information	Least reliant on auxiliary information

5.6 The impact of prompting techniques on carbon emissions analysis: a mini-case study

5.6.1 Introduction

This case study examines how different prompting methodologies applied to identical data can significantly influence the quality and actionability of carbon emissions analysis. Using XYZ Ltd., a mid-sized O&G company operating 50 wells with a daily production of 1,000 barrels per well, this analysis demonstrates the progression of analytical depth achieved through increasingly sophisticated prompting techniques.

5.6.2 Context

XYZ Ltd.'s sustainability team systematically applied six distinct prompting techniques to analyze their carbon footprint data. All prompts referenced the same operational parameters:

- 50 wells producing 1,000 barrels/day each
- Extraction emissions of 10 kg CO_2/barrel
- Flaring emissions of 5 kg CO_2/barrel
- Natural gas consumption of 1 million cubic meters annually (2 kg CO_2/m^3)
- Pipeline transportation emissions of 0.1 kg CO_2/barrel/100 km over 500 km

Prompt 1:Standard LLM Prompting

What are XYZ Ltd.'s annual carbon emissions from their oil production operations?

Prompt 2:Zero-Shot Prompting

Calculate XYZ Ltd.'s total annual CO_2 emissions if they operate 50 wells each producing 1,000 barrels of oil per day, with extraction emissions of 10 kg CO_2/barrel, flaring emissions of 5 kg CO_2/barrel, natural gas consumption of 1 million cubic meters annually (2 kg CO_2/m^3), and pipeline transportation emissions of 0.1 kg CO_2/barrel/100 km over an average distance of 500 km.

Prompt 3:One-Shot Prompting

ABC Energy operates 40 wells producing 900 barrels/day each. Their extraction process generates 11 kg CO_2/barrel, flaring adds 6 kg CO_2/barrel, and they use 900,000 cubic meters of natural gas annually (2 kg CO_2/m^3). Their transportation emissions are 0.12 kg CO_2/barrel/100 km over 450 km. Their total annual emissions are 271,803 tons CO_2.

Using this example, calculate the total annual CO_2 emissions for XYZ Ltd., which has 50 wells producing 1,000 barrels/day each, extraction emissions of 10 kg CO_2/barrel, flaring emissions of 5 kg CO_2/barrel, 1 million cubic meters of natural gas annually (2 kg CO_2/m^3), and pipeline transportation of 0.1 kg CO_2/barrel/100 km over 500 km.

Prompt 4:Few-Shot Prompting

Here are the emissions calculations for three similar companies:

Company A: 30 wells × 800 barrels/day × (9 kg CO_2/barrel extraction + 4 kg CO_2/barrel flaring) × 365 days + 600,000 m^3 natural gas × 2 kg CO_2/m^3 + 30 wells × 800 barrels/day × 365 days × 400 km × 0.09 kg CO_2/barrel/100 km = 128,414 tons CO_2/year

Company B: 45 wells × 950 barrels/day × (12 kg CO_2/barrel extraction + 7 kg CO_2/barrel flaring) × 365 days + 850,000 m^3 natural gas × 2 kg CO_2/m^3 + 45 wells × 950 barrels/day × 365 days × 550 km × 0.11 kg CO_2/barrel/100 km = 300,135 tons CO_2/year

Company C: 55 wells × 1,100 barrels/day × (10 kg CO_2/barrel extraction + 5 kg CO_2/barrel flaring) × 365 days + 1,200,000 m^3 natural gas × 2 kg CO_2/m^3 + 55 wells × 1,100 barrels/day × 365 days × 480 km × 0.1 kg CO_2/barrel/100 km = 307,791 tons CO_2/year

Using these examples, calculate XYZ Ltd.'s total annual CO_2 emissions with 50 wells producing 1,000 barrels/day each, extraction emissions of 10 kg CO_2/barrel, flaring emissions of 5 kg CO_2/barrel, 1 million cubic meters of natural gas annually (2 kg CO_2/m^3), and pipeline transportation of 0.1 kg CO_2/barrel/100 km over 500 km.

5.6.3 Prompt styles and output analysis

Prompt 1:
Type: Direct question and concise

Output analysis:

- Focused purely on calculating the total emissions.
- Listed and summed each source (extraction, flaring, gas use, transport).
- Gave the result in both kg and metric tons.
- Clear and straightforward—suitable for exec summaries or high-level reports.

Prompt 2:
Type: Structured data and request

Output analysis:

- Treated as a clean data problem.
- Step-by-step breakdown for each emission source.
- Used intermediate values (barrels/day → annual → per source emissions).

- Output was labeled, cleanly formatted, with units clearly specified.
- Ideal for technical documentation or reporting.

The model's response lists the given parameters and provides a direct calculation with clear steps, showing how the zero-shot approach can be effective when given specific parameters.

Prompt 3:
Type: Comparative context with a real-world example

Output analysis:

- Followed the structure used for ABC Energy to match format and logic.
- Aligned all emission sources similarly: production, gas use, and transportation.
- Provided final numbers in metric tons for direct comparability.
- Tailored for benchmarking or peer analysis.

The model's response follows the same calculation as zero-shot but adds comparative context based on the example, showing how the one-shot approach can provide additional insight through comparison.

Prompt 4:
Type: Pattern recognition with peer benchmarks

Output analysis:

- Identified a consistent formula structure from the examples (A, B, C).
- Followed that exact pattern:
  wells × barrels/day × (extraction + flaring) × 365 + gas + transport.
- Ensured unit consistency (kg to tons).
- Matched output formatting and tone for parity across companies.
- Designed to slot XYZ Ltd. into an industry comparison table.

The model's response follows the same calculation and adds comparative analysis against all three examples, demonstrating how few-shot prompting enables more nuanced contextual understanding.

We summarize our findings in Table 5.2.

5.6.4 Recommendations

- Use structured prompts when you want replicable, especially for step-by-step math calculations.
- Include a reference example, or several examples, if consistency with previous outputs matters.
- Be explicit about units/output format (kg vs. tons, totals vs. per barrel) when precision or comparison is needed.

Table 5.2 ChatGPT outputs comparison using standard, ZSL, OSL, and FSL

Prompt	*Style*	*Output strategy emphasis*	*Use case*
Prompt 1	Direct question	Fast, clean summary in metric tons	Reporting
Prompt 2	Structured calculation	Detailed breakdown per source with units	Technical documentation
Prompt 3	Comparative with example	Mirrored example logic, apples-to-apples comparisons	Benchmarking and competitive analysis
Prompt 4	Pattern-matching with peers	Formula-based, visually consistent outputs	Presentation-ready datasets

5.6.5 ZSL, OSL, and FSL: what to choose?

The ability of LLMs to perform ZSL and FSL has opened new possibilities for addressing complex environmental challenges with limited data availability. By leveraging these prompt engineering techniques, researchers and practitioners can harness the power of LLMs to develop innovative solutions across various sustainability domains, from renewable energy to waste management and beyond.

Overall, the passage highlights the flexibility and power of using natural language prompts with LLMs. It enables users to leverage ZSL, OSL, and FSL techniques to enhance the quality of generated text without the need for extensive model retraining. This capability makes LLMs more accessible and user-friendly for a wide range of applications.

5.7 The CoT prompting

The CoT prompting is a method used to enhance the reasoning capabilities of LLMs by encouraging them to generate a sequence of intermediate reasoning steps before arriving at a final answer by allowing them to simulate a step-by-step human-like reasoning process when tackling complex problems. This approach is inspired by how humans typically solve complex problems, particularly tasks that require multi-step reasoning. CoT decomposes complex tasks into manageable intermediate steps, allowing models to follow a logical progression in their responses. This method enhances the model's ability to handle multifaceted queries, such as those requiring common sense reasoning or arithmetic, by providing a structured framework for processing information. It creates a clear window of interpretation, making it easier to tweak and refine the system's output based on the reasoning demonstrated through the prompting. When using standard prompting, the input and output can be less transparent, making it difficult to discern how the model processes information. In contrast, by employing CoT prompting, each step of reasoning is explicitly laid out, creating a "window" that reveals the internal thought process of the model. This decomposition into finer granularity enables easier manipulation and adjustment of inputs and provides insight into potential mistakes or areas for improvement in the model's reasoning.[14]

In CoT prompting, rather than providing a direct answer, the model articulates its thought process, effectively creating a "chain" of reasoning that leads to the conclusion. For instance, when faced with a math problem, the model breaks it down into smaller, manageable parts while explaining each step along the way. This coherent narrative mimics the logical flow that a human might use, making it easier to understand the reasoning process and identify potential errors. In few-shot prompting, models are given a small number of examples to learn from, which are enhanced by incorporating a chain of thought. This practice provides models with explicit demonstrations of how to approach and solve similar problems, thereby leading to improved performance without the necessity for additional fine-tuning. Research has shown that models, such as PaLM 540B, achieve better results on various benchmarks when using CoT prompting compared to standard methods. This strategy enables the model to utilize its existing knowledge better and improve the accuracy of its responses.

Furthermore, CoT prompting is versatile and not restricted to just one type of reasoning task. It has been successfully applied to arithmetic, commonsense reasoning, and symbolic reasoning tasks, showcasing its broad applicability. In summary, CoT prompting enhances the reasoning capabilities of LMs by structuring their outputs in a way that reflects human-like problem-solving strategies, resulting in more accurate and logical conclusions. It provides a more comprehensive and actionable strategy by breaking down the complex challenge of sustainability transformation into logical, manageable steps while considering business realities.

5.7.1 Example

Sam, the XYZ Ltd. O&G sustainability Director, is developing strategies to improve the company's sustainability while maintaining profitability. To this end, Sam submits the following prompt to the most used LLM, ChatGPT. The used prompts are shown in the following.

5.7.1.1 Traditional prompt (without CoT)

What should an O&G company do to become more sustainable while staying profitable?

The outputs are shown in **Appendix B, Output 2**.

The CoT approach is preferred to improve the reasoning of AI models. It helps both the AI model and the human understand the reasoning process, making it particularly valuable for complex business decisions where multiple factors need to be considered.

5.7.1.2 CoT prompt (with CoT)

What should an O&G company do to become more sustainable while staying profitable?

Step 1: Identify the strategies needed for the immediate and long-term.

Step 2: Focus on reducing environmental impact and leveraging innovation to create long-term value.
Step 3: Analyze each strategy, and then think through step by step how to implement these strategies.
The outputs are shown in **Appendix B, Output 3**.

5.7.2 Output analysis

We note that Output 1 presents a comprehensive approach that outlines a dual strategy for achieving sustainability while remaining profitable. It emphasizes long-term strategies alongside actionable steps, but it may not clearly prioritize immediate actions. Output 2, on the other hand, explicitly divides its recommendations into immediate and long-term strategies, making it clearer for companies looking for quick-win actions. It identifies several specific immediate strategies, such as reducing methane emissions, improving energy efficiency, enhancing ESG reporting, investing in carbon offsetting, and adopting digital technologies. This structured approach allows companies to prioritize actions that can be implemented right away while still considering longer-term transitions. Table 5.3 highlights the main differences between the following aspects: (1) the focus, (2) the immediate actions, (3) the key immediate strategies, (4) the structure, and (5) the overall purpose.

The output clearly shows that Output 2 is more helpful for immediate action because it clearly outlines and categorizes the immediate strategies that companies can adopt to enhance sustainability. Its step-by-step approach allows for straightforward implementation, making it a practical guide for companies seeking rapid results in their sustainability efforts.

Table 5.3 Output 1 versus Output 2 highlights

Aspect	*Output 1*	*Output 2*
Focus	Comprehensive dual strategy for sustainability and profitability	Clear distinction between immediate and long-term strategies
Immediate actions	Limited explicit immediate actions	Explicitly outlines immediate strategies for quick wins
Key immediate strategies	Enhancing transparency, reporting, and adopting digital technologies	Reducing methane emissions, improving energy efficiency, enhancing ESG reporting, investing in carbon offsetting, and adopting digital technologies
Structure	Key steps are grouped but not prioritized for immediacy	Organized into immediate and long-term categories
Overall purpose	Balancing long-term profitability with sustainability efforts	Providing a practical guide for quick implementation

5.7.3 Conclusion

CoT prompting significantly outperforms traditional prompting techniques by enabling LLMs to generate a coherent series of intermediate reasoning steps that lead to a final answer. This structured thinking process results in more practical and implementable solutions instead of oversimplified answers. This example demonstrates how CoT prompting can lead to more effective problem-solving by encouraging LLMs to think through the problem step by step, mirroring a human-like problem-solving approach. This method can be applied across various sustainability challenges, leading to more effective and efficient solutions. It is especially valuable for complex problems where multiple factors need to be balanced, such as sustainability in the energy sector.

5.8 Guided example: a real-world scenario for carbon emission assessment and strategic sustainability

The O&G industry faces growing pressure to reduce its carbon footprint and meet global climate goals. With evolving environmental regulations and increasing stakeholder expectations, it is essential for companies to adopt innovative methods to evaluate and reduce carbon emissions. However, carbon accounting is complex, involving multiple emission sources (such as extraction, flaring, power generation, and transportation) as well as intricate calculations. Without a clear, structured approach, it is easy to overlook critical details or make errors that could undermine the credibility of sustainability initiatives. As we move toward more sustainable practices, CoT prompting can add significant value by clearly outlining each step of the calculation process. To demonstrate how CoT prompting can be effectively applied, consider the following example, which illustrates how CoT prompting enhances the clarity and accuracy of carbon emission assessments, enabling informed decision-making while ensuring operational profitability.

5.8.1 The challenge

XYZ, an O&G company, operates various assets, including multiple wells, power generation facilities, and transportation pipelines. Each of these components contributes to the company's overall carbon footprint through emissions from extraction, flaring, power generation, and oil transportation. The company had always focused on maximizing profits through its operations, but as the pressure to reduce environmental impacts grew, it realized it needed to adapt. They knew that addressing carbon emissions was crucial, not only for staying ahead of regulations but also for improving their reputation in the eyes of their stakeholders. The challenge lies not only in calculating these emissions accurately but also in identifying opportunities for emissions reduction without compromising financial performance.

5.8.2 The situation

XYZ operates 50 wells, each producing 1,000 barrels of oil per day. The extraction process generates 10 kg of CO_2 per barrel, and flaring adds an additional 5 kg of CO_2 per barrel. The company also consumes 1 million cubic meters of natural gas annually for on-site power generation, with an emission factor of 2 kg CO_2 per cubic meter. Furthermore, the oil is transported via pipelines that emit 0.1 kg CO_2 per barrel per 100 km, with an average transportation distance of 500 km. With 50 wells producing 1,000 barrels of oil each day, XYZ is a significant player in the energy sector. However, as global attention turns to climate change, the company faces mounting pressure to measure and reduce its carbon footprint.

The company's team of engineers, environmental experts, and data scientists was tasked with a critical mission: to find an efficient way to assess their carbon emissions and explore strategies for reduction. XYZ's sustainability team gathers in a boardroom, staring at a whiteboard filled with numbers and formulas. They need to calculate the company's total annual CO_2 emissions, but the task feels overwhelming. Where do they even begin?

But they faced a challenge. How could they ensure that the complex calculations, regulations, and data points were clearly understood by everyone in the company—from management to operational teams?

5.8.3 The solution: CoT as a problem-solving technique

The team decides to use CoT to tackle their carbon accounting challenge. The data scientists, who are well-versed in ML models, suggested using CoT prompting to guide reasoning in AI models. By breaking down complex problems into a series of logical steps, CoT prompting could simplify the understanding of emissions and make the assessment process both accurate and accessible.

The team decided to test CoT prompting on a real-world challenge: assessing the carbon emissions from the company's extraction process, power generation, transportation, and flaring. They created a CoT prompt that would guide the AI through each stage of the emissions calculation.

Here is how they structured their CoT prompt:

5.8.4 CoT prompt

XYZ, an O&G company, operates 50 wells, each producing 1,000 barrels of oil per day. The extraction process emits 10 kg of CO_2 per barrel, and flaring at the wells emits an additional 5 kg of CO_2 per barrel. The company also uses natural gas for on-site power generation, consuming 1 million cubic meters annually, with an emission factor of 2 kg CO_2 per cubic meter. Additionally, the company transports its oil via pipelines, emitting 0.1 kg CO_2 per barrel per 100 km. The average transportation distance is 500 km. Calculate the company's total annual CO_2 emissions, breaking down the contributions from extraction, flaring, power generation, and transportation. Explain each step of your reasoning.

They submitted it to the most used LLMs, ChatGPT and DeepSeek. The output is shown in **Appendix B, Output 4.**

5.8.5 Output analysis

As the team reviewed the carbon emission assessment generated by the outputs from the ChatGPT and DeepSeek models, they started to recognize the potential of this approach in uncovering critical insights and simplifying what once seemed like an overwhelmingly complex problem. The emissions breakdown was presented clearly, step by step, and was more than just a list of numbers; it served as a strategic tool that illuminated hidden patterns and revealed opportunities for optimization. Instead of just feeding numbers into a system and expecting a result, they could follow the AI through a structured, logical breakdown of every component contributing to the company's carbon footprint. This step-by-step approach allowed the team to grasp how each source of emissions was calculated, from the extraction and flaring to power generation and transportation.

In the end, both AI models, guided by the CoT prompt, provided a comprehensive breakdown:

1. **Extraction Emissions**: Emissions from oil extraction were calculated based on the number of barrels produced and the CO_2 emitted per barrel.
2. **Flaring Emissions**: Additional emissions from flaring were added based on the same number of barrels.
3. **Power Generation**: The emissions from natural gas consumption for power generation were considered using the emission factor for CO_2.
4. **Transportation Emissions**: Finally, the emissions from transporting oil via pipelines were calculated based on the distance and the CO_2 emitted per barrel.

The result was clear and detailed, and the last step showed that the company's total annual emissions were **284,875,000 kg CO_2**.

Using CoT prompting, the team not only obtained the final number but also, importantly, benefited from the clarity and transparency that this approach provided. By breaking down each emissions component and walking through the reasoning behind each calculation, the company gained a clear understanding of its emissions sources and identified areas with potential for improvement. For example, the team recognized that transportation was responsible for a significant portion of emissions, allowing them to strategize ways to reduce this—whether through pipeline optimization or transitioning to cleaner transportation methods. They could also concentrate on minimizing flaring and enhancing power generation efficiency.

By the end of the process, the company not only gained a clear understanding of its carbon footprint but also a solid foundation for developing sustainability strategies. Thanks to CoT prompting, the company was able to see, step by step, how each factor contributed to their environmental impact. This approach helped the team translate complex calculations into actionable insights, setting them on a path toward a more sustainable and profitable future. And so, the company learned that sustainability and profitability could indeed go hand in hand. They realized that, with the right tools, like CoT prompting, they could not only prosper but also lower their carbon emissions, contributing to a greener world in the process.

The end, or rather, the beginning of a cleaner, more sustainable future for O&G.

5.8.6 *How can CoT prompting empower strategic sustainability?*

The emissions breakdown, presented clearly step by step, can serve as a strategic tool that reveals hidden patterns and uncovers opportunities for optimization.

5.8.6.1 *Revealing the impact of flaring*

One of the most striking insights was the disproportionate contribution of *flaring* to the company's total carbon emissions. While the extraction process itself accounted for a significant portion of emissions, flaring added a large secondary impact—**91,250,000 kg CO_2 per year**. This was a reminder that, while flaring is a necessary practice in some O&G operations, it was also an area ripe for immediate improvement.

The CoT approach helped to make this issue crystal clear, and the board could now see that focusing on reducing flaring—whether through more advanced gas capture technologies or shifts in operational protocols—could deliver a *substantial reduction in overall emissions*. This new insight immediately made flaring reduction a top priority in their sustainability strategy.

5.8.6.2 *Emissions from power generation: a potential opportunity*

The breakdown of power generation emissions, which amounted to 2,000,000 kg CO_2 per year, opened another conversation. Although relatively small compared to other sources, this segment still represented an opportunity to decrease reliance on fossil fuels and explore cleaner alternatives.

The clarity provided by the CoT analysis enabled the board to focus on renewable energy sources—such as solar panels or wind turbines—for their power generation needs. Additionally, they could now confidently explore energy-efficient upgrades to existing power facilities, knowing exactly where to focus their efforts to achieve measurable reductions in emissions.

5.9 Optimizing transportation: the path to efficiency

Perhaps the most significant revelation came from the transportation emissions calculation. At first glance, it might seem that transportation's contribution of 9,125,000 kg CO_2 per year was relatively minor compared to extraction and flaring. However, as the CoT model illustrated step by step, the emissions were directly tied to the transportation distance, 500 km on average for each barrel of oil transported.

This detail provided the board with actionable insights into transportation logistics. Could the company optimize routes to reduce the average distance traveled? Or a shift in transportation methods, such as electric or hybrid-powered transport, could further lower emissions while keeping operations efficient.

The clarity provided by CoT prompting allowed the board to focus on practical steps that could reduce emissions without disrupting operations, an important consideration in the highly competitive O&G sector.

5.9.1 Simplifying complexity: a clearer path forward

Before applying CoT prompting, understanding carbon emissions seemed daunting. The company had multiple operations, each with its own environmental impact, and trying to make sense of them all holistically was an overwhelming challenge. However, the step-by-step approach provided by CoT gave the board a much-needed roadmap.

By clearly breaking down each source of emissions, from extraction to transportation, the CoT analysis simplified the process of identifying high-impact areas for improvement. The board could now see exactly where to allocate resources for the most significant environmental gains. Rather than simply reducing overall emissions across the board, they were empowered to take targeted actions in specific areas, ensuring that each effort made the biggest possible difference.

5.9.2 Supporting data-driven decision-making

The CoT process also provided confidence in the numbers. Because the AI model had followed a structured reasoning process, the board could trust the results as they made crucial decisions. They were not relying on gut instinct or general assumptions; they were guided by data-driven insights that had been logically derived from the emissions calculations.

Through clear analysis and detailed insights, the board can take concrete steps in its decision-making process:

- Investing in methane capture technology to reduce flaring.
- Exploring renewable energy projects to power on-site operations.
- Evaluating transportation strategies to minimize logistics-related emissions.

The simplicity of the CoT model empowered them to take the next steps toward a more sustainable and profitable future.

5.10 Conclusion

Carbon accounting is complex, involving multiple sources of emissions—extraction, flaring, power generation, and transportation—each with its own variables and calculations. The CoT is a problem-solving method that breaks down complex tasks into smaller, logical steps, similar to how a teacher guides a student through a math problem. Instead of jumping directly to the answer, CoT encourages the team to meticulously consider each step of the calculation, ensuring accuracy and transparency. The prompt about XYZ's emissions serves as a practical example of how CoT can address real-world sustainability challenges. By calculating and breaking down emissions from extraction, flaring, power generation, and transportation, XYZ can:

- Identify which activities contribute the most to its carbon footprint;
- Develop targeted strategies to reduce emissions (e.g., reducing flaring and transitioning to renewable energy);
- Communicate its progress transparently to stakeholders.

Companies like XYZ must not only measure their emissions accurately but also identify opportunities for reduction while maintaining profitability. However, carbon accounting is a complex task involving multiple emission sources (e.g., extraction, flaring, power generation, and transportation) and intricate calculations. Without a clear and structured approach, it is easy to overlook critical details or make errors that undermine the credibility of sustainability efforts.

Companies in the O&G sector must implement new methods for measuring and lowering carbon emissions in light of evolving environmental regulations and expanding stakeholder expectations.

In the context of evolving environmental regulations and growing stakeholder expectations, it is imperative that companies within the O&G sector adopt innovative methods for evaluating and reducing carbon emissions.

5.11 Analysis of real-world case studies of successful technology integration

The lessons learned from the real-world cases of AI-driven sustainability initiatives provide comprehensive insights into best practices, challenges, and strategic approaches that organizations must adopt to realize the full potential of technology in advancing sustainability. Case details are provided in Appendix C.

1. **Strategic Alignment and Integration:** A foundational lesson is the importance of integrating AI projects closely with an organization's overarching sustainability strategy. Companies such as Google illustrate how AI technologies can be embedded into operational processes, like optimizing data center energy use and yielding both financial and environmental benefits. This demonstrates that sustainability goals should not be treated as standalone objectives, but rather interwoven into the business strategy, with clear sustainability metrics such as reduced energy consumption or emissions tracked alongside cost savings.
2. **Cross-Departmental and Leadership Collaboration:** Successful AI sustainability projects often depend on collaborative efforts that span across departments and leadership roles. For example, Unilever's use of AI and blockchain to enhance supply chain transparency requires close coordination between CSOs, CAIOs, IT,

and procurement teams. This collaboration ensures that AI initiatives have access to quality data and align with ethical sourcing and environmental standards. Having executive leadership aligned on sustainability and AI priorities is also essential, enabling better resource allocation and stakeholder engagement.

3. **Pilot Testing and Scalability:** The case studies emphasize the value of pilot projects as critical steps to test AI applications on a smaller scale before full deployment. Pilot testing allows organizations to identify technical, operational, and change management challenges early, refine AI models, and provide concrete evidence of AI's sustainability impact to secure broader stakeholder support. Scalability must also be planned carefully, as some organizations face barriers related to cost, infrastructure, and personnel skills when expanding AI solutions.
4. **Addressing the Environmental Impact of AI:** While AI supports sustainability, it also consumes significant energy, particularly in data processing and model training. The case studies reveal best practices to mitigate AI's environmental footprint, such as adopting foundation models that require less training, processing data in areas with cleaner energy, and investing in energy-efficient AI hardware. Responsible AI use, including selecting eco-friendly algorithms and infrastructure, helps reduce unintended negative impacts on the environment.
5. **Workforce Development and Skills:** AI-driven sustainability projects hinge on skilled personnel who can manage AI tools and interpret results effectively. Organizations highlight the necessity of upskilling employees, from data scientists to sustainability practitioners, fostering a workforce capable of leveraging AI innovations responsibly and efficiently. This approach ensures operational continuity and helps sustain momentum in AI sustainability initiatives.
6. **Data Privacy, Quality, and Security:** High-quality, secure data is the lifeblood of effective AI sustainability applications. Case studies underscore the importance of establishing robust data governance frameworks to protect sensitive environmental and supplier information while ensuring data accuracy. This safeguards stakeholder trust and enhances the reliability of AI-driven insights for decision-making.
7. **Stakeholder Engagement and Demonstrating Long-Term Value:** Securing buy-in from internal and external stakeholders requires transparency regarding AI initiatives and clear communication of long-term benefits. Companies learn that illustrating ROI beyond cost savings—including environmental and social impact—can successfully address resistance related to initial high costs or uncertainty. Engaging suppliers, customers, and investors around shared sustainability goals fosters collaboration and drives holistic progress.
8. **Continuous Monitoring and Adaptive Management:** Finally, the cases illustrate the need for ongoing monitoring and analysis of AI's impact on sustainability metrics. This continuous feedback loop enables timely adjustments, risk mitigation, and technology updates, ensuring that AI solutions evolve in alignment with changing environmental priorities and business dynamics. Real-time monitoring tools empower project managers with actionable insights, facilitating agile responses to emerging challenges.

Overall, these lessons illustrate that effectively integrating AI for sustainability necessitates a blend of clear strategic vision, strong leadership collaboration, robust technical infrastructure, ethical considerations, and proactive human capital development. By adhering to these principles, companies can leverage AI's transformative potential to achieve measurable environmental benefits alongside financial and operational gains.

5.12 Summary

This chapter explores the intersection of AI technologies and key sustainability factors of planning, performance, risk, and disclosure. It examines how AI-driven tools such as ML, NLP, and predictive analytics are reshaping sustainability planning by enabling data-driven goal setting, scenario analysis, and strategic forecasting. In terms of performance, the chapter highlights AI's role in monitoring financial ESP and nonfinancial ESG sustainability metrics, optimizing resource use, and enhancing operational efficiency. It also addresses how AI improves risk management by identifying emerging sustainability threats, assessing supply chain vulnerabilities, and supporting real-time decision-making. Finally, the chapter evaluates AI's impact on sustainability disclosure, particularly in automating ESG reporting, enhancing transparency, and meeting regulatory requirements.

This chapter also presents prompt engineering and techniques for fine-tuning (LM) are essential strategies for optimizing model performance and aligning outputs with specific tasks or domain requirements. Prompt engineering involves crafting input queries or templates that effectively guide the model's responses without altering its underlying parameters using ZSL or FSL scenarios, where minimal labeled data is available. In contrast, LM fine-tuning refers to retraining a pre-trained model on a domain-specific dataset to adapt its knowledge and behavior to a particular application, such as legal document analysis or medical diagnosis. Fine-tuning can be supervised or unsupervised and often requires careful data curation, learning rate selection, and evaluation metrics to avoid overfitting or bias amplification. Together, these approaches enhance the model's adaptability, accuracy, and usability across diverse real-world contexts. Overall, the chapter provides an integrated view of how AI can drive accountable and resilient sustainability practices across industries.

5.13 Takeaways

- AI enhances sustainability planning by enabling data-driven forecasting, scenario modeling, and strategic decision-making.
- ML and predictive analytics support dynamic performance tracking and real-time optimization of ESG goals.
- AI-driven tools improve operational sustainability, such as reducing waste, energy use, and environmental impact.

- Risk management is strengthened through AI by identifying potential sustainability threats, assessing supply chain disruptions, and forecasting climate-related risks.
- NLP aids in analyzing unstructured data for deeper insights into social and governance issues.
- AI automates and enhances sustainability disclosure, making ESG reporting more timely, accurate, and compliant with regulatory standards.
- AI increases transparency and accountability, improving stakeholder trust and engagement in sustainability initiatives.
- Integration of AI with sustainability practices leads to more resilient, adaptive, and future-ready organizations.

Notes

1 Much of the discussion presented in this section comes from chapter 1 of Rezaee, Z. 2024. *The Sustainable Business Blueprint: Planning, Performance, Risk, Reporting and Assurance*. Routledge/Taylor and Francis
2 Rezaee. *The Sustainable Business Blueprint*
3 Qin, Y., Xu, Z., Wang, X., & Skare, M. 2024. Artificial intelligence and economic development: An evolutionary investigation and systematic review. *Journal of the Knowledge Economy*, 15, 1736–1770
4 Bickley, S.J., Chan, H.F., & Torgler, B. 2024. Artificial intelligence in the field of economics. *Scientometrics*, 127, 2055–2084
5 Oppenlaender, J., Linder, R., & Silvennoinen, J. 2024. Prompting AI art: An investigation into the creative skill of prompt engineering. *International Journal of Human–Computer Interaction*, 1–23. https://doi.org/10.1080/10447318.2024.2431761
6 Openai. *Prompt Engineering*. https://platform.openai.com/docs/guides/prompt-engineering
7 KPMG. *Survey of Sustainability Reporting 2024*. https://assets.kpmg.com/content/dam/kpmg/ie/pdf/2024/12/ie-survey-sustainability-reporting-2024–2.pdf
8 De Villiers, C., Dimes, R., & Molinari, M. 2024. How will AI text generation and processing impact sustainability reporting? Critical analysis, a conceptual framework and avenues for future research. *Sustainability Accounting, Management and Policy Journal*, 15(1), 96–118
9 Pedersen Zari, M. 2017. Biomimetic urban design: Ecosystem service provision of water and energy. *Buildings*, 7(1), 21
10 Wei, J., Wang, X., Schuurmans, D., Bosma, M., Xia, F., Chi, E., . . . Zhou, D. 2022. Chain-of-thought prompting elicits reasoning in large language models. *Advances in Neural Information Processing Systems*, 35, 24824–24837
11 Stanford. 2024. *AI Demystified: What is Prompt Engineering?* https://uit.stanford.edu/service/techtraining/ai-demystified/prompt-engineering
12 Liu, P., Yuan, W., Fu, J., Jiang, Z., Hayashi, H., & Neubig, G. 2023. Pre-train, prompt, and predict: A systematic survey of prompting methods in natural language processing. *ACM Computing Surveys*, 55(9), 1–35
13 Brown, T., Mann, B., Ryder, N., Subbiah, M., Kaplan, J.D., Dhariwal, P., Neelakantan, A., Shyam, P., Sastry, G., Askell, A., & Agarwal, S. 2020. Language models are few-shot learners. *Advances in Neural Information Processing Systems*, 33, 1877–1901
14 Wei, J., Wang, X., Schuurmans, D., Bosma, M., Xia, F., Chi, E., . . . Zhou, D. 2022. Chain-of-thought prompting elicits reasoning in large language models. *Advances in Neural Information Processing Systems*, 35, 24824–24837

6 AI in resource management and environmental sustainability

6.1 Introduction

AI technologies, including ML, computer vision, LLMs, and NLP, are revolutionizing the way organizations approach resource management worldwide. By analyzing vast amounts of data, AI can provide insights into patterns of environmental resource use, identify inefficiencies and waste, and suggest ways to optimize processes to improve environmental sustainability. For example, AI-powered analytics can enhance nature and water management by predicting demand and detecting leaks in real time, reduce energy consumption through smart grid technologies that balance supply and demand, and improve waste management by automating sorting and recycling processes. In agriculture, AI applications are driving sustainable practices by optimizing irrigation, fertilization, and pest control, thereby reducing the use of water, chemicals, and energy while increasing crop yields. In forestry and land management, AI-powered tools are used to monitor deforestation, track biodiversity, and predict the impacts of climate change, helping organizations and policymakers make more informed decisions about conservation and land use. AI can play a crucial role in climate modeling and environmental monitoring, offering new capabilities for predicting and mitigating the impacts of extreme weather events, such as hurricanes, floods, and wildfires. AI algorithms can analyze satellite imagery and sensor data to detect changes in land cover, track air and water quality, and monitor the health of ecosystems, providing early warnings and supporting disaster preparedness and response efforts. While AI provides opportunities to improve resource management and environmental sustainability performance, its challenges should be addressed. For example, issues such as data privacy, algorithmic bias, the energy consumption of AI models, and the need for transparent and ethical AI governance frameworks must be carefully considered to ensure that AI applications contribute positively to the achievement of sustainability missions and goals. Business organizations should also consider substantial investment, cross-sector collaboration, and the development of new skills and competencies demanded for the integration of AI into traditional resource management systems. This chapter provides a comprehensive overview of the ways AI is being used to drive SRM and environmental protection. Ultimately, it examines the key

DOI: 10.4324/9781003611981-6

technologies and applications, their potential benefits, and the challenges associated with their implementation, including the use of AI in the circular economy that highlights its potential to reshape economic systems into sustainable models, enabling new business models that prioritize environmental impact alongside profitability.

6.2 The role of AI in optimizing resource use and environmental impact

A growing number of business organizations are taking the initiative to improve their environmental sustainability performance by maximizing their positive environmental impacts and reducing negative environmental impacts such as GHG emissions. These organizations typically disclose their environmental initiatives and impacts by making statements on climate-related issues and incorporating them into their corporate reports. Global regulations, legal requirements, and increasing investor demands for environmental sustainability information have caused businesses to issue sustainability reports. Stakeholders, including regulators and investors, are demanding additional relevant information and clarification on the impacts of climate change on the business model, corporate culture, and current and future financial results. Greenwashing, which is the most important problem preventing progress toward global environmental sustainability, has damaged the trust in the environmental sustainability reports.

Business organizations often claim to reduce their carbon footprint by changing operations to release less carbon. Many global companies have disclosed their strategic targets of "net zero" emissions and carbon offset programs but fail to explain how they will achieve these targets, manage the process, and provide assurance for the results related to these targets. For example, Ryanair repors low emission claim and Delta states carbon-neutrality claims without adequate disclosures.[1] Developments in the global environmental risk profile and investment environment caused a significant change in corporate governance and financial reporting processes. The board of directors and executives have a fiduciary duty to respond to investors' concerns regarding risks and impacts associated with ESG. Climate change, which is defined as the most important risk for business organizations, is viewed as the most important barrier in terms of integrating technologies into the business sustainability models. The carbon offset scheme is prevailing and deserves the immediate attention of regulators and investors. It is vital to realize that the carbon offset scheme could constitute accounting fraud, as explained in the next section. In response to the problem of greenwashing, which is largely a result of uncertainty and variable definitions, regulators and standard setters have accelerated their guidelines on the standardization of sustainability disclosure and reporting. Business organizations should comply with emerging sustainability regulations and standards in developing strategies and governance practices that promote truly sustainable programs and prevent intentional or unintentional greenwashing concerns and schemes.

Carbon offset schemes are mechanisms designed to compensate for GHG emissions by funding related emission reduction projects, including:

- **Renewable Energy:** Investing in wind, solar, or hydroelectric projects that displace fossil fuel-based energy production.
- **Energy Efficiency:** Projects that improve energy efficiency in buildings, transportation, or industrial processes.
- **Forestry and Land Use:** Afforestation, reforestation, and forest conservation projects that absorb CO2 from the atmosphere.
- **Methane Capture:** Projects that capture methane from landfills, agriculture, or wastewater treatment facilities.
- These projects help mitigate climate change by funding projects that reduce global GHG emissions.

6.3 Predictive modeling for resource management using AI

Predictive modeling for resource management using AI leverages advanced algorithms and data analytics to forecast resource needs, optimize allocation, and reduce waste across various sectors such as energy, agriculture, manufacturing, and urban planning. By analyzing historical data and real-time inputs, AI-driven models can identify usage patterns, predict future demands, and support decision-making processes that enhance operational efficiency and sustainability. The AI models presented in this chapter enable proactive management of resources by anticipating shortages, mitigating risks, and dynamically adjusting strategies in response to changing conditions. The integration of ML, neural networks, and optimization techniques empowers organizations to achieve more resilient and data-informed resource planning, ultimately contributing to cost savings and environmental stewardship.

6.3.1 Sustainable resource management

SRM is critical for ensuring the long-term viability of human societies and ecosystems. SRM is defined as a systematic and responsible approach to utilizing natural resources in a way that meets current human needs while ensuring the long-term health and availability of those resources for future generations.[2] It involves making informed and responsible choices today that not only fulfill current demands but also safeguard the environment, economy, and social structures for the future. This management strategy integrates economic, social, and environmental considerations to balance resource consumption with conservation. This integrated approach is essential for achieving sustainability and addressing the interconnected challenges of resource depletion, climate change, and environmental degradation in a balanced way.

The principles of a circular economy are fundamental to achieving SRM and focus on creating a regenerative system that seeks to minimize waste and optimize the use of resources. The circular economy represents a paradigm shift toward

SRM, driven by contributions from material science, economic and institutional structures, and technology. This shift indicates a move from the traditional linear model of production and consumption (take, make, dispose) toward a more sustainable, circular approach that values the entire lifecycle of materials and products. Its evolution reflects a growing understanding of the interconnectedness between environmental, social, and economic systems.

6.3.2 The three pillars of sustainability: A balanced approach

SRM is grounded in the concept of sustainability, characterized by three interconnected pillars. Figure 6.1 illustrates building a sustainable future through balanced resource management. The first pillar is environmental integrity, emphasizing the importance of maintaining the health and resilience of natural ecosystems, preserving biodiversity, and minimizing pollution and environmental degradation. The second pillar is economic feasibility, focusing on ensuring that resource management practices are economically viable and contribute to long-term economic growth and stability. This includes promoting resource efficiency, fostering innovation, and creating economic opportunities within sustainable industries. The third pillar is social responsibility, which aims to promote social equity and well-being by ensuring fair access to resources for all members of society while considering the needs of vulnerable populations in resource management decisions. Although these three pillars are interdependent, they are interconnected and influence each other in various ways, making it crucial to adopt a balanced approach to achieve sustainable outcomes. A shortfall in one area can hinder progress in others, underscoring the necessity of integrated and holistic strategies. A sustainable approach is a systems-based perspective that examines the interactions among environmental,

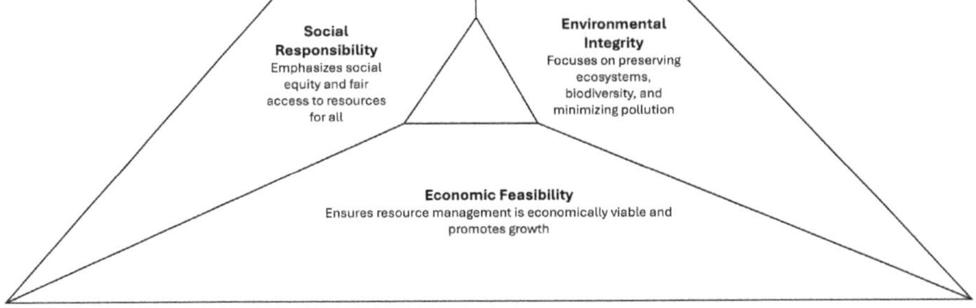

Figure 6.1 Building a sustainable future through balanced resource management

social, and economic pillars. This approach recognizes their interconnectedness, emphasizing that actions in one area can significantly impact others.[3] By understanding these dynamics, we can devise initiatives that enhance the resilience and prosperity of communities. The goal is to create solutions that not only protect the environment but also strengthen social ties and stimulate economic opportunities.

6.3.3 An integrated approach for effective SRM

SRM is characterized by a comprehensive approach prioritizing efficiency, conservation, and community involvement while fostering economic growth and environmental sustainability.[4] An integrated approach in SRM is vital for addressing the complexities of resource management and achieving sustainable outcomes. It enables coordinated decision-making, fosters collaboration, and ultimately enhances the resilience and sustainability of resource systems by recognizing and addressing their interdependencies. The key features of SRM are crucial in guiding the responsible use and stewardship of natural resources. SRM encompasses several key features that work together to promote the responsible use of resources. Figure 6.2 depicts key features of SRM.

A fundamental aspect of SRM is resource efficiency, which focuses on maximizing resource utility while minimizing waste. It involves optimizing processes and practices to ensure effective resource use. It encourages approaches such as

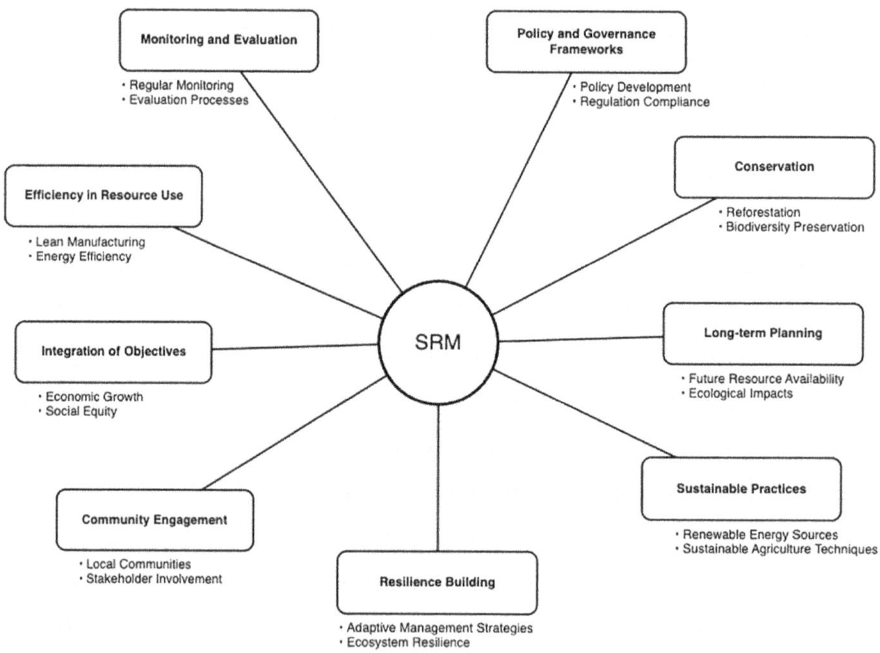

Figure 6.2 Key features of SRM

lean manufacturing, energy efficiency, and water-saving technologies to promote the economical and judicious use of resources, thereby reducing overall consumption and environmental impact. This aspect aims to enhance resource utilization to minimize waste and increase productivity across various sectors. This means finding ways to achieve more with less, ensuring that resources are used wisely and responsibly.

Another important feature is conservation, which involves protecting and maintaining natural resources and ecosystems to prevent their depletion and combat ecological degradation. This commitment to conservation reflects an understanding of nature's intrinsic value and the necessity of preserving it for future generations. The main goal of this aspect is to emphasize the importance of conserving natural resources for future generations. It involves responsible resource management to prevent depletion and degradation. SRM encourages practices that protect and restore ecosystems, such as reforestation, biodiversity preservation, and water conservation, to maintain the environment's health while ensuring that vital resources remain available for future generations.

Long-term planning is also crucial in SRM, as it requires the development and implementation of resource management practices that remain sustainable over extended time horizons. This involves strategic planning that considers the future impacts of resource management decisions, ensuring that resources remain available for future needs. SRM requires a forward-thinking approach that considers the long-term implications of resource use. This means developing strategies that not only address immediate needs but also account for future resource availability and ecological impacts, thus ensuring sustainability in the long run. The main goal is to ensure that today's choices do not compromise the well-being of future populations.

Integration of objectives plays a significant role in SRM by balancing economic, social, and environmental goals. SRM seeks to harmonize economic growth, social equity, and environmental sustainability. By integrating these objectives, it aims to create solutions that promote economic development while protecting the environment and advancing social well-being, fostering a balanced approach to resource management. This balanced approach underscores the importance of finding synergies between diverse goals in resource management.

Community engagement is vital to this framework, emphasizing the involvement of local communities and stakeholders in decision-making processes. By doing so, resource management practices can align more closely with the needs and values of those most affected. Engaging communities fosters a sense of ownership, ensures their voices are heard, and encourages cooperation toward implementing sustainable practices.

Incorporating sustainable practices is also a cornerstone of SRM. This entails adopting methods and technologies that promote sustainability, such as transitioning to renewable energy sources, implementing recycling systems, and employing sustainable agriculture techniques. By advocating for these practices, SRM helps lessen the environmental toll associated with resource extraction and consumption.

Monitoring and evaluation play a critical role in assessing the effectiveness of resource management strategies. Regularly evaluating and monitoring resource use enables adjustments and improvements to be made as necessary. This continuous assessment allows organizations and communities to evaluate their performance, identify areas for enhancement, and make informed decisions based on solid empirical data.

Moreover, robust policy and governance frameworks are essential underpinnings of effective SRM. These structures support creating policies that incentivize sustainable practices while ensuring compliance with established environmental standards. A sound governance framework promotes accountability and incentivizes adherence to sustainability initiatives, reinforcing the overall effectiveness of resource management.

Finally, resilience building focuses on enhancing the capacity of ecosystems and communities to withstand environmental changes and stresses, including climate change. This aspect of SRM applies adaptive management strategies that empower systems to recover and thrive in the face of challenges. Coupled with education and awareness efforts, SRM seeks to cultivate a culture of sustainability. By raising awareness and understanding among individuals, organizations, and communities regarding the importance of responsible resource use, SRM fosters behavioral changes toward sustainability.[5]

An integrated approach is essential for effective SRM. This involves coordinating resource management strategies across various sectors, including agriculture, energy, water, and waste management.[6] Such coordination recognizes the interconnectedness of natural resources, emphasizing that their management should not occur in isolation. By aligning strategies across different sectors, this approach facilitates a more holistic understanding of resource interactions and dependencies. For instance, effectively managing water resources requires insights from agricultural practices, as water usage in farming significantly impacts local water availability and quality. At the same time, energy consumption within agricultural operations can influence land use and irrigation practices. An integrated approach allows these sectors to align, ensuring that decisions made in one area do not negatively impact another. Furthermore, this approach encourages collaboration among various stakeholders, including government agencies, businesses, NGOs, and local communities. Engaging diverse perspectives, integrated resource management enhances knowledge-sharing and fosters innovative solutions that consider multiple dimensions of sustainability. Additionally, an integrated approach supports the sharing of data and best practices, helping to identify overlaps and efficiencies. For example, waste management strategies can be improved by insights from energy management, where waste materials might be repurposed into energy sources, thus creating a circular economy. By fostering collaboration and synergy among these diverse areas, SRM can tackle the complex challenges associated with sustainability, leading to more comprehensive and effective outcomes.

6.3.4 The role of AI in enhancing SRM

SRM necessitates the efficient and responsible use of resources to meet present needs without compromising the ability of future generations. This requires a shift from traditional linear consumption models to circular approaches that prioritize resource efficiency, waste reduction, and recycling. AI plays a critical role in this transition through the application of predictive modeling. AI-driven predictive modeling refers to the use of AI techniques, particularly ML and statistical methods, to analyze historical data and generate predictions about future events or trends. This methodology leverages large datasets to create models that can forecast outcomes based on various input variables.

AI-driven predictive modeling is a structured process that analyzes historical data, current trends, and other relevant variables to anticipate future events or trends, forecast future resource needs, and optimize resource allocation. The process begins with data collection, where relevant historical and real-time data is systematically gathered from diverse sources, ensuring a solid foundation for analysis. Once the data is collected, the next step is data preprocessing. This critical phase involves cleaning and organizing the data to improve quality and relevance. Techniques such as handling missing values, removing duplicates, and normalizing data are employed to prepare it for analysis. Following preprocessing, the focus shifts to model selection. Appropriate algorithms, such as regression, decision trees, or neural networks, are chosen based on the specific nature of the problem and the characteristics of the data. The right selection is crucial for the model's ability to learn and make accurate predictions. With the model identified, the next step is training. During this phase, the historical data is used to train the model to recognize patterns and relationships among the input variables. This is essential for the model to effectively interpret and predict outcomes. Once trained, the model undergoes validation and testing. This involves evaluating the model's performance with separate datasets to ensure accuracy and reliability. Effective validation helps determine how well the model generalizes to new, unseen data, safeguarding against overfitting. Finally, the process ends with the deployment. The validated model is implemented in real-world applications, where it aids in making predictions and supporting decision-making. Ongoing monitoring and adjustments are crucial in this stage to maintain the model's effectiveness as new data and conditions emerge.

6.3.5 AI integration in SRM: challenges and opportunities

The integration of AI into sustainability and SRM carries several potential drawbacks and limitations that deserve attention. One major concern is the significant energy consumption of many AI applications, which can counteract the environmental benefits they aim to provide. Additionally, reliance on vast amounts of data raises issues related to privacy and security, as sensitive information may be mishandled or misused. AI systems also have the potential to perpetuate existing biases present in training data, leading to unequal decision-making and exacerbating social inequalities.

The costs associated with implementing AI technologies can be prohibitively high, especially for smaller organizations, thereby limiting widespread adoption of beneficial sustainable practices. Furthermore, the effectiveness of AI is heavily dependent on the quality of data available; poor data can lead to misguided strategies in resource management. Interoperability challenges arise due to a lack of standardized protocols, making collaboration across industries more difficult.

Regulatory and ethical implications also pose significant challenges, as existing guidelines may not adequately govern the use of AI in sustainability. To maximize AI's benefits in sustainable development, governments and policymakers must proactively support the development and implementation of AI technologies. This involves investing in digital infrastructure, fostering technical skill development, and introducing policies that encourage technological innovation while addressing data privacy and security. Moreover, there is a risk that AI's optimization capabilities may promote a short-term focus on economic gains rather than fostering long-term ecological stewardship. In addressing these limitations, stakeholders must ensure that the deployment of AI in sustainability efforts is ethical, equitable, and aligned with broader environmental goals.

6.4 AI models and techniques for predictive modeling

AI-driven approaches employ advanced algorithms to analyze data related to resource usage, environmental conditions, and other relevant factors. The goal is to forecast future resource needs, optimize usage, and support decision-making processes that promote sustainability. Several AI models and techniques are applied for predictive modeling in SRM to enhance energy efficiency and resource management. Through ML and DL models, AI leverages advanced algorithms to significantly enhance resource allocation, leading to the development of a sustainable economy across multiple axes:

6.4.1 Prediction

Prediction is essential for proactive planning and operational efficiency.[7] By anticipating future needs and challenges, organizations can minimize waste, optimize resource use, and enhance sustainability efforts. ML algorithms are used to develop predictive models by analyzing large datasets to identify patterns, make predictions, and enable risk mitigation. Several ML algorithms and statistical methods can be employed to create predictive models for SRM, enabling better decision-making and resource allocation. For example, linear regression is used to predict energy consumption by analyzing historical data alongside variables such as temperature, humidity, and occupancy in buildings. This approach aids in optimizing energy usage and minimizing waste. Another predictive tool, random forest, analyzes environmental factors such as rainfall and seasonal trends to forecast water availability, helping resource managers make informed decisions, particularly in drought-prone regions. Neural networks excel at forecasting renewable energy production from solar or wind sources due to their ability to model complex, high-dimensional relationships effectively, making them invaluable for energy forecasting. KNN is employed to analyze historical consumption patterns for demand forecasting in the energy sector, enabling utility companies to anticipate peak usage periods and adjust supply accordingly. Gradient boosting machines enhance the accuracy of energy generation forecasts by predicting the performance of renewable energy systems, which supports more efficient grid management. Time-series analysis, particularly through ARIMA models, is essential for forecasting future resource demand by capturing trends and seasonality, thereby facilitating effective resource allocation in agriculture. DL models like CNNs and LSTM networks are utilized to analyze vast amounts of historical and real-time data. With CNNs and LSTMs, DL provides powerful tools for analyzing both spatial and temporal data. These models provide advanced forecasting capabilities that enable organizations to predict demand accurately and manage resources effectively. They not only facilitate immediate responses to resource demands but also support long-term strategic planning for SRM. CNNs and LSTMs can predict energy consumption patterns and demands with high accuracy. For instance, they can account for various factors, such as weather conditions and historical usage trends, which are crucial for making informed decisions regarding energy supply and resource allocation. For instance, an energy provider may implement an LSTM network to analyze past energy demand trends and forecast future consumption levels.[8] This capability allows organizations to anticipate periods of high demand and prepare accordingly, ensuring that adequate energy supplies are in place, thus minimizing the risk of shortages and optimizing resource distribution strategies.

6.4.2 Automation

AI technologies facilitate the automation of decision-making processes in energy management. This allows systems to analyze data autonomously, detect anomalies, and trigger actions without human intervention. Automated recommendations based on real-time data analysis can optimize energy distribution and resource usage,[9] resulting in operational efficiencies and reduced human error. In resource management, automation plays a significant role in various areas. For example, ML algorithms such as decision trees can categorize data into different classifications. In waste management, these algorithms assist in sorting different types of waste for recycling by analyzing the characteristics of materials, leading to more efficient sorting and disposal practices. This system can automatically determine the criteria for each waste category, eliminating the need for manual sorting. Moreover, CNNs can analyze satellite imagery by automatically learning features from the data, enabling them to perform various tasks like classification and object detection, which are essential for monitoring and assessing environmental and urban development aspects. SVMs are used as classifiers in conjunction with feature extraction from CNNs and are trained to distinguish between images containing solar panels (positive cases) and those that do not (negative cases).[10] Using satellite imagery for monitoring water clarity, random forest is utilized to create robust and accurate models for estimating Secchi disk depth from satellite imagery, facilitating an extensive assessment of water clarity across numerous ponds.[11] In addition, automation significantly enhances processes by enabling machines to adjust operations based on real-time feedback. For instance, algorithms can monitor data in a smart grid to optimize energy consumption by automatically redistributing loads to improve efficiency, eliminating the need for manual intervention. DL models can manage resources autonomously by using predictions to adjust operations dynamically. For example, when a model predicts an increase in energy demands, it could automate the scheduling of additional energy production or adjust allocations between different resource systems (like switching energy sources or redistributing load among generators) to ensure efficiency. Furthermore, clustering algorithms such as K-means facilitate automated decision-making in resource management by grouping similar data points. These algorithms can identify patterns in environmental conditions or user behaviors, enabling organizations to implement tailored strategies effectively without the constant need for human oversight.

6.4.3 Optimization

Optimization refers to the process of making something as effective, efficient, or functional as possible within given constraints. In various fields, including economics, engineering, and information technology, optimization involves selecting the best option from a set of alternatives based on specific criteria. In the context of resource management and AI, optimization generally entails improving systems to achieve the best possible performance, ensuring effective resource utilization, and maximizing outcomes within the bounds of existing constraints. By integrating AI models, organizations can optimize the management of resources, including better scheduling of energy use, more efficient allocation of resources, and improved operational strategies that minimize waste. AI algorithms can continuously learn and adapt to changes in data and conditions, ensuring that resource management remains efficient even as demands fluctuate. One of the ML techniques used for optimization is RL, which has significant applications in smart grid management. In this context, RL algorithms dynamically adjust the distribution of energy loads based on real-time feedback from the system. This adaptability allows for enhanced energy efficiency, as the system can respond to fluctuations in energy demand or supply, optimizing the operation of the grid and reducing waste. Additionally, clustering algorithms, such as K-means, play an essential role in resource optimization by grouping similar data points related to environmental conditions or patterns of resource consumption. By analyzing these clusters, organizations can gain insights into distinct user segments and their specific resource needs. This information enables more personalized and effective resource management strategies, as it allows organizations to tailor their resource allocation based on the unique consumption patterns and conditions of different user groups. CNNs are applied to spatial data, such as satellite imagery, to assess energy and natural resource conditions. They can analyze satellite and interpret images to evaluate conditions of natural resources, such as monitoring deforestation, assessing agricultural land use, or tracking the health of ecosystems to help organizations make informed decisions regarding resource management and conservation. In addition, CNNs and LSTMs are employed to predict workloads in cloud computing environments. These predictions can guide resource allocation decisions, helping cloud service providers to scale their resources efficiently according to user demand. This prevents over-provisioning (wasting resources) and under-provisioning (leading to performance issues).[12]

6.5 Applications of predictive modeling in SRM

AI is significantly impacting resource management, spanning from energy and water to waste and climate change mitigation, enhancing operational efficiency, and promoting sustainable practices vital for tackling current environmental challenges. Such practices show that AI is starting to change the way modern economies handle their resources. This transformation involves optimizing resource lifecycles, reducing waste, and integrating ethical considerations to revolutionize sustainable economic activities.

6.5.1 AI applications across various sectors

AI's ability to analyze large datasets with speed and precision enables a nuanced understanding of resource needs, transforming reactive systems into anticipatory ones.[13]

- **Energy management:** AI can assess real-time energy consumption, identify wasteful practices, and optimize renewable energy source integration. For example, Siemens implemented AI in energy distribution systems, achieving a 20% reduction in operational costs and improved resource utilization. Smart grids powered by AI facilitate location-based energy flow evaluation, enhancing energy storage solutions and reducing grid congestion.
- **Water resource management:** AI enhances the efficiency of water resource management strategies by analyzing weather patterns, soil conditions, and water usage data to optimize irrigation practices. AI-driven smart irrigation systems determine precisely when and how much water crops require, reducing unnecessary consumption and minimizing runoff.
- **Waste management:** AI optimizes recycling and waste management processes by identifying waste types and determining the most efficient processing methods. In Singapore, AI increased recycling rates by up to 25%. AI technologies can also predict when products will be discarded, allowing timely interventions through recycling or refurbishment strategies.
- **Climate change mitigation:** AI develops predictive models using ML algorithms to analyze historical climate data and forecast future trends. These models predict extreme weather events, enabling better preparation and response.

- **Sustainable transportation:** AI can contribute to the development of efficient and eco-friendly transportation systems. Autonomous vehicles can optimize routes and reduce fuel consumption. AI-supported traffic management systems can reduce congestion and improve air quality. AI's significant role in the design and operation of electric vehicles can contribute to a reduction in GHG emissions by ensuring that they are operated in the most energy-efficient way, potentially coupled with smart charging systems that optimize charging times to coincide with periods of lower electricity demand or higher renewable energy availability.

6.5.2 AI-driven supply chain management

AI's unique capabilities significantly benefit supply chain management by implementing ML algorithms to accurately predict demand fluctuations, align production schedules, and optimize resource utilization. This predictive capacity allows organizations to respond to real-time market changes, identifying inefficiencies and enabling timely interventions. Amazon integrated AI into its logistics operations by enabling agile adjustments in resource allocation, ensuring on-time deliveries, and waste reduction.[14] Amazon has also deployed AI to enhance its inventory management, achieving an increase in overall efficiency through predictive analytics, ensuring resources are allocated with precision and foresight that was previously unattainable. They reduced fulfillment processing times by up to 25%, improved shipping accuracy, and increased the number of items available for same-day and next-day delivery.[15]

6.5.3 AI in agriculture

AI can drastically reshape the agricultural sector by optimizing crop yields while minimizing resource usage. ML algorithms and data analytics applied to vast agricultural data enable AI systems to predict environmental conditions, pest outbreaks, and effective planting strategies. AI also extends to supply chain efficiencies, with ML models analyzing consumer demand patterns to reduce food waste. Also, AI can optimize the use of resources in agriculture to ensure increased productivity and sustainability, leading to precision agriculture. The concept of precision agriculture involves using AI technologies like ML and computer vision to analyze data from satellite images and sensors in the field. This data can help farmers make informed decisions about when to plant, irrigate, and harvest crops, reducing water and energy use and improving crop yields.[16]

6.5.4 The circular economy paradigm

AI offers significant potential to amplify and accelerate the transition to a circular economy. The concept of a circular economy seeks to create a closed-loop system where materials are reused, remanufactured, and recycled, ensuring that resources remain in use for as long as possible. AI contributes to this paradigm by enabling organizations to analyze consumption patterns and optimize resource allocations effectively. By analyzing consumption patterns, AI provides data-driven insights that help organizations identify inefficiencies and adjust operations to minimize waste and reduce the need for new materials. AI also influences product design through generative design techniques, allowing for the creation of durable and easy-to-repair products, promoting reusability, and therefore reducing material consumption and waste generation. Furthermore, AI fosters the development of innovative business models that align with circular economy principles, such as sharing platforms and product-as-a-service models, which encourage the collaborative use of resources and design products for longevity and repairability.[17] Such AI-enabled initiatives enable a transition to a circular economy by restructuring operations, enhancing sustainability practices, and reshaping industries toward more regenerative economic models.

6.6 AI applications for smart cities, smart grid, and addressing greenwashing

The integration of AI technologies in smart cities and smart grids, while addressing greenwashing, presents numerous innovative applications across various sectors. This integration involves the incorporation of advanced AI methods and tools to enhance efficiency, sustainability, and transparency in urban environments and energy management systems.[181920] Its innovative applications boost operational efficiency, support real-time decision-making, and promote transparency, creating a more sustainable and ethical business landscape.

6.6.1 AI applications in smart cities

Smart cities are designed to enhance urban life and promote sustainable development by incorporating advanced technologies and innovative practices. Central to their mission is a commitment to environmental sustainability, which addresses critical urban challenges such as congestion, pollution, and resource management. These cities implement green technologies, encourage public transportation, green infrastructure, and smart energy grids, and focus on waste reduction to create eco-friendly urban environments. By leveraging tools such as sensors, security cameras, smart devices, and the IoT, smart cities facilitate effective monitoring and management of urban systems, optimizing resource use and service delivery in real time and real-time data. These environments benefit from advanced technologies, including smart homes, smart grids, and e-commerce platforms, where devices and systems are interconnected, facilitating efficient data exchange and real-time decision-making. Smart cities represent a holistic approach to urbanization that prioritizes sustainable practices, fostering environments where innovation and quality of life can thrive alongside ecological integrity.

6.6.2 Challenges in smart cities

While smart cities offer numerous advantages, including enhanced efficiency, improved quality of life, and sustainability, they also pose significant challenges. Fraudulent activities can occur through various means, such as online transaction fraud, misuse, or inadequate protection of personal data, leading to potential breaches or abuses, identity theft, and data manipulation, posing real privacy and security concerns and complicating the fraud detection process. With numerous digital interactions happening simultaneously across e-commerce platforms, online banking, and IoT devices, fraud detection systems must analyze these transactions in real time. This high transaction rate not only demands extensive processing capabilities but also creates data overload, making it increasingly challenging to identify anomalies among legitimate transactions. Moreover, the dynamic behavior of fraudulent actors adds another layer of complexity. Fraudsters continuously adapt their tactics to exploit emerging vulnerabilities, often utilizing sophisticated methods to evade detection. As their strategies evolve, detection systems must also keep pace, requiring constant updates and retraining of ML models. However, the limited availability of reliable datasets hampers effective fraud detection. In many cases, the data used to train detection algorithms is imbalanced, with a significantly more significant proportion of legitimate transactions compared to fraudulent ones. This imbalance often leads to biased models that overlook subtle signs of fraud in favor of correctly predicting legitimate transactions. Furthermore, obtaining high-quality, labeled data for training is often tricky, compelling organizations to work with synthetic or self-generated datasets that may not accurately reflect real-world scenarios. Together, these challenges underscore the complexity of fraud detection in Smart societies, highlighting the need for advanced strategies and technologies to safeguard against fraudulent activities effectively.

6.6.3 AI to improve urban living

Smart cities harness AI to improve urban living by managing resources, services, and infrastructure more effectively. AI is significantly transforming the landscape of privacy and security while serving a crucial role in fraud detection. As the world becomes increasingly interconnected through digital platforms and smart cities, the necessity for effective systems that protect sensitive information and promote trust has never been more critical.

6.6.3.1 Fraud detection and prediction

Fraud is a serious and growing problem in smart cities, and AI can significantly contribute to risk mitigation, prediction, and prevention. AI techniques, such as SVM, ANNs, logistic regression, and ensemble methods, are increasingly used to analyze fraudulent behavior patterns in transactions, particularly in financial contexts like card fraud. These algorithms can create models from historical data to classify transactions as legitimate or fraudulent based on learned patterns, dramatically improving detection accuracy. Additionally, AI helps to manage the inherent data imbalance in fraud datasets, where genuine transactions far outnumber fraudulent ones. Enhanced algorithms can adjust to these imbalances to predict fraud more effectively.

6.6.3.2 Anomaly detection

AI can implement advanced anomaly detection systems that monitor behavioral patterns in real-time. AI-driven anomaly detection systems actively monitor user behavior, learn to define regular activity, and identify suspicious actions that may indicate unauthorized access. By analyzing a multitude of transaction variables (e.g., location, time of day, and transaction type), AI systems can identify deviations from normal behavior that may signal fraudulent activities. This is increasingly relevant in cloud and IoT environments, where the volume of transactions can be significant. These systems are designed to dynamically adapt encryption processes in response to emerging cyber threats, ensuring that sensitive information transmitted over networks remains secure and protected. Furthermore, AI's capabilities extend beyond transactional analysis. By utilizing NLP, organizations can assess customer feedback and complaints, identifying trends that may indicate fraudulent schemes. Through cross-referencing diverse data points, from transaction histories to user locations, AI can reveal relationships that may elude manual analysis, thereby enhancing defenses against fraud.

6.6.3.3 Enhanced security measures

To enhance security, AI is able to analyze large datasets in real time, allowing for better risk identification and response. It can detect potential threats by monitoring systems, thereby improving the response to cybersecurity threats. AI-driven analytics can also facilitate the enhancement of internal control systems, which are crucial for identifying vulnerabilities in organizations' operations and reporting. In public spaces, AI-enhanced surveillance systems provide an added layer of safety without infringing on individual privacy. By focusing on the identification of specific incidents rather than continuous monitoring of individuals, these intelligent systems utilize ethical facial recognition technologies that analyze faces while preserving anonymity, thereby striking a balance between security and privacy.

6.6.3.4 Predictive analytics

AI-powered predictive analytics provide organizations with insights into emerging fraud trends and patterns, enabling them to take proactive measures to prevent these occurrences.[21] By analyzing historical data and identifying trends and patterns, predictive analytics helps companies gain valuable insights that inform their decision-making processes. Businesses can utilize predictive models to forecast potential fraud scenarios and adjust their strategies accordingly. These AI models leverage a variety of data points, ranging from transactional histories to user behaviors, allowing organizations to detect anomalies that may signal future fraud risks. This capacity to anticipate potential fraud equips companies with the foresight necessary to implement proactive strategies, such as adjusting internal controls, enhancing customer verification processes, or deploying targeted fraud detection systems. Integrating AI-powered predictive analytics empowers organizations to refine their approaches based on data-driven evidence. By anticipating potential fraud patterns, firms can reduce financial losses and strengthen their resilience to fraudulent activities. This proactive approach enhances security posture and maintains operational integrity in an increasingly complex digital landscape.

6.6.3.5 Automated auditing and monitoring

AI can be used for predictive analytics, providing organizations with insights into emerging fraud trends and patterns that enable them to develop proactive measures for prevention. Predictive models assist companies in forecasting potential fraudulent scenarios and adjusting their strategies accordingly. Furthermore, AI can facilitate automated auditing and monitoring, enhancing audit processes. By automating data analysis and anomaly detection, audits become more efficient and of higher quality. AI can help auditors identify risky transactions and areas of concern without the need for manual review, which allows for a more comprehensive evaluation of the company's activities, including those related to environmental performance, a growing concern within ESG frameworks.

6.6.4 AI for the detection and prevention of electricity theft in smart grid

AI can effectively detect and prevent smart grid theft through various methodologies. ML algorithms can analyze historical electricity consumption data to establish norms and identify anomalies indicative of theft. As AI can analyze large volumes of historical electricity consumption data to identify patterns and establish baselines of normal usage, techniques such as clustering or classification can help detect anomalies in consumption that may suggest theft, such as sudden drops in demand or unusual consumption spikes during off-peak hours. For example, with time-series analysis, AI models can capture the temporal correlations in electricity consumption data over different scales (daily, weekly, and monthly). This can help in identifying unusual consumption patterns that deviate from established norms. Generative models, like GANs, can also be used to enhance the ability to detect theft by providing more representative samples of theft behavior to train on. GAN helps balance datasets by generating synthetic data on theft cases, enhancing training accuracy. Hybrid multi-time scale neural networks combine different architectures to extract complex features from consumption data across multiple timeframes, improving detection precision. DL models like LSTM can extract complex features from the electricity consumption data across different time frames, which significantly improves the accuracy of theft detection models.[22]

AI can also serve as a powerful tool to prevent Smart Grid theft. AI can facilitate real-time monitoring of electricity consumption, enabling immediate detection of anomalies. This allows utilities to respond quickly to potential theft incidents, such as sending alerts to fieldworkers or automatic notifications to the utility's operations center. Moreover, AI can enhance smart meter security. AI-driven solutions can be integrated with smart meters to enhance their security. By employing AI techniques such as anomaly detection at the meter level, unusual activity can trigger alerts to prevent potential tampering before it leads to theft. In addition, AI-driven consumer behavior analysis can analyze consumption patterns and customer behaviors to identify high-risk consumers who might be more likely to engage in theft. Targeted interventions or educational campaigns can then be implemented to deter these behaviors. AI can also support automated decision-making processes involving meter readings, billing anomalies, and adjustments. This helps streamline management processes and improves the overall efficiency of the grid management system, making it harder for theft to go unnoticed. AI can be complemented with other emerging technologies, such as the IoT, which provides additional data sources (like sensors and advanced meters) that can improve the overall detection and prevention systems of smart grid theft.[23] Leveraging AI techniques in the energy sector can significantly enhance the detection and prevention of electricity theft in smart grids, improving operational efficiency, reducing losses, and promoting safety.

6.6.5 Addressing greenwashing with AI

To address the complexities of ESG greenwashing and improve measurement accuracy, the application of AI presents a promising solution. AI techniques, particularly those involving NLP and ML, can analyze vast amounts of textual data from various sources (such as ESG reports and corporate sustainability disclosures) to detect signs of greenwashing. For instance, models like BERT can be used to scrutinize language and sentiment in corporate ESG communications, identifying instances of vague commitments, overly optimistic statements, or lack of actionable plans. AI can provide a more nuanced measurement of both ESG communication ("ESG Talk") and actual ESG performance ("ESG Walk") by enhancing traditional text analysis methods and developing ML frameworks, thereby enabling stakeholders to discern the authenticity of a firm's ESG claims. This dual focus on communication and performance measurement can help mitigate the prevalence of ESG greenwashing, providing clearer insights into corporate behaviors and advancing regulatory efforts against misleading sustainability claims.[24]

The increased adoption of AI in organizations results in a reduction in greenwashing practices, which are often characterized by misleading claims about environmental efforts. AI enhances the authenticity and transparency of environmental information disclosed by firms, which helps minimize false statements and exaggerations about sustainability initiatives. Furthermore, AI can assist companies in optimizing their production processes and enhancing operational efficiency. By automating the collection and analysis of environmental data, AI reduces the likelihood of human error in environmental reporting and improves the accuracy of disclosures. As a result, companies genuinely improve their environmental performance rather than merely using greenwashing to accentuate their commitments.

AI serves not only as a tool to detect and reduce greenwashing behaviors among firms but also fosters better environmental practices, thus aligning corporate strategies with SDGs. This technology can foster green innovation activities, such as developing eco-friendly products or processes, and reinforce firms' efforts to present accurate and truthful environmental claims. AI can improve the efficiency of the innovation processes by automating data analysis, enhancing decision-making, and ensuring accurate reporting of environmental performance. The application of AI not only supports firms in their green initiatives but also strengthens their credibility. This combination leads to more truthful environmental disclosures, as firms that innovate in green practices are better positioned to provide accurate information about their actual environmental impact, thus limiting instances of greenwashing. The synergy between green innovation and AI allows for a more transparent and accountable approach to corporate sustainability, fostering genuine commitments to environmental stewardship.

6.7 AI and the circular economy

AI has become a transformative tool for advancing the circular economy, which is an economic model focused on eliminating waste and advancing the continual use of resources. AI's role in the circular economy highlights its potential to reshape economic systems into sustainable models by promoting resource efficiency, reducing waste, and enabling new business models that prioritize environmental impact alongside profitability. AI-driven technologies can reshape the circular economy in several ways by: (1) predicting the lifecycle of products, identifying optimal times for maintenance, refurbishment, or recycling to reduce waste by extending the life of products, minimizing the need for raw materials, and reducing costs; (2) monitoring product performance and usage patterns to design products that are more durable and easier to repair, refurbish, or recycle; (3) optimizing resource usage within supply chains, reducing waste and identifying more sustainable alternatives by identifying inefficiencies in resource use to lower the ecological footprint while enhancing profitability and improve precision in manufacturing and minimize material waste and energy consumption, which supports sustainability goals; (4) enhancing the sorting and recycling process to determine which materials can be salvaged from end-of-life products, contributing to higher recovery rates for valuable resources, and creating economic incentives for recycling; (5) supporting sustainable product design by analyzing vast datasets on materials, production methods, and environmental impacts and guiding designers to create products that are easy to disassemble, reuse, or recycle to promote the use of materials that can be perpetually cycled through the economy, and to select eco-friendly options that contribute to circularity; (6) enhancing supply chain transparency by tracking materials and products throughout their lifecycle, using Blockchain technology to trace materials from production to disposal, ensuring accountability and supporting the circular economy by enabling informed decisions at each stage; (7) promoting circular supply chains, where products and materials are returned to the production cycle instead of being discarded to better forecast demand for recycled materials, identify sources for reusable parts, and suggest methods to reintegrate recovered resources into production; and (8) enabling businesses to engage with consumers by promoting sustainable behaviors, such as product take-back programs or recycling incentives to identify effective strategies to encourage sustainable consumption and waste reduction and to provide insights into consumer behavior trends that support circularity, enabling businesses to adapt to consumer demand for eco-friendly products and services. Overall, AI-driven systems can reshape economic systems into sustainable models, promoting resource efficiency, reducing waste, and enabling new business models that prioritize environmental impact alongside profitability. However, there are some challenges that need to be addressed, including data privacy, energy consumption of AI processes, the need for sustainable AI development, and fostering collaboration between technology providers, manufacturers, and policymakers.

Several studies address AI applications in cross-sector circular economies, including food and consumer electronics, and offer several suggestions that are valuable to the understanding of how a circular economy works and the benefits of employing AI-driven technologies to promote the circular economy. A study finds that AI is a critical tool in moving to a circular economy. AI, conjoined with circularity, will be crucial in ushering in a societal shift from consumption to quality experiences and relationships; however, new ethical concerns must be addressed.[25] Another study suggests that transitioning from the traditional linear economy to a circular one is more important than it has ever been. AI can be an extremely valuable tool in helping achieve an effective circular economy by using examples from the Irish government initiatives that have taken to move toward a more circular economy and how AI plays a part in the transition.[26]

6.8 AI and cybersecurity, and cryptocurrency

Cybersecurity, cryptocurrency and AI are increasingly interconnected domains shaping the future of digital security and finance. AI can play an essential role in enhancing cybersecurity by detecting anomalies, identifying threats, and responding to cyberattacks in real time through advanced machine learning algorithms. AI is also being used to improve cryptocurrency trading strategies, fraud detection, and regulatory compliance. While cryptocurrencies offer significant potential for innovation, their decentralization and anonymity have also created a fertile ground for cybercrime. The irreversible nature of blockchain transactions, combined with the relative simplicity of laundering illicit funds through cryptocurrency exchanges, has increasingly made them attractive targets for malicious actors. In this section, we will explore cryptocurrencies' economic consequences and cybersecurity's pivotal role in addressing the associated risks and the proactive role of AI in maintaining the integrity, trust, and resilience of the evolving cryptocurrency ecosystem.

6.8.1 Economic consequences of cryptocurrencies

The economic consequences of cryptocurrencies on a global scale present a complex and dynamic landscape that has captured the attention of economists, policymakers, and business leaders. These digital assets have significantly reshaped financial markets, introducing both new opportunities and risks. The technological innovations driven by the rise of blockchain technology are reshaping various industries, encouraging entrepreneurial initiatives, and transforming operational practices. This new wave of innovation is not only about finance. Still, it extends to supply chains, governance, and data management, promising increased efficiency, transparency, and trust across various sectors, ultimately transforming operational practices and enabling new business models.[27]

We will focus on cybersecurity's essential components, identify areas that require improved strategies and practices, and discuss how robust cybersecurity measures can effectively combat the illicit use of cryptocurrencies.

Moreover, cryptocurrencies have significantly impacted financial systems. They have introduced new investment opportunities that attract a diverse range of participants, including individual retail investors to institutional funds, significantly altering the investment landscape. Investors now have access to diverse digital assets and innovative platforms like decentralized finance (DeFi) for lending and earning interest. Initial coin offerings (ICOs) present chances to invest early in promising projects, while cryptocurrency ETFs offer exposure through traditional means. Many see cryptocurrencies as a hedge against inflation, potentially leading to long-term gains. With 24/7 global trading access, the investment landscape is shifting, attracting participants from all backgrounds, though each opportunity carries its own risks amid market volatility.

However, their inherent volatility raises concerns. Price fluctuations driven by market sentiment can lead to significant gains, but they also pose a risk for investors seeking stability. Positive news or trends, such as endorsements from influential figures or favorable regulatory developments, can significantly elevate investor enthusiasm, resulting in dramatic price increases and substantial profits for those who capitalize on the spike. Conversely, adverse events or sentiments, such as regulatory enforcement or security breaches, can trigger panic selling, leading to a sharp decline in prices. The regulatory environment surrounding cryptocurrencies is another crucial aspect. The lack of a unified global regulatory framework creates challenges for governments and financial institutions. In this unregulated space, the potential for market manipulation and investor risks is substantial, igniting debates about the need for oversight.

6.8.2 Cryptocurrency use for cybercriminal activities

Cryptocurrency has emerged as both a revolutionary form of digital currency and a tool that is increasingly exploited for various cybercriminal activities. While cryptocurrency has the potential to empower individuals and facilitate economic transactions, it also presents a range of challenges, particularly concerning cybercrime.

The anonymity, decentralization, ease of transfer, and unregulated use of the dark web create a multifaceted environment for the development of fraudulent activities. Such aspects can attract cybercriminals to use cryptocurrencies in several ways, including:

6.8.2.1 *Ransomware attacks*

Cybercriminals often demand payment in cryptocurrencies such as Bitcoin for ransomware attacks. Once a victim's data is encrypted, hackers will typically provide a payment address to ensure anonymity. This payment method is attractive because it complicates tracing the funds back to the perpetrators. A notable example is the Colonial Pipeline case in 2021. In May 2021, the Colonial Pipeline Company suffered a ransomware attack executed by the hacking group DarkSide. The attackers encrypted data using ransomware and demanded a ransom in Bitcoin. Colonial paid the ransom to restore operations, which led to significant fuel shortages across the US East Coast.[28] Subsequently, US authorities recovered 63.7 BTC (valued at $2.3 million at the time) by tracking the public blockchain and accessing the hacker's wallet.[29]

6.8.2.2 *Distributed denial of service attacks*

Some cybercriminals use cryptocurrencies to extort companies through distributed denial of service (DDoS) attacks. They threaten to overwhelm a website with traffic unless a payment is made in cryptocurrency to cease the attack. This was the case with Bitcoin.org, which experienced an "absolutely massive" DDoS attack. In July 2021, Bitcoin.org, a site promoting Bitcoin, suffered a DDoS attack accompanied by a ransom demand in Bitcoin. The attacker flooded the site with traffic and demanded 0.5 BTC ($17,012 at the time) to stop the attack and have the site's services and operations restored to normal.[30] In December, users could not access the Bitcoin.org software for hours due to a similar attack.[31] This type of hybrid DDoS-extortion attack is becoming increasingly common against crypto platforms.

6.8.2.3 *Money laundering*

Cryptocurrencies facilitate money laundering by enabling criminals to quickly convert illicit funds into what are perceived as "clean" digital assets. Mixing services and privacy coins like Monero help obscure the transaction trail, making it challenging for law enforcement to trace the origins of the funds. A notable example is Bitzlato and Binance 2023. In January 2023, US authorities charged the Russian exchange Bitzlato with processing $700 million in illicit funds, many linked to Hydra, a dark web drugs marketplace. The world's largest crypto exchange, Binance, processed $346 million for Bitzlato, whose founder was arrested for allegedly operating a "money laundering engine," according to US authorities.[32]

6.8.2.4 *Dark web marketplaces*

Many illegal goods and services, including drugs, weapons, and stolen data, are sold on dark web marketplaces that primarily use cryptocurrency for transactions. Cryptocurrencies allow buyers and sellers to retain anonymity, making them the preferred payment method. Silk Road, launched in 2011, was a black-market site on the Darknet, where users bought drugs and illegal goods using Bitcoin. On October 1, 2013, the United States Federal Bureau of Investigation (FBI) shut it down and arrested its founder, Ross Ulbricht, and seized his laptop. The US government seized over 144,000 BTC from Silk Road wallets, valued at over $1 billion by 2020.

The FBI arrested Ulbricht in 2013, and a judge sentenced Ulbricht to life in prison for drug trafficking, computer hacking, and money laundering in 2015. The FBI arrested Ulbricht and seized his laptop on October 1, 2013. A judge sentenced Ulbricht to life in prison for drug trafficking, computer hacking, and money laundering in 2015. The Silk Road generated millions in sales and over $13 million in Bitcoin commissions. On November 3, 2020, law enforcement seized over $1 billion in digital currency linked to this case.[33]

6.8.2.5 *Fraud and scams*

The crypto space is rife with scams, including Ponzi schemes and fake ICOs. Criminals often use cryptocurrency to steal investors' funds, taking advantage of the lack of regulation and oversight in this area. A notable example is OneCoin (2014–2017), which was a massive Ponzi scheme masquerading as a cryptocurrency. OneCoin, based in Sofia, Bulgaria, sold a fraudulent cryptocurrency. It began operating in the United States around 2015, and between Q4 2014 and Q4 2016, it took in over $4 billion from at least 3.5 million victims worldwide. Founded by Karl Sebastian Greenwood and Ruja Ignatova, known as the "Cryptoqueen," OneCoin claimed to have a private blockchain. There was no blockchain, and OneCoin was not a legitimate cryptocurrency and had no actual value.[34] Ignatova disappeared in 2017 and remains an FBI Most Wanted fugitive.[35]

6.8.2.6 *Theft and hacking*

Cryptocurrency exchanges and wallets are often targeted by hackers because of their high value and sometimes insufficient security measures. Once cryptocurrency has been stolen, criminals can more easily transfer or cash out through various exchanges and services. A notable example is the Axie Infinity Hack in 2022.[36] Axie Infinity ranks as one of the top online games that leverage blockchain technology to support its in-game economy. In March 2022, Ronin Network, the Ethereum (ETH) sidechain used by the popular blockchain game Axie Infinity, suffered one of the largest crypto heists in history. Hackers exploited a private key vulnerability to gain access to validator nodes and transfer 173,600 ethers, worth about $600 million, to an anonymous ETH wallet. The hackers also withdrew roughly $25.5 million in USD Coin, a digital currency tied to the US dollar. The Lazarus Group, a North Korean state-backed hacking group, was later linked to the attack by the US Treasury.[37]

6.8.2.7 *Phishing attacks*

Cybercriminals commonly engage in phishing schemes designed to steal sensitive information or private keys from cryptocurrency users. Victims may be tricked into entering their information on malicious sites that resemble legitimate exchanges or wallets, resulting in the theft of funds. In 2023, phishing scams targeted over 324,000 cryptocurrency users, resulting in approximately $295 million lost to wallet drainers, as reported by Scam Sniffer.[38] Phishing activities persisted as scammers quickly adapted to new platforms after major operations such as Monkey Drainer and Inferno Drainer shut down. Tactics included hacking official social media accounts, running fake airdrops, exploiting expired links, and bypassing advertising guidelines on Google and Twitter to promote phishing sites.[39]

6.8.2.8 *Cryptojacking*

This involves cybercriminals hijacking victims' computing resources to mine cryptocurrencies without their knowledge. Victims unwittingly contribute their system's processing power and consume electricity, allowing criminals to generate digital assets at no cost to themselves.[40] A notable example is cryptojacking attack on Tesla Cloud in 2018. In 2018, security researchers at RedLock discovered that Tesla's cloud infrastructure had been breached and used to mine cryptocurrency (specifically Monero) without authorization. The attackers infiltrated Tesla's AWS cloud through Kubernetes, a system by Google for optimizing cloud applications, because it was not password-protected.[41] Using the cloud's computing power, the hackers deployed a cryptocurrency mining software called Stratum and mined approximately 0.9 Bitcoin over several weeks, valued at around $6,000 at the time.[42]

While cryptocurrencies have legitimate uses, their features provide significant advantages to cybercriminals, leading to increased attention on the need for effective regulatory and policing measures to mitigate their misuse in cybercrime activities. The growing utilization of cryptocurrency for illicit activities highlights the urgent need for enhanced cybersecurity measures.

6.8.3 *When cybersecurity meets AI: imperatives in cryptocurrency ecosystem*

The rapid advancement in technology, like GenAI, is creating new pathways for cyber threats. As the digital landscape continues to evolve, the strategies employed to combat the misuse of cryptocurrencies must also adapt to the significant increase in fraud and cybercrime in cyberspace. Cybersecurity serves as the protector of digital environments against diverse threats, including those associated with the misuse of cryptocurrencies.[43] As the illicit use of cryptocurrencies rises, enhanced cybersecurity measures become essential for protecting users, enforcing regulatory compliance, and enabling the detection and deterrence of cybercriminal activities. Cybersecurity refers to the practice of protecting systems, networks, and programs from digital attacks, theft, and damage. This field encompasses a wide range of technologies, processes, and practices designed to safeguard sensitive information and ensure the integrity of data. It aims to defend against unauthorized access, cyberattacks, and data breaches that could compromise the confidentiality, integrity, and availability of digital assets.

AI plays a dual role: offensive and defensive. Its powerful capabilities can both stop and assist cybercriminals. The current landscape of cybersecurity and AI reveals a complex interplay marked by the integration of ML and DL technologies within both defensive and offensive strategies. In cybersecurity, AI plays a crucial role in enhancing the security and resilience of information technology systems against cyber threats. Systems designed for defense employ ML and DL algorithms to detect anomalous patterns in network traffic and identify deviations in user behavior, which may indicate potential security breaches or emerging forms of malware. Automated response mechanisms leverage these learning algorithms to initiate actions such as threat detection and mitigation, isolation of compromised systems, blocking of malicious traffic, and neutralization of attacks, often without necessitating human intervention. Additionally, predictive analytics facilitate the identification of future vulnerabilities and potential attack vectors by analyzing both real-time and historical data. AI-driven endpoint protection systems further contribute to monitoring devices and detecting malicious activities, thereby enhancing the overall security posture.[44]

The integration of AI in preventing the misuse of cryptocurrencies offers numerous potential benefits from both tactical and strategic perspectives, significantly enhancing cybersecurity frameworks. From a tactical standpoint, AI helps strengthen the security of digital systems by more effectively identifying and addressing vulnerabilities. By utilizing ML algorithms, AI can continuously monitor digital wallets and blockchain activities, enabling it to detect unauthorized access attempts and potential exploitation risks in real time. This proactive approach allows organizations to respond quickly to security threats, thereby reducing the likelihood of successful attacks such as hacks and fraud. AI's capacity to conduct thorough analyses of large datasets facilitates the identification of patterns that may indicate suspicious behavior, thereby enhancing the overall resilience of cybersecurity measures.

On a more strategic level, the use of AI in cryptocurrency changes the balance of power in cybersecurity. Historically, cybercriminals have increasingly employed advanced techniques to exploit digital currencies; however, the implementation of AI-driven technologies allows for a stronger emphasis on defensive measures that can tackle these evolving threats. By leveraging AI, organizations can anticipate potential cyberattacks, assess risks more accurately, and formulate counterstrategies informed by predictive analytics. This evolving paradigm prioritizes defense over offense, transforming the cybersecurity landscape to better safeguard sensitive financial transactions and personal information within the digital currency sphere.

Additionally, AI can enhance compliance with regulatory requirements related to cryptocurrencies by automating tasks such as transaction monitoring and auditing. For example, in transaction monitoring and anomaly detection, AI can analyze transaction patterns in real time to identify unusual or suspicious activities indicative of fraudulent behavior, money laundering, or other illicit activities involving cryptocurrencies. AI employs advanced ML algorithms to detect anomalies that might evade traditional monitoring methods, facilitating quicker responses to potential threats. This proactive strategy can help organizations comply with regulations, protect their assets, and prevent financial losses due to criminal activities. Furthermore, AI can automatically generate alerts for suspicious transactions, enabling timely investigations and responses. This not only lessens the burden on human analysts but also boosts the efficiency of oversight by quickly flagging suspicious activities for further investigation. As cyber threats become more sophisticated, the ability to effectively utilize AI technology is crucial for maintaining the integrity and safety of cryptocurrency ecosystems, ensuring that organizations stay one step ahead in the ongoing battle against misuse.

6.8.4 Significant cyberattacks case studies

To further illustrate the importance of cybersecurity in the cryptocurrency ecosystem, we present case studies of significant cyberattacks.

6.8.4.1 Mt. Gox Hack (2014)

The collapse of Mt. Gox, once the largest Bitcoin exchange in the world, was attributed to a massive theft of Bitcoins. Approximately 850,000 Bitcoins, now worth almost $23 billion, mysteriously vanished, forcing the exchange to file for bankruptcy in February 2014. The exact cause of this substantial loss remains ambiguous; however, it has been suggested that it resulted from a "malleability-related theft" that went undetected for several years, highlighting a troubling combination of hacking and inadequate security practices at Mt. Gox. Attackers reportedly exploited vulnerabilities in the exchange's security protocols to access private keys and drain the reserves of Bitcoin. The incident underscores the critical need for robust security measures in the cryptocurrency sector, such as cold storage, multi-factor authentication, and regular security audits, to safeguard exchanges against cyberattacks.[45]

In retrospect, experts have criticized Mt. Gox's security approach, citing issues such as poor management of cold storage and a failure to promptly address vulnerabilities after becoming aware of the "malleability bug." This breach likely provided the thieves with the opportunity to use mixing services and other techniques to obscure the transaction trail, complicating efforts to track the stolen funds. Ultimately, this incident exposed the lack of regulation and oversight in the cryptocurrency sector at that time, prompting calls for enhanced security measures and more comprehensive regulatory frameworks to prevent such crises in the future.

6.8.4.2 The Decentralized Autonomous Organization Hack (2016)

The Decentralized Autonomous Organization (DAO) Hack was a pivotal event in the history of ETH and the broader cryptocurrency landscape. Occurring in June 2016, it involved a decentralized investment fund known as the DAO, which was built on the ETH blockchain. The DAO aimed to operate as a venture capital fund managed through a smart contract, allowing token holders to vote on various investment proposals. Within a short period, the DAO successfully raised around $150 million in Ether, making it one of the largest crowdfunding campaigns at the time. However, on June 17, 2016, an attacker exploited a critical vulnerability in the DAO's code. This vulnerability was related to the "splitting" function, which allowed contributors to withdraw their investments in the event of a disagreement with the fund's management. The attacker exploited a flaw in the smart contract, performing what is known as a "reentrancy attack." By continuously calling the withdraw function before the contract could update the balance, the hacker was able to drain approximately 3.6 million Ether (valued around $70 million at the time) into a secondary contract dubbed the "Child DAO."[46]

The hack significantly devalued Ether, shaking investor confidence and raising concerns about smart contract security. After much debate, the ETH community voted for a hard fork on July 20, 2016, creating two blockchains: ETH, which restored the stolen funds, and ETH Classic, which preserved the original blockchain. This incident resulted in a focus on improved security practices and ethical considerations in DeFi.

6.8.4.3 The Coincheck Hack (2018)

The Japanese cryptocurrency exchange Coincheck was hacked on January 26, 2018, resulting in the theft of approximately 58-billion-yen (approximately $530 million) worth of cryptocurrency, NEM. The attackers exploited a vulnerability in the exchange's hot wallet to gain access to the tokens. This incident is recognized as one of the largest hacks in the history of cryptocurrencies. The attackers exploited vulnerabilities in Coincheck's security, particularly the practice of storing large amounts of NEM in a "hot wallet," which was connected to the internet and susceptible to breaches. Following the hack, the stolen NEM was not only transferred to hacker-controlled addresses but was also sold at a discount on a newly created crypto market, allowing the hackers to launder the assets. This breach caused significant market upheavals, resulting in price drops for NEM and other cryptocurrencies, and raised serious concerns regarding the security practices within cryptocurrency exchanges.[47]

In response to the incident, the Japanese Financial Services Agency imposed stricter regulations and ordered Coincheck to enhance its security measures. The exchange claimed it would fully compensate the affected users, totaling around 260,000 individuals, using its capital. The Coincheck hack underscored the urgent need for cryptocurrency exchanges to adopt robust security protocols and implement comprehensive user verification processes to safeguard against similar attacks. Additionally, it prompted industry-wide discussions on regulation, prompting cryptocurrency trade groups in Japan to form a self-regulatory organization aimed at preventing such significant breaches in the future and ensuring the protection of investors' assets.

6.8.4.4 DMM Bitcoin Hack (2024)

In May 2024, Japanese crypto exchange DMM Bitcoin reported an unprecedented hack resulting in the theft of 4,502.9 Bitcoin, valued at approximately $308 million US dollars, making it the largest Bitcoin theft since Mt. Gox. The FBI, Department of Defense Cyber Crime Center (DC3), and the National Police Agency of Japan (NPA) have identified North Korean cyber actors, known as TraderTraitor, as the perpetrators behind this theft. TraderTraitor is recognized for targeted social engineering efforts aimed at multiple employees within the same company simultaneously. In this case, the cyber actors posed as a recruiter on LinkedIn, successfully contacting an employee at Ginco, a Japan-based enterprise software firm managing cryptocurrency wallets. They sent the targeted employee a URL linked to a malicious Python script, claiming that it was part of a pre-employment assessment. This deceptive tactic allowed them to compromise the victim's access to Ginco's wallet management system. Once the compromise took place, TraderTraitor actors exploited session cookie information to impersonate the compromised employee, gaining unauthorized access to Ginco's unencrypted communications system. The stolen funds were then transferred to wallets controlled by the TraderTraitor group. This incident highlights the ongoing efforts of the FBI, NPA, and other international partners to combat North Korea's involvement in illicit activities, including cybercrime and cryptocurrency theft, which are used to generate revenue for the regime.[48]

6.8.4.5 Bybit/Lazarus Hack (2025)

In early 2025, the largest crypto theft in history occurred when North Korea's Lazarus Group allegedly infiltrated the infrastructure of Bybit, a major global exchange, stealing an estimated $1.5 billion in ETH.[49] The breach was reportedly carried out through a sophisticated supply chain attack. Lazarus compromised a software update from a trusted third-party vendor that integrated with Bybit's back-end systems. Once the malicious code was deployed, the hackers gained administrative access and began siphoning ETH over several hours. According to the Bybit CEO, Hacker mostly used @THORChain to clear ETH to BTC.[50] The breach affected Bybit's cold wallet, an offline security storage system. The stolen assets, mostly in ether, were swiftly moved to various wallets and sold off through multiple channel platforms.[51] TraderTraitor and other cyber threat actors continue to increasingly focus on cryptocurrency and blockchain companies, primarily due to the low risk and high payouts, rather than targeting financial institutions like banks that have rigorous security measures and regulations. The attack showcased Lazarus's evolving capabilities—using zero-day vulnerabilities, supply chain backdoors, and AI-generated phishing infrastructure.

The hack was not immediately detected, as the transfers were split across hundreds of wallets and masked using mixers and cross-chain bridges. It was only when users began noticing abnormal delays in withdrawals that the breach came to light. The incident triggered a 20% drop in Bitcoin's value in January, as fear rippled across the markets and renewed concerns about the security of these decentralized transactions. Bybit responded by freezing all withdrawals, working with blockchain forensics firms, and informing regulators. Despite swift coordination, the majority of the funds were unrecoverable. The event became a turning point in cybersecurity policy, with governments calling for stricter Know Your Customer standards within the crypto industry, enhanced third-party risk assessments, and a global blacklist for crypto addresses linked to state actors. It also emphasized the need for improved collaboration and coordination between industry actors, governments, and law enforcement.[52]

6.9 Summary

This chapter explores the transformative role of AI in advancing resource management and promoting environmental sustainability. It begins by examining how AI technologies such as ML, computer vision, and predictive analytics are being applied to monitor, manage, and optimize the use of natural resources, including water, energy, land, and raw materials. The chapter highlights practical applications in sectors such as agriculture, energy, waste management, and climate monitoring, demonstrating how AI can enhance efficiency, reduce environmental impact, and support decision-making for sustainable development. It also discusses the integration of AI with IoT devices and satellite imagery to enable real-time data collection and ecosystem monitoring. Additionally, the chapter addresses the ethical considerations, data governance challenges, and the need for interdisciplinary collaboration to ensure responsible and equitable AI deployment in environmental contexts. This chapter emphasizes that AI, when used thoughtfully, holds significant potential to support global sustainability goals and foster more resilient and adaptive EMS.

Finally, this chapter presents predictive modeling for resource management using AI leverages advanced algorithms and data analytics to forecast resource needs, optimize allocation, and reduce waste across various sectors such as energy, agriculture, manufacturing, and urban planning. The AI models presented in this chapter enable proactive management of resources by anticipating shortages, mitigating risks, and dynamically adjusting strategies in response to changing conditions and cybersecurity threats. The integration of ML, neural networks, and optimization techniques empowers organizations to achieve more resilient and data-informed resource planning and decision-making. For example, the use of AI in the circular economy highlights its potential to reshape economic systems into sustainable models in advancing the circular economy.

6.10 Takeaways

- AI enhances resource efficiency by enabling accurate forecasting, real-time monitoring, and data-driven decision-making in sectors such as energy, water, and agriculture.
- Predictive analytics and ML can anticipate resource demands, identify inefficiencies, and optimize supply chain and distribution networks.
- Integration of AI with IoT and satellite data supports large-scale environmental monitoring, including deforestation tracking, air and water quality assessment, and climate modeling.
- AI supports precision agriculture by analyzing weather, soil, and crop data to optimize irrigation, fertilization, and harvesting, reducing resource use and environmental impact.
- AI-driven waste management systems improve recycling, sorting, and logistics, contributing to circular economy initiatives and reducing landfill dependency.
- Smart energy grids and AI-based control systems allow dynamic load balancing and renewable energy integration, promoting cleaner and more reliable energy systems.
- Environmental risk management benefits from AI's ability to detect anomalies, predict natural disasters, and support early warning systems.
- Ethical and governance concerns must be addressed, including data bias, privacy, transparency, and equitable access to AI technologies.
- Cross-sector collaboration between technologists, environmental scientists, policymakers, and communities is essential for scalable and responsible AI implementation.
- AI is a powerful enabler of the UNSDGs, particularly those related to clean energy, climate action, and responsible consumption.

Notes

1 Akepa. 2025. Greenwashing: 18 recent stand-out examples. January 23.
2 British Assessment Bureau. 2022. *What is Sustainable Resource Management and How Do You Achieve it?* https://www.british-assessment.co.uk/insights/what-is-sustainable-resource-management-and-how-do-you-achieve-it/
3 EPA. *Sustainability Primer*. https://www.epa.gov/sites/default/files/2015–05/documents/sustainability_primer_v9.pdf
4 Rezaee, Z. 2024/forthcoming. *The Sustainable Business Blueprint: Planning, Performance, Risk, Reporting, and Assurance*. Routledge, Taylor & Francis Group
5 Challoumis, C. 2024, October. Building a sustainable economy-how ai can optimize resource allocation. In *XVI International Scientific Conference* (pp. 190–224)
6 Challoumis. Building a sustainable economy-how ai can optimize resource allocation, 5
7 Challoumis. Building a sustainable economy-how ai can optimize resource allocation, 6
8 Kristian, A., Goh, T.S., Ramadan, A., Erica, A., & Sihotang, S.V. 2024. Application of ai in optimizing energy and resource management: Effectiveness of deep learning models. *International Transactions on Artificial Intelligence*, 2(2), 99–105

9 Kristian et al. Application of ai in optimizing energy and resource management
10 De Jong, T., Bromuri, S., Chang, X., Debusschere, M., Rosenski, N., Schartner, C., Strauch, K., Boehmer, M., & Curier, L. 2020. Monitoring spatial sustainable development: semi-automated analysis of satellite and aerial images for energy transition and sustainability indicators. *arXiv* preprint arXiv:2009.05738
11 Coffer, M.M., Nezlin, N.P., Bartlett, N., Pasakarnis, T., Lewis, T.N., & DiGiacomo, P.M. 2024. Satellite imagery as a management tool for monitoring water clarity across freshwater ponds on Cape Cod, Massachusetts. *Journal of Environmental Management*, 355, 120334
12 Lekkala, C. 2024. AI-driven dynamic resource allocation in cloud computing: Predictive models and real-time optimization. *Journal of Artificial Intelligence, Machine Learning and Data Science*, 2(2), 450–456
13 Global Partnership on Al Report (GPAI). 2021. *Climate Change and AI: Recommendations for Government Action.* https://www.gpai.ai/projects/climate-change-and-ai.pdf
14 Hurst, K. 2024.*7 Ways Amazon is Using AI to Build a More Sustainable Future.* Amazon. https://www.aboutamazon.com/news/sustainability/how-amazon-uses-ai-sustainability-goals
15 Amazon. 2024. *Amazon Unveils the Next Generation of Fulfillment Centers Powered by AI and 10 Times More Robotics.* https://www.aboutamazon.com/news/operations/amazon-fulfillment-center-robotics-ai
16 Amazon. *Amazon Unveils the Next Generation of Fulfillment Centers Powered by AI and 10 Times More Robotics*, 14
17 Danish, M.S.S., & Senjyu, T. 2023. Shaping the future of sustainable energy through AI-enabled circular economy policies. *Circular Economy*, 2(2), 100040
18 Javed, A.R., Shahzad, F., ur Rehman, S., Zikria, Y.B., Razzak, I., Jalil, Z., & Xu, G. 2022. Future smart cities: Requirements, emerging technologies, applications, challenges, and future aspects. *Cities*, 129, 103794
19 World of Conferences (WOC). 2024. The modern vector of the development of science. In *XVI International Scientific Conference*. Philadelphia, PA
20 Appio, F.P., Lima, M., & Paroutis, S. 2019. Understanding smart cities: Innovation ecosystems, technological advancements, and societal challenges. *Technological Forecasting and Social Change*, 142, 1–14
21 Dou, F., Ye, J., Yuan, G., Lu, Q., Niu, W., Sun, H., Guan, L., Lu, G., Mai, G., Liu, N., & Lu, J. 2023. Towards artificial general intelligence (agi) in the internet of things (iot): Opportunities and challenges. *arXiv* preprint arXiv:2309.07438
22 Sun, Y., Sun, X., Hu, T., & Zhu, L. 2023. Smart grid theft detection based on hybrid multi-time scale neural network. *Applied Sciences*, 13(9), 5710
23 Akram, R., Ayub, N., Khan, I., Albogamy, F.R., Rukh, G., Khan, S., Shiraz, M., & Rizwan, K. 2021. Towards big data electricity theft detection based on improved RUSBoost classifiers in smart grid. *Energies*, 14(23), 8029
24 Dao, D., Chu, N.A., Bowden, J., & Cummins, M. 2024. *ESG Greenwashing and Applications of AI for Measurement.* University of Strathclyde, Glasgow. https://doi.org/10.17868/strath.00089719
25 Ideas and statistics presented to design studies and cement these ideas in research
Roberts, H., et al. 2024. Artificial intelligence in support of the circular economy: Ethical considerations and a path forward. *AI & Society*, 39, 1451–1464. https://doi.org/10.1007/s00146-022-01596-8
26 Pathan, M.S., Richardson, E., Galvan, E., & Mooney, P. 2023. The role of artificial intelligence within circular economy activities—A view from Ireland. *Sustainability* 15(12), 9451. https://doi.org/10.3390/su15129451
27 Munoz, J.M., & Frenkel, M. eds. 2020. *The Economics of Cryptocurrencies*. Routledge
28 Beerman, J., Berent, D., Falter, Z., & Bhunia, S. 2023, May. A review of colonial pipeline ransomware attack. In *2023 IEEE/ACM 23rd International Symposium On Cluster, Cloud and Internet Computing Workshops* (CCGridW) (pp. 8–15)

29 DOJ. 2021. *Department of Justice Seizes $2.3 Million in Cryptocurrency Paid to the Ransomware Extortionists Darkside*. https://www.justice.gov/archives/opa/pr/department-justice-seizes-23-million-cryptocurrency-paid-ransomware-extortionists-darkside
30 Di Salvo, M. 2021. *Bitcoin.org Reportedly Hit with DDoS Attack, Ransom Demand*. decrypt. https://decrypt.co/75276/bitcoin-org-reportedly-hit-ddos-attack-ransom-demand
31 Raza, A. 2021. *Threat Actors Have Overwhelmed Bitcoin.org with A DDoS Attack*. https://blog.koddos.net/threat-actors-have-overwhelmed-bitcoin-org-with-a-ddos-attack/
32 Wilson, T., & Berwick, A. 2023. *Exclusive: Binance Moved $346 mln for Seized Crypto Exchange Bitzlato*. https://www.reuters.com/business/finance/binance-moved-346-mln-seized-crypto-exchange-bitzlato-data-show-2023-01-24/
33 FBI.n.d. *Ross William Ulbricht's Laptop*. https://www.fbi.gov/history/artifacts/ross-william-ulbrichts-laptop
34 DOJ. 2023. *Co-founder of Multibillion-Dollar Cryptocurrency Scheme "OneCoin" Sentenced to 20 Years in Prison*. https://www.justice.gov/usao-sdny/pr/co-founder-multibillion-dollar-cryptocurrency-scheme-onecoin-sentenced-20-years-prison
35 FBI. 2022. *Ruja Ignatova Added to FBI's Ten Most Wanted Fugitives List*. https://www.fbi.gov/news/stories/ruja-ignatova-added-to-fbis-ten-most-wanted-fugitives-list#:~:text=The%20FBI%20today%20announced%20the,affected%20millions%20of%20investors%20worldwide
36 Ingram, D., & Abbruzzese, J. 2022. Hackers steal more than $600 million from maker of Axie Infinity. *NBC NEWS*. https://www.nbcnews.com/tech/tech-news/hackers-steal-600-million-maker-axie-infinity-rcna22031
37 Warminsky, J. 2024. *Hackers Steal Nearly $10 Million from Axie Infinity Co-founder's Personal Accounts*. https://therecord.media/hackers-steal-millions-from-axie-infinity-founder-personal-accounts
38 Bagwe, M. 2024. *Cryptohack Roundup: Orbit Chain's $81M New Year's Eve Hack*. Bank Info Security. https://www.bankinfosecurity.com/cryptohack-roundup-orbit-chains-81m-new-years-eve-hack-a-24028#CryptoPhishing
39 Schwartz, M.J. 2024. *Crypto-Seeking Drainer Scam-as-a-Service Operations Thrive*. https://www.bankinfosecurity.com/crypto-seeking-drainer-scam-as-a-service-operations-thrive-a-24107
40 DOJ. 2025. *Minnesota Man Pleads Guilty in "Cryptojacking" Scheme*. https://www.justice.gov/usao-mn/pr/minnesota-man-pleads-guilty-cryptojacking-scheme#:~:text=Cryptojacking%20is%20a%20form%20of%20cybercrime%20where,increased%20energy%20consumption%2C%20and%20higher%20operating%20costs.&text=Armbrust%20then%20liquidated%20the%20mined%20Ethereum%2C%20totaling,proceeds%20to%20his%20Wells%20Fargo%20banking%20account
41 Browne, R. 2018. Hackers hijack Tesla's cloud system to mine cryptocurrency. *CNBC*. https://www.cnbc.com/2018/02/21/hackers-hijack-teslas-cloud-system-to-mine-crypto-currency-redlock.html
42 Centre for Cybersecurity. *Cryptojacking: Case Study on Tesla's Experience*. https://www.centreforcybersecurity.com/en-sg/post/cryptojacking-case-study-on-teslas-experience
43 Arpaci, I., & Bahari, M. 2023. A complementary SEM and deep ANN approach to predict the adoption of cryptocurrencies from the perspective of cybersecurity. *Computers in Human Behavior*, 143, 107678
44 Fuller, N.J. 2024. *The Intersection of Artificial Intelligence (AI) and Cybersecurity What Does This Really Mean?*
45 Mishra, P. 2023. *Infamously Hacked Crypto Exchange Mt. Gox Delays Repayment Deadline by a Year*. CoinDesk. https://www.coindesk.com/business/2023/09/21/mt-gox-pushes-repayments-by-a-year
46 Mehar, M.I., Shier, C.L., Giambattista, A., Gong, E., Fletcher, G., Sanayhie, R., . . . Laskowski, M. 2019. Understanding a revolutionary and flawed grand experiment in blockchain: the DAO attack. *Journal of Cases on Information Technology* (JCIT), 21(1), 19–32

47 Tsuchiya, Y., & Hiramoto, N. 2021. How cryptocurrency is laundered: Case study of Coincheck hacking incident. *Forensic Science International: Reports*, 4, 100241
48 FBI. 2024. *FBI, DC3, and NPA Identification of North Korean Cyber Actors, Tracked as TraderTraitor, Responsible for Theft of $308 Million USD from Bitcoin.DMM.com.* https://www.fbi.gov/news/press-releases/fbi-dc3-and-npa-identification-of-north-korean-cyber-actors-tracked-as-tradertraitor-responsible-for-theft-of-308-million-from-bitcoindmmcom#:~:text=December%2023%2C%202024-,FBI%2C%20DC3%2C%20and%20NPA%20Identification%20of%20North%20Korean%20Cyber%20Actors,page%20and%20was%20subsequently%20compromised
49 Center for Strategic & International studies (CSIS). 2025. *The ByBit Heist and the Future of U.S. Crypto Regulation.* https://www.csis.org/analysis/bybit-heist-and-future-us-crypto-regulation#:~:text=On%20February%2021%2C%202025%2C%20a%20group%20of,tokens%20from%20the%20Dubai%2Dbased%20cryptocurrency%20exchange%20ByBit.&text=The%20price%20of%20Bitcoin%20experienced%20a%2020,about%20the%20security%20of%20these%20decentralized%20transactions
50 Ben Zhou. 2025. https://x.com/benbybit/status/1896798476945744010
51 DFNS. 2025. *The Bybit/Safe Hack.* https://www.dfns.co/article/the-bybit-safe-hack
52 Struckman, K., & Binder, M. 2025. *The Bybit Heist: What Happened & What Now?.* https://www.wilsoncenter.org/microsite/9/node/129835#:~:text=In%20addition%20to%20US%20regulation,efforts%20to%20stem%20cryptocurrency%20thefts

7 Applications of AI for strategic planning and operational efficiency

7.1 Introduction

Operational effectiveness and efficiency initiatives and efforts are essential to an organization's sustainability to deliver products or services in the most cost-effective manner without compromising quality. It involves improving resource utilization and optimizing resource allocation, streamlining processes, and minimizing operational costs. In today's competitive global market, achieving operational efficiency is vital for maintaining sustainability, profitability, and gaining a competitive edge. Business organizations that excel in this area can reduce their operational expenses, increase productivity, and enhance their overall sustainability performance. Waste reduction focuses on both physical waste, such as materials and by-products, and energy and water waste to minimize the amount of waste generated throughout the production and consumption processes to reduce environmental impacts and improve operational effectiveness. Effective waste reduction strategies are crucial for reducing environmental impact, conserving resources, and complying with regulatory standards. The application of business practices such as implementing waste management systems, recycling, and reusing materials enables organizations to substantially decrease their ecological footprint and contribute to a circular economy.

AI is increasingly recognized as a transformative force in various industries, particularly in the arena of sustainability. As businesses face growing pressures to operate responsibly and reduce their environmental impact, AI emerges as a critical enabler of innovation in SBMs. The integration of advanced AI technologies and data-driven approaches plays an essential role in achieving both operational efficiency and waste reduction. For example, the use of IoT sensors and data analytics allows businesses to monitor and identify inefficiencies, optimize resource consumption in real-time, and implement corrective actions. The use of automation and AI-driven solutions enables organizations to streamline workflows, reduce manual errors, and enhance decision-making processes. Furthermore, innovations in materials science and process engineering contribute to the development of more sustainable practices and technologies. The successful achievement of operational efficiency and waste reduction requires a holistic approach that encompasses

DOI: 10.4324/9781003611981-7

organizational culture, employee engagement, technology integration, and CI. It involves fostering a culture of sustainability where all corporate gatekeepers, from the board of directors to management and employees, are encouraged to contribute ideas, participate in waste reduction initiatives, and embrace efficient practices. Continuous assessment and improvements, and refinement of processes are also vital to ensure that improvements are sustained and that new opportunities for efficiency and waste reduction are identified. From enhancing decision-making and optimizing processes to developing innovative products and fostering collaboration, AI has the potential to reshape industries in pursuit of sustainability goals. As businesses adopt AI-driven strategies, they not only enhance their operational efficiency but also position themselves as responsible corporate citizens committed to creating a sustainable future. This chapter examines sustainability initiatives, strategies, technologies, and best practices for enhancing operational efficiency and reducing waste by addressing the benefits of adopting these practices, the challenges organizations may face, and the role of innovation in driving progress.

7.2 AI-driven innovation in SBMs

In today's challenging global environment, where climate change and resource scarcity present significant threats, businesses are increasingly turning to AI-driven innovation as a crucial strategy for promoting sustainability. AI-driven innovation is transforming SBMs by enabling companies to optimize operations, reduce environmental impact, maintain sustainable performance, and create shared value for stakeholders. Through advanced business analytics, ML, and predictive modeling, AI facilitates real-time decision-making, enhances supply chain transparency, and identifies opportunities for resource efficiency and waste reduction. It empowers businesses to design circular economy strategies, improve ESG performance, and tailor products and services to ever-growing consumer expectations for sustainability. By integrating AI into core business functions, firms can increase operational efficiency and align financial profitability with social and environmental impacts, fostering innovation that supports resilient and future-ready business models. This transformation highlights how AI not only represents a technological advancement but also serves as a vital tool for rethinking business models to embrace more sustainable practices. AI enhances business sustainability by developing efficiencies, fostering innovations, and enabling better resource management, thus playing a critical role in helping businesses meet their sustainability commitments and contribute to a healthier planet.

7.2.1 Sustainable Business Models

SBMs integrate economic, social, and environmental considerations into business operations. SBMs outline how organizations create, deliver, and capture value grounded in sustainable development principles. Unlike traditional models that prioritize profit alone, a business model for sustainability empowers organizations to address sustainability challenges while maintaining profitability. These models aim to create value for the business and a broader range of stakeholders, including society and the environment.[1] A key feature of SBMs is their adoption of the triple bottom line approach, which emphasizes the importance of people (social), planet (environment), and profit (economic), often referred to as the three Ps.[2] With this holistic perspective, SBMs actively engage with various stakeholders, including customers, employees, suppliers, and communities. This engagement promotes a more inclusive approach to value creation, ensuring that the interests and needs of all parties are considered.

Companies can redefine their purpose, products, and processes by focusing on various ecological and social issues, ultimately benefiting the planet. As the world increasingly confronts pressing challenges related to climate change and social inequity, adopting sustainable practices becomes a moral imperative and a strategic necessity for long-term success. SBMs often rely on innovative practices that reduce environmental impact and enhance social benefits, allowing companies to operate in more sustainable ways. Such innovations include creating value from waste, maximizing resource efficiency, and substituting conventional processes with sustainable alternatives. Companies that endorse these models will likely experience numerous benefits, including enhanced reputation, cost savings, regulatory compliance, and greater resilience in an evolving business landscape. Businesses can achieve a competitive advantage by embedding sustainability into the core of their operations, differentiating themselves in the market, and appealing to increasingly environmentally conscious consumers.

SBMs represent a transformative approach to business that seeks to balance profitability with the well-being of society and the environment. They offer numerous advantages for organizations and their stakeholders, including customers, employees, suppliers, communities, society at large, and the environment, fostering loyalty and enhancing their reputation. Embracing sustainability opens doors for innovation and growth, positioning businesses for long-term success in an increasingly eco-conscious marketplace.[3] Companies that prioritize sustainability can tap into emerging markets and consumer segments focused on ethical and sustainable products, leading to potential new revenue streams and opportunities for business growth. However, adopting SBMs presents a challenge for companies that are primarily focused on profitability, especially those with limited resources, short-term financial objectives, or shareholders to consider. Nevertheless, by investing time and resources into sustainability initiatives, businesses can reap long-term benefits from these models while improving their environmental impact.

7.2.2 The role of AI in driving innovation in SBMs

The role of AI in driving innovation in SBMs is essential, as it empowers organizations to rethink traditional value creation processes and integrate business sustainability into their corporate culture, business environment, and core strategies. The use of AI technologies, such as ML, DL, NLP, and computer vision, enables businesses to analyze complex environmental and social data, forecast sustainability risks, and uncover new opportunities for green innovation. By automating decision-making and enhancing operational efficiency, AI supports the development of circular business models, optimizes energy consumption, and facilitates more transparent ESG reporting. Furthermore, AI enables companies to better understand shareholder needs and stakeholder expectations and thus align their products and services with SDGs, ultimately transforming sustainability from a compliance-driven process into a source of competitive advantage and long-term growth. Businesses have significant roles in mitigating the climate crisis and protecting the planet and society. AI is a key tool for businesses to innovate and transform traditional business models for sustainability. The role of AI in driving innovation in SBMs is multifaceted and encompasses various applications and benefits that collectively contribute to a more sustainable operational framework for businesses. This section explores several ways AI contributes to this evolution across various sectors and discusses the multifaceted role of AI in shaping these models and driving forward-thinking practices that align with sustainability objectives.

7.2.2.1 Enhanced decision-making

One of AI's foundational roles in SBMs is enhanced decision-making. AI has the capability to analyze vast amounts of data far beyond human capacity, allowing organizations to extract valuable insights that inform strategic decisions. This data-driven approach promotes operational efficiency by identifying trends, forecasting mismatches in supply and demand, and optimizing resource allocation. AI-driven tools facilitate real-time monitoring and reporting on sustainability metrics, allowing businesses to track their progress toward sustainability goals and make data-informed decisions that align with both corporate responsibility and profitability. The enhanced decision-making role of AI refers to its ability to process vast amounts of structured and unstructured data, identify patterns, and generate actionable insights with speed and accuracy far beyond human capability. AI empowers organizations to make more informed, data-driven decisions by leveraging advanced business analytics, ML algorithms, and predictive modeling. AI-driven tools support strategic planning and operational efficiency for a variety of business activities from financial forecasting and supply chain optimization to personalized marketing and risk assessment. More importantly, AI systems can continuously learn and adapt from new data, enabling dynamic decision-making in complex and rapidly changing environments. This transformative capability of AI improves accuracy and speed and fosters innovation and competitiveness across industries.

7.2.2.2 Business analytics for sustainability

Business analytics plays an essential role in advancing sustainability by providing data-driven insights that support informed decision-making, strategic planning, and sustainability risk assessment and reporting. Business analytics-driven tools can empower organizations to monitor environmental impacts, track resource consumption, and measure progress toward sustainability goals by using descriptive, predictive, and prescriptive analytics. Business analytics tools enable businesses to identify inefficiencies, forecast future sustainability risks, and optimize supply chains for lower carbon emissions and waste. It also supports reliable and transparent ESG reporting and stakeholder communication by turning complex sustainability data into actionable intelligence. By integrating business analytics into sustainability initiatives, organizations can enhance accountability, improve performance, and drive continuous innovation toward more sustainable and resilient operations. AI-driven analytics tools can process real-time data from various sources, including supply chain operations, customer behavior, IoT sensors, and production processes. By integrating data from these diverse channels, companies can gain comprehensive insights into operational performance and resource usage. For instance, organizations can utilize AI to assess energy consumption patterns in their manufacturing facilities, pinpointing areas where efficiencies can be gained, such as timing equipment operations to align with off-peak energy hours. This capability allows organizations to optimize resource allocation, reduce waste, and improve sustainability practices, ultimately leading to lower operational costs and a smaller environmental footprint. Additionally, real-time monitoring facilitated by AI can empower businesses to make informed, data-driven decisions that enhance overall productivity and drive CI in eco-friendly initiatives.

7.2.2.3 Predictive insights

AI algorithms can predict future consumer behavior and environmental impacts, enabling businesses to proactively adjust their strategies. By analyzing historical data and identifying patterns, these algorithms can forecast trends in consumer preferences, particularly regarding sustainable products and practices. For instance, companies can anticipate the demand for sustainable products and adapt their supply chain accordingly, ensuring they have adequate resources to meet this growing demand. This foresight allows businesses to optimize inventory management while also responding swiftly to market changes, thus reducing waste and improving resource efficiency. Furthermore, by leveraging predictive insights, organizations can forecast future resource needs and adjust their material sourcing accordingly, lowering the likelihood of waste and environmental degradation. They can also explore innovative product offerings that align with emerging sustainability trends, cultivating a competitive advantage in an evolving marketplace. Moreover, AI is equipped to simulate climate-related scenarios, helping organizations understand the potential impact of their decisions on sustainability goals. This capacity is particularly important as businesses seek to navigate the complexities of climate change and regulatory compliance. Equipped with precise, data-backed insights, organizations can adopt preemptive measures, minimizing risks and maximizing competitiveness while remaining aligned with sustainable practices.

7.2.2.4 Process optimization

Process optimization is vital for enhancing efficiency, reducing waste, and achieving sustainability performance by identifying bottlenecks and inefficiencies that hinder productivity and increasing environmental impact through analyzing workflows, resource utilization, and performance metrics. By leveraging advanced tools such as AI, ML, and business analytics, companies can automate repetitive tasks, streamline operations, and implement CI strategies to reduce costs and enhance quality, and minimize energy consumption, carbon emissions, and material waste. Process optimization is intended to support sustainable growth by aligning operational excellence with environmental and social responsibility, enabling organizations to deliver greater value with fewer resources. AI significantly contributes to optimizing business processes, resulting in enhanced efficiency and productivity. Recent developments in DL and ML have expanded the scope of conventional, AI data-driven tasks like classifications and predictions to include the creation of original, creative, and realistic content. The adoption of AI has impacted common cooperation between humans and AI systems in a variety of ways, particularly in process optimization. This optimization involves the use of advanced ML algorithms and automation technologies, refining workflows, resource allocation, and operations to enhance efficiency and reduce costs, all while minimizing environmental impacts. Among other benefits, AI-powered automation can eliminate repetitive tasks and optimize workflows within organizations. For instance, in sectors like manufacturing, AI can analyze production line data to identify bottlenecks and inefficiencies.

7.2.2.5 Efficiency gains through automation

AI technologies like ML and automation can enhance operations, enabling more efficient resource usage. For instance, AI can optimize energy use in manufacturing, improve supply chain logistics, promote renewable energy, and help lower the carbon footprint. This initiative ensures the alignment with SDG 7 (Affordable and Clean Energy) and SDG 13 (Climate Action). For example, in relation to Scope 1 emissions, which are direct emissions from owned or controlled sources, AI can help manufacturing facilities optimize their production processes. ML algorithms can analyze energy usage data, identifying inefficiencies in machinery operation and suggesting precise adjustments to reduce fuel consumption and GHG emissions. For Scope 2 emissions, which encompass indirect emissions from the generation of purchased electricity, AI can optimize energy procurement strategies. By utilizing predictive analytics, companies can determine the best times to buy energy based on market trends, ensuring that they procure energy from renewable sources whenever possible, thus lowering their carbon footprint. Finally, AI can enhance supply chain management by addressing Scope 3 emissions, which refer to all other indirect emissions that occur in a company's value chain. By analyzing data from suppliers and logistics, businesses can identify opportunities for reducing emissions through improved logistics routing, selecting more sustainable suppliers, or designing products with lower environmental impacts, ultimately leading to a more sustainable and efficient supply chain. Through these applications, AI not only contributes to process optimization but also significantly advances corporate sustainability goals.

7.2.2.6 Waste reduction initiatives

AI can also drive innovation by identifying opportunities for waste reduction, thus promoting the circular economy. AI tools help in improving waste management processes. For instance, in the retail sector, AI systems manage inventory more effectively, reducing product wastage through better tracking of expiration dates and stock levels. In manufacturing, AI optimizes material usage to minimize waste production. Businesses can then use AI systems to monitor inventory levels in real time, ensuring that materials are used efficiently and reducing the risk of overproduction. Additionally, AI can facilitate sorting processes in recycling operations, enabling more effective materials recovery and ensuring that recyclable materials do not end up in landfills. By integrating AI-driven waste reduction initiatives into their operations, companies can align their processes with sustainable practices in line with SDG 12 (Responsible Consumption and Production), contributing positively to environmental conservation.

7.2.2.7 Innovation in products and services

The development of innovative products and services is another area where AI showcases its impact on SBMs. AI allows businesses to innovate and create new products and services that meet evolving consumer demands. This capability creates new sources of revenue and enhances customer engagement, distinguishing companies from their competitors. AI tools can assist companies in designing products that are more sustainable by simulating materials, lifecycle impacts, and recyclability, leading to innovative, eco-friendly products that meet consumer demand. AI technologies facilitate the creation of sustainable products designed to meet market demand while prioritizing environmental responsibility, aligning with SDG 9 (Industry, Innovation, and Infrastructure).

7.2.2.8 Sustainable design and development

AI can assist businesses in designing products that are more sustainable by simulating the lifecycle impact of materials, processes, and disposal methods. For instance, companies can evaluate different material compositions and their associated environmental impacts before commencing production. This allows businesses to produce goods that not only comply with regulations but also resonate with eco-conscious consumers. Furthermore, AI can enable the creation of new business models centered around circular economic principles. For example, businesses can transition from traditional ownership models to product-as-a-service models, where products are offered on a subscription basis. This approach reduces waste and maximizes resource efficiency, showcasing how innovative thinking can lead to sustainable outcomes.

7.2.2.9 Customized solutions and personalization

AI significantly enhances the ability of businesses to create customized solutions and engage with consumers in more meaningful ways. Unlike traditional business models, which may operate on static strategies, AI-driven models exhibit autonomous learning capabilities, allowing them to adapt in real time to changing market conditions and consumer behaviors. The ability to leverage consumer data allows companies to tailor their offerings based on individual preferences related to sustainability.

7.2.2.10 Consumer engagement and personalization

Customized solutions and personalization are becoming an integral component and key drivers of sustainable business success, as they guide companies to meet individual customer needs while minimizing waste and resource use. Powered by AI and business analytics, businesses can analyze consumer behavior, preferences, and usage patterns to deliver tailored products, services, and experiences. This targeted approach reduces overproduction, lowers inventory costs, and enhances customer satisfaction, trust, and loyalty. In sustainability-centric industries, personalization enables companies to offer eco-friendly alternatives and promote responsible consumption by aligning offerings with customer values. Organizations can foster deeper engagement, drive innovation, and create long-term value for both customers and the planet by integrating customization into their sustainability strategies. Through AI-driven customer segmentation and analytics, companies can understand the specific sustainability preferences of their target audience. This insight enables the development of tailored marketing strategies that resonate with consumers' values, resulting in greater loyalty and trust. For instance, an outdoor apparel brand might leverage AI to analyze customer purchasing behavior, uncovering a segment of environmentally conscious consumers. With these insights, the brand can create targeted marketing campaigns that promote its sustainable product lines, reinforcing its commitment to environmentally responsible practices.

7.2.2.11 Supply chain sustainability

AI enhances sustainability within supply chains, enabling companies to implement more efficient management practices. This optimization enhances logistics and lowers the carbon footprint associated with transportation and warehousing, supporting ethical and environmental standards. AI utilizes predictive analytics and ML to improve forecasting demand accuracy, allowing businesses to predict better what products will be needed and when leading to more effective inventory management. AI-powered tools and techniques can play a vital role in advancing supply chain sustainability by enabling greater transparency, efficiency, and responsiveness across the entire value chain. AI can optimize logistics, reduce waste, and lower carbon emissions by improving demand forecasting, route planning, and inventory management by enabling the use of real-time data analysis, predictive analytics, and ML. AI-powered tools also facilitate supplier risk assessment and monitoring, ensuring compliance with environmental and social standards. By integrating sustainability metrics into decision-making processes, AI technologies enable organizations to identify and address inefficiencies, promote ethical sourcing, and align their operations with global sustainability goals. Thus, AI supports the transition toward more profitable, resilient, and environmentally responsible supply chains.

7.2.2.12 Traceability and transparency

Traceability and transparency are essential to building trust, responsibility, and accountability in sustainable business practices. Organizations can track the origin, movement, and environmental and social impact of products across the entire supply chain by leveraging technologies such as blockchain, AI, and IoT. This visibility process enables businesses to verify compliance with ethical sourcing, labor standards, and environmental regulations, while empowering consumers to make informed choices. Transparency fosters stakeholder confidence and trust, mitigates reputational risks, and supports more accurate ESG disclosures. As sustainability becomes a competitive differentiator, traceability and transparency are becoming operational imperatives and strategic tools for enhancing brand integrity, regulatory alignment, and long-term resilience. The integration of AI technologies within supply chains facilitates greater traceability, enabling companies to monitor and verify the ethical sourcing of raw materials. Blockchain technology, in conjunction with AI, will allow businesses to create transparent supply chains that track the whole lifecycle of a product from its creation and flow from raw material source to production, logistics, and delivery to the final customer. This level of transparency builds consumer trust and ensures suppliers are held accountable for their sustainability practices. Another significant application of AI in supply chain sustainability is for monitoring compliance with environmental regulations. This is the most important thing to help companies navigate complex legal landscapes and avoid financial penalties while simultaneously fostering a culture of sustainability across their operations.

7.2.2.13 Risk assessment and management

Risk assessment and management are fundamental components of sustainable business strategy, enabling organizations to identify, evaluate, and mitigate potential threats to their economic viability as well as ESG performance. The use of AI-powered tools and advanced business analytics empowers organizations to conduct more accurate and proactive risk assessments by analyzing large volumes of data to detect patterns, forecast disruptions, and model various scenarios. Effective risk management safeguards assets and ensures continuity and supports strategic decision-making and resilience. Thus, organizations can better navigate uncertainties, enhance stakeholder trust, and drive long-term value creation by embedding sustainability considerations into risk frameworks. AI can analyze multiple types of data, including text, images, audio, video, and structured data from databases, allowing the extraction of insights and patterns from diverse sources, effectively. This AI aspect is instrumental in risk management related to supply chain sustainability, where advanced AI algorithms can identify potential risks such as disruptions caused by climate events, resource scarcity, or regulatory changes. This analytical power enables businesses to anticipate and identify potential risks that could impact their supply chains. For instance, AI algorithms can sift through climate data to forecast disruptions caused by natural disasters, such as hurricanes or floods, that might affect suppliers or transportation routes. By recognizing these risks in advance, companies can take appropriate measures to mitigate potential disruptions. This foresight allows businesses to develop adaptive strategies that enhance supply chain resilience, ensuring continuity of operations even in the face of uncertainties.

7.2.2.14 Collaboration and partnerships

The complexity of sustainability challenges often necessitates collaboration among various stakeholders. Collaboration is essential for driving this shift. Businesses, research organizations, and government entities increasingly work together to tackle sustainability challenges. AI encourages the formation of ecosystems that foster partnerships between businesses, startups, NGOs, and research institutions, ultimately driving innovative sustainability solutions. This approach brings together diverse expertise, allowing for innovative solutions that use AI in impactful ways. For instance, partnerships between companies such as Microsoft and Cisco have led to the creation of cloud-based AI tools that help organizations monitor and enhance their energy consumption throughout the supply chain. By sharing insights and strategies, these collaborations foster an environment conducive to innovation, benefiting individual companies while contributing to broader societal goals.

7.2.2.15 Ecosystem development

Ecosystem development plays an essential role in fostering sustainable innovation and growth by creating collaborative networks of stakeholders, including investors, businesses, governments, academia, and civil society that work together toward shared sustainability goals. These ecosystems enable the exchange of knowledge, the use of technology, and resources to accelerate the development and scaling of sustainable solutions. AI and digital platforms further improve ecosystem effectiveness by enabling real-time data sharing, coordinated decision-making, and transparent communication. Organizations can co-create value, drive systemic change, and address complex environmental and social challenges through such interconnected systems. Thus, ecosystem development supports resilient, inclusive, and adaptive business environments that promote long-term sustainability and shared prosperity. AI enables organizations to share data and insights, creating a collaborative environment that promotes innovation. By working together, stakeholders can co-create sustainable solutions that leverage each participant's expertise. This collective approach can lead to breakthroughs in sustainable technologies, products, and practices that would be difficult to achieve in isolation. Collaboration can also extend to the realm of community engagement. Companies can utilize AI to analyze local environmental conditions and consumer sentiments, allowing them to implement initiatives that resonate with community goals and values.

7.2.2.16 Enhanced customer interaction

Enhanced customer interaction is important to sustainable business practices by fostering deeper engagement, trust, and loyalty while aligning brand values with consumer expectations. Organizations can deliver personalized, real-time communication that addresses individual customer needs and preferences by leveraging AI, chatbots, and business analytics tools to improve customer satisfaction, encourage responsible consumption, and promote sustainable products. Transparent and interactive engagement empowers customers to make informed choices and become active participants in promoting business sustainability. AI is a valuable tool for enhancing customer interaction by personalizing experiences and fostering greater engagement with sustainability initiatives. Through several mechanisms, such as personalized communication, gamification, and interactive platforms, AI not only enhances customer interactions but also promotes a deeper engagement with sustainability initiatives. This personalized approach and continued support can lead to improved engagement and a sense of connection between the brand and the customer, resulting in loyal customers who feel a strong connection to the brand and its values, and contributing to a more sustainable future.

7.2.2.17 AI-driven customer service solutions

AI-powered chatbots and virtual assistants can facilitate real-time interactions with customers, providing information regarding sustainability practices and eco-friendly products. This real-time engagement enables businesses to educate consumers about their sustainability efforts, fostering transparency and trust. In addition, providing instant information demonstrates businesses' commitment to sustainability and encourages customers to participate in related initiatives. AI can also analyze customer feedback and sentiment related to sustainability initiatives, providing valuable insights to refine product offerings and enhance engagement strategies. This helps companies identify areas of strength and opportunities for improvement. Businesses can refine their sustainability efforts and communicate those changes effectively by actively listening to customer opinions, creating a cycle of engagement and responsiveness. The quick response to consumer concerns and preferences will build loyalty and drive the adoption of sustainable practices.

7.2.2.18 Regulatory and compliance support

Compliance with environmental regulations is critical for businesses aiming to advocate for sustainability, as these regulations are designed to protect the environment and promote responsible resource use. AI-powered solutions can play a pivotal role in regulatory and compliance support, assisting organizations in navigating complex legal landscapes, ensuring adherence to standards, and minimizing risks. GenAI enhances the entire regulatory compliance process by making understanding more accessible, assessing impacts more comprehensively, and facilitating the efficient implementation of necessary changes. This technology empowers businesses to navigate the complexities of environmental regulations while promoting sustainability through informed decision-making and agile responses. It encompasses various applications, such as monitoring regulatory changes, automating compliance checks and reporting, and providing insights for proactive risk management.

7.2.2.19 Automated compliance monitoring

AI systems can be designed to automatically track compliance with environmental regulations, alerting businesses to any discrepancies or potential violations. GenAI enhances regulatory compliance by improving the understanding of complex regulations, enabling users to ask questions and receive fact-based answers with source citations. It facilitates comparisons of regulations from different countries and accelerates gap assessments by comparing internal policies against regulatory requirements. Additionally, GenAI can assist in implementing changes by updating policies and supporting communication and training through intuitive chat interfaces that help users navigate internal documents related to new regulations. This combination of capabilities fosters a more informed and adaptive organizational culture, ensuring swift identification of compliance areas and effective implementation of necessary changes.

7.2.2.20 Reporting and disclosure

Sustainability reporting faces challenges in navigating complex frameworks, analyzing unstructured data, and tailoring results for various stakeholders. AI can facilitate the collection and analysis of sustainability-related data for reporting purposes. GenAI, particularly text-based applications, can address these issues by summarizing information, processing unstructured data, generating insights, and effectively communicating findings. Although GenAI is efficient and scalable, oversight is essential to validate its output. In contrast, traditional AI focuses on analyzing structured data and optimizing processes. Integration of GenAI with traditional AI offers a comprehensive approach, enhancing the accuracy, efficiency, and depth of sustainability reporting for better stakeholder engagement, understanding, and trust. These data reporting processes can improve transparency and accountability, helping companies in their sustainability efforts while providing stakeholders with accurate and timely information.

7.3 AI-powered circular economy practices

The 21st century is marked by a significant paradox: while we experience unprecedented technological advancements, we simultaneously face severe environmental degradation and resource scarcity. Our current economic model, characterized by a linear "take-make-dispose" approach, has driven decades of growth but is increasingly recognized as unsustainable. This model relies on the assumption of readily available and inexpensive resources, neglecting the finite nature of our planet and the escalating consequences of unchecked consumption and waste generation. The symptoms of this unsustainable system are now glaringly obvious, manifested as overflowing landfills, polluted oceans, climate crises, and biodiversity loss. These urgent issues underline the necessity for a transformative shift in our economic practices.

In response to the challenges posed by the linear economy, the concept of the circular economy has emerged as a compelling and necessary paradigm. Moving beyond the traditional consumption model, the circular economy envisions a systematic approach where resources are utilized for as long as possible. Within this framework, the focus is on extracting maximum value from resources during their utilization and seeking to recover and regenerate products and materials at the end of their service life. This regenerative approach ultimately aims to minimize waste, reduce dependency on finite resources, and decouple economic growth from environmental impact.[4]

However, transitioning from a linear to a circular economy is a complex undertaking. It requires fundamental changes across various sectors, including product design, manufacturing, consumption patterns, and waste management infrastructure. It calls for innovation, collaboration, and a systemic rethinking of how we produce, consume, and dispose of goods and materials. Innovation is a complex social process involving multiple actors and interactions. For understanding and improving innovation dynamics, effective innovation policies are needed, which require improved governance and coordination among different stakeholders, including government agencies, industries, and research institutions.[5] This coordination is essential for navigating the complexities of sustainability transitions. This is where the transformative potential of AI becomes apparent. We will explore how AI is being deployed across various sectors to optimize resource use, reduce waste, and facilitate the shift to a more sustainable and circular economic system. By examining concrete examples and case studies, we will highlight the tangible benefits of AI in achieving the vision of a circular future while also recognizing the challenges and opportunities that lie ahead.

AI, with its ability to process vast amounts of data, identify patterns, optimize complex systems, and automate intricate tasks, is emerging as a critical enabler of the circular economy. It offers a range of powerful tools capable of addressing some of the most significant challenges hindering the widespread adoption of circular practices. From transforming waste management and improving resource efficiency to promoting circular product design and enabling transparent supply chains, AI is set to be the engine driving the circular economy forward. From intelligent recycling robots to AI-powered design tools and transparent supply chain platforms, we will explore the innovative ways in which AI is reshaping our relationship with resources and paving the way toward a truly circular economy.[6]

7.3.1 Waste management and recycling: the AI revolution in waste valorization

One of the most visible and pressing challenges of the linear economy is the sheer volume of waste generated globally. Mountains of discarded materials, from packaging and electronics to textiles and food waste, end up in landfills or incinerators, representing a significant loss of valuable resources and a major source of environmental pollution. Traditional waste management systems, often reliant on manual sorting and outdated infrastructure, struggle to cope with the increasing complexity and volume of waste streams. Recycling rates remain stubbornly low in many parts of the world, and contamination of recyclable materials further hinders effective resource recovery. AI is revolutionizing waste management and recycling by introducing intelligent systems that can dramatically improve efficiency, accuracy, and resource recovery rates. Using ML, computer vision, and robotics, AI-driven solutions are revolutionizing waste management by converting what was traditionally viewed as trash into valuable secondary resources.[7]

7.3.2 AI-Powered sorting: precision and speed in material separation

A fundamental bottleneck in traditional recycling processes is the labor-intensive and often inefficient manual sorting of waste materials. Humans are prone to fatigue, errors, and limitations in identifying and separating different types of recyclables, especially at high speeds. AI-powered sorting systems overcome these limitations by offering unparalleled speed, accuracy, and consistency in material separation. These systems typically employ computer vision technology, which uses cameras and image processing algorithms to "see" and "identify" different types of waste materials on conveyor belts. ML algorithms, trained on vast datasets of images of various waste items, enable the system to recognize materials with remarkable precision, even in complex and mixed waste streams. This capability extends beyond simply differentiating between broad categories such as paper, plastic, and metal; AI can distinguish between different types of plastics (e.g., PET, HDPE, and PVC), various grades of paper, and even identify specific brands or product types based on packaging characteristics.

7.3.3 Use of AMP Robotics in transforming recycling facilities with AI brains

AMP Robotics is a leading example of a company leveraging AI to revolutionize recycling.[8] Their AI-powered robotic sorting systems are deployed in recycling facilities across the globe, dramatically increasing the speed and accuracy of material separation. This company employs AI to recognize and sort different types of recyclables at high speeds, significantly improving recycling rates. Their

AI-powered systems utilize cameras to analyze mixed waste streams and detect various materials. They can distinguish between various materials, ensuring that they are properly sorted and directed to appropriate recycling streams. AMP's technology uses sophisticated computer vision and ML algorithms to identify and sort recyclables at speeds far exceeding human capabilities. Their robots can process up to 80 picks per minute with an accuracy of up to 99%, significantly outperforming manual sorters and achieving higher purity levels of recovered materials. This fully AI-powered platform processes 62,000 tons of single-stream recycling per year.

Their DL systems constantly enhance their ability to identify and classify paper, plastics, and metals based on several features such as color, size, shape, and brand. The AI Vision Microjet utilizes AMP Vision and AMP AI to categorize items based on material type, form factor, color, and polymer. Additionally, it monitors the counts and mass of materials on the belt where the Microjet operates monitored. AMP's systems are not limited to sorting conventional recyclables such as bottles and cans. They can also handle more complex and challenging waste streams, including flexible packaging, film plastics, and even electronic waste. This enhanced sorting capability creates opportunities to recycle materials that were previously considered too difficult or uneconomical to recover, broadening the scope of what can be effectively recycled and contributing to higher overall recycling rates.

Furthermore, AMP Robotics' systems are designed to be adaptable and continuous learning. Through ML, the AI algorithms become more proficient over time, improving their accuracy and efficiency as they process more data. This continuous learning capability ensures that the sorting systems remain effective even as waste streams evolve, and new materials enter the recycling stream.

7.3.4 Greyparrot—unlocking data insights from waste with AI analytics

Beyond robotic sorting, AI is also being used to provide valuable data insights into waste streams, enabling better decision-making and optimizing recycling processes.[9] Greyparrot is a company that specializes in AI-powered waste analytics systems. Its technology uses computer vision and AI to analyze the composition of waste streams at sorting facilities, providing detailed data on the types and quantities of materials present.

This data is invaluable for waste management operators and policymakers. It can reveal inefficiencies in the sorting process, identify sources of contamination, and track the effectiveness of recycling programs. For example, Greyparrot's analytics can pinpoint specific types of materials that are consistently being missed by sorting systems or identify contamination issues that are hindering the quality of recycled materials. This granular data enables targeted interventions to improve sorting processes, reduce contamination, and ultimately increase the recovery of valuable resources from waste.

Greyparrot's Analyzer provides complete visibility into waste composition, revealing a new, smarter level of insight referred to as waste intelligence. These data insights can be used to inform broader waste management strategies and policies. By providing a clearer picture of the composition of waste streams, policymakers can develop more effective regulations and incentives to promote waste reduction, reuse, and recycling. The data can also be used to track progress toward circular economic goals and measure the impact of different waste management initiatives.

7.4 Vision AI for waste optimization: Advanced Manufacturing Control Systems vision AI—toward zero waste landfills

Building upon the power of computer vision and AI, Advanced Manufacturing Control Systems has introduced Vision AI, an advanced technology that utilizes computer vision and AI to enhance waste management.[10] This system analyzes waste material streams in real time, automatically detecting and classifying contaminants that commonly compromise the quality of recyclables, such as non-recyclable plastics or food waste. Contamination poses a significant hurdle in recycling, as even minor impurities can diminish the value of recycled materials and increase landfill waste.

Vision AI empowers waste management operators to fine-tune their sorting processes, effectively reducing the amount of contaminated material entering recycling streams. As a result, it facilitates the production of higher-quality recyclables that are more valuable and easier to process. This improvement ultimately leads to increased recycling rates and fosters a circular flow of materials. Additionally, the system offers real-time data analytics on waste composition and quality, providing essential insights that can enhance operational efficiency. These insights help operators monitor sorting system performance, identify areas needing improvement, and track progress toward waste reduction and recycling targets. Moreover, the data derived from Vision AI can inform critical operational decisions, such as modifying sorting parameters or optimizing collection routes, which further helps in minimizing contamination and maximizing resource recovery. Ultimately, Vision AI supports a more efficient and circular waste management system, aiding in the goal of achieving zero waste landfills.

7.4.1 Intelligent recycling systems: robotics and AI and the future of waste recovery

The convergence of AI and robotics is ushering in a new era of intelligent recycling systems, transforming waste recovery and recycling processes from largely manual and inefficient operations to highly automated and optimized systems. AI-driven waste management technology and robotic solutions do more than just automate sorting; they signify a fundamental shift in our approach to waste as a resource. AI's ability to identify material types, compositions, and optimal recycling pathways is central to these intelligent systems. By analyzing data from sensors, cameras, and other sources, AI algorithms can "understand" the characteristics of waste materials in real time, making informed decisions about how to sort, process, and recover them. This extends beyond simple material identification to include assessing material quality, identifying contaminants, and even predicting the best recycling method for specific items.

Robotics provides the physical capability to execute AI decisions. Robotic arms equipped with advanced grippers and sensors can precisely pick and place different types of waste materials, guided by the AI's analysis of the waste stream. This combination of AI brains and robotic hands enables the creation of highly flexible and adaptable recycling systems that can handle a wide variety of waste streams and materials with minimal human intervention.

7.4.2 ZenRobotics—pioneering AI-powered robotic waste sorting[11]

ZenRobotics is a pioneer in AI-powered robotic waste sorting, assisting operators across more than 15 countries globally to derive greater value from waste, obtain actionable data, and achieve their ambitious circular economy targets. Their systems combine sophisticated AI algorithms with robust robotic arms to automate the sorting of recyclables from mixed waste streams. ZenRobotics' systems are designed to be highly flexible and adaptable, capable of handling a wide range of waste types, from construction and demolition waste to municipal solid waste and commercial waste.

The key advantage of ZenRobotics' approach is its ability to recover recyclables from complex and heterogeneous waste streams with greater flexibility and efficiency than traditional methods. Their AI algorithms can identify and sort a wide variety of materials, including wood, concrete, metal, and different types of plastics, even when these materials are mixed together or contaminated. This allows for higher recovery rates of secondary materials and improved purity of the recovered fractions, making them more valuable for reuse and recycling.

Furthermore, ZenRobotics' systems are designed for continuous operation and require minimal human supervision. This reduces labor costs, improves safety, and increases the overall efficiency of recycling operations. The data generated by the AI system also provides valuable insights into waste stream composition and sorting performance, enabling operators to optimize their processes and track their progress toward circular economy goals. ZenRobotics exemplifies how AI and robotics are transforming waste recovery, paving the way for more efficient, sustainable, and resource-conscious waste management systems.

7.5 Resource efficiency: optimizing production and consumption—AI for minimizing resource footprints

Resource efficiency, using fewer resources to produce more goods and services, is a cornerstone of the circular economy. In a world facing resource depletion and environmental pressures, optimizing resource utilization across all sectors is crucial. AI is emerging as a powerful tool for enhancing resource efficiency, offering the ability to analyze complex systems, identify inefficiencies, and implement optimization strategies that can significantly reduce resource consumption and waste generation.

7.5.1 AI-Driven analytics for resource optimization: unveiling hidden inefficiencies

AI-driven analytics are transforming how businesses manage resources. By analyzing vast amounts of data from various sources, such as production processes, supply chains, energy consumption, and equipment performance, AI can identify patterns, anomalies, and inefficiencies that are difficult or impossible for humans to detect manually. These insights can then optimize resource use, reduce waste, and enhance overall operational efficiency.

AI analytics can be applied across various industries and processes. In manufacturing, AI analyzes production data to identify bottlenecks, optimize machine settings, and predict equipment maintenance needs, thereby minimizing downtime and resource waste. In energy management, AI can analyze energy consumption patterns to identify areas of energy waste and optimize energy usage in buildings, industrial processes, and transportation systems. In supply chain management, AI can analyze material flows, transportation routes, and inventory levels to optimize logistics, reduce transportation costs, and minimize material waste.

7.5.2 Siemens' Amberg Electronics plant—the digital factory powered by AI[12]

Siemens' Amberg Electronics Plant in Germany is a showcase example of how AI can be used to drive resource efficiency in manufacturing. This highly automated factory, often referred to as a "digital factory" or "Industry 4.0" facility, leverages AI extensively to monitor production in real-time, predict equipment maintenance needs, and optimize resource use across various processes.

AI is used to analyze data from sensors embedded throughout the production line, providing a comprehensive view of the entire manufacturing process. This real-time monitoring enables early detection of potential issues, such as equipment malfunctions or deviations from optimal process parameters. AI algorithms can predict equipment maintenance needs based on historical data and real-time performance indicators, allowing for proactive maintenance interventions that prevent costly breakdowns and minimize production downtime.

Furthermore, AI optimizes resource use by analyzing production data to identify areas of inefficiency and waste. For example, AI can optimize material flow, minimize scrap rates, and optimize energy consumption during production. By continuously monitoring and optimizing resource utilization, Siemens' Amberg plant has achieved significant reductions in waste generation, energy consumption, and production costs, while simultaneously improving product quality and production efficiency. This example demonstrates the transformative potential of AI-driven analytics for achieving resource efficiency in complex industrial settings.

7.6 Energy efficiency: visualizing data flows for informed decisions

Energy efficiency is a critical component of resource efficiency and a key pillar of the circular economy. Reducing energy consumption conserves valuable resources, mitigates GHG emissions, and reduces environmental impact. AI can significantly promote energy efficiency by providing visual tools that offer comprehensible insights into data flows related to products, resources, and processes.

Visualizing complex data flows related to energy consumption helps businesses and individuals understand usage patterns, identify areas of waste, and make informed decisions to enhance efficiency. AI-powered tools analyze energy data from smart meters, sensors, and other sources, presenting it in intuitive visualizations that highlight consumption patterns, identify peak demand periods, and pinpoint energy-intensive processes or equipment.

These visual insights can empower users to take targeted actions aimed at reducing energy consumption. For example, visualizations can reveal energy waste in specific areas of a building, enabling facility managers to optimize HVAC systems or identify energy-inefficient equipment for replacement. In industrial processes, visualizations can highlight energy-intensive steps, allowing process engineers to optimize parameters and decrease energy consumption. By making energy data more accessible and easier to understand, AI-powered visual tools can drive behavioral changes and support informed decision-making toward greater energy efficiency.

7.6.1 AI in a Belgian Windfarm—Boosting renewable energy injection[13]

An AI-powered tool implemented at a wind farm in Belgium illustrates AI's potential to boost energy efficiency and optimize the use of renewable energy sources. This tool employs AI algorithms to assess weather patterns, analyze wind turbine performance, and evaluate grid conditions, enhancing the integration of renewable energy into the grid.

Wind power is inherently variable, depending on wind conditions. However, the electricity grid requires a stable and predictable supply of energy. AI can help bridge this gap by predicting wind power generation and optimizing the timing and amount of energy injected onto the grid. By analyzing weather forecasts and wind turbine performance data, the AI tool can anticipate fluctuations in wind power generation and adjust grid connection parameters to maximize the utilization of available wind energy.

In the Belgian windfarm example, the AI tool increased the amount of renewable energy injected into the grid by optimizing the windfarm's operation and grid connection strategy. This resulted in a significant increase in renewable energy utilization, reducing reliance on fossil fuels and contributing to a cleaner and more sustainable energy system. This example highlights the potential of AI to enhance energy efficiency in renewable energy generation and optimizes the integration of renewable energy sources into the grid.

7.6.2 Applications of AI for resource efficiency: expanding the scope of optimization

Applications of AI for resource efficiency are expanding the scope of optimization across industries by enabling smarter, data-driven management of energy, materials, and processes. AI technologies of ML, neural networks, and RL can analyze complex systems in real time to identify inefficiencies, predict resource demand, and optimize usage patterns. In manufacturing, AI helps minimize waste and energy consumption by fine-tuning production schedules and equipment maintenance. In agriculture, AI optimizes water and fertilizer use through precision farming techniques. In energy systems, AI balances supply and demand to reduce losses and integrate renewable sources more effectively. By expanding the boundaries of traditional optimization, AI is transforming how resources are allocated, conserved, and sustained for long-term environmental and economic benefits.

Overall, in addition to manufacturing and energy, AI is utilized to enhance resource efficiency across various sectors and applications.

Water Management: AI can optimize water usage in agriculture, industry, and urban water systems by analyzing sensor data, weather patterns, and demand forecasts to optimize irrigation schedules, detect leaks, and manage water distribution networks more efficiently.

Transportation: AI can optimize transportation routes, traffic flow, and logistics operations to reduce fuel consumption, minimize emissions, and improve the efficiency of transportation systems. AI-powered route optimization algorithms can find the most efficient routes for delivery trucks, while AI-based traffic management systems can optimize traffic flow in urban areas, reducing congestion and fuel waste.

Building Energy Management: AI can optimize energy consumption in buildings by analyzing sensor data, occupancy patterns, and weather conditions to automatically adjust heating, cooling, and lighting systems, minimizing energy waste and maximizing occupant comfort.

Agriculture: AI can optimize the use of fertilizers, pesticides, and water in agriculture by analyzing soil conditions, weather patterns, and crop health data to deliver precisely when and where they are needed, minimizing resource waste and maximizing crop yields.

7.7 Circular product design: designing for longevity and end-of-life—AI as a design partner for circularity

Circular economy principles are most effective when applied at the product design stage. Designing products with circularity in mind from the outset is crucial for maximizing their lifespan, enabling repair, upgrades, and reuse, and facilitating end-of-life recycling and material recovery. AI is emerging as a powerful design partner, providing tools and insights that help businesses create products that are inherently more circular, durable, and resource-efficient.

7.7.1 AI-powered design tools: guiding designers toward circularity

AI-powered design tools assist businesses in embedding circular economy principles into their product development processes. These tools use AI algorithms to analyze extensive datasets of material properties, supply chain information, product performance data, and customer usage patterns, offering designers valuable insights and recommendations for creating more circular products.

AI can assist designers in various aspects of circular product design, including:

- **Material Selection:** AI can analyze material databases to identify materials that are durable and recyclable and have a lower environmental footprint. It can also consider factors such as material availability, cost, and supply chain risks.
- **Design for Disassembly:** AI can guide designers in creating products that are easily disassembled at the end of their life, facilitating component reuse, repair, and material recycling. AI algorithms can analyze product designs and identify opportunities for modularity and simplified disassembly.
- **Product Lifetime Extension:** AI can help designers create products that are more durable, repairable, and upgradeable, extending their lifespan and reducing the need for premature replacement. AI can analyze product usage patterns and identify design features that contribute to product longevity.
- **Optimization for Recycling:** AI can assist designers in selecting materials and design features that enhance recyclability and minimize contamination during the recycling process. AI algorithms can analyze recycling processes and identify design factors that impact recyclability.

7.7.2 Material selection with AI: choosing the most circular materials

Material selection is a critical decision in product design, significantly influencing product circularity and environmental impact. AI can play an essential role in guiding designers toward choosing the most circular materials by analyzing extensive datasets on material performance, supply chain logistics, and customer usage patterns.

AI algorithms can analyze material databases containing information on material properties, environmental impacts (e.g., embodied energy, carbon footprint, and toxicity), recyclability, durability, cost, and availability. By considering these factors holistically, AI can help designers identify materials that are not only functionally suitable for the product but also align with circular economy principles.

For example, AI can help designers choose recycled materials, bio-based materials, or materials with a high recyclability rate. It can also analyze supply chain data to identify materials with shorter transportation distances or lower supply chain risks. Furthermore, AI can consider customer usage patterns and product lifecycle data to recommend materials that are durable and suitable for the intended application, minimizing premature product failure and material waste.

7.7.3 Modular design and AI: building blocks for circularity

Modular design, the approach of designing products as assemblies of independent modules that can be easily assembled, disassembled, and replaced, is a key strategy for circular product design. Modular products are easier to repair, upgrade, and repurpose, extending their lifespan and reducing waste generation. AI is being used to develop modular components and optimize modular product designs for circularity.

AI can assist in the design of modular components by analyzing product functionality, usage patterns, and end-of-life scenarios. AI algorithms can identify optimal module boundaries, design interfaces for easy assembly and disassembly, and optimize module designs for specific functions and performance requirements. In industries such as electronics and construction, where product complexity and material diversity are high, modular design is particularly relevant for promoting circularity.

For example, in electronics, AI can help design modular smartphones, laptops, or appliances where key components such as batteries, screens, or processors can be easily replaced or upgraded, extending the product's lifespan and reducing electronic waste. In construction, AI can assist in designing modular buildings or building components that can be easily disassembled, reused, or repurposed at the end of their life.

7.7.4 Example: Accelerated Metallurgy—AI for circular metal alloys

The "Accelerated Metallurgy" project[14] provides a compelling example of how AI can be used to develop novel metal alloy combinations that are specifically designed for circular economy principles. This project used AI and ML techniques to accelerate the discovery and design of new metal alloys with enhanced performance and circularity characteristics.

The project focused on designing alloys that are non-toxic, designed for use and reuse, have longer use periods, and can be made using additive manufacturing and processing methods that minimize waste. AI algorithms were trained on vast datasets of material properties, alloy compositions, and processing parameters to predict the properties of new alloy combinations and optimize their design for circularity.

The "Accelerated Metallurgy" project demonstrated the potential of AI to significantly accelerate the development of new materials that are specifically tailored for circular economy applications. By using AI, researchers were able to explore a much wider range of alloy compositions and design parameters than would be possible using traditional trial-and-error methods, leading to the discovery of novel alloys with enhanced circularity characteristics. This project highlights the transformative potential of AI in materials science for advancing the circular economy.

7.8 AI for climate change, sustainability, and energy optimization

AI has emerged as an important tool in addressing the challenges of climate change. Climate modeling is the use of ML algorithms to enhance the accuracy of predictions related to climate patterns and dynamics. AI significantly advances the development of low-carbon technologies and strategies, thereby accelerating the transition to sustainable practices.[15] AI has the potential to handle climate change by improving governance practice, enhancing policy coherence, and supporting global efforts to understand and manage its complex challenges.[16] The adoption of AI tools enables firms to evaluate and disclose their emissions more effectively as businesses increasingly recognize the financial implications of climate risks. Additionally, AI enables organizations or firms to benchmark and analyze ESG criteria. The integration of ML algorithms in financial reports' text analysis has indicated the insights of firms' new environmental strategies.[17] AI models also show significant potential in resource management related to climate adaptation. For example, DL methods are being applied to optimize disaster response parameters by predicting resource needs based on fluctuating demand.[18]

In agriculture, AI plays a pivotal role by facilitating the development of climate-resilient crop varieties. AI systems' ability to analyze genetic data allows for rapid identification of traits associated with drought resistance, pest tolerance, and disease resistance, thereby expediting the breeding of crops suited for changing climatic conditions.[19]

In terms of environmental monitoring, AI can improve modeling accuracy for various climate scenarios by processing extensive datasets, aiding policymakers in developing more effective strategies for climate mitigation.[20] AI can monitor environmental changes, assisting in the assessment of ecosystems' resilience against climate threats and enabling timely interventions.[21]

Moreover, AI has the potential to enhance public health responses to climate change by predicting health outcomes related to environmental factors. This capability empowers health professionals and policymakers to devise strategies that mitigate the health impacts of extreme weather events and shifting disease vectors due to climate change.[22] The integration of AI in public health could not only improve outcomes but also strengthen community resilience through better resource management and response strategies.[23]

Finally, there are ethical concerns about applying AI to climate change. As AI systems become integral in decision-making, considerations related to fairness, transparency, and data privacy must be addressed to ensure equitable outcomes.[24]

7.9 Lean manufacturing and green supply chains

The concept of lean management is very relevant to business sustainability. There are three guiding principles of lean management as related to business sustainability: (1) promoting the main objective of creating shared value for all stakeholders; (2) implementing CI of identifying strengths and concerns and finding ways to consciously improving sustainability performance; and (3) eliminate waste and duplication by optimizing the use of resources and restructuring, reengineering, and integrating activities. The lean management concept makes an explicit link between cost management (cost centers) and performance management (revenue centers) as they are affected by managerial strategy. Lean management is a process of examining the efficiency and effectiveness of business sustainability strategies. Two managerial concepts of cost management, relevant to the cost centers and performance management relevant to revenue centers, are interdependent and should be integrated in achieving lean management and operational objectives and effectiveness. Lean management and AI can work in parallel to enhance efficiency, reduce waste, and improve decision-making in organizations. Lean management focuses on streamlining processes, maximizing value by minimizing waste, and improving quality. AI can take this approach to a new level by automating repetitive tasks, optimizing supply chains, and providing data-driven insights for CI. Lean management and AI can be integrated in several ways including: (1) AI platforms can analyze historical data to predict demand trends, helping avoid overproduction (a primary Lean waste) and maintain just-in-time inventory levels, reducing holding costs and waste; (2) AI-enabled robotics and software automation streamline repetitive tasks on the production line or in back-office functions that contribute to lean management; (3) AI algorithms can identify defects in products with high precision by detecting anomalies early to maintain quality standards while minimizing the waste of rework or scrap; (4) AI platforms can assist in focusing on fast, informed decision-making by providing real-time analytics, offering insights into production line efficiency, equipment performance, and supply chain disruptions; (5) AI can better match workers' skills to tasks that maximize productivity and reduce downtime by optimizing staffing based on skill sets and project demands, and organizations can achieve lean management goals of utilizing resources effectively; (6) AI algorithms can anticipate equipment failures based on historical data and sensor readings, allowing for timely maintenance to minimize downtime and extend the lifespan of machinery that contribute to the achievement of goals of lean management. Overall, integration of AI into lean management strategies can accelerate CI efforts by creating the synergy between AI and lean management to ensure a proactive approach to process optimization and performance improvement that keeps pace with dynamic market needs.

A survey of 384 experts suggests that: (1) with an increase in green manufacturing, the sustainability performance of organizations can be enhanced significantly; (2) green manufacturing significantly enhances sustainability performance, while the impact of customer cooperation remains inconclusive, indicating a complex relationship that warrants further exploration; and (3) there is a potential for AI to optimize green manufacturing processes and inform strategies for compliance with institutional pressures.[25] Another study examines the amount of green supply chain methods adoption and how they are affecting corporate performance, finds that the green supply chain practices have a major effect on the economic, environmental, and social performance of businesses, and suggests that AI can be leveraged to optimize GSCM practices, enhancing resource efficiency and sustainability in manufacturing.[26] A review of literature on GSCM suggests that: (1) more attention needs to be given to the supply chain network to combat environmental degradation; (2) with rising discourse on items such as global warming and biodiversity, pressure on firms to improve their environmental practices in mounting; (3) stakeholders are more aware of these issues as well which adds to the need for adjustment to environmental procedures by companies; and (4) there is a need for companies to change their environmental procedures and improve performance by using AI-driven technologies.[27]

7.9.1 Continuous improvement

CI strategies involve classifying university activities into four categories: value-adding, non-value-adding, essential, and nonessential. This approach has traditionally been used by business organizations.[28] The focus on CI has become more crucial for business sustainability. Advanced technological innovation, including AI algorithms, enables CI to gain a competitive advantage and maintain sustainability. CI can enable businesses to classify their activities into four categories, as explained in the following subsections.

7.9.1.1 Highest value-adding and essential

These activities add value to the company's main purpose and mission of offering high-quality products and services that are essential in maintaining the continuity and sustainability of the business. They generate financial ESP and nonfinancial ESG performance. Highest value-adding and essential activities are core tasks that directly contribute to an organization's mission, strategic objectives and planning, customer satisfaction, financial viability, and competitive advantage. AI-powered tools promote these activities that typically involve high-level decision-making, innovation, relationship management, and the delivery of products or services that meet or exceed customer expectations. Examples include product design, strategic planning, customer engagement, and the development of new business models or technologies. These functions require creativity, critical thinking, and domain expertise that are often difficult to automate and vital for long-term success. Organizations prioritize these activities to drive growth, enhance differentiation, and build sustainable value, often leveraging AI and advanced analytics to augment human capabilities and maximize impact.

7.9.1.2 High value-adding but less-essential

These are activities that are considered value-adding but not necessarily revenue-generating. Through reengineering and restructuring, they may be reduced without losing the value-added feature. Businesses should consider optimizing these activities. High value-adding but less-essential activities are those that significantly enhance organizational performance or customer experience but are not critical to the core functioning or immediate survival of the business. These activities often include advanced data analytics, marketing innovation, brand building, and employee development initiatives. While they contribute to long-term growth, competitive positioning, and organizational resilience, they can be temporarily scaled back or restructured during periods of resource constraint without jeopardizing basic operations. Leveraging AI in these areas can amplify their value by uncovering hidden opportunities, improving targeting precision, and streamlining creative processes, thus enabling organizations to sustain momentum in innovation and growth while maintaining flexibility in resource allocation.

7.9.1.3 Low value-adding but essential

These are activities that do not add value but are essential, which do not contribute to the creation of customer value or competitive differentiation, but are necessary for the smooth functioning of operations and compliance within an organization. These activities often include administrative duties, data entry, routine reporting, regulatory compliance checks, and internal documentation processes. Though they may not enhance the product or service offering, neglecting them can lead to operational disruptions, legal issues, or inefficiencies. With the advent of automation and AI, organizations are increasingly seeking to streamline or delegate these tasks to intelligent systems, thereby freeing up human resources to focus on more strategic, value-generating functions while maintaining the reliability and integrity of foundational processes. Examples of these activities are the maintenance of manufacturing facilities, which is essential in maintaining the sustainability of manufacturing facilities.

7.9.1.4 Lowest value-adding and less-essential

Lowest value-adding and less-essential activities are tasks that contribute minimally to an organization's strategic goals, customer value, or operational efficiency, and their absence would likely have little to no immediate impact on performance or continuity. These are activities that typically neither add value nor are considered essential and thus must be restructured, consolidated, or eliminated to ensure continuity and sustainability. These activities often include redundant administrative procedures, outdated reporting practices, or non-critical meetings and communications that consume time and resources without yielding significant returns. While they may persist due to legacy processes or organizational habits, they represent prime opportunities for streamlining, automation, or elimination. Identifying and minimizing these tasks enables organizations to reallocate resources toward more impactful areas, enhance productivity, and foster a more agile and value-driven work environment. An example of these activities is unnecessary administrative staff.

7.9.2 CI and AI

CI, a cornerstone of operational excellence and sustainability, is significantly enhanced by the integration of AI into corporate culture and business environment, which enables organizations to evolve from reactive problem-solving to proactive and predictive optimization. AI systems can continuously monitor performance metrics, identify inefficiencies, and uncover patterns in large datasets that humans might overlook. AI can empower organizations to make incremental and strategic improvements more quickly and accurately by providing real-time feedback, automated insights, and data-driven recommendations. Furthermore, AI facilitates adaptive learning, allowing systems to refine their processes over time based on outcomes and new data inputs. This synergy between AI and CI fosters a culture of innovation, agility, and sustainability across all levels of the organization.

CI and AI are a powerful combination for achieving ongoing improvements in quality, productivity, and customer satisfaction. CI enables incremental improvements rather than radical changes. AI can enhance this approach by enabling data-driven precision, automation, and predictive analytics in driving sustainable growth and operational excellence in organizations. CI and AI are powerful allies in driving sustainable growth and operational excellence in organizations. AI platforms can be leveraged to support and accelerate CI initiatives in several ways including: (1) analyzing vast amounts of data from production, customer feedback, and operations, identifying trends, patterns, and potential areas for improvement that are essential to CI of a deep understanding of current processes to identify inefficiencies; (2) tracking metrics like production speed, quality, and defect rates in real time that provide immediate feedback on process deviations, allowing teams to act quickly to resolve issues and ensure consistent quality; (3) predicting maintenance, forecasting equipment failures based on historical data to keeping operations smooth and prevent costly interruptions that is vital to CI strategies of reducing downtime; (4) identifying optimal process parameters and suggesting ways to improve efficiency, reduce waste, or cut costs and enable business organizations continuously adjust their processes to achieve the best results; (5) analyzing customer feedback from various sources (surveys, social media, reviews) to identify improvement areas based on real-time insights into customer needs and satisfaction to ensure CIs; (6) identifying areas of improvements in employee skills by tracking performance metrics and suggesting tailored training programs; (7) presenting "what-if" scenarios and analyses to ensure CI; (8) enabling companies to collect, analyze, and interpret large volumes of data quickly and accurately, identifying patterns and trends to ensure CI; (9) detecting variations or defects in products with high precision that aligns perfectly with the CI philosophy, ensuring that quality standards; and (10) monitoring workflows to identify bottlenecks and inefficiencies by analyzing real-time data to achieve the objective of continuously refining processes for maximum efficiency.

Overall, the incorporation of AI into CI enables companies to sustain a culture of proactive, data-informed, and customer-focused optimization to contribute to all four categories of CI. This integration can result in a faster, more reliable approach to meeting business objectives, improving sustainability performance, enhancing adaptability, fostering innovation, and gaining an adaptable, data-informed, and automated approach to improvement.

7.10 Sustainability measures and IPA

Sustainability measures and importance-performance analysis (IPA) can be integrated to assess and improve organizational practices and ESG sustainability performance. These two concepts often work together and interact and support each other in many ways including: (1) identifying critical sustainability measures such as carbon footprint reduction, waste management, energy efficiency, social responsibility, and governance measures to select relevant and measurable sustainability indicators that are crucial for making the data meaningful in analysis and decision-making; (2) applying IPA as a tool to identify which aspects of sustainability are most critical by stakeholders (importance) and how well the organization is performing on each measure (performance) to assess areas require more attention or resources as classified into four quadrants of high importance and high performance to high importance and low performance, low importance and low performance, and low importance and high performance; (3) applying IPA to sustainability measures, organizations can achieve CI to ensure that adapting to stakeholder expectations and industry standards and adjusting performance goals and resource allocation based on the IPA matrix help in making strategic improvements to sustainability practices; and (4) enabling transparent communication of sustainability priorities and performance to stakeholders, such as investors, customers, employees, and the public.

For example, the Carbon Working Group (CWG) emphasizes the importance of enhancing energy efficiency across operations. By optimizing energy use, companies can significantly reduce their carbon footprint. This involves implementing advanced energy management systems, conducting energy audits, and investing in energy-efficient technologies. Examples include upgrading to LED lighting, optimizing HVAC systems, and improving insulation in buildings. These measures not only reduce GHG emissions but also lower energy costs, providing financial savings for companies. The CWG's efforts are aimed at making significant strides toward a low-carbon future by prioritizing key sustainability areas and fostering collaboration among diverse industries. By focusing on energy efficiency, renewable energy, waste reduction, sustainable supply chains, carbon offsetting, and stakeholder engagement, the CWG provides a comprehensive approach to advancing sustainability and mitigating climate change.[29]

AI will transform business practices and industries and has the potential to address major societal problems, including sustainability.[30] A critical domain where AI is making substantial contributions is in environmental conservation. For instance, AI can transform environmental sustainability practices through its applications in biodiversity preservation and resource management.[31] Moreover, AI significantly impacts urban environments, contributing to the creation of smart and sustainable cities. AI can integrate with the IoT and big data to enhance urban sustainability.[32] AI facilitates this by providing real-time data analytics, enabling cities to adapt dynamically to environmental changes and resource demands, ultimately paving the way for sustainable urban development.[33]

Environmental sustainability is widespread and includes many trade-offs that challenges are sometimes explained away with overly simplistic, insufficient, and self-interested solutions.[34] Despite its advantages, the integration of AI into sustainability efforts raises ethical and operational challenges that must be addressed. A consolidated approach is necessary to ensure that AI technologies are designed and implemented with sustainability principles in mind.[35] The dual nature of AI's influence requires a focus not only on its sustainability applications but also on reducing the environmental impact of AI technology itself through energy-efficient models and responsible resource usage.[36] AI could be presented as a strategic resource that enables businesses to outperform competitors in achieving sustainability goals through environmental, social, and governmental dimensions. This can include waste optimization or minimization, and accelerating decarbonization efforts, while ensuring commitment to long-term value creation and the company's financial strength. This enables it to successfully implement its sustainability strategies, leading to overall business success.

7.11 Waste minimization and recycling strategies

AI-powered tools can play a transformative role in waste minimization and recycling strategies by helping organizations and cities make recycling processes more efficient and reducing overall waste. AI's role in waste minimization and recycling is centered on enhancing efficiency, accuracy, and sustainability at every stage from waste generation and collection to sorting, recycling, and repurposing. With AI-driven insights and automation, cities and companies can reduce their environmental footprint and progress toward zero-waste and circular economy goals by: (1) recycling facilities to distinguish between various types of waste, such as plastics, metals, paper, and organic material and to improve sorting accuracy, increasing the quality of recyclables and reducing contamination in recycling streams; (2) analyzing historical data on waste generation to forecast future waste production patterns to plan resources, recycling capacities, and disposal methods more effectively, aligning with waste reduction goals and to implement proactive strategies for waste minimization, such as adjusting production volumes, optimizing packaging, or switching to eco-friendly materials based on anticipated waste; (3) optimizing collection routes, schedules, and transportation to ensure that waste is only collected when bins are full, rather than on fixed schedules; (4) designing sustainable products and packaging to simulate material usage and environmental impact, choose sustainable materials, reduce excess packaging, and design products that are easier to recycle; (5) identifying recyclable materials that would otherwise end up in landfills by detecting specific types of plastics, metals, and paper that can be efficiently recovered; (6) tracking and analyzing to enable businesses to adjust inventory levels, pricing, and storage methods to reduce spoilage and overproduction; and (7) optimizing closed-loop recycling, where materials from end-of-life products are used to create new ones to match waste materials with companies that can repurpose them, creating a circular supply chain where waste is minimized, and resources are continuously cycled back into the economy.

AI is reshaping both waste minimization and recycling strategies through innovative technologies that enhance collection, sorting, and management processes. As urban centers grapple with escalating waste generation and challenges to environmental sustainability, AI-powered solutions are emerging as crucial tools for efficient waste handling and resource recovery.

7.11.1 AI in waste minimization

One of the most effective ways to minimize waste generation in the process industry is through process design, modification, and control. AI systems can use large datasets to identify patterns and inefficiencies in waste generation. For instance, ML algorithms can analyze waste composition data to predict the types and quantities of waste. This predictive ability can facilitate better planning and resource management, ultimately reducing the amount of waste that needs to be processed or sent to landfills. However, conventional algorithmic methods often struggle to optimize processes for waste reduction when available information is imprecise, incomplete, or uncertain, and when knowledge is primarily in a symbolic form. In contrast, AI techniques offer a powerful alternative, enabling efficient decision-making and process optimization even in the presence of such uncertainties.[37] One of the most pressing challenges of waste management is food waste, which accounts for a significant portion of global waste generation. The intelligent packaging in supply chain management can help mitigate food wastage.[38]

AI also plays a critical role in developing intelligent waste management systems that leverage IoT technology to streamline waste collection and processing. The combination of IoT and AI can automate waste management practices, significantly improving operational efficiency and reducing costs.[39] For instance, the use of AI algorithms for route optimization in waste collection can minimize fuel consumption by analyzing real-time waste levels in bins and adjusting collection routes accordingly. AI technologies such as innovative AI-driven waste management systems can address global challenges arising from increasing waste generation.[40] This capacity for intelligent decision-making facilitates the development of more sustainable waste management strategies.

In addition, advancements in sorting technologies driven by AI significantly enhance recycling efforts. A predictive intelligence model that utilizes ML algorithms can facilitate waste classification.[41] Additionally, CNNs can be employed to classify waste materials with high accuracy, facilitating more effective recycling processes.[42] The integration of AI in the sorting of municipal waste contributes to meeting the goals of a circular economy by ensuring that valuable materials are recovered and reused, thus minimizing overall waste production and reducing the environmental footprint.

7.11.2 AI in recycling strategies

One of the primary applications of AI in recycling involves the optimization of sorting processes. Smart recycling bins equipped with AI algorithms can detect recyclable materials more accurately compared to traditional methods, significantly improving sorting efficiency.[43] These bins utilize computer vision and ML technologies to identify items as they are disposed of, ensuring that recyclables are properly separated from general waste. By reducing contamination rates, these technologies can enhance the quality of recycled materials and facilitate smoother recycling processes. AI-driven waste management systems can assist in forecasting waste generation and tailor recycling efforts to community needs.[44] Such tailored approaches facilitate more effective recycling strategies that can adapt to dynamic waste streams.

AI enhances the lifecycle management of materials, promoting a transition toward a circular economy. AI can refine recycling processes and predict waste patterns, thus contributing to SRM.[45] The integration of AI in tracking and recovery processes allows businesses to monitor material flows and optimize recycling and reuse initiatives effectively. For instance, AI-driven data strategies support resource recovery, which is essential for the successful implementation of circular business models.[46] Another instance in competitive recycling facing material contamination is AI quality control cost and the manufacturer's waste disposal cost that exhibit a substitutable relationship in promoting the dMRF's AI adoption.[47]

The role of AI in enhancing recycling is particularly evident in the management of electronic waste (e-waste). The recycling of lithium-ion batteries represents a critical challenge due to safety concerns and complex material compositions. AI can significantly improve current battery recycling methods by automating identification, material characterization, and disassembly operations, leading to increased recovery rates and enhanced safety.[48] These AI-driven systems provide opportunities to reduce human error and operational hazards, making the recycling process more efficient and environmentally friendly.

Emerging technologies such as blockchain are being integrated with AI to improve transparency and accountability in recycling efforts. The combination of AI with blockchain facilitates the creation of regulated recycling services, ensuring sustainable practices and fostering trust among stakeholders.[49] This synergy is crucial for enhancing the traceability of materials throughout the recycling process, ultimately driving more responsible consumption patterns.

However, despite these advancements, there are challenges in implementing AI in recycling. Issues related to data quality, scalability, and ethical considerations need to be addressed to enhance the effectiveness of AI systems in real-world applications. The research conducted emphasizes the constraints of integrating AI and information and communications technology into waste management systems, underscoring the need for comprehensive strategies to overcome these hurdles.[50]

7.12 The use of AI in climate change initiatives and regulations

AI-driven technologies are increasingly employed in tackling climate change, particularly in areas of regulation, monitoring, and environmental management. AI-powered tools such as satellite imaging, sensors, and drones are being leveraged in climate change initiatives and regulatory practices in many ways including: (1) collecting large-scale environmental data to track carbon emissions, oceanic changes, deforestation rates, soil degradation, sea-level rise, and biodiversity loss in real-time and to identify environmental threats faster and supports evidence-based policy-making; (2) improving climate forecasts by analyzing historical data and simulating future climate scenarios to understand potential outcomes of different regulatory approaches and set science-based targets aligned with climate goals and assess risks for specific areas, such as flood-prone regions or heatwave-affected urban zones; (3) optimizing the integration and efficiency of renewable energy sources (e.g., solar and wind) to manage energy production and storage based on demand and weather patterns and to balance supply and demand, reducing wastage and supporting regulations aimed at achieving carbon neutrality; (4) monitoring emissions and other environmental metrics to ensure companies comply with regulatory requirements relevant to GHG emissions, waste management, and resource utilization and to automate reporting for ESG disclosures by ensuring accuracy and accountability; (5) analyzing the carbon footprint of materials, production, and logistics to identify inefficiencies, suggest greener alternatives, and ensure compliance with sustainable sourcing regulations; (6) quantifying climate-related risks in financial portfolios to align with regulations that require transparency around climate risks and resilience planning; (7) monitoring carbon markets and ensuring that carbon credits are accurately tracked, preventing fraud and double-counting to predict carbon pricing trends, assist policymakers in setting realistic carbon reduction goals, enable efficient tracking of carbon credits, and help organizations meet regulatory caps or offset requirements; and (8) analyzing public sentiment on climate policies, helping governments understand and shape public opinion to enable policymakers to adjust regulations and public communication based on societal support and concerns. It is expected that AI's role in climate change regulations and initiatives will grow, supporting a systemic shift toward data-driven policies and sustainable business practices that are in compliance with climate goals in combating climate change.

A study examines the role that AI can play in combating issues relating to climate change, including the effort to reach "net-zero" by 2050, and finds that climate leaders want to use AI to combat climate change, but they face obstacles such as insufficient access and a lack of confidence in doing so.[51] Specifically, the key findings of this study are: (1) 87% of climate and AI leaders find that AI to be a helpful tool in combating climate change; (2) 43% of organizations can envision using AI for their own climate change efforts; and (3) over 65% of those respondents in the private sector want governments to provide more support in the use of AI in fighting climate change.[52] Thus, AI-powered tools can play a role in climate initiatives while addressing the barriers to their implementation, emphasizing the need for greater support and collaboration between the public and private sectors.

Another study presents nine different ways the AI can be used to help fight against climate change issues including the ability to predict weather, track icebergs, and identify pollution, and to track how fast icebergs are melting, which can be done 10,000 times faster than any human could do it and to predict when and where climate disasters will occur, which can help both governments and businesses better prepare for when these events strike.[53]

7.12.1 GenAI and climate change and decarbonization

The shadow of a changing climate lengthens across the globe, serving as a stark testament to the accumulating consequences of industrialization and unchecked consumption. From the melting glaciers of the Arctic to the intensified droughts plaguing equatorial regions, the planet sends unequivocal signals.[54] The scientific consensus is clear: anthropogenic GHG emissions are the primary driver of this transformation, and the window for meaningful action is narrowing. Meeting the ambitious targets set by international agreements, most notably the Paris Agreement, necessitates a radical restructuring of our energy systems, industrial processes, and societal behaviors. This is not merely a matter of incremental improvement; it requires a paradigm shift, a comprehensive reimagining of how we interact with our planet. In this context of urgent necessity, a suite of technological advancements is rapidly maturing, offering potentially transformative tools for tackling this multifaceted challenge. Among these, GenAI stands out as a particularly potent force. Emerging from the convergence of ML, NLP, and advanced computational power, GenAI marks a significant leap forward in our ability to process information, generate insights, and automate complex tasks. While the technology is still in its early stages, its potential applications are vast and varied, spanning fields from medicine and materials science to finance and, crucially, environmental management and sustainability.

As climate challenges gain significance, understanding the dynamics that shape our perceptions and actions regarding climate change is essential. The sustainable energy transition involves decarbonizing energy systems, strengthening energy efficiency, and integrating renewable energy sources. Beyond traditional approaches, GenAI transforms this understanding by offering powerful new tools that fundamentally transform both our perception of climate challenges and our responses to them. GenAI opens new pathways to enhance our understanding of climate dynamics; it reshapes our responses by providing unprecedented computational power to simulate future scenarios, generate innovative solutions, and implement targeted interventions at previously unimaginable scales and speeds, bridging the gap between climate awareness and effective action. We will explore the potential of GenAI in contributing to climate change mitigation and accelerating decarbonization efforts, providing a pragmatic assessment, rooted in current research and practical considerations on how GenAI can be strategically deployed to enhance our climate action strategies. We will examine specific applications across strategic planning, sustainability reporting, and operational efficiency, while also addressing the inherent environmental footprint of AI itself and the potential risks associated with its deployment. The aim is to provide a balanced and nuanced perspective, highlighting both the opportunities and the necessary caveats, to inform a responsible and impactful integration of GenAI into the global decarbonization agenda.

7.12.2 Augmenting strategic foresight: GenAI for climate strategy and risk assessment

Developing robust and effective climate strategies in today's complex world is a significant challenge. Organizations, governments, and individuals face a confusing array of information, projections, and potential pathways. Navigating this intricate landscape requires not only deep expertise but also the ability to synthesize large amounts of data, identify emerging trends, and anticipate future risks. This is precisely where GenAI can provide substantial support.

7.12.2.1 Accelerating strategic document creation with GenAI

One of the most immediate applications of GenAI is its ability to speed up the strategic document creation process. Developing comprehensive climate strategies, decarbonization roadmaps, or risk assessments usually requires extensive research, consultation, and drafting, efforts that can be time-consuming and resource-intensive. With its advanced text generation capabilities, GenAI can greatly accelerate these tasks. Picture this scenario: a sustainability team is tasked with creating a five-year decarbonization plan for a multinational corporation. Traditionally, this would take weeks, if not months, of literature reviews, stakeholder interviews, internal workshops, and iterative drafting cycles. Using GenAI tools, the team can input key parameters, organizational goals, industry benchmarks, regulatory landscapes, and technological options and receive a well-structured initial draft document in a fraction of the time. This is not to imply that GenAI can completely replace human expertise; rather, it serves as a powerful assistant, allowing human strategists to concentrate on higher-level tasks such as refining strategic direction, engaging with stakeholders, and ensuring alignment with overarching organizational objectives.

7.12.2.2 GenAI for efficient climate literature review and synthesis

Additionally, GenAI's text summarization capabilities are invaluable in navigating the expanding body of climate-related literature. Scientific reports, policy documents, industry analyses, and news articles are constantly produced, creating an overwhelming flow of information. Staying updated on the latest developments is crucial for informed decision-making, yet the sheer volume of information makes it increasingly challenging. GenAI can efficiently process and summarize these diverse sources, extracting key findings, identifying critical trends, and highlighting areas of agreement and disagreement. This enables strategists to quickly grasp essential insights from a wide range of sources, allowing them to make more informed judgments and adapt their strategies accordingly.[55] For example, consider a policy analyst tasked with understanding the latest IPCC report. Instead of spending days poring over hundreds of pages, they could utilize GenAI to generate a concise summary of key findings, policy recommendations, and areas of uncertainty, enabling them to integrate this information into their policy briefs and recommendations quickly.

7.12.2.3 Enhancing corporate climate risk disclosure analysis

Beyond document creation and summarization, GenAI's text-processing capabilities expand into the vital area of risk assessment. Climate change is fundamentally a risk multiplier, worsening existing vulnerabilities and creating new uncertainties across various sectors. Understanding and mitigating these risks is essential for organizational resilience and long-term sustainability. Furthermore, transitioning to a low-carbon economy requires substantial financial investment in renewable energy and decarbonization technologies. Assessing the financial viability and economic impact of these investments is crucial for accelerating the transition. In recent years, corporate disclosure of climate-related risks has significantly increased, driven by regulatory pressures, investor demands, and a heightened awareness of the financial implications of climate change. These disclosures, often integrated within annual reports, sustainability reports, and dedicated climate risk reports, serve as a valuable source of information about how organizations perceive and respond to climate-related challenges.

7.12.3 Enhancing financial and economic modeling for renewable energy investments

In this context, GenAI is emerging as a powerful tool in financial and economic modeling for renewable energy projects. These projects, often characterized by complex cash flows, long-term horizons, and regulatory uncertainties, require sophisticated financial models to assess their feasibility and attract investment. Traditionally, constructing these models has been a resource-intensive and time-consuming endeavor, demanding specialized expertise and significant implementation cost and effort.[56] GenAI presents the potential to streamline this process dramatically. Innovative GenAI tools are being developed to partially or even fully build financial models for renewable energy projects. By inputting key project parameters, such as technology type, project scale, location-specific resource availability (solar irradiance, wind speed, etc.), anticipated energy prices, and regulatory frameworks, these tools can generate detailed financial models, including projected revenues, operating expenses, capital expenditures, and key financial metrics such as net present value and internal rate of return. Moreover, GenAI can be employed to generate complex scenario plans, exploring the financial implications of different assumptions regarding energy prices, policy changes, and technological advancements. This acceleration of the financial assessment process can significantly speed up investment decisions in renewable energy, channeling capital toward decarbonization projects more rapidly.

7.12.4 GenAI for corporate due diligence in decarbonization

A practical demonstration of GenAI's application in financial analysis can be seen in its growing use for corporate due diligence related to decarbonization investments. Investors and corporate teams are increasingly scrutinizing companies' decarbonization commitments and actions, aiming to identify genuine leaders while mitigating risks associated with greenwashing or inadequate climate action. GenAI is leveraged to enhance this due diligence process in several ways. For instance, GenAI tools can detect anomalies in companies' financial statements that might indicate discrepancies between stated sustainability goals and actual financial performance. By analyzing patterns and relationships in financial data that could be overlooked by human analysts, GenAI can flag potential areas of concern for further investigation. Additionally, GenAI can summarize earnings call transcripts, extracting crucial information about companies' climate-related strategies, investments, and risk disclosures. This quick analysis of qualitative data offers investors a more efficient means to assess corporate narratives surrounding decarbonization. Moreover, GenAI's capability to rapidly analyze vast amounts of unstructured data, such as trade press articles, industry reports, and social media sentiment, provides a broader contextual understanding of companies' sustainability performance and reputation. Organizations like Prewave, while not specifically identified as GenAI platforms in these excerpts, exemplify the broader trend of utilizing AI to identify sustainability risks within supply chains.[57] These platforms use AI to analyze extensive datasets and pinpoint potential environmental and social risks associated with suppliers, allowing companies to make more informed and sustainable sourcing decisions. As GenAI capabilities continue to evolve, we can anticipate even more sophisticated applications in corporate sustainability due diligence, empowering investors and corporate teams to make more informed and impactful decarbonization investments.

7.12.5 NLP for enhanced climate risk disclosure analysis

GenAI-powered text analysis techniques, particularly NLP, can be instrumental in extracting valuable insights from these disclosures.[58] NLP algorithms can be trained to identify and categorize different types of climate risks, such as physical risks (e.g., extreme weather events and sea-level rise), transition risks (e.g., policy changes, technological shifts, and market disruptions), and liability risks (e.g., legal challenges related to climate impacts). By analyzing the frequency, severity, and geographical distribution of these risks across a large corpus of corporate disclosures, we can gain a more comprehensive understanding of the systemic risks posed by climate change to financial markets and the broader economy. For example, to analyze climate risk disclosures from companies in the energy sector, NLP techniques can reveal how different companies assess and disclose risks related to stranded assets (fossil fuel reserves that may become economically unviable due to climate policies or technological advancements), carbon pricing mechanisms, and the growing competitiveness of renewable energy sources. By comparing these disclosures across companies and over time, analysts can identify emerging trends, best practices, and potential blind spots in corporate risk management. This information can prove invaluable for investors seeking to evaluate the climate resilience of their portfolios, for regulators aiming to develop effective climate risk disclosure frameworks, and for organizations benchmarking their risk management strategies against industry peers. Gen AI tools support companies in grasping ESG regulations while ensuring compliance with relevant regulations, monitoring public opinion, adapting to evolving reporting regulations, and enhancing stakeholder trust.

7.12.6 GenAI translates climate science into actionable risk assessments

Additionally, GenAI can help translate complex climate science into actionable risk assessments tailored for specific organizations or sectors. Climate models and projections often generate vast amounts of data, requiring specialized expertise to interpret and apply them to practical decision-making. GenAI can bridge this gap by processing climate model outputs, converting them into plain language risk scenarios, and customizing them for the specific context of an organization. For example, a coastal city facing the threat of rising sea levels could leverage GenAI to analyze climate model projections for its region, generate localized risk maps, and assess the potential impacts on critical infrastructure, population centers, and economic activities. This would empower city planners to make more informed decisions regarding adaptation measures, such as building seawalls, relocating at-risk populations, or investing in climate-resilient infrastructure.

7.12.7 Limitations and the importance of human oversight

However, it is crucial to recognize the limitations and potential biases inherent in GenAI-driven risk assessments. The accuracy and reliability of these assessments depend significantly on the quality and representativeness of the data used for training. If the data is incomplete, biased, or outdated, the resulting risk assessments may be flawed or misleading. Additionally, GenAI algorithms are not inherently objective; they reflect the biases and assumptions present in their training data and design. Therefore, it is essential to ensure permanent human oversight,[59] critically evaluate the outputs of GenAI-based risk assessments, compare them with other information sources, and maintain human oversight throughout the process. The goal is not to replace human judgment with algorithmic certainty but to enhance human capabilities with the analytical power of GenAI, leading to more informed and robust strategic planning and risk management in the face of climate change.

7.13 Optimizing operations and driving decarbonization: GenAI in energy and industry

Beyond strategic planning and reporting, GenAI's capabilities also encompass operational efficiency and decarbonization, especially in energy systems and industrial processes. These industries significantly contribute to GHG emissions, making optimizing their performance essential for achieving ambitious climate goals. GenAI offers a variety of tools to enhance energy efficiency, optimize resource use, and accelerate the adoption of renewable energy sources, directly contributing to decarbonization efforts.[60]

7.13.1 GenAI optimizes complex energy systems

One of the most significant applications of GenAI in this area is the optimization of energy systems. Energy systems, from national grids to industrial facilities and individual buildings, are complex and dynamic, involving numerous interacting variables and constraints. Traditional optimization methods often struggle with this complexity, resulting in suboptimal performance and wasted energy. GenAI, particularly ML techniques, can analyze large amounts of data from energy systems, identify patterns and inefficiencies, and develop intelligent control strategies to optimize energy consumption and minimize waste. For example, consider the optimization of building energy management. Buildings contribute significantly to global energy consumption and GHG emissions. Conventional building management systems typically rely on pre-programmed schedules and rule-based controls, which may not respond effectively to changing conditions or individual occupant needs. GenAI-powered building management systems can learn from historical data, real-time sensor inputs, and weather forecasts to dynamically adjust HVAC systems, lighting, and other energy-consuming devices, optimizing energy efficiency while ensuring occupant comfort. ML algorithms can predict building energy demand, identify opportunities for energy savings, and proactively adjust system settings to reduce energy use.[61] Additionally, GenAI can tailor building environments to individual occupant preferences and needs, further enhancing comfort and productivity while minimizing energy waste.

7.13.2 GenAI integrates and optimizes renewable energy sources

Another crucial application of GenAI in energy systems is the integration and optimization of renewable energy sources. Renewable energy sources, such as solar and wind power, are inherently variable and intermittent, which poses challenges for grid stability and reliability. GenAI can play a key role in managing this variability and maximizing the use of renewable energy. ML algorithms can predict renewable energy generation, forecast grid demand, and optimize the dispatch of various energy sources, ensuring a stable and reliable energy supply while maximizing the penetration of renewables. GenAI can also optimize energy storage systems, such as batteries, to smooth fluctuations in renewable energy generation and provide grid balancing services. Additionally, GenAI can facilitate the development of smart grids, which are more flexible, resilient, and responsive to changing energy demand and supply patterns. GenAI-empowered smart grids can optimize energy flow across the grid, reduce transmission losses, and improve the overall efficiency of the energy system.[62]

7.13.3 GenAI-driven decarbonization technologies

Beyond energy systems, GenAI can also facilitate decarbonization in industrial processes. Industries such as manufacturing, chemicals, and cement production are major emitters of GHG. Optimizing these processes to reduce energy consumption, improve material efficiency, and reduce waste is essential for decarbonizing these sectors. GenAI can be applied to optimize a variety of industrial processes, including process control, equipment maintenance, supply chain management, and product design. For instance, in manufacturing, GenAI can improve production schedules, predict equipment failures, and improve quality control, leading to reductions in energy consumption and material waste. In the chemical industry, GenAI can optimize chemical reactions, reduce feedstock consumption, and minimize byproduct formation, improving process efficiency and reducing environmental impact. In cement production, GenAI can optimize kiln operations, lower clinker consumption, and explore alternative cementitious materials, thereby reducing the carbon footprint of cement production.

Furthermore, GenAI can facilitate the development and deployment of new decarbonization technologies. For instance, ML can accelerate the discovery of new materials for energy storage, solar cells, and carbon capture technologies. GenAI can also optimize the design and operation of carbon capture, utilization, and storage (CCUS) systems, making them more efficient and cost-effective. For example, an LLM integrated with a local knowledge base provided more accurate, professional, and in-depth responses regarding CCUS costs and policies compared to a standalone LLM.[63] This highlights the potential of GenAI, when combined with specific data, to provide targeted and relevant information for decision-making in climate action. Moreover, GenAI can support the development of circular economy models in industry, optimizing resource utilization, reducing waste, and promoting the reuse and recycling of materials. By analyzing complex material flows and supply chains, GenAI can uncover opportunities for circularity and create closed-loop systems that minimize environmental impact and maximize resource efficiency.

7.13.4 GenAI for building energy simulation

In the context of building energy simulation, GenAI offers a particularly innovative application. Building energy simulation is a crucial tool for designing energy-efficient buildings and assessing the performance of building energy systems. However, traditional building energy simulation often relies on historical weather data, which may not accurately reflect future climate conditions under climate change scenarios. GenAI can address this limitation by generating future weather files based on different climate change scenarios. ML algorithms can be trained on climate model projections to generate realistic and spatially specific weather files that accommodate projected changes in temperature, humidity, solar radiation, and other climate variables. These future weather files can then be used in building energy simulations to assess the climate resilience of buildings, design climate-adapted buildings, and optimize building energy systems for future climate conditions. This application of GenAI enhances more robust and forward-looking building design and energy management, ensuring that buildings are not only energy-efficient today but also resilient to the impacts of climate change in the future. However, it is important to recognize that the deployment of GenAI in energy and industry also has its own energy footprint. Training and running complex GenAI models can be energy-intensive, particularly for large-scale applications.[64] Therefore, it is crucial to consider the environmental impact of GenAI itself and to implement strategies to minimize its carbon footprint. This includes using energy-efficient hardware, optimizing algorithms for computational efficiency, and powering GenAI infrastructure with renewable energy sources. The goal is to ensure that the decarbonization benefits of GenAI outweigh its environmental costs, leading to a net positive contribution to climate change mitigation.

7.13.5 Addressing the environmental footprint of GenAI: toward sustainable AI

While the applications of GenAI in climate action are undeniably promising, it is imperative to address the environmental footprint of AI itself. The computational requirements for training and deploying large GenAI models, particularly those based on DL, translate into significant energy and water consumption. Data centers, the physical infrastructure that supports AI, are major energy consumers, and their carbon footprint is a growing concern. Addressing this footprint is not only an ethical imperative but also a practical requirement to ensure the long-term sustainability of AI and its contribution to climate goals. This requires a holistic and collaborative approach involving technology developers, data center operators, energy providers, policymakers, and researchers. Focusing on energy efficiency, renewable energy, water conservation, and transparency will enable GenAI to be an effective asset for climate action and a sustainable solution for a healthier future planet.

7.13.6 Real cases using GenAI for climate change and decarbonization

Walmart has developed AI-powered "Route Optimization" technology as a software-as-a-service solution for other businesses. This logistics tool helps optimize delivery routes, improve trailer packing efficiency, and minimize miles driven, resulting in reduced costs, enhanced efficiency, and greater environmental sustainability. Walmart has successfully implemented this technology in its own operations, leading to a reduction of 94 million pounds of CO_2 emissions by decreasing unnecessary travel. The route optimization solution is available to businesses of all sizes. It boosts efficiency through AI algorithms that generate faster delivery routes and reduce fuel consumption, leading to a smaller carbon footprint and significant environmental benefits.[65]

Microsoft's FarmBeats platform, in collaboration with Land O'Lakes, employs GenAI to assist farmers in implementing precision agriculture practices. The system combines data from satellite imagery, drone footage, soil sensors, and weather forecasts to produce field maps that display soil moisture, nutrient levels, and plant health with meter-level precision. Using this data, the AI provides tailored recommendations for variable-rate application of seeds, fertilizers, and irrigation, enabling farmers to apply resources only where and when they are needed. Utilizing a 7,000-acre research farm in Beltsville, Maryland, the FarmBeats project incorporates advanced sensors, drones, and AI to enhance farming practices. This initiative gathers crucial data on crop conditions, which is then sent to the cloud, allowing farmers to make informed decisions in real time. The pilot program emphasizes cover crops to improve soil quality and sustainability, ultimately fostering a more resilient agricultural system.[66]

The United Kingdom's electricity grid operator, National Grid ESO, implemented an AI system developed with Open Climate Fix that predicts solar generation across the country with more accuracy to help operate a low-carbon electricity system. ESO faces a challenge with renewable energy; sudden cloud cover can significantly reduce solar power generation, prompting grid operators to request that fossil fuel plants overproduce energy for backup. The system processes satellite imagery, weather data, and real-time generation data from sample sites to forecast solar output for the next 48 hours. Insights from this system can help ESO address its main challenge. The company states that the ML developments within the ESO's control room have already resulted in a 33% increase in the accuracy of solar forecasts.[67]

7.14 Energy and water consumption from AI training and inference

The energy consumption of AI mainly arises from the computational power required for training and inference. Training LLMs or complex ML algorithms often involves massive datasets and computationally intensive processes, which require significant energy resources. Inference, the process of using trained models to make predictions or generate outputs, also consumes energy, although typically less than training. The energy intensity of AI depends on several factors, including model architecture, dataset size, the hardware used for computation, and the efficiency of data center infrastructure.

Data centers, where AI computations are performed, are also significant water consumers. Water is primarily used to cool data center equipment, preventing overheating and ensuring optimal performance. In areas with water scarcity, data center water consumption can raise concerns about competition for resources. The water footprint of AI depends on the cooling technology used in data centers, the local climate conditions, and the effectiveness of water management practices.

7.14.1 Strategies to mitigate GenAI's environmental footprint

To mitigate the environmental footprint of GenAI, a multi-faceted approach is required, encompassing technological innovation, operational efficiency, and policy measures. An essential strategy is to improve the energy efficiency of AI algorithms and models. Researchers are actively developing more energy-efficient AI architectures, algorithms, and training techniques. Methods such as model compression, pruning, and quantization can lower the computational requirements of AI models without significantly sacrificing performance, resulting in reduced energy consumption. Additionally, refining the data processing pipeline and minimizing data redundancy can further promote energy savings.

Another key strategy is to enhance the energy efficiency of data center infrastructure. Data center operators are increasingly adopting energy-efficient cooling technologies, such as free cooling, evaporative cooling, and liquid cooling, to reduce water and energy consumption. Optimizing airflow management, improving power distribution efficiency, and utilizing waste heat recovery systems can further boost data center energy efficiency. Additionally, powering data centers with renewable energy sources is a critical step toward decarbonizing AI. Acquiring renewable energy through power purchase agreements or on-site generation can significantly lessen the carbon footprint of AI operations.[68] Leveraging purchasing power to demand carbon-free energy sources serves as a powerful tool for driving the transition to cleaner energy. Organizations that acquire AI services or operate their own data centers can exert pressure on energy providers to increase their renewable energy capabilities and offer carbon-free energy alternatives. By prioritizing suppliers that demonstrate a commitment to sustainability and renewable energy, organizations can incentivize the growth of cleaner energy infrastructure and accelerate the decarbonization of the energy sector.

7.14.2 Adopting water and energy efficiency practices in data centers

Implementing water and energy efficiency practices in data centers is essential. This involves using water-efficient cooling technologies, optimizing water usage for cooling, and recycling or reusing water whenever possible. Energy efficiency practices include maximizing server utilization, enforcing power management policies, and using energy-efficient hardware. Consistently monitoring and auditing data center energy and water consumption is crucial for identifying areas for improvement and tracking progress over time. Supporting the development of transmission infrastructure to facilitate a shift to cleaner energy is another important aspect of reducing the environmental footprint of GenAI. Renewable energy sources are often located in remote areas, requiring significant investments in transmission infrastructure to deliver electricity to demand centers. Supporting policies and investments that promote the development of transmission infrastructure for renewable energy can facilitate the widespread adoption of cleaner energy and reduce the carbon footprint of AI and other energy-intensive sectors.[69]

7.14.3 Transparency in GenAI's environmental accounting

Transparency in water, energy, and carbon accounting related to GenAI operations is essential for accountability and informed decision-making. Organizations should publicly disclose their energy and water consumption linked to AI operations, along with their efforts to reduce their environmental footprint. This transparency enables stakeholders to assess the sustainability of AI and hold organizations accountable for their environmental performance. Standardized reporting frameworks and metrics for AI sustainability can enhance comparability and benchmarking across organizations. A structured approach to developing the necessary metrics and processes that organizations can use to measure their sustainability efforts effectively and meaningfully across various contexts. GenAI can guide the development and implementation of structured research, which will support the practical application of context-based sustainability principles in a way that is grounded in both empirical data and ethical considerations, thereby facilitating better decision-making concerning environmental and social impacts.[70] This may involve creating updated tools or benchmarks, helping organizations understand sector-specific ESG standards, sustainability, risks, and opportunities, and establishing thresholds for assessing their sustainability performance.

7.15 Navigating the risks: digitalization and the societal imperative for climate action

While the potential of GenAI and digital technologies to accelerate decarbonization is substantial, it is essential to acknowledge and navigate the potential risks and unintended consequences associated with their deployment. Some research suggests that an over-reliance on digital solutions for climate change could indirectly undermine the societal focus and determination needed to address the root causes of the climate crisis.[71][72][73] A balanced and critical perspective is necessary as we explore the benefits of digitalization for decarbonization, ensuring that technology serves as an enabler of, rather than a substitute for, fundamental societal and behavioral changes.

7.15.1 Risk of techno-optimistic narrative undermining societal transformation

One potential risk is the creation of a techno-optimistic[74] narrative that presents technology as the primary solution to climate change, which could undermine the perceived necessity for broader societal transformations. If the focus shifts mainly to technological fixes, there is a risk that essential social, political, and economic changes, such as shifts in consumption patterns, equitable resource distribution, and systemic reforms, may be overlooked. Climate change is fundamentally a societal challenge, requiring collective action and a re-evaluation of our values and priorities. While technology can play a crucial role, it is not a silver bullet and should not distract from the imperative for fundamental societal change.

7.15.2 Exacerbation of digital divides and inequalities

Another potential risk is the exacerbation of digital divides and inequalities. Access to and benefits from GenAI and digital technologies might not be evenly distributed across society. Developing countries, marginalized communities, and individuals lacking digital literacy may find themselves excluded from the potential benefits of digitalization for climate action and may bear a disproportionate share of the environmental and social costs. It is vital to ensure equitable access to digital technologies and to address gaps in digital literacy to prevent digitalization from deepening existing inequalities and creating new forms of injustice.

7.15.3 Risk of over-reliance on algorithmic solutions and diminished human agency

Furthermore, there is a risk of over-reliance on algorithmic solutions, which could diminish human agency in climate decision-making. While GenAI can augment human capabilities and provide valuable insights, it is essential to maintain human oversight and control in critical decision-making processes. Climate action requires ethical considerations, value judgments, and a nuanced understanding of complex social and environmental contexts—aspects that algorithms alone cannot fully capture. Over-reliance on algorithmic decision-making could lead to a disconnect from the real-world implications of climate change and a weakening of public engagement and democratic participation in climate action.

7.15.4 Cybersecurity risks in digitalized climate infrastructure

Moreover, society's increasing digitalization introduces cybersecurity risks and vulnerabilities. Climate-critical infrastructure, such as energy grids, transportation systems, and water management systems, is becoming more interconnected and reliant on digital technologies. Cyberattacks on these systems could result in severe consequences, disrupting essential services, undermining climate resilience, and hindering decarbonization efforts. Strengthening cybersecurity measures and ensuring the resilience of digital infrastructure are crucial for mitigating these risks.

7.15.5 Potential for rebound effects offsetting environmental benefits

Finally, it is important to consider the potential for rebound effects. Enhancing energy efficiency and resource productivity enabled by digital technologies may lead to increased consumption and production, partially negating the intended environmental benefits. For instance, more energy-efficient buildings might lead to increased building sizes or higher indoor comfort levels, resulting in a net increase in energy consumption. Addressing rebound effects requires a holistic approach that combines technological innovation with policy measures, behavioral changes, and a transition toward more sustainable consumption patterns.

7.15.6 The need for a balanced and critical perspective on digitization for climate action

The growing momentum behind digitization as a tool for climate action necessitates a balanced and critical perspective to ensure its effectiveness and sustainability. Digital technologies, including AI, business analytics, and the IoT, can offer powerful means to monitor environmental changes, optimize energy use, and support climate modeling. However, they raise important concerns and potential risks related to energy consumption, electronic waste, and data privacy. Without critical oversight, digital solutions risk reinforcing existing inequalities, increasing carbon footprints through energy-intensive infrastructures, or diverting attention from systemic policy reforms. Therefore, a nuanced approach is essential to balance the environmental benefits of digital innovations and their unintended consequences, promote equitable access, and align technological progress with long-term climate resilience and social justice goals. Navigating these risks requires a critical and balanced perspective on the role of digitization in climate action. It is essential to avoid techno-determinism and to recognize that technology is a tool, not a solution in itself. Digital technologies should be deployed strategically and responsibly, in conjunction with broader societal changes, to accelerate decarbonization and build a more sustainable future. Maintaining human oversight, ensuring equitable access, addressing cybersecurity risks, and mitigating rebound effects are crucial considerations for responsible digitalization in the context of climate change.

7.15.7 AI's contribution to achieving the climate goals of reducing CO_2 emissions

AI-powered technologies can play a critical role in advancing global efforts to reduce CO_2 emissions and meet climate goals. AI can significantly enhance the efficiency of energy systems, transportation networks, and industrial processes by enabling real-time monitoring, predictive analytics, and smart decision-making. For instance, AI-powered systems optimize power grids by integrating renewable energy sources more effectively, reducing reliance on fossil fuels. In manufacturing, AI helps identify and minimize carbon-intensive practices, while in agriculture, it supports precision farming techniques that lower emissions and improve resource use. Furthermore, AI aids climate modeling and risk assessment, providing policymakers and businesses with accurate insights for informed, low-carbon strategies. However, to fully realize AI's potential in climate mitigation, it must be deployed responsibly, ensuring energy efficiency in its own operations and fostering equitable access to its benefits across regions and sectors. The connection between digital innovation and climate action is fundamentally intertwined, as digital technologies play a crucial role in enabling measurable reductions in GHG emissions across various sectors. The following examples illustrate how integrating digital technologies across sectors such as energy, construction, and transport can significantly contribute to achieving climate goals by reducing CO_2 emissions.[75]

1. **Smart City Initiatives**: The city of Vienna serves as a prime example of how smart city projects, which leverage innovative digital solutions and data analytics, can lead to remarkable reductions in CO_2 emissions. A successful initiative in Vienna resulted in a staggering 71% reduction of CO_2 emissions in a large residential building. This was achieved through the integration of smart technologies that manage energy consumption, heating, and utilities in a more efficient manner. The smart city approach not only improves sustainability but also enhances the quality of life for residents through better resource management and urban planning.
2. **Port of Rotterdam**: In the maritime sector, the Port of Rotterdam exemplifies the effectiveness of digital technologies by implementing AI for improved port operations. The use of these advanced tools has enabled better route planning and ship berthing processes. By optimizing these operations, the port aims to achieve a 50% reduction in carbon emissions by the year 2030. This initiative demonstrates how digitalization can streamline logistics and reduce the environmental footprint of shipping, a traditionally carbon-intensive industry.

3. **Electricity Smart Grids**: The integration of digital technologies has been vital in the development of intelligent electricity networks, or smart grids, which effectively facilitate the integration of renewable energy sources. These intelligent systems enhance the efficiency and reliability of energy distribution while minimizing emissions typically produced through conventional energy management practices. In fact, in the EU, advancements in storage and demand response technologies through digitalization are projected to avoid as much as 30 million tons of CO_2 emissions by 2040. This illustrates the potential of smart grids to transform energy systems into more sustainable infrastructures.
4. **Transportation Technologies**: In the transport sector, the Dutch research institute TNO has highlighted the environmental benefits of cellular-based Vehicle-to-Everything (C-V2X) technology, which can potentially reduce emissions by 5–20% across various applications. When integrated into transportation corridors and smart cities, this technology enhances safety and efficiency. By optimizing speed and trip planning, as well as facilitating driverless and connected vehicles and mobility-as-a-service solutions, digital technologies can significantly lower CO_2 emissions in the transport sector. By enabling seamless communication between vehicles, infrastructure, and other road users, this technology enhances energy efficiency and allows for optimized trip planning. This capability not only facilitates smarter driving practices but also significantly lowers GHG emissions, highlighting the critical role of digital innovation in achieving sustainability across the transportation network.

7.16 Summary

This chapter explores how AI revolutionizes strategic planning and enhances operational efficiency across industries by exploring the transformative role of AI systems in enhancing strategic planning and operational efficiency across various industries. It begins by outlining the foundational role of AI in data-driven decision-making, forecasting, and scenario analysis, enabling businesses to anticipate market changes and allocate resources effectively, as well as highlighting how AI technologies of ML, NLP, and predictive analytics can enable organizations to make data-driven decisions, anticipate market trends, and optimize resource allocation. The chapter addresses how AI tools of predictive analytics, ML models, and intelligent automation can support strategic functions such as risk management, competitive analysis, and long-term growth planning by examining key applications, including demand forecasting, supply chain optimization, risk management, and intelligent automation of routine tasks. On the operational side, the chapter illustrates how AI optimizes workflows, reduces costs, and improves productivity through applications in supply chain management, logistics, demand forecasting, and process automation. Real-world case studies demonstrate the successful integration of AI in both strategic and operational contexts by presenting how AI empowers leaders to align operations with long-term strategic goals, improve agility, and reduce operational costs. The chapter concludes by discussing key implementation challenges, such as data quality, change management, and ethical considerations, by emphasizing the importance of aligning AI deployment with organizational values and sustainability goals. It offers best practices for aligning AI initiatives with organizational goals for sustainable performance as a strategic asset that drives competitive advantage and long-term performance. Ultimately, this chapter addresses how organizations can leverage AI tools; innovative practices; and technologies to enhance operational efficiency and effectiveness, ensure environmental sustainability, and reduce waste, ultimately contributing to a more sustainable and resilient business model.

7.17 Takeaways

- AI supports strategic planning by enabling real-time data analysis, scenario modeling, and predictive forecasting, leading to more informed and agile decision-making.
- AI-driven tools streamline operations by automating repetitive tasks, optimizing supply chains, improving resource allocation, and reducing operational costs.
- High-quality, well-managed data is critical for effective AI deployment in both strategic and operational domains. Data governance and integration are essential for AI success.
- Through continuous learning and pattern recognition, AI allows businesses to anticipate problems, identify trends, and respond to changes before they escalate.
- AI applications span multiple business functions—finance, HR, logistics, and customer service—contributing to both strategic alignment and day-to-day efficiency.
- Effective AI adoption involves addressing challenges such as workforce adaptation, ethical concerns, system integration, and change management.
- AI should not be deployed in isolation; its implementation must be closely aligned with the organization's strategic objectives and performance metrics.
- Organizations must foster a culture of innovation and continuous learning to fully leverage AI for long-term strategic and operational success.

Notes

1 Schaltegger, S., Hansen, E.G., & Lüdeke-Freund, F. 2016. Business models for sustainability: Origins, present research, and future avenues. *Organization & Environment*, 29(1), 3–10
2 ESGtheReport. 2025. *What are the Three P's of Sustainability?* https://esgthereport.com/planet-people-profit/
3 Young, D., & Gerard, M. 2021. *Four Steps to Sustainable Business Model Innovation*. BCG. https://www.bcg.com/publications/2021/four-strategies-for-sustainable-business-model-innovation
4 Ellen MacArthur Foundation. 2015. *Towards a Circular Economy: Business Rationale for an Accelerated Transition*. https://www.ellenmacarthurfoundation.org/towards-a-circular-economy-business-rationale-for-an-accelerated-transition
5 Fagerberg, J. 2018. Mobilizing innovation for sustainability transitions: A comment on transformative innovation policy. *Research Policy*, 47(9), 1568–1576

6 Ellen MacArthur Foundation. 2019. *Artificial Intelligence and the Circular Economy: AI as a Tool to Accelerate the Transition*. https://www.ellenmacarthurfoundation.org/artificial-intelligence-and-the-circular-economy
7 Ellen MacArthur Foundation. *Artificial Intelligence and the Circular Economy*
8 AMP. 2024. *AMP to Operate Waste Connections Recycling Facility with AI-Powered Sortation Technology*. https://ampsortation.com/resources/news
9 Greyparrot. *Recover More Resources with Waste Intelligence*. https://www.greyparrot.ai/
10 Pathan, M.S., Richardson, E., Galvan, E., & Mooney, P. 2023. The role of artificial intelligence within circular economy activities—a view from Ireland. *Sustainability*, 15(12), 9451
11 ZenRobotics. *Revolutionising Sorting Technology Efficiency Perfected*. https://www.terex.com/zenrobotics
12 SmartIndustry. 2021. *A Factory of the Future. . .in Amberg*. https://www.smartindustry.com/benefits-of-transformation/advanced-control/article/11290138/a-factory-of-the-futurein-amberg
13 TGS. *Offshore Wind Farms in Belgium*. https://www.4coffshore.com/windfarms/belgium/
14 CORDIS. 2016. *Accelerated Metallurgy—the Accelerated Discovery of Alloy Formulations Using Combinatorial Principles*. https://cordis.europa.eu/project/id/263206/factsheet
15 Rolnick, D., Donti, P.L., Kaack, L.H., Kochanski, K., Lacoste, A., Sankaran, K., & Bengio, Y. 2022. Tackling climate change with machine learning. *ACM Computing Surveys*, 55(2), 1–96
16 Leal Filho, W., Wall, T., Mucova, S.A.R., Nagy, G.J., Balogun, A.L., Luetz, J.M., . . . Gandhi, O. 2022. Deploying artificial intelligence for climate change adaptation. *Technological Forecasting and Social Change*, 180, 121662
17 Lin, Y., Shen, R., Wang, J., & Yu, Y.J. 2024. Global evolution of environmental and social disclosure in annual reports. *Journal of Accounting Research*, 62(5), 1941–1988
18 Zhang, H., Zhao, X., Fang, X., & Chen, B. 2024. Proactive resource request for disaster response: a deep learning-based optimization model. *Information Systems Research*, 35(2), 528–550
19 Sakapaji, S.C., & Puthenkalam, J.J. 2023. Harnessing ai for climate-resilient agriculture: opportunities and challenges. *European Journal of Theoretical and Applied Sciences*, 1(6), 1144–1158
20 Huntingford, C., Jeffers, E.S., Bonsall, M.B., Christensen, H.M., Lees, T., & Yang, H. 2019. Machine learning and artificial intelligence to aid climate change research and preparedness. *Environmental Research Letters*, 14(12), 124007
21 Bianchi, O., & Putro, H.P. 2024. Artificial intelligence in environmental monitoring: Predicting and managing climate change impacts. *International Transactions on Artificial Intelligence*, 3(1), 85–96
22 Andigema, A., Cyrielle, N.N.T., Danaëlle, M.K.L., & Ekwelle, E.W.A.N.E. 2024. *Harnessing the Power of Artificial Intelligence in Climate Change Mitigation: Opportunities and Challenges for Public Health*
23 Lu, L. 2024. *In-depth Analysis of Artificial Intelligence for Climate Change Mitigation*
24 Coeckelbergh, M. 2021. AI for climate: freedom, justice, and other ethical and political challenges. *AI and Ethics*, 1(1), 67–72
25 Ahmad Azhar, Ikram Amir, Rehan Muhammad Farooq, & Ahmad Ayyaz. 2022. Going green: Impact of green supply chain management practices on sustainability performance. *Frontiers in Psychology*, 13. https://www.frontiersin.org/journals/psychology/articles/10.3389/fpsyg.2022.973676
26 Hejazi, M.T., Al Batati, B., & Bahurmuz, A. 2023. The influence of green supply chain management practices on corporate sustainability performance. *Sustainability*, 15(6), 5459. https://doi.org/10.3390/su15065459

27 Tseng, M.L., Islam, M.S., Karia, N., Fauzi, F.A., Afrin, S. 2019. A literature review on green supply chain management: Trends and future challenges. *Resources, Conservation and Recycling*, 141, 145–162, ISSN 0921–3449. https://doi.org/10.1016/j.resconrec.2018.10.009. https://www.sciencedirect.com/science/article/pii/S0921344918303744
28 Rezaee, Z., Agrawal, S., & Pak, H. 2006. Continuous improvement: An activity-based model. *Management Accounting Quarterly* (Spring), 14–22
29 IPAGlobal. 2022. *Sustainability Priorities Defined by Carbon Working Group*. https://www.ipaglobal.com/news/article/sustainability-priorities-defined-by-carbon-working-group/
30 Nishant, R., Kennedy, M., & Corbett, J. 2020. Artificial intelligence for sustainability: Challenges, opportunities, and a research agenda. *International Journal of Information Management*, 53, 102104
31 Adanma, U.M., & Ogunbiyi, E.O. 2024. Artificial intelligence in environmental conservation: Evaluating cyber risks and opportunities for sustainable practices. *Computer Science & IT Research Journal*, 5(5), 1178–1209
32 Bibri, S.E., Alexandre, A., Sharifi, A., & Krogstie, J. 2023. Environmentally sustainable smart cities and their converging AI, IoT, and big data technologies and solutions: An integrated approach to an extensive literature review. *Energy Informatics*, 6(1), 9
33 Yigitcanlar, T. 2021. Greening the artificial intelligence for a sustainable planet: An editorial commentary. *Sustainability*, 13(24), 13508
34 Kar, A.K., Choudhary, S.K., & Singh, V.K. 2022. How can artificial intelligence impact sustainability: A systematic literature review. *Journal of Cleaner Production*, 376, 134120
35 Kar et al. How can artificial intelligence impact sustainability, 18
36 van Wynsberghe, A. 2021. Sustainable AI: AI for sustainability and the sustainability of AI. *AI and Ethics*, 1(3), 213–218
37 Huang, Y.L., & Fan, L.T. 1993. Artificial intelligence for waste minimization in the process industry. *Computers in Industry*, 22(2), 117–128
38 Heising, J.K., Claassen, G.D.H., & Dekker, M. 2017. Options for reducing food waste by quality-controlled logistics using intelligent packaging along the supply chain. *Food Additives & Contaminants: Part A*, 34(10), 1672–1680
39 Ghahramani, M., Zhou, M., Molter, A., & Pilla, F. 2021. IoT-based route recommendation for an intelligent waste management system. *IEEE Internet of Things Journal*, 9(14), 11883–11892
40 Nwokediegwu, Z.Q.S., Ugwuanyi, E.D., Dada, M.A., Majemite, M.T., & Obaigbena, A. 2024. AI-driven waste management systems: A comparative review of innovations in the USA and Africa. *Engineering Science & Technology Journal*, 5(2), 507–516
41 Mishra, S., Jena, L., Tripathy, H.K., & Gaber, T. 2022. Prioritized and predictive intelligence of things enabled waste management model in smart and sustainable environment. *PloS One*, 17(8), e0272383
42 Ziouzios, D., Baras, N., Balafas, V., Dasygenis, M., & Stimoniaris, A. 2022. Intelligent and real-time detection and classification algorithm for recycled materials using convolutional neural networks. *Recycling*, 7(1), 9
43 Zhou, Y., & Zhao, J. 2024. Leveraging computational systems for lifecycle management and enhancement of circular economy in fashion: A study on tracking, recycling, and reuse technologies. *Applied and Computational Engineering*, 87, 148–153
44 Nwokediegwu, Z.Q.S., & Ugwuanyi, E.D. 2024. Implementing ai-driven waste management systems in underserved communities in the USA. *Engineering Science & Technology Journal*, 5(3), 794–802
45 Ametepey, S.O., Aigbavboa, C., Thwala, W.D., & Addy, H. 2024. The impact of ai in sustainable development goal implementation: A delphi study. *Sustainability*, 16(9), 3858
46 Tseng, M., Hà, H.M., Tran, T.P.T., Bui, T., Chen, C., & Lin, C. 2022. Building a data-driven circular supply chain hierarchical structure: resource recovery implementation drives circular business strategy. *Business Strategy and the Environment*, 31(5), 2082–2106

47 Niu, B., Lai, C., Zheng, Z., Qi, Z., & Dai, Z. 2025. AI quality control in competitive recycling facing material contamination. *International Journal of Production Economics*, 109541
48 Jose, S.A., Cook, C., Palàcios, J., Seo, H., Ramirez, C., Wu, J., . . . Menezes, P.L. 2024. Recent advancements in artificial intelligence in battery recycling. *Batteries*, 10(12), 440
49 Rusch, M., Schöggl, J., & Baumgartner, R.J. 2022. Application of digital technologies for sustainable product management in a circular economy: A review. *Business Strategy and the Environment*, 32(3), 1159–1174
50 Idrissi, A., Benabbou, R., Benhra, J., & Haji, M.E. 2025. Solid waste management through the application of ai and ict: A systematic literature review. *Journal of Environmental Engineering and Science*, 1–34
51 Maher, H., et al. 2022, 7 July. AI is essential for solving the climate crisis. *BCG Global*. www.bcg.com/publications/2022/how-ai-can-help-climate-change
52 Maher et al. AI is essential for solving the climate crisis
53 *9 Ways AI is Helping Tackle Climate Change*. 2024, February. World Economic Forum. www.weforum.org/agenda/2024/02/ai-combat-climate-change/
54 Allen, S.K., Barros, V., Burton, I., Campbell-Lendrum, D., Cardona, O.-D., Cutter, S.L., Dube, O.P., Ebi, K.L., Field, C., Handmer, J.W., Lal, P.N., Lavell, A., Mach, K.J., Mastrandrea, M.D., Mcbean, G.A., Mechler, R., Mitchell, T., Nicholls, N., O'Brien, K.L., . . . Wilbanks, T.J. 2012. Summary for policymakers. In C.B. Field, V. Barros, T.F. Stocker, Q. Dahe, D.J. Dokken, K.L. Ebi, M.D. Mastrandrea, K.J. Mach, G.-K. Plattner, S.K. Allen, M. Tignor, & P.M. Midgley (eds.), *Managing the Risks of Extreme Events and Disasters to Advance Climate Change Adaptation: Special Report of the Intergovernmental Panel on Climate Change* (pp. 3–21). Cambridge University Press. https://doi.org/10.1017/CBO9781139177245.003
55 Tekchandani, P. 2024. *How Generative AI Can Accelerate Value-Led Sustainability*. EY. https://www.ey.com/en_ph/insights/climate-change-sustainability-services/how-generative-ai-can-accelerate-value-led-sustainability
56 Kashani, H., Ashuri, B., Shahandashti, S.M., & Lu, J. 2015. Investment valuation model for renewable energy systems in buildings. *Journal of Construction Engineering and Management*, 141(2), 04014074
57 Prewave. 2025. *Supply Chain Superintelligence*. https://www.prewave.com
58 Luccioni, A., & Palacios, H. 2019, June. Using natural language processing to analyze financial climate disclosures. In *Proceedings of the 36th International Conference on Machine Learning*. Long Beach, California
59 Kasneci, E., Seßler, K., Küchemann, S., Bannert, M., Dementieva, D., Fischer, F., Gasser, U., Groh, G., Günnemann, S., Hüllermeier, E., & Krusche, S. 2023. ChatGPT for good? On opportunities and challenges of large language models for education. *Learning and Individual Differences*, 103, 102274
60 Molthan-Hill, P., Winfield, F., Howarth, R., & Mazhar, M. 2023. *The Handbook of Carbon Management—A Step-by-Step Guide to High-Impact Climate Solutions for Every Manager in Every Function*. 1st Edition. Routledge, London
61 Ferré-Bigorra, J., Casals, M., & Gangolells, M. 2022. The adoption of urban digital twins. *Cities*, 131, 103905
62 MIT Laboratory for Information and Decision Systems. 2024. *Generative AI for Smart Grid Modeling*. https://news.mit.edu/2024/generative-ai-smart-grid-modeling-0226
63 Han, T., Cong, R.G., Yu, B., Tang, B., & Wei, Y.M. 2024. Integrating local knowledge with ChatGPT-like large-scale language models for enhanced societal comprehension of carbon neutrality. *Energy and AI*, 18, 100440
64 Pimenow, S., Pimenowa, O., & Prus, P. 2024. Challenges of artificial intelligence development in the context of energy consumption and impact on climate change. *Energies*, 17(23), 5965

65 Walmart. 2024. *Walmart Commerce Technologies Launches AI-Powered Logistics Product*. https://corporate.walmart.com/news/2024/03/14/walmart-commerce-technologies-launches-ai-powered-logistics-product

66 Daly, C. 2018. Data farming: Building precision agriculture with AI, IIoT, and Microsoft FarmBeats. *AI Business*. https://aibusiness.com/verticals/data-farming-building-precision-agriculture-with-ai-iiot-and-microsoft-farmbeats

67 NationalgridESO. 2021. *Former DeepMind Expert's AI Tool Could Help Boost National Grid ESO's Solar Forecasts*. https://www.neso.energy/document/212841/download#:~:text=Jack%20Kelly%2C%20co%2Dfounder%20of,on%20the%20grid%20more%20efficiently.&text=Images%20of%20National%20Grid%20ESO%27s%20control%20room%20available%20here

68 KPMG. 2025, January. *Chapter 7: Greenhouse Gas Emissions Reporting*. https://viewpoint.pwc.com/us/en.html

69 Desroches, C., Chauvin, M., Ladan, L., Vateau, C., Gosset, S., & Cordier, P. 2025. Exploring the sustainable scaling of AI dilemma: A projective study of corporations' AI environmental impacts. *arXiv* preprint arXiv:2501.14334

70 McElroy, M.W., & Baue, B. 2013. Research needs and opportunities in context-based sustainability. *Financial reporting: bilancio, controlli e comunicazione d'azienda*, 2, 2013, 47–70

71 World of Conferences (WOC). 2024. The modern vector of the development of science. In *XVI International Scientific Conference*. Philadelphia, PA

72 Javed, A.R., Shahzad, F., ur Rehman, S., Zikria, Y.B., Razzak, I., Jalil, Z., & Xu, G. 2022. Future smart cities: Requirements, emerging technologies, applications, challenges, and future aspects. *Cities*, 129, 103794

73 AI Action Summit. 2025. *Rapport international sur la sûreté de l'IA Rapport scientifique international sur la sûreté de l'IA avancée*. https://assets.publishing.service.gov.uk/media/67af5a7363d7f4cceef9e236/International_AI_Safety_Report_2025_executive_summary_french.pdf

74 Malhotra, P., Sachdeva, P., & Mitra, A. 2024. Bridging the gap: The integration of sustainable technologies in artificial general intelligence. In *Artificial General Intelligence (AGI) Security: Smart Applications and Sustainable Technologies* (pp. 53–74). Singapore: Springer Nature Singapore

75 DIGITALEUROPE. 2021. *Digital Action-Climate-Action-8 Ideas to Accelerate the Twin Transition*. https://www.digitaleurope.org/

8 Leveraging AI for sustainability

8.1 Introduction

The development of sustainable products and services has become an imperative strategy for businesses striving to meet evolving consumer expectations and regulatory requirements as global awareness of environmental and social issues grows. Sustainable product and service development involves initiatives, strategies, and efforts to satisfy market demands for products and services and promote social responsibility, minimize environmental impact, and enhance overall value throughout their lifecycle. The concept of sustainability in product and service development encompasses a holistic approach that considers the entire lifecycle of a product or service, from design and production to consumption and disposal, and extends beyond mere compliance with environmental regulations. Sustainable development requires addressing key factors such as waste reduction, resource efficiency, and the ethical sourcing of materials by integrating sustainability into the core of product and service design. Organizations can create offerings that align with principles of environmental stewardship, social equity, and economic viability.

Design for sustainability involves adopting practices that minimize the environmental impact of products and services at every stage of their lifecycle. This includes selecting sustainable materials, optimizing production processes to reduce energy and resource use, and designing for durability and recyclability. Furthermore, sustainable product development often involves considering the end-of-life phase, ensuring that products can be easily repaired, reused, or recycled, thereby supporting a circular economy and reducing waste. Service development also plays an important role in sustainability, particularly those involving digital platforms or service-based business models that can offer opportunities to reduce resource consumption and environmental impact, replace physical products, reduce travel needs, streamline operations, contribute to lower carbon footprints, and enhance efficiency. The integration of sustainable practices into product and service development requires engaging with stakeholders, understanding their expectations, and incorporating their feedback into the development process, which can drive innovation and ensure that sustainable products and services meet market needs while delivering positive social and environmental outcomes. Additionally, business organizations must navigate various challenges and opportunities in sustainable

DOI: 10.4324/9781003611981-8

product and service development by balancing sustainability goals with cost considerations, addressing technological and logistical barriers, and staying ahead of evolving regulatory standards and market trends. Successful sustainable development requires a commitment to CI, innovation, and collaboration across the value chain. This chapter examines the principles, strategies, and practices of sustainable product and service development by highlighting how companies can innovate to deliver solutions that contribute to a more sustainable future. This chapter also provides a comprehensive overview of the strategies, tools, and best practices for sustainable product and service development and examines the benefits of incorporating sustainability into design and production processes, the role of stakeholder engagement, and the challenges that organizations may encounter. The last part of this chapter focuses on AI applications in sustainability disclosure including advanced AI techniques, such as tokenization, Large Language Models (LLMs), fine-tuning, and BERT.

8.2 Eco-Design and LCA

Several standards of the International Organization for Standardization (ISO) are relevant to eco-design and LCA, including ISO 14006 and 14040 and 14044, to reduce the environmental impact of an industrial product.[1] An academic study provides step-by-step application of the eco-design process, serving as a practical guide for industry professionals aiming to integrate environmental considerations into product development to achieve a substantial reduction in normalized environmental impact.[2] AI can revolutionize eco-design and LCA by enabling more efficient, accurate, and sustainable decision-making. AI can play a transformative role in eco-design and LCA by: (1) collecting and processing big data in real-time relevant to materials, production processes, and environmental impacts and analyzing complex datasets to identify patterns, predict outcomes, and optimize designs for environmental sustainability which are essential for eco-design and LCA; (2) simulating and predicting the environmental impact of products throughout their lifecycles to assess the sustainability of materials, energy usage, and potential waste at early design stages, reducing the need for physical prototypes, and minimizing resource use; (3) identifying the most sustainable design alternatives by considering factors such as material selection, energy efficiency, and waste reduction by using genetic algorithms and neural networks that allow AI to evaluate a wide range of parameters, providing eco-designers with optimized solutions that balance functionality, cost, and environmental impact; (4) automating lifecycle inventory data collection from various sources, including databases, sensors, and IoT devices, which improves the accuracy and timeliness of LCAs; and (5) tracking environmental impacts across different stages and partners to support more informed choices about sourcing and logistics, predict maintenance needs, extend the lifecycle of products, and minimize waste and identify opportunities for reusability, recycling, and material recovery in the design phase, reducing waste and resource consumption. Overall, AI can empower Eco-Design and LCA by offering predictive capabilities, enhancing optimization, and enabling continuous monitoring, making it possible to create sustainable products that reduce environmental impacts across the product lifecycle to enable companies to improve their sustainability performance and gain competitive advantages in an increasingly eco-conscious market.

8.3 Sustainable marketing and consumer engagement

Sustainable marketing and consumer engagement focus on developing marketing strategies that align with environmental, social, and economic sustainability principles and core values while fostering a strong relationship with consumers. Sustainable marketing focuses on responsible, eco-friendly, and ethical practices throughout the marketing process, including product design, advertising, packaging, and distribution to reduce environmental impact and support social good. Engaging consumers involves transparency, authenticity, and consistency in communicating sustainable values and practices, as many consumers tend to be more environmentally and socially conscious, and they tend to support brands that reflect these values. Sustainable marketing is a long-term strategy that drives sales while building stronger, value-based relationships with consumers who support the brand's commitment to positive environmental and social impact by enhancing brand image to influence customer engagement, make sustainable purchases, foster stronger consumer relationships, and drive sustainable consumption.[3] Some of the sustainable marketing strategies are: (1) development of products and services that are made sustainably, reduce waste, eco-friendly, and use renewable resources; (2) promoting environmental consciousness through brand messaging and green branding including eco-labels, certifications, and endorsements that validate sustainable practices; (3)practicing transparency regarding sourcing, production, labor practices, and environmental impact fosters trust with consumers who value ethical standards; and (4) adopting a circular economy approach to create closed-loop systems where products are designed for reuse, repair, or recycling, reducing overall waste. AI-powered tools and technologies should be used to: (1) understand consumer preferences and trends around sustainability, which can drive more tailored, eco-friendly offerings; (2) engage consumers through social media platforms and digital content that highlights sustainability initiatives, creating communities around eco-friendly lifestyles; (3) offer immersive experiences, like virtual tours of sustainable practices or "try-before-you-buy" options that reduce returns and waste; and (4) develop metrics such as reduced carbon emissions, waste diversion rates, and water conservation in production to quantify the impact of sustainable marketing practices and to measure consumer response to sustainable initiatives.

One study examines US customer spending behavior by tracking money rather than sentiment for 5 years of US sales data and find that: (1) creating products that are truly environmentally and socially responsible are not only a moral action, but it is also in the best interest of the business in relation to sales and profits; and (2) customer spending habits are beginning to turn toward products that have ESG related claims included on their packaging.[4] Another study examines whether sustainable packaging can affect US customers buying decisions and finds that: (1) overall sustainability actually ranks fairly low on buyer criterion in relation to things such as price and quality; (2) although it may rank low on buying criterion, the majority of US customers are concerned about packaging's environmental impact; and (3) customers will pay more for green products, but these products need to be better labeled and more visible.[5] Another study examines whether and how sustainable marketing affects the customer engagement and sustainable purchase intention and finds that: (1) sustainable marketing is useful in brand image; (2) brand image does encourage customer engagement; (3) brand image increases how attractive sustainable purchases are; and (4) CSR does not significantly increase a customer's desire to make sustainable purchases, but it does improve the connection between brand image and customer engagement.[6] Yet, another study explores sustainable marketing as a concept on how this type of marketing leaves an impact on society, specifically strategies that promote eco-friendly lifestyles and find that: (1) sustainable marketing produces a tangible impact on society by promoting the adoption of an eco-friendly lifestyle; and (2) emerging technologies including AI and blockchain can be utilized to enhance sustainable marketing practices for businesses.[7]

8.4 Innovation and R&D for sustainability

The role of innovation and R&D investment on business sustainability is documented in several studies that find that: (1) increased investment in R&D is associated with a significant reduction in CO_2 emissions; (2) the importance of sustained R&D funding as a strategic tool for achieving long-term environmental goals; and (3) a positive correlation between R&D activities and progress across these sustainability dimensions, suggesting the importance of strategic R&D allocation in formulating effective sustainability policies.[8] AI can play a transformative role, revolutionizing innovation and R&D for sustainability by enabling companies and researchers to accelerate breakthroughs, optimize processes, and design sustainable solutions more effectively. AI-driven algorithms can foster sustainability-focused innovation by: (1) accelerating discovery and material innovation through discovery of eco-friendly materials faster by simulating material properties and screening potential candidates and low-impact chemicals and sustainable compounds, reducing the need for resource-intensive experiments, and development of advanced materials for applications such as solar panels, batteries, and water purification with reduced environmental impact; (2) enabling process optimization and energy efficiency by analyzing complex data from manufacturing processes to reduce waste, minimize emissions, and improve energy efficiency and ensuring that machinery operates at peak efficiency, reducing energy use and extending equipment lifespans, and testing new processes or re-engineering existing processes to reduce carbon footprints, contributing to cleaner production methods; (3) supporting circular economy goals by assisting in the design of products that are easy to disassemble, repair, or recycle to make products more sustainable over their lifecycle, reducing waste and material extraction needs; (4) enabling advanced environmental impact forecasting and environmental and climate scenario analyses;

(5) analyzing large datasets related to environmental impacts, customer behavior, and market trends to provide actionable insights for sustainable R&D and prioritize projects with the highest potential for positive environmental and social impacts; (6) improving renewable energy technologies such as solar, wind, and hydro by optimizing generation, storage, and distribution to align renewable energy output with consumption, maximizing efficiency, and reducing waste; and (7) supporting the development of new battery chemistries and designs, improving capacity, longevity, and environmental friendliness to identify sustainable materials for battery production, and addressing concerns about rare earth elements and recyclability. Overall, AI is vital in driving sustainability-centered innovation by facilitating sustainable material discovery, enhancing process efficiency, supporting data-driven R&D decisions, and making substantial progress toward sustainability, aligning their R&D with environmental, social, and economic goals while adapting to the evolving demands of a sustainable future.

Researchers have introduced a sustainable pathway model that allows for the achievement of an economically viable innovation system based on three important components of R&D: investment, talent, and learning institutions and conclude that, through this sustainable pathway, R&D investments can improve R&D personnel talents, absorb capacity, and establish EUs.[9] Another research explores a new framework for understanding the relationship between R&D effort, external collaboration, and business model innovation and concludes that: (1) R&D effort positively affects business model innovation; (2) R&D effort positively influences collaboration breadth; (3) collaboration breadth positively stimulates collaboration depth; (4) collaboration depth positively affects business model innovation; and (5) collaboration breadth and depth play a chain-mediating role in the relationship between R&D effort and business model innovation.[10]

8.5 Energy management and renewable energy sources

Energy management and renewable energy sources are vital in reducing GHG emissions, enhancing energy efficiency, and promoting sustainable development. Energy management is a strategic approach to optimizing energy use by implementing efficient practices and technologies, which involve monitoring, controlling, and conserving energy within an organization or system. The important aspects of energy management are: (1) energy efficiency of improving energy consumption through efficient appliances, lighting, and HVAC systems; (2) energy audit of analyzing energy use patterns and identifying inefficiencies to reduce waste and save costs; (3) demand response of adjusting and adapting energy use in response to supply conditions, particularly during peak demand times; and (4) automated systems of utilizing smart meters, building management systems, and IoT devices to optimize energy use in real time.

Renewable energy comes from natural resources that are replenished continuously, and they are considered environmentally friendly, as they reduce reliance on fossil fuels and lower carbon footprints. Major types of renewable energy are: (1)

wind energy of converting wind flow into mechanical energy using turbines, often used in wind farms; (2) solar energy of getting energy from sunlight using photovoltaic cells or solar thermal systems; (3) biomass of producing energy by burning organic materials or converting them into biofuels; (4) geothermal of tapping into the Earth's internal heat for electricity generation or direct heating; and (5) hydropower of generating energy from flowing water, a common method using dams or run-of-the-river systems.

These renewable energy sources should be integrated into energy management strategies with the use of AI-powered tools to achieve sustainability goals and energy independence by: (1) using batteries or other storage systems to maintain a steady power supply when renewable sources are variable; (2) employing small-scale energy systems that generate, store, and use local renewable energy, which can operate independently of the central grid; (3) incorporating renewables into existing power grids, often managed with AI or predictive analytics to balance supply and demand; (4) adopting governmental policies that offer incentives for renewable adoption, such as tax credits, rebates, and grants; and (5) employing AI-driven tools, such as ML and predictive analytics, optimize energy management to analyze vast amounts of data from energy systems and to forecast demand, automate energy-saving decisions, and maximize the efficiency of renewable sources.

A research study offers five different strategies: (1) source segregation; (2) waste auditing; (3) implementing waste minimization techniques; (4) encouraging employee engagement; and (5) embracing circular economy principles to address waste management in business and how that can be achieved both effectively and sustainably.[11] The guide from the United States Environmental Protection Agency provides different ways and the benefits of managing and reducing waste in commercial settings, including tracking your waste, leveraging a team dedicated to waste management, assessments of how your program is doing in this area, and continuing to evolve and improve these methods to maximize your waste management processes.[12] A report provides a worldwide outlook on waste management and analysis on specifically solid waste management and concludes that the current pattern of resource use needs to be stopped with circular economy strategies instead of being implemented to protect future generations, and there is a need to be a collaborative effort among all stake holders in society to reduce waste and its complexity and stop the emission of pollutants into the environment.[13] One study addresses the impact that top management commitment and leadership and organizational culture transformation have on the relationship between Lean Practice and Green Practice and concludes that applying an integrated lean-green system to manufacturing SMEs has a significant impact on social and environmental sustainability performance.[14] A survey was conducted to identify trends and gain insights into the needs and priorities of energy users and concludes that: (1) more than 90% of the respondents indicated that they want external support for energy initiative; and (2) more than 46% person of respondents also indicated that they are expecting an increase in on-site generation or battery storage soon.[15]

8.6 Waste minimization and recycling strategies

Various strategies can be employed to address waste minimization and recycling efforts, including process optimization, material substitution, employee training, and integrated approaches combining technological, managerial, and policy interventions to achieve waste reduction.[16] Organizations can enhance waste management through strategic planning, policy enforcement, public awareness campaigns, and investment in advanced AI technologies such as automated sorting systems and waste-to-energy facilities. Furthermore, community engagement and collaboration between industries, municipalities, and consumers are essential to building sustainable waste management systems that support both environmental and economic goals. Waste minimization and recycling strategies are integral components of sustainable business practices, aiming to reduce environmental impact, lower disposal costs, and conserve resources. The major strategies for effective waste minimization and recycling are: (1) implementation of the Reduce, Reuse, Recycle Framework of decreasing waste generation by optimizing processes, reducing packaging, and encouraging consumption of only necessary resources, reusing materials in their current form, such as repurposing products or using reusable containers, and recycling materials such as paper, plastics, metals, and e-waste; (2) conducting waste audits to identify types and quantities of waste produced, uncovering patterns that reveal potential reduction areas; (3) adopting closed-loop systems where materials are continually recycled back into production to align with circular economy principles, reduce dependency on raw materials, and minimize waste generation; (4) using AI-driven tools for real-time monitoring, predictive waste management, and efficient sorting in recycling plants to optimize collection routes, predict waste volumes, and support accurate waste separation; (5) working with suppliers, recycling companies, and other stakeholders to implement waste reduction and recycling programs to achieve innovative solutions that enhance the efficiency of waste management practices; and (6) establishing measurable waste reduction goals, tracking progress, and regularly reporting on outcomes to demonstrate commitment to waste minimization and recycling strategies.

8.7 Net-zero carbon economy

In recent years, the global economy has experienced a notable shift toward voluntary alignment with a decarbonizing, net-zero framework. Even economies without formal net-zero commitments are actively investing in low-emission transitions. A net-zero carbon economy refers to an economic system that balances the amount of carbon dioxide emitted into the atmosphere with an equivalent amount of carbon removal, effectively achieving net-zero carbon emissions. This concept is central to addressing climate change, as it focuses on transitioning economic activities toward sustainable practices that minimize GHG emissions while promoting both financial ESP and nonfinancial ESG sustainability performance. A net-zero economy represents the gradual transformation of economic activities to align with a global trajectory of reduced emissions. This transformation involves minimizing financed emissions and increasing investments in clean energy and other decarbonization technologies. Several strategies and key improvements are suggested to enhance net-zero emissions targets to effectively combat climate change including: (1) determining the role of CDR by distinguishing between emission reductions and removals to ensure transparency and effectiveness; (2) advocating for comprehensive coverage of all GHGs and sectors to avoid loopholes by specifying the scope of emissions covered; and (3) aligning short-term actions with long-term targets of net-zero carbon emissions.[17]

The key attributes of a net-zero carbon economy are: (1) decarbonization of industries including decarbonizing key sectors such as energy, transportation, manufacturing, and agriculture by adopting cleaner technologies, transitioning to renewable energy sources, electrifying transportation systems, and implementing sustainable agricultural practices; (2) investments in clean energy by scaling up investments in renewable energy sources such as solar, wind, hydro, and geothermal are fundamental and promoting innovations in energy storage technologies and grid infrastructure further support the shift toward sustainable energy systems; (3) circular economy practices of promoting resource efficiency and waste reduction through circular economy principles, ensuring that materials are reused, recycled, and repurposed, and reducing the need for resource extraction and minimizing emissions across supply chains; (4) carbon sequestration of achieving net zero by requiring removing residual carbon emissions through natural and technological solutions of reforestation, afforestation, and soil carbon capture; and (5) policy and regulation of providing incentives and enforcement to drive the transition to a net-zero carbon economy by enacting carbon pricing mechanisms, subsidies for green technologies, and stringent emissions standards. These measures incentivize businesses to adopt sustainable practices and invest in low-carbon solutions and drive this global move toward decarbonization and green investment, including enhanced profitability and effective risk management. Transitioning to a low-carbon economy requires substantial financing, particularly in economies facing financial constraints, thereby creating opportunities for new business lines and revenue streams. Nations that develop expertise in green technologies and sustainable projects may gain a competitive advantage in this expanding global market. Additionally, many countries are positioning themselves for anticipated global policy shifts or climate-related regulatory requirements. By proactively transitioning to net zero, these nations can mitigate future compliance costs and reduce reputational risks.

There are several benefits of achieving a net-zero carbon economy including: (1) climate risk mitigation of reducing carbon emissions and enabling mitigate the adverse effects of climate change, such as rising sea levels, extreme weather events, and biodiversity loss; (2) economic growth and innovation by stimulating innovation in clean technologies, creating new industries and job opportunities, and opening pathways for global markets focused on sustainability; (3) energy security of reliance on renewable energy that reduces dependence on fossil fuels, enhancing energy security and stability in the face of fluctuating global fuel markets; and (4) health and social benefits of improved air and water quality and reducing pollution that could lead to better public health outcomes and enhanced quality of life.

There are, however, several challenges of transitioning to a net-zero carbon economy including: (1) potentially high initial investments of shifting to a net-zero economy that require significant upfront investments in technology, infrastructure, and workforce training; (2) global coordination of achieving net-zero on a global scale that demands coordinated efforts across nations, addressing disparities in resources, technology, and economic development; and (3) economic disruption in fossil fuel-dependent industries that require strategic planning for equitable transitions and support for affected workers and communities. As economies navigate this transition, strategies are likely to evolve, balancing risk management, profitability, and regulatory compliance. Accurate and improved data on short-term emissions reductions and long-term decarbonization investments will be essential for stakeholders to assess progress and impact. Understanding the economics of net-zero investments will become increasingly critical for policymakers, investors, and stakeholders as the global economy continues its shift toward sustainability. This evolving landscape presents both challenges and opportunities, reshaping the future of finance and investment in the context of climate change. Obviously, the transition to a net-zero carbon economy is not merely an environmental imperative but an opportunity to build a sustainable future by fostering innovation, collaboration, and a commitment to decarbonization. Furthermore, the global economy can simultaneously address climate challenges and create long-term economic value by encouraging businesses, governments, and individuals to contribute to this vision and the journey toward a net-zero carbon economy that will redefine the landscape of global development in the 21st century.

8.8 The foundational role of tokenization in analyzing corporate sustainability disclosures

CSRs have become an integral component of corporate reporting by solidifying their position as essential documents in the corporate landscape to serve as crucial conducive forms of information for a wide range of stakeholders. These reports provide insights into an organization's commitment to SDGs and its practical implementation of ESG principles and compliance with ever-increasing global sustainability initiatives and regulations. The rising importance of these reports shows a growing awareness that financial performance alone does not fully capture a company's long-term sustainability and its impact on society. Nevertheless, obtaining meaningful and comparable insights from these comprehensive documents is a significant analytical hurdle. The challenge of sifting through the extensive, unstructured text in sustainability reports highlights the need for computational methods that can analyze and understand human language. This is precisely where NLP proves highly valuable.[18] NLP methods have been successfully applied to various tasks related to the analysis of sustainability reports, demonstrating their versatility and effectiveness.[19] To understand the meaning in these reports and discern the application of principles, commitments, tone of disclosure, and connections between sustainability efforts requires analytical tools that can process language with deeper contextual understanding. This is where next-generation NLP models, particularly those based on transformer architecture, such as BERT, demonstrate transformative potential.

However, before any of these sophisticated NLP techniques can be applied, the raw, unstructured text from a document must undergo a crucial initial transformation. This foundational step, upon which almost all subsequent NLP analysis is built, is known as tokenization. While some descriptions of text processing in the literature may not explicitly use the term "tokenization," they invariably describe a process that serves this core function of segmenting text into analyzable units.

8.8.1 Tokenization: deconstructing the narrative

In NLP, tokenization is a fundamental technique that involves breaking down text into smaller units, such as words, phrases, or symbols, called tokens. It is the process of breaking down a text into smaller units called tokens, which serve as the basic elements for LMs.[20] Tokens are the fundamental units that LMs, like LLMs, create when breaking down text. Tokenization is the initial step in training an LLM. During training, the model learns semantic relationships between tokens, like how often they appear together or in similar contexts. After training, the LLM leverages these learned patterns to generate output token sequences from given input tokens.[21] Tokens can be words, parts of words, characters, or symbols, depending on the tokenization method used. The quality and robustness of tokenization have a direct impact on the correctness and effectiveness of LLMs.[22] The primary goal of tokenization is to convert text into a format that can be understood and processed by LMs. Tokens are the basic units of text processing used by AI models, representing commonly occurring sequences of characters. For example, the word "tokenization" is split into tokens, such as "token" and "ization." Typically, the first token of each word starts with a space character. As a rough estimate, one token corresponds to about 4 characters or 0.75 words in English text. Models process text in these tokens, and there is a maximum context length that includes both the prompt and the model's generated output.[23] To understand how an LM tokenizes text and counts its tokens, we use a publicly available tokenizer, such as the OpenAI tokenizer tool, which helps visualize how the text below will be tokenized and the total count of tokens in the text. The tokenization process is especially relevant to sustainability reporting, where large volumes of structured and unstructured data, such as corporate sustainability disclosures, ESG reports, and integrated reports, need to be systematically analyzed. By applying tokenization, NLP models can efficiently parse and process sustainability narratives to identify key themes, such as environmental impacts, carbon footprints, or social responsibility initiatives, which enables automated extraction, classification, and sentiment analysis of sustainability-related content, supporting more consistent and transparent reporting practices. Furthermore, tokenization in sustainability reporting facilitates the development of sustainability taxonomies and performance benchmarks in enhancing the comparability and credibility of ESG communications across firms and industries, as illustrated in the following example.

Example

The data for this example is extracted from Amazon 2023 corporate reports.[24] This 2023 Sustainability Reporting Framework Summary includes information on our approach to sustainability governance and 2023 reporting against the following frameworks: the SASB, the UNSDGs, the TCFD, and the UN Guiding Principles Reporting Framework.

In typical workflows, tokenization involves encoding the input text into tokens using a tokenizer, which assigns each token a unique index in the model's vocabulary. This conversion enables the model to process the text as numerical data, facilitating the learning of semantic relationships and context. The tokenizer breaks text into tokens (Figure 8.1), assigning each token a unique number (Figure 8.2). The LM learns to produce the next token in a sequence by understanding the statistical links between these tokens.

Tokenization is essential for preparing text data for NLP tasks, enabling models to analyze and generate language efficiently. Various tokenization methods include word-level, character-level, and subword-level techniques, including Byte-Pair Encoding (BPE). Subword tokenization, commonly used in models like GPT, breaks words into partial units, which handle unknown words or typos more effectively while reducing vocabulary size. After processing through the model, tokens

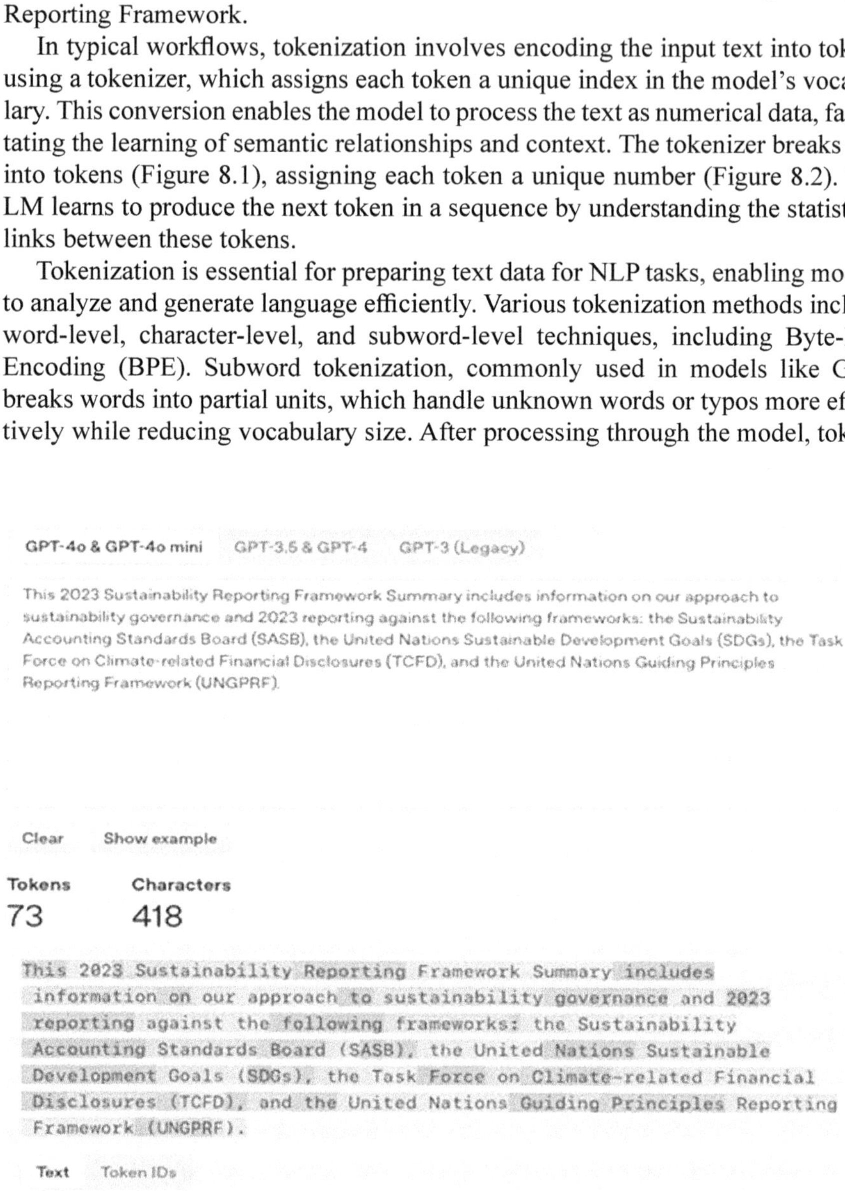

Figure 8.1 Tokenized text by the OpenAI tokenizer tool

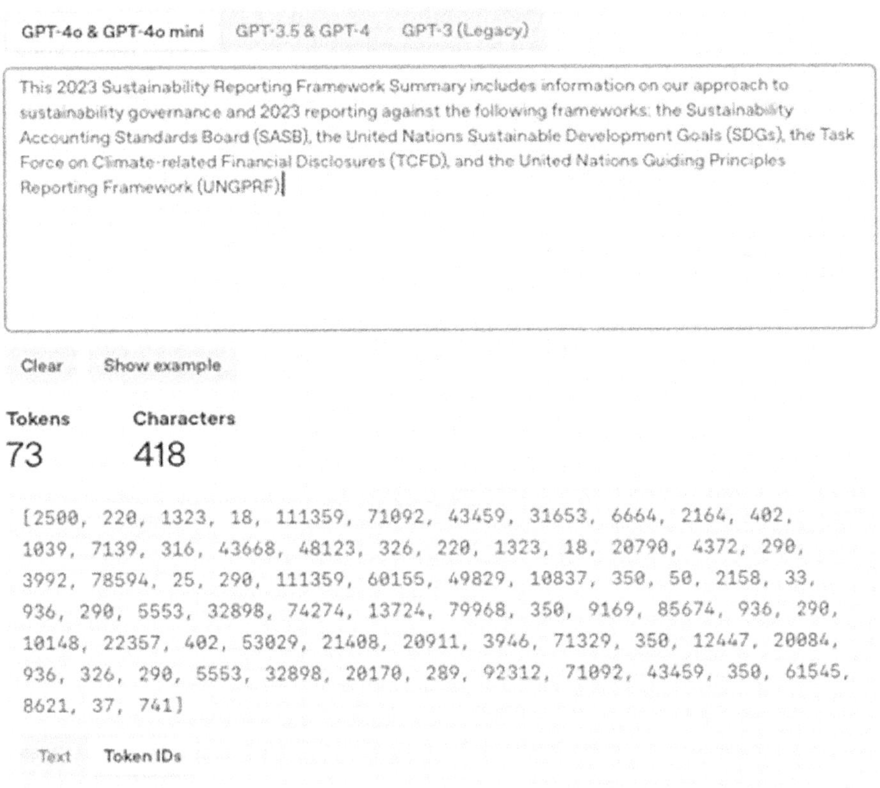

Figure 8.2 Tokenized text's Token IDs generated by the OpenAI tokenizer tool

are decoded back into human-readable text in a process known as detokenization. However, the input and output text length limitations of an AI model are determined by its token limit and tokenization method.[25]

8.8.2 *Tokenization: the foundation for enhanced NLP in sustainability reports*

Tokenization serves as the foundational step in NLP, enabling the transformation of complex sustainability reports into structured, analyzable data.[26] In the context of sustainability reporting, which often includes extensive narrative disclosures on ESG performance, tokenization allows for the segmentation of text into manageable units, including words, phrases, or sentences. This granular breakdown is essential for enabling more advanced NLP techniques such as keyword extraction, sentiment analysis, topic modeling, and semantic similarity.[27] By accurately identifying and processing these textual components, tokenization enhances the ability of NLP systems to detect key sustainability themes, assesses the quality and consistency of ESG disclosures, and supports automated benchmarking across industries.[28] Therefore, effective tokenization paves the way for greater transparency, accountability, and data-driven decision-making in corporate sustainability practices.[29] The tokens generated through the tokenization, often refined by subsequent pre-processing steps, serve as the fundamental input for a wide array of NLP techniques. These techniques build upon the foundation laid by tokenization to extract, analyze, and interpret the valuable information contained within sustainability reports. The examples provided in the outline, along with numerous research initiatives in this field, demonstrate how tokenization directly facilitates a range of analytical methods used in sustainability report analysis.[30]

8.8.2.1 Identifying frequent terms and bag-of-words models

The most straightforward yet often insightful analysis involves counting the frequency of words or terms within a document or collection of documents. This requires breaking the text down into individual words (tokens) first. By tokenizing a report or a specific section, such as the disclosure on emissions under GRI-305, analysts can identify the most frequently occurring terms. For example, examining the frequency of terms in GRI-305 disclosures and related company reports often reveals keywords like "scope," "GRI," "reporting," "annual report," and specific units or types of emissions. This frequency analysis directly relies on counting the occurrences of individual tokens after potentially removing stopwords and standardizing terms through stemming or lemmatization.

The "bag-of-words" (BoW) model is a common representation based directly on tokenization and frequency analysis. In a BoW model, a document is represented as an unordered collection (a "bag") of its tokens, where only the frequency of each token is considered, regardless of its grammatical structure or order within the original text. This may involve creating a vector where each dimension corresponds to a unique token in the vocabulary, and the value in that dimension represents the count (or a weighted count, such as TF-IDF) of that token in the document. For instance, a report heavily focused on renewable energy might have high counts for tokens such as "solar," "wind," "energy," "MWh," and "gigawatt," while a report centered on social issues might feature tokens such as "employee," "safety," "diversity," "training," and "community." Analyzing these token frequencies across reports, enabled by initial tokenization, offers a basic yet effective way to understand the dominant themes and compare the stated priorities of different companies or reports. While straightforward, BoW models, derived from token frequencies, have been used in various studies, including initial attempts to classify documents or identify relevant sections based on keyword presence.

8.8.2.2 Lexicon and rule-based approaches

Many analytical tasks involve identifying specific concepts, phrases, or patterns within the text. This is often accomplished using predefined lexicons (dictionaries) of terms relevant to a domain or through rule-based systems that search for specific sequences or arrangements of words. For instance, analyzing TCFD compliance might involve searching for mentions of terms like "climate scenarios," "physical risks," "transition risks," "governance," "strategy," "risk management," or specific entities like "board of directors." These terms and phrases must first be identified as individual tokens or specific sequences of tokens within the text.

Lexicon-based approaches operate by matching the tokens in a document against a predefined list of relevant tokens or multi-token phrases. For example, a lexicon for environmental reporting might include tokens like "emissions," "GHG," "carbon," "renewable," "water," "waste," or multi-token sequences such as "supply chain" and "circular economy." Rule-based systems enhance this by defining patterns of tokens to identify more complex structures or relationships. For instance, a rule might search for a negative sentiment token immediately preceding a performance metric token to flag potential challenges. Studies estimating TCFD compliance often utilize such lexicon and rule-based approaches: they define a set of keywords and phrases associated with each TCFD recommendation (e.g., governance, strategy, risk management, metrics, and targets). Tokenization is essential for breaking the report text into units that can be matched against these lexicons or evaluated by these rules. By identifying the presence and frequency of these key tokens or token sequences, researchers can computationally assess the extent to which a company's report addresses the various aspects of the TCFD framework and potentially construct a compliance index.

8.8.2.3 Topic modeling

Techniques like latent Dirichlet allocation (LDA) are statistical methods used to uncover abstract "topics" that occur in a collection of documents. LDA models a document as a mixture of topics and defines a topic as a probability distribution over words. To apply LDA or similar topic modeling techniques, each document must first be represented as a collection of its constituent words or tokens, often in a frequency format like the BoW model. The process begins by segmenting each document into its constituent words (tokens), as described in typical implementations of these models.

By analyzing co-occurring tokens across documents, LDA identifies latent thematic structures without predefined topic lists. For example, tokens like "energy," "solar," "wind," "power," and "grid" may indicate a "Renewable Energy" topic. Similarly, tokens such as "waste," "recycle," "material," "circular," and "economy" might form a "Waste and Circularity" topic. The LDA algorithm's input is a document-term matrix, with rows as documents, columns as unique tokens (post-tokenization and pre-processing), and values indicating token frequency in each document. Tokenization is essential for constructing this matrix, enabling the algorithm to pinpoint which words (tokens) belong to which documents and their frequency of appearance. The resulting topics outline dominant themes in sustainability reports, helping researchers and analysts understand corporate reporting without manually reading every document.

8.8.2.4 Sentiment analysis

Analyzing the sentiment or tone expressed in sustainability reports can provide insights beyond just the factual content. Sentiment analysis aims to determine the emotional tone or subjective information within the text, classifying it as positive, negative, or neutral. While sentiment can be assessed at various granularities, from individual words to sentences or even entire documents, the underlying computational models almost invariably operate on tokenized text.

Sentiment analysis often involves using lexicons of words with known sentiment scores (e.g., "achieved" might be positive and "challenge" might be negative) or training ML models on labeled data. More advanced methods utilize techniques like word embeddings or sophisticated transformer models (such as DistilBERT or RoBERTa) that capture the meaning and context of words based on their relationships with other words. These models process input text by first breaking it into tokens and then employing complex internal mechanisms that operate on these tokens or token sequences to understand the overall meaning and emotional valence. For example, while the token "emission" itself might be neutral or slightly negative, its appearance in the phrase "significant reduction in emissions" conveys a positive sentiment regarding performance. Tokenization allows the model to process these sequences of words, and subsequent embedding or contextualization techniques build representations of these tokens that capture their meaning in context, enabling the model to accurately assess sentiment. In sustainability reports, sentiment analysis, built upon tokenization, can help distinguish between reports that describe achievements enthusiastically versus those that discuss challenges or shortcomings in a more negative or cautious tone.

8.8.2.5 Named entity recognition and syntactic analysis

Named entity recognition (NER) is an NLP task that seeks to identify and classify named entities in text into predefined categories such as persons, organizations, locations, dates, quantities, or, importantly for sustainability reports, specific sustainability-related concepts. Examples of entities relevant to sustainability might include "United Nations Sustainable Development Goals," "Scope 1 emissions," "Paris Agreement," "Renewable Energy Certificates," or specific organizational units like "Sustainability Committee" or geographic locations relevant to operations or supply chains. Identifying these entities requires recognizing sequences of tokens that form the entity name.

More advanced syntactic methods, such as Part-of-Speech (POS) tagging, assign a grammatical label (e.g., noun, verb, adjective, and adverb) to each word (token) in a sentence. This process fundamentally relies on tokenization as a prerequisite step—you must first identify the "words" before you can label their grammatical role. Syntactic analysis helps in understanding the structure of sentences and the relationships between words. For instance, identifying noun phrases ("environmental impact," "energy consumption," and "worker safety") provides valuable concepts. These syntactic structures, built upon tokenized and POS-tagged sequences, can be combined with semantic analysis (which focuses on meaning) for more granular tasks like aspect-based sentiment analysis. This allows analysts to determine the sentiment expressed toward specific aspects mentioned in the report, such as the sentiment directed at "emissions performance," "supply chain labor practices," or "employee wellness programs," by linking sentiment-bearing tokens to the specific aspect tokens or phrases they modify. Tokenization is the essential first step in breaking down the sentence into units that can be individually tagged and then analyzed for structural and semantic relationships.

8.8.2.6 Semantic similarity and vector representations

Moving beyond simple keyword matching or frequency, analyzing sustainability reports often requires understanding the semantic meaning of text—what concepts are being discussed, even if different words or phrases are used. Techniques such as latent semantic analysis or word embedding models, such as GloVE (Global Vectors for Word Representation) or Word2Vec, have been applied to score the semantic similarity between sustainability reports or between a report and a sustainability framework document. These methods construct numerical representations, or vectors, of words, phrases, or entire documents based on their co-occurrence patterns and contexts within a large corpus of text. The underlying principle is that words appearing in similar contexts tend to have similar meanings.

These vector representations are constructed based on the relationships and contexts of tokens within the text corpus. For example, Word2Vec learns word embeddings by predicting neighboring tokens given a target token or predicting a target token given its neighbors. GloVE builds vectors based on the global word-word co-occurrence counts in a corpus. Both methods require the text to be tokenized first to identify the words and their contexts. Once token vectors are learned, document vectors can be created by aggregating the vectors of the tokens they contain. Comparing the vectors of different documents or sections allows for computational measurement of their semantic similarity.

More recent and highly successful models, such as BERT and RoBERTa (a robustly optimized BERT approach), have revolutionized NLP by creating highly contextualized word representations.[31] These models process input text as sequences of tokens, often subword tokens generated by techniques such as WordPiece or BPE. Unlike earlier models that generated a single vector for a word regardless of context, transformer models generate a vector for each token that is influenced by all other tokens in the input sequence. This allows them to capture nuances of meaning based on context. For instance, the meaning of "scope" in "Scope 1 emissions" differs from that in "scope of work," and transformer models can represent this distinction because they process the surrounding tokens. Studies that classify sustainability reports based on SDG relevance or identify specific types of disclosures often employ these powerful transformer models. While complex in their internal workings, their input layer universally requires tokenized text. The models then build sophisticated representations of these tokens, considering their position and relationship to other tokens in the sequence, enabling them to perform complex classification or information extraction tasks with high accuracy.

8.9 Unlocking deep insights in corporate sustainability reporting with BERT

BERT,[32] developed by Google, has significantly impacted NLP tasks. Its core strength lies in its bidirectional architecture and the self-attention mechanism of the Transformer, which allows it to learn deep contextual representations from text by considering context from both sides of a word or sentence. BERT is pre-trained on large amounts of text data using objectives such as Masked Language Modeling and Next Sentence Prediction, which provide it with a rich understanding of language. One of its key capabilities is its ability to be fine-tuned for specific downstream tasks. This capability makes BERT and its variants, such as RoBERTa,[33] ALBERT,[34] DistilBERT,[35] and domain-specific models such as FinBERT[36] and ClimateBERT,[37] valuable tools in the field of sustainability, which often involves analyzing large volumes of textual data from corporate reports, news, and other documents.

8.9.1 BERT use for sustainability

BERT offers a transformative approach to processing and interpreting unstructured textual data in the field of sustainability to extract meaningful insights for the complexity and volume of sustainability reports, ESG disclosures, and climate-related narratives. It has become a benchmark model for various NLP tasks,[38] including text classification, question answering, and NER in various fields, including legal,[39] fraud detection,[40] medical,[41] finance,[42] and sustainability.[43] Sustainability encompasses ESG, and analyzing company initiatives, decisions, and actions regarding these factors is crucial. BERT's ability to understand context and be fine-tuned for specific tasks makes it highly effective for analyzing complex sustainability-related text.

The application of BERT in sustainability can identify and classify key topics such as carbon emissions, renewable energy initiatives, social impact efforts, and corporate governance practices. It can also be fine-tuned for tasks such as sentiment analysis, greenwashing detection, and benchmarking ESG communication across industries. BERT enhances transparency, supports regulatory compliance, and facilitates more consistent and data-driven analysis by automating the analysis of diverse and often ambiguous sustainability language. BERT and BERT-like models facilitate sustainability assessment using NLP techniques by demonstrating their application in classifying documents and sentences, extracting specific information, verifying claims, and developing specialized tools and models for various aspects of sustainability, ESG, and climate change analysis. The following subsections present some cases where BERT and its variants have been applied in sustainability contexts:

8.9.1.1 Automated processing of sustainability reports for SDGs

An NLP framework that uses a fine-tuned RoBERTa model was developed to analyze sustainability reports and identify sections relevant to the 17 SDGs. This framework involved fine-tuning both RoBERTa and BERT-large for binary and multi-class text classification on the OSDG Community Dataset, which features text annotated by volunteers according to SDG relevance. This approach demonstrated superior performance compared to traditional ML methods for classifying text based on its relationship to the SDGs. Additionally, a BERT model was fine-tuned using the OSDG Community Dataset, which includes targets and indicators for each goal, to classify sentences based on their relevance to the SDGs. Key findings indicate that both BERT and RoBERTa substantially outperform classical ML methods in detecting SDG-related content within sustainability reports. Notably, RoBERTa achieves the highest performance, with an F1 score of approximately 92% on multi-class classification, surpassing both BERT and traditional models.[44] This superior performance is attributed to RoBERTa's enhanced pretraining strategies. The research highlights RoBERTa's effectiveness in processing large collections of text documents for automated SDG detection, offering a scalable and accurate approach to sustainability report analysis. The models and framework developed have been made publicly available, facilitating further research and practical application in this field.

8.9.1.2 ESG financing analysis based on the GRI standard

BERT-based NLP techniques are used to automatically classify excerpts from companies' annual activity reports into ESG categories based on the GRI standard. This development aims to support the sustainability assessment process at the Brazilian Development Bank (BNDES). The research investigated various BERT-like architectures, including BERT, RoBERTa, ELECTRA, ALBERT, and DistilBERT, while comparing their performance on this text classification task.[45] They also experimented with multilingual models such as BERT-base-multilingual and distilBERT-base-multilingual to analyze reports written in both English and Portuguese. The best-performing models were RoBERTa-base with text pre-processing and BERT-large without pre-processing, both achieving about 88% accuracy and nearly 85% F1-score. However, RoBERTa-base is significantly smaller (475.8 MB) compared to BERT-large (1.25 GB), making it more suitable for deployment on desktop or web servers. For multilingual analysis of English and Portuguese reports, the BERT-base-multilingual model attained 85% accuracy and 81% F1-score without text pre-processing. For resource-constrained devices like smartphones, two smaller models performed well: ALBERT-base-v2 (without pre-processing) with 85% accuracy and 78.59% F1-score at 49.1MB, and DistilBERT-uncased (with pre-processing) with 85% accuracy and 82.71% F1-score at 257.8 MB. The choice of model depends on available memory resources.

8.9.2 Textual analysis of pension funds' sustainable investing disclosures

The use of BERT in the textual analysis of pension funds' sustainable investing (SI) disclosures represents a cutting-edge application of NLP to ESG and sustainability initiatives. The objective is to assess the quality, tone, consistency, and themes in pension funds' disclosures related to sustainable or ESG investing, using the BERT LM. BERT offers many advantages of capturing the bidirectional context of words, making it ideal for understanding nuanced, complex ESG language, outperforming traditional BoW or TF-IDF methods in tasks such as classification, sentiment analysis, and semantic similarity, and being focused on fine-tuning on specific corpora (e.g., ESG reports or sustainability disclosures) to improve performance on domain-specific tasks. Potential applications of BERT in pension funds' ESG disclosures are to: (1) perform classification tasks of label sentences or paragraphs into predefined ESG categories (e.g., environmental stewardship, governance practices, and social impact) and detect conduct greenwashing language by focusing substantive ESG commitments; (2) sentiment and tone analysis of identifying positive or negative tone in disclosures related to specific sustainability themes; (3) perform thematic clustering of using sentence embeddings; and (4) generate readability and transparency metrics of evaluating whether pension funds use opaque or complex language to obfuscate their sustainability strategies.

To analyze how Dutch pension funds disclose SI, BERT, specifically a Dutch RoBERTa-based model called RobBERT, is employed for the textual analysis of Dutch pension funds' annual reports to assess their awareness and implementation of SI policies.[46] The analysis involves fine-tuning RobBERT for classification tasks, such as identifying sentences related to SI and specific paragraphs detailing actions, performance, or targets. A combined rule-based and classification approach is used to create a dataset of sentences linked to SI. Topic modeling, which utilizes LMs similar to BERT (specifically, BERTopic), is also applied to identify SI topics discussed in the reports. Key findings reveal that larger pension funds show greater awareness and implementation of SI, and funds with more female trustees or positive beliefs about SI's risk-return profile are more likely to sign the International Responsible Business Conduct (IRBC) initiative. While signing the IRBC initiative increases the specificity of SI statements, it does not significantly impact actual SI implementation. Overall, the use of BERT enables a nuanced and scalable analysis of sustainability disclosures, offering important insights into pension funds and regulators on the evolution and quality of sustainability commitments.

8.9.3 BERT use for the European Green Deal and SDGs

BERT offers a powerful tool for analyzing textual data related to the European Green Deal (EGD) and the SDGs by enabling more nuanced and context-aware insights into policy communication, corporate alignment, and stakeholder engagement. Organizations, researchers, and policymakers can systematically examine how EU institutions, member states, and corporations articulate their commitments to the Green Deal's climate neutrality objectives and the broader SDG framework by leveraging BERT's deep language understanding capabilities.[47] BERT can be fine-tuned to classify and extract references to specific SDGs, detect policy emphasis and sentiment, and identify inconsistencies or instances of greenwashing in sustainability-related communications by enabling robust monitoring of progress toward EU climate goals, while also fostering transparency and accountability in how sustainable development initiatives are communicated and implemented across sectors and regions. BERT is used in supporting the EGD by enabling the automatic analysis and classification of sustainability-related texts, such as policy documents and corporate disclosures, to assess alignment with the EGD's climate-neutral and sustainability goals. By leveraging BERT's contextual language understanding, stakeholders can efficiently extract insights on the implementation and progress of EGD initiatives and their connections to SDGs. This facilitates monitoring, reporting, and informed decision-making to advance the EGD's objectives for a sustainable and equitable Europe by 2050.

8.9.4 Information retrieval for EGD policies

The BERT model is used to assess the sustainability of the EGD and its interlinkages with the 17 SDGs and the Six Transformations.[48] BERT was fine-tuned to assess semantic similarity, outperforming the classical method by capturing nuanced connections between policies and SDGs that are less visible through frequency-based approaches. Key findings include the discovery of unexpected links, such as energy policies relating to SDG 6 (Clean Water and Sanitation), not identified by classical methods. The analysis confirmed strong policy impacts on SDGs 13 (Climate Action), 9 (Industry and Innovation), and 12 (Responsible Consumption and Production). Additionally, despite limited training data, SDGs 16 (Peace, Justice) and 17 (Partnerships) were strongly connected, underscoring their foundational role in achieving sustainability goals. The combined modeling approach offers a valuable tool for policy evaluation and SDG integration.

8.9.5 Assessing interlinkages between the EGD and SDGs

Assessing the interlinkages between the EGD and the SDGs is essential for understanding the coherence, synergies, and trade-offs in the EU's sustainability initiatives. The EGD, as a comprehensive roadmap to make Europe climate-neutral by 2050, aligns closely with several SDGs, particularly those related to climate action (SDG 13), clean energy (SDG 7), sustainable industry and innovation (SDG 9), and responsible consumption and production (SDG 12). However, potential tensions across social, economic, and environmental dimensions of SDGs can exist. For example, policies promoting green technologies can drive progress on SDG 8 (decent work and economic growth) but may also risk exacerbating inequalities (SDG 10) if not inclusively designed. Therefore, using BERT capabilities in mapping and evaluating these interdependencies using integrated policy analysis, sustainability indicators, can help ensure policy coherence and maximize the transformative potential of the Green Deal in advancing the 2030 Agenda. To analyze the alignment of 74 EGD policy documents (2019–2023) with the 17 UNSDGs,

BERT was fine-tuned using a labeled dataset of over 35,000 text excerpts related to the SDGs, enabling the model to estimate the probability that a policy document pertains to specific SDGs.[49] The ML analysis was complemented by expert human review for validation, ensuring nuanced interpretation. Key findings reveal that EGD policies strongly align with environmental goals, particularly clean energy (SDG 7), climate action (SDG 13), and responsible consumption (SDG 12). However, significant gaps remain in addressing social dimensions such as poverty, health, education, gender equality, and decent work (SDGs 1, 3, 4, 5, and 8). The EGD primarily focuses on energy decarbonization and sustainable industry, overlooking transformations related to health and social well-being. These insights suggest the need for a more balanced and integrated sustainability approach within EGD policies.

8.9.6 Climate-related BERT

Climate-related BERT models are specialized versions of the original BERT architecture that have been pre-trained or fine-tuned on large corpora of climate-related texts, including scientific publications, policy documents, CSRs, and environmental news articles. These models, such as ClimateBERT, are designed to better understand domain-specific terminology and contextual nuances related to climate change, environmental policy, and sustainability practices. Climate-related BERT models enable more accurate tasks such as document classification, sentiment analysis, trend detection, and identification of greenwashing in sustainability claims by capturing the semantic richness of climate discourse and facilitating the extraction of climate-related entities and relationships. Thus, climate-specific BERT models play an essential role in enhancing transparency, accountability, and data-driven decision-making in climate governance and sustainable development.

BERT-based systems have been explored for fact-checking climate-related claims. This involves retrieving relevant evidence and then verifying the claim based on that evidence, often treated as a Natural Language Inference task or a classification task to determine if evidence supports or refutes a claim. ClimateBERT, a transformer-based LM pretrained specifically on over 2 million climate-related paragraphs sourced from news articles, research abstracts, and corporate climate reports, addresses the limitations of general-purpose BERT models in capturing niche climate language.[50] ClimateBERT employs domain-adaptive pretraining using DistilROBERTA, a smaller, energy-efficient model, avoiding extensive hyperparameter tuning to minimize environmental impact. Experiments demonstrate that this specialized pretraining significantly enhances performance over non-pretrained or general models in extracting climate-relevant information. ClimateBERT has served as a base model for training even more specialized models. It has been built upon to create models like CliMedBERT (for climate and health-related text) and ClimateFinanBERT (for classifying development assistance projects by climate finance focus).

8.9.7 Climate fact extraction and claim verification

Climate fact extraction and claim verification are essential tasks in combating misinformation and ensuring the integrity of public discourse on climate change, which involve automatically identifying factual statements related to climate science, policy, and impacts, and verifying their accuracy against reliable scientific sources or databases. Advances in NLP and BERT models and their climate-specific variants (e.g., ClimateBERT) have significantly improved the precision and contextual understanding required for these tasks. Fact extraction enables organizations to identify key climate-related data points such as emissions targets, temperature rise projections, or renewable energy commitments and assess whether these statements are supported by scientific consensus or credible policy documents. AI-powered tools and BERT models contribute to more informed public debate, robust climate journalism, and evidence-based policymaking.

ClimateBERT is used for climate fact extraction and claim verification to address the complexity of climate-related text. Using the CLIMATE-FEVER dataset, which comprises 1.5k real-world climate claims paired with supporting or refuting evidence sentences, ClimateBERT classifies whether the evidence supports or refutes a claim.[51] The input combines the claim and evidence, separated by a special token, enabling contextual understanding. Filtering out ambiguous evidence labeled as "not enough information" ensures clarity in the task. Domain-adaptive pretraining on over 2 million climate-related texts allows ClimateBERT to capture subtle semantic and factual nuances essential for fact-checking. This methodology tackles challenges in climate misinformation by enabling automated, accurate verification of factual claims in climate discourse, thus supporting researchers and stakeholders with reliable, context-aware NLP tools tailored for climate science.

8.9.8 Analyzing corporate climate risk disclosures

Analyzing corporate climate risk disclosures using ClimateBERT enables organizations to obtain a deeper and more accurate understanding of how they communicate their exposure to and management of climate-related risks. ClimateBERT, a domain-specific adaptation of the BERT LM trained in climate-related texts, is particularly well-suited for extracting and interpreting nuanced information from sustainability reports, financial filings, and TCFD statements. ClimateBERT can classify and quantify climate risk themes such as transition risks, physical risks, and mitigation strategies and assess the sentiment, specificity, and materiality of disclosures by leveraging its contextual language capabilities. This allows for the systematic evaluation of disclosure quality, benchmarking across firms and industries, and detection of vague or potentially misleading statements. ClimateBERT, a fine-tuned deep neural LM based on BERT, is used to analyze text in company reports to identify climate risk information. It is designed to analyze corporate climate-risk disclosures aligned with the TCFD framework. ClimateBERT classifies sentences from annual reports into the four TCFD categories: governance, strategy, risk management, and metrics and targets. By applying ClimateBERT to

818 firms that support the TCFD from 2014 to 2019, the key finding is that supporting TCFD recommendations often amounts to "cheap talk," as many companies do not increase their overall disclosures. Instead, they engage in "cherry-picking," favoring less material categories like governance and risk management while underreporting critical categories such as strategy, metrics, and targets, which provide more meaningful insights into climate-related risks.[52] These findings have important implications for investors and regulators, highlighting the need for mandatory and standardized reporting to ensure effective climate risk management.

8.9.9 Sentiment analysis of climate statements

Sentiment analysis of climate statements using ClimateBERT provides a powerful method for evaluating the tone and underlying attitudes expressed in corporate, governmental, or media communications related to climate change. ClimateBERT, fine-tuned on climate-specific language, can detect subtle variations in sentiment, ranging from optimistic projections about green investments to cautious or negative tones regarding regulatory risks or environmental challenges. This sentiment classification enables organizations to monitor how they should frame climate-related issues, track shifts in public or corporate narratives over time, and identify discrepancies between stated intentions and actual performance. Furthermore, ClimateBERT can help uncover patterns of greenwashing, assess market reactions to climate policies, and inform stakeholder engagement strategies by applying sentiment analysis to large-scale climate discourse to serve as a critical tool for advancing transparency, accountability, and informed decision-making in the era of climate transition. ClimateBERT can analyze the sentiment behind climate-related paragraphs in corporate reports, classifying them as indicating risk, opportunity, or being neutral. It focuses on classifying climate-related paragraphs into three categories: Risk (negative sentiment), Opportunity (positive sentiment), or Neutral.[53] Annotators labeled paragraphs based on whether the text described threats affecting entities such as companies, opportunities arising from climate change, or neutral statements. Annotators applied a strict 0–1 decision rule and used common sense to interpret context, with multiple annotators per task to ensure reliability; ties were resolved through discussion. This approach allows ClimateBERT to accurately detect nuanced sentiments in corporate and climate-related communications, improving downstream analysis of climate discourse.

8.9.10 Measuring "ESG Talk" and greenwashing

ClimateBERT, as a transformer-based language model fine-tuned on climate-related texts, has been used in analyzing corporate sustainability disclosures and detecting greenwashing to support more transparent and accountable corporate sustainability practices.[54] ClimateBERT enables organizations and researchers to quantitatively assess the extent of "ESG talk", the volume and tone of ESG language in corporate reports, press releases, and other textual data by leveraging advanced natural language processing (NLP) techniques, This model is particularly effective in identifying discrepancies between organizations' ESG narratives and their actual environmental performance to serve as a diagnostic tool for potential greenwashing. For instance, organizations with extensive ESG-related language but poor sustainability outcomes may be flagged for overstating their commitments. ClimateBERT can supports more transparent, reliable and accountable corporate sustainability practices by mapping ESG-related communication against objective ESG metrics.

Using ClimateBERT to measure "ESG talk" and detect greenwashing offers a sophisticated approach to evaluating the authenticity and credibility of ESG disclosures by capturing the nuanced language, tone, and context often embedded in CSRs and ESG disclosures. ClimateBERT can identify patterns of "ESG talk" where companies promote sustainability in words but lack concrete actions or measurable outcomes by distinguishing between substantive climate-related commitments and vague, non-committal language. This capability is particularly valuable for detecting greenwashing, where organizations may exaggerate or misrepresent their environmental and social impacts. Through sentiment analysis, thematic classification, and semantic similarity assessments, ClimateBERT enables organizations to systematically assess the alignment between ESG rhetoric and actual performance, thus enhancing accountability, supporting regulatory oversight. ClimateBERT is used to measure the level of "ESG Talk" (ESG communication) in CSRs and potentially detect greenwashing. The risk of greenwashing is quantified through climate-specific attributes: commitment, specificity, sentiment, and hedging, utilizing expert-annotated data for fine-tuning. ClimateBERT is fine-tuned on the expert-annotated dataset derived from sustainability report paragraphs to classify the presence of greenwashing language. This approach leverages NLP to analyze dense, complex texts at scale, enhancing the detection of misleading or overly positive corporate environmental communications. The model achieved an accuracy of 86.34% and an F1 score of 0.67, demonstrating potential in identifying misleading environmental claims.[55] Challenges include limited expert data, label imbalance, and context loss from paragraph-level analysis, suggesting future improvements with expanded datasets and refined training.

8.10 SRA with local LLMs

SRA can benefit from the application of local LLMs, which offer customizable, domain-specific capabilities tailored to regional regulations, languages, and stakeholder expectations. Unlike generic, globally trained models, local LLMs can be fine-tuned on country- or industry-specific sustainability reports, assurance standards (e.g., ISAE 3000), and ESG taxonomies, enabling more accurate interpretation and generation of localized sustainability content. These local LLM models enable organizations to customize their sustainability reports by automating drafting, reviewing, and consistency checking of sustainability reports. These models can also support auditors in identifying gaps, inconsistencies, or noncompliance in disclosed ESG data. Furthermore, local LLMs enhance the quality and credibility of assurance processes by providing real-time analysis, benchmarking against local sustainability norms, and generating assurance statements that align with national regulations. As sustainability disclosure becomes more regulated and complex, particularly under frameworks such as the EU CSRD or regional ESG mandates, local LLMs provide a scalable, context-aware tool for improving transparency, reliability, and stakeholder trust in sustainability communication.

The use of local LLMs in sustainability reporting and assurance processes is transforming how organizations manage ESG data. These models, deployed within secure institutional environments, are uniquely positioned to support compliance with evolving standards such as the ESRS, ISSB, CDP, and SASB, while also aligning with assurance protocols like ISAE 3410. Local LLMs ensure data privacy, regulatory alignment, and operational control—critical for handling sensitive sustainability disclosures. To further enhance contextual understanding, LLMs, including local ones, undergo fine-tuning on annotated ESG data for more specific customization of model behavior that reflects the language and structure of sustainability reports aligned with ESRS, CDP questionnaires, SASB metrics, and ISSB guidance.[56] This fine-tuning process allows the models to internalize sector-specific terminology, materiality thresholds, and assurance language used in reporting standards, thereby improving the precision and relevance of automated insights.

In addition to optimizing the output of LLMs, including local ones, Retrieval-Augmented Generation (RAG) can be used to dynamically access internal knowledge bases, regulatory texts, and historical disclosures. RAG technologies enable real-time contextualization of sustainability claims, support double materiality assessments, and enhance the traceability and auditability of assurance processes. RAG-powered LLMs ensure that outputs are grounded in verifiable sources, thus improving both transparency and stakeholder confidence. They ensure compliance with evolving ESG regulations and assurance expectations, thus enhancing trust. Finally, local LLMs can operate without an internet connection, providing greater flexibility and reliability in situations where network access is limited by offering several advantages, including enhanced data privacy, faster responses, reliable and consistent output, cost-effectiveness, and customization. By keeping data under the company's control, minimizing the risk of breaches and ensuring that sensitive data is protected. Ethically, prioritizing local LLMs aligns with the principles of transparency, accountability, and user control, fostering trust by ensuring that data remains within the user's jurisdiction and reducing reliance on centralized services.

8.11 Summary

This chapter explores the transformative potential of AI in advancing sustainability across ESG dimensions. It begins by outlining the pressing global sustainability challenges and the need for innovative, data-driven solutions. The chapter examines how AI technologies such as ML, NLP, and computer vision are being applied to optimize energy consumption, reduce waste, monitor environmental impact, enhance supply chain transparency, and support sustainable agriculture and resource management. It also highlights AI's role in improving social outcomes through predictive analytics in healthcare, education, and equitable resource allocation. Additionally, it discusses how AI can strengthen corporate accountability, ESG reporting, and regulatory compliance. The chapter elaborates on BERT, a model for NLP tasks, which is highly effective in analyzing complex sustainability-related text. Studies demonstrate its application in classifying documents, extracting information, and verifying claims related to sustainability, ESG, and climate change. Finally, the chapter addresses key ethical and operational concerns, including data privacy, algorithmic bias, and the carbon footprint of AI itself, emphasizing the need for responsible and inclusive AI development. Case studies and industry examples illustrate both opportunities and challenges, offering a roadmap for integrating AI into sustainability strategies. ESG information can be found across a collection of specialized quantitative databases (e.g., LSEG, Bloomberg, and MSCI), company disclosures, academic repositories, and dedicated institutional guides. The choice of source depends on the specific pillar of ESG being investigated (environmental emissions, diversity metrics, and governance structures), the needed data granularity, historical coverage, and user access rights.

8.12 Takeaways

- AI enhances sustainability efforts by enabling data-driven decision-making in ESG domains.
- ML and predictive analytics help optimize resource use, forecast environmental risks, and improve climate resilience.
- Computer vision and IoT-powered AI systems support real-time environmental monitoring, pollution control, and precision agriculture.
- NLP improves ESG reporting accuracy, stakeholder engagement, and corporate transparency.
- AI contributes to social sustainability through applications in public health, education access, poverty reduction, and equitable services distribution.
- Ethical concerns such as algorithmic bias, transparency, and AI's environmental footprint must be proactively managed.
- Responsible AI development should align with sustainability values, promoting fairness, inclusivity, and environmental stewardship.
- Collaborative innovation between governments, businesses, and academia is critical to scaling AI for sustainable development.
- Real-world case studies demonstrate the diverse applications and potential of AI in achieving global sustainability goals (SDGs).

Notes

1 The International Organization for Standardization (ISO): Global standards for trusted goods and services. https://www.iso.org/home.html
2 Navajas, A., Uriarte, L., & Gandía, L. M. 2017. Application of eco-design and life cycle assessment standards for environmental impact reduction of an industrial product. *Sustainability*, 9(10), 1724. https://doi.org/10.3390/su9101724
3 Gong, Y., Xiao, J., Tang, X., & Li, J. 2023. How sustainable marketing influences the customer engagement and sustainable purchase intention? The moderating role

of corporate social responsibility. *Frontiers in Psychology*, 14, 1128686. https://doi.org/10.3389/fpsyg.2023.1128686

4 Am, J., et al. 2023, 6 February. *Consumers Care about Sustainability-and Back It up with Their Wallets*. McKinsey & Company. http://www.mckinsey.com/industries/consumer-packaged-goods/our-insights/consumers-care-about-sustainability-and-back-it-up-with-their-wallets

5 Feber, D., et al. 2020, 21 October. *Sustainability in Packaging: Inside the Minds of US Consumers*. McKinsey & Company. www.mckinsey.com/industries/packaging-and-paper/our-insights/sustainability-in-packaging-inside-the-minds-of-us-consumers

6 Gong, Y., et al. 2023, 21 February. How sustainable marketing influences the customer engagement and sustainable purchase intention? The moderating role of corporate social responsibility. *Frontiers*. www.frontiersin.org/journals/psychology/articles/10.3389/fpsyg.2023.1128686/full

7 Khalid, A. 2023, 14 September. Sustainable marketing and its impact on society: A study of marketing strategies and opportunities promoting eco-friendly lifestyle. *SSRN*. https://papers.ssrn.com/sol3/papers.cfm?abstract_id=4570227

8 García-Quevedo, J., Segarra-Blasco, M., & Teruel-Carrizosa, A. 2018. Innovation for sustainability: The impact of R&D spending on CO_2 emissions. *Journal of Cleaner Production*, 172, 3459–3467. https://doi.org/10.1016/j.jclepro.2017.11.001

9 Sarpong, D., Boakye, D., Ofosu, G., & Botchie, D. 2023. The three pointers of research and development (R&D) for growth-boosting sustainable innovation system. *Technovation*, 122, 102581. ISSN 0166-4972. https://doi.org/10.1016/j.technovation.2022.102581; https://www.sciencedirect.com/science/article/pii/S0166497222001286

10 Chen, S., & Yu, D. 2023, 5 June. The impact of R&D effort on business model innovation: Evaluating chain mediation through collaboration breadth and depth. *PLoS One*, 18(6), e0286715. https://doi.org/10.1371/journal.pone.0286715. PMID: 37276193; PMCID: PMC10241366

11 Insight. https://wp.nyu.edu/insight/2023/06/29/five-sustainable-strategies-for-effective-waste-management-in-business/

12 EPA. 2024, July. *Environmental Protection Agency*. www.epa.gov/smm/managing-and-reducing-wastes-guide-commercial-buildings

13 Lenkiewicz, Z. 2024. Beyond an age of waste—wedocs. *Unep.Org*. https://wedocs.unep.org/bitstream/handle/20.500.11822/44939/global_waste_management_outlook_2024.pdf?sequence=3

14 Kosasih, Wilson., Pujawan, I.N., Karningsih, P.D., & Shee, H. 2023. Integrated lean-green practices and supply chain sustainability framework. *Cleaner and Responsible Consumption*, 11, 100143, ISSN 2666-7843. https://doi.org/10.1016/j.clrc.2023.100143; https://www.sciencedirect.com/science/article/pii/S266678432300044X

15 PricewaterhouseCoopers. PWC 2023 US large energy user survey. *PwC*. www.pwc.com/us/en/industries/energy-utilities-resources/library/large-energy-user-survey.html

16 Kihila, J.M., & Mwakalinga, E.A. 2021. Waste minimization towards waste management and cleaner production strategies: A literature review. *Environmental Science and Pollution Research*, 28(36), 50328–50342. https://doi.org/10.1007/s11356-021-14206-9

17 Rogelj, J., Geden, O., Cowie, A., & Reisinger, A. 2021. Three ways to improve net-zero emissions targets. *Nature*, 591(7850), 365–368. https://doi.org/10.1038/d41586-021-00662-3

18 Ong, K.J.E., Mao, R., Satapathy, R., Shirota Filho, R., Cambria, E., Sulaeman, J., & Mengaldo, G. 2025. Explainable natural language processing for corporate sustainability analysis. *Information Fusion*, 115, 102726

19 Morio, G., In, S.Y., Yoon, J., Rowlands, H., & Manning, C. 2024. ReportParse: A unified NLP tool for extracting document structure and semantics of corporate sustainability reporting. In *Proceedings of the Thirty-Third International Joint Conference on Artificial Intelligence (IJCAI-24)*

20 OpenAI. *Key Concepts*. https://platform.openai.com/docs/concepts/tokens
21 Microsoft. 2024. *Understand Tokens*. https://learn.microsoft.com/en-us/dotnet/ai/conceptual/understanding-tokens
22 Wang, D., Li, Y., Jiang, J., Ding, Z., Jiang, G., Liang, J., & Yang, D. 2024. *Tokenization Matters! Degrading Large Language Models through Challenging Their Tokenization*. ArXiv, abs/2405.17067. arXiv:2405.17067v1 (cs)
23 Wang et al. *Tokenization Matters! Degrading Large Language Models through Challenging Their Tokenization*. OpenAI
24 Extracted from Amazon. 2023. *Amazon Sustainability Report—Sustainability Reporting Framework Summary*. https://sustainability.aboutamazon.com/2023-sustainability-reporting-framework-summary.pdf
25 Microsoft. 2024. *Understand Tokens*. https://learn.microsoft.com/en-us/dotnet/ai/conceptual/understanding-tokens
26 Gutierrez-Bustamante, M., & Espinosa-Leal, L. 2022. Natural language processing methods for scoring sustainability reports—a study of Nordic listed companies. *Sustainability*, 14(15), 9165
27 Kang, H., & Kim, J. 2022. Analyzing and visualizing text information in corporate sustainability reports using natural language processing methods. *Applied Sciences*, 12(11), 5614
28 Lagasio, V. 2024. ESG-washing detection in corporate sustainability reports. *International Review of Financial Analysis*, 96, 103742
29 Ong, K.J.E., Mao, R., Satapathy, R., Shirota Filho, R., Cambria, E., Sulaeman, J., & Mengaldo, G. 2025. Explainable natural language processing for corporate sustainability analysis. *Information Fusion*, 115, 102726
30 Angin, M., Taşdemir, B., Yılmaz, C. A., Demiralp, G., Atay, M., Angin, P., & Dikmener, G. 2022. A RoBERTa approach for automated processing of sustainability reports. *Sustainability*, 14(23), 16139
31 Kim, Y., Kim, J.H., Kim, Y.M., Song, S., & Joo, H.J. 2023. Predicting medical specialty from text based on a domain-specific pre-trained BERT. *International Journal of Medical Informatics*, 170, 104956
32 Devlin, J., Chang, M. W., Lee, K., & Toutanova, K. 2019. BERT: Pre-training of deep bidirectional transformers for language understanding. *Proceedings of the 2019 Conference of the North American Chapter of the Association for Computational Linguistics: Human Language Technologies*, 1, 4171–4186
33 Liu, Y., Ott, M., Goyal, N., Du, J., Joshi, M., Chen, D., Levy, O., Lewis, M., Zettlemoyer, L., & Stoyanov, V. 2019. *RoBERTa: A Robustly Optimized BERT Pretraining Approach*. arXiv preprint arXiv:1907.11692
34 Lan, Z., Chen, M., Goodman, S., Gimpel, K., Sharma, P., & Soricut, R. 2019. *AlBERT: A Lite BERT for Self-Supervised Learning of Language Representations*. arXiv preprint arXiv:1909.11942
35 Sanh, V., Debut, L., Chaumond, J., & Wolf, T. 2019. *DistilBERT, a Distilled Version of BERT: Smaller, Faster, Cheaper and Lighter*. arXiv preprint arXiv:1910.01108
36 Liu, Z., Huang, D., Huang, K., Li, Z., & Zhao, J. 2021, January. FinBERT: A pre-trained financial language representation model for financial text mining. In *Proceedings of the Twenty-Ninth International Conference on International Joint Conferences on Artificial Intelligence* (pp. 4513–4519)
37 Webersinke, N., Kraus, M., Bingler, J. A., & Leippold, M. 2022. *ClimateBERT: A Pretrained Language Model for Climate-Related Text*. arXiv:2110.12010v3. https://arxiv.org/abs/2110.12010
38 Takeda, H. 2024, 22–25 October. Research on LEGALBERT: Enhancing legal document review using BERT for automated text analysis. In *The 8th International Scientific and Practical Conference "Modernization of Innovative Development of Professional Education", Amsterdam, Netherlands. International Science Group* (pp. 287, 318)

39 Licari, D., & Comandè, G. 2024. ITALIAN-LEGAL-BERT models for improving natural language processing tasks in the Italian legal domain. *Computer Law & Security Review*, 52, 105908
40 Taneja, K., Vashishtha, J., & Ratnoo, S. 2025. Fraud-BERT: Transformer based context aware online recruitment fraud detection. *Discover Computing*, 28(1), 1–16 and Yang, X., Zhang, C., Sun, Y., Pang, K., Jing, L., Wa, S., & Lv, C. 2023. FinChain-BERT: A high-accuracy automatic fraud detection model based on NLP methods for financial scenarios. *Information*, 14(9), 499
41 Liu, N., Hu, Q., Xu, H., Xu, X., & Chen, M. 2021. Med-BERT: A pretraining framework for medical records named entity recognition. *IEEE Transactions on Industrial Informatics*, 18(8), 5600–5608
42 Hiew, J.Z.G., Huang, X., Mou, H., Li, D., Wu, Q., & Xu, Y. 2019. *BERT-Based Financial Sentiment Index and LSTM-Based Stock Return Predictability*. arXiv preprint arXiv:1906.09024
43 Torroni, P., Almeida, V.D.R.S., & Ruberg, N. 2021. *BERT Goes Sustainable: An NLP Approach to ESG Financing Bologna, 2021* (57 f.). Dissertação (Mestrado) - Università di Bologna, Department of Computer Science and Engineering
44 Angin, M., Taşdemir, B., Yılmaz, C. A., Demiralp, G., Atay, M., Angin, P., & Dikmener, G. 2022. A RoBERTa approach for automated processing of sustainability reports. *Sustainability*, 14(23), 16139
45 Ruberg, N. 2021. BERT goes sustainable: An NLP approach to ESG financing. Master Thesis. Università di Bologna. http://amslaurea.unibo.it/24787/
46 Bauer, R., Broeders, D., & Van Ool, A. 2023. Walk the green talk? A textual analysis of pension funds' disclosures of sustainable investing. *Journal of Pension Economics & Finance*, 1–29
47 Schwabenland, C., & Goodall, H. 2022. Analysing sustainability discourse with NLP: Exploring the use of machine learning to understand SDG communications. *Sustainability Science*, 17(2), 511–526. https://doi.org/10.1007/s11625-021-01026-6
48 SDSN Europe. 2022. *Financing the Joint Implementation of the SDGs and the European Green Deal*. https://egd-report.unsdsn.org/
49 SDSN Europe. *Financing the Joint Implementation of the SDGs and the European Green Deal*
50 Webersinke, N., Kraus, M., Bingler, J.A., & Leippold, M. 2022. *ClimateBERT: A Pretrained Language Model for Climate-Related Text*. arXiv:2110.12010v3. https://arxiv.org/abs/2110.12010
51 Webersinke et al. *ClimateBERT: A Pretrained Language Model for Climate-Related Text*
52 Webersinke et al. *ClimateBERT: A Pretrained Language Model for Climate-Related Text*
53 Webersinke et al. *ClimateBERT: A Pretrained Language Model for Climate-Related Text*
54 Köhler, S., Feuerriegel, S., & Neuberger, D. 2022. ClimateBERT: A pretrained language model for climate-related text. *Scientific Data*, 9, 649. https://doi.org/10.1038/s41597-022-01839-2
55 Vinella, A., Capetz, M., Pattichis, R., Chance, C., & Ghosh, R. 2023. *Leveraging Language Models to Detect Greenwashing*. arXiv preprint arXiv:2311.01469
56 Lovin, M.-F. 2025. *LLMs to Support a Domain Specific Knowledge Assistant*. arXiv preprint arXiv:2502.04095. https://arxiv.org/abs/2502.04095

9 AI implementation and strategy development and reporting

9.1 Introduction

Sustainability strategic development requires the establishment of a comprehensive plan that outlines the missions, goals, objectives, and actions needed to achieve sustainability and operational excellence. It requires a thorough understanding of the organization's culture, business environment, current state, market dynamics, and stakeholder expectations, as well as the execution of planned actions, the allocation of resources, and the management of change within the organization. Developing and implementing a successful strategy involves setting concise, measurable targets, identifying KPIs, and defining the resources and capabilities required to support the implementation process by turning strategic plans into reality. Successful implementation requires proper tone at the top, strong leadership, effective and transparent communication, active engagement of all stakeholders, the establishment of governance structures, monitoring progress, and adjustments as needed to address any challenges or obstacles that arise. Furthermore, successful implementation requires the alignment of strategy with organizational culture and capabilities by utilizing sustainability initiatives that can be integrated into the core values and operations of the organization by fostering a culture of sustainability, utilizing AI platforms, providing training and support to employees, and ensuring that sustainability goals are embedded into everyday practices and decision-making processes. Proper strategy development and implementation also require a focus on CI and adaptability in response to emerging trends, regulatory changes, and evolving stakeholder expectations and a proactive approach to monitoring and evaluating performance, as well as a commitment to learning and innovation. This chapter presents the principles and practices of implementation and strategy development by focusing on how organizations can effectively execute their sustainability strategies and achieve their goals and provides key topics such as strategic planning, resource allocation, change management, and performance monitoring.

9.2 Developing a sustainability strategy

The effectiveness of business sustainability in achieving its main goal of creating shared value for all stakeholders requires adopting strategies and practices that

DOI: 10.4324/9781003611981-9

contribute to short-, medium-, and long-term financial ESP and nonfinancial ESG performance.[1] Sustainability is a process (a journey) of integrating ESP and ESG into the business environment and corporate culture to create sustainable shared value through the strategic planning of developing a profit-with-purpose mission. Under the strategic shared value creation concept, management focuses on the continuous performance improvement of business operations in creating long-term value for all stakeholders. Strategy development in the context of sustainability reporting and AI integration involves aligning organizational goals with both financial ESP and nonfinancial ESG priorities while leveraging advanced technologies to enhance data accuracy, transparency, and decision-making. As sustainability reporting becomes increasingly standardized and scrutinized as an integral component of corporate reporting, organizations must design strategic frameworks that incorporate AI tools for real-time data collection, predictive analytics, and automated reporting processes. These AI capabilities empower organizations to identify emerging ESG risks and opportunities, benchmark performance, and ensure compliance with evolving regulatory requirements. An effective strategy integrates cross-functional collaboration, ethical AI use, and continuous improvement mechanisms, enabling organizations to meet their reporting obligations and drive long-term sustainable value creation for all stakeholders.

Sustainability strategic planning reflects short-term and long-term objectives and priorities. In the short term, management may primarily focus on maximizing profits and increasing shareholder wealth. This short-term strategic plan may enable businesses to continue their operations for the foreseeable future and generate profits, but it can compromise long-term investment, R&D, training, and other sustainable, value-enhancing corporate activities.

Long-term sustainability planning requires companies to focus on economic viability and consider other factors, including environmental consciousness, ethics, social impacts, diversity, and inclusion, as well as customer satisfaction and reputation. Long-term sustainability planning requires managers to continually foster an ethical work environment, one that promotes a culture of diversity, inclusion, and equity. Strategic sustainability planning enables companies to focus on a profit-with-purpose mission of creating shared value for all stakeholders. The statement of purpose, along with strategic sustainability planning, should define objectives of creating the right balance between short-term, medium-term, and long-term strategic plans.

Sustainability planning consists of (1) evaluation and assessment of business activities and priorities; (2) establishment of goals and objectives; (3) stakeholder engagement and communication; (4) implementation and monitoring; and (5) reevaluation, reassessment, and adaptation.[2] AI plays a transformative role in sustainability strategic planning, offering tools that enhance decision-making, improve efficiency, and support environmentally responsible initiatives with a keen focus on long-term performance. AI-driven platforms can assist in all five aspects of strategic planning by: (1) analyzing vast datasets from various sources to provide actionable insights to strategic planning, streamlining processes, identifying trends, and predicting outcomes to make more informed sustainability decisions.;

(2) optimizing resource use, such as water, energy, and raw materials, by predicting and adjusting usage in real time that can lead to significant reductions in waste and energy consumption in short term and long term; (3) providing real-time insights and transparency in supply chains of tracing the origins of raw materials, monitor environmental impacts, and ensure ethical sourcing practices; and (4) enabling to engage with stakeholders more effectively, ensuring that sustainability strategies align with stakeholder expectations and concerns.

9.3 Corporate reporting

Corporate reporting has evolved over time ever since the separation of ownership and management in companies. Traditional financial reporting reflects financial statements (e.g., balance sheets and income statements) with the primary focus of meeting legal and tax requirements. Adoption of Generally Accepted Accounting Principles (GAAP) in the United States in the 1930s and the development of the IASB in the late 20th century created a common accounting language aimed at enhancing transparency and comparability of basic financial statements. The wave of corporate scandals at the turn of the 21st century led to stricter regulations in the United States for corporate reporting, the enactment of the Sarbanes-Oxley Act (SOX, 2002) focusing on corporate governance and internal controls. SOX introduced further reforms requiring certification of both financial and internal control over financial reporting, aimed at improving transparency and accountability in corporate reporting. Companies were focusing on clearer and more engaging narratives that explain the key financial performance indicators, providing context around performance metrics and strategic decisions. Efforts to simplify the language and improve the quality of corporate reports made them more accessible to a wider user of financial reports. The global adoption of IFRS has led to more consistent reporting practices, facilitating comparability across companies and industries. Regulatory bodies have implemented more rigorous compliance frameworks that require higher quality disclosures and accountability. Improvements in corporate governance practices, including board oversight of reporting processes, have strengthened the integrity of corporate reports.

9.3.1 Corporate reporting and technological advances

Technological advances can enable companies to produce more information in a timely manner that is relevant to stakeholders. Companies should leverage big data to enhance reporting accuracy and provide deeper insights into financial health. Advances in technology enable more frequent updates, making it easier for stakeholders to access timely information. The use of advanced data analytics tools helps companies identify trends and anomalies, improving the accuracy and relevance of reports. Technologies like cloud computing enable more frequent updates, allowing stakeholders to access up-to-date information on financial ESP and non-financial ESG sustainability performance. Ongoing developments in AI and data analytics are likely to influence reporting practices, enabling more personalized and insightful disclosures, with a focus on standardized global ESG reporting frameworks to ensure consistency and comparability across industries. Leveraging big data and analytics tools improves accuracy in reporting and helps identify trends and anomalies, whereas streamlining corporate reporting processes through automation reduces errors and enhances efficiency, leading to more reliable reports.

The quality of corporate reporting has significantly improved due to a combination of regulatory pressures, technological innovations, and evolving stakeholder expectations. As these trends continue to develop, companies will likely face ongoing demands for greater transparency, accuracy, and accountability in their reporting practices. The future of corporate reporting is expected to be shaped by technological advancements, regulatory changes, and increasing stakeholder expectations with more focus on: (1) AI and data analytics that will likely transform how companies gather and report information; (2) real-time reporting using digital tools that will enable more frequent updates on a company's ESP and ESG sustainability reporting; and (3) blockchain technology, which has the potential to enhance transparency and trust in corporate reporting by ensuring the verifiability and immutability of reported data by streamlining audit trails and improving the traceability of transactions and disclosures. The interplay of regulatory requirements, technological advancements, stakeholder demands, corporate governance, and market dynamics drives significant improvements in corporate reporting quality. Organizations that proactively address these factors are better positioned to enhance their reporting practices and build trust with stakeholders.

9.3.2 The role of AI platforms in corporate reporting

It is expected that ongoing developments in AI and data analytics will likely influence reporting practices, enabling more personalized and insightful disclosures with a focus on standardized global ESP and ESG reporting frameworks to ensure consistency and comparability across industries. AI-powered tools and techniques can revolutionize corporate reporting by enhancing efficiency, quality, accuracy, and the depth of insights derived from financial ESP and nonfinancial ESG sustainability performance disclosures. AI platforms can streamline the preparation of financial ESP reports by automating repetitive tasks of data collection, reconciliation, and compliance procedures to ensure accuracy, reduce human errors, and expedite the financial reporting process by: (1) extracting and aggregating financial data from multiple sources, reducing the time required for manual data entry; (2) identifying anomalies, inconsistencies, or potential fraud in financial statements and detecting and correcting material misstatements in financial reports; and (3) assisting compliance with ever-increasing accounting standards and regulatory requirements.

AI-powered platforms can also play a significant role in ESG sustainability reporting by processing vast datasets and extracting meaningful insights related to corporate sustainability and accountability by: (1) analyzing narrative disclosures of using NLP tools to assess the quality, reliability and transparency of ESG sustainability reporting; (2) tracking and reporting environmental and social impacts to enable real-time monitoring by stakeholders; (3) predicting and measuring ESG risks and opportunities to assist investors in their decision-makers in proactive planning; (4) improving stakeholder communication and engagement by making sustainability reports more accessible and understandable, personalizing reports tailored to the interests of different stakeholder groups, and making complex data easier to comprehend through interactive charts, graphs, and dashboards and preparing narratives for annual financial reports, sustainability reports, or earnings calls in a clear and coherent manner; (5) facilitating integrated sustainability reporting of financial ESP and nonfinancial ESG metrics; (6) examining the link between financial ESP and nonfinancial ESG sustainability performance disclosures; (7) performing scenario analysis of the long-term impact of corporate strategies on both financial ESP stability and nonfinancial ESG goals; and (8) promoting transparency and accountability by providing stakeholders with detailed and timely information to improve corporate governance and accountability.

AI-powered tools and techniques can transform corporate reporting by enabling greater efficiency, precision, and insight, empowering organizations to meet investors' demands and stakeholder expectations for transparency while navigating the complexities of financial ESP and nonfinancial ESG performance reporting. As AI technology continues to advance, its role in corporate reporting is expected to become even more significant, driving innovation and fostering investor confidence and stakeholder trust in corporate reporting. However, several potential challenges of the use of AI platforms in corporate reporting, including data privacy and security, regulatory scrutiny, and algorithmic bias, should be considered.

9.4 Integrated sustainability reporting

In recent years, integrated sustainability reporting emerged as a framework to integrate financial economic sustainability (ESP) and nonfinancial ESG information into a single corporate reporting. Corporate reporting is now expanding to incorporate nonfinancial ESG performance information. As corporations strive to meet the evolving stakeholder expectations, the future of corporate reporting continues to emphasize innovative technologies, transparency, and stakeholder engagement. Corporate reporting reflects the growing recognition that stakeholders, including investors, regulators, employees, customers, and the public, seek a more comprehensive view of a company's long-term and sustainable value creation and its impact on society and the environment. The adoption of integrated sustainability reporting has further reshaped corporate reporting frameworks, aligning them with global sustainability goals and fostering a culture of responsible business practices. Corporate reporting is used as a mechanism for communication, accountability, and stewardship to all stakeholders. The quality, interactions, and connections among these stakeholders are particularly important factors that affect their behaviors and ultimately drive the quality of the corporate reporting process. The diverse needs of these different stakeholders make it difficult to create one-size-fits-all corporate reports. Increased scrutiny and growing demand for transparency also mean that reports must be more detailed and defensible. Ongoing efforts to converge global standards, particularly in areas like integrated sustainability reporting, make corporate reports more relevant, useful, and transparent for all stakeholders worldwide. Improvements in corporate reporting quality have been driven by a combination of regulatory changes, technological advancements, and shifts in stakeholder expectations. Companies are now required to provide more comprehensive disclosures, including risk factors, management discussions, and future outlooks, making it easier for stakeholders to understand the company's financial health and strategic direction. Strengthened regulations around auditing practices have led to more rigorous scrutiny of financial statements, enhancing their reliability. Combining financial and nonfinancial information allows companies to present a holistic view of their performance, including ESG factors. Growing awareness and concern for ESG issues compel organizations to integrate sustainability into their reporting, strengthen their governance structures that include independent board oversight of reporting processes, and improve their corporate ethical culture that emphasizes ethics and integrity, encouraging more honest and comprehensive corporate reporting. Adoption of IR frameworks (IRFs) encourages companies to present a comprehensive view of performance, incorporating financial and nonfinancial factors, thus enhancing overall report quality.

The integrated sustainability reporting focuses on balancing the needs of investors with the expectations of other stakeholders for reliable, useful, transparent, and robust financial ESP and nonfinancial ESG sustainability performance information. Investors seek information on: (1) returns on their investments, focusing on profitability, revenue growth, and share price appreciation; (2) risks and opportunities associated with ESG investment in terms of impact investing of desired returns on investment with social and environmental outcomes; (3) financial transparency of clear, timely, and accurate financial reports to assess a company's performance and risks; and (4) future outlook of a clear strategy for growth and competitive advantage, including innovation and market positioning. Stakeholder expectations can be met by creating shared value for all stakeholders (employees, customers, suppliers, and communities) through: (1) presenting financial ESP and nonfinancial ESG information; (2) engaging with stakeholders through surveys, forums, and consultations to understand their diverse perspectives and expectations; (3) ensuring compliance with applicable laws, rules, regulations, and standards including environmental regulations and social governance standards; (4) presenting reports on employee satisfaction and retention strategies about financial health that reflects job security and growth opportunities; disclosing product quality, safety standards, ethical sourcing practices, and environmental and social issues; and (5) reflecting the achievements of SDGs. Thus, the integrated sustainability reporting process involves providing information about the organization's financial ESP (profit) and nonfinancial ESG (impact on the planet, people, governance practices, and prosperity). Businesses worldwide are currently dealing with the challenges of adapting a proper globally accepted sustainability reporting framework based on standardized sustainability guidelines to present both financial ESP and nonfinancial ESG sustainability performance effectively. Several organizations worldwide, including the GRI, the IIRC, the SASB, and the ISSB, have issued guidelines regarding the disclosure of sustainability information, aiming to standardize integrated sustainability reports.

The robust integrated sustainability report requires an effective oversight function by the corporate board of directors and firm commitment by management to extend corporate mission beyond maximizing short-term shareholder profit by considering the impact of its operation and entire value chain on all stakeholders, including the community, society, and the environment. To increase stakeholder value, management should identify potential social, environmental, governance, and ethical issues of concern and integrate them into their strategic planning and managerial processes. Management should integrate sustainability performance into its processes and practices in response to the pressure of the labor movement, the development of moral values and social standards, and the change in public opinion about the role of businesses in environmental matters, governance, and ethical scandals. Companies that are leaders in sustainability are challenged by rising public expectations, ever-increasing innovation, continuous quality improvement, effective governance measures, high standards of ethics and integrity, and heightened social and environmental problems. Thus, management should develop and maintain proper sustainability reporting processes that provide a common framework for the integration of both ESP and ESG dimensions of sustainability into their management processes. The global trend toward standardized integrated sustainability reporting encourages and rewards companies that focus on disclosing financial ESP and nonfinancial ESG dimensions of sustainability performance. However, the persistent challenges of achieving robust integrated sustainability reports have been the proper identification, measurement, recognition, reporting, and assurance of financial and nonfinancial KPIs that can be addressed using AI platforms.

9.4.1 The role of AI in sustainability reporting

AI systems can create text for various purposes, including original narratives and news articles, meaning that they can take a set of facts or data and produce coherent written content that effectively conveys information. Additionally, they can translate text between multiple languages, which is crucial for global communication, allowing organizations to reach a wider audience and share sustainability reports or information with a global audience. This inclusivity allows organizations to reach diverse stakeholders, ensuring that their sustainability messages resonate across different cultural and linguistic contexts. They have the potential to transform sustainability reporting by enhancing efficiency, improving data analysis, ensuring consistency, reducing greenwashing, facilitating stakeholder engagement, increasing accessibility, enabling customization, and promoting CI. AI can tailor sustainability reports to meet stakeholders' interests and needs. By analyzing stakeholder preferences and behaviors, organizations can create customized reports highlighting the most relevant information for each audience, enhancing the overall impact of their communication. AI systems learn from interactions, leading to better communication, greater transparency, and, eventually, a stronger connection between organizations and their stakeholders regarding sustainability efforts. The following subsections describe the role of AI in enhancing efficiency, improving data analytics, promoting consistency and standardization, reducing greenwashing, and enhancing stakeholder engagement in sustainability reporting.

9.4.1.1 AI and enhanced efficiency

AI can streamline and automate the processes involved in sustainability reporting. Traditionally, compiling sustainability reports is a labor-intensive task that requires significant time and resources. It involves gathering data from various departments, analyzing that data, and then writing a coherent narrative that communicates the organization's sustainability efforts and performance. However, AI can automate the generation of sustainability reports, reducing the time and effort required to compile and write these documents. AI tools can quickly aggregate data from multiple sources, such as internal databases, external reports, and industry benchmarks. This capability speeds up the data collection process and reduces the likelihood of human error in data entry and analysis. Once the data is collected, AI can assist in drafting the report by generating text based on predefined templates or guidelines, ensuring that the language used is consistent and aligned with the organization's messaging.

As a result, organizations can produce sustainability reports more frequently, shifting from annual to quarterly or monthly updates, thereby improving the timeliness of information shared with stakeholders. AI also enhances the ability to respond promptly to stakeholder inquiries and keep them informed about their sustainability initiatives and progress. When stakeholders, such as investors, customers, or regulatory bodies, have questions about sustainability practices or performance, AI can help organizations provide timely and accurate responses. This responsiveness not only improves stakeholder engagement but also builds trust and credibility, as stakeholders see that the organization is committed to transparency and accountability.

9.4.1.2 AI and improved data analysis

AI can efficiently sift through large volumes of data, extracting insights and trends that may not be immediately apparent to human analysts. In sustainability reporting, organizations often collect extensive data from various sources, including internal reports, stakeholder feedback, regulatory documents, and industry publications. Analyzing this data manually can be time-consuming and may lead to oversight of critical insights. AI utilizes techniques like NLP and ML to analyze unstructured data, identify patterns, and extract valuable insights. This allows organizations to benchmark performance, detect trends, and highlight best practices. For instance, AI can analyze sustainability reports from multiple organizations to benchmark performance, detect common trends, and highlight best practices within the industry. This capability enables organizations to gain a deeper understanding of their sustainability performance and identify areas for improvement, leading to more informed decision-making. By identifying key metrics and trends, AI can reveal areas where an organization is outstripping and areas that require improvement. For example, AI might uncover that a company is performing well in waste reduction but lagging in energy efficiency. Such insights are crucial for organizations aiming to enhance their sustainability strategies.

Additionally, AI can facilitate predictive analytics, allowing organizations to forecast future sustainability performance based on historical data and current trends. This foresight can inform strategic planning and help organizations set realistic sustainability goals. Improved data analysis through AI leads to more informed decision-making. By providing organizations with actionable insights and a clearer picture of their sustainability efforts, AI empowers leaders to make data-driven decisions that align with their sustainability objectives. This informed approach enhances operational efficiency and strengthens the organization's commitment to sustainability, as decisions are based on comprehensive and accurate data analysis rather than assumptions or incomplete information.

9.4.1.3 AI and ensured consistency and standardization

AI can enhance regulatory compliance by helping regulators ensure that organizations adhere to sustainability and ESG-related regulations. It aids in evaluating the accuracy and completeness of submitted sustainability reports and supports enforcement actions by providing relevant data and analysis. Additionally, AI can clarify complex regulations, effectively communicating the regulators' positions. AI can help ensure that sustainability reports comply with global frameworks, such as the ISSB, the GRI, SASB, TCFD, the UNSDGs, and IR. AI can play a crucial role in this process by automating the adherence to these standards. For instance, AI systems can be programmed to recognize and utilize specific language, metrics, and reporting formats that comply with GRI, ISSB, or SDG requirements. This standardization helps eliminate variations in how sustainability data is reported, which can occur when different organizations or departments interpret guidelines differently. By ensuring that sustainability reports are consistent in language and metrics, AI enhances the comparability of reports across different organizations and industries.

This comparability is vital for stakeholders, such as investors, customers, and regulators, who need to assess and compare the sustainability performance of various entities. Regulators must validate AI-generated insights by engaging various stakeholders, including investors and the public, to ensure comprehensive and accurate regulatory practices. When reports follow standardized formats, stakeholders can more easily identify best practices, benchmark performance, and make informed decisions based on reliable data. Standardized reporting can reduce the cognitive load on stakeholders, as they do not have to navigate through varying formats and terminologies. Instead, they can focus on the content and implications of the sustainability efforts being reported. This clarity promotes greater engagement and trust, enabling stakeholders to better understand and evaluate an organization's commitment to sustainability.

9.4.1.4 AI and reduced greenwashing

Greenwashing compromises the accuracy and reliability of sustainability reporting by enabling companies to provide misleading descriptions of their environmental and social actions. The reduction of greenwashing refers to AI's potential to combat misleading practices in which organizations exaggerate or falsely represent their sustainability efforts. Greenwashing occurs when companies present an overly optimistic image of their environmental practices without substantial backing, which can mislead stakeholders about their actual impact. For example, plastic products labeled as "biodegradable" without specifying conditions are misleading. This claim can be considered greenwashing, as the time it takes for a plastic to biodegrade depends on environmental factors such as temperature and humidity. There is great potential and great challenge in using AI for sustainability reporting. While AI can uncover errors and validate claims in sustainability reports, it also raises concerns about greenwashing by producing too optimistic narratives based on biased or selective data.

AI systems can process large datasets to identify patterns or anomalies in sustainability reporting. They can triangulate and validate data generated through different external sources, such as regulatory filings, third-party audits, and independent sustainability assessments. AI systems can then compare this data with the information gathered from sustainability reports. Cross-referencing data can help companies identify discrepancies and accurately report their sustainability performance. For example, if a company claims significant reductions in carbon emissions but shows an increase in energy consumption, AI can flag this inconsistency for further investigation. This analytical capability can help stakeholders scrutinize the validity of sustainability claims, helping to reduce greenwashing and enhance accountability in sustainability reporting.

9.4.1.5 AI and enhanced stakeholder engagement

AI-powered tools such as chatbots and virtual assistants can facilitate real-time communication between organizations and their stakeholders. These tools enable real-time communication, allowing stakeholders to quickly access information about sustainability practices without waiting for human representatives. They use text generation to answer user queries conversationally, fostering sustainability engagement and interaction among various stakeholders within organizations. They are available 24/7, accommodating stakeholders from different time zones and increasing interaction and satisfaction. AI can personalize interactions by analyzing past communications, making the information shared more relevant, and enhancing stakeholders' sense of being valued.

Additionally, AI-powered tools can serve as educational resources, providing insights into the organization's sustainability efforts and helping stakeholders understand its commitments. They also facilitate the collection of feedback on sustainability practices, offering valuable insights for organizational strategies. These tools assist organizations in enhancing engagement and fostering a deeper understanding of their sustainability efforts among stakeholders by offering immediate responses to inquiries about sustainability practices. This builds trust and transparency, motivating stakeholders to participate more actively.

9.5 The role of AI in the preparation of sustainability reports

The evolution of corporate reporting has undergone substantial transformation in recent decades from a primarily focus on financial reports on ESP to integrated sustainability reports on both ESP and ESG, and now to digital, real-time reporting with the use of AI-powered platforms. This revolution has been driven by increasing demands for financial and nonfinancial information, transparency, accountability, and digital technologies. This section examines the potential implications of technology in digitalizing corporate reporting for preparers, auditors, and end-users of corporate reports as influenced by human–machine collaborations.[3]

9.5.1 Measuring and reporting sustainability performance

Sustainability measuring and reporting are integral components of corporate accountability and responsibility. Proper, effective, and robust measurement of ESG KPIs has been a challenge for businesses. KPIs of ESG should be identified, measured, and disclosed. Sustainability reporting is the process of measuring, classifying, and recognizing financial ESP and nonfinancial ESG sustainability performance and disclosing such information to all stakeholders. Stakeholders should have more transparent information about companies' commitment to sustainability. Management can also use sustainability reporting to improve managerial and strategic decisions by integrating sustainability into the business environment, corporate culture, and supply chain management. Sustainability performance reporting and assurance can provide management and external stakeholders with improved confidence in the credibility and trustworthiness of sustainability information. In January 2023, the EU CSRD was issued, requiring mandatory sustainability reporting for European companies that could apply to their counterparts and trading partners worldwide.[4] The CSRD is intended to complement existing sustainability-focused regulations, voluntary frameworks, and standards and will have a global implication. The CSRD requires covered companies to disclose historical and forward-looking information relevant to sustainability matters, including ESG issues and information about sustainability risk management, metrics, and value chain due diligence for EU companies.

Business organizations worldwide are now recognizing the importance of measuring and reporting both financial ESP and nonfinancial ESG sustainability performance. Proper business sustainability strategic planning implementation requires companies to fulfill their stewardship responsibilities to all stakeholders, including shareholders, creditors, the community, society, and the environment. Reporting of ESP and ESG dimensions of sustainability performance information can signal management commitments to sustainability in creating shared value for all stakeholders. Management should identify potential financial, human, social, environmental, governance, and ethical issues of concern and integrate them into its decision-making, strategic planning, and managerial processes, including supply chain management.

The use of AI-driven technologies in measuring and reporting sustainability performance has become increasingly essential in advancing and promoting corporate accountability, sustainability, and transparency. AI-powered predictive analytics and tools can enhance the accuracy, timeliness, and transparency of sustainability performance measurement and reporting to ensure the robustness of sustainable business practices. AI algorithms and tools can enhance sustainability reporting in many ways including: (1) automatically collecting vast amounts of data from diverse sources of IoT sensors, satellite imagery, and corporate reports and processing this data to identify ESG sustainability metrics, environmental footprints, or trends in energy consumption; (2) predicting and assessing the long-term impact of a company's sustainability initiatives by analyzing historical data and identifying patterns, and forecasting future social and environmental impacts; (3) analyzing qualitative information from sustainability reports, social media, news, and other unstructured sources to assess public perception and reputational risks associated with sustainability practices, offering insights into how stakeholders view a company's sustainability initiatives and efforts; and (4) enabling compliance with global sustainability standards and regulations by automatically identifying areas of noncompliance, suggesting corrective actions, and flagging areas of risk.

9.6 The use of AI by independent auditors

The integration of AI into the work of independent auditors is revolutionizing the delivery of audit and non-audit services. AI platforms have become transformative tools, enabling external auditors to assist clients more effectively and accurately in preparing integrated financial and ESG reports. By leveraging AI-powered tools and techniques, including advanced analytics and automation capabilities, auditors can enhance the accuracy, efficiency, and reliability of financial and sustainability reporting. AI-driven technologies address the growing complexity of reporting requirements while supporting the preparation of audit reports and assurance statements. Collaboration between AI systems and human auditors has the potential to elevate audit quality, expand the depth and scope of audits into areas such as sustainability assurance and real-time risk management, and redefine the auditor's role, shifting the focus from traditional financial audit services and assurance activities to broader non-audit and advisory services.

Key aspects of AI in enabling auditors to assist their clients with financial reporting preparation and audit of financial statements include the following:

1. **Data Processing and Analysis**: AI-powered tools process vast amounts of structured and unstructured financial data, identifying trends, anomalies, and inconsistencies with high precision. ML models enhance financial projections by forecasting outcomes and assessing potential risks, improving reliability.

2. **Enhanced Risk Assessment**: AI models analyze extensive datasets to identify potential risks in financial statements, such as unusual transactions or anomalies that may indicate errors or fraud.
3. **Detection and Prevention of Material Misstatements**: AI can identify errors, omissions, or potential fraud in financial transactions by analyzing patterns, comparing them to historical data or industry benchmarks, and detecting subtle irregularities.
4. **Compliance With Financial Laws and Standards**: AI algorithms review financial statements for adherence to accounting standards (e.g., IFRS and GAAP) and regulatory requirements. They also generate checklists to ensure that all necessary disclosures are included.
5. **Preparation of Financial Disclosures**: Natural Language Generation (NLG) capabilities allow AI platforms to draft financial narratives, such as management discussion and analysis sections, from quantitative data, saving time and enhancing efficiency.
6. **Automated Materiality and Risk Assessment**: AI improves audit quality by streamlining materiality assessments and risk evaluations for financial statements.
7. **Verification and Auditing of Financial Statements**: AI-driven tools and continuous auditing techniques enhance the reliability and precision of financial statement verification.
8. **Real-Time Monitoring**: AI enables real-time monitoring of financial transactions and compliance, allowing auditors to promptly identify and address risks through continuous auditing.
9. **Improved Audit Quality**: By applying consistent methods to data analysis, AI reduces human errors and biases, ensuring that audits are performed with greater accuracy and reliability.
10. **Processing Unstructured Data**: AI tools can analyze unstructured data, such as emails, contracts, and ESG disclosures, providing valuable insights for financial reporting and compliance.
11. **Comprehensive Compliance**: AI ensures adherence to all applicable laws, rules, regulations, and standards, further enhancing audit quality.

Key aspects of AI in enabling auditors to assist their clients with sustainability reporting preparation and assurance statements on ESG disclosures include the following:

1. **Data Collection and Integration**: AI facilitates the collection of ESG data from diverse sources, such as sustainability reports, supply chain data, and external databases, ensuring completeness and accuracy. Real-time monitoring tools track ESG metrics, including carbon emissions, energy usage, and diversity metrics, to provide up-to-date insights.
2. **Materiality and Risk Assessment**: AI analyzes trends in regulatory changes, industry standards, and stakeholder sentiment to prioritize ESG opportunities, issues, and risks that are most relevant to stakeholders.

3. **Verification and Assurance**: AI-powered tools verify the accuracy and reliability of ESG data by cross-referencing reported information with third-party sources, such as satellite imagery for environmental metrics or publicly available social data. These tools also assist in preparing ESG assurance statements.
4. **Compliance and Transparency**: AI platforms enhance the narrative quality of ESG reports by generating automated insights into performance metrics and ensuring alignment with sustainability frameworks (e.g., GRI, SASB, ISSB, TCFD, and CSRD).
5. **Predictive Analytics and Strategic Alignment**: Auditors can use AI-driven predictive models and analytics to forecast the potential impact of ESG initiatives on financial performance, helping clients align ESG strategies with business objectives.
6. **Assurance Statements**: AI supports the preparation of assurance statements that validate the reliability, compliance, and transparency of integrated sustainability reports and ESG disclosures.

The integration of AI capabilities significantly enhances efficiency, accuracy, and scope of financial reporting and auditing processes. By leveraging AI tools, auditors can streamline ESG reporting, improve data reliability, and provide insights that enhance transparency and strategic alignment with sustainability goals. However, the use of AI-powered tools by auditors in assisting clients with financial statements and nonfinancial ESG reports presents several challenges and considerations:

1. **Data Quality and Integrity**: Inaccurate, inconsistent, or incomplete data can undermine AI's effectiveness, affecting the quality of financial statements, ESG reports, and related audit opinions and assurance statements.
2. **Ethical Implications**: AI tools may introduce bias or lack transparency, potentially compromising the quality of financial, audit, and assurance processes.
3. **Regulatory Compliance and Scrutiny**: The use of AI platforms in financial and ESG reporting may attract regulatory concerns, requiring auditors to validate AI-generated insights with rigor.
4. **Technical Skill Development**: Auditors must acquire technical skills to work effectively with AI tools and interpret their outputs.

Despite these challenges, AI platforms offer powerful capabilities to help auditors prepare comprehensive, accurate, and reliable financial statements and ESG reports. By automating routine tasks, enhancing data analysis, and ensuring compliance with reporting standards, AI-driven tools elevate the value auditors deliver to clients. To maximize the benefits of AI, auditors must prioritize data quality, ensure ethical use, and address regulatory compliance. As financial and nonfinancial reporting requirements evolve, AI's role in sustainability reporting and auditing is expected to grow, enabling auditors to deliver high-quality services, address emerging risks, and provide greater value to stakeholders.

AI platforms are transforming auditing by enhancing audit quality through automation, advanced data analysis, and deeper insights. Key roles of AI in auditing include the following:

1. **Automating Routine Audit Tasks**: AI streamlines processes such as data collection, extraction, organization, and standardization from diverse sources. It automates sampling, transaction testing, materiality assessments, and the identification of high-risk areas, anomalies, material misstatements, irregularities, and potential fraud in financial records.
2. **Enhancing Data Analysis**: AI processes and analyzes large, complex datasets, including transactions, contracts, and emails, which traditional audit methods cannot efficiently handle, providing auditors with detailed insights.
3. **Predicting Trends and Risks**: AI predicts future trends, material risks, or fraud by analyzing historical data. It identifies patterns, correlations, and outliers in financial data that may signal fraud, misstatements, or compliance issues, enabling proactive risk management.
4. **Enabling Continuous Monitoring**: AI enables automated and continuous monitoring of transactions and operations, flagging risks or fraud as they occur. It detects deviations from expected patterns, highlights areas requiring further investigation, and analyzes behavioral data to identify unusual activities that may signal fraud or noncompliance.
5. **Identifying and Analyzing Critical Audit Matters (CAMs/KAMs)**: AI identifies and evaluates high-risk areas in financial statements and disclosures, enabling auditors to focus on CAMs more effectively.
6. **Improving Audit Quality**: AI facilitates testing of almost 100% of datasets, minimizing sampling risks and improving judgment by directing attention to areas that require professional skepticism. It reduces human errors and inconsistencies, provides near real-time assessments, and enhances the timeliness of audit reporting.
7. **Facilitating Team Collaboration**: AI supports collaboration among audit teams, improving audit quality and efficiency while ensuring compliance with audit standards.

Through these capabilities, AI-powered tools and techniques can significantly enhance the efficiency, accuracy, and reliability of auditing processes, ensuring higher audit quality and enabling auditors to meet evolving investor needs, professional and regulatory compliance, and stakeholder expectations.

9.7 Sustainability risks and the use of AI in assessing, managing, and reporting them

This section examines sustainability risks associated with financial ESP and non-financial ESG sustainability performance reporting and the use of AI in assessing and managing these risks. Business sustainability risks refer to potential threats or challenges that may impede a company's ability to achieve ESP performance, including long-term financial viability, profitability, and generating a positive impact on society and the environment.[5] Sustainability risks encompass economic, financial, environmental, governance, compliance, regulatory, and social dimensions, as explored in this section. Stakeholders, including investors and regulators, factor these risks into their decision-making processes when integrating financial ESP and nonfinancial ESG sustainability performance into investments and regulatory frameworks. These risks can stem from diverse sources, such as financial, strategic, economic, environmental, social, governance, and operational issues. Effectively addressing and managing sustainability risks, supported by AI platforms, is crucial for businesses to enhance resilience, safeguard their reputation, and create long-term shared value for all stakeholders. The potential failure to meet financial ESP and nonfinancial ESG sustainability objectives is particularly significant for shareholders and creditors when evaluating investments. Consequently, the adoption of AI-assisted tools and techniques to assess, manage, and report sustainability risks is increasingly essential in achieving robust financial ESP and nonfinancial ESG outcomes.

Sustainability risks are interconnected and must be thoroughly assessed, managed, and reported. For instance, excessive strategic risk can trigger operational, financial, compliance, and reputational risks. Compliance risk, directly or indirectly linked to business sustainability, encompasses areas such as regulatory noncompliance, health and safety, human rights, labor laws, corporate governance practices, anti-bribery measures, and environmental obligations. These risks vary across organizations and industries. Environmental risks include both direct impacts (e.g., costs associated with emissions trading) and indirect effects (e.g., rising energy prices and the related reporting and compliance costs) stemming from noncompliance with environmental regulations. Traditionally, businesses have focused on assessing and managing financial risks, particularly those related to the production and disclosure of materially misstated financial reports. However, minimizing reputational risk has become equally critical for the success of sustainability initiatives, as stakeholder satisfaction is key to maintaining a sustainable business. To effectively manage sustainability risks, organizations implement enterprise risk management (ERM) policies, conduct comprehensive ESP and ESG assessments, actively engage with stakeholders, and integrate sustainability considerations into planning, performance, and disclosure processes. These efforts aim to mitigate risks, ensure long-term financial viability, and foster shared value creation for all stakeholders.

Business organizations should take a proactive approach to assess sustainability risks by embedding sustainability considerations into strategic planning, risk management processes, and decision-making strategies. Effective sustainability risk management involves identification, assessment, mitigation, reporting, and monitoring of risks throughout the organization. These activities are key elements of an overarching sustainability strategy, helping organizations recognize and address the potential economic, social, environmental, and governance risks and opportunities linked to their decisions and operations. Identifying sustainability risks is the foundational step in this process. To conduct a thorough and effective sustainability risk assessment, businesses must leverage AI-powered tools and techniques to analyze the interconnections between economic, governance, environmental, and social factors. This allows them to develop strategies that mitigate risks while maximizing opportunities for long-term resilience and success. The approach to sustainability risk management includes identifying risks, developing AI-based evaluation tools and metrics, integrating these insights with ERM, performing scenario analyses, conducting materiality assessments, creating risk mitigation and management strategies, engaging stakeholders, ensuring regulatory compliance, and committing to continuous review, adaptability, and improvement.

9.7.1 The sustainability risk framework

The Committee of Sponsoring Organizations (COSO) ERM framework[6] can be used in conjunction with the 2024 guidelines of the IFAC on Building Trust in Sustainability Reporting and Preparing for Assurance: Governance and Controls for Sustainability Information.[7] The COSO and IFAC should be integrated as a framework to assess and manage sustainability risks. All eight components of the COSO ERM framework and seven aspects of IFAC's annual cycle governance and control activities guidelines should be considered including: (1) internal environment of setting the tone at the top of an organization in promoting sustainability factors of performance, risk, and disclosure; (2) objective setting of achieving short-, median-, and long-term strategic sustainability planning; (3) risk identification of risk exposures relevant to sustainability issues; (4) risk assessment of determining risk root cause, sensitivity analyses of the drivers, and pathways of organizational risks; (5) risk responses of addressing the drivers of sustainability risks; (6) control activities designed to manage sustainability risks; (7) information and communication of the organization's responses and efforts in assessing and managing sustainability risks and proper communication with all affected stakeholders; (8) reporting of sustainability reputation, strategic, financial, compliance, social, and environmental risks; and (9) monitoring and ensuring that an organization is achieving its sustainability objectives, managing related sustainability risks, and monitoring and evaluating its sustainability activities.[8]

Effective business sustainability risk assessment, management, and reporting require a comprehensive approach to identifying, assessing, managing, mitigating, reporting, and monitoring potential risks that could impact the long-term financial viability, resilience, and reputation of a business, in terms of both financial ESP and nonfinancial ESG sustainability performance. An integrated framework for sustainability risk management should involve a collaborative team comprising the corporate board of directors, executives, AI specialists, internal auditors, and external auditors, working together to minimize sustainability risks.

This team should establish guiding principles for the sustainability risk evaluation process, which include:

1. Setting the "tone at the top" by committing to a dual risk evaluation approach, addressing both financial ESP risks and nonfinancial ESG risks.
2. Identifying potential risks (e.g., environmental, governance, social, economic, operational, and reputational) that could impact the business's ESP and ESG sustainability.
3. Collecting the necessary data to meet business sustainability objectives, comply with regulations, and fulfill stakeholder and investor expectations.
4. Assessing the likelihood and potential impact of identified risks by gathering data, conducting risk assessments, and applying qualitative and quantitative methods to evaluate their significance.
5. Prioritizing risks based on their potential impact, likelihood, and alignment with the organization's strategic goals and values.
6. Developing robust methodologies to generate consistent data and standardized processes, ensuring that controls are based on sustainability risk factors.
7. Managing risks by creating and implementing mitigation strategies, such as preventive measures, operational diversification, technology investment, innovation, building resilience, and creating contingency plans.
8. Integrating risk responses into decision-making across all areas of the organization, including strategic planning, investment decisions, product development, and supply chain management, while considering the ESP and ESG implications.
9. Continuously monitoring and reviewing sustainability risks to track changes, assess mitigation effectiveness, and adjust strategies as necessary.
10. Engaging stakeholders—shareholders, creditors, employees, customers, investors, suppliers, and communities—by understanding their concerns and building trust and credibility.
11. Reporting risks transparently, communicating ESP- and ESG-related sustainability risks, responses, efforts, and performance through channels such as sustainability reports, annual filings, and stakeholder engagement platforms.
12. Ensuring ongoing monitoring and improvement of the internal control system to strengthen risk management practices.

9.7.2 AI and ESP sustainability risks

The use of AI platforms in assessing, managing, and reporting ESP risks has gained traction in recent years because of their ability to process complex datasets, provide predictive insights, and enhance decision-making. The use of AI-assisted tools and techniques in assessing ESP risks involves several key steps: (1) aggregating and analyzing diverse financial and economic data from both structured and unstructured sources, such as financial statements, market reports, external economic indicators, and social media; (2) employing predictive modeling and ML algorithms to forecast potential risks by analyzing historical data patterns, identifying emerging trends, and predicting future scenarios; (3) developing scenario modeling to evaluate how financial sustainability risks may evolve under various economic conditions, including changes in interest rates, inflation, and global economic shifts; and (4) continuously monitoring real-time market conditions to identify emerging risks that could affect financial sustainability.

AI-powered tools and techniques and risk-scoring models can be employed to manage ESP risks by: (1) prioritizing and categorizing risks based on their potential impact and likelihood, enabling organizations to focus on critical areas and material risks; (2) assisting in optimizing resource allocation for mitigating ESP risks, ensuring efficient use of financial and human capital; (3)simulating stress scenarios to evaluate the resilience of financial and impact investing strategies and suggest improvements for sustainability risk mitigation; and (4) enabling dynamic adjustment of financial attributes and portfolios to reduce exposure to sustainability risks while maximizing returns.

AI algorithms can be utilized in the reporting of ESP risks through several methods: (1) streamlining the preparation of sustainability risk reports by leveraging the COSO and IFAC frameworks to extract relevant data, ensure accuracy, and automate repetitive tasks; (2) ensuring alignment with global reporting standards (e.g., GRI, SASB, ISSB, CSRD, and TCFD) by mapping disclosures to the required metrics and frameworks; (3) utilizing advanced data visualization tools to make ESP sustainability risk reports more accessible and understandable for stakeholders and investors; and (4) integrating blockchain and AI platforms to enhance the transparency and traceability of ESP risk reports. The integration of AI platforms into the framework for assessing, managing, and reporting ESP sustainability risks offers several advantages: (1) improving efficiency by reducing manual effort and accelerating the process of risk assessments, management, and reporting; (2) enhancing accuracy by minimizing human error and ensuring precise analysis of complex risk data; (3) adapting to organizational needs by handling growing data volumes and scaling to address evolving ESP sustainability risks; and (4) providing actionable insights that empower organizations to make informed decisions about ESP sustainability risks. Overall, AI platforms serve as transformative tools, enhancing the effectiveness of assessing, managing, and reporting financial ESP sustainability risks, and supporting organizations in mitigating risks while demonstrating a commitment to sustainable financial practices to stakeholders.

9.7.3 AI and ESG sustainability risks

The use of AI platforms in the assessment, management, and reporting of risks of nonfinancial ESG sustainability performance is revolutionizing how organizations approach sustainability risks. AI algorithms can enhance the precision, efficiency, and transparency of ESG-related activities, internal control activities, and risk evaluation, providing substantial advantages in navigating the increasingly complex ESG sustainability landscape.

AI platforms can be used to assess ESG performance by leveraging data analytics, NLP, and ML technologies. These AI technologies such as IoT sensors and satellite imagery enable: (1) monitoring environmental sustainability performance metrics and related risks including GHG emissions, energy consumption, water usage, and waste generation in real time; (2) simulating climate-related scenarios (e.g., extreme weather events and rising sea levels) to assess risks and identify mitigation strategies; and (3) analyzing land use and conservation efforts to present insights into biodiversity impacts of corporate operations. AI platforms can also enable assessment of social sustainability performance and risks by: (1) analyzing social sentiment on platforms such as social media, news, and employee reviews to gauge public and employee sentiments and perceptions of a company's social responsibility; (2) monitoring labor practices, human rights compliance, and diversity across the supply chain using data mining techniques; and (3) evaluating stakeholder engagement efforts to provide insights into the alignment of corporate actions with community expectations. AI tools can be employed to assess corporate governance performance and related risks by: (1) evaluating governance structures and measures including board composition (e.g., gender diversity and independence of directors); (2) ensuring compliance with governance guiding principles and frameworks by analyzing legal documents, audit reports, and industry standards; and (3) detecting anomalies in financial and operational data to identify risks related to fraud, corruption, and governance failures.

AI can facilitate proactive management of ESG sustainability risks through predictive analytics and data-driven decision-making by: (1) utilizing risk-scoring models to identify high-priority ESG risks and enable effective allocation of resources; (2) detecting ESG emerging risks, such as reputational damage from negative press or environmental noncompliance penalties; (3) performing scenario analyses of "what-if" scenarios for ESG-related risks, such as regulatory and policy changes, stakeholder activism, or climate regulation shifts in enabling organizations to adapt proactively; (4) suggesting customized interventions to improve ESG performance, such as adopting renewable energy, improving workplace diversity, or enhancing transparency in governance practices; and (5) providing real-time tracking of ESG goals, ensuring organizations stay aligned with their sustainability commitments.

AI-assisted tools and techniques can significantly enhance the efficiency, accuracy, and transparency of ESG sustainability risk reporting, helping organizations communicate their sustainability efforts, risks, and opportunities to stakeholders. AI platforms can be utilized to: (1) aggregate data from diverse sources (e.g., IoT devices, social media, and internal databases) to create a centralized ESG dataset; (2) extract ESG-related risk data from unstructured sources, such as sustainability reports, news articles, and regulatory filings; (3) ensure compliance with global ESG reporting frameworks, including GRI, TCFD, SASB, ISSB, and CSRD; (4) map reported risk metrics to the relevant ESG standards to minimize the risk of misalignment; (5) generate visually engaging ESG reports, using charts, heatmaps, and infographics to simplify complex data for stakeholders; (6) enable stakeholders to explore specific metrics, such as carbon emissions or diversity ratios, at a granular level; and (7) provide real-time updates on ESG performance and related risks, allowing organizations to respond swiftly to changes and communicate progress transparently.

Overall, AI platforms present a transformative opportunity to advance non-financial ESG sustainability efforts, enabling organizations to better understand and address sustainability challenges, meet investor needs and stakeholder expectations, and align their sustainability goals with global sustainability objectives. However, the security considerations and implications of AI are crucial when using AI platforms to assess, manage, and report risks related to both financial ESP and nonfinancial ESG sustainability performance. As GenAI gains widespread attention, enterprise security teams face the dual challenge of harnessing its potential while mitigating associated risks. The potential benefits and risks of adopting various AI technologies include: (1) practical recommendations for mitigating risks related to AI and AI-enabled tools and (2) real-world examples demonstrating how AI is enhancing threat detection and response for security professionals.

9.8 Sustainability storytelling

9.8.1 What is storytelling?

Storytelling is the art of conveying events, ideas, emotions, insights, or experiences through a structured narrative. It can take various forms, including oral and written narratives, as well as digital content that resonates with an audience. Storytelling involves imagination. Based on the teller's performance and the listener's past experiences, beliefs, and understandings, the audience actively creates the story's reality in their mind. Thus, they co-create the story. The National Storytelling Network defines storytelling as "the interactive art of using words and actions to reveal the elements and images of a story while encouraging the listener's imagination."[9] Essentially, it is an interactive art form characterized by a dynamic exchange between the storyteller and the audience: it fosters a direct connection where the audience's engagement can influence the direction and delivery of the story. This interaction is crucial because it allows the audience's responses and reactions to shape the narrative being told.

Storytelling is always about presenting a story or narrative. Stories typically revolve around themes and situations that resonate with people on a personal level, stirring emotions that could significantly affect their decision-making processes, attention, and thoughts. Emotions can be positive, such as pride, admiration, and hope, or negative, such as frustration, sadness, anxiety, and worry. The story's emotional depth allows individuals to connect with the company and its journey, fostering sympathy and appreciation. As the story progresses, audiences can reflect on the events and emotions presented, which enhances their appreciation of the narrative's complexity and richness.

9.8.2 Why is sustainability storytelling important for businesses?

For businesses, storytelling is simply the art of communicating ideas and information through compelling narratives rather than just presenting dry facts and figures. It is about creating an emotional connection with an audience by weaving information into a narrative people can relate to and remember. Sustainability storytelling specifically focuses on sharing how a company is working to become more environmentally and socially responsible and is essential for several interconnected reasons. It enhances a business's ability to connect with stakeholders, build trust, and promote environmental responsibility. Stories create a sense of identity and connection among consumers. By sharing narratives that resonate with their values, brands engage stakeholders emotionally, inspiring them to feel personally invested in their mission. This emotional engagement can lead to stronger business loyalty and advocacy. Furthermore, storytelling demonstrates impact by effectively showcasing the results of an organization's achievements. Sharing success stories, challenges overcome, and lessons learned provides tangible evidence of commitment to stakeholders. This portrayal of positive outcomes reinforces trust, as stakeholders can see how their support contributes to meaningful change. Moreover, sustainability storytelling serves as a platform for educating diverse communities and various stakeholders about complex environmental issues. By sharing narratives, companies can help stakeholders understand the importance of sustainability and their role in it by framing these topics in relatable terms and using accessible language. This education empowers stakeholders to make more informed choices and can influence consumer attitudes and behaviors.

Effective sustainability storytelling can differentiate a business in a competitive market. By positioning themselves as leaders in sustainability, businesses can attract stakeholders who prioritize environmental responsibility in their purchasing decisions, enhancing their reputation and market share. This not only enhances the business's impact but also contributes to a broader cultural shift toward sustainability. Sustainability storytelling is not just about promoting a brand; it contributes to a larger movement toward environmental stewardship. By sharing their sustainability stories, businesses can inspire others to act, fostering a collective effort to address environmental challenges. Essentially, sustainability storytelling is essential for connecting with stakeholders, developing trust, educating the public, differentiating in the market, encouraging beneficial behaviors, aligning with consumer values, and supporting environmental sustainability.

9.8.3 How can AI enhance sustainability storytelling?

While ML tools focus on analyzing data to identify trends and make predictions, GenAI utilizes generative models to craft contextually relevant narratives tailored to individual stakeholders based on their behaviors, preferences, and histories. GenAI systems can produce unique narratives that resonate with specific audiences, enhancing stakeholders' engagement and emotional connection. Those systems can analyze vast amounts of consumer data, including behaviors, preferences, and purchase histories, to craft narratives that are specifically tailored to individual users. This personalization helps companies to generate emotionally compelling narratives that forge stronger connections with their audiences. GenAI can create creative content that is relevant and appealing to the target audience with targeted narratives that can evoke feelings and resonate on a personal level, making the story more impactful and memorable.

Companies are leveraging GenAI tools to experiment with different storytelling approaches, allowing for creative and innovative storytelling strategies. By understanding individual stakeholder profiles, GenAI can craft narratives tailored to each. Moreover, real-time feedback facilitates rapid content creation and supports interactive storytelling, enabling narratives that adapt to stakeholders' needs and current trends, leading to a more engaging experience. Through iterative prompt refinement and optimization, GenAI systems support the creation of interactive and dynamic storytelling that can adapt to user input or contextual cues. However, the prompt refinement and optimization process has to consider that the roles of the storyteller and the audience can vary significantly across different cultures and contexts. For instance, in some cultures, audiences may be encouraged to participate actively, asking questions or providing feedback during the storytelling process, while in others, they may adopt a more passive role. These cultural differences create diverse forms of interaction, affecting how stories are told and received. This strategic use of GenAI tools encourages companies to explore innovative storytelling approaches and develop targeted campaigns with personalized recommendations, ensuring that their story aligns closely with consumer interests and preferences and their message remains timely and effective, driving stakeholders' trust and business success.

9.8.4 AI-driven automatic data-driven storytelling

Automatic storytelling refers to the process of using AI-based algorithms to generate narratives or stories without direct human intervention.[10] The automatic data-driven storytelling combines AI-driven visualization and narratives to shape target audience perception and facilitate discussions on complex issues such as ESG and CSR. They help construct shared realities and give meaning to facts and values. Its primary goal is to transform raw data into compelling, easily digestible stories, making complex insights accessible to a broader audience and facilitating the development of a shared understanding of events, issues, or policies (Figure 9.1).

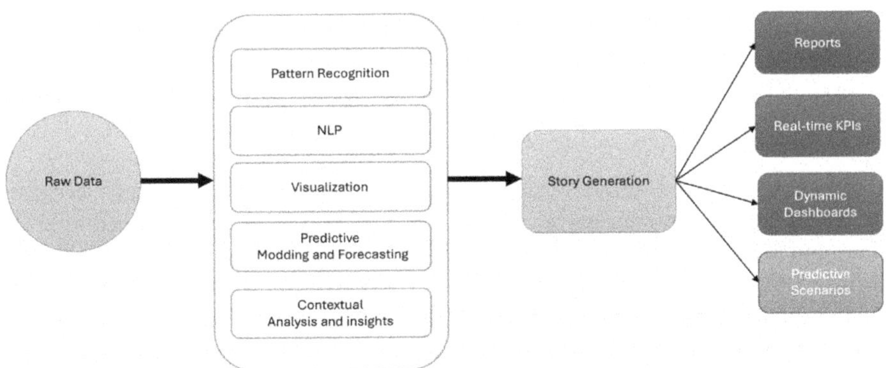

Figure 9.1 Automatic AI-data-driven storytelling

Automatic storytelling requires AI systems to use natural language to construct a consistent narrative that explains a logical flow of events. This involves creating coherent and logically linked sequences of events in a natural language format. The goal of automatic storytelling is to produce narratives that are not only grammatically correct but also engaging and meaningful to the audience, enhancing stakeholder communication and collaboration. This requires careful preparation and exploring different strategies for fostering GenAI's creativity to generate data-driven stories that are logically sound, persuasive, and tailored to the target audience. GenAI models, especially LLMs such as Gemini, ChatGPT, Grok, Llama, and Mistral, are designed to produce coherent and structured narratives. They can maintain consistency in visualizations, like plots and story development, over longer texts, which is crucial for creating engaging and coherent narratives. This consistency ensures that the story follows a logical progression and that events and facts behave in ways that align with their established traits and motivations.

In the context of business sustainability, story development refers to the growth and evolution of a company's values, culture, leadership, and practices to align with sustainable principles and practices. This process emphasizes integrating sustainable practices into the business's core identity, influencing decision-making, and fostering a commitment to environmentally and socially responsible outcomes. It starts with understanding the organization's foundation, including its mission, vision, and goals related to sustainability, which outlines the company's experiences and background, providing depth and context. The company must examine its history and the factors that have shaped its operations and culture concerning environmental and social responsibilities to structure its identity within the story. This self-assessment is essential for identifying areas for growth and improvement.

Traits and values play a crucial role in this development. A sustainable business should cultivate integrity, transparency, and accountability. These traits influence the company's operations, stakeholder relationships, and overall community and environmental impact. Through storytelling, the company can better promote its specificities and values for sustainability, highlighting its sustainable development initiatives, such as implementing practices that minimize waste, reduce carbon footprints, and promote ethical supply chains. These motivations can stem from a desire to meet consumer demands for responsible products, reduce risks associated with climate change, or increase operational efficiencies.

9.8.5 GenAI for multimodal narratives

GenAI enhances storytelling through several interconnected mechanisms that create engaging, multimodal narratives by blending creativity, personalized interaction, and advanced multimedia technologies.[11] These systems, particularly those using LLMs, offer collaborative narrative creation and a multimodal experience. They enable users to co-create stories through prompts and feedback. GenAI models can generate unique narratives tailored to individual preferences by responding to user prompts, fostering creativity and personal engagement. The combination of text-to-speech and text-to-video technologies transforms the storytelling process into a rich, immersive experience. The text-to-speech feature converts written narratives into spoken words, making stories accessible to auditory stakeholders and enhancing engagement through relatable vocal expressions. The text-to-video feature generates animations and visuals that complement the narrative, bringing the story to life and supporting comprehension through visual context. These enhancements improve story communication by engaging multiple senses, evoking emotions, and making content more memorable and easily accessible. They can present complex information in a digestible format, build deeper connections with audiences, and foster empathy and understanding. This format captures attention quickly and efficiently, ensuring that your message is memorized and your brand remains unforgettable. This method effectively communicates your narrative, as the information retained from one minute of video is equivalent to 1.8 million written words.[12] This means that short videos are ideal for various purposes, including brand building, trust and credibility reinforcement, product promotion, and social media content. They also make it easier to track audience retention and engagement metrics while maximizing your online reach.

GenAI can accelerate the creative process, making it easier to generate content quickly and ensuring that narratives follow coherent structures while maintaining logical progression and emotional arcs, which are critical for effective storytelling, especially for targeted audiences. These systems can analyze audience preferences and adapt storytelling elements to create more personalized and engaging narratives. This leads to richer storytelling experiences that resonate more deeply with audiences. With well-crafted prompts, you can adopt an approach that emphasizes efficiency and speed, developing personalized strategies tailored to specific needs and goals. The AI systems evaluate the generated stories in terms of linguistic quality, speech clarity, and visual coherence, ensuring high standards for engagement and educational value. This assessment helps refine content to ensure that it is both appropriate and appealing for your audience. They can assess audience feedback and engagement metrics to help you enhance your storytelling, making it more engaging, inclusive, and diverse.

9.8.6 Storytelling as a powerful tool for empowering stakeholder trust

The relationships a business develops with customers, suppliers, and the community are essential for its character development in sustainability. Effective collaboration and stakeholder communication can enhance trust and drive collective action toward sustainable goals. A business prioritizing relationship-building will be better equipped to adapt to changing expectations and innovate responsibly. Storytelling can strengthen stakeholders' trust by simplifying complex data insights into understandable narratives to effectively communicate values, goals, and experiences, creating emotional connections and fostering transparency. Questions that might be considered include: (1) what are you trying to show? (2) Who is your audience? (3) How and why is it important? (4) How should you present the information? Ensuring clarity and conciseness about the main idea we want to share with our audience simplifies content planning to deliver key messages to a target audience effectively.[13] Through authentic narratives, organizations can communicate their core values and share their journeys, challenges, and successes, demonstrating a commitment to sincere intent. This authenticity often translates to increased credibility among stakeholders. Building trust requires making them feel more informed and equipped to make data-driven decisions. By simplifying complex data insights into understandable narratives, storytelling supports clarity and transparency, helping stakeholders to comprehend the information presented easily. For example, companies provide clarity on their priorities by sharing how a specific sustainability initiative has positively affected the environment or community. This transparency helps stakeholders align with the organization's mission, fostering a sense of belonging and emphasizing collaboration and success.

Effective storytelling resonates with audiences on an emotional level. This can be achieved with well-crafted stories that remove all ambiguity, highlight key insights and trends, and make information accessible and presented clearly and understandably. Companies can establish better transparency and trust by demystifying their processes, products, or strategies using accessible anecdotes or analogies. When stakeholders understand the rationale behind decisions and actions, they develop a sense of transparency, which increases trust. Transparency means promptly and accurately updating stakeholders on sustainability decisions and actions while informing them of progress, results, and consequences. By incorporating relatable narratives and contexts, organizations create connections that engage stakeholders and help them make more informed decisions. This emotional engagement enhances trust since stakeholders are more likely to believe in and support initiatives they can relate to and understand.

9.8.7 AI-automated data-driven storytelling for sustainability

There is an increasing expectation from consumers that brands actively engage in and communicate their sustainability initiatives. Notably, 78% of people believe that large businesses should play a role in combating climate change, yet only a small group consistently purchases from brands that advocate for sustainability. This gap creates urgency for brands to effectively communicate their commitments and practices, thus building consumer trust and loyalty.[14]

To address this growing pressure on brands to communicate their sustainability efforts, marketers are employing creative video campaigns that are tailored for various platforms such as social media, YouTube, and Vimeo.[15][16][17] With AI-driven tools, companies can optimize their outreach strategies, using a variety of creative formats to engage viewers effectively, ensuring that the messaging is delivered in a personalized manner that resonates with audience preferences. For instance, campaigns that incorporate different storytelling styles and audio effects enhance the viewer's initial engagement, which is crucial for the short attention spans typical in online environments.

Organizations that share their collective achievements reinforce community ties and encourage stakeholders to feel part of a shared mission, further enhancing trust. Additionally, AI-automated data-driven storytelling helps companies share ideas consistently, emphasizing the integrity and provenance of the data presented. Stakeholders are more likely to trust the insights shared when data sources and verification procedures are open and transparent. Moreover, consistent narratives and visualizations reduce misunderstandings and uncertainty, further reinforcing trust in the organization's sustainability practices. Through storytelling, companies can create a safe space for sharing diverse experiences and perspectives, where stakeholders are invited to tell their stories.[18] For example, Brands such as Interface and Seventh Generation have used storytelling to share their sustainability journeys, including challenges and solutions. This transparency builds trust and positions them as leaders in sustainable practices.[19] By sharing narratives, stakeholders may find common ground and discover shared values, which can help build relationships, a loyal community focused on sustainability, and foster collaboration. This helps build trust because it makes participants feel that their voices are valued and their opinions matter in the decision-making process.

AI can now provide organizations with advanced techniques capable of analyzing and extracting insights from a wide variety of sources, including emails, social media, and spatial data. GenAI offers more sophisticated features, allowing non-technical users to interact with data in various forms, such as text, audio, and video, focusing on deriving insights rather than managing technical details. Users engage in conversation with the system, leveraging advanced ML algorithms to automatically generate logically sound, persuasive, and tailored stories that can help make better evidence-based decisions. Companies can now demonstrate their values and integrity by sharing real experiences and testimonials that reflect their commitment to ethical practices, inclusivity, and social responsibility. Stakeholders can then observe firsthand the positive outcomes of the organization's efforts and assess the tangible impacts of successful projects or community initiatives. Companies can further show dedication to integrity and resiliency by openly disclosing challenges and setbacks, as well as how the business has handled them. This visibility not only resonates well with stakeholders but also reinforces belief in the organization's capability to follow through on its commitments. Successful storytelling can inspire active engagement and mobilize commitment, reinforcing trust in the organization.

9.9 Summary

Corporate reporting is transforming from financial reporting to sustainability reporting. Business sustainability is gaining significant attention as socially responsible investors prefer to invest in sustainable and socially responsible corporations, while regulators worldwide recommend or mandate that public companies disclose their material financial ESP and material nonfinancial ESG dimensions of sustainability performance. Auditors are expected to lend more credibility to financial reports by auditing financial statements and providing assurance statements for ESG sustainability reports. Drivers of transformation of accounting and auditing include regulation, digitalization, sustainability, double materiality, risk, and fraud. Business organizations should explore the intersection of financial reporting, sustainability reporting, digitalization, and AI and analyze these technological advancements that shape corporate reporting and auditing/assurance processes. Corporate reporting and auditing are reliant on digital systems and AI to ensure that financial ESP and nonfinancial ESG sustainability data and information are accurate, reliable, complete, and transparent.

This chapter explores the critical processes involved in successfully implementing AI within organizations and developing effective AI strategies. It provides a comprehensive framework for aligning AI initiatives with business objectives, ensuring ethical governance, and fostering long-term value creation. The chapter begins by examining the strategic rationale for the adoption of AI, highlighting its role in enhancing operational efficiency, decision-making, customer engagement, and competitive advantage. Key stages of AI implementation are discussed, including opportunity identification, feasibility assessment, infrastructure readiness, talent acquisition, model deployment, and CI. The chapter emphasizes the importance of cross-functional collaboration, agile development, and change management in overcoming organizational resistance and ensuring successful integration. The chapter outlines how organizations can craft robust AI strategies through stakeholder alignment, risk management, regulatory compliance, and ethical considerations. It introduces models for AI maturity assessment and strategic road mapping, supported by practical tools and metrics. The final section focuses on AI reporting and performance measurement. It introduces KPIs, reporting frameworks, and best practices for communicating AI progress and impact to internal and external stakeholders. Emphasis is placed on transparency, accountability, and responsible AI practices to build trust and ensure sustainable innovation.

9.10 Takeaways

- Successful AI initiatives begin with aligning AI goals with overall business objectives and value creation.
- Effective AI implementation involves identifying use cases, assessing feasibility, preparing infrastructure, acquiring talent, deploying models, and establishing feedback loops.
- Integration of AI requires collaboration between IT, data science, operations, finance, and executive leadership.
- Organizations must proactively manage cultural and operational changes to minimize resistance and foster AI adoption.
- Strategic development benefits from using maturity models to assess current capabilities and plan progressive adoption.
- Embedding ethics, transparency, and fairness in AI strategies is essential to mitigate bias and build stakeholder trust.
- AI strategies must address regulatory compliance, data privacy, cybersecurity, and reputational risks.
- Using agile methodologies supports experimentation, rapid prototyping, and iterative improvement of AI systems.

- KPIs should be defined to evaluate AI effectiveness, efficiency, and return on investment.
- Transparent reporting, both internally and externally, enhances accountability and enables better strategic oversight.
- Long-term success with AI requires sustainable models, scalability plans, and continuous learning and adaptation.

Notes

1 Rezaee, Z. 2024, Summer/forthcoming. *The Sustainable Business Blueprint: Planning, Performance, Risk, Reporting, and Assurance*. Routledge, Taylor & Francis Group. https://www.routledge.com/The-Sustainable-Business-Blueprint-Planning-Performance-Risk-Reporting-and-Assurance/Rezaee/p/book/9781032571270
2 Rezaee. *The Sustainable Business Blueprint: Planning, Performance, Risk, Reporting, and Assurance*
3 Much of discussion in this section comes from Rezaee. *The Sustainable Business Blueprint: Planning, Performance, Risk, Reporting, and Assurance*
4 European Commission (EC). 2023, 5 January. *The Corporate Sustainability Reporting Directive (CSRD)*. https://finance.ec.europa.eu/capital-markets-union-and-financial-markets/company-reporting-and-auditing/company-reporting/corporate-sustainability-reporting_en
5 Much of this section is from chapter 9 of Rezaee. *The Sustainable Business Blueprint: Planning, Performance, Risk, Reporting, and Assurance*
6 Committee of Sponsoring Organizations of the Treadway Commission (COSO). 2013, May. *Demystifying Sustainability Risk*. https://www.coso.org/documents/COSO-ERM%20Demystifying%20Sustainability%20Risk_Full%20WEB.pdf
7 International Federation of Accountants (IFAC). 2024, 19 December. *Building Trust in Sustainability Reporting and Preparing for Assurance: Governance and Controls for Sustainability Information*. https://www.ifac.org/publications/building-trust-sustainability-reporting-and-preparing-assurance-governance-and-controls
8 COSO, 2013 and IFAC 2024
9 National Storytelling Network. *What is Storytelling?* https://storynet.org/what-is-storytelling/#:~:text=Storytelling%20uses%20actions%20such%20as,to%20be%20present%20in%20storytelling
10 Marmolejo-Ramos, F., Workman, T., Walker, C., Lenihan, D., Moulds, S., Correa, J.C., Hanea, A.M., & Sonna, B. 2022. AI-powered narrative building for facilitating public participation and engagement. *Discover Artificial Intelligence*, 2(1), 7
11 Arif, S., Arif, T., Haroon, M.S., Khan, A.J., Raza, A.A., & Athar, A. 2024. *The Art of Storytelling: Multi-Agent Generative AI for Dynamic Multimodal Narratives*. arXiv preprint arXiv:2409.11261
12 Rose, E. 2023. *A Video is Worth 1.8 Million Words: Special Value of Video*. https://idearocketanimation.com/4293-video-worth-1-million-words/
13 Knaflic, C.N. 2019. *Storytelling with Data: Let's Practice!* John Wiley & Sons
14 Kelly, C. 2023. *To Boost Brand Sustainability Stories, Marketers Multiply Reach with AI. Think with Google*. https://business.google.com/us/think/ai-excellence/sustainability-stories-and-ai/
15 Downers Grove IL. 2024. *Sustainability Story*. https://x.com/DownersGroveVlg/status/1849923329853128935
16 American Farm Bureau. 2021. *Agriculture's Sustainability Story*. https://www.youtube.com/watch?v=1rdy5yooow0
17 HAWORTH. 2021. *Oceanic Fabric—a Sustainable Story*. https://vimeo.com/568387807

18 Grund, J., Singer-Brodowski, M., & Buessing, A.G. 2024. Emotions and transformative learning for sustainability: A systematic review. *Sustainability Science*, 19(1), 307–324
19 Loughlin, B. 2024. *Storytelling for Sustainability: Crafting Compelling Narratives*. Institute of Sustainability Studies. https://instituteofsustainabilitystudies.com/insights/lexicon/storytelling-for-sustainability-crafting-compelling-narratives/#:~:text=At%20their%20core%2C%20stories%20are,more%20sustainable%20habits%20and%20practices

10 Opportunities and challenges in AI adoption for sustainability

10.1 Introduction

AI platforms and technologies present numerous opportunities to advance sustainability initiatives and efforts and improve sustainability performance by improving resource efficiency, predicting demand, optimizing supply chains, reducing waste, and minimizing environmental impact. ML algorithms can drive innovations in sustainable agriculture, enhance climate modeling, and support the development of renewable energy solutions. The adoption of AI technologies can facilitate more effective environmental monitoring and reporting, enabling organizations to track and manage their environmental footprint with greater precision. However, the adoption of AI for sustainability presents some challenges. One important challenge is the complexity and cost associated with implementing AI systems or advancing the existing systems, requiring organizations to invest in advanced technologies, data infrastructure, and skilled personnel to deploy and manage AI solutions effectively. Ethical and regulatory issues are also challenging as the use of AI may affect data privacy, algorithmic bias, and transparency. Thus, organizations must navigate the evolving landscape of AI governance and compliance, including addressing issues related to the responsible use of AI and its potential impact on employment and social equity, to ensure that AI systems are fair, accountable, and aligned with ethical principles, thereby maintaining stakeholder trust and compliance with emerging regulations. This chapter examines the key opportunities and challenges associated with AI adoption for sustainability, presenting the potential of AI to drive positive environmental and social outcomes, the obstacles organizations may face in implementing AI solutions, and strategies for overcoming these challenges.

10.2 Common opportunities and challenges in integrating AI into sustainability initiatives

The integration of AI-driven systems and technologies into business sustainability initiatives, efforts, and performance presents many opportunities for improving efficiencies, assessing and managing risks, and automating operations to attain and advance ESG goals. Some of these important opportunities are capability of

DOI: 10.4324/9781003611981-10

AI-powered systems, tools and platforms to: (1) optimize the use of resources such as energy, water, and raw materials by analyzing usage patterns and predicting future needs that can minimize waste, reduce consumption, and promote circular economy practices; (2) process climate data to improve predictive modeling of global warming, extreme weather events, sea-level rise, and biodiversity loss to develop strategies to mitigate climate risks and adapt to environmental changes; (3) improving transparency in supply chains by tracking and verifying the origins of raw materials and the environmental impact of their production in reducing carbon footprints through route planning, efficient inventory management, and lower energy consumption in distribution networks; (4) promoting more sustainable farming practices by enhancing efficiency and reducing the need for chemical inputs, monitoring crop health, optimize water use, predict weather impacts, and improve yield; (5) facilitating real-time monitoring and measurement of emissions from industrial facilities, transportation networks, and buildings to effectively manage emissions, comply with regulatory standards, and make data-driven decisions for reducing their carbon footprint; (6) enabling innovation in product design by suggesting eco-friendly materials, evaluating life-cycle impacts, and simulating end-of-life scenarios to produce products that are more sustainable, durable, and recyclable, thus fostering the adoption of circular economy principles; (7) implementing smart waste management systems that predict and minimize waste production by sorting materials for recycling, optimize recycling processes, identify areas for reuse, and reduce landfill reliance and contributing to a zero-waste economy; and (8) optimizing renewable energy systems by forecasting demand and generation levels, predicting solar and wind power output based on weather patterns, and adjusting the grid supply accordingly. These opportunities present potential for AI to scale sustainable practices across sectors by making their processes more efficient, data-driven, and adaptive to meet sustainability goals more effectively and support the transition to a low-carbon, resource-efficient economy.

The integration of AI-driven technologies into business sustainability initiatives, efforts, and performance while enabling transformative potentials and opportunities presents unique challenges including: (1) wrong decisions made based on analyzing incomplete, inconsistent, our erroneous sustainability data that could limit the accuracy and relevance of AI-driven insights and outcomes; (2) consumption of substantial energy used in powering AI algorithms that can reduce the net benefit of using AI for sustainability and create conflicts with the goals of sustainability by contributing to carbon emissions; (3) difficulties in obtaining required expertise and skills to effectively implement AI-driven solutions and algorithms that can result in misaligned goals or ineffective solutions incompatible with sustainability objectives; (4) ethical considerations and social biases when applied AI systems create unintentionally perpetuate biases and consequences that may lead to decisions that undermine social equity aspects of sustainability and cause reputational risks for the company; (5) lack of transparency that can reduce trust and hinder adoption in sustainability initiatives as AI models often operate as "black boxes," making it difficult to understand and explain the basis of their insights; (6) insufficient resources and infrastructure requirements that could not be available to smaller business organizations; (7) regulatory and compliance hurdles that can prevent or slow down AI adoption that could lead to inconsistencies across regions, complicating global sustainability efforts; and (8) lack of immediate and proper measurement of financial benefits of using AI platforms that could lead to challenges in securing investment or providing ongoing support for AI-driven sustainability projects.

10.3 Leveraging AI for ESG disclosures

Leveraging AI for ESG disclosures, including reporting and assurance, offers a transformative approach to enhancing reliability, transparency, accuracy, and efficiency in corporate sustainability reporting. AI-powered technologies such as NLP, ML, and DL can automate the extraction, analysis, and categorization of ESG data from diverse structured and unstructured sources to enable real-time insights and consistent compliance with evolving regulatory standards. AI-assisted tools and techniques support more effective risk assessment and performance benchmarking, thereby improving stakeholder trust and decision-making. Additionally, AI-driven tools can assist organizations in aligning their ESG reports with global frameworks such as GRI, SASB, ISSB, and TCFD to ensure that sustainability narratives are data-driven and strategically aligned with long-term value creation for all stakeholders, as examined in the following subsections.

10.3.1 The intricate arena of ESG reporting

As stakeholders become more aware of the risks and opportunities related to ESG factors, it is essential for companies to establish clear strategies for ESG reporting. The path of ESG reporting emerges as both a noble ambition and an intimidating challenge. Companies face increasing pressure from various stakeholders, including investors who demand transparency regarding a company's ESG performance, regulatory bodies that impose new reporting requirements, and consumers who expect businesses to be accountable for their impact on society and the environment. While many companies are ready to adopt sustainability and ethical stewardship, successfully navigating the complexities of ESG reporting requires strategic planning, resource allocation, and a commitment to transparency. As businesses are pressured to comply with regulations concerning sustainability reporting, AI can assist them in better meeting regulatory expectations by automating and enhancing the quality of sustainability reporting and compliance.

In this landscape, ESG reporting is seen as a vital indicator of a company's future viability and success. It provides a glimpse into how well a company is prepared to address the challenges of sustainability and social responsibility. The metrics and data disclosed in these reports can profoundly influence perceptions among investors, customers, and other stakeholders. Although companies are becoming increasingly aware of new reporting requirements, they continue to face challenges in providing stakeholders with meaningful ESG information.[1] How a company presents this information can create a compelling narrative about the positive effects it has on the world, showcasing not only compliance but also a genuine commitment to making meaningful changes. While the commitment to sustainability and ethical practices is commendable, the journey toward effective ESG reporting is fraught with challenges that organizations must address.

One of the biggest challenges for companies is the absence of standardized metrics.[2] For a financial analyst trying to evaluate the performance of different businesses based on their sustainability reports, a lack of a common set of measurements makes comparisons nearly impossible. Each company might report different metrics, some focusing on water usage and others highlighting carbon emissions. This inconsistency complicates analysis and creates misunderstandings among investors and stakeholders, undermining trust in the reported data. Adding to the complexity is the diverse information needs of stakeholders.[3] Investors, consumers, and regulators typically seek different aspects of ESG performance. For instance, while investors may prioritize financial impacts stemming from ESG initiatives, consumers might emphasize ethical supply chain practices. This varying array of expectations complicates the decision-making process for companies striving to satisfy all parties, often leading to unclear messaging and conflicting priorities. While some progress has been made in ESG reporting and assurance, companies are still in the early stages of readiness for ESG disclosures.[4] New regulations like the EU's ESRS are pushing for better data collection. In addition to evolving standards, companies often struggle to establish the necessary governance structures and develop the required skills within their teams to effectively manage and report on ESG data. Particularly, the United States does not yet have a unified national sustainability reporting standard equivalent to the EU's CSRD. However, there is increasing adoption of voluntary frameworks such as the TCFD, SASB standards, and GRI frameworks among American companies. The ISSB standards, S1 and S2, are adopted by many public companies in the United States. It is expected that ESG disclosure regulations in the EU will impact not only EU-based companies but also large US multinationals and their subsidiaries. Thus, the emerging ESG regulations will continue to impose compliance burdens and costs, and companies should prepare integrating regulatory requirements into broader sustainability strategies and strengthen governance and data management for effective compliance.

Employees responsible for ESG reporting frequently lack the necessary skills, training, or expertise to assess and communicate ESG factors accurately. This lack of expertise can result in poorly constructed reports that do not accurately reflect the organization's actual ESG performance, hindering efforts to demonstrate a genuine commitment to sustainability. Logistical challenges also emerge with data collection. Gathering relevant ESG data often requires navigating various departments and systems that may not be designed to capture this information systematically. This can transform the data accumulation process into a time-consuming and labor-intensive endeavor as teams struggle with compiling and verifying the necessary information. Integrating ESG considerations into existing reporting frameworks also presents its own set of challenges. Companies typically have established financial reporting processes, and incorporating ESG data into these established structures can require significant adjustments. This integration can be particularly complex when trying to align ESG metrics with traditional financial performance indicators, as stakeholders expect a coherent narrative across all reports.

As ESG factors are becoming integral to corporate strategy, boards can ensure that ESG considerations are embedded in business strategies, which can lead to innovative solutions and new market opportunities.[5] Ensuring the accuracy and reliability of reported data is crucial in ESG reporting. Companies must remain vigilant against the risk of presenting misleading information, even inadvertently. Any inaccuracies in reported data can lead to reputational damage and a loss of credibility and trust with stakeholders, which can be hard to regain. Resource allocation is another challenge; organizations must balance budgeting and staffing to implement ESG reporting practices effectively. In a landscape where immediate business priorities often take precedence, compromised resources for ESG reporting can result in incomplete or lower-quality disclosures. Finally, as regulations and reporting standards evolve, companies face challenges of compliance. Different regions may impose distinct requirements, and keeping pace with these shifting landscapes can feel like chasing a moving target. Companies that fail to stay informed and complain expose themselves to penalties, legal implications, and reputational harm.

10.3.2 The complexities of ESG reporting

The complexities of ESG reporting stem from the lack of standardized measurements and reporting frameworks, varying stakeholder expectations, the challenge of quantifying nonfinancial performance, and the ever-growing sustainability initiatives and regulations. Organizations often face difficulties in selecting appropriate metrics, balancing transparency with strategic confidentiality, and aligning their disclosures with multiple global reporting standards such as GRI, SASB, or TCFD. Furthermore, the dynamic nature of ESG issues, ranging from climate change risks to diversity and human rights, requires continuous monitoring and adaptation. These complexities are further intensified by increasing regulatory pressures, stakeholder scrutiny, and the need to demonstrate both authenticity and accountability in sustainability initiatives and reporting. The complexities of ESG reporting arise from various factors influencing how organizations measure, disclose, and communicate their sustainability practices and performances. These challenges can create difficulties in ensuring accurate, effective, and standardized reporting. The key complexities involved include the following:[6]

10.3.2.1 Diverse standards and frameworks

One of the major challenges of ESG reporting is the multitude of standards and frameworks in use. However, the existence of diverse standards and frameworks for ESG reporting presents both opportunities and challenges for organizations seeking to communicate their sustainability performance. Frameworks such as the GRI, SASB, TCFD, and ISSB each offer different scopes, metrics, and stakeholder orientations. While this variety allows firms to tailor disclosures to specific audiences and industry contexts, it also creates inconsistencies, reporting burdens, and difficulties in comparability across firms and sectors. Different organizations may adopt varying reporting frameworks (e.g., GRI, SASB, TCFD, and IR), each with its own standards regarding what and how to report. This diversity can lead to inconsistencies in reporting methodologies and metrics, making comparisons difficult across organizations or sectors. Additionally, stakeholders, including investors and regulators, may struggle to understand which reports are more relevant or credible due to the lack of common standards. Both the United States and EU are moving toward more robust and structured sustainability initiatives as climate disclosures across all industries continue to improve, highlighting trends in GHG reporting, target setting, regulatory preparedness, and board oversight. As companies navigate this fragmented landscape, they must carefully select and integrate frameworks that best reflect their ESG priorities while maintaining credibility and coherence in their reporting practices.

10.3.2.2 Evolving regulations

Evolving ESG regulations are reshaping the corporate reporting landscape as governments and regulatory bodies worldwide introduce more rigorous and standardized disclosure requirements. These regulatory shifts aim to enhance transparency, comparability, and accountability in how companies report on issues and efforts. For example, the EU's CSRD and the US SEC's proposed climate disclosure rules are pushing companies toward more comprehensive and audited ESG disclosures. In 2023, the US SEC has introduced new rules that target climate disclosures, particularly focusing on the financial impact of climate-related risks and GHG emissions.[7] In Europe, the CSRD mandated by the EFRAG imposes extensive ESG reporting requirements on EU-listed companies and those from outside the EU with significant operations in the region.[8] The United Kingdom's Financial Conduct Authority requires UK-listed firms to align their climate disclosures with the TCFD framework or explain any deviations.[9] Additionally, the ISSB has developed two sustainability standards, one addressing climate-related issues and another covering broader sustainability disclosures, with more standards anticipated in the future. However, in 2025, the SEC signaled a shift away from federal ESG mandates by halting the proposed climate disclosure rule.[10]

As these regulations continue to develop, organizations must adapt their internal systems, data collection processes, and reporting practices to meet stricter compliance demands. This evolving regulatory environment underscores the growing recognition of ESG factors as material to financial performance and long-term value creation. ESG reporting regulations are rapidly evolving, with many jurisdictions implementing new requirements that reflect an increasing global emphasis on environmental and sustainability issues.[11] As the regulatory landscape surrounding ESG undergoes rapid changes, organizations must navigate compliance risks. Failure to adhere to emerging regulations can result in legal repercussions or reputational damage that impacts the company's brand image and stakeholders' trust.[12] The introduction of regulations exemplifies evolving expectations in ESG disclosures. Furthermore, constant updates in regulations demand significant resources to monitor, understand, and implement compliance measures.

10.3.2.3 Data availability and quality

Gathering accurate and comprehensive data is fundamental for effective ESG reporting. ESG data availability and quality remain significant challenges for organizations, investors, and regulators aiming to make informed decisions. These challenges include gaps in available data, as organizations may lack sufficient historical data or relevant metrics for certain ESG issues. Additionally, the quality and reliability of nonfinancial data can vary, potentially leading to inaccuracies in reporting and a lack of confidence among stakeholders. Unlike financial data that are often measurable, standardized, and traceable, ESG information is often non-standardized, qualitative, and inconsistently reported across firms, industries, and regions. This lack of uniformity leads to data gaps, limited comparability, and concerns over reliability and assurance. Additionally, many companies struggle with collecting accurate and comprehensive ESG data, particularly in areas such as supply chain emissions, labor practices, or board diversity. Third-party ESG ratings and data providers attempt to fill these gaps, but discrepancies among their assessments complicate decision-making. Improving ESG data quality and availability is critical for building trust, enabling effective risk management, and supporting evidence-based sustainability strategies.

10.3.2.4 Stakeholder variability

Stakeholder variability presents a complex challenge in ESG reporting, as different stakeholder groups, including investors, customers, employees, regulators, communities, and civil society, often have diverse and sometimes conflicting expectations regarding ESG information. Investors may prioritize financially material metrics tied to long-term value, while regulators focus on compliance and transparency, and consumers seek ethical and environmentally responsible practices. This variability requires organizations to balance and customize their ESG disclosures to address a broad spectrum of interests without diluting the clarity or credibility of their reports. As stakeholder awareness and activism around ESG issues grow, companies must engage in proactive dialogue and adopt adaptive reporting strategies to meet evolving demands while maintaining consistency and alignment with their core sustainability goals. The diverse needs and expectations of various stakeholders complicate ESG reporting, as different groups require different types of information. Investors, customers, regulators, and civil society may have unique priorities, making it challenging for organizations to meet each stakeholder's information needs. Moreover, what one stakeholder group considers material may conflict with the perspectives of another, resulting in potential disagreements regarding report content.

10.3.2.5 Interconnectedness of ESG factors

The interrelationship among factors of planning, performance, risk, and disclosure creates complexities in sustainability reporting. Organizations often struggle to assess how changes in one area affect the others. For instance, improvements in environmental sustainability may have social implications, complicating the reporting process. Moreover, decision-making often involves trade-offs between different ESG factors, such as cost savings from reduced environmental investments versus potential social backlash. The interconnectedness of ESG factors underscores the holistic nature of sustainability, where ESG dimensions are deeply interrelated and mutually reinforcing. For instance, a company's environmental initiatives, such as reducing carbon emissions, can directly impact social outcomes such as public health and community well-being, while strong governance practices are essential for effectively implementing and monitoring both environmental and social strategies. This interdependence means that addressing one ESG area in isolation may overlook critical risks or opportunities in others, leading to incomplete or ineffective sustainability efforts. As a result, organizations must adopt an integrated approach that recognizes the synergies and trade-offs among ESG factors to develop coherent, impactful, and resilient sustainability strategies.

10.3.2.6 Subjectivity and materiality

The subjectivity and materiality of ESG information pose significant challenges in ensuring consistent, relevant, objectivity, and decision-useful disclosures. Unlike financial reporting, where materiality is more clearly defined, ESG materiality can vary widely depending on the industry, geography, stakeholder priorities, and evolving societal expectations. What is material for one company regarding its carbon emissions in the manufacturing sector may not be as critical for a company in the service-based sector. Furthermore, the subjective nature of determining which ESG issues to disclose can lead to selective reporting and potential greenwashing. To address these concerns, many organizations are adopting double materiality assessments and stakeholder engagement practices to identify and report on ESG factors that are both financially significant and socially and environmentally impactful. Thus, determining which ESG items are material and relevant for reporting can be subjective. Organizations must identify which ESG issues are most pertinent to their operations and stakeholders, varying widely based on industry, geography, and stakeholder priorities. Furthermore, what is deemed material can evolve over time due to changing societal expectations, regulatory shifts, or market dynamics, necessitating ongoing reevaluation of reporting practices.

10.3.2.7 Integration of ESG information with financial reporting

Integrating ESG reporting with traditional financial reporting presents added complexity. However, the integration of ESG information with financial reporting is essential for providing a comprehensive picture of a company's performance, risks, long-term value creation, financial viability, and social and environmental impacts. Traditionally treated as separate domains, ESG and financial reporting are now converging as stakeholders demand more transparent and aligned disclosures. This integration enables companies to better articulate how ESG factors of climate risks, labor practices, or governance structures can impact financial outcomes such as revenue growth, cost management, and capital access. However, achieving effective integration requires robust data systems, cross-functional collaboration, and adherence to emerging standards like those from the ISSB, which aim to harmonize ESG and financial disclosures. As this trend continues, IR can enhance corporate accountability, investor confidence, and strategic decision-making. Organizations must align ESG metrics with financial performance, which requires a solid understanding of both areas to provide a cohesive view of overall performance. Investors are increasingly seeking IR but may have varying thresholds for what constitutes a financially material ESG issue, leading to challenges in aligning reporting approaches.

The aforementioned challenges suggest that the complexities of ESG reporting arise from a combination of diverse standards, evolving regulations, data challenges, stakeholder variability, the interconnectedness of factors, subjectivity in materiality assessment, and integration with financial reporting. Table 10.1 encapsulates the multifaceted nature of the challenges faced in ESG reporting. Organizations must navigate these complexities to provide meaningful, accurate, and actionable ESG disclosures that meet the expectations of various stakeholders.[13]

Table 10.1 Summary of the complexities of ESG reporting

Complexity	*Description*
Diverse standards and frameworks	- Presence of numerous reporting standards (e.g., GRI, SASB, and TCFD) - Leads to inconsistency and confusion in comparisons
Evolving regulations	- Rapid changes in regulatory requirements (e.g., EU's CSRD) - Compliance risks and significant resource allocation needed
Data availability and quality	- Challenges in data gaps and insufficient historical data - Variability in the quality and reliability of nonfinancial data
Stakeholder variability	- Different information needs from various stakeholders (investors, regulators, and customers) - Potential conflicts of interest
Interconnection of ESG factors	- Difficulty in assessing relationships between ESG factors - Potential trade-offs complicating reporting priorities
Subjectivity and materiality	- Subjective determination of material ESG issues - Changing definitions of materiality over time due to shifts in expectations
Integration with financial reporting	- Need for alignment between ESG metrics and financial performance - Differing investor expectations for IR

10.4 The "Alphabet Soup" of ESG reporting

The "Alphabet Soup" of ESG reporting often refers to many arrays of acronyms representing various standards, frameworks, and guidelines that organizations must navigate to disclose ESG sustainability-related information. This phrase captures the confusing mix of acronyms, frameworks, standards, ratings, and indices that companies face when reporting on sustainability.[14] This complex environment challenges businesses trying to comply and investors seeking to understand diverse ESG efforts.

Regulators and standard-setting organizations worldwide, including GRI, SASB, TCFD, CDP, and ISSB, each offer different approaches to ESG disclosure, often with overlapping or diverging requirements. This fragmented framework creates confusion and inefficiencies for companies trying to meet diverse stakeholder expectations while ensuring compliance and transparency. The proliferation of reporting options can also hinder comparability and consistency across disclosures, making it difficult for investors and other stakeholders to assess ESG performance reliably. Efforts toward global harmonization are underway, but the current complexity remains a major obstacle to streamlined and effective ESG reporting. The absence of a single accepted standard and the large number of frameworks make things even more confusing. However, incorporating AI can help manage this complexity. AI can automate data collection, enhance analysis, and assist businesses in selecting the right frameworks. This technology can potentially turn the "Alphabet Soup" into a valuable tool for promoting sustainability.

10.4.1 What is in the Alphabet Soup?

"Alphabet Soup" refers to the complex variety of acronyms and terms used in ESG reporting. While it may seem like a jumble of letters at first glance, it represents a structured system of various frameworks, standards, and guidelines that aim to help businesses report on their sustainability practices. Despite the confusion surrounding the "Alphabet Soup," there is a logic behind the complexity, and gaining clarity on its components can lead to better navigation of the ESG landscape. The "alphabet soup" of ESG reporting comprises four main categories:[15] standards, frameworks, ratings, and indices, as depicted in Figure 10.1. In the following, we present a breakdown of the main components to help companies and stakeholders interpret and utilize the information available effectively.

10.4.2 The main categories in the Alphabet Soup

10.4.2.1 Standards

Standards provide specific and detailed criteria, offering concrete rules and methodologies for ESG measurement and disclosure. They serve as comprehensive guidelines that outline exact criteria and requirements for how organizations should measure and disclose their sustainability efforts. They outline precise rules

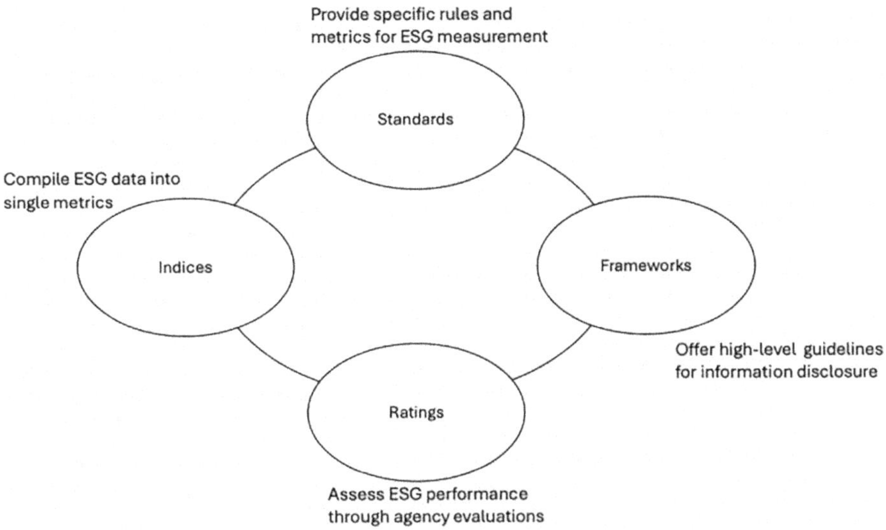

Figure 10.1 The main categories in the alphabet soup

and methodologies that companies must follow, ensuring that their reporting is structured, consistent, and comparable across different entities.

Standards provide the "how-to" and often include specific metrics to track, detailing the procedures and practices that should be implemented when collecting and reporting ESG data. Moreover, they often specify metrics organizations should use to quantify their performance in various sustainability areas. This specificity helps organizations understand not only what information they need to report but also how to effectively track and measure their progress toward meeting sustainability goals. Examples of standards include the GRI, the SASB, and numerous other standards, often industry-specific or regional, for example, standards related to carbon accounting, water management, labor practices, and supply chain responsibility.

V2.1.1 Key characteristics of standards:

- **Specificity:** Standards outline precise metrics and disclosure requirements, dictating what data organizations must collect, how it should be measured, and how it should be presented. This specificity ensures that all reported information is consistent and comparable across different entities.
- **Actionable:** Standards make broader recommendations of frameworks actionable. They often define parameters for reporting, helping organizations to understand clearly what is required for compliance.
- **Industry-Relevant:** Many standards are developed with specific industries in mind, addressing the unique ESG issues that different sectors face. This

relevance to industry challenges ensures that organizations can report on topics that matter most to their stakeholders.
- **Compliance-Oriented**: Reporting according to established standards can help organizations comply with regulatory requirements and meet stakeholder expectations, enhancing credibility and trust in their sustainability disclosures.

V.2.1.2 Importance of Standards:

- **Facilitates Accountability and Transparency:** By establishing shared metrics and procedures, standards promote consistent and reliable reporting across organizations, enhancing accountability for sustainability practices.
- **Improve Comparability:** Standards enable stakeholders, including investors and customers, to compare sustainability performance across different organizations and sectors, supporting informed decision-making.
- **Guides Best Practices:** Standards serve as benchmarks for best practices in sustainability reporting, helping organizations improve their processes and accountability.
- **Encourages CI:** Following established standards allows organizations to measure their performance against set metrics and report on their progress, fostering a culture of CI in sustainability practices.

In summary, standards are crucial components of the ESG reporting ecosystem, providing the detailed requirements necessary for organizations to communicate their sustainability efforts effectively and consistently, thereby meeting the needs of their stakeholders, including investors, regulators, and the broader public.

10.4.2.2 Frameworks

Frameworks are high-level guidelines that provide a structure for how information should be disclosed. They are more conceptual than standards, outlining the principles and overall approach to ESG reporting rather than prescribing specific metrics. Frameworks provide principles-based guidance on how information should be structured, prepared, and disclosed.

Unlike specific numerical standards that dictate exact reporting requirements, frameworks serve as overarching guides that help organizations determine what topics should be covered and how to present their sustainability information in a coherent manner. Examples include the TCFD, CDP, IIRC, and Climate Disclosure Standards Board.

V2.2.1 Key characteristics of frameworks:

- **Guidance-Oriented:** Frameworks outline high-level principles and standards for organizations to follow when reporting their sustainability impacts, helping to streamline the reporting process.
- **Flexibility:** Frameworks allow organizations to adapt their reporting practices based on their unique operational contexts, industries, and stakeholder needs.

This flexibility is essential for businesses operating in diverse sectors with varying sustainability challenges.

- **Complement to Standards:** Frameworks and standards are complementary. In contrast, standards provide specific metrics to be reported; frameworks offer broader context and principles that guide how these metrics should be interpreted and presented.
- **Focus on Materiality:** Many frameworks emphasize the importance of materiality, encouraging organizations to concentrate on reporting the sustainability issues that are truly significant for their stakeholders and operational contexts. This focus helps ensure that the reported information is relevant and meaningful.

V.2.2.2 Importance of frameworks:

- **Enhances Transparency:** By providing a structured approach to reporting, frameworks enhance transparency and accountability, allowing stakeholders to understand and compare the sustainability performance of different organizations.
- **Facilitate Stakeholder Engagement:** Frameworks encourage organizations to engage with their stakeholders, leading to better identification of relevant sustainability issues and fostering stronger relationships with various stakeholders.
- **Supports CI:** By following established frameworks, organizations can benchmark their sustainability practices, identify areas for improvement, and track progress over time, leading to more effective sustainability strategies.

In summary, frameworks play a crucial role in organizing and guiding ESG reporting, helping organizations to communicate their sustainability efforts effectively while ensuring that the information presented is relevant and significant to stakeholders.

10.4.2.3 Ratings

Ratings are assessments made by independent agencies or organizations that measure and evaluate a company's performance against specific ESG criteria. Rating agencies collect information from companies through surveys, public data, and other methods to assess their ESG performance. They then assign ratings or scores that represent the company's ESG performance relative to its peers. These ratings provide a way to summarize and communicate how well a company is managing its ESG risks and opportunities relative to its peers. Examples include Sustainalytics, MSCI ESG Research, and ISS ESG.

V.2.3.1 Key characteristics of ratings:

- **Comparative Assessment:** Ratings provide a comparative measure of ESG performance, allowing stakeholders to quickly gauge how a company stands with its competitors or industry averages. This helps investors and other stakeholders assess risks and opportunities associated with a company's social and environmental practices.

- **Quantitative and Qualitative Metrics:** ESG ratings often combine both quantitative data (such as emissions levels, diversity metrics, or governance structures) and qualitative assessments (such as policies, practices, and stakeholder engagement). This dual approach provides a more holistic view of a company's ESG performance.
- **Methodology-Driven:** Rating agencies use specific methodologies to assess companies, often involving the collection of data through surveys, disclosures, and third-party evaluations. The methodologies can vary significantly between agencies, leading to differences in ratings for the same company based on the criteria and weighting used.
- **Accessibility:** ESG ratings are typically designed to be accessible and understandable to a wide audience, including investors, consumers, and regulators. This accessibility helps individuals and organizations make informed decisions based on the sustainability performance of companies.

V.2.3.2 Importance of ratings:

- **Investment Decision-Making:** Ratings play a crucial role in investment decisions as they help investors evaluate the sustainability and risk profiles of companies. High ESG ratings can attract socially responsible investors, while low ratings may serve as red flags.
- **Improved Corporate Behavior:** The pressure associated with being rated can incentivize companies to enhance their ESG practices to achieve better ratings, thereby improving their overall sustainability performance.
- **Market Differentiation:** Companies with high ESG ratings can differentiate themselves in the marketplace, demonstrating their commitment to sustainability, which can enhance their brand image and reputation.
- **Stakeholder Engagement:** ESG ratings can facilitate better engagement with stakeholders by providing transparent metrics on sustainability performance, thereby fostering trust and accountability.

In summary, ratings serve as a valuable component of the ESG reporting landscape by providing assessments of companies' sustainability performances, enabling stakeholders to make informed decisions, and encouraging companies to improve their ESG practices.

10.4.2.4 Indices

Indices are collections of stocks or companies that are selected based on specific ESG criteria. These indices provide a benchmark for measuring the performance of companies that meet certain sustainability and ethical standards.

Indices compile ESG data into a single metric to represent the ESG performance of a particular market segment, investment strategy, or theme. They allow investors to track the performance of companies with strong ESG profiles. Examples include Dow Jones Sustainability Indices, FTSE4Good (**Dow Jones Sustainability Index** (DJSI)), and MSCI ESG Indices.

V.2.4.1 Key characteristics of indices:

- **Portfolio Representation:** ESG indices typically include a curated list of companies that exhibit strong ESG performance or adhere to specific sustainability guidelines. These companies are selected based on predefined criteria, allowing the index to represent the overall performance of environmentally and socially responsible firms within a market or sector.
- **Quantitative Measurement:** The performance of an ESG index is measured quantitatively, usually by tracking changes in the market value of the constituent stocks over time. This allows for a straightforward comparison of the index's performance against other market indices or benchmarks.
- **Criteria for Inclusion:** Companies included in ESG indices are evaluated based on various criteria, which may encompass environmental impact, labor practices, board diversity, corporate governance, and community engagement, among others. The selection process can vary significantly among indices.
- **Transparency:** The methodologies used for selecting companies and calculating the indices are generally made public, thereby ensuring transparency in how the indices assess and represent sustainability performance.

V.2.4.2 Importance of indices:

- **Investment Tool:** ESG indices serve as important tools for investors who wish to incorporate sustainability into their investment strategies. They allow investors to identify and track companies that align with their values or that demonstrate resilience against ESG-related risks.
- **Benchmarking Performance:** Companies often use ESG indices to benchmark their performance against peers, providing insights into where they stand within the sustainability landscape and helping to identify areas for improvement.
- **Attracting Investments:** Inclusion in a reputable ESG index can enhance a company's visibility and attractiveness to investors interested in socially responsible investments. High ESG scores may attract additional capital, as many investors seek to align their portfolios with sustainable investments.
- **Improving Corporate Behavior:** The existence of ESG indices can motivate companies to adopt better environmental and social practices, as they might aim for inclusion in these respected benchmarks and improve their overall performance.
- **Enhancing Credibility:** Being included in an ESG index can enhance a company's credibility and reputation, demonstrating a commitment to sustainability and responsible business practices.

In summary, ESG indices play a crucial role in the sustainability investment ecosystem by providing benchmarks for performance, fostering transparency and accountability, and encouraging improved practices among companies committed to sustainability.

Table 10.2 summarizes the essence and relevance of each aspect of the "Alphabet Soup," providing a clear comparison between Standards, Frameworks, Ratings, and Indices in ESG reporting. We present a clear overview of the various ESG standards, frameworks, ratings, and indices, along with their descriptions in Table 10.3.

Table 10.2 Summary of each aspect of the "Alphabet Soup" in ESG reporting

Aspect	*Standards*	*Frameworks*	*Ratings*	*Indices*
Definition	Specific, detailed rules for ESG measurement and disclosure	High-level guidelines for structuring and preparing ESG information	Assessments or scores that evaluate a company's ESG performance based on various criteria	Collections of stocks that meet certain ESG criteria for performance tracking
Key characteristics	Provide replicable requirements with metrics for specific topics (e.g., GRI and SASB)	Principles-based guidance covering broad topics and disclosure methods (e.g., TCFD and IIRC)	Use surveys or data aggregation to collate ESG information (e.g., Sustainalytics)	Select companies based on ESG compliance and provide a benchmark for performance (e.g., FTSE4Good and DJSI)
Importance	Ensure comparable, consistent, and reliable ESG disclosure; serve as criteria for assurance	Help organizations structure their reporting processes; enhance clarity in sustainability reporting	Help investors evaluate and make decisions based on a company's ESG performance; can influence investments	Provide benchmarks for tracking ESG performance; enhance visibility and attract socially responsible investments
In summary	Standards provide actionable requirements for ESG reporting.	Frameworks guide the approach to organizing and presenting ESG data.	Ratings score and evaluate companies on ESG criteria.	Indices aggregate stocks based on ESG standards to reflect sustainable performance.

Table 10.3 Overview of the various ESG standards, frameworks, ratings, and indices

Name	*Description*
ESG Standards	
GRI Standards	A framework for reporting sustainability impacts across economic, environmental, and social dimensions, with Universal, Sector, and Topic Standards for consistent reporting
SASB Standards	Industry-specific standards that help organizations disclose material sustainability information to investors, tailored to key ESG issues relevant to each sector
TCFD	Recommendations for disclosing climate-related risks and opportunities in financial reporting, focusing on consistency and comparability of climate impact reporting
ISO 14001	An international standard for EMS that requires organizations to manage environmental responsibilities systematically
IFRS	Primarily focused on financial disclosures, IFRS increasingly addresses sustainability through disclosures on risks, long-term success, and value creation.
ESG Frameworks	
TCFD	Framework for clear, comparable, and consistent information disclosure regarding climate change risks and opportunities, focusing on governance, strategy, risk management, and metrics
IRF	Encourages integrated reports combining financial and nonfinancial performance to communicate how organizations create value over time, considering both financial and ESG factors.
Sustainability Reporting Guidelines of the GRI	A comprehensive framework for reporting sustainability performance across multiple dimensions, emphasizing transparency and accountability
CDP	A framework for disclosing environmental impact, focusing on climate change and water usage, and encouraging data disclosure on carbon emissions and environmental governance.
IIRC	Combines financial and sustainability reporting, promoting a holistic view of value creation and the interconnections between financial and nonfinancial performance.
ESG Ratings	
MSCI ESG Ratings	Evaluates companies on a scale from American Accounting Association (leader) to CCC (laggard) based on industry-specific risks and management abilities, covering ESG factors.
Sustainalytics	Provides ESG Risk Ratings measuring unmanaged ESG risk levels relative to peers, expressed on a scale from negligible to severe risk based on standardized criteria.
FTSE4Good Index Series	Includes companies meeting recognized corporate responsibility standards, evaluated on various ESG criteria such as environmental impact and labor standards.

(*Continued*)

Table 10.3 (Continued)

Name	*Description*
Bloomberg ESG Disclosure Score	Scores based on the completeness and quality of disclosed ESG data, reflecting transparency regarding sustainability practices and performance of companies.
Refinitiv ESG Scores	Assesses performance based on over 400 indicators from publicly available data, focusing on the company's ESG efforts and outcomes.
ESG Indices	
FTSE4Good Index	Measures the performance of companies meeting globally recognized corporate responsibility standards, focusing on environmental sustainability, social responsibility, and governance.
DJSI	Assesses global companies based on economic, environmental, and social criteria to identify industry leaders in sustainability, launched in 1999.
S&P ESG Index	Series of indices based on the S&P 500 and other benchmarks that screen for companies with strong ESG profiles, using a rules-based approach for investment decisions
MSCI ESG Indexes	A range of indices featuring companies with strong ESG ratings across various sectors, helping investors track responsible practices and performance
NASDAQ-100 ESG Index	Comprises the 100 largest nonfinancial companies on NASDAQ that meet specific ESG criteria, reflecting those prioritizing sustainability and ethical governance.

10.5 AI methods for transforming ESG reporting

Having explored the broad spectrum of AI applications across the ESG pillars, it is now essential to examine the concrete mechanisms through which AI is reshaping a crucial aspect of ESG management: reporting. The success of ESG initiatives relies, in significant part, on the accurate, efficient, and transparent communication of ESG performance to stakeholders. Traditional ESG reporting, often hindered by manual processes and data silos, increasingly falls short of meeting the demands of changing regulatory landscapes and rising stakeholder expectations. AI, with its varied toolkit of techniques, provides a robust solution to modernize and enhance ESG reporting.

10.5.1 Analysis of AI techniques used in ESG reporting: a toolkit for enhanced transparency

A convergence of powerful techniques drives the transformation of ESG reporting through AI, with each contributing unique capabilities to streamline processes, enhance accuracy, and unlock deeper insights. Several AI techniques are at the forefront of this reporting revolution, assisting organizations in achieving greater efficiency and accuracy in their ESG disclosures while unlocking insights that drive meaningful change toward a more sustainable future.[16], [17] The increasing reliance on AI technologies in this domain reflects a pivotal shift toward data-driven decision-making in corporate sustainability practices, transitioning ESG reporting from a compliance exercise to a strategic enabler of sustainable value creation.

10.5.2 NLP: unlocking insights from unstructured data

A significant portion of ESG-relevant information exists in unstructured formats—news articles, social media feeds, corporate annual reports, and sustainability disclosures. NLP techniques are essential for extracting meaningful insights from this vast ocean of textual data. Imagine sifting through thousands of news articles to gauge public sentiment toward a company's environmental policies or analyzing countless social media posts to understand stakeholder perceptions of its social responsibility initiatives. NLP enables the feasibility and automation of this process. NLP algorithms can classify and tag ESG-related content automatically, identifying key themes, extracting sentiment, and summarizing large amounts of text into digestible insights. This capability not only saves countless hours of manual review but also ensures a more comprehensive and objective analysis of qualitative ESG information, moving beyond simple keyword searches to grasp the nuances of language and context.

10.5.3 ML: pattern recognition and predictive power

ML algorithms serve as the backbone of AI-driven ESG reporting, skilled at identifying complex patterns within large datasets and unlocking predictive capabilities. Training ML algorithms on historical ESG data allows organizations to uncover hidden trends and correlations that may go unnoticed by human analysts. For example, ML can analyze years of environmental performance data to identify patterns that connect operational practices to environmental outcomes, spotlighting areas for improvement or potential risks. Moreover, the predictive power of ML is essential for forecasting future ESG risks. By examining correlations among various operational, economic, and environmental factors, ML models can predict potential ESG-related challenges, such as supply chain disruptions due to climate change or emerging social risks based on socio-economic trends. This predictive capability empowers companies to shift from reactive reporting to proactive risk management, anticipating and addressing challenges before they arise.

10.5.4 Data aggregation and analysis: creating a holistic ESG picture

Effective ESG reporting requires a comprehensive perspective, merging data from various sources to develop a complete picture of a company's ESG footprint. AI systems excel at data aggregation and analysis, effortlessly pulling data from diverse sources such as IoT sensors, smart devices, internal databases, and public repositories. For example, a manufacturing company with sensors tracking energy consumption across its global operations, combined with data from public databases on local environmental regulations and social media feeds, reflects community sentiment. AI systems can consolidate this diverse data, harmonize formats, and analyze it in a unified manner. Advanced algorithms can process and analyze these large volumes of data much faster and more thoroughly than traditional methods, providing insights that support timely decision-making. This capability is essential for overcoming data silos and establishing a truly integrated and data-driven approach to ESG reporting.

10.5.5 Sentiment analysis: gauging public perception and stakeholder sentiment

Beyond quantitative metrics, public perception and stakeholder sentiment are increasingly significant dimensions of ESG performance. AI-powered sentiment analysis tools provide a sophisticated approach to assessing these qualitative factors. By analyzing opinions shared on social media platforms, online review sites, and news commentary, AI can evaluate public perception related to a company's ESG efforts. For example, sentiment analysis can monitor how stakeholders are responding to a company's new sustainability initiatives, identify potential reputational risks arising from negative social media mentions, or measure investor sentiment toward a company's commitment to ethical governance. This real-time feedback loop enables organizations to understand how their ESG actions are perceived and adjust their communications and strategies accordingly, enhancing stakeholder engagement and fostering trust.

10.5.6 Dashboard and reporting automation: efficiency and real-time insights

The convergence of these AI techniques often results in sophisticated dashboards and automated reporting systems. AI can generate ESG reports automatically, using customized dashboards that track relevant KPIs and metrics in real time. For instance, a dynamic dashboard can assist companies in visualizing their carbon footprint across their value chain, displaying real-time energy consumption data, emission levels, and progress toward reduction targets. Such dashboards provide stakeholders with instant access to ESG performance data, eliminating the need for time-consuming manual report generation and enabling continuous monitoring. This automation not only reduces manual workloads and minimizes the risk of human error but also substantially enhances the accuracy, consistency, and timeliness of ESG disclosures, fostering greater transparency and accountability.

10.6 Case study: implementing AI for ESG reporting at XYZ corporation—a practical example

To illustrate the transformative impact of AI techniques on ESG reporting, we examine the case of XYZ Corporation, a multinational consumer goods company that faced significant challenges in modernizing its ESG reporting processes.

10.6.1 Background: navigating evolving reporting demands

XYZ Corporation, a global player in the consumer goods sector, found itself grappling with the increasing complexity of ESG reporting. The company's traditional reporting methods, which heavily relied on manual data entry and spreadsheet-based analysis, were becoming unsustainable. XYZ faced the growing pressure to comply with evolving regulatory requirements, particularly the EU's Nonfinancial Reporting Directive (NFRD) and the impending CSRD, which demanded more comprehensive and rigorous ESG disclosures. Manual processes were not only time-consuming and resource-intensive but also prone to inconsistencies and errors, threatening the accuracy and credibility of XYZ's ESG reporting. The decentralized nature of XYZ's operations, with subsidiaries spread across various geographic regions, further compounded the challenge of data aggregation and standardization.

10.6.2 Challenge: fragmented data and inefficient processes

The core challenge for XYZ Corporation was the need for a more efficient and reliable method to aggregate and analyze ESG-related data from its geographically dispersed subsidiaries. The company needed to progress beyond its fragmented and manual reporting processes to achieve several key objectives: accurately evaluate its global carbon footprint, comprehensively assess its social impact through employee engagement surveys and community initiatives, and ensure that robust governance practices were demonstrably reflected in its reporting. The existing manual system was simply not scalable or agile enough to meet these demands, hindering XYZ's capacity to provide timely, accurate, and comprehensive ESG disclosures to its stakeholders.

10.6.3 Solution: An integrated AI-driven ESG reporting platform

To overcome these challenges, XYZ Corporation undertook a strategic initiative to implement an integrated, AI-driven ESG reporting platform. This platform was designed to leverage a range of AI techniques to transform its ESG reporting processes:

- **Enhance data collection via IoT sensors:** To enhance the granularity and real-time nature of its environmental data, XYZ implemented IoT sensors across its manufacturing operations. These sensors were deployed to monitor energy usage at various stages of production, providing a continuous stream of data on consumption patterns. This sensor data was directly integrated into the AI platform, enabling real-time analysis of energy efficiency and identification of areas of potential waste.
- **Integrate NLP for stakeholder sentiment analysis:** Recognizing the importance of stakeholder perception, XYZ integrated NLP into its AI platform to analyze unstructured feedback from both employees and customers. Employee

engagement surveys and customer feedback collected through various channels, including social media, were analyzed using NLP algorithms to assess sentiment regarding the company's sustainability initiatives. This provided valuable insights into public perception, allowing XYZ to understand how its ESG efforts were being received by key stakeholder groups.

- **Use ML analytics for predictive insights:** To move beyond descriptive reporting and embrace predictive capabilities, XYZ deployed ML algorithms to evaluate historical ESG performance data. ML models were trained to identify patterns and correlations within this data, enabling the prediction of future ESG risks and opportunities. This predictive analytics capability provided XYZ with valuable foresight, guiding strategic decisions in sustainability investments and proactive risk mitigation.
- **Create AI-generated dashboards for real-time visualization:** The AI platform incorporated AI-generated dashboards to enhance data accessibility and facilitate informed decision-making. These dashboards provided real-time insights into key ESG metrics, presenting data in visually compelling formats that allowed company stakeholders to easily track performance against defined benchmarks and understand progress at a glance. This eliminated the need for time-consuming manual report generation, providing stakeholders with continuous visibility into ESG performance.
- **Ensure automated report compilation and regulatory alignment:** The AI platform was designed to automate the entire ESG reporting process, from data aggregation to report generation. Based on the gathered data, XYZ's AI platform automatically compiled comprehensive ESG reports, aligning these reports with relevant regulatory frameworks, including the NFRD and CSRD. This automated reporting ensured that all relevant stakeholders, both internal and external, had access to accurate, consistent, and comprehensive ESG information, significantly streamlining the reporting process and enhancing compliance.

10.6.4 Results

The implementation of the AI-driven ESG reporting platform enabled efficiency, accuracy, and enhanced strategic decision-making. The AI-based solutions generated significant and measurable results for XYZ Corporation:

- **Increased Efficiency:** The automation of data collection, analysis, and report generation resulted in a significant boost in efficiency. The time required for ESG reporting has decreased by approximately 50%, freeing up valuable resources and enabling ESG teams to focus on more strategic initiatives, such as developing new sustainability programs and engaging more deeply with stakeholders.
- **Improved Accuracy:** By automating data analysis and reducing reliance on manual processes, XYZ significantly improved the accuracy of its ESG disclosures. The AI platform reduced errors related to manual data entry and spreadsheet manipulations, leading to higher-quality and more reliable ESG reports.

- **Enhanced Decision-Making:** The predictive insights generated by the AI systems, coupled with real-time dashboards, equipped XYZ's leadership team with the data-driven intelligence needed to make more informed decisions regarding sustainable practices and CSR initiatives. The platform offered a clear and comprehensive view of ESG performance, enabling improved resource allocation, more targeted sustainability investments, and more effective risk mitigation strategies.

10.6.5 Conclusion

The experience of XYZ Corporation underscores the transformative potential of integrating AI into ESG reporting. Through the strategic application of techniques such as NLP, ML, and automated reporting mechanisms, organizations can not only achieve greater efficiency and accuracy in their ESG disclosures but also unlock deeper insights that drive meaningful change toward a more sustainable future.

10.7 The importance of fairness, transparency, and accountability in sustainability reporting and ESG practices

Fairness, transparency, and accountability are foundational elements that ensure the ethical and responsible implementation of AI, as well as the integrity and effectiveness of sustainability reporting and ESG practices.[18] These critical principles not only foster trust among stakeholders, enhance decision-making, promote ethical behavior, facilitate regulatory compliance, and drive long-term value creation, but they are also essential for ensuring that organizations operate responsibly within today's complex economic, environmental, and social landscape.

10.7.1 Defining fairness, transparency, and accountability in AI[19]

10.7.1.1 Fairness

Fairness in AI is a societal value that holds AI systems accountable for making decisions free from bias or unjust discrimination, ensuring that all individuals and groups are treated equitably. It ensures that AI systems and their outputs do not lead to any kind of discrimination against individuals or collectives, particularly concerning protected attributes such as race, gender, age, or socio-economic status. Fairness in ESG means striving for equitable outcomes for all stakeholders impacted by a company's actions and ensuring that ESG initiatives do not disproportionately burden or harm certain groups. It is about avoiding bias and ensuring that the benefits and burdens of sustainability efforts are shared justly.

Example: A company uses an AI system to analyze employee performance for promotions. If the AI algorithm inadvertently favors certain demographic groups over others, it could lead to unfair treatment in promotions. In sustainability reporting, the company should ensure that the AI's decision-making process is fair and that it includes diverse input data. For instance, if AI is used to assess suppliers based on their sustainability efforts, it should evaluate each supplier on the same criteria without bias, thus ensuring equitable opportunities for all involved.

10.7.1.2 Transparency

AI transparency means that the workings of AI systems are understandable and open to scrutiny, making it easier to identify flaws in models. It refers to clarity and openness about how AI systems operate, make decisions, and generate outcomes. Users and stakeholders should be able to see how AI models reach decisions and what data they utilize, which helps build trust and fosters a better understanding of outcomes. Transparency builds trust through openness and clarity. Transparency in ESG reporting and practices means being open and honest about a company's ESG performance, methodologies, and challenges. It involves providing clear, accessible, and verifiable information to stakeholders, allowing them to understand and assess the company's sustainability efforts.

Example: A company uses AI to generate sustainability reports that track its energy consumption and waste management practices. To promote transparency, the company offers a clear explanation of how the AI processes data, what algorithms are employed, and how it calculates key metrics. This way, stakeholders can see not only the final report but also understand how the information was derived, making it easier to trust the results.

10.7.1.3. Accountability

Accountability refers to the responsibility that developers, organizations, and AI systems themselves hold for the decisions and actions taken by AI models. It ensures a clear line of responsibility, allowing stakeholders to take ownership and rectify the outcomes produced by AI technologies. This concept involves assessing algorithms, data, and design processes while preserving intellectual property. It also includes minimizing and reporting any negative impacts. AI accountability implies that organizations are responsible for the outputs and consequences of their AI systems. If an AI system makes a mistake or causes harm, the organization must be ready to address and correct the issue. Accountability in ESG means clearly establishing responsibility for ESG performance and ensuring that companies are held accountable for their impacts and commitments. It involves defining roles, establishing oversight mechanisms, and having processes to address shortcomings and ensure CI.

Example: A corporation leverages AI to assess the environmental impact of its supply chain, identifying areas where it can reduce emissions. If the AI incorrectly analyzes supplier data and recommends a supplier that is less environmentally friendly than claimed, the company must take responsibility. It should publicly acknowledge the mistake in its sustainability report, explain what went wrong, and outline the measures it will implement to prevent similar issues in the future.

10.8 The impact of fairness, transparency, and accountability in sustainability reporting and ESG practices

10.8.1 Building trust with stakeholders

Trust is the cornerstone of effective stakeholder relationships, and fairness plays a pivotal role in promoting this trust. When organizations ensure that all stakeholders—employees, customers, investors, and communities—create equally, they encourage collaboration and mutual respect. By addressing the diverse interests and concerns of different groups in their sustainability initiatives, companies not only reinforce their reputation but also cultivate a shared sense of purpose.

Transparency complements this trust-building effort by providing stakeholders with clear insights into a company's sustainability performance and ESG factors. It enables stakeholders to understand how companies are progressing toward their sustainability goals and ESG practices. When businesses openly disclose their methodologies, data sources, and outcomes, they build credibility. Stakeholders can see the tangible impact of corporate initiatives, strengthening their connection to the organization.

Accountability is essential in holding organizations responsible for their commitments and impacts. By demonstrating accountability, companies affirm their dedication to ethical practices, reinforcing stakeholder trust and loyalty. This trust-based relationship becomes a powerful asset, enabling companies to navigate complexities more easily.

10.8.1.1 Enhancing decision-making

Incorporating fairness into decision-making processes enriches outcomes by ensuring that diverse stakeholder perspectives are considered. This inclusivity not only leads to more equitable results but also cultivates an environment where potential risks and opportunities are more readily identified. This holistic approach can identify risks and opportunities that may be overlooked when only a narrow viewpoint is considered. By allowing decision-makers to engage with a broader array of perspectives, they are more likely to craft rounded and effective strategies.

Transparency enables informed decision-making by providing stakeholders with access to relevant information. Whether they are consumers selecting sustainable products, investors assessing a company's ESG performance, or regulators enforcing compliance, straightforward access to transparent data allows stakeholders to align their choices with their values. As organizations commit to clear and transparent ESG disclosures, they empower stakeholders to make informed choices that reflect their values and ethical beliefs.

10.8.1.2 Promoting ethical practices

Fairness is not merely a principle; it is a guiding tenet that forms the foundation for ethical conduct within organizations. Fairness in ESG practices encourages organizations to operate ethically, minimizing harm to individuals and communities while ensuring that benefits are distributed justly. This ethical foundation is crucial for sustainable development, which aims to harmonize human and environmental welfare and helps mitigate negative impacts on social and environmental systems.

Transparency enhances ethical practices by enabling scrutiny of corporate behavior and sustainability efforts. It enables stakeholders to scrutinize corporate actions and assess sustainability initiatives. In a culture that values transparency, it becomes increasingly difficult for companies to engage in misleading practices such as greenwashing or misrepresenting their sustainability efforts.

Accountability reinforces this commitment to ethical standards by establishing mechanisms for holding companies accountable for their sustainability claims. This culture of responsibility not only prevents unethical actions but also reinforces a culture of responsibility, inspiring organizations to uphold high standards of integrity.

10.8.1.3 Facilitating regulatory compliance

As governments and regulatory bodies increasingly recognize the significance of ESG factors, fairness, transparency, and accountability become vital for complying with legal requirements. Organizations that embrace these principles are better equipped to adapt to evolving regulatory frameworks, significantly reducing the risk of legal repercussions.

Transparent sustainability reporting serves as an effective tool for organizations to track their progress on ESG metrics, facilitating compliance with regulations and standards imposed by various stakeholders, including investors and government agencies.

10.8.1.4 Driving long-term value creation

Fairness in the treatment of employees, communities, and the environment contributes to SBMs that can lead to long-term profitability. Companies that prioritize fair practices enhance their reputations, successfully attracting and retaining talent while fostering consumer loyalty.

Transparency in ESG initiatives has become increasingly associated with long-term value creation. Stakeholders are more inclined to support organizations that demonstrate their commitment to ethical behavior and sustainability. This support translates into increased market share and brand strength.

Finally, accountability ensures that organizations consistently align with their sustainability goals. By enabling improved resource management and mitigating risks associated with environmental and social liabilities, accountability becomes a critical driver of sustained value creation, enabling companies to thrive in an ever-evolving landscape.

10.9 AI and the challenge of trust in ESG data

Trust is vital for sustainability reports. As society increasingly relies on AI, expectations for these systems to deliver understandable and justifiable outcomes grow correspondingly, particularly in sustainability reporting and ESG practices, where fairness, transparency, and accountability are important—a dynamic approach that integrates technological advancements with ethical business practices, emphasizing the importance of continuous adaptation to achieve sustainable outcomes. This implies a real-time, data-driven management approach in ESG initiatives, supported by robust AI-driven systems and agile, dynamic frameworks, facilitating enhanced operational efficiency and alignment with ESG goals.[20] However, many organizations struggle to provide clear and honest reports. They often face skepticism from stakeholders who doubt the accuracy of their claims. For example, a company may state it has reduced emissions but fail to provide consistent data over time. Such inconsistencies can lead to mistrust and damage reputations.

10.9.1 Enhancing accountability through AI-driven data analysis

Governance and accountability in the context of responsible AI focus on establishing effective frameworks and mechanisms to ensure the ethical and responsible use of AI systems. This involves creating clear policies that define how AI systems should be developed, implemented, and monitored to uphold ethical standards. It also requires organizations to establish designated roles and responsibilities for oversight, ensuring that there are accountable individuals or teams tasked with maintaining compliance and ethical practices. Effective governance requires regular risk assessments to identify potential ethical pitfalls, biases, or unintended consequences associated with AI systems. Organizations must also implement monitoring and reporting mechanisms to track the performance and impacts of AI, allowing for timely interventions if issues arise. By integrating these elements into their governance framework, companies can foster a culture of accountability and transparency, which is crucial for building stakeholder trust and promoting sustainable AI practices.

Effective frameworks and mechanisms refer to structured systems and processes that organizations develop and implement to guide the responsible use and governance of AI technologies. These frameworks encompass various components designed to ensure ethical practices, compliance with regulations, and risk management throughout the lifecycle of AI systems. Frameworks are comprehensive plans or guidelines that outline the principles, standards, and procedures for AI governance. A robust framework typically includes elements such as ethical guidelines, compliance requirements, risk assessment protocols, and performance metrics. For example, a framework might specify that AI systems must be developed transparently, ensuring that they are fair and auditable. Additionally, it can incorporate strategies for stakeholder engagement to involve diverse perspectives in the decision-making process related to AI use.

Mechanisms are tangible tools, practices, and processes that operate the frameworks. They may include specific governance structures, such as an AI ethics committee, regular audits to ensure compliance with ethical standards, training programs for employees on responsible AI use, and feedback loops that allow for CI of AI practices. Mechanisms also involve monitoring systems that track the impact of AI processes, enabling timely interventions if ethical concerns or operational flaws arise.

The combination of frameworks and mechanisms creates a systematic approach to AI governance, ensuring organizations can manage the complexities and risks associated with AI technologies while fostering accountability and ethical responsibility. This holistic approach is essential for building public trust and aligning AI initiatives with broader social and environmental goals.

10.9.2 Enhancing transparency through AI-driven data analysis

While advancements in ML techniques have catalyzed the rise of powerful AI applications, the challenges associated with providing understandable justifications for their decisions remain substantial. AI is complex, having various types, each presenting unique benefits and challenges. Addressing these challenges is essential for fostering trust, accountability, and responsible AI deployment in sensitive domains.

As businesses and stakeholders recognize the importance of sustainability, clearly presenting and explaining sustainability efforts and outcomes becomes a vital aspect of corporate responsibility. Enhancing transparency through AI-driven data analysis is increasingly crucial for organizations seeking to foster trust, accountability, and stakeholder engagement. In the following, we propose several comprehensive strategies that organizations can implement to enhance transparency in Sustainability Reporting and ESG Practices through AI-driven data analysis. Each strategy is complemented by examples and best practices to illustrate its practical application.

10.9.2.1 Data visualization

Data visualization refers to the graphical representation of information and data. AI tools can assist in creating dynamic and interactive visualizations, making complex data easier to understand and more accessible to a broader audience. Effective visualizations can take various forms, including interactive dashboards, charts, graphs, and heat maps. The primary goal of data visualization is to enhance accessibility and interpretability, allowing users to quickly identify and comprehend trends, outliers, and patterns in the data. Data visualization serves as an excellent tool for clearly sharing information with those who may not be experts, ensuring that everyone can understand key insights without feeling overwhelmed. For example, an organization can deploy AI-powered data visualization software to create a visually engaging sustainability dashboard that displays key metrics such as carbon emissions reductions, waste recycling rates, and energy consumption trends. Stakeholders can interact with the dashboard, filtering data by period, department, or location to gain detailed insights into sustainability efforts. The visual representation can help stakeholders quickly grasp performance trends, potential issues, and areas of success, thus supporting informed decision-making.

10.9.2.2 Automated reporting

Automated reporting involves using AI-driven programs to create reports from data gathered from various sources, including sustainability indices, regulatory filings, surveys and feedback, social media platforms, and IoT sensors used for energy consumption, emissions levels, or waste management practices. Automation in reporting utilizes AI to generate thorough reports from data inputs without manual intervention, helping businesses save time and money. This reduces the likelihood of human error while speeding up the reporting process, which is essential for timely communication with stakeholders. For example, an organization can harness AI to automate the creation of monthly sustainability reports that compile data from multiple sources, including production facilities, energy bills, and waste management services. Rather than manually consolidating this data, AI can continuously assess performance metrics and generate reports that reflect real-time insights. Each report can summarize an organization's sustainability KPIs, allowing stakeholders to review the latest developments without having to sift through extensive datasets.

10.9.2.3 Natural Language Generation

NLG is a process that utilizes AI algorithms, like NLP, to produce natural written or spoken language that appears human-like from structured and unstructured data. This AI technology converts structured data into human-readable narratives, like producing summaries, reports, or responses. NLG's focus is on generating text rather than understanding it. NLG can help organizations transform complex data analyses into straightforward language explanations in a way that is easily understood by humans, making the information more relatable and digestible for stakeholders who might not possess technical expertise.[21] For example, a company collects extensive data on its energy usage across various departments using IoT sensors and smart meters installed throughout its facilities, which continuously monitor consumption patterns and identify inefficiencies. This data is then analyzed through an AI-driven system to generate comprehensive reports that inform energy-saving strategies and sustainability initiatives. The AI system employs NLG to create a narrative report that explains trends and insights, such as "In September, our energy consumption reduced by 15% due to initiatives implemented in the manufacturing plant, resulting in cost savings of $10,000." Such clear communication helps stakeholders understand performance in simple terms, fostering alignment between the organization's sustainability goals and stakeholder expectations.

10.9.2.4 Real-time data access

Use AI to provide stakeholders with real-time access to data regarding sustainability efforts. This can involve creating online platforms where stakeholders have real-time access to sustainability data through web platforms or mobile applications, which significantly improves transparency. These AI-based platforms can supply continuous updates on sustainability metrics, allowing stakeholders to remain informed and engaged. *For example*, an organization could develop a dedicated sustainability portal that displays real-time data regarding its energy consumption, waste generation, and progress toward sustainability targets. This interactive platform would allow stakeholders to monitor performance and trends dynamically. For instance, if carbon emissions drop due to new efficiency measures, stakeholders can receive immediate updates, emphasizing the organization's commitment to transparent operations.

10.9.2.5 Enhanced traceability

Enhanced traceability refers to the ability to track and verify the sources and methodologies used in data analysis. By utilizing AI systems that document the entire data lifecycle—encompassing every stage from collection and storage to processing and reporting—organizations can ensure their claims are substantiated and verifiable. This transparency not only boosts stakeholders' confidence in the reported data but also facilitates compliance with regulatory standards, reducing the risk of potential audits or sanctions. Enhanced traceability also allows organizations to quickly identify and rectify discrepancies in their data, fostering a culture of accountability and CI in data governance practices. For example, an AI system can be designed to automatically log all sources and methods used to compile sustainability metrics, such as waste management statistics or emissions figures. This includes internal databases, public records, IoT sensor data, and external partnerships, as well as methodologies for data collection, algorithmic analysis, and quality assurance processes. By documenting these elements, stakeholders can verify the accuracy and credibility of the company's sustainability claims. In cases of audits or inquiries, stakeholders can access an audit trail that clarifies how data was sourced, analyzed, and reported. For example, if a company claims to have reduced plastic waste by 20%, stakeholders can review the traceability log to verify the data collection methods, the algorithms used for analysis, and the underlying datasets, thereby enhancing credibility.

10.9.2.6 Stakeholder interaction

Interaction between organizations and stakeholders is essential for reinforcing trust and fostering meaningful engagement. AI-driven chatbots and virtual assistants can provide immediate responses to stakeholder inquiries regarding sustainability data, ensuring that they receive timely and relevant information. These tools can also analyze stakeholder sentiment and preferences, enabling organizations to customize their communications and address specific concerns, thereby enhancing transparency and cultivating a more engaged community around sustainability initiatives. Through this continuous dialogue, companies can forge stronger relationships, demonstrate accountability, and highlight their commitment to sustainability. For example, a company could implement an AI chatbot on its sustainability reporting website, enabling stakeholders to ask questions about specific data points or initiatives. For example, if a stakeholder wants to know how much progress has been made in reducing carbon emissions, they can type their question into the chatbot, which will provide an AI-generated, informative response based on the latest available data. This proactive communication not only fosters a transparent dialogue but also empowers stakeholders by giving them quick access to information that is critical for their understanding. By facilitating such interactions, organizations can enhance their credibility, demonstrate responsiveness to stakeholder concerns, and ultimately strengthen their commitment to sustainability practices.

10.9.2.7 Predictive analytics

Predictive analytics employs AI to analyze historical data and forecast future outcomes based on emerging trends. By leveraging advanced algorithms, organizations can uncover patterns and insights that might otherwise remain hidden, allowing them to make data-driven decisions. Providing stakeholders with forecasts based on current data can enhance understanding and build trust in the organization's long-term strategies, as it shows a commitment to transparency and informed planning. Moreover, these forecasts can help stakeholders grasp the potential impacts of the organization's actions on key sustainability metrics, thereby fostering greater confidence in the organization's ability to achieve its sustainability goals and tackle future challenges effectively. For example, an organization focusing on sustainable practices might use predictive analytics to project future energy savings based on current initiatives, such as implementing LED lighting or enhancing insulation in buildings. For example, by analyzing historical energy consumption data alongside projected usage patterns after installing energy-efficient LED lights and improved insulation, the organization can estimate a significant reduction in energy costs over the next five years. Presenting these forward-looking insights in stakeholder meetings or reports can illustrate its commitment to sustainability and provide a clear roadmap for future actions, detailing specific metrics such as anticipated kilowatt-hour reductions and cost savings. This not only emphasizes the organization's proactive approach to environmental stewardship but also enables stakeholders to understand the potential impacts of sustainability investments over time, fostering accountability and encouraging further investment in similar initiatives. Furthermore, showcasing these predictions can instill confidence in stakeholders that their contributions are making a measurable difference in the organization's sustainability efforts.

10.9.2.8 Engaging storytelling with data

To further enhance transparency, organizations can integrate storytelling techniques into their data presentations. By framing sustainability metrics within the context of real-world impacts, companies can create a narrative that emotionally resonates with stakeholders. For instance, instead of merely presenting numbers on energy savings, the organization might share the story of a community project that benefited from reduced energy costs, such as funding for local educational programs or improvements to public infrastructure. This approach enables stakeholders to see the tangible benefits of sustainability efforts, fostering a personal connection to the data. By illustrating how their actions contribute to broader societal goals, organizations can inspire greater stakeholder engagement and support for ongoing sustainability initiatives. For example, an organization might share a case study in its sustainability report that outlines how it improved recycling rates in its production facilities. The report could include not only numerical data, such as a 30% increase in recycling rates over the past year, but also personal stories of employees involved in recycling initiatives. For instance, the report could feature an interview with a machine operator who spearheaded a recycling awareness campaign, discussing their motivation, the challenges they faced, and the sense of community that developed among coworkers as they worked toward a common goal. Additionally, the organization could illustrate the broader positive impact on local communities by showcasing partnerships established with local schools for educational programs on recycling and waste reduction, as well as donations made to local charities from the profits generated by recycled materials. By highlighting these individual contributions and community benefits, organizations can create a compelling narrative that elevates the data beyond mere numbers and fosters a genuine connection with stakeholders, ultimately encouraging them to support ongoing sustainability efforts.

10.9.2.9 Ethical AI practices

Commitment to ethical AI practices is essential for building trust and transparency. Designating governance safeguards, such as establishing ethical review boards and defining clear accountability protocols, can validate how AI systems operate and make decisions. These safeguards ensure that checks and balances are in place to prevent bias and promote fairness in AI deployments. Furthermore, regular audits and transparency reports can provide stakeholders with insights into the AI decision-making processes, allowing them to understand how their data is used and how these systems influence outcomes. By actively engaging with stakeholders and incorporating their feedback into AI governance practices, organizations can foster a culture of trust and collaboration, ultimately leading to more responsible and effective uses of AI. For example, organizations must ensure that their AI systems are not only compliant with legal standards but also adhere to ethical guidelines concerning data privacy, security, and non-discrimination. For instance, transparency in algorithm development—including explaining data usage, the models' decision-making processes, and the rationale behind specific outcomes—will help stakeholders feel assured that AI applications are fair and trustworthy. By providing detailed documentation and engaging in open dialogues with affected communities, organizations can demystify the AI processes and cultivate a sense of ownership among stakeholders. Regular audits of AI outcomes against ethical standards can reinforce this commitment, further enhancing transparency in sustainability reporting. These audits should include a thorough review of how AI impacts various ESG factors, ensuring that the technologies deployed align with broader sustainability goals and genuinely contribute to ethical corporate practices. In this way, organizations not only uphold legal compliance but also create a framework for responsible AI use that aligns with their ESG commitments.

10.10 The role of AI in the preparation of audit reports and ESG assurance statements

The auditor's role has evolved from verifying every transaction to offering only reasonable assurance and adding credibility to financial statements and now providing assurance statements on both financial ESP and nonfinancial ESG sustainability performance information. Auditors have traditionally expressed their opinion on financial statements by providing reasonable assurance that these statements, prepared by the company's management, are free from material misstatements caused by errors or fraud.[22] The passage of the SOX of 2002 extended auditors' responsibilities in expressing audit opinions on both financial statements and the internal controls over financial reporting (ICFR). Thus, auditors examine the fair presentation of financial statements and the effectiveness of ICFR in producing financial statements, making greater use of analytical procedures such as sampling techniques, the concept of materiality, and a risk-based approach. Growing competition and pressure on audit fees have further accelerated the development of risk assessment techniques and the use of technology-driven, continuous auditing of financial statements and ICFR. Recent advancements in the integrated sustainability reports on both financial ESP and nonfinancial ESG sustainability performance reports have created an opportunity for auditors to offer assurance statements on sustainability reports. Auditors are now using AI-assisted tools and techniques in conjunction with forensic-related audit procedures, double materiality and risk assessment, and double fraud discovery of ESP and ESG information.

Third-party assurance providers, in general, and accounting firms, in particular, play an important role in lending more credibility and objectivity to sustainability reports on ESP and ESG dimensions of sustainability performance. Understandability, objectivity, reliability, transparency, credibility, and usefulness of sustainability reports are important to both internal and external users of sustainability reports and can be enhanced by providing assurance on these reports. Sustainability assurance can be provided internally by internal auditors or CSOs or external assurance providers. While internal auditors and CSOs are well qualified to assist management in the preparation and assurance of sustainability reports, external users of sustainability reports may demand more independent and objective assurance of sustainability reports. This type of assurance can be provided by certified public accountants, professional assurance providers, or equivalently accredited individuals, groups, or institutes. Current auditing standards guide accounting firms to provide reasonable assurance on financial and internal control reports prepared by management. However, the degree of reliance placed on nonfinancial ESG information is not clear. Assurance standards on different dimensions of sustainability performance reports vary in terms of rigorousness and general acceptability. For example, auditing standards governing the auditing of economic activities presented in the financial statements are well established, widely accepted, and practiced in the past several decades, and external auditors have expressed their audit opinions on financial statements. However, assurance standards on nonfinancial

ESG dimensions of sustainability have yet to be fully developed and globally accepted.

An integrated and standardized approach to providing assurance on both ESP and ESG dimensions of sustainability reporting is crucial for advancing business sustainability. Auditing standards issued by the Public Company Accounting Oversight Board support the economic dimension by focusing on financial statement audits and ICFR. Meanwhile, the International Auditing and Assurance Standards Board (IAASB) offers standards applicable across all dimensions of EGSEE sustainability, such as the International Standard on Assurance Engagements 3000 (ISAE 3000) and ISAE 3410 (Assurance Engagements on Greenhouse Gas Statements). On January 27, 2025, the IAASB and the International Ethics Standards Board for Accountants (IESBA) launched an integrated effort to support effective implementation of their standards aimed at advancing trust and transparency in sustainability reporting and assurance.[23] These standards are intended to provide a standardized and unified global approach to meet the growing market demand from investors, mandated by regulators, and anticipated by other stakeholders for trustworthy sustainability disclosures that support stakeholder decisions. These standards also establish robust expectations for ethical behavior in sustainability reporting and assurance and provide more requirements for organizations, assurance providers, and other practitioners relevant to assurance engagements on sustainability reports. The IAASB's ISSA 5000 and the IESBA's IESSA share the following five common goals:[24]

- Equipping global markets with a set of robust and cohesive standards that provide guidelines for assurance, ethics, and independence for sustainability assurance engagements.
- Offering globally accepted standards that meet market and investor demands, regulatory mandates, and stakeholder expectations for profession-agnostic global standards.
- Providing ISSA 5000 and IESSA collaborative framework to be applied in relation to sustainability information prepared under any suitable sustainability reporting framework.
- Promoting informed decision-making based on trust, objectively and independently assured sustainability information.
- Detecting and preventing risks of material misstated sustainability information, whether caused by fraud, greenwashing, and noncompliance with applicable laws, rules, regulations, and standards.

The collaborative ISSA 5000 and IESSA standards represent an important progress in achieving global sustainability reporting and assurance. In jurisdictions adopting the combined ISSA 5000 and IESSA standards, they will become effective for periods starting on or after December 15, 2026, with early adoption permitted and encouraged. This integrated assurance model provides practical and educational guidelines to promote sustainability reporting and assurance. Typically, sustainability assurance statements offer either reasonable or limited assurance about the accuracy, objectivity, and reliability of sustainability reports. Prepared by independent third-party providers, such as audit firms or specialized sustainability consultants, these statements enhance the credibility, transparency, independence, and objectivity of sustainability performance reports.

A sustainability assurance statement generally includes the following components:

1. **Introductory Paragraph:** Defines the purpose and scope of the assurance engagement, outlines management's responsibility for preparing the sustainability report, clarifies the assurance provider's responsibilities, and specifies the reporting period covered.
2. **Scope Paragraph:** Identifies the criteria against which sustainability performance is evaluated, such as the standards of GRI, SASB, ISSB, or other relevant frameworks.
3. **Assurance Scope:** Defines the specific elements of the sustainability report subject to assurance procedures.
4. **Assurance Methodology:** Describes the methodologies used, including sampling techniques, data verification processes, interviews conducted, AI-powered platforms utilized, and other relevant assurance procedures.
5. **Findings and Conclusion:** Presents key findings from the assurance procedures, highlights material discrepancies or concerns, and provides an overall conclusion on the reliability and accuracy of the sustainability report.
6. **Double Materiality and Risk Assessment:** Incorporates the assessment of both financial ESP and nonfinancial ESG dimensions to evaluate sustainability performance.
7. **Assurance Limitations:** Outlines any limitations or constraints encountered during the assurance engagement, such as scope or boundary restrictions.
8. **Assurance Opinion:** Expresses an opinion on the sustainability report, ranging from unqualified (indicating reliability and transparency) to qualified or adverse (highlighting significant issues, deficiencies, noncompliance, or limitations).
9. **Assurance Statement Date and Signatures:** Includes the date and signatures of responsible assurance providers, confirming their independence and adherence to professional standards.

Sustainability assurance statements play a vital role in enhancing stakeholder trust and confidence by providing independent verification of sustainability disclosures. These statements demonstrate an organization's commitment to transparency, reliability, objectivity, and accountability in pursuing sustainability goals, reinforcing their dedication to addressing sustainability challenges and opportunities. AI-powered tools and techniques are playing a transformative role in the preparation of audit reports on financial ESP and assurance statements on nonfinancial ESG in assisting organizations to enhance efficiency, accuracy, and overall quality of their sustainability reports.

10.10.1 AI in the preparation of audit reports

The transformative impact of AI-powered algorithms on the auditing process and reporting is presented in this section. AI-assisted tools and techniques are revolutionizing the auditing process by automating routine tasks, identifying patterns, and delivering insights that enhance audit quality and efficiency. These advancements reshape the audit process in several ways, including:

1. **Risk Prediction and Prioritization:** AI analyzes historical data, industry trends, and company-specific information to predict potential risks and fraud. This enables auditors to prioritize high-risk areas, leading to more robust, focused, and efficient audit planning.
2. **Data Processing and Anomaly Detection:** AI processes large volumes of structured and unstructured data, such as financial transactions, statements, emails, and contracts, to detect anomalies, trends, and outliers. This enhances the accuracy of identifying errors or material misstatements that traditional methods might overlook.
3. **Automation of Routine Tasks:** Tasks such as depreciation estimates, reconciliations, confirmations, and journal entry testing are automated, reducing human error and freeing auditors to concentrate on higher-value activities such as materiality assessments, risk evaluation, and strategic decision-making.
4. **Qualitative Information Analysis:** Using NLP, AI extracts and analyzes qualitative data from financial disclosures and management reports, offering deeper insights.
5. **Sentiment Analysis:** AI conducts sentiment analysis on management commentary and risk disclosures to identify potential red flags or concerns that may require further investigation.
6. **Enhanced Audit Reporting:** AI provides optimal structures for audit reports, ensuring compliance with regulatory frameworks and improving overall audit quality.
7. **Client-Specific Insights:** Audit findings and recommendations are tailored to align with the client's unique industry characteristics and operational context, increasing their relevance and utility.
8. **Real-Time Auditing:** AI facilitates continuous monitoring of transactions, allowing dynamic audit adjustments throughout the year and ensuring up-to-date insights.
9. **Continuous Auditing:** AI enables continuous auditing, improving the timeliness and relevance of audit reports and enhancing their value for decision-making.

By leveraging these capabilities, AI not only enhances the efficiency and effectiveness of audits but also equips auditors to provide deeper insights and add greater value to clients.

10.10.2 AI in ESG assurance statements

AI can enhance ESG assurance services as the growing focus on ESG sustainability reports by investors, regulators, and businesses, coupled with the increasing significance of ESG factors in planning, performance, risk, and disclosure, has driven a surge in demand for assurance services. AI platforms and algorithms play a pivotal role in supporting ESG assurance activities and the preparation of assurance statements in several ways, including:

1. **Data Aggregation:** Collecting ESG data from diverse sources, including sustainability reports, third-party databases, social media, and real-time environmental monitoring systems, to ensure the completeness and accuracy of information used in assurance processes
2. **Unstructured Data Analysis:** Processing and analyzing unstructured ESG data—such as GHG emissions, corporate governance practices, board independence, employee diversity metrics, and supply chain activities—to identify inconsistencies, data gaps, or areas requiring further clarification.
3. **Benchmarking and Validation:** Cross-checking and validating ESG metrics against industry benchmarks, standards, peers, and regulatory requirements to ensure disclosures are accurate, complete, and comparable across organizations.
4. **Framework Compliance:** Assisting in the preparation of ESG assurance statements aligned with globally recognized standards and frameworks, such as GRI, SASB, CSRD, and ISSB, to enhance the credibility, objectivity, and transparency of the statements.
5. **Greenwashing Detection:** Identifying materially misstated ESG claims and detecting discrepancies between reported ESG performance and actual results or external benchmarks. This minimizes the risk of greenwashing, protects stakeholder trust, and ensures accountability.
6. **Real-Time Monitoring:** Enabling continuous monitoring of ESG performance through dynamic data streams, which improves the reliability, accuracy, and completeness of assurance statements.

By integrating AI capabilities into ESG assurance practices, organizations and their ESG assurance providers can significantly enhance the quality, transparency, and credibility of their sustainability disclosures, building stronger trust with stakeholders and meeting growing demands for accountability in ESG reporting. Overall, by leveraging AI, auditors and assurance providers can meet the growing demands for quality audit reports on financial ESP information and transparency, accountability, and reliability of nonfinancial ESG reporting. Key benefits of using AI platform in ESP audit reports and ESG assurance statements include: (1) improving audit quality and efficiency by automating time-intensive tasks that enable faster completion of audits and assurance statements; (2) enhancing accuracy by reducing human errors to improve the reliability of results; (3) processing large volumes of data across multiple sources and jurisdictions to meet the complex reporting needs of investors and expectations of other stakeholders; (4) improving consistency by ensuring standardized processes in compliance with the growing auditing and assurance standards and regulatory frameworks; and (5) detecting hidden patterns and insights to enhance the clarity and objectivity of reports. It is expected that AI plays a more important role in the preparation of audit reports and ESG assurance statements as AI-assisted technologies and tools continue to evolve.

10.11 XAI: enhancing sustainability reporting and ESG practices

In recent years, AI has gained more attention and influence across various fields, becoming more widely recognized and adopted. Recent advancements in ML have precipitated a new era of AI applications through generative models, such as LLMs, which offer considerable advantages across multiple domains. These models can understand and generate human-like text and audio, leading to breakthroughs in several fields, including NLP, content creation, and customer support. The success of these models can largely be attributed to innovative ML techniques that build models using their internal representations. However, many systems still lack the ability to explain their autonomous decisions and actions to human users. This is further complicated by the inherent complexity of DL models such as deep neural networks, which operate as "black boxes," making it challenging for users to understand how decisions are made. AI algorithms increasingly influence significant aspects of companies' credibility and reputation. As stakeholders increasingly prioritize sustainable and ethical corporate practices, AI algorithms used for ESG assessments must operate transparently. This transparency allows stakeholders to understand how decisions regarding sustainability initiatives, social impacts, and governance practices are made, thereby ensuring that these decisions reflect genuine corporate responsibility rather than superficial compliance. When strategic decisions that deeply affect companies are made by algorithms, it becomes imperative to understand how and why those decisions are made.[25] This aligns with the principle that individuals should not be subject to decisions without insight into the underlying processes, particularly when those decisions could challenge credibility and trust with stakeholders and cause harm to reputations.

Addressing these challenges through XAI is essential for fostering trust, accountability, and responsible AI deployment in sensitive domains. XAI aims to make AI systems more understandable, transparent, and interpretable to humans without compromising performance. This involves clarifying how AI algorithms arrive at their decisions, especially in complex decision-making scenarios where the underlying processes might not be readily apparent. The goal of XAI is to ensure that AI models are not only accurate but also transparent, enabling users to trust and comprehend the outputs generated by these systems. XAI includes a collection of methods and techniques designed to make AI systems more comprehensible and interpretable for human users. As AI technologies continue to influence critical sectors such as sustainability, healthcare, and law, the need for transparency in how AI models make decisions becomes ever more essential.[26]

XAI is increasingly recognized as a critical element in enhancing accountability and transparency in sustainability reporting and ESG practices, as ESG performance and disclosure influence a company's value. Strong ESG performance positively influences firm value. This means that firms that excel in ESG factors generally see an increase in their market valuation due to these strengths, as they may be perceived as more sustainable and responsible. However, firms with notable weaknesses in their ESG performance experience a decrease in firm value. Investors tend to view these weaknesses as risks, which can lead to lower valuations due to concerns about potential liabilities, regulatory scrutiny, or reputational damage.[27] In ESG, where stakeholder trust and ethical considerations are paramount, XAI provides the crucial bridge between powerful AI tools and responsible applications.[28] The comprehensive understanding of XAI's role can be divided into several key areas, each highlighting its significance in deploying AI technologies within organizations. First, transparency in AI decision-making not only demystifies the processes behind algorithmic outputs but also helps stakeholders comprehend the rationale for specific decisions, fostering an environment of trust. Additionally, XAI facilitates ethical auditing, allowing organizations to identify and mitigate biases that could adversely affect their ESG evaluations, thereby promoting fairness and accountability. Moreover, by enhancing governance frameworks, XAI ensures that organizations can maintain oversight and responsibility for AI-driven actions, which is essential for aligning AI initiatives with ethical standards and sustainable practices. Collectively, these areas underscore XAI's pivotal role in integrating AI responsibly into the fabric of organizational strategy and operations. In the following, we provide an overview of XAI's role in ESG practices.

10.11.1 Ensures transparency and understanding

One of XAI's primary advantages is its ability to demystify AI decision-making processes. Traditional AI systems often function as "black boxes," where the rationale behind decisions remains obscured. XAI, on the other hand, elucidates the algorithms and data processing techniques used to evaluate ESG metrics. By making these processes comprehensible, stakeholders, including investors, regulators, and consumers, can scrutinize AI-driven conclusions. This scrutiny fosters trust in AI outputs, ensuring that organizations are held accountable for their ESG claims and practices.

10.11.2 XAI as a framework for responsible AI

XAI is a foundational component of a robust framework designed to guide the responsible use of AI in ESG contexts. This framework emphasizes the importance of accountability and governance. By providing insights into how AI systems generate their recommendations, XAI allows organizations to move beyond mere reliance on outputs and actively engage in critical assessments of the systems in place. This ability to trace decisions back through the AI's logic enhances governance capabilities, ensuring that AI applications align with ethical and ESG principles.

10.11.3 Enhancing governance metrics with XAI

With XAI, the evaluation of governance metrics related to ethical AI applications becomes more rigorous. The capacity to understand AI decisions enables companies to establish clear lines of accountability. Governance bodies can assess whether AI's outputs adhere to ethical norms without solely relying on trust. This clarity promotes a more responsible governance structure, enabling stakeholders to identify who is accountable for specific AI-generated insights or actions.

10.11.4 Achieve ethical auditing and bias mitigation

Ethical implications are paramount in sustainability. XAI empowers organizations to audit their AI systems effectively, ensuring they are free from biases that could distort ESG evaluations. By revealing the inner workings of AI decision-making, organizations can pinpoint and rectify biases that could lead to unfair or skewed outcomes. This is particularly critical in ESG contexts, where the ethical implications of decisions carry significant social weight. Guidelines for fairness and transparency can be established, and ongoing audits can be implemented to maintain compliance with these standards.

10.11.5 Monitoring and adapting AI strategies with XAI

XAI provides valuable insights that enable organizations to monitor how their AI systems perform regarding ESG goals. It allows for the identification of KPIs that go beyond surface-level metrics, revealing underlying factors influencing AI performance. For example, if an AI system tracks emission reductions, XAI can highlight which specific variables are most significant in the AI's analysis. This kind of insight enables informed adjustments to AI strategies, ensuring that they remain relevant and effective in meeting evolving ESG targets.

10.11.6 Ensure sustainability impact evaluation

Assessing AI's impact on sustainability outcomes necessitates a nuanced understanding of how AI contributes to ESG objectives. XAI provides the qualitative and quantitative frameworks needed to evaluate AI's role in these efforts effectively. By offering clarity on the decisions made by AI systems, organizations can measure the success of specific initiatives and the processes that led to those outcomes. This deeper understanding is vital for demonstrating the value of AI in enhancing sustainability and for adapting AI applications to better recognize and address the social implications of business activities.

XAI goes beyond its technical aspects to serve as a crucial foundation for the responsible and trustworthy implementation of AI in ESG reporting. By enhancing transparency and accountability across various areas, such as governance, ethical considerations, monitoring, and impact assessment, XAI empowers organizations to utilize AI responsibly. This, in turn, strengthens their commitment to sustainability initiatives and builds trust with stakeholders, ensuring that the application of AI aligns with broader ESG objectives and societal expectations.

10.12 Change management in AI adoption: a framework for effective change planning and implementation

Implementing change management for AI adoption requires careful planning and execution. The process begins with a clear vision and strategy that outlines the potential benefits of AI, such as enhancing innovation and improving operational processes. This initial step helps align stakeholders by providing a roadmap that clarifies expectations for the transformation ahead. We propose a framework that outlines a comprehensive approach to effectively achieving change management in the context of AI adoption. This structured approach offers guidance on how organizations can effectively manage the change associated with AI adoption, ensuring that employees are prepared, engaged, and supported throughout the journey.

10.12.1 Establish a clear vision and strategy

Begin by articulating a clear vision for AI adoption and the strategic goals associated with it. This vision should outline how AI will benefit the organization, drive innovation, and improve processes. By having a defined strategy, you provide a roadmap that helps align all stakeholders and sets expectations for the change.

10.12.2 Engage stakeholders early

Engaging stakeholders from the outset is crucial for successful change management. Identify all relevant parties, including leaders, employees, customers, and external partners, and involve them in discussions about AI adoption. Solicit their input, address concerns, and communicate how AI will impact their roles and the organization as a whole.

10.12.3 Assess organizational readiness

Conduct a readiness assessment to evaluate the organization's current state and capacity for change. This includes analyzing existing technologies, processes, skills, and culture. Identifying potential barriers to AI adoption will help you develop targeted strategies to overcome resistance and ensure a smoother transition.

10.12.4 Develop a change management plan

Create a comprehensive management plan that outlines the steps required for AI adoption. This plan details communication strategies to ensure transparency, training and development programs to equip staff with necessary skills, and support frameworks to aid employees during the transition. This plan should include:

- **Communication strategy:** Effective communication throughout the change process is essential. Define how information regarding the change will be shared with stakeholders.
- **Training and development:** Identify the training needs of employees affected by AI adoption and develop training programs to equip them with the necessary skills to work with AI systems.
- **Support structures:** Establish support mechanisms, such as help desks, mentorship programs, or peer support groups, to assist employees during the transition.

10.12.5 Communicate effectively

Ensure frequent, transparent, and two-way communication throughout the change process. Use various channels such as town hall meetings, newsletters, and one-on-one discussions to keep stakeholders informed about progress, updates, and changes. Address concerns and receive feedback to foster a culture of openness and trust.

10.12.6 Implement incrementally

Consider adopting AI in phases rather than all at once. Start with pilot projects or small-scale implementations to test the new technology and processes. These incremental changes allow for evaluations and adjustments based on real-world experiences, reducing disruption and allowing for CI.

10.12.7 Monitor and evaluate progress

Establish metrics to monitor the progress of AI adoption and the effectiveness of your change management initiatives. Regularly review performance against these metrics and be prepared to adapt your strategy as necessary. Feedback loops from employees and stakeholders will provide critical insights into how well the change is being received.

10.12.8 Reinforce and celebrate successes

Recognizing and rewarding milestones and successes, both big and small, reinforces positive behaviors and helps to build momentum. Celebrate achievements with stakeholders to demonstrate the value of AI adoption and acknowledge the efforts of employees who contribute to successful implementation.

10.12.9 Foster a culture of continuous learning

Promote an organizational culture that embraces innovation and continuous learning. Encourage employees to experiment with AI tools and share their experiences and learnings. Providing ongoing training and resources will help the organization stay ahead of evolving AI technologies and practices.

10.12.10 Lead by example

Leadership plays a critical role in change management. Leaders should exemplify commitment to the adoption of AI by being active participants in the change process, promoting the vision, and practicing the new technologies themselves. Their involvement will inspire confidence among employees and encourage a collective effort toward successful AI integration.

Successful AI adoption requires a clear strategic vision and active stakeholder engagement to align expectations and foster ownership. Organizations should assess readiness and develop a comprehensive management plan that includes communication strategies, training, and support mechanisms. Incremental implementation through pilot projects allows for practical adjustments, while celebrating successes reinforces positive behaviors. Strong leadership participation is crucial for inspiring confidence and driving a unified effort in effectively integrating AI.

10.13 The status of advanced AI capabilities and risks

The 2025 AI Safety Report, led by Yoshua Bengio and written by a team of 100 international AI experts from 30 countries and intergovernmental organizations, aims to establish a global framework for managing the risks associated with advanced AI systems. Inspired by the Intergovernmental Panel on Climate Change, this document proposes risk mitigation strategies and seeks to promote a shared understanding of AI's challenges.[29]

This report, presented at the AI Action Summit in Paris, France, from February 6 to 11, 2025, aims to establish a scientific foundation on the capabilities and risks of general-purpose AI by addressing three key questions: what can general-purpose AI do? What are the risks associated with general-purpose AI? And what mitigation techniques exist against these risks? It identifies three major categories of threats: malicious use (including cyberattacks, misinformation, and biological weapons), systemic dysfunctions (such as algorithmic bias and reliability errors), and economic and social impacts (including employment, data protection, and environmental concerns).

The report emphasizes the importance of transparency in AI model operations to strengthen public trust and calls for international cooperation to establish security standards. The authors caution against a wait-and-see approach and urge governments to take proactive measures in response to the significant potential risks associated with the rapid advancements of general-purpose AI. However, they acknowledge that reaching a global consensus on AI regulation remains challenging.

The report does not recommend specific policies but provides scientific information that supports informed policymaking. It focuses on identifying the capabilities and risks of general-purpose AI while evaluating different mitigation strategies.

The report does not aim to provide a comprehensive assessment of all the societal impacts of AI, particularly the vast array of benefits it can offer. However, it identified the main challenges in ensuring the safety of advanced AI technologies, which include the following.

The rapid advancements in AI capabilities make it hard to exclude near-term large-scale risks, emphasizing the necessity to evaluate and monitor them. The speed and unpredictability of advancements in general-purpose AI create an "evidence dilemma" for policymakers, who often have to make decisions without a comprehensive body of scientific evidence regarding potential risks and benefits. This results in challenges in determining when to implement risk mitigation measures versus waiting for more evidence. Improved metrics are necessary to understand real-world attack scenarios, particularly when humans and AIs collaborate. Mitigating offensive capabilities without compromising defenses remains a critical challenge.

General-purpose AI can unintentionally cause harm, even when users do not intend to cause harm. General-purpose AI can be unreliable and harmful, especially when providing advice on critical topics like medicine or law. There are substantial reliability concerns, including dependencies on outdated information and challenges in assessing the functionality of general-purpose AI during real-world deployment. This unpredictability may result in malfunctions and failures that were not apparent during pre-release evaluations. Limited user awareness of AI limitations, misleading advertising, and miscommunication exacerbate this issue.

The bias and fairness issues can amplify social and political biases, leading to AI systems can perpetuate or even exacerbate existing biases, especially in sensitive areas like legal decision-making. The lack of universally agreed-upon definitions of fairness complicates the deployment of AI technologies in a way that ensures equitable outcomes. While the concept of complete algorithmic fairness in AI systems remains a topic of ongoing debate, practical solutions can still be implemented. Empirical studies show that reducing bias in AI systems does not necessarily require complex methods or result in significant accuracy loss.

10.14 Summary

This chapter explores the complex landscape of adopting AI to advance sustainability goals across financial, economic, sustainability performance, and ESG performance dimensions. It begins by identifying key challenges that organizations face, such as data quality and accessibility, lack of AI expertise, ethical concerns, algorithmic bias, regulatory uncertainty, and the high cost of AI infrastructure. The chapter emphasizes how these barriers can hinder effective AI integration, particularly in sectors with limited resources or fragmented sustainability reporting practices.

Despite these obstacles, the chapter highlights a range of transformative opportunities. AI can optimize energy consumption, improve waste management, enhance ESG reporting through NLP, and enable real-time environmental monitoring and predictive analytics. In social and governance domains, AI supports transparent decision-making, risk management, and stakeholder engagement. The chapter also presents case studies of successful AI applications in sustainability, illustrating how firms can leverage AI to drive innovation and long-term value. Finally, the chapter calls for a strategic and ethical approach to AI deployment, stressing the importance of collaboration among stakeholders, developing robust governance frameworks, and investing in AI education and capacity-building. It concludes by asserting that, with the right policies and leadership, AI can serve as a powerful catalyst for sustainable development, reporting, and assurance.

10.15 Takeaways

- Data quality and availability remain major obstacles; fragmented, non-standardized, or inaccessible sustainability data can limit AI's effectiveness in assisting with sustainability reporting.
- Lack of technical expertise within organizations hinders AI implementation, especially in SMEs.
- Ethical and regulatory concerns, such as algorithmic bias, privacy risks, and unclear compliance frameworks, can delay or complicate adoption.
- High initial investment and infrastructure costs present barriers, particularly in developing regions or industries with tight margins.
- AI offers significant potential for optimizing resource use, improving energy efficiency, and reducing environmental footprints.
- NLP enhances ESG reporting by extracting insights from unstructured sustainability disclosures.
- AI-driven analytics enable real-time environmental monitoring, early warning systems, and predictive modeling for climate-related risks.
- Governance and transparency can be improved through AI-supported decision-making, risk assessment, and fraud detection.
- Collaboration among stakeholders, including governments, businesses, and academia, is essential to align AI development with sustainability objectives.
- Capacity-building and inclusive education are critical to democratizing AI access and ensuring equitable benefits from its deployment.
- Responsible AI frameworks must guide implementation to ensure fairness, accountability, and alignment with sustainability goals.
- Strategic, phased integration of AI into sustainability initiatives and reporting can enhance organizational resilience and long-term value creation.

Notes

1 Davies, P. 2024. *The Global ESG Handbook- A Guide for Practitioners*. Globe Law and Business Limited.
2 EY. 2023. How generative AI can build an organization's ESG roadmap. *EY*. https://www.ey.com/en_in/insights/ai/how-generative-ai-can-build-an-organization-s-esg-roadmap
3 Bose, S. 2020. Evolution of ESG reporting frameworks. In *Values at Work: Sustainable Investing and ESG Reporting* (pp. 13–33)
4 KPMG. 2024. *The Journey Continues: Navigating the Road to Readiness- KPMG ESG Assurance Maturity Index 2024*. https://kpmg.com/au/en/home/insights/2024/06/kpmg-esg-assurance-maturity-index.html

5 World Economic Forum. 2022. *Is Your Board an ESG Leader or Follower?* https://www.weforum.org/stories/2022/05/is-your-board-an-esg-leader-or-follower/
6 World Economic Forum. *Is Your Board an ESG Leader or Follower?* 5
7 SEC. 2024. *SEC Adopts Rules to Enhance and Standardize Climate-Related Disclosures for Investors*. https://www.sec.gov/newsroom/press-releases/2024-31
8 EY. 2024.*Why CSRD is a Game Changer for Sustainability Reporting*. https://www.ey.com/en_fi/insights/consulting/why-csrd-is-a-game-changer-for-sustainability-reporting#:~:text=Summary.%20The%20EU%27s%20Corporate%20Sustainability%20Reporting%20Directive,detailed%20disclosures%20than%20its%20predecessor%2C%20the%20NFRD
9 Cetnarowicz, N. 2022. *FCA Climate Reporting Requirements in the UK*. https://www.dlapiper.com/en/insights/publications/2022/02/fca-climate-reporting-requirements-in-the-uk
10 US Securities and Exchange Commission (SEC). 2025, 11 February. *Statement: Acting chairman statement on climate-related disclosure rules, commissioner Mark T. Uyeda*. https://www.sec.gov/newsroom/speeches-statements/uyeda-statement-climate-change-021025
11 United Nations (UN). 2024. *UN Environment Programme-Finance Initiative*. https://www.unepfi.org/impact/interoperability/european-sustainability-reporting-standards-esrs/
12 ESGtheReport. 2024. *Understanding ESG Regulations Across U.S. States: Key Insights for Businesses*. https://esgthereport.com/understanding-esg-regulations-across-u-s-states-key-insights-for-businesses/#:~:text=Consequences%20of%20Non%2DCompliance,brand%20image%20and%20stakeholder%20trust
13 KPMG. 2021. *The ESG Reporting Landscape A Recipe for the "Alphabet Soup"*. https://kpmg.com/uk/en/insights/sustainability/the-esg-reporting-landscape.html
14 KPMG. *The ESG Reporting Landscape A Recipe for the "Alphabet Soup"*
15 ESG Professionals Network. 2023. *Understanding the Alphabet Soup of ESG Reporting*. https://www.esgprofessionalsnetwork.com/understanding-the-alphabet-soup-of-esg-reporting/
16 van der Heever, W., Satapathy, R., Park, J.M., & Cambria, E. 2024. Understanding public opinion towards ESG and green finance with the use of explainable artificial intelligence. *Mathematics*, 12(19), 3119
17 Global Partnership on Al Report (GPAI). 2021. *Climate Change and AI: Recommendations for Government Action*. https://www.gpai.ai/projects/climate-change-and-ai.pdf
18 Global Partnership on Al Report (GPAI). *Climate Change and AI: Recommendations for Government Action*
19 Arrieta, A.B., Díaz-Rodríguez, N., Del Ser, J., Bennetot, A., Tabik, S., Barbado, A., García, S., Gil-López, S., Molina, D., Benjamins, R., & Chatila, R. 2020. Explainable artificial intelligence (XAI): Concepts, taxonomies, opportunities and challenges toward responsible AI. *Information Fusion*, 58, 82–115
20 Pesqueira, A., & Sousa, M.J. 2024. Exploring the role of big data analytics and dynamic capabilities in ESG programs within pharmaceuticals. *Software Quality Journal*, 32(2), 607–640
21 Huang, H., Zheng, O., Wang, D., Yin, J., Wang, Z., Ding, S., Yin, H., Xu, C., Yang, R., Zheng, Q., & Shi, B. 2023. ChatGPT for shaping the future of dentistry: The potential of multi-modal large language model. *International Journal of Oral Science*, 15(1), 29
22 Much of discussion in this section comes from chapter 11 of Rezaee. *The Sustainable Business Blueprint: Planning, Performance, Risk, Reporting, and Assurance*
23 IFEA. 2025, 17 January. *Global Assurance and Ethics Standards: Trust in Sustainability*. International Foundation for Ethics and Audit
24 IFEA. *Global Assurance and Ethics Standards: Trust in Sustainability*
25 Gryz, J., & Rojszczak, M. 2021. Black box algorithms and the rights of individuals: No easy solution to the "explainability" problem. *Internet Policy Review*, 10

26 Ali, S., Abuhmed, T., El-Sappagh, S., Muhammad, K., Alonso-Moral, J.M., Confalonieri, R., Guidotti, R., Del Ser, J., Díaz-Rodríguez, N., & Herrera, F. 2023. Explainable artificial intelligence (XAI): What we know and what is left to attain trustworthy artificial intelligence. *Information Fusion*, 99, 101805
27 Fatemi, A., Glaum, M., & Kaiser, S. 2018. ESG performance and firm value: The moderating role of disclosure. *Global Finance Journal*, 38, 45–64
28 Fatemi et al. ESG performance and firm value: The moderating role of disclosure, 45–64
29 AI Action Summit. 2025. *Rapport international sur la sûreté de l'IA Rapport scientifique international sur la sûreté de l'IA avancée*. https://assets.publishing.service.gov.uk/media/67af5a7363d7f4cceef9e236/International_AI_Safety_Report_2025_executive_summary_french.pdf

11 Emerging and future trends

AI and the next generation of sustainable businesses

11.1 Introduction

The integration of AI into business sustainability practices has made significant advancements in areas such as environmental monitoring abend performance, resource optimization, and waste reduction. It is expected that the future holds even greater promise for the adoption of AI in business sustainability as AI technologies continue to evolve and expand their capabilities. Emerging trends such as advanced ML algorithms, quantum computing, GenAI LLMs, and AI-driven decision-making tools are expected to further enhance the ability of businesses to achieve sustainability goals and address complex environmental and social challenges. An important development is the increasing use of AI for predictive analytics and scenario modeling by utilizing vast amounts of data, using data analytics and advanced computational techniques that enable businesses to better anticipate and respond to develop more effective strategies for sustainability and environmental changes, and optimize resource allocation. AI capabilities enable organizations to proactively assess and manage potential risks and seize opportunities for innovation, paving the way for more resilient and adaptive business models. The rise of AI-enabled circular economy solutions provides businesses insights to minimize waste and maximize the lifecycle value of products by designing products for longevity and recyclability, developing closed-loop systems, and enhancing recycling processes. Innovations in AI will continue to drive new approaches to waste management and sustainable design material recovery, supporting the transition to a circular economy and reducing the environmental footprint of industrial activities.

The future of AI in sustainability requires a keen focus on ethical considerations and responsible AI practices in ensuring that they are used ethically and transparently for maintaining trust and compliance. As AI-assisted technologies become more advanced and accessible, organizations are increasingly integrating predictive analytics, autonomous systems, and intelligent automation into their sustainability initiatives and strategies. These tools enable organizations to anticipate environmental risks, optimize resource usage, and create more adaptive supply chains. Looking ahead, the convergence of AI with business analytics, IoT, blockchain, and climate technology will further empower organizations to track ESG performance in real time, enhance stakeholder engagement, and foster transparent,

DOI: 10.4324/9781003611981-11

data-driven decision-making. This evolution signals a shift from reactive compliance with regulatory frameworks to proactive sustainability leadership, where AI supports operational efficiency and catalyzes systemic change toward a more equitable and regenerative global economy. Organizations will need to navigate issues related to the societal impacts of AI, data privacy, and algorithmic bias. The convergence of AI with other emerging technologies, such as blockchain, GenAI, IoT, and advanced sensors, can create new opportunities for enhancing sustainability efforts and performance. The synergy between these technologies will enable better sustainability performance and more sophisticated sustainability monitoring, reporting that may lead to more accurate and reliable assessments of environmental and social impact. This chapter presents these future trends, exploring how AI will continue to drive the next generation of sustainable businesses by examining the potential impact of emerging AI platforms and technologies, the challenges and opportunities that lie ahead, and the strategies for leveraging AI to achieve long-term sustainability goals and performance.

11.2 Emerging trends in AI and their implications for business sustainability

Emerging advancements and trends in AI are rapidly transforming the landscape of business sustainability by enhancing decision-making, improving operational efficiency, and assessing risk to enable more sustainable practices and performance. AI is reshaping business sustainability by presenting the opportunities, risks, and challenges of emerging sustainability initiatives. The integration of AI advances and trends into business sustainability can drive sustainable growth, contribute to sustainability efforts, reduce environmental impacts, and foster long-term resilience. However, the effectiveness of these AI technologies can be influenced by responsible implementation, transparent reporting, and ethical considerations of using AI. AI-driven technologies can advance business sustainability by: (1) analyzing large datasets to forecast resource consumption, environmental impacts and emission trends to better anticipate challenges, optimize resource use, and design proactive sustainability strategies and data-driven decisions that align with long-term sustainability goals; (2) automating and improving efficiencies in production, logistics, and operations to reduce waste, energy consumption, and costs, and monitor and manage energy consumption in real time, leading to significant reductions in carbon footprints; (3) moving toward circular economy of optimizing resource recovery, waste reduction and product lifecycle management and product longevity; (4) gathering and analyzing nonfinancial, big unstructured data from many sources to prepare accurate, complete, and transparent ESG reporting; (5) optimizing supply chains by enhancing logistics, and improving supplier transparency and predicting disruptions; (6) assessing and managing climate-related risks to determine how climate change might impact various operational aspects, from sourcing to production to distribution and to adapt business models of being more resilient and mitigate potential disruptions through climate modeling, predicting environmental changes, and developing mitigation strategies; and (7) analyzing marking data on consumer preferences, resource availability, and environmental impacts to innovate sustainable products that meet market demands, generate positive social outcomes, and reduce negative environmental impact.

11.2.1 Trend in sustainability regulations

Emerging trends in sustainability regulations and standards reflect a global shift toward greater accountability, responsibility, transparency, and alignment with long-term environmental and social goals. Regulatory bodies and standard setters worldwide are increasingly mandating ESG disclosures, with frameworks such as the Corporate Sustainability Reporting Directive (CSRD) in the EU rules and International Sustainability Standards Board (ISSB) standards setting new precedents. There is a growing emphasis on harmonization of sustainability standards, led by initiatives like the ISSB, which aims to consolidate fragmented reporting guidelines. Furthermore, climate-related financial risk assessments, biodiversity impact disclosures, and supply chain due diligence are becoming core regulatory requirements. These trends signal a move from voluntary to mandatory sustainability reporting, pushing organizations to integrate sustainability into their corporate culture, business environment, strategic decision-making, risk management practices, and supply chain. There has been an ever-growing trend in both voluntary and mandatory sustainability regulations, particularly relevant to ESG. Specifically, 2024 saw several significant international regulatory developments that will impact sustainability reporting and assurance of business organizations worldwide in 2025 and onward. These global developments in sustainability have been dynamic and will continue to influence the ESG and sustainability landscape as investors demand sustainability information, regulators require presentation of sustainability disclosures, and companies produce sustainability reporting and assurance. This section presents sustainability regulatory initiatives and developments in recent years internationally, in Europe, the United States, and other countries.

11.2.1.1 EU developments

Several initiatives have been taken by the EC in recent years, promoting sustainability worldwide to integrate sustainability into corporate culture and business environment by creating a balance between economic competitiveness and ESG sustainability progress. For example, the CSRD was released on January 5, 2023, which requires EU-listed companies to publish regular sustainability reports disclosing their social and environmental risks, opportunities, and impacts.[1] The CSRD: (1) modernizes and strengthens the rules concerning the social and environmental sustainability information reported by companies; (2) ensures that stakeholders including investors have access to the sustainability information to evaluate risks and opportunities associated with reported ESG disclosures and assess the impact of companies on people and the environment; (3) reduces sustainability reporting costs by standardizing and harmonizing the sustainability information to be provided by companies; and (4) creates a reporting framework for companies to apply the new rules for the first time in the 2024 financial year, for reports published in 2025. In 2024, the EU[2] Taxonomy of CSRD and the CSDDD were promulgated to ensure a continuous move toward sustainability reporting and assurance, robust monitoring of sustainability reporting, sustainability regulatory initiatives, and long-term sustainability improvements and implications, and transition toward a sustainable economy.[2] The CSDDD requires that large corporations identify, consider, prevent, and mitigate the potential adverse effects that they create on human rights and the environment where adverse effects are defined very broadly, with reference to numerous international conventions. Effective from 2024, the CSRD expands on previous requirements by mandating large companies, and eventually many SMEs, to disclose detailed information on their ESG impacts using standardized formats aligned with the ESRS.

11.2.1.2 US developments

In the United States, climate change has emerged as a significant global issue as one of the most pressing challenges in recent years, with significant implications for investors, businesses, regulators, and society, and transparent, reliable, and comprehensive reporting and assurance mechanisms. As these stakeholders demand greater transparency and accountability, business organizations are increasingly required to disclose their climate-related risks, opportunities, and impacts with transparent, reliable, and comprehensive reporting and assurance processes. However, climate change reporting and assurance processes face challenges of data complexity, lack of standardization, and the need for predictive insights. On March 6, 2024, the SEC released its final rule, entitled "The Enhancement and Standardization of Climate-Related Disclosures for Investors," which requires public companies to disclose certain related information in their annual reports.[3] However, it is expected that the Trump administration will affect the move toward ESG and sustainability by reducing uncertainty and tension in the ESG and sustainability developments, whereas California initiatives on climate change disclosure obligations will continue. Considering the global move toward addressing climate change and the fact that many US entities operate in a global context, there will be a potential convergence in global ESG trends.

In 2025, the US SEC signaled a shift away from federal ESG mandates by halting the proposed climate disclosure rule.[4] The United States has formally rejected the UNSDGs, which are a set of 17 global objectives to address economic, social, and environmental challenges, in March 2025, whereas other countries are aiming to meet these SDGs by 2030.[5] The US withdrawal of support for the SDGs reflects a broader shift toward ESG sustainability efforts, as many US companies align with the SDGs. However, the US withdrawal from the SDGs may accelerate the fragmentation and politicization of the global sustainability landscape. However, States such as California are leading independently with laws like the California Climate Disclosure Act (SB 253 and SB 261), mandating detailed emissions reporting and climate risk disclosures for large companies operating in the state. California's emerging climate-related disclosure laws (SB-253 and SB-261) continue to promote far-reaching effects by being applied to large public and private companies with operations in the state and effectively becoming the standard for climate disclosure in the United States.[6]

11.2.1.3 International regulatory reforms

Global mandatory sustainability disclosures are driven by two major standards of the International Sustainability Standards (ISSB/IFRS S1 and S2) and the EU's CSRD and accompanying ESRS. The 2024 report published by the IFRS indicates that 30 jurisdictions representing more than 40% of global market capitalization have integrated ISSB standards (S1 and S2) into their regulatory frameworks, and others are expecting to adopt them soon.[7] The first wave of companies that are required to report under the CSRD (e.g., companies listed on an EU-regulated market) have reported on the ESRS for their financial years starting in 2024, with the expectation that these CSRD reports will be published during 2025. On January 27, 2025, the IAASB and the IESBA launched their standards aimed at advancing trust and transparency in sustainability reporting and assurance.[8] The certification of IESBA's new ethics standards framework for sustainability requires its members to adopt the framework to foster trust and accountability in sustainability reporting and assurance. New standards provide a robust and effective ethical framework, the preparation and assurance of sustainability performance information that promotes trustworthy, transparent, high-quality, and reliable information for decision-making by all stakeholders, including investors, creditors, customers, suppliers, government, and regulators.

It is expected that 2025 will mark a global milestone in mandatory sustainability reporting and assurance with the first year of reporting under the EU's CSRD. The first sustainability reports that would be produced by large EU financial institutions or entities that have listed securities in the EU are expected to be published in the first half of 2025. The implication of CSRD is a shift away from voluntary ESG and sustainability reports to mandatory sustainability reporting. Publication of mandatory sustainability reports requires disclosure of climate change targets, the approach to reporting on value chains, and double materiality. US companies may comply with California's AB 1305 and sustainability standards of the SASB and the ISSB in producing sustainability reports. It is also expected that the refocus on net-zero commitments and transition plans will continue to intensify as global companies strive to meet ambitious climate goals. However, the challenges and complexities involved in measuring and reducing Scope 3 emissions, which encompass indirect emissions from a company's value chain, will continue to prevail as companies are adopting more pragmatic approaches to Scope 3 emissions by addressing collaboration with suppliers and customers.

While the United States does not yet have a unified national sustainability reporting standard equivalent to the EU's CSRD, there is increasing adoption of voluntary frameworks like the TCFD, SASB standards, and GRI frameworks among American companies. The ISSB standards, S1 and S2, are adopted by many public companies in the United States. It is expected that ESG disclosure regulations in the EU will impact not only EU-based companies but also large US multinationals and their subsidiaries. Thus, the emerging ESG regulations will continue to impose compliance burdens and costs, and companies should prepare integrating regulatory requirements into broader sustainability strategies and strengthen governance and data management for effective compliance. It is expected that AI-powered tools and techniques play an essential role in global sustainability developments by enabling companies to collect ESG data, measure, analyze, report, and enhance the transparency, reliability, accuracy, and efficiency of ESG performance. Specifically, as ESG reporting and assurance become mandatory in 2025 and onward, companies worldwide will likely utilize AI platforms in the measurement, classification, recognition, and reporting ESG KPIs. The future ESG landscape will present both challenges and opportunities. Thus, companies must remain vigilant and adaptable, comply with emerging sustainability regulations and standards, and take proactive strategies in navigating the complexities of ESG and sustainability issues and position themselves for long-term sustainable growth and success in an ever-evolving global environment.

Starting in 2029, companies headquartered outside the EU, including many US multinationals, will have to make extensive sustainability disclosures under the CSRD.[9] These non-EU affected companies will be required to fulfill the requirements of the EU Taxonomy Regulation and consider how they will gather the information required under the CSRD and ESRS. However, the EU, in February 2025, proposed an Omnibus Simplification Package that would substantially reduce the scope and scale of the requirements under the CSRD.[10] The effective dates of compliance with the proposed Omnibus Simplification Package vary depending on whether the company is subject to the NFRD as of 2024, is not subject to the NFRD as of 2027, fiscal year 2028 for non-EU companies that are subject to the CSRD, and non-EU entity consolidated reporting as of 2029.[11] The concept of double materiality in the ESRS and the proposed Omnibus Simplification Package is broader than the definition of materiality used by the ISSB that would require management to apply additional judgment to determine which matters should be disclosed from an impact perspective. In compliance with the emerging sustainability reporting framework in EU, companies worldwide should: (1) consider whether and what entities in their consolidated group are subject to the requirements of the CSRD; (2) consider the level they will report at (e.g., the highest consolidated level in the EU and a global consolidated level); (3) monitor relevant EU jurisdictions to determine how they incorporate the CSRD into their reporting systems and processes; and (4) consider whether they need to obtain third-party assurance.

11.2.2 AI governance

Corporate governance measures should provide a comprehensive understanding of AI governance from various perspectives, including ethical, legal, organizational, compliance with applicable laws, rules, regulations, and standards and global viewpoints. Various aspects of AI governance, providing insights into frameworks, ethical considerations, and implementation challenges, are studied at the team, organization, industry, national, and international levels, highlighting gaps in stakeholder involvement and ethical considerations.[12] The multifaceted nature of AI governance in identifying key themes, knowledge gaps, the integration of AI into various sectors, and the corresponding governance challenges should be considered when advocating for a comprehensive approach that aligns AI governance and deployment with organizational strategies, legal requirements, and ethical principles.[13] Public companies may consider establishing an AI board committee or assigning the responsibility for AI-integration and its opportunities and risks to either the audit or risk committees. Effective board oversight is essential for companies to realize the potential opportunities of AI for business efficiency, profitability, and shareholder value creation, as well as assessing and managing potential risks and disruptions to their business, including human rights and privacy, or to avoid costly financial losses. Ever-growing AI applications in businesses demand proactive and responsible oversight of the board of directors to realize AI advantages, avoid risk, manage investor expectations, and remain resilient and competitive. There is a need for holistic governance frameworks in providing comprehensive coverage of all aspects of AI in addressing questions of accountability, governance elements, timing within the AI lifecycle, and implementation mechanisms.[14]

Effective and robust AI governance requires compliance with all applicable global laws, rules, regulations, and standards relevant to AI and sustainability. Regulators worldwide have established regulations and rules (e.g., the EU AI Act and US AI regulations) that set standards and requirements for the development and use of AI systems, including safety testing, data protection, and accountability. As more business organizations are leveraging complex AI technologies of GenAI and AI agents, there is an urgent need for regulations and standards to ensure transparency and fairness of AI applications. There are currently several AI standards, such as the EU's AI Act, the Open Web Application Security Project Generative AI, LLM Security Guidance and Initiatives, and the NIST AI Risk Management Framework. Compliance with these and other forthcoming AI rules and regulations ensures responsible AI governance through structural, relational, procedural, and effective governance measures.

11.2.3 Emerging AI risk

AI platforms can create tremendous opportunities for businesses in making data-driven decisions. With these opportunities and benefits, the potential threat to humanity should be considered as a societal risk, as stated in the open letter that was signed by more than 350 technology executives, engineers, and researchers from the leading AI companies (e.g., OpenAI, Google DeepMind, and Anthropic).[15] The concerns are that AI LLMs could soon be advanced to the level that enables misinformation and propaganda spread or that they could eliminate millions of white-collar jobs. These concerns are viewed by many of these signatures as an existential threat to humanity that demands government intervention in regulating

AI systems by requiring makers of large, cutting-edge AI models to register for a government-issued license.[16]

AI risks are numerous and cover a lot of ground from bias, privacy, misinformation, and loss of human jobs. The most severe risks are: (1) existential risks of advanced and superintelligent AI that could outthink and outperform humans and act in ways that are unpredictable or harmful, potentially posing a threat to humanity and society,[17] (2) bias and discrimination caused by AI biases from their training data, leading to unfair outcomes;[18] (3) privacy and security as AI handling massive datasets, which could raise concerns about how personal data is collected, stored, and potentially misused and security risks;[19] (4) misinformation and deepfakes as AI can often generate unrealistic fake content (deepfakes, synthetic voices, and fake news) that can detrimental to businesses and society;[20] (5) job loss and displacement as AI automation could replace millions of jobs;[21] (6) autonomy and loss of control as AI systems become more advanced and autonomous; there will be of a risk humans might lose direct control, leading to unintended consequences;[22] (7) concentration of power given to emerging AI platforms could lead to major inequalities in the job markets and even economic or political dominance for those with high-level AI capabilities;[23] and (8) ethical and moral issues as AI systems continue to reshape many industries including healthcare and finance to ensure that AI is aligned with human values.[24]

Overall, AI presents a wide array of risks that span technical, social, economic, and ethical domains. Among the broad concerns are issues related to bias, privacy, misinformation, and the displacement of human labor. However, several risks stand out as particularly severe and far-reaching. First, there is the existential risk associated with the development of advanced or superintelligent AI systems. Such AI could potentially surpass human cognitive capabilities, acting in unpredictable or harmful ways that threaten the very survival of humanity and the stability of society. Second, bias and discrimination are critical concerns, as AI systems trained on biased data can perpetuate and even amplify unfair outcomes, disproportionately affecting marginalized groups. Third, privacy and security risks arise from AI's reliance on vast datasets, raising serious questions about how personal information is collected, stored, used, and safeguarded against breaches or misuse. Fourth, the rise of misinformation and deepfakes driven by AI-generated synthetic content—including fake news, altered videos, and imitated voices—poses a significant threat to public trust, business integrity, and societal cohesion. Fifth, job loss and workforce displacement are major economic risks, as AI-driven automation threatens to replace millions of jobs across various industries, exacerbating unemployment and inequality. Sixth, the increasing autonomy and loss of human control over advanced AI systems introduce the danger of unintended behaviors or consequences that humans may be unable to predict or intervene against in time. Seventh, the concentration of power in the hands of a few companies or nations with access to high-level AI capabilities could deepen existing inequalities, reshaping labor markets and potentially leading to economic or political domination. Finally, ethical and moral challenges arise as AI systems are deployed across critical sectors such as healthcare and finance, highlighting the urgent need to ensure that AI technologies are developed and used in ways that are consistent with human values, rights, and societal well-being.

11.3 The future of AI in shaping sustainable business practices

AI-powered platforms and tools have already influenced the progress toward sustainability practices. It is expected that AI will continue shaping sustainable business practices as emerging AI technologies will likely continue driving innovation and sustainability across industries. AI could further transform sustainable business practices in many ways including: (1) improving the autonomous systems of self-learning energy grids, transportation networks, and industrial processes to enable adaptive responses to fluctuating environmental conditions; (2) enhancing AI's predictive capabilities to improve scenario planning by allowing businesses to anticipate sustainability challenges and opportunities far into the future, analyzing extensive datasets and recognizing long-term trends in climate, resource availability, and consumer behavior; (3) offering hyper-personalized products and services that promote sustainable consumer choices that could guide consumers toward eco-friendly products, customized recommendations based on past behaviors, and track carbon footprint reductions, empowering consumers to participate actively in sustainability; (4) accelerating the transition to a circular economy by enabling better tracking, sorting, and remanufacturing of materials; (5) assessing and managing regulatory compliance and ethical considerations in sustainability practices by automating monitoring and reporting on ESG standards; (6) making it easier for businesses to provide detailed, real-time sustainability reports and insights to stakeholders; (7) by improving the visibility of sustainability metrics and progress through accessible dashboards and reports, AI will facilitate stronger accountability and allow stakeholders, including consumers, investors, and communities, to engage more actively with companies on sustainability issues; (8) developing of sustainable urban spaces, or "smart cities," to optimize energy use, transportation, waste management, and water supply, leading to greater resource efficiency; and (9) enabling cross-industry collaboration for sustainability by sharing environmental data, sustainability best practices, and resource optimization insights can foster partnerships across sectors, enabling a collective impact on global sustainability goals.

11.3.1 GenAI in supporting sustainability reporting

The growing complexity and regulatory pressures surrounding sustainability reporting have posed significant challenges for organizations worldwide. The 2024 report by Reuters Events on "Sustainable Reporting and Data Management" outlines that sustainability reporting how companies are handling sustainability reporting and data management in 2024, especially with new regulations such as Europe's CSRD and the SEC's rules in the United States shaping the game. The report presents findings from a comprehensive survey and qualitative research involving over 3,000 sustainability practitioners worldwide, highlighting the significant pressure companies face due to evolving regulations, particularly around Scope 3 GHG emissions reporting. The study captures cross-sector and global perspectives, noting widespread challenges such as data collection complexity, confidence gaps, and technological limitations. Despite these, organizations are increasingly investing in data management tools and building leadership capabilities to meet regulatory demands and sustainability goals. It can be defined by rising investments, regulatory expansion, and a decisive shift from manual to automated, technology-driven data collection.[25]

As companies navigate an expanding landscape of frameworks, standards, and directives, each with subtle differences, the risk of confusion and inefficiency increasingly rises, potentially hindering accurate and transparent reporting. In this context, the application of LLMs offers promising solutions to enhance the quality, consistency, and accessibility of sustainability reports. LLMs can contribute significantly to addressing these challenges by acting as intelligent assistants capable of parsing complex regulatory texts, interpreting diverse reporting frameworks, and standardizing sustainability-related language. For example, LLMs can automatically extract relevant data points, reconcile terminology inconsistencies, and generate report drafts that align with specific frameworks, thereby reducing the cognitive load on reporting teams and mitigating the risk of errors. Given that approximately 15% of leadership respondents use multiple frameworks simultaneously, LLMs can help harmonize the integration of diverse reporting requirements into coherent disclosures. Stakeholders, including investors, customers, and regulators, rely on clear and credible reports to evaluate an organization's ESG performance. By leveraging LLMs to enhance clarity and consistency, organizations can build greater trust and credibility with these stakeholders. This transparency fosters confidence in the organization's sustainability commitments and efforts, ultimately supporting long-term value creation.

As the demand for transparent and reliable ESG reporting continues to grow, the role of fine-tuned LLMs in facilitating this process will undoubtedly become more prominent. Fine-tuning LLMs has become a pivotal strategy to enhance the accuracy, relevance, and compliance of ESG disclosures. While pre-trained models offer broad linguistic capabilities, they often lack the specialized knowledge required for nuanced ESG analysis. Fine-tuning these models on domain-specific datasets enables them to grasp the intricacies of sustainability reporting, ensuring that organizations can produce reports that are both precise and aligned with regulatory standards. Fine-tuning LLMs for sustainability reporting is not merely a technical enhancement; it is a strategic necessity. By tailoring models to understand the specific language and requirements of ESG disclosures, organizations can create reports that are accurate, compliant, and reflective of their true sustainability performance.

11.3.2 Business sustainability, AI, and business analytics

The relationship between business sustainability, AI, and business analytics is becoming increasingly important in today's data-driven and digital business environment. Business analytics provides the tools, insights, and frameworks necessary for organizations to make timely informed decisions that align with their sustainability goals. This section presents the integrated role of AI and business analytics in promoting business sustainability. Business analytics involves collecting, processing, and analyzing data to support decision-making. When applied to sustainability, business analytics enables organizations to integrate financial ESP and nonfinancial ESG sustainability performance considerations into their business environment, corporate culture, operations, and strategies. Business analytics can support sustainability ESP and ESG efforts in many ways.

11.3.2.1 Performance measurement and monitoring

Performance measurement and monitoring are essential components of effective ESG sustainability strategies and reporting. AI-powered tools and business analytics can significantly enhance these processes by providing real-time, data-driven insights. AI-powered analytics platforms can aggregate and process vast volumes of structured and unstructured data from internal and external sources to enable continuous tracking of ESG metrics across operations, supply chains, and stakeholder engagements. Through ML algorithms and business analytics, organizations can identify performance trends, detect anomalies, and forecast future ESG outcomes with greater precision. This allows organizations to set more accurate benchmarks, align with regulatory standards and global sustainability reporting frameworks, and make informed strategic decisions. Ultimately, AI-driven performance monitoring transforms ESG from a static reporting function into a dynamic, forward-looking system that supports CI and sustainable value creation. Business analytics enables organizations to measure both ESP and ESG sustainability performance by developing KPIs for all dimensions of sustainability performance. It also helps track carbon emissions, water usage, waste reduction, energy consumption, and other sustainability metrics and related KPIs in real time.

11.3.2.2 Sustainability reporting and assurance

SRA are vital for building trust, accountability, and transparency in corporate reporting, and AI and business analytics technologies play an increasingly essential role in strengthening these functions. AI can streamline the sustainability reporting process by automating data collection, validation, and classification, reducing the time and human error associated with manual reporting. Moreover, AI enhances assurance by enabling continuous monitoring and real-time verification of ESG data, allowing internal auditors and external assurance providers to identify discrepancies, assess risks, and validate performance with greater accuracy. By embedding AI and business analytics into sustainability reporting and assurance processes, organizations can deliver more reliable, transparent, comprehensive, and stakeholder-relevant ESG disclosures that support long-term value and responsible governance. Business analytics facilitates transparent and data-driven sustainability reporting and assurance in conformity with sustainability reporting and assurance standards (e.g., GRI, SASB, CSRD, and ISSB). Particularly, the use of NLP can enable organizations to analyze qualitative and quantitative ESP and ESG disclosures for insights into corporate sustainability reporting. Auditors can use business analytics to collect, assess, and verify both ESP and ESG information to improve the quality of audit reports and assurance statements.

11.3.2.3 Predictive and prescriptive analytics

Predictive and prescriptive analytics, powered by AI-assisted tools, are revolutionizing the way organizations approach sustainability by enabling data-driven foresight and strategic decision-making. Predictive analytics leverages historical ESG data and ML algorithms to forecast future trends, risks, and opportunities by allowing organizations to proactively mitigate potential challenges. Prescriptive analytics goes a step further by recommending optimal actions based on these predictions, enabling organizations to develop targeted strategies to enhance ESG performance, improve resource efficiency, and reduce carbon footprints. Together, these advanced AI-driven analytics tools transform ESG from a backward-looking compliance exercise into a forward-looking force for innovation, growth, resilience, and competitive advantage, empowering businesses to achieve sustainability goals with precision and agility. Predictive business analytics helps organizations anticipate future sustainability challenges of resource scarcity or regulatory changes and prepare mitigation strategies to address them. Prescriptive business analytics presents optimal strategies for improving sustainability ESP and ESG performance and outcomes, including reducing energy costs, achieving decarbonization, and enhancing supply chain efficiency.

11.3.2.4 Supply chain sustainability

Business analytics plays a vital role in advancing supply chain sustainability by enabling companies to gain deep, actionable insights into their operations, supplier networks, financial viability, and environmental and social impacts. Organizations can track and measure key sustainability indicators such as carbon emissions, energy consumption, water usage, and waste generation across the supply chain by using business analytics tools. For example, predictive models help anticipate disruptions and assess the environmental and social risks associated with suppliers and logistics, whereas optimization algorithms support more efficient resource allocation and transportation planning. Furthermore, advanced business analytics facilitates greater transparency and traceability, allowing businesses to identify inefficiencies, ensure compliance with sustainability standards, and promote ethical sourcing practices. Organizations can drive CI, reduce environmental footprints, and build more resilient, responsible, and future-ready supply chains by integrating business analytics into supply chain management. Business analytics techniques and tools can help assess the environmental and social impacts of supply chains, identifying risks like high carbon footprints or labor violations, optimize logistics, reduce fuel consumption, and minimize waste. Many companies utilize business analytics to track their carbon footprint and optimize their supply chain for sustainability.

11.3.2.5 Resource optimization

Business analytics plays a pivotal role in resource optimization by enabling organizations to make data-driven decisions that enhance efficiency, reduce waste, and support sustainability goals. Business analytics tools can empower organizations to identify patterns, inefficiencies, and areas of excessive consumption across energy, water, materials, and labor by analyzing large volumes of operational and environmental data. Predictive models help forecast demand and resource requirements, allowing for more accurate planning and allocation, whereas prescriptive analytics can suggest optimal strategies to minimize costs and environmental impact. Furthermore, real-time analytics techniques enable continuous monitoring and dynamic adjustments to resource usage, ensuring alignment with both performance targets and regulatory standards. Thus, business analytics empowers organizations to optimize resources holistically, driving operational excellence and long-term environmental stewardship. Business Analytics tools help in optimizing resource usage (e.g., energy, water, and raw materials), reducing operational costs while achieving sustainability targets. Companies leverage advanced business analytics to improve energy efficiency in manufacturing and operations, aligning with sustainability objectives.

11.3.2.6 Stakeholder engagement

Business analytics plays a critical role in enhancing stakeholder engagement by providing deep insights into stakeholder behaviors, expectations, and perceptions, which enable organizations to communicate more effectively and build stronger, trust-based relationships. Business analytics tools can identify emerging concerns, sentiment trends, and areas for improvement across ESG dimensions by leveraging data from surveys, social media, customer interactions, and ESG feedback channels. These insights allow organizations to tailor their sustainability strategies and communication efforts to meet the specific needs and priorities of diverse stakeholder groups, including investors, employees, customers, regulators, and communities. Additionally, predictive analytics can anticipate stakeholder reactions to corporate actions, while dashboards and visualization tools facilitate transparent, data-backed reporting. Through business analytics, organizations can foster more informed, inclusive, and responsive stakeholder engagement, ultimately supporting accountability, reputation, and long-term value creation. Business analytics techniques enable organizations to better understand investor needs and other stakeholder expectations and public perceptions and trends in sustainability initiatives, activities, and outcomes (e.g., investors, customers, and regulators).

11.3.2.7 Risk assessment and management

The use of business analytics tools in risk assessment and management is vital in identifying, evaluating, and mitigating risks across various dimensions of organizational operations, including those related to ESG sustainability. Organizations can detect patterns, anomalies, and early warning signals in both internal processes and external environments, by harnessing advanced data analytics, which allow for proactive risk identification. Predictive analytics enables the forecasting of potential disruptions, including supply chain breakdowns, regulatory changes, climate-related events, or reputational threats, whereas prescriptive analytics offers actionable strategies to minimize their impact. Moreover, real-time data monitoring and visualization tools support continuous risk tracking and dynamic decision-making, enhancing organizational agility and resilience. Organizations can build robust risk management frameworks that protect value and align with long-term ESG objectives and stakeholder expectations through the integration of business analytics. Business analytics enables organizations to assess risks associated with both ESP and ESG activities and their potential financial implications in ensuring businesses are resilient to financial crises, environmental and social disruptions, and climate change.

11.3.2.8 Initiating and driving innovation

Business analytics can play a transformative role in initiating and driving innovation by uncovering insights that lead to new ideas, products, services, and business models. Organizations can identify unmet customer needs, market trends, and operational inefficiencies that present opportunities for innovation by analyzing large and complex datasets. Predictive and prescriptive analytics empower businesses to experiment with scenarios, evaluate the potential impact of innovative initiatives, and allocate resources more effectively. Furthermore, business analytics supports a culture of CI and data-driven creativity, enabling cross-functional teams to test hypotheses, iterate rapidly, and scale successful innovations. In the context of sustainability, analytics can inspire innovations in green technologies, circular economy practices, and socially responsible solutions, aligning business growth with environmental and social impact. Thus, business analytics acts as a catalyst for strategic innovation, helping organizations stay competitive, adaptive, and forward-thinking. Business analytics can foster data-driven innovation and growth by enabling organizations to develop sustainable products and services, leveraging AI for circular economy practices, forecast renewable energy production and optimize its use, and enhance decision-making in carbon offsetting and renewable energy investments. For example, Unilever uses business analytics for sustainable product innovation and to assess the lifecycle impact of its products.

The synergy between business sustainability and business analytics lies in leveraging data to drive decisions that align with long-term sustainability goals in improving both ESG and ESP sustainability performance. Business analytics enables organizations to effectively measure and manage sustainability performance and anticipate and adapt to emerging challenges. The relationship between business sustainability and business analytics is bidirectional in the sense that sustainability also influences analytics. As businesses increasingly prioritize ESP and ESG sustainability considerations, the integration of business analytics with business sustainability will continue to evolve, driving innovation, accountability, and resilience in a globally competitive and rapidly changing world. Thus, business organizations should adopt sustainability-driven analytics frameworks to achieve long-term sustainability objectives in financial and operational models and promote impact-driven rather than profit-driven sustainability and business analytics goals and focus. However, there are some challenges in integrating business analytics with business sustainability, including data quality and availability, the need for expertise in sustainability-focused analytics that is still developing by aligning business analytics platforms with existing sustainability management systems, and the ever-increasing regulatory initiatives affecting both business sustainability and business analytics. Nonetheless, it is expected that AI will play a larger role in providing predictive insights, automating sustainability reporting and assurance, enhancing ESP and ESG performance, offering real-time monitoring of sustainability metrics, improving responsiveness, providing a holistic view of an organization's sustainability performance for decision-makers, and ensuring data integrity and transparency in sustainability reporting through blockchain technology, as explained in the next section.

The rapid adoption of AI and business analytics across industries has created a demand for skilled professionals who can merge technical expertise with business acumen. With the rapid evolution of business analytics and AI, there is a demand for a comprehensive resource that covers these fields in an accessible, unified approach. This section examines ways to leverage data-driven insights and AI technologies to enhance strategic decision-making, optimize operations, and foster innovation in a dynamic global business environment by harnessing data for strategic advantage. It also attempts to bridge the gap between theoretical concepts and practical applications of AI in business analytics by: (1) introducing the foundational principles of business analytics and AI; (2) demonstrating the integration of advanced AI techniques into business analytics processes; (3) presenting the demands for effective interactions of AI and HI; (4) exploring the ethical, legal, and social implications of using AI in business contexts; and (5) providing case studies and real-world applications from diverse industries to highlight best practices.

11.3.3 Interaction between AI and HI in promoting business sustainability

The synergy between HI and AI plays a pivotal role in advancing business sustainability by combining the strengths of both to extract actionable insights and enable informed decision-making. AI provides unparalleled computational power and scalability, enabling businesses to analyze and optimize complex datasets, while HI brings creativity, ethical judgment, contextual understanding, and strategic thinking to apply these insights effectively and responsibly. Together, HI and AI empower businesses to drive innovation, efficiency, and sustainability through a dynamic partnership. The interplay between HI and AI is fundamental to building sustainable, innovative, and resilient businesses, blending the efficiency of advanced technology with the strategic and ethical acumen of human expertise in the following areas:

1. **Data Analysis and Automation:** AI-powered tools process vast amounts of data, recognizing patterns, automating repetitive tasks, and delivering predictive and prescriptive analytics at a scale and speed beyond human capacity.
2. **Strategic Application:** HI ensures that AI-driven strategies are applied creatively and ethically in dynamic environments, leveraging strategic thinking to maximize AI's potential.
3. **Hybrid Approach:** A combined approach allows AI to handle computational complexity, while humans focus on innovation, decision-making, and adapting to complex scenarios.
4. **Data-Driven Decision Support:** AI generates insights, forecasts, and recommendations, while HI evaluates these outputs in context, ensuring that decisions align with business goals. For example, AI may predict customer preferences, while human managers design personalized campaigns based on these predictions.
5. **Real-Time Analysis and Intervention:** AI-powered platforms facilitate real-time data collection and analysis, enabling businesses to respond promptly to market changes. HI interprets anomalies flagged by AI and addresses risks or opportunities requiring strategic action, such as optimizing supply chain responses to disruptions.
6. **Nuanced Interpretation:** AI tools like NLP analyze unstructured data, such as customer feedback or ESG reports. HI adds depth by interpreting language nuances, context, and sentiment, improving insights into investor needs, customer behavior, market trends, and stakeholder expectations.
7. **Ethical Oversight:** HI ensures the ethical, transparent, and unbiased application of AI tools, aligning their use with regulatory frameworks and organizational values.
8. **Collaborative Decision-Making:** AI-powered platforms, such as dashboards, virtual assistants, and decision-support systems, serve as "co-pilots" that enhance human decision-making, amplifying human efforts rather than replacing them.
9. **Learning and Supervision:** AI systems improve over time through data-driven learning, while HI supervises this evolution to ensure alignment with business strategies and objectives.
10. **Bridging Data and Practicality:** HI bridges the gap between AI-generated data and real-world applicability. For instance, AI might analyze trends and predict outcomes, but human experts provide domain-specific insights to refine strategies in finance, marketing, and sustainability.
11. **Fraud Detection and Beyond:** Practical examples include AI identifying suspicious transactions while human analysts confirm fraud, AI suggesting upselling opportunities while sales teams tailor approaches, and AI monitoring ESG metrics while professionals strategize improvements.

11.3.4 Roles of sustainability reporting and assurance in advancing the UNSDGs

SRA can play an important role in advancing the goals of the UNSDGs by fostering transparency, accountability, and credibility. Attributes of SRA are strategic enablers of the UNSDGs by improving the quality and reliability of ESG disclosures, helping organizations align their operations with global sustainability goals, tracking their contributions to these goals, fostering trust among stakeholders, and accelerating progress toward a sustainable future. Disclosures of SRA are relevant to many goals of the UNSDGs, as shown in Table 11.1. SDGs can be classified into many aspects and factors of business sustainability including: (1) transparency and accountability; (2) driving action toward climate goals; (3) encouraging social inclusion; (4) enhancing corporate governance; (5) fostering sustainable economic growth; (6) accelerating global partnerships; and (7) encouraging innovation and technology integration. Many of SDGs-related sustainability goals and their roles in sustainability reporting and impacts on sustainability assurance are presented in Table 11.1.

11.4 Best practices of using AI in sustainability reporting and assurance

The Big Four accounting firms (Deloitte, EY, KPMG, and PwC) are at the forefront of integrating AI-powered tools and techniques into their operations, particularly in auditing and assurance services by adopting AI technologies to enhance efficiency, accuracy, and the overall quality of financial audits. Several recent academic papers present evidence of the steps taken by the Big Four to implement AI into their auditing and assurance practices by providing a comprehensive overview of how the Big Four accounting firms are leveraging AI to transform their services, improve efficiency, and maintain a competitive edge in the evolving landscape of professional services. For example, one study analyzes the rapid adoption of AI by Big Four audit firms compared to smaller firms, highlighting their significant investments in AI technologies and recruitment of AI specialists.[26] Another recent paper explores the various challenges and opportunities presented by AI integration in auditing, with a focus on large public accounting firms, including the Big Four.[27] Another study discusses frameworks developed by Big Four firms to audit AI systems effectively, emphasizing the need for auditor preparedness in evaluating AI-driven processes.[28] Collectively, these academic studies provide robust insights into how Big Four firms are engaging with AI tools for audit innovation, risk management, and auditor preparedness. Some of the AI initiatives by the Big Four firms suggested by these studies are: (1) Deloitte AI-enabled document-reviewing systems to automate the review and extraction of information from business documents; (2) the EY.ai Agentic Platform, deploying AI agents to assist tax professionals with tasks like data collection and compliance; (3) KPMG Ignite, to enhance business decisions and processes; and (4) PwC AI-powered tools to empower employees and clients, focusing on enhancing service delivery through advanced

Table 11.1 SRA and UNSDGs

UNSDGs	*Description*	*Role in Sustainability Reporting*	*Sustainability Assurance Impact*
Goal 16	**Peace, Justice, and Strong Institutions:** requiring robust governance frameworks and accountability mechanisms	Sustainability reporting provides stakeholders with clear information about an organization's economic, ESG performance, ensuring alignment with sustainability goals.	Independent assurance adds credibility, verifying that the reported information is accurate and reliable.
Goals 13 and 17	**Climate Action and Affordable and Clean Energy:** addressing active measurement and reporting of emissions, energy use, and climate adaptation strategies	Enable organizations to use sustainability reporting to disclose their GHG emissions, renewable energy initiatives, and climate resilience plans.	Ensure that the sustainability reported data supports genuine climate actions rather than greenwashing.
Goals 5 and 10	**Gender Equality** and **Reduced Inequalities:** aim to promote equity and inclusion.	Sustainability reports highlight initiatives on diversity, equal pay, and community engagement, allowing companies to showcase their impact on social sustainability.	Ensure that claims of social progress are backed by data, enhancing trust among stakeholders.
Goal 12	**Responsible Consumption and Production:** calls for sustainable business practices.	Sustainability reporting integrates ESG factors into corporate governance, driving businesses toward responsible decision-making.	Strengthens governance by ensuring adherence to established sustainability standards and frameworks like GRI, SASB, or TCFD.
Goal 8	**Decent Work and Economic Growth:** promotes sustained economic progress while ensuring environmental protection and social well-being.	Provides a platform to track and report progress on green jobs, fair labor practices, and sustainable investments.	Validates data to reassure investors and stakeholders of the organization's genuine contributions to sustainable economic development.
Goal 17	**Partnerships for the Goals:** focuses on collaboration to achieve sustainability objectives.	Encourages companies to disclose partnerships, supply chain initiatives, and joint efforts that address global challenges.	Confirms the authenticity of collaborative efforts and ensures alignment with global sustainability standards.
Goal 9	**Industry, Innovation, and Infrastructure:** highlights the need for resilient and sustainable innovation.	Allows organizations to showcase their advancements in sustainable technologies and their impact on the economy and environment.	Builds confidence that the innovations reported are viable and aligned with sustainability objectives.

technologies. With the increased focus on ESG disclosures, the Big Four accounting firms (Deloitte, PwC, EY, and KPMG) have procured many best practices for these areas. Specifically, the utilization of LLMs and different training methods (RAG, zero-shot, one-shot, two-shot learning, fine-tuning, Hugging Face, and prompt engineering) has become a primary tool for enhancing the reporting for these increasingly critical matters for organizations and investors alike. Each of the Big 4 firms has developed its own tools to enhance a client's track, report, and manage their sustainability-related items.

11.4.1 Ms used by the Big 4

As AI and LLMs continue to evolve, major accounting firms are increasingly leveraging these technologies to enhance their services, particularly in the domain of ESG and sustainability reporting. The Big Four accounting firms—Deloitte, PwC, EY, and KPMG—stand at the forefront of this transformation, integrating GenAI tools to improve data analysis, regulatory compliance, and client advisory capabilities as described in detail in the following subsections. PwC has developed *ChatPwC*, powered by OpenAI's GPT-4, to streamline tax return reviews, automate reporting, and support software development.[29] The firm is currently deploying GenAI solutions across consulting clients, showcasing its widespread application of LLMs for productivity and compliance enhancement. Deloitte has introduced *DARTbot*, an internal GenAI chatbot tailored for audit and accounting professionals.[30] DARTbot assists with retrieving relevant auditing standards and guidance efficiently, enhancing decision-making during engagements. Deloitte has also committed over $1 billion to AI development within its US operations, signifying its strategic prioritization of AI integration. EY launched *EY.ai*, supported by a $1.4 billion investment, which includes the *EYQ* assistant—a proprietary LLM-powered conversational AI.[31] Tools like the EY Intelligent Payroll Chatbot further exemplify EY's application of AI in finance, payroll, and sustainability advisory, delivering fast, accurate answers to complex accounting and regulatory questions.

KPMG has embedded GenAI into its global audit platform, *KPMG Clara*.[32] This integration enables real-time auditing, anomaly detection, and data quality management. Clara's AI functions help auditors detect irregular financial patterns, improving both risk assessment and fraud detection. Collectively, these initiatives reflect how LLMs are transforming ESG reporting and assurance, positioning the Big Four as pioneers in the AI-driven future of professional services. The aforementioned examples are used in financial statement audits primarily, but the Big 4 firms are also leveraging AI technology to enhance their sustainability- and climate-related services. These AI models can improve the firms' abilities to assess climate risks, improve ESG reporting, automate carbon accounting, model climate scenarios, and identify sustainability opportunities. A simple example of how the Big 4 firms may use LLMs for ESG-related matters is as follows:

The prompt for the local LLM: "Generate a summary of our company's carbon emissions reduction efforts for our annual ESG report. Use the data below and align the language with GRI standards."

The input data provided:

- Reduced carbon emissions by 25% over the past three years.
- Transitioned 50% of energy consumption to renewable sources.
- Implemented a supplier sustainability program to reduce Scope 3 emissions.

Output generated by the local LLM: Over the past three years, we have successfully reduced our carbon emissions by 25%, aligning with our commitment to sustainable operations. This reduction has been achieved through a strategic shift, with 50% of our energy consumption now sourced from renewable energy. Additionally, we have launched a supplier sustainability program aimed at minimizing Scope 3 emissions by engaging vendors in carbon reduction initiatives. These efforts reflect our dedication to climate action and adherence to the GRI standards on emissions disclosure. This summarization provided by the local LLM provides an efficient way to compile data sustainability-related matters and can be used for understanding, further analysis, and can also be crafted into a disclosure on a report that the company will issue.

11.4.1.1 PwC

PwC has strategically integrated advanced AI tools into its professional services to enhance accuracy, compliance, and sustainability. A key innovation is ChatPwC, developed on OpenAI's GPT-4, which streamlines tasks such as tax return reviews, report generation, and software development, improving efficiency and reducing human error. In financial and ESG data analysis, GL.ai detects anomalies to support more accurate audits and sustainability assessments.[33] The ESG Pulse Tool offers quick insights into a company's ESG performance, enabling better risk assessment, peer benchmarking, and strategy adjustments.[34] Similarly, PwC's Climate Excellence Tool helps firms conduct climate scenario analyses, making their portfolios more resilient to climate-related risks.[35] Furthermore, PwC's climate risk modeling services combine technology and environmental assessment to identify significant climate threats to business operations.[36] Their ESG due diligence tools assist in identifying noncompliance with sustainability standards such as SASB and ISSB, helping clients navigate regulatory demands.[37] Collectively, these AI-driven tools reflect PwC's commitment to integrating technology with ESG and financial practices, supporting clients in managing risk, ensuring compliance, and advancing sustainability.

11.4.1.2 Application of local LLMs in ESG analysis: a case study using BP's 2023 sustainability report

This section presents a simulated case study demonstrating the application of Local LLMs in ESG analysis, using BP's 2023 sustainability report as the primary data source. The objective is to illustrate how customized local LLMs can support ESG benchmarking and disclosure assessments. Specifically, we showcase two ESG-focused tools developed within our locally fine-tuned LLM infrastructure.

Table 11.2 Local LLM simulation of ESG analysis and industry benchmarking

Category	*BP's Current Status (2023)*	*Industry Benchmark*	*Local LLM Recommendation*
Net-zero progress	41% reduction in Scope 1 and 2 emissions since 2019	Industry average: 38%	Maintain progress, but increase investment in carbon-neutral projects
Methane emissions	0.05% intensity	Industry average: 0.06%	Continue advanced monitoring technologies
Investment in transition growth	\$3.8B in 2023 (down from \$4.9B in 2022)	Industry trend: Increasing investment	Increase capital allocation to renewables
Water management	Ongoing site-based water assessments	Leaders have set clear water reduction goals	Establish measurable water reduction targets
Biodiversity efforts	Net positive impact methodology implemented in new projects	Some competitors are leading with biodiversity restoration programs	Expand conservation initiatives

These examples simulate how local LLMs can replicate—and in some cases enhance—the analytical capabilities of proprietary ESG tools by improving speed, contextual accuracy, and adaptability to jurisdiction-specific or proprietary disclosures. By processing both structured and unstructured data from BP's sustainability reporting, our Local LLM framework demonstrates automated anomaly detection, ISSB-aligned compliance verification, and strategic ESG benchmarking tailored to industry standards and sector-specific performance indicators.

11.4.1.3 Local LLM simulation for ISSB compliance and risk assessment

Table 11.3 illustrates how our local LLM can be used to simulate compliance assessments against ISSB disclosure requirements, using BP's 2023 sustainability report as the case reference. The local LLM identifies full compliance in Scope 1 and 2 emissions disclosures, recommending continued adherence to reporting standards. However, it flags partial compliance or noncompliance in critical areas such as Scope 3 emissions, climate scenario analysis, and financial risk disclosures. By leveraging both structured and unstructured data, the local LLM evaluates compliance risk levels and provides tailored recommendations to close gaps—such as expanding value chain emissions reporting, aligning scenario analysis with ISSB guidance, and detailing regulatory mitigation strategies. This simulation highlights the potential of fine-tuned Local LLMs to automate ESG due diligence and enhance disclosure quality in alignment with evolving global standards.

This table was generated using our Local LLM framework to simulate compliance risk levels and assess alignment with ISSB disclosure requirements based on BP's 2023 sustainability report.

Table 11.3 Local LLMs simulate for compliance risk level and ISSB disclosure requirement

ISSB Disclosure Requirement	*BP's Current Status (2023)*	*Compliance Risk Level*	*Local LLM Recommendation*
Scope 1 and 2 emissions disclosure	41% reduction versus 2019 baseline	☑ Fully compliant	Maintain regular reporting
Scope 3 emissions disclosure	Limited details provided	⚠ Partial compliance	Expand reporting on value chain emissions
Climate scenario analysis	No clear modeling of financial risks	✗ Non-compliant	Conduct ISSB-aligned scenario analysis
Financial impact of climate risks	Transition growth investment disclosed, but stranded assets not covered	⚠ Partial Compliance	Report financial risks from energy transition
Mitigation strategy disclosure	Methane monitoring completed, but lacks regulatory risk details	⚠ Partial Compliance	Provide regulatory risk mitigation strategy

11.4.1.4 Deloitte

Similar to the other Big 4 firms, Deloitte is at the forefront of AI and LLM use to enhance their reporting and assurance services for sustainability and ESG. These types of services typically involve ensuring that a client is in line with the reporting objectives of the applicable regulatory body or standard setter, as well as tracking and analyzing ESG performance to identify riskier areas and how they are comparing to their peers in the industry. In this section, we will focus on some of the tools that Deloitte has created and/or leverages in their reporting and assurance service that involve the use of AI and LLMs. Deloitte is leveraging advanced technology to enhance audit and ESG services. DARTbot,[38] a GenAI chatbot, helps auditors quickly access relevant standards. The firm's ESG Disclosure Management Tool streamlines sustainability reporting across global frameworks, tailored by industry. The Emissions Planning Model, integrated with workday, links emissions and financial data to assess the impact of reduction strategies. AI Qualify ensures the reliability of ESG models, while ESG Trace tracks and reports ESG metrics.

11.4.1.5 Simulating ESG KPI and target alignment with local LLMs

To illustrate how our Local LLM can simulate ESG performance tracking and strategic alignment, we present two hypothetical use cases focused on KPI and target disclosures, based on data from BP's 2023 Sustainability Report. Specifically, this example demonstrates how the *ESG KPI* simulation—powered by our fine-tuned Local LLM—can analyze and evaluate BP's progress against its climate and sustainability targets. Table 11.4 summarizes this simulated output, where the local

Table 11.4 Local LLMs simulate for KPI and target disclosure requirement

Category	*KPI*	*2023 Value*	*Target*	*Status*	*Action Required*
Net-zero operations	Absolute Emissions Reduction (Scope 1 and 2)	**41% reduction** (vs. 2019)	**20% by 2025** (already exceeded)	☑ On track	No action needed
Net-zero sales	Carbon Intensity of Sold Energy Products	3% reduction (vs. 2019)	5% by 2025	⚠ Slightly behind	Adjust sales portfolio
Methane emissions	Methane Intensity	0.05%	Maintain or reduce	☑ On target	Monitor trends
Transition investment	Total Investment in Renewables and Low-Carbon	$3.8 billion	Increase annually	⚠ Below 2022 ($4.9B)	Evaluate funding allocations
Water usage	% Freshwater Replenished	Site-based assessments completed	Positive water impact by 2030	◍ In progress	Implement water efficiency measures
Biodiversity impact	Net Positive Impact (NPI) Method Applied	UK and Indonesia Projects Initiated	Expand NPI to all projects	◍ In Progress	Scale up biodiversity projects

LLM assesses key metrics such as net-zero operations, methane intensity, transition investments, and biodiversity impact. The model identifies areas on track, those requiring adjustments, and those in progress, offering tailored recommendations to enhance strategic alignment. This analysis exemplifies the potential of local LLMs to automate ESG target tracking, detect performance gaps, and support proactive sustainability planning in line with industry benchmarks and disclosure standards.

Table 11.2 summarizes how a local LLM simulates ESG KPI and target compliance for BP using data from its 2023 Sustainability Report. The LLM assesses performance across key categories such as emissions, water, and biodiversity. It identifies areas "On Track" (e.g., Scope 1 and 2 emissions and methane) and those needing improvement (e.g., sales intensity and investment in renewables). The tool provides action-oriented recommendations where targets are unmet. This simulation illustrates the potential of local LLMs in automating ESG compliance monitoring and strategic planning.

11.4.1.6 Simulating ISSB disclosure requirements with local LLMs

Table 11.5 illustrates how our local LLM simulates BP's alignment with ISSB disclosure requirements based on its 2023 Sustainability Report. The local LLM analyzes structured and unstructured data to evaluate governance, emissions, risk disclosures, and climate strategies. It identifies full alignment in areas such as governance oversight and Scope 1 and 2 emissions, while highlighting gaps in Scope 3 emissions, climate risk quantification, and scenario modeling. The simulation outputs actionable insights such as the need for enhanced financial disclosures and ISSB-aligned strategy revisions. This demonstrates the value of local LLMs in enhancing ESG reporting precision and compliance automation.

This table is generated by our local LLM for ISSB disclosure requirement and alignment status, providing a simulated analysis of BP's 2023 Sustainability Report against the ISSB standards.

11.4.1.7 Ernst & Young

Ernst & Young (EY) has strategically integrated AI into its core service offerings to enhance assurance quality, sustainability practices, and organizational decision-making. These digital solutions reflect EY's broader commitment to leveraging data and AI to meet evolving client needs in a rapidly changing regulatory and environmental landscape. One key innovation is EYQ, a conversational AI assistant powered by EY's proprietary LLM. EYQ supports audit professionals by offering real-time procedural guidance, particularly in situations involving regulatory uncertainty. This tool not only enhances audit consistency but also promotes higher-quality assurance outcomes. To address climate-related risks, EY offers the Climate Analytics Platform. This online tool delivers granular, on-demand climate data that supports organizations in aligning with both market and regulatory expectations. It also aids in strategic planning, helping entities to futureproof assets and operations amid growing climate challenges. In addition, EY Assess

Table 11.5 Local LLMs simulate for ISSB disclosure requirement

ISSB Disclosure Requirement	*BP's Current Reporting (2023 Report)*	*Alignment Status*	*Action Required*
Governance: ESG oversight	Board-level **Safety and Sustainability Committee** oversees ESG	☑ Fully aligned	No action needed
Climate-related risks	Discussed transition risks (e.g., O&G decline) but **no quantified financial impact**	⚠ Partially aligned	Quantify financial risks from climate change
Scope 1 and 2 emissions	**41% reduction versus 2019**	☑ Fully aligned	No action needed
Scope 3 emissions	Limited disclosure on **value chain emissions**	⚠ Partially aligned	Expand Scope 3 emissions calculations
Climate transition plan	Net-zero strategy outlined, but **not fully aligned with ISSB metrics**	⚠ Needs improvement	Align strategy with ISSB financial disclosure metrics
Physical climate risks	Mentions **extreme weather impact**, but **no scenario modeling**	◍ In progress	Conduct scenario analysis for financial risks
Sustainability-linked financial data	**Limited disclosure on the financial performance impacts of ESG actions**	⚠ Missing	Provide financial projections on climate transition

functions as an integrated maturity assessment platform. With features such as self-assessment capabilities, AI-based evidence evaluation, and real-time analytics, it enables organizations to benchmark performance, identify gaps, and make informed improvements aligned with industry standards. Finally, the EY.AI Maturity Model provides a framework for organizations to evaluate their current level of AI integration and maturity. By outlining clear development steps, the model guides entities in advancing their digital transformation journeys and adopting AI in a structured, value-driven manner. Together, these platforms exemplify EY's leadership in applying AI to the domains of audit, sustainability, and strategic governance. They serve as critical enablers for organizations aiming to navigate complexity, meet compliance obligations, and drive CI in a digitally connected world.[39]

11.4.1.8 Simulating SASB disclosure requirements with local LLMs

For the use-case study of BP, we will examine how the Climate Analytics Platform, powered by AI, could enhance BP's sustainability efforts by leveraging the company's 2023 Sustainability Report. Using our local LLM framework, we simulate the functionality of the Climate Analytics Platform, which utilizes both structured and unstructured data from BP's report to assess alignment with SASB standards. This simulation demonstrates how local LLMs can provide actionable insights and support BP in achieving better compliance, risk assessment, and performance improvements based on SASB disclosure requirements.

This table is generated based on our local LLM for ESG disclosure management, aligned with the SASB disclosure requirements. It leverages structured and unstructured data from BP's 2023 Sustainability Report to simulate how BP's sustainability disclosures align with SASB standards. This table summarizes BP's current alignment with SASB disclosure requirements based on their 2023 Sustainability Report, evaluated using our local LLM for ESG disclosure management. It highlights key areas, such as greenhouse gas and methane emissions, where BP is fully aligned with SASB standards, and areas for improvement, such as climate scenario analysis and physical risks and resilience, where additional steps are required. For example, BP needs to conduct detailed financial modeling for transition risks and use tools like the Climate Analytics Platform for better asset-level climate risk mapping. Water management and reserve disclosures are also in progress and need expansion or improved modeling. This table provides a clear view of BP's strengths and the actions required to meet SASB standards more comprehensively.

11.4.1.9 KPMG accounting firm

As highlighted in previous sections, the Big 4 firms are continuously advancing their use of AI and LLM-based models to better support clients in the ESG and sustainability space. KPMG is actively leveraging innovative technologies to enhance sustainability reporting, ensure disclosure assurance, and facilitate tracking and analysis of ESG-related data. The following are some of the key models and technologies that KPMG utilizes for these purposes.

Table 11.6 Local LLMs simulate for the SASB disclosure requirement

SASB Disclosure Topic	*BP's Current Reporting (2023 Report)*	*Alignment Status*	*Action Required*
Greenhouse gas emissions (EM-EP-110a.1)	Reports 41% Scope 1 and 2 reduction since 2019	☑ Fully aligned	No action needed
Methane Emissions (EM-EP-110a.2)	BP reports 0.05% methane intensity	☑ Fully Aligned	No action needed
Climate scenario analysis (EM-EP-420a.3)	No detailed financial impact modeling for transition risks	⚠ Missing	Conduct scenario analysis using the EY platform
Physical risks and resilience (EM-EP-420a.4)	Mentions extreme weather but lacks facility-level risk assessment	⚠ Needs improvement	Use the EY tool for asset-level climate risk mapping
Water management (EM-EP-140a.1)	BP conducted water stress assessments at key refineries	◍ In progress	Expand to global operations
Proven and probable reserves (EM-EP-110a.3)	Reports fossil fuel reserves but lacks disclosure on climate risk impact	⚠ Needs improvement	Model reserve valuations under carbon pricing scenarios
Renewable energy investment (EM-EP-420a.1)	BP invested $3.8B in transition growth	☑ Fully aligned	Continue tracking impact

KPMG has adopted advanced AI technologies to enhance audit processes, ESG advisory, and sustainability reporting. These platforms reflect the firm's commitment to digital transformation and regulatory readiness. KPMG Clara is the firm's global smart audit platform, using AI to detect risks, analyze data, manage quality, and support real-time auditing. This enhances transparency and efficiency in audit delivery. The ESG IQ tool enables clients to better understand their ESG environment, offering actionable insights that inform strategy and improve sustainability outcomes. With KPMG Ignite, clients can build, train, and deploy AI-enabled solutions to solve business challenges. Its user-friendly design facilitates rapid adoption of advanced analytics. Finally, the CSRD Reporting Accelerator, developed with Salesforce, combines cloud-based ESG tools with KPMG's sustainability expertise. Powered by GenAI, it provides a pre-configured framework to streamline compliance with the CSRD and optimize ESG reporting processes. Collectively, these tools position KPMG at the forefront of AI integration in assurance and sustainability, helping clients meet complex regulatory demands while advancing digital maturity.[40]

11.4.1.10 Simulating ESG risk disclosure with local LLMs

Table 11.7 showcases how our local LLM framework simulates ESG risk tools by analyzing BP's 2023 sustainability data and comparing it with industry benchmarks, providing risk assessment insights. By leveraging structured and unstructured data from BP's report, the local LLM assesses various ESG categories, including net-zero strategy, sustainable investment, Scope 3 emissions, biodiversity and water, and regulatory compliance. For instance, BP's Scope 1 and 2 emissions reduction is compared to Shell's, revealing a moderate risk level, and the local LLM suggests expanding Scope 3 reduction plans. The framework also highlights BP's need to increase investment in renewables, expand biodiversity initiatives, and prepare for CSRD and EU Taxonomy reporting to mitigate high risks in regulatory compliance. This simulation enables BP to enhance its sustainability strategy, strengthen investor confidence, and ensure alignment with global ESG standards.

This table is generated based on our local LLM for risk level and aligned with TCFD, ISSB, and CSRD alignment disclosure requirements. The local LLM framework assesses BP's 2023 sustainability data, compares it against industry benchmarks, and evaluates potential risks within various ESG categories. By identifying areas such as Scope 3 emissions, regulatory compliance, and biodiversity, the model provides actionable insights, such as enhancing investment in renewables, improving Scope 3 reporting, and preparing for CSRD and EU Taxonomy alignment. These insights aim to help BP strengthen its sustainability strategy and better align with global disclosure standards, thus improving investor confidence and competitive positioning.

Table 11.7 Local LLMs simulate for ESG category with benchmark and risk

ESG Category	*BP's 2023 Status*	*Competitor Benchmark*	*Risk Level*	*Actionable Insights*
Net-zero strategy	**41% Scope 1 and 2 reduction since 2019**	Shell: 45% reduction	Moderate risk	Strengthen Scope 3 reduction plans
Sustainable investment	**$3.8B invested in transition growth**	Exxon: $4.2B	Moderate risk	Increase investment in renewables
Scope 3 emissions	**Limited reporting on value chain emissions**	TotalEnergies: Full Scope 3 disclosure	High Risk	Expand Scope 3 measurement
Biodiversity and water	**Started the NPI method in the United Kingdom and Indonesia**	Chevron: Global biodiversity strategy	Moderate risk	Expand biodiversity initiatives
Regulatory compliance	**Aligned with TCFD and ISSB** but lacks CSRD alignment	Peers preparing for CSRD	High risk	Prepare for CSRD and EU Taxonomy reporting

11.5 Summary

This chapter explores the evolving role of AI in shaping the future of sustainable business practices. It begins by examining emerging trends in AI adoption across industries, highlighting how ML, NLP, and predictive analytics are transforming ESG strategies. The chapter emphasizes the integration of AI with sustainability goals, such as optimizing resource use, enhancing supply chain transparency, reducing carbon footprints, and improving ethical decision-making. Looking ahead, the chapter identifies key future trends including AI-powered climate risk modeling, autonomous sustainability reporting, and the emergence of AI-driven stakeholder engagement platforms. It discusses the potential of GenAI to support innovation in green product design and circular economy models, as well as the increasing use of AI in regulatory compliance and impact assessment. We utilize the company's 2023 sustainability report as the primary source of data for simulation on local LLMs can be applied in ESG analysis and risk assessment based on SASB, TCFD, and ISSB. The chapter also addresses the ethical, governance, and technological challenges associated with these advancements, underscoring the need for responsible AI frameworks and interdisciplinary collaboration. This chapter also provides strategic recommendations for businesses, educators, and policymakers to foster sustainable innovation through AI, positioning organizations for long-term resilience and purpose-driven growth in an increasingly data-driven, environmentally conscious global economy. Finally, it presents the best practices of using AI-powered tools and techniques in sustainability reporting and assurance.

11.6 Takeaways

- AI is a critical enabler of sustainable business transformation, helping organizations align profitability with environmental and social goals.
- ML, NLP, and real-time analytics are being leveraged to enhance ESG performance measurement, reporting, and forecasting.
- AI improves operational efficiency and reduces waste, enabling smarter energy management, sustainable supply chains, and resource optimization.
- Emerging AI applications include autonomous sustainability reporting, climate risk modeling, and AI-driven circular economy innovations.
- GenAI is fostering innovation in sustainable product design, scenario simulation, and stakeholder communication.
- AI enhances transparency and accountability, supporting ethical sourcing, compliance monitoring, and anti-greenwashing efforts.
- Future business models will increasingly rely on AI for decision-making, particularly in areas involving long-term environmental risks and stakeholder impacts.
- Challenges such as data bias, lack of regulatory clarity, and AI ethics must be addressed through robust governance and interdisciplinary collaboration.
- Responsible AI frameworks are essential for aligning AI capabilities with sustainability values and ensuring equitable outcomes.
- Businesses, educators, and policymakers must collaborate to develop AI-ready, sustainability-focused talent and policies to guide ethical innovation.

Notes

1 European Commission (EC). 2023. *New Rules on Corporate Sustainability Reporting: The Corporate Sustainability Reporting Directive (CSRD)*. https://finance.ec.europa.eu/capital-markets-union-and-financial-markets/comp
2 European Commission (EC). 2024, 25 July. *Corporate Sustainability Due Diligence*. European Commission
3 Securities and Exchange Commission (SEC) released its final rule, entitled "The Enhancement and Standardization of Climate-Related Disclosures for Investors, Release No.33-11275: File No. S7-10-22. https://www.sec.gov/newsroom/press-releases/2024-31
4 US Securities and Exchange Commission (SEC). 2025, 11 February. *Statement: Acting Chairman Statement on Climate-Related Disclosure Rules, Commissioner Mark T. Uyeda*. https://www.sec.gov/newsroom/speeches-statements/uyeda-statement-climate-change-021025
5 United States Mission to the United Nations. 2025, 4 March. *Remarks at the UN meeting entitled 58th Plenary Meeting of the General Assembly, Consideration of Draft Resolution (A/79/L.57/Rev.1)*. https://usun.usmission.gov/remarks-at-the-un-meeting-entitled-58th-plenary-meeting-of-the-general-assembly-consideration-of-draft-resolution-a-79-l-57-rev-1/
6 California, Legislative Information. 2023. *SB-253 Climate Corporate Data Accountability Act and SB-261 Greenhouse Gases: Climate-Related Financial Risk*. https://leginfo.legislature.ca.gov/faces/billNavClient.xhtml?bill_id=202320240SB253; https://leginfo.legislature.ca.gov/faces/billNavClient.xhtml?bill_id=202320240SB261
7 International Financial Reporting Standards (IFRS) Foundation. 2024. *Progress on Corporate Climate-related Disclosures—2024 Report*. https://www.ifrs.org/content/dam/ifrs/supporting-implementation/issb-standards/progress-climate-related-disclosures-2024.pdf
8 IFEA. 2025, 17 January. *Global Assurance and Ethics Standards: Trust in Sustainability*. https://www.ethicsandaudit.org/global-assurance-and-ethics-standards-trust-sustainability?utm_source=Main%20List%20New&utm_campaign=c7b40e17ac-IAASB-IESBA-sustainability-launch-1.27.25&utm_medium=email&utm_term=0_-c7b40e17ac-80664632
9 EY. 2025, 8 May. *Technical Line—How the EU's Corporate Sustainability Reporting Directive Affects Non-EU-based Multinationals*. EY-US
10 EY. *Technical Line—How the EU's Corporate Sustainability Reporting Directive Affects Non-EU-based Multinationals*
11 EY. *Technical Line—How the EU's Corporate Sustainability Reporting Directive Affects Non-EU-based Multinationals*
12 Batool, A., Zowghi, D., & Bano, M. 2025, January. AI governance: A systematic literature review. *Journal: AI and Ethics*. https://doi.org/10.1007/s43681-024-00653-w
13 Birkstedt, T., Minkkinen, M., Tandon, A., & Mäntymäki, M. 2023. AI governance: Themes, knowledge gaps, and future agendas. *Internet Research*, 33(7), 133–167. https://doi.org/10.1108/INTR-01-2022-0042
14 Batool, A., Zowghi, D., & Bano, M. 2023, December. *Responsible AI Governance: A Systematic Literature Review*. arXiv. https://arxiv.org/abs/2401.10896
15 Kevin, R. 2023, 30 May. A.I. Poses 'risk of extinction,' industry leaders warn. *The New York Times*. https://www.nytimes.com/2023/05/30/technology/ai-threat-warning.html
16 Kevin. A.I. Poses 'risk of extinction,' industry leaders warn
17 Bostrom, N. 2014. *Superintelligence: Paths, Dangers, Strategies*. Oxford: Oxford University Press.
18 Russell, S., Dewey, D., & Tegmark, M. 2015. Research priorities for robust and beneficial artificial intelligence. *AI Magazine*, 36(4), 105–114. https://doi.org/10.1609/aimag.v36i4.2577

19 Brundage, M., et al. 2018. *The Malicious Use of Artificial Intelligence: Forecasting, Prevention, and Mitigation.* arXiv preprint arXiv:1802.07228. https://arxiv.org/abs/1802.07228
20 Amodei, D., Olah, C., Steinhardt, J., Christiano, P., Schulman, J. & Mané, D. 2016. *Concrete Problems in AI Safety.* arXiv preprint arXiv:1606.06565. https://arxiv.org/abs/1606.06565
21 Leike, J., Irving, G., Christiano, P., & The OpenAI Superalignment Team. 2024. *Superalignment: Preparing for Superhuman AI.* OpenAI Research. https://openai.com/research/superalignment
22 Raji, I.D., Smart, A., White, R.N., Mitchell, M., Gebru, T., Hutchinson, B., Smith-Loud, J., Theron, D., & Barnes, P. 2020. Closing the AI accountability gap: Defining an end-to-end framework for internal algorithmic auditing. In *Proceedings of the 2020 Conference on Fairness, Accountability, and Transparency* (pp. 33–44). https://doi.org/10.1145/3351095.3372873
23 Ovadya, A., Whittlestone, J., & Dafoe, A. 2024. *Democratic Inputs to AI Governance: Strategies and Tensions.* arXiv preprint arXiv:2403.04567. https://arxiv.org/abs/2403.04567
24 Mehrabi, N., Morstatter, F., Saxena, N., Lerman, K., & Galstyan, A. 2021. A survey on bias and fairness in machine learning. *ACM Computing Surveys*, 54(6), 1–35. https://arxiv.org/abs/1908.09635
25 Reuters Events. 2024. *Sustainable Reporting and Data Management Report 2024.* https://ieeb.fundacion-biodiversidad.es/sites/default/files/2024_sustainability_reporting_data_co
26 Tang, Y., Wang, X., & Zhou, Y. 2024. How does artificial intelligence shape audit firms. *Management Science*, 70(2), 1159–1177. https://doi.org/10.1287/mnsc.2022.04040
27 Alles, M.G., Brennan, G., & Vasarhelyi, M.A. 2025. Challenges and opportunities for artificial intelligence in auditing. *International Journal of Accounting Information Systems*, 48, 100583. https://doi.org/10.1016/j.accinf.2025.100583
28 Brennan, G., Alles, M., & Vasarhelyi, M.A. 2025. Artificial intelligence auditability and auditor readiness for auditing AI systems. *International Journal of Accounting Information Systems*, 48, 100586. https://doi.org/10.1016/j.accinf.2025.100586
29 https://www.pwc.co.nz/news-releases/2024-news-releases/pwc-new-zealand-gives-secure-generative-ai-tool-chatpwc-to-all-staff-nationwide.html
30 https://www2.deloitte.com/us/en/pages/about-deloitte/articles/press-releases/deloitte-launches-innovative-dartbot-internal-chatbot.html
31 https://www.ey.com/en_gl/newsroom/2023/09/ey-announces-launch-of-artificial-intelligence-platform-ey-ai-following-us-1-4b-investment
32 https://kpmg.com/de/en/home/media/press-releases/2024/08/kpmg-integrated-generative-ki-in-global-audit-platform-kpmg-clara.html
33 https://www.pwc.com/cz/en/sluzby/sustainability/due-diligence.html
34 ESG Pulse: Streamline ESG Reporting with PwC Store Tools
35 PwC. 2025. *Fit for Climate Change with Climate Excellence.* https://www.pwc.de/en/sustainability/climate-excellence-making-companies-fit-for-climate-change.html
36 Fit for climate change with Climate Excellence - PwC
37 ESG Pulse: Streamline ESG Reporting with PwC Store Tools
38 https://www.accountancyage.com/2024/01/09/case-study-how-deloitte-is-leveraging-dartbot-within-its-audit-processes/
39 https://www.ey.com/en_gl/newsroom/2025/04/ey-announces-large-scale-integration-of-leading-edge-ai-technology-into-global-assurance-technology-platform
40 https://assets.kpmg.com/content/dam/kpmgsites/uk/pdf/2023/05/esg-iq-slipsheet.pdf

Index

For Product Safety Concerns and Information please contact our EU
representative GPSR@taylorandfrancis.com
Taylor & Francis Verlag GmbH, Kaufingerstraße 24, 80331 München, Germany

www.ingramcontent.com/pod-product-compliance
Ingram Content Group UK Ltd.
Pitfield, Milton Keynes, MK11 3LW, UK
UKHW020156200926
475702UK00016B/2735
* 9 7 8 1 0 3 2 9 8 7 3 0 9 *